Chambers
Concise Dictionary
of Scientists

Albert Einstein in the 1930s

Reproduced from an oil painting by his friend and doctor in Berlin, Janos Plesch, by courtesy of Professor P. H. Plesch.

Chambers
Concise Dictionary
of Scientists

David Millar, Ian Millar,
John Millar and Margaret Millar

1/1/24/5/89

CHAMBERS
CAMBRIDGE

CAMBRIDGE   EDINBURGH

NEW YORK   NEW ROCHELLE   MELBOURNE   SYDNEY

Published jointly by W & R Chambers Ltd and
The Press S_ndicate of the University of Cambridge, 1989

W & R Chambers Limited
43-45 Annandale Street, Edinburgh EH7 4AZ, and
The Press Syndicate of the University of Cambridge
The Pitt Building, Trumpington Street, Cambridge CB2 1RP
32 East 57th Street, New York, NY 10022, USA
10 Stamford Road, Oakleigh, Melbourne 3166, Australia.

British Library Cataloguing in Publication Data

Chambers concise dictionary of scientists.
1. Scientists, to 1980's. Biographies. Collections
I. Millar, Ian
509.2'2

ISBN 1-85296-354-9

Cover photograph by Dave Harrold
Cover design by James Hutcheson
Typeset by Pillans & Wilson Specialist Litho Printers Ltd. Edinburgh
Printed in Great Britain by Richard Clay Ltd, Bungay, Suffolk

Contents

Preface

The biographies in this book cover men and women whose names are famous in the physical, life, earth and space sciences, and in mathematics. The people profiled are linked, in many cases by name, with scientific laws, units, and effects, chemical reactions, diseases, and mathematical methods, and we include these. We have also included those explorers, engineers, physicians and surgeons who were substantial innovators as applied scientists; scientists whose distinction lies in their use of established techniques are not included. Neither are teachers, administrators, social scientists, in general, nor philosophers.

In recording major discoveries in science, the book covers much of the history of science. Science, however, is not merely a series of clearly successful investigations by talented individuals. Many investigations are valuable precisely because they set a challenge which leads to new evidence, which then establishes a new view—but only until this in turn is modified. In a sense there is no stable final position embodied in scientific 'laws', only a present state of experiment and theory; laws in science are not proved, but they can be firmly disproved; our body of well-received scientific knowledge is that which still, despite challenge, survives.

Scientific ideas reflect, and are part of, the attitudes and needs of their time and place; the study of the history of science in isolation is convenient but, in a sense, false. Some trends are clear. For example, early anatomy is much linked with the Italian Renaissance interest in art; while, in contrast, it was technical skill of a different kind which later introduced and developed three devices which have been of vast importance in science: the telescope, microscope, and spectroscope, in their various forms. It is also clear that ideas and devices often have no single discoverer. In such cases, we have tried to select the individual who made something workable, and who knew that this had been achieved.

In many areas of science, the major outlines were drawn in the 19th century, and much work in the 20th century has been directed towards developing this inheritance. So, a number of our entries deal with men (and some women) born in the 19th century. However, although the overall shape of biology, chemistry, geology and physics dates from then, it is at the interfaces between them that much 20th-century science has grown. Nuclear physics, molecular biology, computer science and space science are essentially 20th-century creations and many of our entries are for people working in these newer areas. This raises some difficulties; for example, many ideas of modern physics and mathematics are complex, and appreciation of them requires specialist knowledge; while the high cost of 'big science' has led to extensive team-work, in which it is not always possible to select key individuals in a traditional manner. Thus, it may be very difficult to write a book like this in the 21st century; but we believe it is still possible and useful to make the attempt now.

Acknowledgements

We have used too many sources of information to list them here. Autobiographies and biographies have been used where these are available; most of the living scientists have been able to check the accounts given of them and their work, and we are grateful to them for doing this. The *Dictionary of Scientific Biography* (editor-in-chief, C. C. Gillispie, published by Charles Scribner's Sons, New York, 1970-80, 16 vols.), has been much consulted, as have the *Biographical Memoirs of Fellows of the Royal Society* and the *Nobel Lectures*.

We are indebted to Professor T. E. Allibone, CBE, FRS, for permission to reproduce the photograph of Chadwick and Kapitsa, and to Professor P. H. Plesch for the frontispiece portrait of Einstein. We are particularly grateful also to Mr R. P. Moore, and to Professor P. C. Kendall and other friends and colleagues in the University of Keele who have helped in a number of ways: especially Mr F. M. J. Doherty, Professor W. Fuller, Professor I. M. L. Hunter, Dr E. D. Morgan, Mr M. J. Phillips, Mrs M. G. Pritchard, Mr D. B. Thompson, and Dr H. S. Torrens; and to Mrs Stella Pierce of Industriarts of Bath for locating engraved portraits, and Mr Xu Hourong of the Central Translation Bureau of the People's Republic of China for translations. We are grateful also to all our subjects who located and loaned portraits of themselves, most of which are published here for the first time. The photograph of Stephen Hawking is reproduced by permission of Manni Mason's Pictures. We are much indebted to Alastair Fyfe Holmes of Chambers who has been so encouraging and helpful at every stage.

Conventions and Symbols

Dates of scientists before Christ (BC) are usually not precisely known, and the dates we give are approximate. The entries are listed in the alphabetical order of their surnames. Translations of names from other alphabets can often be made in more than one way, and we give the most usual form. Names with prefixes are listed in the form commonly used; e.g., van de Waals (not Waals), and Liebig (not von Liebig). Where a man has multiple forenames, his lesser-used names are bracketed. When a scientist is mentioned in another's entry and also has an entry of his own, the name is first given in italic type. Scientific laws, units, effects, reactions and diseases which are linked with names of scientists are indicated in bold type for ease of location within the entry. Being often modest, scientists did not generally give their own names to these things; this was done by others. Laws are expressed in modern form, replacing words which are now outdated by their modern equivalents.

In giving the nationalities of scientists, we have usually used modern names for countries, and we have taken some note of where they spent their lives; e.g. Einstein, born in Ulm, went to school in Munich (also in Germany) and to college in Switzerland where he worked until he was over 50, before moving to the US; he became an American citizen 10 years later. We describe him as a German-Swiss-American theoretical physicist. For early scientists, the description 'Greek' is used for those of Hellenic culture and who wrote in Greek; some lived in Sicily, Asia Minor or Egypt. Again, 'Arabic' is used in a similar sense for Arabic writers; nationality in our modern sense is inappropriate here also.

In some cases, the name entry covers more than one member of a family, either through the generations (e.g. the Monros) or through marriage (the Coris) or as siblings (the Herschels).

Teamwork has become very common in the 20th century. In such cases, the research has been outlined in one entry only, with cross-references to the principal co-workers who did not necessarily play a smaller part. We do not normally list the prizes and honours awarded, except Nobel Prizes. Book titles are usually given in English translation, except for a few classics. Where we note that a man or woman was educated in a named city, we normally mean in the university or polytechnic there.

The International System of Units (SI) is used; and for chemical names the form now most used by chemists (which is not always the IUPAC preferred name) is given.

Certain symbols are defined as needed; a list of common symbols is given on p. 10.

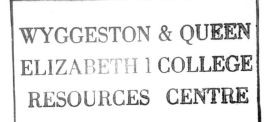

c	velocity of light in vacuum
e	unit of electronic charge
g	acceleration of free fall due to gravity (in vacuum)
h	Planck constant
K	thermodynamic temperature unit (kelvin)
kg	kilogram (SI unit of mass)
km	kilometre
m	metre (SI unit of length)
n	neutron
N_Λ	Avogadro constant
p	proton
p	pressure
s	second (SI unit of time)
t	tonne (megagram, i.e. 1000 kg)
STP	standard temperature and pressure; 298 K and 760mm Hg.
T	temperature (on absolute scale)
V	volume
A.U.	astronomical unit of distance; the mean Earth-Sun distance

Mathematical symbols

ln	logarithm to base e
log	logarithm to base 10
π	pi; ratio of circumference to diameter of a circle
$=$	equal to
$\neq$	not equal to
$\approx$	approximately equal to
$<$	less than
$>$	greater than
$\leqslant$	less than or equal to
$\geqslant$	greater than or equal to
$\ll$	much less than
$\gg$	much greater than
ab	a multiplied by b
a/b	a divided by b
$|a|$	magnitude of a (without regard to sign)
a^n	a raised to power n
i	$(-1)^{1/2}$
Σ	sum of the terms
e	base of Napierian logarithms, 2.71828 . . . (Euler's number)
exp x or e^x	exponential of x

List of Illustrations

A

ABBE, Ernst
1840-1905

German physicist and developer of optical instruments

Abbe was professor of physics and Observatory Director at Jena. He worked on optical theory, and with Carl Zeiss (an instrument maker) and Otto Schott (a glass maker) was able to improve several devices. These include the **Abbe condenser** for converging light on microscope specimens; the achromatic lens, which is free from colour distortion (1886); and the **Abbe refractometer**. From 1888 he was the sole owner of the Zeiss company, whose optical instruments were of the highest standard.

ABEGG, Richard
1869-1910

German physical chemist

Abegg's Rule (for which he is best remembered) states that each element has a positive valence and a negative valence, whose sum is 8. This idea reflects in primitive form the 'octet rule', i.e., the trend shown by most elements of the 2nd and 3rd (short) periods to attain an outer octet of electrons, but even as a mnemonic it applies only to elements of the 4th to 7th Periodic Groups.

ABEL, (Sir) Frederick (Augustus)
1827-1902

British chemist: expert on military explosives

An early pupil of *Hofmann* at the Royal College of Chemistry, he became chemist to the War Department in 1854. He showed that guncotton (obtained by nitrating cotton) could be made safe by removing traces of acid, which if not removed led to instability. In 1889 with *Dewar* he invented 'cordite', a mixture of guncotton and nitroglycerin gelatinized with propanone and petroleum jelly, which became the standard British military propellant. It produces little smoke on firing, an important advantage in a battlefield.

ABEL, John Jacob
1857-1938

American biochemist: detected adrenalin, and crystallized insulin; isolated amino acids from blood

An Ohio farmer's son, Abel studied very widely in Europe before returning to Johns Hopkins University, equipped with a wide knowledge of chemistry, biology and medicine, as professor of pharmacology. He studied the adrenal hormone now known as adrenalin; and in 1926 first crystallized insulin and showed it was a protein and contained zinc. He was the first to isolate amino acids from blood, in 1914. He did this by passing blood from an artery through a cellophane tube immersed in saline; the amino acids dialysed through the tube, and the blood was returned to a vein of the animal. The proof that amino acids are present in blood is fundamental in animal biochemistry; and the method used led the way towards dialysis in the treatment of kidney disease.

ABEL, Neils Henrik

1802-1829

*Norwegian mathematician: pioneer of
group theory; proved that no algebraic
solution of the general fifth-degree equation
exists*

Abel was the son of a Lutheran minister.
In 1821 he went to Oslo to study at the
university, but his father's death forced
him to give this up in order to support the
large family of which he was the eldest; he
was extremely poor throughout his life. In
1825 he visited Germany and France, and
with Leopold Crelle founded Crelle's
Journal in which much of his work was
published, since Abel could not persuade
the French Academy of Sciences to do so.
Having failed to find a university post in
Germany, and with his health failing due
to tuberculosis, he returned to Norway,
where he died shortly afterwards aged 26.
Two days later a letter from Crelle
announced that the professorship of
mathematics at Berlin, one of the most
prestigious posts in the mathematical
world, had been awarded to him.

Despite his tragically early death Abel
largely founded the theory of groups, and
in particular commutative groups which
were later known as **Abelian groups**. He
also showed that the general fifth degree
equation is not solvable algebraically
(ironically *Gauss* threw this proof away
unread when Abel sent it to him). He
revolutionized the important area of elliptic integrals with his theory of elliptic and
transcendental functions, and contributed to the theory of infinite series.

ADAMS, John Couch

1819-1892

*English astronomer: predicted existence of
Neptune*

As the son of a tenant farmer, Adams
had financial problems in entering Cam-

bridge, but his career was successful and
he remained there throughout his life.

By 1820 it had become apparent to
astronomers that the motion of Uranus
could not be explained by *Newton's* law of
gravitation and the influence of the known
planets alone, since a small but increasing
perturbation in its orbit had been
observed. Whilst still an undergraduate,
Adams proved that the deviation had to be
due to the influence of an eighth, undiscovered, planet. He sent his prediction for
its position to *Airy*, the Astronomer
Royal, who was sceptical of its value and
ignored it. Only when *Leverrier*, in
France, announced similar results nine
months later did Airy initiate a search by
James Challis at the Cambridge Observatory, based on Adams's prediction. The
planet, now named Neptune, was however found first by Johann Galle in Berlin
in 1846, using Leverrier's figures. A bitter
controversy about the credit for the
prediction soon developed. Adams's
precedence was eventually recognized,
despite his taking no part in the debate.
He turned down the subsequent offers of a
knighthood and the post of Astronomer
Royal.

ADAMS, Walter Sydney

1876-1956

*American astronomer: discovered first white
dwarf star*

Adams was born in Syria, where his
American parents were missionaries, but
he returned with them when he was nine
and was educated in the US and in
Europe.

Adams's work was principally concerned with the spectroscopic study of
stars. He showed how dwarf and giant
stars could be distinguished by their
spectra, and established the technique of
spectroscopic parallax to deduce a star's
distance. In 1915 he observed the spectrum of Sirius B, the faint companion of
Sirius, and discovered it to be an exceptionally hot star. Since it is only eight

light-years distant he realized that it must therefore be very small (otherwise it would be brighter), and hence of very high density. Sirius B proved to be a 'white dwarf', and the first of a new class of stellar objects; such stars are the final stage in the evolution of stars of similar mass to the Sun, and which have collapsed to form extremely dense objects.

Adams also searched for the relativistic spectral shift expected from a heavy star's presumed intense gravitational field. This he succeeded in finding in 1924, thereby proving his hypothesis about the nature of Sirius B and strengthening the case for *Einstein's* general relativity theory as well. Adams spent most of his working life at the Mount Wilson Observatory in southern California, and was its Director from 1923 until 1946.

ADDISON, Thomas
1793-1860

British physician: a founder of endocrinology

A graduate in medicine from Edinburgh and London, his early work included the first clear descriptions of appendicitis, lobar pneumonia, and the action of poisons on the living body. In 1855 his small book *On the Constitutional and Local Effects of Disease of the Supra-renal Capsules* described two new diseases: one is 'pernicious' anaemia; the other, also an anaemia, is associated with bronzing of the skin and weakness, and is known as **Addison's disease**. He found that cases of the latter showed post-mortem changes in the suprarenal capsules (one on top of each kidney). Later, physiological studies by others showed that the supra-renal capsules are glands, now known as adrenal glands and which produce a complex group of hormones. Addison's disease was the first to be correctly attributed to endocrine failure (i.e., disorder of the ductless glands of internal secretion).

ADRIAN, (Baron) Edgar Douglas
1889-1977

English neurophysiologist: showed frequency code in nerve transmission

Adrian began his research in physiology in Cambridge before World War I, but in 1914 he speedily qualified in medicine and tried to get to France. In fact he was kept in England working on war injuries, and his later work was a mixture of 'pure' research and applications to medical treatment.

In the 1920s he began his best-known work. Already, crude methods were available for detecting electrical activity in nerve fibres. Adrian used thermionic valve amplifiers to reliably record nerve impulses in a single nerve fibre, and to show that they do not change with the nature or strength of the stimulus, confirming his friend K. Lewis's work of 1905 on this 'all or none' law. He went on to show that a nerve transmits information to the brain on the intensity of a stimulus by frequency modulation, i.e., as the intensity rises, the number of discharges per second (perhaps 10-50) in the nerve also rises: a fundamental discovery. He then worked on the brain, using the discovery by *Berger* in 1924 that electrical 'brainwaves' can be detected.

From 1934 he studied these brainwave rhythms, which result from the discharge of thousands of neurons and which can be displayed as an electroencephalogram (EEG). Within a few years the method was widely used to diagnose epilepsy cases, and later to locate lesions, e.g., those due to tumours or injury.

Adrian was linked with Trinity College Cambridge for nearly 70 years and did much to advance neurophysiology. He was a very popular figure; as a student he was a skilful night roof-climber, an excellent fencer, and he sailed and rock-climbed until late in life. He helped to organize a famous hoax exhibition of modern pictures in 1913. He was never solemn, moved very quickly, and claimed his own brainwaves were as rapid as a

15

rabbit's; as a motorist his quick reflexes alarmed his passengers. When in a hurry he would use a bicycle in the long dark basement corridors of the Physiological Laboratory. He shared a Nobel Prize in 1932.

AGASSIZ, Jean Louis Rodolphe

1807-1873

Swiss-American naturalist and glaciologist: proposed former existence of Ice Age

Agassiz owed much of his scientific distinction to the chance of his birth in Switzerland. He studied medicine in Germany, but zoology was his keen interest. He studied under *Cuvier* in Paris, and then returned home and worked with enthusiasm on fossil fishes, becoming the world expert on them (his book describes over 1700 ancient species of fish).

Holidaying in his native Alps in 1836 and 1837, he formed the novel idea that glaciers are not static, but move. He found a hut on a glacier which had moved a mile over 12 years; he then drove a straight line of stakes across a glacier, and found they moved within a year. Finding rocks which had been moved or scoured, apparently by glaciers, he concluded that in the past, much of Northern Europe had been ice-covered. He postulated an 'Ice Age' in which major ice sheets had formed, moved, and were now absent in some areas; a form of catastrophism, in contrast to the extreme uniformitarianism of *Lyell*. We now know that a series of ice ages has occurred.

In 1846 Agassiz was invited to the US to lecture, enjoyed it, and stayed to work at Harvard. He found evidence of past glaciation in North America; it too had undergone an Ice Age. His studies on fossil animals could have been used to support *Darwin's* ideas on evolution, but in fact Agassiz was America's main opponent to Darwin's view that species had evolved.

AGRICOLA, Georgius

1494-1555

German mineralogist, geologist and metallurgist: described mining and metallurgical industries of 16th century

His name is the Latinized form of Georg Bauer (both surnames are 'farmer' in English). Born in Saxony, Agricola trained in medicine in Leipzig and in Italy. The link between medicine and minerals led to his interest in the latter, and his work as a physician in Saxony put him in ideal places to develop this interest, and to extend it to mining and metal extraction by smelting, and related chemical processes. His book *The Nature of Fossils* (1546) classifies minerals in perhaps the first comprehensive system. Later he wrote on the origin of rocks, mountains, and volcanoes. His best-known book, *On the Subject of Metals* (De re metallica, 1556) is a fine illustrated survey of the mining, smelting and chemical technology of the time. An English edition (1912) was prepared by the American mining engineer H. C. Hoover (who became President of the US, 1929-33) and his wife.

AIRY, (Sir) George Biddell

1801-1892

English geophysicist and astronomer: proposed model of isostasy to explain gravitational anomalies

Airy was successful early in life, his talent and energy leading to his appointment as Astronomer Royal in 1835, a post he held for 46 years. He much extended and improved the astronomical measurements made in Britain. Airy's researches were in the fields of both optics and geophysics. He experimented with cylindrical lenses to correct astigmatism (a condition he suffered from himself); and he studied the **Airy discs** in the diffraction pattern of a point source of light.

In geophysics he proposed that mountain ranges acted as blocks of differing thickness floating in hydrostatic equilibrium in a fluid mantle, rather like icebergs in the sea. He was thus able to explain gravitational anomalies that had been observed in the Himalayas, as due to the partial counteraction of the gravitational attraction of the topography above sea level with that of a deep 'root' extending into the mantle. The model of isostasy satisfactorily explains the gravity field observed over mountainous terrain in much of the world.

Airy was arrogant and unlucky in his failings, now almost better known than his successes. He failed to exploit *Adams*'s prediction of a new planet Neptune; he was against *Faraday*'s idea of 'lines of force' (a fruitful intuition, in fact): and although he expended great effort to ensure precise measurements of the transits of Venus, observed in 1874 and 1882, the results failed to give accurate measurements of the scale of the solar system because Venus's atmosphere makes the timing of its apparent contact with the Sun's disc uncertain.

ALFVÉN, Hannes Olof Gösta
1908-

Swedish theoretical physicist: pioneer of plasma physics

Hannes Alfvén

Educated at Uppsala, Alfvén worked in Sweden until 1967, when he moved to California. Much of his work was on plasmas (gases containing positive and negative ions) and their behaviour in magnetic and electric fields. In 1942 he predicted magnetohydrodynamic waves in plasmas (**Alfvén waves**) which were later observed. His ideas have been applied to plasmas in stars, and to experimental nuclear fusion reactors. He shared a Nobel Prize in 1970 for his pioneering theoretical work on magnetohydrodynamics.

ALHAZEN
c.965-1038

Egyptian physicist: made major advances in optics

Alhazen's major work was in optics. He rejected the older idea that light was emitted by the eye, and took the view that light was emitted from self-luminous sources, was reflected and refracted and perceived by the eye. His book *The Treasury of Optics* discusses lenses (including that of the eye), plane and curved mirrors, colours, and the camera obscura (pin-hole camera).

His career in Cairo was nearly disastrous. Born in Basra, he saw in Cairo the annual flooding of the Nile, and got the Caliph al-Hakim to sponsor an expedition to southern Egypt with the object of controlling the river and providing an irrigation scheme. Alhazen's expedition showed him only the difficulties, and on his return he realised that the Caliph would probably ensure an unpleasant death for him. To avoid this, he pretended to be mad, and maintained this successfully until the Caliph died in 1021. Alhazen then considered studying religion, before turning fully to physics in middle age. His mathematical and experimental approach is the high point of Islamic physics, and his work in optics was not surpassed for 500 years.

17

AL-KHWARIZMI
c.800-c.850

Persian mathematician: introduced modern number notation

Little is known of al-Khwarizmi's life; he was a member of the Baghdad academy of science, and wrote on mathematics, astronomy and geography. His book *Algebra* introduced that name, although much of the book deals with calculations. However, he gives a general method (**al-Khwarizmi's solution**) for finding the two roots of a quadratic equation $ax^2+bx+c=0$ (where $a\neq0$); he showed that the roots are $x_1=[-b+(b^2-4ac)^{1/2}]/2a$ and $x_2=[-b-(b^2-4ac)^{1/2}]/2a$

In his book *Calculation with the Hindu Numerals* he described the Hindu notation (misnamed 'Arabic' numerals) in which the digits depend on their position for their value, and include zero. The term 'algorithm' (a rule of calculation) is said to be named after him. The notation (which came into Europe in a Latin translation after 1240) is of huge practical value, and its adoption is one of the great steps in mathematics. The ten symbols (1 to 9 and 0) had almost their present shape by the 14th century, in surviving manuscripts.

ALPHER, Ralph Asher
1921-

American physicist: (with Robert Herman) predicted microwave background radiation; and synthesis of elements in early universe

A civilian physicist in World War II, Alpher afterwards worked in US universities and in industry. He is best known for his theoretical work concerning the origin and evolution of the universe. In 1948, Alpher, together with *Bethe* and *Gamow*, suggested for the first time the possibility of explaining the abundances of the chemical elements as the result of thermonuclear processes in the early stages of a hot, evolving universe. This work became known as the $\alpha\beta\gamma$ ('alpha, beta, gamma') theory. As further developed in a number

Ralph A. Alpher

of collaborative papers with R. Herman over the years, and in another important paper with Herman and J. W. Follin, Jr., this concept of cosmological element synthesis has become an integral part of the standard 'big bang' model of the universe, particularly as it explains the universal abundance of helium. The successful explanation of helium abundance is regarded as major evidence of the validity of the model. While this early work on forming the elements has been superseded by later detailed studies involving better nuclear reaction data, the ideas had a profound effect on later developments.

Again in 1948, Alpher and Herman suggested that if the universe began with a 'hot Big Bang', then the early universe was dominated by intense electromagnetic radiation, which would gradually have 'cooled' (or red-shifted) as the universe expanded, and today this radiation should be observed as having a spectral distribution characteristic of a black body at a temperature of about 5 K (based on then-current astronomical data). At that time radio astronomy was not thought capable of detecting such weak radiation. It was not until 1964 that *Penzias* and *R. W. Wilson* finally observed the background radiation. It was realised later that evidence for this radiation had been available in 1942 in the form of observed temperatures of certain interstellar molecules. The existence of this background radiation (current observed value 2.73 K), whose peak intensity is in the microwave region of the spectrum, is widely regarded as a major cosmological discovery, and as strong evidence for the validity of the 'big bang' model, a model to which Alpher, Gamow and Herman contributed the pioneering ideas.

ALTER, David

1807-1881

American physicist: contributed to spectral analysis

A physician and inventor as well as a physicist, Alter was one of the earliest investigators of the spectrum. In 1854 he showed that each element had its own spectrum, conclusively proved a few years later by *Bunsen* and *Kirchhoff* in their pioneer research on the *Fraunhofer* lines. He also forecast the use of the spectroscope in the domain of astronomy.

ALVAREZ, Luis Walter

1911-1988

American physicist: developed the bubble-chamber technique in particle physics

Alvarez was a student under *Compton* at Chicago, and then joined *Lawrence* at the University of California at Berkeley in 1936. He remained there, becoming professor of physics in 1945.

Alvarez was an unusually prolific and diverse physicist. He discovered the phenomenon of **orbital electron capture**, whereby an atomic nucleus 'captures' an orbiting electron, resulting in a nuclide with a lower proton number. In 1939, together with *Bloch* he made the first measurement of the magnetic moment of a neutron. During the Second World War

he worked on radar, developing such devices as microwave navigation beacons and radar landing approach systems for aircraft, and also worked on the American atomic bomb project. In 1947 he built the first proton linear accelerator, and later developed the liquid hydrogen bubble-chamber technique for detecting charged sub-atomic particles, which in turn led to a great increase in the number of known particles. For this he received the Nobel Prize for physics in 1968.

He was ingenious in the application of physics to a variety of problems. He used the X-ray component of natural cosmic radiation to show that Chephren's pyramid in Egypt had no undiscovered chambers within it; and he used physics applied to the Kennedy assassination evidence to confirm that only one killer was involved. With his son Walter, a geologist, he studied the problem of the catastrophe of 65 000 000 years ago which killed the dinosaurs and other fossil species; they concluded from tracer analysis that a probable cause was Earth's impact with an asteroid or comet, resulting in huge fires and/or screening of the Sun by dust. His interest in optical devices led him to found two companies; one to make variable focus spectacle lenses, devised by him to replace his bifocals; the other to make an optical stabilizer, which he invented to avoid shake in his cine camera and in binoculars. He was an engaging and popular personality.

AMICI, Giovan Battista

1786-1868

Italian microscopist: improved the compound microscope

Trained as an engineer and architect in Bologna, Amici became a teacher of mathematics but was soon invited to Florence to head the observatory and science museums there. His interest from his youth was in optical instruments, especially microscopes. At that time compound microscopes were inferior to simple types, partly because of aberrations and also because of the false idea that enlargement was the dominant target of design. Amici devised in 1818 a catadioptric (mirror) design which was free of chromatic aberration, and used it to observe the circulation of protoplasm in *Chara* cells; at once he became distinguished as an optician and as a biologist. By 1837 he had a design with a resolving power of 0.001 mm, a numerical aperture of 0.4 and able to magnify 6000 times. His objectives had up to six elements; and he invented the technique of immersion microscopy, using oil.

He also much improved telescopes, but his main interest remained in biology, where he made the notable discovery of the fertilization of phanerogams, observing in 1821 the travel of the pollen tube through the pistil of the flower.

AMONTONS, Guillaume
1663-1705

French physicist: discovered interdependence of temperature and pressure of gases

In his teens Amontons became deaf, and his interest in mechanics seems then to have begun. He later improved the design of several instruments, notably the hygrometer, the barometer, and the constant-volume air thermometer. In 1699 he discovered that equal changes in the temperature of a fixed volume of air resulted in equal variations in pressure, and in 1703 seemed near to suggesting that at a sufficiently low temperature the pressure would become zero. Unfortunately his results were ignored, and it was almost a century later before *Charles* rediscovered the relationship. His work on the thermal expansion of mercury, however, contributed to the invention of the mercury thermometer by *Fahrenheit*.

AMPÈRE, André Marie
1775-1836

French physicist and mathematician: pioneer of electrodynamics

Ampère was a very gifted child, combining a passion for reading with a photographic memory and linguistic and mathematical ability. He was largely self-taught. His life was disrupted by the French Revolution when, in 1793, his father, a Justice of the Peace, was guillotined, along with 1500 fellow citizens in Lyons. For a year Ampère seems to have suffered a state of shock; he was aged 18. Ten years later, his adored young wife died following the birth of his son. His second marriage, undertaken on the advice of friends, was a disaster. His professional life ran more smoothly.

In 1802 Ampère was appointed to the first of a series of professorships, and in 1808 was appointed Inspector-General of the university system by Napoleon, a post he retained until his death.

Ampère was a versatile scientist, interested in physics, philosophy, psychology and chemistry, and made discoveries in this last field that would have been important had he not been unfortunate in being pre-empted by others on several occasions. In 1820 he was stimulated by *Oersted*'s discovery, that an electric current generates a magnetic field, to carry out pioneering work on electric current and electrodynamics. Within months he had made a number of important discoveries: he showed that two parallel wires carrying currents flowing in the same direction attracted one another, whilst when the currents ran in opposite directions they were repelled; he invented the coiled wire solenoid; and he realised that the degree of deflection of Oersted's compass needle by a current could be used as a measure of the strength of the current, the basis of the galvanometer. Perhaps his most outstanding contribution, however, was in 1827, when he provided a mathematical formulation of electromagnetism, notably **Ampère's law**, which relates the magnetic force between two wires to the product of the currents flowing in them and the inverse square of the distance between them. It may be generalized to describe the magnetic force generated at any point in space by a current flowing along a conductor. The SI unit of electric current, the **ampere** (sometimes abbreviated to **amp**) is named in his honour. Its definition is: the ampere is that steady current which, when it is flowing in each of two infinitely long, straight, parallel conductors which have negligible areas of cross-section and are 1 metre apart in a vacuum, causes each conductor to exert a force of 2×10^{-7} N on each metre of the other.

ANAXIMANDER (of Miletus)

611-547 BC

Ionian (Greek) natural philosopher: suggested Earth was curved body in space

A pupil of *Thales*, Anaximander's writings are now lost, but he is credited with a variety of novel ideas. He was the first Greek to use a sundial (long known in the middle east), and with it found the dates of the two solstices (shortest and longest days) and of the equinoxes (the two annual occasions when day and night are equal). He speculated on the nature of the heavens and on the origin of the Earth and of man. Realizing that the Earth's surface was curved, he believed it to be cylindrical (with its axis east to west); and he was probably the first Greek to map the whole known world. He visualized the Earth as poised in space (a new idea).

ANDERSON, Carl David

1905-

American physicist: discovered the positron and the muon

Anderson, the only son of Swedish immi-grants, was educated in Los Angeles, and the California Institute of Technology, where he remained for the rest of his career.

Anderson discovered the positron accidentally in 1932 (its existence had been predicted by *Dirac* in 1928). As a result, Dirac's relativistic quantum mechanics and theory of the electron were rapidly accepted, and it became clear that other antiparticles existed. Anderson shared the 1936 Nobel Physics Prize with *V.F.Hess* for this discovery.

Anderson discovered the positron while studying cosmic rays, which he did by photographing their tracks in a cloud chamber in order to find the energy spectrum of secondary electrons produced by the rays. A lead plate divided the chamber so that the direction of movement of the particles could be deduced (they are slowed or stopped by the lead). Also, a magnetic field was applied to deflect particles in different directions according to their charge and by an amount related to their mass. Many positive particles were seen which were not protons; they were too light and produced too little ionization. Anderson identified their mass as about that of an electron, concluding that these were positive electrons, or positrons. The discovery was confirmed by *Blackett* and G. Occhialini the following year.

Anderson discovered another elementary particle within the same year, again by observing cosmic ray tracks. It had unit negative charge and was 130 times as heavy as an electron, and seemed a possible confirmation of *Yukawa*'s theory of a particle communicating the strong nuclear force (now called a pi-meson or pion). However a series of experiments by Anderson in 1935 revealed that it was not, and the role of this mu-meson (or muon), as it is now called, remained unclear. The true pi-meson was first found by *Powell* in 1947. Positrons and all types of meson are short-lived particles.

ANDERSON, Phillip Warren

1923-

American physicist: discovered aspects of the electronic structure of magnetic and disordered systems

Anderson studied at Harvard, doing doctoral research with *Van Vleck* and spending 1943-45 involved in antenna engineering at the Naval Research Laboratory. Anderson's career has been largely with Bell Telephone Laboratories, but he became professor of physics at Princeton in 1975, and he also held a visiting professorship at Cambridge, England (1967-75). Under Van Vleck, Anderson worked on pressure broadening of spectroscopic lines. In 1958 he published a paper on electronic states in disordered media, showing that electrons would be confined to regions of limited extent (**Anderson localization**) rather than be able to move freely. In 1959 he constructed a model explaining 'super-exchange', or the way in which two magnetic atoms may interact via an intervening atom. In 1961 he published important work on the microscopic origin of magnetism in materials. The **Anderson model** is a quantum mechanical model that describes localized states and their possible transition to freely mobile states. This model has been used widely to study magnetic impurities, superconducting transition temperatures and related problems. Also, during his work on superconductivity and superfluidity, Anderson worked on the possible superfluid states of ^{3}He. For these investigations of electronic properties of materials, particularly magnetic and disordered ones, Anderson shared the 1977 Nobel Prize for physics.

ANDREWS, Roy Chapman

1884-1960

American naturalist and palaeontologist

Andrews's career was mostly spent with the American Museum of Natural History, New York, and with its expeditions (especially to Asia) to collect specimens. His more dramatic finds included the fossil remains of the largest land mammal yet found, the *Paraceratherium*, a relative of the rhino which stood 5.5 m high at the shoulder; and the first fossil dinosaur eggs. He had a special interest in whales and other cetaceans (aquatic mammals) and built up a fine collection of them; and he found evidence of very early human life in central Asia.

ANDREWS, Thomas

1813-1885

Irish physical chemist: showed existence of critical temperature and pressure for fluids

The son of a merchant, Andrews studied chemistry and medicine in Scotland. In Paris he studied chemistry under *Dumas* and at Giessen he studied under *Liebig*. In Belfast he first practised medicine, and later became professor of chemistry. He proved that 'ozone' is an allotrope of oxygen (i.e., a different form of the element; ozone was later shown to be O_3; ordinary oxygen is O_2). He was a fine experimenter, and is best known for his work on the continuity of the liquid and gaseous states of matter (1869). Using carbon dioxide, he showed that above its 'critical temperature' (31°C) it cannot be liquefied by pressure alone. This example suggested that at a suitably low temperature, any gas could be liquefied, as was later demonstrated by *Cailletet*.

ANFINSEN, Christian Boehmer

1916-

American biochemist: made discoveries related to the shape and activity of enzymes

Educated at Swarthmore and Harvard, Anfinsen afterwards worked at Harvard and from 1950 at the National Institutes in Bethesda, Maryland. In 1960 *Moore and W. Stein* found the sequence of the 124 amino acids which make up ribonuclease, and it became the first enzyme for which

Nobel Prizewinners of 1972 who received honorary degrees at the University of Pennsylvania in 1973: *left to right*, Gerald M. Edelman, Martin Meyerson (President of the University), Christian Anfinsen and John Robert Schrieffer.

the full sequence was known. However, it was clear that enzymes owe their special catalytic ability not only to the sequence of amino acid units, but also to the specific shape adopted by the chain-like molecule. Anfinsen showed that if this shape is disturbed, then it can be restored merely by putting the molecule into the precise environment (of temperature, salt concentration, etc.,) favourable for it, when it spontaneously takes up the one shape (out of many possibilities) which restores its enzymic activity. He deduced that all the requirements for this precise three-dimensional assembly must be present in the chain sequence; and he showed that other proteins behaved similarly. He shared the Nobel Prize for chemistry with Moore and Stein in 1972.

ÅNGSTRÖM, Anders Jonas
1814-1874

Swedish spectroscopist: detected hydrogen in the Sun

Ångström was educated at Uppsala, and taught physics at the university there until his death. He was an early spectroscopist, and deduced in 1855 that a hot gas emits light at the same wavelengths at which it absorbs light when cooler; this was proved to be so in 1859 by *Kirchhoff*. From 1861 he studied the Sun's spectrum, concluding that hydrogen must be present in the Sun, and mapping about 1000 of the lines seen earlier by *Fraunhofer*. A non-SI unit of length, the Ångström (Å) is 10^{-10} m; it was used by him to record the wavelength of spectral lines.

APOLLONIUS (of Perga)
c.260-190 BC

Greek mathematician: wrote classic treatise on conic sections

Apollonius was a student in Alexandria and later taught there, specializing in geometry. Of his books, one survives, *On Conic Sections*. It deals with the curves formed by intersecting a plane through a double circular cone (see diagram). These are the circle, ellipse, parabola and hyperbola (the last three were named by Apollonius). Much of the book on the

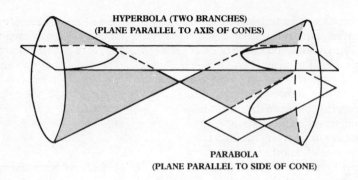

HYPERBOLA (TWO BRANCHES)
(PLANE PARALLEL TO AXIS OF CONES)

PARABOLA
(PLANE PARALLEL TO SIDE OF CONE)

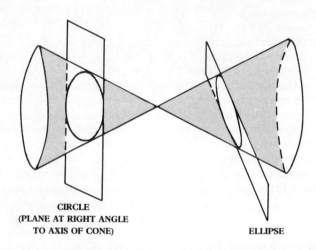

CIRCLE
(PLANE AT RIGHT ANGLE
TO AXIS OF CONE)

ELLIPSE

properties of conics is original; it represents the high point of Greek geometry, and although at the time the work appeared to have no uses, *Kepler* later found the planets moved in ellipses, and the curves now have many applications in ballistics, rocketry and engineering.

Apollonius was also interested in astronomy and especially in the Moon, and proposed a theory of epicycles to describe the sometimes apparently retrograde motions of the outer planets.

APPLETON, (Sir) Edward Victor
1892-1965

British physicist: pioneer of ionospheric physics; discovered reflective layers within the ionosphere

Appleton studied physics at Cambridge,

but it was service in World War I as a signals officer which led to his interest in radio. In 1924 he was appointed professor of experimental physics at King's College, London. In 1939 he was appointed secretary of the Department of Scientific and Industrial Research, and later became Vice-Chancellor of Edinburgh University.

In 1901 *Marconi* had transmitted radio signals across the Atlantic, to the astonishment of many in the scientific community who believed that since electromagnetic radiation travels in straight lines, and the Earth's surface is curved, this was not possible. Shortly afterward, A. E. Kennelly and *Heaviside* proposed a reflecting layer of charged particles in the atmosphere as the explanation. In a classic experiment in 1925, Appleton became the first to demonstrate beyond doubt the existence of such a reflecting layer within the ionosphere. He transmitted signals between Bournemouth and Cambridge (a distance of 170 km); and by slowly varying the frequency and studying the received signal, he showed that interference was occurring between the part of the signal which travelled in a straight line from transmitter to receiver (the direct, or ground, wave) and another part which was reflected by the ionosphere (the sky wave). Measurement of the interference, caused by the different path lengths, enabled him to measure the height of the reflecting layer, about 70 km. This was the first radio distance measurement. This layer is now known as the **Heaviside layer** or **E layer**. Further work revealed a second layer above the first, which is now called the **Appleton layer** or **F layer**. The E layer is more effective after dark, since the Sun's ultraviolet rays interact with the ionosphere, which is why distant radio stations are more readily picked up at night. For his achievements Appleton received the Nobel Prize for physics in 1947.

ARAGO, Dominique François Jean

1786-1853

French physicist

Beginning his career as a secretary at the Bureau de Longitudes, Arago went with *Biot* to Spain in 1806 to complete the geodetic measurements of an arc of the meridian. The return journey was eventful as the ship was wrecked and he was almost enslaved at Algiers. He made distinguished researches in many branches of physics, and in 1838 suggested a crucial experiment to decide between the particle and wave theories of light, by measuring its speed in air and in water. The experiment was tried by *Foucault* in 1850 and pointed to the wave theory.

Arago was the first to discover that other substances than iron have magnetic properties. He worked on the velocity of sound from 1818 to 1822. He also discovered the production of magnetism by electricity: a piece of iron, surrounded by a coil of wire, was briefly magnetized by passing a current from either a capacitor or a voltaic cell through the coil.

ARCHIMEDES (of Syracuse)

c.287-212 BC

Sicilian Greek mathematician and physicist: pioneer of statics and hydrostatics

A member of a wealthy noble family, Archimedes studied in Alexandria but returned to Syracuse in Sicily, whose King Hieron II was a relative. Archimedes was the finest scientist and mathematician of the ancient world, but little is firmly known of his life, although legends exist. He is known to have used experiments to test his theories, which he then expressed mathematically. He devised weapons against the Roman fleet when it attacked Syracuse in 215 BC; the Romans took the city in 212 BC and Archimedes was killed. Cicero found and restored his tomb in 75 BC.

In mathematics, Archimedes used geometrical methods to measure curves and the areas and volumes of solids (e.g. the volume of a sphere, $4\pi r^3/3$); he used a close approximation for π (he showed it to be between 223/71 and 220/70) and developed his results without the use of the calculus (which came nearly 2000 years later). He used a new notation to deal with very large numbers, described in his book *Sand-Reckoner*.

In applied mathematics, he created mechanics; his innovations ranged from the directly practical (e.g. the compound pulley and the Archimedian screw) to derivations of the theory of levers and centres of gravity, forming the basic ideas of statics. He founded hydrostatics, contributing ideas which included specific gravity, and the **Archimedes principle**: this states that when a body is wholly or partly immersed in a fluid, it experiences a buoyant force (upthrust) which shows itself as an apparent loss of weight, equal to the weight of fluid displaced. (The fluid can be liquid or gas).

Gauss thought that Archimedes had only *Newton* as a mathematical equal.

ARISTARCHUS (of Samos)

c.320-c.250 BC

Greek astronomer: proposed heliocentric cosmology, and made first estimate of astronomical distances

Although little is known of the life of Aristarchus, he was perhaps the first to propose that the Earth moved around the Sun, in contrast to the accepted thinking of his day. He also attempted to estimate the relative distances of the Sun and the Moon, utilizing the fact that when the Moon is exactly half light and half dark it forms a right angle with the Earth and the Sun. Although his result was wildly inaccurate, it was the first experimental attempt at measuring an astronomical distance. His work makes him the most original of the Greek astronomers, and in the modern view the most successful. His heliocentric scheme was made precise by *Copernicus* in the 16th century.

ARISTOTLE

384-322 BC

Athenian (Greek) philosopher and naturalist: provided philosophical basis of science which proved dominant for 18 centuries

Son of the court physician at Macedon, Aristotle was orphaned early and moved to Athens, where he became Plato's finest pupil. In 342 BC he returned to Macedon as tutor and then adviser to Philip II's son Alexander, who became Alexander the Great. Later he became a public teacher in Athens, using a garden he owned (the Lyceum). His collected lectures cover most of the knowledge of the time in science, and some other fields such as logic and ethics (but not mathematics), and include much of Aristotle's own work in zoology and anatomy. He was a first-class naturalist and marine biologist; whereas his record of older views in physics and cosmology contained many misguided, although defensible, ideas. Aristotle's books survived in the Arab world, and re-entered Christian Europe in Latin translation in the 12th and 13th centuries. It was no fault of the writer that his books were accorded almost divine authority, and some of the erroneous ideas were not easily displaced (e.g., that bodies 'outside the sphere of the Moon' are perfect and unchanging). His status as a major figure in philosophy has never changed.

ARRHENIUS, Svante August

1859-1927

Swedish physical chemist: proposed theory of ionic dissociation

Arrhenius came from a family of farmers, and his father was an estate manager and surveyor. He attended Uppsala University and did very well in physical science, and then moved to Stockholm to work for a higher degree on aqueous solutions of electrolytes (acids, bases and salts); he concluded that such solutions conduct a current because the electrolyte exists in the form of charged atoms or groups of atoms (positive cations, and negative anions) which move through the solution when a current is applied. He obtained good evidence for this during the 1880s but his theory was only slowly accepted, especially in Sweden. (Since then, further evidence has substantially confirmed his views, and has also shown that salts are largely ionic even in the solid state.) In 1903 he was awarded the Nobel Prize for chemistry. His work was surprisingly varied, and included immunology, cosmic physics, and the first recognition of the **'greenhouse effect'** (heat gain by the atmosphere due to carbon dioxide). He also studied the effect of temperature on the rates of chemical reactions, and showed that

$$k = A \exp(-E/RT)$$

where k is the rate constant for the reaction, A is the frequency factor, E is the activation energy for the reaction, R is the gas constant, and T the Kelvin temperature (this is the **Arrhenius equation**).

ASTON, Francis William
1877-1945

English chemical physicist: invented mass spectrograph

After graduating in chemistry in Birmingham, Aston worked for three years as a chemist in a nearby brewery. In his leisure at home he designed and made an improved vacuum pump, and in 1903 he turned to physics as a career, working on discharge tubes in Birmingham, and from 1909 in Cambridge as *J.J. Thomson*'s assistant. They worked on the 'positive rays' which Thomson had found to be generated within one part of a vacuum tube through which an electric discharge is passed. Aston and Thomson believed that their experiments on positive rays from tubes containing neon gas showed it to contain atoms with masses of about 20 and 22 units. Proof of this, and extension of the work, was interrupted by World War I.

Aston's war work at the Royal Aircraft Establishment linked him with a talented group of physicists, including F. A. Lindemann, G. I. Taylor, *E. D. Adrian*, H. Glauert, and *G. P. Thomson*. Soon after the war he devised a mass spectrograph which was able to separate atoms of similar mass, and measure these masses accurately (his third spectrograph to 1 in 10^5; now, 1 in 10^9 is easily available on commercial machines). Aston showed clearly that over 50 elements consisted of atoms of similar but different relative atomic mass (e.g., for S; 32, 33 and 34)

but the same atomic number (i.e., nuclear charge). The **Aston rule** is that the masses are approximately integers; the apparent deviations of relative atomic masses of the elements from integers results from the presence of isotopes.

Aston found that isotopic masses are not exactly integral (by about 1 per cent) and he related the discrepancy (the '**packing fraction**') to the force binding the nucleus together. Atomic energy generation from nuclear reactions, on Earth or in the stars, can be calculated from packing fractions.

The modern mass spectrograph has played a central part in nuclear physics and radiochemistry, and more recently in exact analysis in organic chemistry. Aston was a 'one device' investigator, but he chose a device whose value has been immense.

He was a shy man, a poor teacher, with a passion for sports and for sea travel. He won the Nobel Prize for chemistry for 1922.

AUER, Carl (Baron von Welsbach)
1858-1929

Austrian chemist: invented the gas mantle

Auer studied at Vienna Polytechnic and at Heidelberg, the latter under *Bunsen*.

In 1885 Auer succeeded in showing that the lanthanide 'element' didymium was actually a mixture of two new elements, praseodymium and neodymium. He is perhaps better known, however, as the inventor of the gas mantle, a fabric net impregnated with thorium oxide and cerium which glows incandescent when heated in a gas flame. Hitherto, the gas lighting had relied on the luminescence of the flame itself. Unfortunately, the invention of electric lighting had made his invention largely redundant within a few years. Following an unsuccessful attempt to improve *Edison*'s bulb with an osmium filament, he later found another use for cerium, as an alloy with iron as the 'flint' of gas lighters.

AUGER, Pierre Victor

1899-

French physicist: discovered the Auger effect

Auger was educated at the École Normale Supérieure, and subsequently became professor of physics at the University of Paris. After World War II he held a succession of posts in French and European science administration, and was director general of the European Space and Research Organisation at his retirement.

Auger is remembered for his discovery in 1925 of the **Auger effect**, in which an atom absorbs energy in the form of an X-ray photon, and loses it by emitting an electron. **Auger spectroscopy** utilizes the effect to yield information about the electronic structure of atoms, particularly if they form part of a crystal.

AVERY, Oswald (Theodore)

1877-1955

American bacteriologist: showed that genetic material of bacterial chromosomes is DNA

Born in Canada, Avery went to New York when he was ten and remained there for his working life; he qualified in medicine at Columbia in 1904, and from 1913 researched in bacteriology at the Rockefeller Institute Hospital. His special interest was pneumococci (the bacteria causing pneumonia). In 1928 he was intrigued by the claim of the British microbiologist F. Griffith that a non-virulent, 'rough' (i.e., unencapsulated) pneumococcus could be transformed into the virulent smooth (capsulated) form in the mouse, by the mere presence of some of the dead (heat-killed) smooth bacteria.

Avery found this so strange that he repeated the work, and also showed in 1944 that the substance which caused the transformation is deoxyribonucleic acid (DNA). Prudently, he did not go on to surmise that genes are simply DNA, which was surprising enough to be accepted only slowly after 1950 and formed the basic idea of molecular biology.

AVOGADRO, (Lorenzo Romano) Amedio (Carlo)

1776-1856

Italian physicist: proposed a method for finding molecular formulae of gases

Trained in law like his forefathers and working as a lawyer for some time, after 1800 he turned to science and held professorships in physics for much of his life. His fame now rests on one brilliant and important idea. He considered *Gay-Lussac's* law of combining volumes and with little evidence offered a daring explanation for it in 1811. His idea, **Avogadro's law**, was that 'equal volumes of all gases, under the same conditions of temperature and pressure, contain the same number of smallest particles'. There is now ample evidence that he was right; in some cases (e.g., the noble gases) the smallest particles are atoms; for most other gases, they are combinations of atoms (molecules). The law gives a direct method of finding the molecular formula of a gas, and such a formula in turn gives the relative atomic masses of the elements present in it. Avogadro's law shows that the simple gases hydrogen and oxygen are diatomic (H_2 and O_2) and that water is H_2 (and not HO as *Dalton* believed). However, the law was largely rejected or ignored for 50 years (although *Ampère* accepted it) until *Cannizzarro* in 1860 convinced a Chemical Congress at Karlsruhe of its value.

The SI base unit of amount of substance is the **mole** (which is related to Avogadro's law). The mole is defined as containing as many elementary entities (usually atoms or molecules, and specified for each case) as there are atoms in 0.012 kg of carbon-12. Thus for a compound, 1 mole has a mass equal to its relative molecular mass in grams. The number of entities in a mole, the **Avogadro constant**, N_A, is 6.022×10^{23} mol^{-1}; and 1 mole of any ideal gas, at STP., (standard temperature and pressure) has a molar volume of 22.415 dm^3.

For example: since the relative atomic masses ('atomic weights') of carbon and oxygen are 12 and 16 respectively, a mole of carbon dioxide (CO_2) will weigh $12+(2\times16)=44$ g, and will have a volume at STP close to 22.4 dm^3.

B

BAADE, Wilhelm Heinrich Walter
1893-1960

German-American astronomer: classified stars into different population types; his work gave larger estimates for the size and the age of the universe

Educated in Germany at Göttingen, he was on the staff of the University of Hamburg for 11 years before moving to the US in 1931.

Baade spent World War II at the Mount Wilson and Palomar Observatories studying the Andromeda galaxy (as a German immigrant he was excluded from military service). He used the 100 inch telescope and had the advantage of the wartime blackout of Los Angeles, which cleared the night sky. He identified two fundamentally distinct classes of stars in the galaxy—hot young blue stars in the spiral arms of the galaxy, which he called Population I stars, and older redder stars in the central region, which he called Population II. This distinction was to prove fundamental to theories of galactic evolution.

He showed that Cepheid variable stars found in Andromeda, whose period/luminosity relationship had been discovered 30 years earlier by *Leavitt* and quantified by *Shapley* as a means of calculating their distance, could also be divided into the two categories. In 1952 he demonstrated that Leavitt and Shapley's period/luminosity relationship was only valid for Population I Cepheids, and calculated a new relationship for Population II Cepheids. *Hubble*, in the 1920s, had used the Cepheid variable technique to calculate the distance of the Andromeda galaxy as 800 000 light years, from which he estimated the age of the

universe to be two billion years. However, Hubble's estimate proved to have depended upon Population II Cepheids, for which the original period/luminosity relationship was invalid; using his new relationship Baade showed that Andromeda was more than 2000 000 light years away and that the universe was therefore at least five billion years old. (This revised time scale came as a relief to geologists, who had estimated the age of the Earth as three to four billion years or more.)

Baade also discovered two asteroids, Hidalgo and Icarus, which strangely are those with (respectively) orbits which take them farthest and nearest to the Sun of all known asteroids. He also worked on supernovae and the optical identification of radio sources.

BABBAGE, Charles
1792-1871

British mathematician and computer scientist: inventor of the programmable computer

Babbage graduated from the University of Cambridge in 1814, becoming professor of mathematics there in 1828. Although doing much useful work on the theory of functions and algebra, his primary interest was in developing a calculating machine that could produce and print mathematical tables without error. He completed his first attempt at this in 1833, a 'difference engine' which was used to compile tables of logarithms from 1 to 108 000.

He then turned his attention to designing an 'analytical engine' that was to be capable of executing any sequence of arithmetic instructions. Although never finished, many of the basic principles of modern computers, in particular the use of a 'program' input by punched cards to specify the sequence of instructions, and a memory to hold the results, owe their origins to this machine. Babbage was assisted in this work by Lady Ada Lovelace (daughter of Lord Byron, the poet), who spent much time publicizing his ideas and designing programs for the hypothetical machine (the US Defense Department programming language ADA is named after her). When government funding ceased, the two of them spent a great deal of time trying to invent an infallible system for predicting winners of horse races, and lost a great deal of money in the process.

BABCOCK, Horace Welcome
1912-

American astronomer: made first measurements of stellar magnetic fields

Horace Babcock is the son of Harold Delos Babcock, also an astronomer, in collaboration with whom his most profit-

Horace W. Babcock in 1954

able work was done. Both worked at the Mount Wilson Observatory, Horace as Director from 1964 to 1978. It had been known since 1896 that some spectral lines are 'split' in the presence of strong magnetic fields (the *Zeeman effect*), and in 1908 *Hale* had shown that light from sunspots is split in this way, and that magnetic fields of up to 0.4 tesla in strength must be present in sunspots. A generalized solar magnetic field could not, however, be detected at that time.

In 1948 the Babcocks developed equipment for measuring the Zeeman splitting of spectral lines far more precisely than had hitherto been possible. This allowed them to detect the Sun's magnetic field, which is about 10^{-4} T in strength. They discovered that the Sun's magnetic poles periodically flipped polarity, and went on to measure the magnetic fields of many other stars. Some of these were found to be 'magnetic variables', their field strength varying by several teslas over periods as short as a few days.

BACKUS, John
1924-

American computer scientist: developed first high-level computer language

Born in Philadelphia and educated at Columbia, Backus has been closely associated with IBM for much of his career.

World War II gave a great stimulus to the development of electronic computers, but until the early 1950s they still had to be programmed in a very basic fashion. Backus demonstrated the feasibility of high-level computer languages, in which a problem could be expressed in a readily understandable form, which was then converted into the basic instructions required by the computer via a 'compiler'. In 1954 he published the first version of FORTRAN (FORmula TRANslator), and by 1957 it was commercially available for use on IBM computers. High-level languages have greatly aided the use of

31

John Backus

almost mechanically; Bacon was antagonistic to imaginative speculation. His ideas were certainly influential in science and probably even more in philosophy. His personality was unattractive and his writings abstruse, but his confidence that nature could be understood and even controlled was important, and as a critic and a prophet his role in the scientific development of the following centuries is significant. His own direct scientific work was limited; the best example being his conclusion on the nature of heat, which by argument and thought-experiments he decided was 'an expansive motion restrained, and striving to exert itself in the smaller particles'.

computers in solving scientific problems, and FORTRAN itself remains the most widely used scientific programming language.

BACON, Francis (Baron Verulam, Viscount St Albans)

1561-1626

English statesman and natural philosopher: advocate of inductive method in science

Son of a statesman and courtier, Bacon was trained in law to follow the same path; with much effort and little scruple, he succeeded and held office under James I, finally becoming Lord High Chancellor in 1618. Convicted of taking bribes, he was banished from Court and office in 1621.

His views of scientific method were influential, and were expressed in a series of books and essays. He criticized *Aristotle* and the deductive method, and advocated 'induction', in which emphasis is on the exhaustive collection of scientific data (with careful choice and the exclusion of extraneous items) until general causes and conclusions emerge,

BACON, Roger

c.1214-1292

English philosopher and alchemist: supporter of the experimental method in science

Probably a member of a wealthy family, Bacon studied at Oxford under Grosseteste and in Paris, and joined the Franciscan Order as a monk about 1247. He was not himself an experimentalist nor a mathematician (although he did some work in optics), but he saw that these two approaches were needed for science to develop; and he foresaw a control of nature by man, as his namesake *Francis Bacon* was also to foresee 350 years later. He made imprecise predictions on mechanical transport on land, above and below the surface of the sea, and in the air; on circumnavigation of the globe, and robots. He had a wide knowledge of the science of the time, together with alchemy, and was thought to have magic powers. He knew of gunpowder, but did not invent it. He saw theology as the supreme area of knowledge, but his difficult personality led to conflict with his colleagues. Among 13th century thinkers, his attitude to science is nearest to that of the present day.

BAEKELAND, Leo Hendrik

1863-1944

Belgian-American industrial chemist: intro-duced Bakelite, the first widely used synthetic plastic

Baekeland became an academic chemist in his native Ghent, but a honeymoon visit to the US led him to settle there from 1889, working as an independent consultant. From 1893 he made 'Velox' photographic paper, but sold out to Kodak in 1899. A few years later he studied the already-known reaction of phenol C_6H_5OH with methanal, H.CHO. Under suitable condi-tions the dark solid product is a ther-mosetting resin, rigid and insoluble. Baekeland manufactured it from 1909, and mixed with fillers as 'Bakelite', it has been much used for moulded electric fittings. It is now known to be a highly cross-linked three-dimensional polymer of high relative molecular mass, consist-ing largely of benzenoid rings linked by methylene (-CH_2-) groups at their 1-, 3-, and 5- positions.

BAER, Karl Ernst von

1792-1876

Estonian embryologist: discoverer of the mammalian ovum

Baer's wealthy family was of German descent, so it was natural for him to study in Germany after graduating in medicine at Dorpat in Estonia. He taught at Königsberg in Germany from 1817 to 1834, when he moved to St Petersburg (now Leningrad). His best-known dis-coveries, however, were made in Königs-berg. There, in 1826, he studied the small follicles discovered in the mammalian ovary by R. de Graaf in 1673, and named after him; they had often been assumed to be mammalian eggs. Baer showed that the Graafian follicle of a friend's bitch con-tained a microscopic yellow structure which was the egg (ovum). He identified structures within the embryo (the ferti-lized and developing egg), including the notochord, a gelatinous cord which devel-ops into the backbone and skull in the vertebrates, and he found the neural folds (which later form the central nervous system). In 1817 C. H. Pander had noted three layers of cells in the vertebrate embryo, which were to be named by *Remak* in 1845 as ectoderm (outer skin), mesoderm (middle skin) and endoderm (inner skin). These 'germ layers' each develop into specialized organs later (e.g., the mesoderm forms muscles and bones); Baer emphasized that the embryos of various species are at first very similar, and may not be distinguishable; and that as it develops, the embryo of a higher animal passes through stages which resemble stages in the development of lower animals. This idea was later to be fruitful in embryology and in evolution theory.

Baer led expeditions to Arctic Russia to collect plant and animal specimens, stu-died fishes, and collected human skulls (in 1859 he suggested that human skulls might have a common ancestral type, but he never supported *Darwin*'s ideas). His fame rests on his position as a founder of modern embryology.

BAEYER, Adolf von

1835-1917

German organic chemist: master of classical organic synthesis

Baeyer's life spanned a period of rapid change in science and technology; from *Faraday's* laws of electrolysis to X-ray crystallography, and from the first rail services to regular air transport. His father was a Prussian soldier who became a General. The boy was a keen chemical experimenter; which prompted a poet visiting the family to write a verse on the dreadful smells he caused. When Baeyer was twelve he made his first new sub-stance, the beautiful blue crystalline car-bonate $CuNa_2(CO_3)_2.3H_2O$; and he cele-brated his 13th birthday by buying a lump of the bronze-purple dye, indigo.

After his military service in 1856 he went to study chemistry in Germany's best-known laboratory, that of *Bunsen* in Heidelberg. However his interest soon focused on the organic side, which Bunsen had given up, and so he joined *Kekulé* as his first research student. His first independent work was done during twelve years spent teaching organic chemistry in a small Berlin technical college. He moved from there to Strasbourg and then to Munich, working there for 40 years.

Baeyer was a hugely talented organic chemist, with an instinctive feel for structures and reactions. He was an experimenter who saw theory as a tool which was easily expendable after use: he wrote 'I have never planned my experiments to find out if I was right, but to see how the compounds behave'. His preference was for simple equipment, mainly test-tubes and glass rods; he was suspicious even of mechanical stirrers. He had no superior as an organic chemist in his Munich period, and all the best men in the field worked with him.

His successes included the structure and synthesis of indigo. His work on the purine group began with studies on uric acid, and included the synthesis of the useful drugs, the barbiturates (named, he said, after a lady friend named Barbara). Other work dealt with hydrobenzenes, with terpenes, and with the sensitively explosive polyalkynes. It was in connection with the latter that he devised his **strain theory** to account for the relative stabilities of carbocyclic rings, which in modified form is still accepted. Absent-minded and genial, he was very popular with his students. He won the Nobel Prize in 1905.

BAILY, Francis

1774-1844

English astronomer: discovered Baily's beads

Baily was a stockbroker and amateur astronomer. He observed the phenomenon known as **Baily's beads** seen during total solar eclipses where, for a few seconds just before and after totality, brilliant beads of light are seen around the edge of the Moon. These are caused by the Moon's irregular surface allowing rays of sunlight to shine fleetingly down suitably aligned lunar valleys. Baily observed the effect during the solar eclipse of 1836.

BAIRD, John Logie

1888-1946

Scottish electrical engineer: television pioneer

Son of a Presbyterian minister, Baird was educated in Glasgow, almost completing a course in electrical engineering. His poor health made a career difficult, and several ventures failed, including making and selling foods, boot-polish and soap. After a serious illness in 1922 he devoted himself to experimentation and developed a crude TV apparatus, able to transmit a picture and receive it over a range of a few feet. The first real demonstration was within two attic rooms in Soho in early 1926. In the following year he transmitted pictures by telephone line from London to Glasgow, and in 1928 from London to New York. In 1929 his company gave the first BBC TV transmissions, soon achieving daily half-hour programmes with synchronized sound and vision. He used a mechanical scanning system, with 240 lines by 1936, but then the BBC opted to use the Marconi-EMI electronic scanning system, with 405 lines. Baird also pioneered colour, stereoscopic and big screen TV, and ultra-short-wave transmission. Television has no single inventor, but to Baird is due its first commercial success, although his methods have largely been replaced.

BALMER, Johann Jakob

1825-1898

Swiss mathematician: discovered relationship between hydrogen spectral lines

Son of a farmer, Balmer studied in Germany and, from 1850, taught in a girls school in Basle. Rather late in life he became interested in spectra, and reported his first research when aged 60. The lines in the Sun's spectrum had earlier seemed to be randomly scattered, but *Kirchhoff* had shown that if the spectrum of an individual element was considered, this was not so; for example, the spectrum of hydrogen consists of lines which converge with diminishing wavelength, λ. Balmer found in 1884 that one set of the hydrogen lines fitted the relation $\lambda = A\ m^2/(m^2-4)$ where m has integral values 3, 4, 5 ... for successive lines, and A is a constant. This is the **Balmer series**; originally empirical, it pointed to the need to find an explanation for the data, which led through *Rydberg*'s work to *Bohr*'s theory and to quantum theory.

BALTIMORE, David
1938-

American molecular biologist: discovered reverse transcriptase enzyme

Baltimore studied chemistry at Swarthmore and later at the Massachusetts Institute of Technology and Rockefeller University; in 1972 he became professor of biology at MIT, and later director of the Whitehead Institute at Cambridge, Massachusetts. In 1968 Baltimore showed how the polio virus replicates, with some detail on how its RNA core and protein coat are formed. In 1970 he announced his discovery of the enzyme 'reverse transcriptase' which can transcribe RNA into DNA, and does so in some tumour viruses. This was a novel finding; the 'central dogma' of molecular biology, due to *Crick*, is the scheme: DNA→RNA-→protein, in which the first arrow is designated transcription, and the second translation. Before Baltimore's work it had been assumed that the converse of transcription did not occur. Baltimore shared a Nobel Prize in 1975 with H. Temin who had independently discovered the same enzyme.

BANKS, (Sir) Joseph
1743-1820

English naturalist and statesman of science

Educated at Harrow, Eton and Oxford, Banks was wealthy and able to indulge his interest in science; he was a passionate and skilful botanist, and this took him on several major expeditions, at his own expense. The best known of these began in 1768; young Banks had learned that *Cook* was to sail to the south Pacific to observe the transit of Venus in 1769, and realized this would be a great opportunity to see entirely new plants and animals. He joined the expedition, which lasted three years, with his staff of eight, and returned with a large collection of new specimens to find himself a celebrity. The voyage was the first to be organised and equipped for biological work, even though the Government's secret plan was political—to secure a territorial advantage over the French. Banks brought back 1300 new plant species, as well as the idea that Botany Bay would form a suitable penal settlement.

He became President of the Royal Society in 1778 and held the post for 42 years, as the dominant personality in

David Baltimore about 1974

British science. His successes included the introduction of the tea plant in India (from China) and breadfruit in the Caribbean (after a frustrated first attempt in which HMS *Bounty*, carrying the breadfruit, was diverted by a mutiny). Banks did much to establish the Botanic Garden at Kew, which he planned as a major collecting centre and source of advice on all aspects of plants.

BANTING, (Sir) Frederick
1891-1941

Canadian physiologist: co-discoverer of insulin

Banting studied in Toronto for the church, but after a year changed to medicine, and after graduation in 1916 he joined the Canadian Army Medical Corps, winning an MC for gallantry in action in 1918. After the war he set up a practice in London, Ontario, and also worked part-time in the physiology department of the university at London.

Diabetes mellitus is a disease in which glucose appears copiously in the blood and urine, disturbing the metabolism. It is not curable, and until Banting's work it was always fatal. It was known that the disease is linked to failure of the pancreas, and probably to the cells in it known as the islets of Langerhans. In 1921 Banting devised a possible method for obtaining from these islets the unknown hormone which was suspected of controlling glucose levels, and whose absence would cause the disease. J. J. R. Macleod, professor of physiology at Toronto, gave him the use of a university laboratory, experimental dogs, and a recently qualified assistant, C. H. Best, to try the method while Macleod himself went on holiday. In 1922, after eight months' work, they announced their success. Extracts of a hormone (insulin) were obtained, and with the help of a chemist, J. B. Collip, these extracts were purified sufficiently to inject and treat diabetic patients. The effect was dramatic, and since 1923 millions of diabetics have led manageable lives using insulin to control their glucose levels. Industrial production of insulin (from pig pancreas) began in 1923.

In 1923 a Nobel Prize was awarded to Banting and to Macleod. Banting was furious at the omission of Best and shared his half-prize with him; Macleod shared his with Collip. Banting became a professor at Toronto. When World War II began he joined an army medical unit and researched on war gases, but was killed in an air crash in Newfoundland. In 1926 insulin was isolated in pure form, but it was a generation later before *Sanger* deduced its chemical structure, and 1966 before it was made by synthesis; it is a protein molecule, built of 51 amino acid units.

BARDEEN, John
1908-

American physicist: co-inventor of the transistor and contributor to the BCS theory of superconductivity

Bardeen comes from an academic family, and studied electrical engineering at the University of Wisconsin. He worked as a geophysicist for three years at the Gulf Research Laboratories, before obtaining a PhD in mathematical physics at Harvard under *Wigner* in 1936. Following periods at the University of Minnesota and the Naval Ordnance Laboratory, Bardeen joined a new solid state physics group at Bell Telephone Laboratories at the end of the Second World War. His major creative work then began, and continued after his move from Bell to a professorship at the University of Illinois in 1951. Bardeen together with *Brattain* and *Shockley* received the Nobel Prize for physics in 1956, for the development of the point-contact transistor (1947). He won the Nobel Prize again in 1972, shared with *Cooper* and *Schrieffer*, for the first satisfactory theory of superconductivity

John Bardeen in 1972

(1957), now called the **BCS theory**. Bardeen thereby became the first man to receive the Nobel Physics prize twice.

Superconductivity was discovered in 1911 by *Kamerlingh-Onnes*. A metal brought into this state by low temperature (< 15 K) expels magnetic field and will maintain electric currents virtually indefinitely (it shows zero resistance). Work in 1950 had revealed that the critical temperature is inversely proportional to the atomic mass of the metal, and Bardeen inferred that the oscillations of the metal lattice must be interacting with the metal conduction electrons. Cooper (1956) at the University of Illinois showed that electrons can weakly attract one another by distorting the metal lattice around them, forming a bound pair of electrons (Cooper pair) at low temperature when thermal vibrations are much reduced. Bardeen, Cooper and Schrieffer then assumed that a co-operative state of many pairs formed, and that these pairs carried the superconducting current. The members of a pair have a common momentum, and the scattering of one electron by a lattice atom does not change the total momentum of the pair so that the flow of electrons continues indefinitely.

The BCS theory not only greatly revived interest in superconductivity, but showed how quantum effects can give rise to unusual phenomena even on a macroscopic scale.

BARKHAUSEN, Heinrich Georg
1881-1956

German physicist: developed early microwave components

Barkhausen moved from his studies at Bremen and Göttingen to Dresden, where he became professor of electrical engineering. His early research established the theory of the amplifier valve (1911), and he went on to discover the **Barkhausen effect** (1919). This is the discontinuous way in which the magnetization of a piece of ferromagnetic material rises under an increasing applied field. It occurs because a ferromagnet is made up of many magnetic domains, and these change direction or size in a sudden manner.

His work on ultra high frequency oscillators and early microwave components was done in 1920 with K. Kurz, and was rapidly developed for military radar during World War II.

BARNARD, Edward Emerson
1857-1923

American astronomer: discovered Amalthea and Barnard's star

Despite a background of poverty and poor schooling, Barnard became a professional astronomer with great skill as an observer; he discovered a variety of interesting celestial objects. By the time he was 30 he had found more than ten comets, and in 1892 he discovered Amalthea, the first new satellite of Jupiter to be discovered for nearly three centuries. In 1916 he discovered the star with the largest proper motion, a red star six light-years away which moves across the sky at 10.3 seconds of arc per year, and which is now known as **Barnard's star**. With M. Wolf, he showed that 'dark nebulae' were clouds of dust and gas.

BARR, Murray Llewellyn

1908-

Canadian geneticist

Working in 1949 with a research student in the medical school at London, Ontario, Barr found that a characteristic small mass of chromatin can be detected in the nuclei of the nerve cells of most female mammals, but it is absent in the males. So this **'Barr body'** provides the marker in a simple test for the sex of an individual; previously sex could be detected at cell level only by examining chromosomes in dividing cells. It allows the sex of a foetus to be found long before birth, which is valuable if a parent carries a sex-linked genetic disorder. Barr also devised methods using a smear of cells from a patient's mouth, to locate chromosomal defects such as certain types of hermaphroditism.

BARTHOLIN, Erasmus

1625-1698

Danish mathematician: discovered double refraction of light

Bartholin qualified in medicine in Leiden and Padua (his father and brother were both distinguished anatomists) and he taught medicine and mathematics at Copenhagen from 1656. His pupils included *Roemer*, and Prince George who married the English Queen Anne. In 1669 he described in a book his study of the crystals of Iceland spar (a form of calcite, $CaCO_3$) including his discovery that it produces a double image of objects observed through it. He realized that the crystals split a light ray into two rays by what he called ordinary and extraordinary refraction. He gave no theory of this double refraction, which much puzzled other physicists; *Huygens* argued that the effect supported the wave theory of light, rather than *Newton*'s idea that light consisted of particles. In the early 19th century, work by E. Malus and *Fresnel* on polarized light made double refraction easier to understand.

BARTLETT, Neil

1932-

English-American inorganic chemist: prepared first noble gas compounds

Bartlett studied in Newcastle upon Tyne and later worked in Canada and the US. Although it had been previously accepted that the noble gases were not chemically reactive (the valence theory of chemical bonding being in accord with this), Bartlett used platinum hexafluoride PtF_6, a highly reactive compound, to prepare xenon hexafluoroplatinate $Xe^+[PtF_6]^-$

Neil Bartlett

(he had shown in 1961 that blood-red PtF_6 combined with oxygen to give a red salt $O_2{}^+PtF_6{}^-$). Since 1962 many other compounds, mainly of krypton and xenon, have been made using the noble gases.

BARTON, (Sir) Derek (Harold Richard)

1918-

English organic chemist: distinguished for work on stereochemistry and organic natural products

Educated at Imperial College, London, Barton returned there as professor for over 20 years and in 1985 became professor at Texas A & M University. In 1950, he deduced that some properties of organic molecules depend on their conformation; that is, the particular shape adopted by a molecule as a result of rotations about single carbon-carbon bonds. The study of these effects (**conformational analysis**) is applied mainly to six-membered carbon rings, where usually the conformers easily convert into each other; this interconversion is not easy

Derek Barton in 1950

if the rings are fused, e.g., in steroids. Reactivity can be related to conformation in many such molecules. Barton has studied many natural products, mainly phenols, steroids, and antibiotics. He won a Nobel Prize (with O. Hassel, who also studied six-membered carbon rings), in 1969.

BASOV, Nikolai Gennediyevitch

1922-

Soviet physicist: invented the maser and laser

After service in the Red Army during World War II, Basov studied in Moscow, and obtained his doctorate in 1956. Remaining there, he became head of his laboratory in 1962.

From 1952 onwards Basov developed the idea of amplifying electromagnetic radiation by using the relaxation of excited atoms or molecules to release further radiation. His colleague A. Prokhorov had studied the precise microwave frequencies emitted by gases, and together they produced (1955) molecular beams of excited molecules which would amplify electromagnetic radiation when stimulated by incident radiation. Such a device is known as a **maser** (Microwave Amplification by Stimulated Emission of Radiation). The 1964 Nobel Prize for Physics went to Basov, Prokhorov and *Townes* (who did similar independent work in the US) for the invention of the maser.

Rather than selecting excited molecules from a beam, Basov and Prokhorov found a way of using a second radiation source to 'pump' the gas into an excited state (the 'three-level' method). Basov then invented the **laser** (Light Amplification by Stimulated Emission of Radiation; 1958) and even achieved the effect in semiconductor crystals. He has since worked on the theory of laser production in semiconductors and on pulsed lasers, and on the interaction of light with matter.

BATESON, William
1861-1926
English geneticist: a founder of genetics

Bateson was described as a 'vague and aimless boy' at school and he surprised his teachers by getting first-class honours in science at Cambridge in 1883. He then spent two years in the US. He returned to Cambridge, taught there, and in 1910 became director of the new John Innes Institution. From the time of his US visit he was interested in variation and evolution, and by 1894 he had decided that species develop not continuously by gradual change, but evolve discontinuously in a series of 'jumps'. To support his view against opposition, be began breeding experiments, unaware of *Mendel*'s work of 1866. When the latter was rediscovered in 1900, Bateson saw that it gave support for his 'discontinuity' theory and he translated and publicized Mendel's work, and extended it to animals by his own studies on the inheritance of comb shape in fowls. He showed that *Garrod*'s work on human inborn errors of metabolism had a Mendelian interpretation. He also found that some genes can interact; so that certain traits are not inherited independently, which is in conflict with Mendel's laws. This interaction results from 'linkage', that is genes being close together on the same chromosome, as *Morgan* and others showed. Bateson coined the word 'genetics'; but he never accepted the ideas of natural selection, or of chromosomes.

fly *Drosophila*; as a result of this work, ingeniously transplanting eye buds in the larvae, they suspected that genes in some way controlled the production of the eye pigment. When he returned to the US, to a job at Stanford, he met the microbiologist E. L. Tatum, and in 1940 they decided to use the pink bread fungus *Neurospora crassa* for a study of biochemical genetics. It grew easily, reproduced quickly, and has an adult stage which is haploid (only one set of chromosomes) so that all mutant genes show their phenotypic expression. (*Drosophila*, like other higher organisms, has two genes for every character, so dominant genes can mask recessives). Beadle and Tatum exposed *Neurospora* to X-rays to produce mutations, and then examined the mutant strains to find their ability or inability to synthesize a nutrient needed for their own growth. They concluded that the function of a gene is to control production of a specific enzyme; they did not know that *Garrod* had reached the 'one gene-one-enzyme' idea 30 years earlier by studying human metabolic disease. The value of their work was in providing an experimental method allowing biochemical genetics to develop. It did so speedily, and their central idea remains unchallenged. More precisely, we would now say that one functional unit of DNA controls the synthesis of one peptide chain. Beadle, Tatum and *Lederberg* shared a Nobel Prize in 1958.

BEADLE, George Wells
1903-
American geneticist: pioneer of biochemical genetics

Born on a farm at Wahoo, Nebraska, Beadle first planned to return there after graduation, but became an enthusiast for genetics and was persuaded to work for a doctorate at Cornell on maize genetics. In 1935 he worked with B. Ephrussi in Paris on the genetics of eye-colour in the fruit

BEAUFORT, (Sir) Francis
1774-1857
British hydrographer: inventor of Beaufort wind scale

Born in Ireland, Beaufort joined the Royal Navy at an early age and saw active service for over 20 years. In 1806 he proposed the **Beaufort wind scale**, ranging from 0 for dead calm to 13 for a full storm, and specifying the amount of sail that a ship should carry in each situation. It was officially adopted by the Admiralty some 30 years later. In 1829 Beaufort became hydrographer to the Royal Navy.

BEAUMONT, William
1785-1853

American surgeon: made pioneer studies of human digestive physiology

Beaumont was a farmer's son who became a village schoolmaster and later qualified in medicine. In the war of 1812 he became an army surgeon.

In 1822 at Fort Mackinac a young Canadian trapper was accidentally shot by a duck gun at close range, producing gross abdominal wounds and an opening into the stomach. Beaumont was nearby, saved his life, and tended him for two years. He was left with a permanent fistula (opening) into the stomach. Beaumont employed him and for ten years was able to study digestion rather directly. Gastric juice could be obtained, and the lining of the stomach examined easily, and its movements, and the effects of different diets and emotions. Beaumont's 238 observations gave a firm basis to the physiology of gastric digestion. The work also suggested to *Bernard* the value of artificial fistulas in experimental physiology, using animals. The trapper lived to age 82, greatly outliving his surgeon.

BECKMANN, Ernst Otto
1853-1923

German chemist: discovered a rearrangement reaction, and a method for determining relative molecular mass in solution

Beginning as an apprentice pharmacist, Beckmann turned to chemistry with success, being professor at three universities before appointment as first director of the Kaiser Wilhelm Institut für Chemie at Berlin-Dahlem in 1912. His distinction began in 1886, when he discovered the **Beckmann rearrangement**; the reaction of ketoximes with acid reagents to give a substituted amide, often in high yield:

$$RR'C=NOH \rightarrow R'CONHR$$

The reaction has been used to prepare some amides, and also in studies on stereochemistry and on reaction mechanism. Beckmann's work led him to seek a general method for finding the relative molecular mass of a reaction product; and he devised a method, using **Raoult's law**, by measuring the rise in boiling point of a solvent caused by dissolving in it a known amount of the substance whose molecular mass is required. To measure this small temperature rise, he devised the **Beckmann thermometer**, which has a reservoir for adjusting its range, and will measure accurately a small rise in temperature.

BECQUEREL, Antoine Henri
1852-1908

French physicist: discoverer of radioactivity

Like his father and grandfather before him, Becquerel studied physics, and like them he was interested in fluorescence; he also succeeded to the posts they had held in Paris. Educated mainly at the École Polytechnique, he became professor of physics there in 1895. Partly by chance, he found in 1896 that a uranium salt, placed on a wrapped photographic plate, caused this to blacken. He soon found that this did not require light; that it was due to the uranium only, and that the radiation was not reflected like light. He found it was able to ionize air. Although similar to the X-rays discovered in 1895 by *Roentgen*, it was not the same. His work was soon confirmed, and was the starting point for all studies on radioactivity. He shared the Nobel Prize for physics in 1903 with the *Curies*. His other studies, on magnetic effects and on light absorption by crystals, were valuable; but his work on radioactivity gave physics a new direction.

Radiotherapy (later used to treat cancer) began with his observation that radium carried in his pocket produced a burn. The SI unit of radioactivity is the becquerel (Bq) defined as an activity of one disintegration per second.

BEDDOES, Thomas
1760-1808

English physician and chemist: mentor of Humphry Davy

A man of wide talents, Beddoes studied classics, modern languages, science and medicine at Oxford, and in 1788 was appointed Reader in Chemistry there. However, his sympathy with the French revolutionaries caused his resignation in 1792. He then turned to medicine, and linked this with his interest in the new gases ('airs') discovered in the previous few years, several by his friend *Priestley*. With the help of friends he set up his Medical Pneumatic Institution in Bristol, to study the therapeutic uses of gases. In 1798 he appointed the 19-year-old *Davy* to join him. A year later they observed the anaesthetic potential of N_2O (unhappily neglected for half a century). Beddoes then guided Davy in his early work on electrochemistry, as well as introducing him to influential friends in science and in literature. In 1801 Davy left for the Royal Institution and soon Beddoes also left for London and returned to medical practice. Beddoes's greatest discovery was Davy (as Davy's was *Faraday*), but although much overshadowed by his pupil, Beddoes's own talents, probably partly unutilized, were real. His Institution was perhaps the first specialized institute of a type now common.

BEDNORZ, (Johannes) Georg
1950-

Swiss physicist: co-discoverer of a new class of superconductors

Nobel prizes have usually been awarded many years after the work which led to them; but the Prize won by Bednorz and K. A. Müller of the IBM Zürich Research Laboratory at Rüschlikon in 1987 followed quickly on their work on novel electrical superconductors. Superconductivity, the absence of resistance shown by some metals near 0 K, had been observed by *Kamerlingh-Onnes* in 1911, and a theory of it was devised by *Bardeen* and others (the BCS theory) in 1957. The effect was seen to be of immense value in electronic devices if materials could be found in which it occurs above, say, 77 K (the b.p. of liquid nitrogen, an easily obtainable temperature). In 1986, Bednorz and Müller showed that a mixed-phase oxide of lanthanum, barium and copper superconducted above 30 K, much above any previous temperature for this effect. A special meeting of the American Physical Society in New York in 1987 on superconductivity became known as the 'Woodstock of physics' and oxides of the type M-Ba-Cu-O (with M a rare earth metal, usually lanthanum or yttrium) were then announced which showed superconductivity up to 90 K.

Bednorz graduated at Münster in 1976 and worked for his doctorate under Müller at IBM Zürich, where he had joined the research staff in 1982.

BEEBE, Charles William
1877-1962

American naturalist: pioneer of deep-sea exploration

Graduating from Columbia (New York) in 1898, Beebe's first interest was in ornithology and he joined the staff of the New York Zoological Society. After service as a fighter pilot in World War I, he returned in 1919 to direct the Society's Department of Tropical Research. Further work on birds was overtaken by his interest in deep-sea exploration. In his 'bathysphere' he reached a record depth of about 1000 m near Bermuda in 1934, and later went even lower. He found that light was absent below 600 m, and discovered previously unknown organisms at these depths. A. Piccard later went even deeper.

BEHRING, Emil von
1854-1917

German bacteriologist: co-discoverer of diphtheria antitoxin

Behring studied at Berlin and after qualifying in medicine joined the Army Medical Corps. In 1889 he became assistant to *Koch*, and from 1895 he was professor of hygiene at Marburg. It was already known that the bacteria causing tetanus produced a chemical **toxin** which was responsible for much of the illness of the patient; the toxin could be obtained from a culture. In 1890 Behring worked with *Kitasato* and showed that blood serum from an animal with tetanus could, if injected into other animals, give them a temporary resistance to the disease and so contained an antitoxin. Similar antitoxic immunity was found with diphtheria, then a major killer of children; this part of his work was done with *Ehrlich*. A diphtheria antitoxin to protect human patients was soon made (best from the blood serum of an infected horse) and found to be protective, and also to be useful for those already having the disease; it was possibly first used on an infected child on Christmas night, 1891, in Berlin.

Behring was awarded the first Nobel Prize in medicine or physiology for this work, in 1901. In 1913 he showed that a mixture of toxin and antitoxin gives more lasting immunity than the antitoxin alone, and later methods for preventing the disease used this method, until it in turn gave way to the use of toxoid (which is toxin treated with formalin, introduced by G. Ramon in 1923). Since then, large-scale immunization of young children has given good control over the disease.

Much honoured, Behring ranks high in medical science; but he was always a lone researcher with few pupils, with much of his energy spent in disputes and in his unsuccessful search for a vaccine against TB.

BEILSTEIN, Friedrich Konrad
1838-1906

German-Russian encyclopaedist of organic chemistry

A student of organic chemistry under several of the masters of the subject in Germany, Beilstein was lecturer at Göttingen and later professor at St Petersburg. His own researches were modest. He is remembered for his *Handbook of Organic Chemistry* (1881) which formed a substantially complete catalogue of organic compounds. The compilation (in many volumes) has been continued by the German Chemical Society, and is of great value to organic chemists.

Beilstein's test for halogen in an organic compound is quick and useful. An oxidized copper wire is coated with the compound and heated in a gas flame. If the flame is coloured blue-green, halogen is probably present. However, some nitrogen compounds give the colour, so the test is only decisive if negative.

BELL, Alexander Graham
1847-1922

Scottish-American speech therapist: inventor of the telephone

The son and grandson of speech therapists, Bell followed the same interest but he also studied sound waves and the mechanics of speech. He emigrated to Canada in 1870 and moved to the US in 1871. From 1873 he was Professor of Vocal Physiology at Boston, and could experiment on his belief that if sound wave vibrations could be converted into a fluctuating electric current, this could be passed along a wire and reconverted into sound waves by a receiver. Success produced the 'telephone' patented by him in

1876, and the start of the AT & T company. Soon *Edison* much improved Bell's telephone transmitter. Bell made other improvements in telegraphy; improved Edison's gramophone; worked with *Langley* and on Curtis's flying machines; and founded the journal *Science*.

BELL, (Sir) Charles
1774-1842

Scottish anatomist and surgeon: pioneer of neurophysiology

Bell learned surgery from his elder brother John (a distinguished surgeon and anatomist) and at Edinburgh University. He moved to London in 1804 and became well known and liked as a surgeon and lecturer on surgery. He treated wounded from the battles of Corunna and Waterloo. From 1807 he showed that nerves are not single units, but consist of separate fibres within a common sheath; that a fibre conveys either sensory or motor stimuli, but not both (i.e. it transmits impulses in one direction only); and that a muscle must be supplied with both types of fibre. In this way Bell began modern neurophysiology. His work was as fundamental and as revolutionary as that of *Harvey* on the circulation of the blood. Later he discovered the long thoracic nerve (Bell's nerve); and he showed that lesions of the seventh cranial nerve produce facial paralysis (**Bell's palsy**).

BELL, Susan Jocelyn (Burnell)
1943-

British astronomer: discovered first pulsar

In August 1967, when Bell was a research student at Cambridge working with *Hewish*, they noticed an unusually regular radio signal on the 3.7-metre wavelength radio telescope. Further detailed studies revealed bursts of radio energy at a very constant interval of just over a second. It was proved that the source was not man-made, nor a signal from some form of

S. Jocelyn Bell (Burnell)

intelligent life elsewhere in the universe (an idea which was dropped when several other pulsars were discovered): and it was soon proposed by *Gold*, and is now widely accepted, that the source is a rapidly rotating neutron star, or pulsar, emitting a beam of radio waves in an analogous fashion to a lighthouse.

BENEDEN, Edouard van
1846-1910

Belgian embryologist and cytologist: discovered that the number of chromosomes per cell is constant for a particular species

Beneden followed his father in taking charge of zoology teaching at Liège in 1870. His course of teaching was based largely on his own researches, which he did not publish, but one of his students published them after Beneden's death. He showed in the 1880s that the number of chromosomes is constant in the cells of an animal body (except the sex cells) and the number is characteristic of the species (e.g., 46 in each human cell). He worked particularly with the chromosomes in the cell nuclei of an intestinal worm from horses; these chromosomes are conveniently large and few (four in the body cells, two in the sex cells). He found that the chromosome number is not doubled in the formation of the sex cells (the ova and spermatozoa) so that these have only half the usual number (a process called **meiosis**). When they unite, the normal number is restored, with results in accord with *Mendel*'s work in genetics. In fact Beneden misinterpreted some of his observations, which were clarified by the work of *Weismann* and *de Vries*.

BENTHAM, George
1800-1884

English plant taxonomist

Son of a wealthy naval architect, Bentham became interested in botany at 17. He was trained in law and worked as secretary to his uncle, the philosopher Jeremy Bentham, from 1826-32. Thereafter, his studies in botany took up all his time; in 1854 he gave his herbarium and library to Kew Gardens, and worked there for the rest of his life. His *Plant Genera* (3 vols., 1862-83) written with *Hooker* has continued to be a standard work for British botanists; but he also wrote other floras, e.g., the 7-volume *Australian Flora*.

BERG, Paul
1926-

American molecular biologist: discovered first transfer RNA, and pioneered recombinant DNA techniques

Educated in the US, Berg held chairs from 1970 at both Washington University (St Louis) and Stanford. In 1955 *Crick* had suggested that the biosynthesis of proteins from amino acids, under the control of an RNA template, involved an intermediate 'adaptor' molecule. He thought it possible that a specific adapter exists for each of the 20 amino acids. The next year Berg identified the first adaptor, now called a **transfer RNA**; it is a small RNA molecule which transfers a specific amino acid, methionine.

Later, Berg developed a method for introducing selected genes into 'foreign' bacteria, thereby causing the bacteria to produce the protein characteristic of the cells from which the genes had been taken. This technique of **recombinant DNA technology** ('genetic engineering') is of value because it can give a convenient bacterial synthesis of a desired protein such as insulin or interferon. However, it offers the potential danger that novel pathogens might be created, by accident or otherwise, and Berg was influential in warning of this problem. He shared a Nobel Prize in 1980.

BERGER, Hans
1873-1941

German psychiatrist: pioneer of electroencephalography (EEG)

Berger studied physics for a year at Jena, but then changed to medicine, and later specialized in psychiatry. He worked on the physical aspects of brain function (e.g., its blood circulation, and its temperature) to try and relate these to mental states; and in 1924 he recorded the electric currents he detected on the exposed brain of a dog. Then he found he could detect currents through the intact skull from his family as well as from patients with brain disorders, and from 1929 he published on this. He described the alpha rhythm (ten cycles per second, from certain areas of the brain at rest) and he recognized that the method could be useful in the diagnosis of diseases of the brain; since then this EEG method has become routinely used in neurological and psychiatric cases, especially since *Adrian*'s work from 1934 onwards.

BERGERON, Tor Harold Percival
1891-

Swedish meteorologist: explained mechanism of precipitation from clouds

After studying at Stockholm and Leipzig, Bergeron worked at the Bergen Geophysical Institute with *Bjerknes*. In 1947 he was appointed professor of meteorology at the University of Uppsala. His principal contribution to the subject was to suggest, in 1935, a mechanism for the precipitation of rain from clouds. He proposed that ice crystals present in the cloud grew by condensation of water vapour onto their surfaces, and that at a certain size they fell, melted, and produced rain. His ideas were soon borne out by the experimental studies and observations of W. Findeisen, and are now known as the **Bergeron-Findeisen theory**.

BERGIUS, Friedrich Karl Rudolf

1884-1949

German industrial chemist: devised conversion process from coal to oil

Son of a chemical manufacturer, Bergius studied under *Nernst* and *Haber*. After five years in teaching, he worked in the chemical industry from the start of the First World War to the end of the Second World War. His interest in high-pressure reactions of gases developed under Haber. Realizing that petroleum (crude mineral oil) differs from coal in the higher hydrogen content and lower relative molecular mass of the oil, Bergius developed a method (the **Bergius process**) for the conversion, by heating a mixture of coal dust and oil with hydrogen under pressure, with a catalyst. Hydrogen is taken up, and the product is distilled to give petrol (gasoline). The process was much used in Germany in World War II. Bergius also developed industrial syntheses for phenol and ethane-1,2-diol.

BERGSTRÖM, Sune

1916-

Swedish biochemist

Educated at the Royal Caroline Institute in Stockholm, Bergström returned there as professor of biochemistry in 1958. His interest has been focused on the **prostaglandins**, a group of related compounds whose biological effects were first noted in the 1930s. Their effects are complex, but a common feature is their ability to induce contraction of smooth muscle, and their high potency (10^{-9} g can be effective); originally found in human semen, they have since been found in many cells (one rich source is the Caribbean sea whip coral). Bergström first isolated two prostaglandins in pure form, in the 1950s. In 1962 they were shown to have a general structure pattern of a five-carbon ring with chains on adjacent carbon atoms, and much medicinal chemistry has been devoted to them since.

BERNARD, Claude

1813-1878

French physiologist: pioneer of experimental medicine and physiological chemistry

Bernard was the child of vineyard workers, and he remained fond of country life; later he spent his time in either a Paris laboratory or, during the harvest, in the Beaujolais vineyards. His schooling was provided by his church, and at 19 he was apprenticed to an apothecary. His first talent was in writing for the theatre, but he was urged to qualify in a profession and chose medicine. He qualified for entry with some difficulty, and emerged from his training in Paris as an average student. Then as assistant to *Magendie* he found his talent in experimental medicine. He never practised as a physician, and an early problem for him was how to make a living. He solved this by marrying a successful Paris physician's daughter and living on the dowry until he succeeded to Magendie's job, in 1852. His marriage was unhappy.

Bernard's discoveries were wide-ranging; many depended on his skill in vivesection, using mainly dogs and rabbits. In digestion he showed the presence of an enzyme in gastric juice; the nervous control of gastric secretion and its localization; the change of all carbohydrates into simple sugars before absorption; and the role of bile and pancreatic juice in the digestion of fats. He noted that the urine of herbivores is alkaline, and that of carnivores is acid, and he pursued the comparisons that these observations suggested. This led him to find that nutrition is complex, and involves intermediate stages and synthesis as well as transport. He discovered glycogen, and sugar production by the liver. He studied the nervous system and discovered the vasomotor and vasoconstrictor nerves. Beginning with an attempt to prove *Lavoisier's* simple ideas on animal combustion, Bernard showed that in fact the oxidation producing animal heat is indirect, and occurs in all tissues and not simply in the lungs. He studied the action of curare and other paralysing poisons and showed their use in experimental medicine. His approach to research was essentially modern; he combined experimental skill with theory, and had a valuable talent for noting experimental results which were not in accord with existing ideas and which led to fruitful new concepts. Perhaps his greatest contribution to physiology was the idea that life is dependent on a constant internal environment (**homeostasis**); cells function best within a narrow range of osmotic pressure and temperature, and bathed in a fairly constant concentration of chemical constituents such as sugar and metallic ions.

BERNOULLI, Daniel
1700-1782

Swiss mathematician: pioneer of hydrodynamics and kinetic theory of gases

This extraordinary family, in the century before and the century after Daniel's birth, produced eleven substantial mathematicians in four generations. Most of them worked mainly in applied mathematics and analysis, had talents in some other areas from astronomy to zoology, and quarrelled vigorously with their relatives.

Daniel studied medicine in Switzerland and Germany and qualified in 1724, and published some major work in mathematics in the same year. In 1725 he was appointed professor of mathematics in St Petersburg, but found conditions in

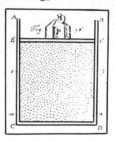

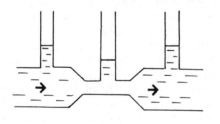

Bernoulli's principle: above left, liquid flow through a constricted tube. Lower left, air flow supporting a wing: air has a longer path above the wing than below it, so it moves faster above, and its pressure is lower above the wing. Hence there is an uplift acting on the wing. Lower right: the trajectory of a golf shot. The dimpled, spinning ball counteracts gravity for much of its flight. Upper right: diagram from Daniel Bernoulli's *Hydrodynamics* (1738) in which kinetic theory is used to show that pV is constant for a gas (Boyle's law). (In reality, the average distance between gas molecules is about 300 times the molecular diameter at STP, i.e. much more than in the diagram in relation to the apparent size of the 'atoms').

Russia primitive and returned to Basle in 1733 as professor of anatomy and botany, and later, of physics. He worked on trigonometry, calculus, and probability. His work on hydrodynamics used *Newton*'s ideas on force applied to fluids, and advanced both theory and a range of applications. One of his results (**Bernoulli's principle**) deals with fluid flow through pipes of changing diameter and shows that pressure in a narrow section (see diagram) is lower than in the wider part, contrary to expectation. A closely related effect leads to the uplift of an aircraft wing; since the distance from leading edge to rear edge is greater over the top of the wing than below it, the air velocity over the top must be higher and therefore its pressure is lower; the result is uplift. Again, when a golf ball is driven off, the loft of the club causes the ball to spin, and the resulting airflow gives it lift so that it has an asymmetric flight, rising in nearly a straight line. As the spin decreases, the lift diminishes and then the ball moves into a path like that of a thrown ball.

Daniel also proposed a mental model for gases, showing that if gases consist of small atoms in ceaseless rapid motion colliding elastically with each other and the walls of their container, *Boyle*'s experimental law should result. This was both a very early application of the idea of atoms, and the origin of the **kinetic theory of gases**.

BERTHELOT, Marcellin Pierre Eugène

1827-1907

French chemist: pioneer in organic synthesis, and in thermochemistry

As the son of a Paris physician, Berthelot saw the city life of the poor and the sick and was often unwell himself. His life was successful from school prizes to worldwide honours in old age, but his early impressions remained, and at 71 he wrote 'I have never trusted life completely'.

Originally a medical student, he turned to chemistry early. Previously, organic chemistry had been concerned with compounds derived from living nature, and little synthesis had been attempted. From 1854 Berthelot used synthetic methods in a systematic way, and built up large molecules from simple starting compounds. Thus he made methanol from methane, methanoic acid from carbon monoxide, ethanol from ethene, and fats (glycerides) from propane-1,2,3-triol and organic acids. He made ethyne from hydrogen passed through a carbon arc; and benzene from ethyne. The former idea of a 'vital force' was banished; organic chemistry became simply the chemistry of carbon compounds, and organic chemists had a new basis for their thinking and an emphasis on synthesis, increasingly making compounds (as Berthelot did) which do not occur in nature. In the 1860s he studied the velocity of reactions; and, later, the heat they evolved (thermochemistry). He concluded that reactions are 'driven' in the direction which evolves heat. (In fact, the matter is not as simple as this, as *Gibbs* showed.) He also worked on physiological chemistry, and on explosives (he discovered the 'detonation wave').

He was scientific adviser during the siege of Paris by the Prussians in 1870, and later was a Senator, and Foreign Minister in 1895. He died a few hours after his wife, and the two had the unique state honour of a joint burial in the Panthéon.

BERTHOLLET, (Compte) Claude Louis

1748-1822

French chemist: worked on a range of inorganic problems

Originally a physician, Berthollet moved to chemistry and was an early staff member of the École Polytechnique, but was not an effective teacher. He was a friend of Napoleon, and joined him in the attack on Egypt in 1798. In 1814 he helped depose Napoleon 'for the good of France', and was made a peer by Louis XVIII. In chemistry, he was an early supporter of *Lavoisier*'s ideas; his research examined the nature of ammonia, the sulphides of hydrogen, hydrogen cyanide, and cyanogen chloride, and the reactions of chlorine. He deduced that some acids did not contain oxygen (unlike Lavoisier's view). He discovered $KClO_3$, but his use of it in gunpowder destroyed a powder mill in 1788. His work on bleaching fabrics with chlorine, and on dyes and steel-making, was more successful.

He believed that chemical affinity resembled gravitation in being proportional to the masses of the reactants; he was wrong, but his work foreshadowed that by *Guldberg*. Similarly, he had a courteous conflict with *Proust*, attacking the latter's law of constant composition. For long, Proust's views seemed to have prevailed entirely, but since 1935 'berthollide' compounds of slightly variable composition have been proved to exist. Berthollet's chemical instincts were usually good, and even when they were not, the debate led to a valuable outcome.

BERZELIUS, (Baron) Jöns Jacob
1779-1848

Swedish chemist: dominated chemical theory for much of his lifetime

Orphaned, Berzelius was brought up by relatives. He was interested in natural history and medicine was his chosen career from his schooldays. After studying medicine he graduated at Uppsala in 1802. He had read and experimented in chemistry under J. Afzelius and his interest focused upon the subject. The wars against France (1805-9 and 1812-14) gave him financial freedom because the need for military surgeons led to an increase in pay for the medical faculty in Stockholm where Berzelius held the chair of Medicine and Pharmacy from 1807 (renamed chair of Chemistry and Phar-

macy in 1810). In 1808 he became a member of the Swedish Academy of Sciences. Berzelius married late in life; he was 56 and his bride 24; as a wedding gift the king of Sweden made him a baron.

Berzelius provided the first major systemization of 19th century chemistry, including the first accurate table of relative atomic masses (for 28 elements in his list of 1828); the reintroduction and use of modern 'initial letter' symbols for elements; concepts including isomerism and catalysis, and the division of the subject into organic and inorganic branches and his theory of dualism, based on his work in electrochemistry. This theory proved first a spur and later an inhibitor to further development, but can now be seen as a precursor to the later division of elements into the electropositive and electro-negative classes. He was the discoverer of three new elements (selenium, cerium and thorium).

For many years Berzelius was a uniquely dominant figure in chemistry, with great influence through his research, his year-book on advances in chemistry, and his many pupils.

BESSEL, Friedrich Wilhelm
1784-1846

German astronomer and mathematician: made first measurement of a star's distance by parallax; detected that Sirius has a companion; introduced Bessel functions

As a young trainee accountant in Bremen, Bessel prepared for travel by studying navigation and then astronomy. This in turn took him, aged 26, to be director of the new Königsberg Observatory.

Much of Bessel's work deals with the analysis of perturbations in planetary and stellar motions. For this purpose he developed the mathematical functions which now bear his name, publishing his results in 1824 in a paper on planetary perturbations. **Bessel functions** have subsequently proved to have wide application in other areas of physics. In 1838 he was the first to announce the measurement of a star's distance by measurement of its parallax. Stellar parallax is the displacement the nearer stars should show (relative to distant ones) over time, because they are viewed at varying angles as the Earth moves across its orbit. Such parallax had not been observed previously; *Copernicus* suggested that this was because all stars are so distant that the parallax is immeasurably small. Bessel was able to measure the parallax of the binary star 61 Cygni as 0.3″ (0.3 arc seconds) and thus found its distance to be 10.3 light-years (within 10% of the present value). Around the same time he observed a small wave-like motion of Sirius, and suggested that it was the result of the gravitational influence of an unseen orbiting companion; the faint companion Sirius B was subsequently detected by Alvan Clark, a telescope lens maker, in 1862. Bessel also succeeded in computing the mass of the planet Jupiter by analysing the orbits of its major satellites, and showed its overall density to be only 1.35. He suggested that irregularities in the orbit of Uranus were caused by the presence of an unknown planet, but died a few months before the discovery of Neptune.

BESSEMER, (Sir) Henry

1813-1898

English engineer and inventor: developed a process for the manufacture of cheap steel

Bessemer's father was an English mechanical engineer at the Paris Mint who returned to England during the French Revolution. Bessemer first gained some knowledge of metallurgy at his father's type foundry. It was a time of rapid progress in industrial manufacture and Bessemer was interested in all new developments. Largely self-taught, he became a prolific inventor.

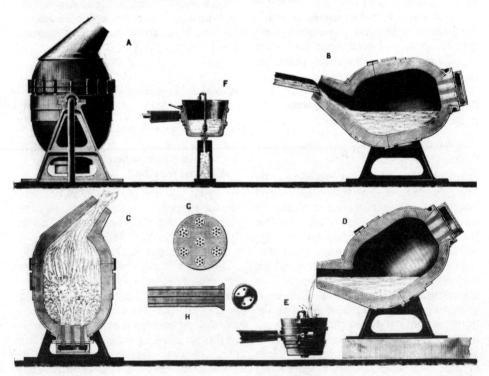

The first form of Bessemer moveable converter and ladle.

When he was 20 he produced a scheme for the prevention of forgeries of impressed stamps used on documents; these forgeries were then costing the Government some £100 000 per year. The Stamp Office adopted his suggestion, but did not reward him. It was an experience he did not forget.

Horrified at the price of hand-made German 'gold powder' purchased for his sister's painting, he devised a method of manufacturing the powder from brass. Unable to patent the process, for secrecy he designed a largely automatic plant, workable by himself and his three brothers-in-law. From this he made enough money to cover the expenses of his future inventions, which included improvements in sugar cane presses and a method for the manufacture of continuous sheet glass.

The Crimean War directed Bessemer's interest to the need for a new metal for guns. Cast-iron (pig iron) which contains carbon and other impurities, is brittle, and the relatively pure wrought-iron was then made from pig iron by a laborious and time-consuming method. Steel (iron with a small amount of carbon) was made in small quantities with heavy consumption of fuel and so was costly. He developed the **Bessemer process** for making cheap steel without the use of fuel, reducing to minutes a process which had taken days. Bessemer steel was suitable for structural use, and was cheap enough to use for this, which greatly helped the industrial development then in progress; as well as being of value for railway systems and the machine-tool industry. The Bessemer process consisted of blowing air through molten crude iron, oxidizing carbon to blow-off gas, and silicon and manganese to solid oxides. For this purpose he designed the **Bessemer converter**, a tiltable container for the molten metal, with holes for blowing air through its base. Some early users of his process were unable to reproduce his results, which led to legal disputes over royalty payments to him. The failures were due to ores containing phosphorus; Bessemer had by chance used iron ore free from phosphorus. This problem of phosphorus impurities in some ores was solved in 1878 by Thomas and Gilchrist. Mushet also improved the process, by the addition of an alloy of iron, manganese and carbon.

Bessemer set up his own steel works in Sheffield, using phosphorus-free ore. During his lifetime the Bessemer process was appreciated more abroad. Andrew Carnegie made his fortune by it in the US, but the British steel manufacturers were loath to acknowledge its success. Bessemer was knighted in 1879.

BETHE, Hans Albrecht

1906-

German-American physicist: proposed mechanism for the production of stellar energy

In 1939 Bethe proposed the first detailed theory for the formation of energy by stars through a series of nuclear reactions, having the net result that four hydrogen nuclei are converted into a helium nucleus and radiated fusion energy. The process (sometimes known as the 'carbon cycle' due to the key part played in it by carbon-12) gives good agreement with observation for some types of stars. Bethe also contributed, with *Alpher* and *Gamow*, to the α-β-γ theory of the origin of the chemical elements during the origin of the universe (see *Alpher* for an account).

BICHAT, (Marie-Francois) Xavier

1771-1802

French pathologist: founder of animal histology

Bichat followed his father in studying medicine. His studies were interrupted by a period in the army, and he returned to Paris at the height of the Terror in 1793. From 1797 he taught medicine, and in 1801 worked in Paris's great hospital, the Hôtel-Dieu. He was struck by the fact that various organs consist of several components or 'tissues' and described 21 of them (such as connective, muscle, and nerve tissue). He saw that when an organ is diseased, usually it was not the whole organ but only certain tissues which are affected. He distrusted microscopes and did not use one for most of his work; and cell theory was yet to come. Bichat's work, done with great intensity during the last years of his short life, had much influence in medical science. It formed a bridge between the 'organ pathology' of *Morgagni* and the later 'cell pathology' of *Virchow*; and the study of tissues (histology) has been important ever since.

BIFFEN, (Sir) Rowland Harry

1874-1949

English geneticist and plant breeder

Biffen graduated at Cambridge in 1896, and after an expedition to south and central America studying rubber production, he returned to Cambridge to teach agricultural botany. He was to dominate the subject there for a generation. In 1899 he began cereal trials intended to select improved types, then a chance process. A year later *Mendel*'s neglected work of the 1860s on plant genetics at last became known. Biffen quickly saw that plant-breeding could be rationalized; and he guessed that physiological traits might be inherited, as well as the morphological traits studied by Mendel. In 1905 he showed this was the case for resistance by wheat to yellow rust, a fungal disease; it is inherited as a simple Mendelian recessive. Since then, improvement of crop plants by hybridization has been widespread. Biffen's own wheat variety 'Little Joss' was unsurpassed for 40 years.

BIOT, Jean Baptiste

1774-1862

French physicist: pioneer of polarimetry

A child during the French Revolution, Biot joined the artillery at 18, but soon left to study mathematics, and at 26 was teaching physics at the Collège de France. His research showed variety. With *Gay-Lussac* he made an early balloon ascent (1804) and made meteorological and magnetic observations up to 5 km; his nerve failed for a second attempt. He made a number of geodetic and astronomical expeditions, visiting Spain and the Orkneys.

His famous work is on optical activity. He showed, for the first time, that some crystals of quartz rotated the plane of polarized light, while other crystals rotated it to the same extent, but in the opposite direction. In 1815 he showed that some liquids (e.g., turpentine) will also rotate plane polarized light, and later he observed the same effect with some solids when dissolved in water (e.g., sugar; and tartaric acid). He realized that this ability of some substances in solution must mean that the effect is a molecular property ('optical activity'). He showed (**Biot's law**) that the amount of rotation of the plane of polarization of light passing through an optically active medium is proportional to the length of its path; and to the concentration, if the medium is a solution of an active solute in an inactive solvent; and that the rotation is roughly inversely proportional to the square of the wavelength of the light.

Polarimetry (measurement of optical activity) was pioneered by Biot, and after 1870 proved of great value in gaining information on molecular configuration (shape). Later still, the variation in optical rotation with the wavelength of the polarized light was also found to be useful in locating molecular shape.

Biot was a man of great talent, as was seen by his older friend *Laplace*; and in his old age Biot saw and appreciated the talent of his young friend *Pasteur*.

BIRKELAND, Kristian Olaf Bernhard

1867-1917

Norwegian physicist: devised process for nitrogen fixation

Birkeland studied physics in Paris,

Geneva and Bonn before returning to his native Oslo to teach at the Christiania University. He studied the aurora borealis, and in 1896 suggested (correctly) that it resulted from some charged solar radiation becoming trapped in the Earth's magnetic field near the arctic pole. His theory was partly based on an experiment with a magnetized model of the Earth, which he placed in a beam of electrons in a cathode ray tube; he found luminous effects near the poles which resembled aurorae. However, he is best known as co-discoverer of the **Birkeland-Eyde process**. This was designed to meet the shortage of nitrate fertilizer, and used *Cavendish*'s observation of 1784 that atmospheric nitrogen and oxygen combined in an electric spark to give nitrogen monoxide, NO. The process used an electric arc spread by a magnetic field, and the NO was mixed with air and water to give nitric acid; it was used (with the benefit of cheap Norwegian hydro-electricity) from 1903 to 1928.

BIRKOFF, George David
1884-1944

American mathematician: proved the ergodic theorem of probability theory

After taking his first degree at Harvard, and a doctorate on boundary problems at Chicago, Birkoff taught at Michigan and Princeton. He became an assistant professor at Harvard in 1912 and a full professor there at 35 in 1919, retiring in 1939.

An early interest in differential and difference equations allowed Birkoff to apply matrix methods generally for the first time. He studied dynamics and *Poincaré*'s celestial mechanics, and in 1913 obtained a now famous proof of Poincaré's 'last geometrical theorem' on the three-body problem.

Collaboration with *von Neumann* gave rise to the 'weak form' of the ergodic theorem, which was shortly followed by von Neumann's discovery of the 'strong form'. Ergodicity refers to whether a dyna-

mical system will develop over time so as to return exactly to a previous configuration. In 1938 Birkhoff published several papers on electromagnetism and also argued that better alternatives to *Einstein*'s general theory of relativity were possible.

Overall Birkhoff is acknowledged as the greatest American mathematician of the early 20th century; he excelled as a teacher and in developing celestial mechanics and the analysis of dynamical systems.

BJERKNES, Vilhelm Firman Koren
1862-1951

Norwegian meteorologist: pioneer of dynamical meteorology

Bjerknes's father was professor of mathematics at the Christiania University (now Oslo), and Bjerknes himself held professorships at Stockholm and Leipzig before founding the Bergen Geophysical Institute in 1917. Through his hydrodynamic models of the atmosphere and the oceans Bjerknes made important contributions to meteorology, and in 1904 showed how weather prediction could be achieved numerically using mathematical models. During World War I Bjerknes established a network of weather stations throughout Norway, the results allowing him and his collaborators (which included his son, Jacob, and *Bergeron*) to develop their theory of polar fronts. They demonstrated that the atmosphere is composed of distinct air masses with different characteristics, the boundaries between such air masses being called 'fronts'. Their **Bergen frontal theory**, as it became known, explains how cyclones are generated over the Atlantic where warm and cold air masses meet.

BLACK, (Sir) James
1924-

British pharmacologist: designer of novel drugs

A graduate in medicine from St Andrews, Black was a university lecturer there, in

Malaya and in Glasgow before working in pharmacology first with ICI, and later with Smith Kline and French and with Wellcome. At the time of his Nobel Prize in 1988 he had been professor of analytical pharmacology at King's College Hospital Medical School, London, from 1984.

He is best known for two major contributions to medicine. His work on beta blockers was based on the theory that heart muscle has specific beta receptors which respond to hormonal control; Black reasoned that if these sites could be blocked, the effect of the hormones on the heart would be inhibited and its workload reduced; and he was able to find a very satisfactory antagonist, propranolol, in 1964. Since then such beta-blockers have been much used to control heart disease and hypertension. He went on to devise a comparatively rational approach to the control of stomach ulcers; he deduced in 1972 that a particular type of histamine receptor is located on the wall of the gut and stimulates acid secretion in the stomach, and then found a compound (cimetidine) which blocked the action of these H2 receptors, so curbing stomach acidity and allowing healing. Black's successes much encouraged a rational approach in medicinal chemistry, as well as having provided drugs of value in two major areas.

BLACK, Joseph
1728-1799

Scottish physician, chemist and physicist: pioneer of modern chemical logic; discoverer of latent heat and specific heat

Black was born in Bordeaux, where his Scots-Irish father was a wine merchant. Joseph was educated in Belfast, Glasgow and Edinburgh. Finally, he studied medicine. His work for his MD degree, expanded in a paper of 1756, is his major contribution to chemistry; it is a model of experiment and logic. In particular, he saw the importance of recording changes of weight, and he recognized the impor-

tance of gases. He studied the cycle of changes we would now express in formulae as follows (note that Black knew his compounds by the names given in parentheses; formulae and atomic theory came much later, but he understood the key relationships between the compounds):

$$CaCO_3 \text{ (limestone)} + heat \rightarrow CaO \text{ (quicklime)} + CO_2 \text{ (fixed air)}$$
$$CaO + H_2O \rightarrow Ca(OH)_2 \text{ (slaked lime)}$$
$$Ca(OH)_2 + CO_2 \rightarrow CaCO_3 + H_2O$$

Black showed that fixed air (CO_2) is produced by respiration and fermentation, and by burning charcoal; that it behaves as an acid (e.g., in neutralizing an alkali) and he deduced its presence in small quantities in the atmosphere. He was a very popular lecturer at Glasgow and later in Edinburgh; one of his pupils was Benjamin Rush, who became the first professor of chemistry in America.

He taught *Lavoisier*'s new views on chemistry when they appeared, but his own research moved to physics. About 1763 he showed that heat is necessary to produce a change of state from solid to liquid, or liquid to vapour, without a rise in temperature; e.g., ice at $0°$ requires heat to form water at $0°$. He called this 'latent heat'. On this basis, he went on to distinguish clearly between heat and temperature; and he examined the different heat capacity of substances. Thus in physics, as in chemistry, he provided basic ideas essential for the subject to advance.

BLACKETT, (Baron) Patrick Maynard Stuart
1897-1974

English physicist: used an improved Wilson cloud chamber to make discoveries using cosmic rays

Blackett, the son of a stockbroker, was educated at Osborne and Dartmouth Naval Colleges and saw action at sea in the battles of the Falkland Islands (1914) and

Jutland (1916). He then studied physics at Cambridge, and continuing in research, made the first cloud chamber photographs (1924) of the transmutation of nitrogen into oxygen-17 by bombardment with alpha particles (helium nuclei). He was appointed to professorships in London (1933), Manchester (1937) and finally Imperial College, London (1953). During World War II Blackett pioneered the use of operational research to produce economies in military resources, including work on submarine warfare, and also invented a new bomb-sight for aircraft. After the war he was active in public affairs, opposing the growing role of nuclear weapons. He was awarded the Nobel Prize for physics in 1948.

The prize winning work was the construction, with G. Occhialini, of a cloud chamber that underwent vapour expansion and took a photograph when two aligned Geiger counters were triggered. Blackett used the apparatus to identify the first positron to be seen following their prediction by *Dirac*; however while he sought further experimental confirmation *C. D. Anderson*'s discovery of the positron was published first.

He was made a life peer in 1969.

BLACKMAN, Frederick Frost
1866-1947

English plant physiologist: demonstrated that gas exchange occurs through leaf stomata

Blackman was the eldest son in a family of eleven, and followed his father in studying medicine. However, he never practised; he had been a keen botanist since his schooldays, and in 1887 he moved to Cambridge as a science student, stayed to teach, and never left.

In 1895 he showed experimentally that gas exchange between plant leaves and the air occurs through the stomata; it had been believed since 1832, but not proved, that these pores are the entry points for the exchange. In 1905 he put forward the

principle of limiting factors: where a plant process depends on several independent factors, the overall rate is limited by the rate of the slowest factor. This idea was offered by *Liebig* in the 1840s, but Blackman demonstrated it clearly by work on the effect of temperature, light, and carbon dioxide availability on photosynthesis in the aquatic willow moss.

BLOCH, Felix
1905-

Swiss-American physicist: invented nuclear magnetic resonance spectrometry

Bloch was educated at Zürich and Leipzig, but following a short period of teaching in Germany moved to the US in 1933. He spent the rest of his career at Stanford.

The theory of solid-state physics and of how electrons behave in solids was advanced by Bloch's research. The Bloch wavefunction describes an electron which is moving freely in a solid, and the term **Bloch wall** describes the boundary between two magnetic domains in a ferromagnetic material.

In 1946 Bloch introduced the **nuclear magnetic resonance** (nmr) technique, also developed independently by *Purcell*. Many types of atomic nucleus possess a magnetic moment and quantum mechanics indicated that the moment could only adopt one of a number of possible orientations with respect to an applied magnetic field. Each orientation requires a different energy and so transitions from one state to another can be accomplished if a photon of electromagnetic radiation (of radio frequencies) is absorbed. The magnetic moments of the proton and neutron were measured by this method, and since then many complex molecules have been studied. The energy state of the nucleus gives information about its atomic neighbours in the molecule because of the effect of the surrounding electrons. Bloch shared the 1952 Nobel Prize for physics with Purcell, and the nmr method has since become a powerful analytical technique in chemistry.

BODE, Johann Elert
1747-1826

German astronomer: publicized numerological relationship between planetary distances

Although Bode was director of the Berlin Observatory for almost 40 years and constructed a notable star atlas, his fame rests, strangely enough, on his popularization of a relationship discovered by someone else. In 1772 Johann Daniell Titius pointed out that the members of the simple series 0,3,6,12,24,48,96, when added to 4 and divided by 10, give the mean radii of the planetary orbits in astronomical units, surprisingly accurately (even though only six planets were known at the time). An astronomical unit (AU) is the mean distance of Earth from the Sun. Through Bode's publicizing of the relationship it became named after him. It played a part in the discovery of Uranus, the asteroid belt (the fifth 'planet'), and Neptune (although its results are hopelessly inaccurate for Neptune and Pluto). It has never been proved whether **Bode's law** has any real meaning, or is merely coincidental; if the latter, it is a remarkable coincidence. Bode was also responsible for the naming of the planet Uranus.

BOGOLIUBOV, Nikolai Nikolaevich
1909-

Soviet mathematical physicist: contributed to quantum theory and the theory of superconductivity

Bogoliubov has worked at the Academy of Sciences in the Ukraine and at the Soviet Academy of Sciences. He has contributed new mathematical techniques to physics and the **Bogoliubov transformation**, by which variables are changed in quantum

field theory, is named after him. A distribution function describing non-equilibrium processes is due to him, as are many developments in parallel to the BCS theory of superconductivity.

BOHR, Neils (Henrik David)
1885-1962

Danish theoretical physicist: put forward the quantum theory of the electronic structure of atoms

Bohr's family was distinguished, his father was professor of physiology at Copenhagen and his younger brother Harald a gifted mathematician. Neils and Harald were both footballers to a professional standard, and both Neils and his son Aage (born in 1922) won the Nobel Prize for Physics, in 1922 and 1975 respectively.

After Bohr had finished his doctorate at Copenhagen (1911) he spent eight months with *J. J. Thomson* in Cambridge, who was not attracted by Bohr's ideas on atomic structure, and so he moved to join *Rutherford* at Manchester, and spent four years there. Rutherford's model of the atom (1911) envisaged electrons as spread around the central positive nucleus, but according to classical physics this system would be unstable. Bohr countered this difficulty by suggesting that the electron's orbital angular momentum about the nucleus can only adopt multiples of a certain fixed value, i.e., it is quantized. Radiation is then only emitted or absorbed when an electron hops from one allowed orbit to another. On this basis Bohr calculated in 1913 what the emission and absorption spectra of atomic hydrogen should be, and found excellent agreement with the observed spectrum as described by *Rydberg* and *Balmer*.

In 1916 Bohr returned to Copenhagen and two years later became the first director of its Institute of Theoretical Physics. This became the focal centre for theoretical physics for a generation, in which physicists throughout the world co-operated in developing quantum theory. In that first year Bohr established the 'correspondence principle': that a quantum description of microscopic physics must tend to the classical description for larger dimensions.

His 'complementarity principle' appeared in 1927: there is no sharp separation between atomic objects and their interaction with the instruments measuring their behaviour. This is in keeping with de Broglie's belief in the equivalence of wave and particle descriptions of matter; Heisenberg's uncertainty principle and Born's use of probability waves to describe matter also fit naturally with this principle.

Rutherford's work had developed nuclear physics to the point by the 1930s where Bohr could apply quantum theory to the nucleus also. This was held to be of neutrons and protons coupled strongly together like molecules in a liquid drop (1936). The very variable response of nuclei to collisions with neutrons of different energies could then be explained in terms of the possible excited states of this 'liquid drop'. By 1939 Bohr and G. V. Wheeler had a good theory of nuclear fission, and were able to predict that uranium-235 would be a more appropriate isotope for fission (and, as Einstein pointed out, an atomic bomb) than uranium-238.

By the autumn of 1943 Bohr was in danger in occupied Denmark (his mother was Jewish) and he chose to escape to Sweden in a fishing boat. He was then flown to England in the bomb-bay of a Mosquito aircraft. Before he left Denmark he dissolved the heavy gold medal of his Nobel Prize in acid; the inconspicuous solution escaped detection in occupied Denmark and was later reduced to metal and the medal recast from it. After his escape, he joined the atomic bomb programme. In 1944 he lobbied Roosevelt and Churchill on the danger inherent in atomic weapons and the need for agreements between the West and the USSR. This led to his organizing the first Atoms for Peace Conference in Geneva in 1955. At his death in 1962 Bohr was widely acknowledged as the foremost theoretician of this century after Einstein.

The Bohr model of the atom gave a good 'fit' with the observed spectra only for the simplest atoms (hydrogen and helium) and it was much modified later, but the concept was a milestone for physics and for chemistry. Similarly, the liquid drop model of the nucleus was to be much developed by others, and notably by Aage Bohr.

Unlike many physicists who have shaped their ideas alone, Bohr refined his ideas in discussions, which often became monologues. He was very popular with his fellow physicists, who produced a five-yearly Journal of Jocular Physics in his honour to celebrate his birthdays.

BOLTWOOD, Bertram Borden
1870-1927

American radiochemist: developed understanding of uranium decay series

Growing up fatherless, but in an academic family, Boltwood studied chemistry at Yale and then in Munich and Leipzig. From 1900 he operated a laboratory as a consultant on analytical and related problems. From 1904 he worked on radiochemistry, from 1906 at Yale, and became America's leading researcher on this. He did much to bring about understanding of the uranium decay series, to improve techniques in radiochemistry, and to introduce Pb:U ratios as a method for dating rocks.

BOLTZMANN, Ludwig Eduard
1844-1906

Austrian physicist: established classical statistical physics, and related kinetic theory to thermodynamics

Boltzmann grew up in Wels and Linz, where his father was a tax officer. He obtained his doctorate at Vienna in 1866, and held professorships during his career at Graz, Vienna, Munich and Leipzig.

Theoretical physics in the 1860s was undergoing great changes following the establishment by *Clausius* and *Kelvin* of the Second Law of Thermodynamics, the kinetic theory of gases by Clausius and *Maxwell* and the theory of electromagnetism by Maxwell. Boltzmann extended the kinetic theory, developing the law of equipartition of particle energy between degrees of freedom and also calculating how many particles have a given energy, the **Maxwell-Boltzmann distribution**.

Furthermore, Boltzmann used the mechanics and statistics of large numbers of particles to give definitions of heat and entropy (a measure of the disorder of a system). He showed that the entropy S of a system is related to the probability W (the number of 'microstates' or ways in which the system can be constructed) by $S = k \log W$ (**Boltzmann's equation**), where k is **Boltzmann's constant** ($k = 1.38 \times 10^{-23}$ JK^{-1}). Other contributions were a new derivation of *Stefan*'s law of black body radiation; and his work on electromagnetism.

Throughout his life Boltzmann was prone to depression, and this was intensified by attacks from the logical positivist philosophers in Vienna, who opposed atomistic theories of phenomena. However, he attracted students who became distinguished and had both many friends and honours. Depressed by lack of acceptance of his work, Boltzmann killed himself whilst on holiday on the Adriatic coast.

BONDI, (Sir) Hermann

1919-

Austrian-British mathematical physicist and astronomer: proponent of the steady-state theory for the origin of the universe

Bondi was born in Vienna and had his schooling there, and then studied at Cambridge where he held academic posts

Hermann Bondi in 1959

and in 1954 was appointed professor of mathematics at King's College, London. From 1967 to 1984 he was in the public service (European Space Agency, Defence, Energy, Natural Environment Research Council). He has been Master of Churchill College Cambridge, since 1983.

Bondi has worked in many areas of theoretical physics and astronomy, especially the theory of gravitation (gravitational waves etc.,). He is best known as one of the originators, with *Gold* and *Hoyle*, of the steady-state theory of the universe, according to which the universe looks the same at all times. On this basis it is considered to have no beginning and no end, with matter being spontaneously created from empty space as the universe expands, in order to maintain an unchanging uniform density. Although the theory enjoyed support for a number of years, the discovery of the cosmic microwave background in 1964 by *Penzias* and *R. W. Wilson* gave conclusive support to the rival 'big bang' theory. However, in provoking new lines of discussion, the steady-state theory made an important contribution to modern cosmology.

BOOLE, George
1815-1864

British mathematician: developed mathematical treatment of logic

Largely self-taught, Boole was a schoolteacher for a number of years before being appointed professor of mathematics at Queen's College, Cork, in 1849. His early work concerned the theory of algebraic forms, but it is for his pioneering of the subject of mathematical logic that he is best known. In 1847 he developed a form of algebra (**Boolean algebra**) that could be used to manipulate abstract logical functions, and which for the first time bridged the hitherto separate disciplines of mathematics and formal logic. Boolean algebra was essential to the development of digital computers from the principles established by *Babbage*, and has important applications in other fields such as probability and statistics.

George Boole

BORDET, Jules
1870-1961

Belgian immunologist: a founder of serology

Bordet graduated in medicine in Brussels in 1892 and taught there from 1901. While working at the Pasteur Institute in Paris in 1898 he found that if blood serum is heated to 55°C, its antibodies are not destroyed but its ability to destroy bacteria is lost. He deduced that some heat-sensitive component of serum is necessary, which *Ehrlich* called complement. In 1901 Bordet showed that this is used up when an antibody reacts with an antigen, a process called **complement fixation** and of importance in immunology. Ehrlich thought that each antigen had its own complement; Bordet thought there was only one. We now know that the immune system contains nine varieties of complement, each an enzyme system which is responsible for the destruction of a range of pathogens. For this and his other work on immunity, Bordet was awarded the Nobel Prize in 1919.

BORN, Max
1882-1970

German physicist: invented matrix mechanics and put forward the statistical interpretation of the wavefunction

Max Born was the son of a professor of anatomy at the University of Breslau, and following the death of his mother when he was four, he was brought up by his maternal grandmother. He studied at Breslau, Heidelberg, Zürich and Cambridge, gaining his PhD at Göttingen (1907). He remained there as a teacher, becoming professor of physics in 1921 and establishing a centre of theoretical physics second only to the Neils Bohr Institute in Copenhagen. As a Jew he left Germany for Cambridge in 1933, becoming a professor in Edinburgh and finally returning in retirement to Göttingen in 1953. In 1944 he was awarded the Nobel Prize for physics for his fundamental contributions to quantum mechanics, together with W. Bothe.

Initially Born's research interests were lattice dynamics, and how atoms in solids hold together and vibrate. The **Born-Haber** cycle of reactions allows calculation of the lattice energy of ionic crystals.

However, in 1923 the old quantum theory established by *Planck, Einstein, Bohr* and *Sommerfeld* remained inconsistent and unable to account for many observations. *De Broglie* then made the startlingly apt suggestion that particles possess wave-like properties (1924) and Born, *E. P. Jordan, Heisenberg* and *Pauli* in collaboration rapidly developed a sequence of important ideas. With Jordan, Born constructed (1925) a method of handling quantum mechanics using matrices (matrix mechanics) and this was the first consistent version of the new quantum mechanics. *Dirac* subsequently took this, and the equivalent wave mechanics due to *Schrödinger*, and blended them into a single theory (1926).

Born also put forward the probability interpretation of the wavefunction. In Schrödinger's wave mechanics a particle is represented by a wave packet, which unfortunately disperses in time. Born's solution was to state that the wave guides the particle in the sense that the square of the amplitude of the wavefunction is the probability of finding a particle at that point. Einstein opposed a move from deterministic to statistical physical laws and Born and Einstein discussed the issue from time to time over many years.

Born is buried in Göttingen where his gravestone displays his fundamental equation of matrix mechanics:

$$pq - qp = h/2\pi i$$

where p is the momentum operator, q the position operator and h Planck's constant.

BORODIN, Aleksander

1833-1887

Russian chemist and musician

Trained as a chemist in St Petersburg, Borodin later travelled in Europe and from 1864 held a professorship in the Russian Academy. His work was mainly in organic chemistry, where he devised methods for fluorinating organic compounds in the 1860s, and he worked on reactions of aldehydes. He showed that both polymerization and condensation of aldehydes occurs, and in this way made aldol and, from it, crotonaldehyde. His method for analysing urea was long used by biochemists.

He is well known as a composer, notably of the heroic opera *Prince Igor*, and of many songs.

BOSE, Satyendra Nath

1894-1974

Indian physicist: discovered the quantum statistics of particles of integral spin

An education at Presidency College in Calcutta led Bose to a lectureship at the Calcutta University College of Science, and another at the University of Dacca when it was formed in 1921. During his research career he made significant advances in statistical mechanics and quantum statistics, the description of all forces by a single field theory, X-ray diffraction and the interaction of electromagnetic waves with the ionosphere.

In 1924 Bose derived *Planck's* black body radiation law without the use of classical electrodynamics which Planck had needed to use. Bose was able to obtain two years leave for research and travel, and in Europe he met *de Broglie, Born* and *Einstein*. Einstein took up Bose's work and formed a general statistics of quantum systems from it (the **Bose-Einstein statistics**) which describes particles of integral spin, which may multiply occupy the same quantum state. Such particles are now known as **bosons**. An equivalent statistics for spin-½ particles which are limited to one particle per quantum state is called the **Fermi-Dirac statistics**, and the particles are called **fermions**.

BOUGUER, Pierre
1698-1758

French physicist and mathematician: pioneer of photometry

A child prodigy, being appointed teacher of hydrography at Havre at the age of 15, Bouguer is chiefly remembered for laying the foundations of photometry. He invented the heliometer, and later a photometer with which he compared the luminosities of the Sun and the Moon. He discovered that the intensity of a collimated beam of light in a medium of uniform transparency decreases exponentially with the length of its path through the medium, a result now known as **Bouguer's law** (but often incorrectly attributed to J. H. Lambert).

In geophysics the correction required to adjust gravity measurements to sea level (approximately 0.1 mgal per metre of rock) is known as the **Bouguer correction**, following his work on gravity in the Andes in 1740.

BOURBAKI, Nicholas

French group of mathematicians

This name was used as a pseudonym by an anonymous but eminent club of mainly French mathematicians. The membership of about 20 was not constant, but undoubtably included several men of great creative ability; retirement at age 50 was required. 'Bourbaki' published 33 parts of an encyclopaedic survey of modern mathematics during 1939-67.

The treatment was formalized and abstract, required expert mathematical knowledge, and was most influential in its earlier years. The attempt made by the group to persuade their readers that Bourbaki was a person failed; and the austerity of their work eventually reduced its popularity among French mathematicians, despite its elegant sophistication.

BOUSSINGAULT, Jean-Baptiste Joseph
1802-1887

French chemist: pioneer of experimental agricultural chemistry

After a school career lacking distinction, Boussingault entered the École des Mines at Saint-Étienne and soon after graduation was employed to direct a mine in Venezuela. During his ten years there he travelled and reported on the geology and geography of the area to the Institut de France, and on his return was appointed professor of chemistry at Lyons. His main work afterwards was in agricultural chemistry. He showed that legumes (peas, beans, etc.,) can secure nitrogen from the air (actually via root bacteria), whereas most plants, and all animals, cannot secure nitrogen from the air and must obtain it from their food. His work on the nutritional value of foods opened an area of study which later led to major discoveries on metabolism and on the vitamins. He found iodine in salt deposits claimed by South American Indians to be curative for goitre, which led him to suggest the use of iodine in treatment, but this was not taken up for many years.

BOVERI, Theodor Heinrich
1862-1915

German cytologist: did basic work on relation of chromosomes to heredity

Boveri began his university life as a student of history and philosophy at Munich, but soon changed to science, and later taught zoology and anatomy at Munich and Würzburg. By 1884 it was known (largely from *Beneden's* work) that in sexual reproduction the nuclei of spermatozoon and ovum provide equal numbers of chromosomes in the fusion which is the central feature of fertilization; that the chromosome number is constant for a given species; and that heredity is dependent on the nucleus. Boveri confirmed and extended Beneden's work on cell division using the roundworm *Ascaris*, and went on to study sea-urchin eggs. He was able to show that embryos which are deficient in chromosomes develop abnormally into the new individual; and that normal development requires not only an appropriate number of chromosomes for the species, but a particular selection of chromosomes. This implied that each chromosome carried in some way certain specific determiners for growth and development, and by 1910 it was fairly widely accepted that the chromosomes are the vehicles of heredity.

BOVET, Daniel

1907-

Swiss-French-Italian pharmacologist: introduced anti-histamines, and curare-type muscle relaxants for surgery

After qualifying in Geneva, Bovet went to the Pasteur Institute in Paris, later moving to Rome. In Paris he was a member of a group who showed that the antibacterial drug Prontosil owed its effect to its conversion in the body to sulphanilamide, which is the parent of the sulphonamide group of drugs. Sulphanilamide was cheap, unpatented, and its derivatives have been widely used against streptococcal infections.

Later Bovet found compounds which antagonize the action of histamine; this opened the way to widespread use of such antihistamines for the relief of allergic symptoms and related conditions (such as the common cold). A visit to Brazil began his interest in the Indian nerve poison curare; later he made simpler synthetic compounds which have a usefully short-

acting curare-type activity. These have been much used as muscle relaxants in surgical operations since 1950. Bovet received a Nobel Prize in 1957.

BOWEN, Ira Sprague

1898-1973

American astronomer: explained spectral lines seen in nebulae

In the 1860s *Huggins* had observed spectral lines in nebulae that did not correspond to any known element. In 1928 Bowen was able to explain these as being due to doubly and triply ionized oxygen and nitrogen atoms, and not to a previously unknown element as had been thought. It is the transition from such highly excited atomic states to more stable forms that gives the characteristic red and green emission colours of nebulae.

BOWEN, Norman Levi

1887-1956

Canadian geologist: used experimental petrology to reveal stages in formation of igneous rocks

The son of English immigrants, Bowen entered Queen's University in Kingston as a student in 1903, and later worked there, and at the Geophysical Laboratory at Washington DC, and at Chicago. His main work was in experimental petrology. From 1915 he studied the crystallization of natural and synthetic minerals under controlled conditions of temperature and pressure; and he linked these results with field observations of igneous rocks. He was able to deduce a crystallization series, in which differentiation occurs through the separation of crystals in stages from fused magma. The geochemistry of rock-forming silicates is complex, but Bowen's work allowed the pattern of their behaviour to be understood in general terms, and was summarized in his book *The Evolution of Igneous Rocks* (1928).

BOYER, Herbert Wayne

1936-

American biochemist: developed recombinant DNA technique to synthesize proteins

A graduate of Pittsburgh, Boyer became professor of biochemistry at the University of California at San Francisco in 1976. He showed in 1973 that a functional DNA can be constructed from two different gene sources, by splicing together segments of two different plasmids from the *E.coli* bacillus (plasmids are deposits of extrachromosomal DNA found in some bacterial strains). The result of this recombinant RNA technique, known as a chimera, was then inserted into *E.coli* and was found to replicate and to show traits derived from both the original plasmids. By the late 1970s the method was in use by Boyer and others to give biological syntheses of costly proteins such as insulin and growth hormone.

BOYLE, Robert

1627-1691

British chemist: established the study of chemistry as a separate science, and gave a definition of an element

The youngest of the 14 children of the first Earl of Cork, Boyle was educated

Robert Boyle

by a tutor at home (Lismore Castle) and at Eton. He showed an ability in languages before the age of eight, and in his interest in algebra he found a useful distraction during convalescence (he was to suffer ill-health throughout his life). His education was continued with a Grand Tour of France and Italy (1638-44), accompanied by his brother Francis and a tutor. In Italy he studied the work of the recently deceased *Galileo*. On the death of his father, Boyle retired to live simply on his estate at Stalbridge in Dorset, where he took no part in the English Civil War then raging.

Boyle moved to Oxford in 1654. He worked on an improved air-pump (which *Hooke* made for him), showing for the first time that Galileo was correct in his assertion that all objects fall at the same velocity in a vacuum. His most famous experiment was with trapped air compressed in the end of a closed shorter end of a U-shaped tube, by the addition of mercury to the open longer end of the tube, which showed that the volume of air halved if the pressure was doubled. The work was published (1660) and became known as **Boyle's law** (in Britain and the US; credited to *Marriotte* in France): it states that for a fixed mass of gas at constant temperature, the pressure and volume are inversely proportional i.e., pV=constant.

With the publication of *The Sceptical Chymist* (1661), Boyle prepared the way for a more modern view of chemistry, which put aside alchemical ideas and the Aristotelian doctrine of the four elements. He proposed the notion of elements as 'primitive and simple, or perfectly unmingled bodies' and that elements could be combined to make compounds and that compounds could be divided into their elements. Later *Lavoisier* used this approach experimentally; but it was Boyle who changed chemical attitudes and prepared the way for *Priestley* and Lavoisier to create the Chemical Revolution. He also believed in the atomic theory, and the importance of the shape of the atoms; his views here were taken from older writers. Boyle was a founder member of the Royal Society.

BOYS, (Sir) Charles Vernon
1855-1944

English experimental physicist: ingenious inventor of sensitive instruments

Educated at Cambridge and an FRS, Boys distinguished himself as a clever and original experimenter. In 1895 he designed a torsion balance which was an improvement on previous models and with this he determined the value of *Newton*'s constant of gravitation, thus arriving at a value of 5.5270 for the mean density of the Earth. He invented the micro-radiometer, a combination of a thermocouple and a delicate suspended-coil galvanometer, and with it he was able to measure the heat radiation from the Moon and planets. He proved that the surface temperature of Jupiter is low. He used quartz fibres instead of silk for delicate suspension instruments and obtained them by shooting from a bow and arrow with the molten quartz attached. He also designed a calorimeter to measure the thermal power of coal gas, and he designed a camera with moving lens with which he obtained some remarkable photographs of lightning flashes.

BRADLEY, James
1693-1762

English astronomer: discovered stellar aberration; obtained first accurate measurement of speed of light, and direct proof of Earth's motion

Bradley was *Halley*'s successor as Astronomer Royal. Whilst attempting to observe parallax in the position of γ Draconis (caused by the Earth's movement across the diameter of its orbit), Bradley found that the star did indeed appear to move, but that the greatest contrast was between September and March, not between December and June, as would be expected from parallax. He deduced that the movement (aberration) he saw was related to the ratio of the velocity of light to the velocity of the Earth about the Sun (the latter is about 30 km s^{-1}, and the ratio about 10 000 to 1). This discovery allowed him to estimate the speed of light to be $3.083 \times 10^8 \text{ m s}^{-1}$, which is more accurate than *Roemer*'s value. It also gave the first direct evidence for the Earth's motion about the Sun. Bradley also discovered nutation, the wobble of the Earth's axis caused by the changing gravitational attraction of the Moon due to its slightly inclined orbit. It was not until *Bessel*'s work, a century later, that stellar parallax was observed.

BRAGG, (Sir) William Henry
1862-1942

English physicist: discovered characteristic X-ray spectra; and developed (with his son) X-ray diffraction methods for determining crystal structures

Bragg is unusual among noteworthy researchers, in that his first significant research was done when he was over 40. However, he had as co-worker after 1912 his son Lawrence (see entry below) and their success brought a Nobel Prize in 1915; they are the only father-son pair to share one. William studied at Cambridge and did so well in mathematics that he was appointed professor in Adelaide in 1886.

In 1904 he gave a major lecture on the new subject of radioactivity, and was spurred by this to research on the subject. In 1909 he took up his duties as professor at Leeds and there began work on X-rays, inspired by *von Laue*'s recent work.

In 1913 Bragg found that when X-rays are generated by the impact of high-energy electrons on a platinum target, then as well as a continuous spectrum of X-rays there is also produced some X-ray lines whose position is characteristic of the metal target. *Moseley* was shortly to use

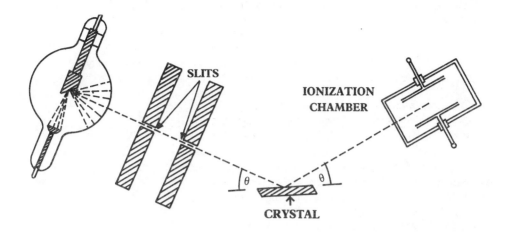

The Bragg method for studying the diffraction of X-rays by crystals. A narrow beam of X-rays from the X-ray tube (left) strikes the crystal, and an ionization chamber was used to find the position of the diffracted beam.

these X-ray spectra in a valuable way. Bragg, with his son Lawrence, went on to examine the wavelengths of X-rays by using crystals (see entry below); their method founded X-ray crystallography.

W. H. Bragg moved to University College London in 1915, worked on submarine detection in World War I, and became Director of the Royal Institution in 1923.

BRAGG, (Sir) William Lawrence
1890-1971

British physicist: founder with W. H. Bragg of X-ray crystallography

Born in Adelaide, W. L. Bragg studied mathematics there and at Cambridge, and in 1910 moved his interest to physics. Like his father, he was attracted by *von Laue*'s observation that X-rays could be diffracted by crystals. Bragg showed that the condition for diffraction by a crystal with lattice planes (layers of atoms) d apart, for X-rays of wavelength λ and angle of incidence θ, is that $n\lambda = 2d \sin \theta$ (**Bragg's law**) where n is an integer. The atomic layers of a crystal acted as mirrors, reflecting X-rays, with interference resulting from reflections at different layers when the angle of incidence met the above condition. Using an X-ray goniometer made by the father (who had taken instruction in instrument making in Adelaide) the pair were able to measure X-ray wavelengths; and then to measure d, the interatomic distance, in crystals of diamond, copper, sulphur and salts such as KCl (which they found contained only ions, and no molecules). Previously crystallography had been concerned with the angles at the exterior of crystals; now X-ray crystallography could study their atomic interior.

At 25, Lawrence Bragg was the youngest Nobel prizewinner, sharing the prize in 1915 with his father. In 1919 he became professor at Manchester and in 1938 at Cambridge. He developed methods whereby X-ray diffraction by crystals (giving on a photographic plate or film a pattern of spots whose position and intensity could be measured) can be used to determine electron density within the crystal, and therefore the position of the atoms. Modern metallurgy, crystallography and molecular biophysics owes much to his methods and to those of his co-workers in Cambridge. Like his father he became Director of the Royal

Institution (in 1954); did much to popularize science; and was knighted.

BRAHE, Tycho (*or* Tyge)

1546-1601

Danish astronomer: produced important star catalogue; the greatest pre-telescopic observer

Brahe, son of a nobleman, was brought up by a childless uncle who effectively kidnapped him, gave him a good education, and planned a political career for him. However, young Tycho at 14 saw the partial solar eclipse of 1560 and devoted his life to astronomy thereafter.

Brahe was without doubt the greatest astronomical observer of the pre-telescopic era. In 1572 he observed a nova (exploding star) in Cassiopeia, the first to be visible to the naked eye since 134 BC, and demonstrated that it was a 'fixed' star, and outside the solar system. (It was brighter than Venus for more than a year.) This was cosmologically very important, as it had been believed since *Aristotle's* time that the stars were eternal and immovable. His observations made his reputation. In 1577 the patronage of the King of Denmark, Frederick II, made possible his second great achievement. Frederick gave him the island of Hven as a gift for life, with funds to build the observatory of Uraniborg; Brahe furnished it with the best and largest instruments available, many of them designed by himself. He devoted the next 20 years to measuring the positions of 777 stars with unprecedented accuracy, thus providing an invaluable body of information for later astronomers, particularly *Kepler*.

In 1596 Frederick's successor, Christian IV, forced Brahe to leave Hven. After three years of travelling he settled in Prague, sponsored by the mad Emperor of the Holy Roman Empire, Rudolph II. He was given a castle near Prague as an observatory, and acquired the young Kepler as his assistant; the association was very fruitful, although stormy. Two years

Tycho Brahe, wearing his artificial nose

later Brahe died, leaving Kepler to publish their star catalogue, the *Rudolphine Tables*, in 1627. Talented, energetic, eccentric and quarrelsome, Brahe lost most of his nose in a duel when at 19 he fought over a mathematical dispute; his false nose, made by himself from silver, can be seen in contemporary portraits. The nova of 1572 is known as 'Tycho's star' and the best-known of lunar craters is also named after him. The magnificent Uraniborg observatory was destroyed by fire in the Thirty Years War.

BRATTAIN, Walter Houser

1902-1987

American physicist: co-inventor of the transistor

Born in China, Brattain grew up in the State of Washington on a cattle ranch, and gained his PhD in physics at Minnesota in 1929. In the same year he joined the talented team at Bell Telephone Laboratories, and soon began work on the surface properties of semiconductors; at first he used copper(I) oxide, but during World War II silicon became available, and this and germanium offered better prospects. Working with *Bardeen* and *Shockley*, and using a mix of theory and experiment, the **point-contact transistor** was developed by 1947; it used a thin germanium crystal, and both rectified and amplified current. For many purposes, the days of the vacuum tube or thermionic valve were numbered, and the silicon micro-chip, smaller, cheaper, and requiring less power, moved towards the dominant place it has held in electronics ever since. Brattain was very much a practical physicist, with a special interest in surfaces. When he left Bell in 1967, he went on to study the lipid surfaces of biological membranes at Whitman College, where he had once been a student. He shared a Nobel Prize with Bardeen and Shockley in 1956.

BRAUN, Karl Ferdinand

1850-1918

German experimental physicist: introduced crystal diodes, and the cathode-ray oscilloscope

Braun studied at Marburg and Berlin and taught at Tübingen and Strasbourg. In 1874 he found that some crystalline semiconductors (e.g., PbS) could be used as rectifiers to convert AC to DC. He used this from 1900 in his crystal diodes, which made possible the crystal radio receiver. He also modified a cathode ray tube so that its electron beam was deflected by a changing voltage; the resulting cathode-ray oscilloscope has been much used in scientific work and is also the basic component of a TV receiver.

He shared a Nobel Prize with *Marconi* in 1909.

BREIT, Gregory

1899-1981

Russian-American physicist: made contributions in quantum mechanics and nuclear physics

Breit moved to America at the age of 16 and finished his doctorate at Johns Hop-

kins University at 22. After several years of travelling, with posts at Leiden, Harvard and Minnesota, he gained a position at the Carnegie Institute, Washington. His later years were spent at New York, Wisconsin and Yale. With *Tuve* he measured the height and density of the ionosphere by reflecting short bursts of radio waves from it, which was essentially the first use of radar imaging.

However, Breit's major research was in quantum mechanics, nuclear physics and the interaction of electrons and photons (quantum electrodynamics) often in collaboration with *Wigner*. The formula giving the absorption cross-section of a nucleus as a function of energy of incoming particles is known as the **Breit-Wigner formula**.

BRENNER, Sydney

1927-

South African-British molecular biologist: co-discoverer of triplet nature of genetic codons

Educated in South Africa and at Oxford, Brenner in 1957 joined the MRC's Molecular Biology Laboratory at Cambridge, becoming its director in 1980.

In the 1950s Brenner did notable work in showing that the triplets (codons) of bases in DNA chains, each of which were believed to code for a specific amino acid destined for protein synthesis, do not form an 'overlapping' code. Thus in a sequence . . . ATCGCATAG . . . the codons could be ATC, GCA, TAG . . . but not ATC, TCG, CGC. . . . By 1961 *Brenner, Crick* and others had confirmed that codons are triplets (and not, for example, quadruplets) and that neither overlapping nor 'punctuation marks' appeared to exist in the code. In the same year Brenner and others also demonstrated that the ribosomes, which require an instructional code to carry out their task of protein synthesis, receive it in the form of a special type of RNA, messenger RNA (mRNA).

In the 1970s he began intensive studies of the nervous system of a type of nematode worm. Although less than 1 mm long, its nervous system is complex and roughly 100 genes contribute to the make-up of its nervous system. Most mutants of the worm show variations in the nervous system which can be informative, and Brenner's work has involved slicing a worm into up to 20 000 serial sections for electron microscopy in order to define the anatomy of the system, and ultimately to relate molecular biology to its visible structure and development.

BREWSTER, (Sir) David
1781-1868

Scottish physicist: discovered polarization by reflection

Trained for the church, Brewster after graduation turned to physics. He produced much factual, non-speculative work on the reflection, absorption and polarization of light. When light is reflected from a non-metallic surface, partial polarization occurs. As the angle of incidence is increased towards a glancing angle the polarization increases, passes through a maximum (the **Brewster**, or polarization, **angle**) and then decreases. **Brewster's law** states that the tangent of the Brewster angle is equal to the refractive index of the reflecting substance (1815). The Brewster angle and the angle of refraction sum to a right angle.

Brewster improved the optics of lighthouses, invented the kaleidoscope, and helped to found the British Association for the Advancement of Science.

David Brewster

BRIDGMAN, Percy Williams
1882-1961

American experimental physicist: studied effects of very high pressure on materials

A Harvard graduate, Bridgman stayed there in a variety of positions until retirement. Most of his research was concerned with very high pressures, for which he designed special equipment. He showed that most liquids become more viscous under high pressure; and that some solid compounds (e.g., ice) and solid elements (e.g., phosphorus) then exist in novel forms. He achieved pressures of 10^{10} N m^{-2}.

The **Bridgman effect** is the absorption or evolution of heat when an electric current passes through an anisotropic crystal. He was awarded the Nobel Prize in 1946.

BRIGGS, Henry
1556-1630

English mathematician: introduced 'common logarithms' (i.e., to base 10)

Educated at Cambridge, Briggs became professor of mathematics at Oxford in 1620. Noted for his work on logarithms which did more than anything to popularize their use, he suggested the decimal base instead of the Naperian, and undertook the tedious work of calculating and preparing the tables, which extended to the fourteenth place of decimals. He also introduced the method of long division which is in common use. His *Logarithmical Arithmetic* was published in 1624.

BRIGHT, Richard
1789-1858

English physician: pioneer user of clinical biochemistry

Bright studied and wrote on botany, zoology, geology and medicine, and travelled widely in Europe, from Iceland to Hungary. Working thereafter as a physician in London, he showed that disease can in some cases be linked with body chemistry and with post-mortem findings. He is best known for his recognition that kidney disease (nephritis) is linked with dropsy (accumulation of fluid in the body) and with the presence of albumin in the urine. The term **Bright's disease** was formerly used to cover the non-supperative inflammatory renal (i.e., kidney) diseases, which show these symptoms. Bright was also a skilful artist and travel writer.

BROENSTED, Johannes Nicolaus
1879-1947

Danish physical chemist

Broensted qualified in chemical engineering in 1897, and then in chemistry in 1902 in Copenhagen. He taught there from 1905. He worked mainly in electrochemistry and reaction kinetics, applying thermodynamics to chemical problems. He is best known for a definition of acids and bases, due to him (and independently and concurrently in 1923 to T. M. Lowry of Cambridge). This, the **Broensted-Lowry definition**, defines an acid as a substance with a tendency to lose a proton, and a base as a substance that tends to gain a proton.

BRONGNIART, Alexandre
1770-1847

French geologist and palaeontologist: pioneer of stratigraphic geology

Brongniart spent some time as an army engineer before being appointed, in 1800, director of the famous porcelain factory at Sévres, a post he was to hold all his life with considerable success. At the beginning of the 19th century, working with *Cuvier*, he pioneered stratigraphic geology, being the first to use the fossils contained within a geological stratum to identify and date that layer. In 1811 they published a classic study of the geology of the Paris Basin, setting out the Tertiary rocks in order and classifying them according to the fossils they contained. Brongniart was also amongst the first to recognize strata containing alternately freshwater and sea-water molluscs, and to interpret this as indicating periodic changes in sea level, an important discovery.

BROOM, Robert
1866-1951

British-South African physician and palaeontologist: confirmed significance of Australopithecus *as a hominid, and proved his bipedality*

After graduating in medicine from Glasgow in 1889, Broom practised general medicine in Australia for some years before moving to South Africa in 1897. In 1934 he gave up medicine and was appointed palaeontologist at the Transvaal Museum, Pretoria.

Something of an eccentric (he buried dead Bushmen in his garden, exhuming them when decomposed), Broom did much to clarify the classification of the fossil reptiles of Africa. In 1936, at the age of 69, he turned his attention to hominid fossils, and was almost immediately successful in finding at Sterkfontein a skull of *Australopithecus africanus*, a hominid first identified by *Dart* in 1924. Two years later a small boy brought him the jaw of another early hominid, *Australopithecus robustus*, now believed to have lived about 1-2 million years ago. These two finds convinced a hitherto sceptical scientific community of the significance of Dart's earlier claim of *Australopithecus africanus* as an ancestor of man. In 1947, when over 80, Broom found a partial skeleton of *Australopithecus* that included the pelvis, giving the first conclusive evidence that he had walked upright.

BROWN, Herbert Charles
1912-

American chemist: introduced organoboranes for organic synthesis

Brown was born in London, but his family emigrated to Chicago in 1914. He obtained a university education with difficulty, but his talent secured a professorship at Purdue in 1947 which he held until retirement in 1978. His researches included studies on carbocations and on steric effects, and especially on boron compounds. He was co-discoverer of sodium borohydride ($NaBH_4$) and pio-

Herbert C. Brown with his Nobel gold medal in 1979

neered its use for the reduction of organic compounds; and he found a simple way of making diborane (B_2H_6) and discovered its addition to unsaturated organic molecules to form organoboranes. The latter are of great value in organic syntheses, the sequence of reactions being known as **hydroboration**. He was awarded a Nobel Prize in 1979.

BROWN, Robert
1773-1858

Scottish botanist: named cell nucleus, and advanced plant taxonomy

While on service as an army medical officer, Brown met *Banks* and as a result joined the Flinders expedition to Australia in 1801: This lasted five years; Brown as naturalist collected 4000 plant species, and spent five years classifying them. In doing so he established the main differences between gymnosperms and angiosperms, and he also observed an essential part of living cells which he named the nucleus (1831). In 1827 he noticed that a suspension of pollen grains in water showed, under the microscope, continuous erratic movement. He found this also with other small particles (for example, of dyes). He had no explanation for this **Brownian movement**, but much later it was recognized as due to the molecular motion of the liquid; this was the first evidence for the existence of molecules which was based on direct observation, rather than on deduction.

BRUCE, (Sir) David
1855-1931

Scottish microbiologist: investigated undulant fever and sleeping sickness

Bruce belongs to a tradition of military medical men who worked on tropical diseases in an age of colonial concern. He studied medicine at Edinburgh, and joined the Army Medical Service in 1883. The next year he was posted to Malta.

There he studied undulant fever (now brucellosis) and in 1886 he isolated the causal bacterium. Later he and his assistants showed that unpasteurized goat's milk carried the infection to the garrison there, and control followed. Later still it was found that the same organism caused contagious abortion in cattle, and that it can be transmitted by a variety of animals.

In 1894 Bruce went to South Africa to study nagana, another disease of cattle, and soon showed it to be carried by the tsetse fly, and to be due to a trypanosome, a protozoal parasite now named as *T.brucei*. Soon Bruce and others showed that the human disease known as African sleeping sickness (trypanosomiasis) is due to the same organism, transmitted in the same way by the bite of the tsetse fly.

In 1912 Bruce was promoted to Surgeon-General and in World War I was Commandant of the Royal Army Medical College. His research was always carried out with his wife, Mary Elizabeth, a skilled microscopist. She shared all his work, including two years in a primitive hut in the Zululand bush studying nagana, and a period as theatre nurse during the siege of Ladysmith, with Bruce as the surgeon.

BRUNEL, Isambard Kingdom

1806-1859

British civil engineer: pioneer designer of large steamships

Brunel revealed a talent for drawing and grasp of geometry by the age of six. His father, Sir Marc Isambard Brunel, having fled his native France and the Revolution for America before settling in Britain, educated his son in England, Normandy and Paris. Brunel joined his father in his engineering projects and in 1825 helped him to construct the first tunnel under the Thames (designed for foot passengers but later used by the London Underground). Isambard Brunel (Kingdom was his mother's surname) was a short man with a commanding presence, an ability to lead and a capacity for hard work which contributed to his early death. He confessed to self-conceit.

In 1830 Brunel won the competition for a design for the Clifton Suspension Bridge, his first independent work. He was appointed engineer of the Great Western Railway in 1833. He surveyed the route, designed tunnels, bridges and the termini at Paddington and Temple Meads, Bristol. Then Brunel turned to the design of steamships to cross the Atlantic, the problem being carriage of sufficient fuel for the distance. Brunel realized that capacity for fuel increased with the cube of the ship's size; its power requirement increased with the square of the size, so a big enough vessel could succeed. He built the *Great Western* in oak in traditional manner, to make an extension to the Great Western Railway; it made the crossing to New York in 15 days in 1838. He designed and built the *Great Britain*, an iron-hulled, screw-driven vessel which was then the largest vessel afloat. He went on to design the *Great Eastern* to carry 4 000 passengers around the world without refuelling. Immense, double skinned with ten boilers, the ship was beset with financial and other problems from the start; it was eventually used to lay the Atlantic cable of 1865.

The great liners which dominated intercontinental travel for a century stemmed from Brunel's confident approach to large-scale ship construction based on steel.

BRUNO, Giordano

1548-1600

Italian philosopher: supporter of Copernican (heliocentric) system

Bruno entered but later left the Dominican Order, and spoke and wrote supporting radical views on religion, the infinity of space, the motion of the Earth, and the Copernican system. He travelled widely in Europe, was arrested by the Inquisition (1592) and after a lengthy trial refused to recant. Details of the trial have been destroyed, but Bruno was burned at the stake in 1600. It is usually believed that this event influenced *Galileo* in favour of recanting when he was similarly charged with heresy and supporting the heliocentric system, in 1633.

BUCHNER, Eduard
1860-1917

German organic chemist: showed that fermentation does not require living cells

Buchner's elder brother Hans (see below), first interested and guided him in science, succeeding so well that Eduard studied botany under *Naegeli* and chemistry under *Baeyer* and became the latter's assistant. From 1893 he was professor at Kiel, and after several moves, at Würzburg from 1911 until he was killed in action in World War I.

Until Buchner's work in 1897, it had been believed that fermentation required intact living yeast cells. Buchner tested this view by grinding yeast cells with sand, and pressing from the mixture a cell-free extract. This extract when added to sugar solution, caused fermentation to ethanol and CO_2 much as would yeast cells. The vitalist view was defeated. Buchner named the active principle 'zymase'. We now call such biological catalysts 'enzymes', and recognize that they are proteins, highly specific in action, and involved in nearly all biochemical changes. Buchner won the Nobel Prize for chemistry in 1907. His brother Hans Buchner (1850-1902) worked in bacteriology, and showed that protein in blood serum was important in immunity.

BUFFON, (Comte) Georges-Louis
1707-1788

French naturalist and polymath: surveyed much of biology and had early ideas on evolution of species

Buffon's mother was rich, and despite his father's desire that Buffon should study law, it is likely that he studied medicine and mathematics. A duel made him leave France in 1730 for two years, but on his return he became active in scientific and financial circles; he was highly energetic and both increased his fortune and contributed to most of the sciences of the time. His range was vast; he translated *Hales* and *Newton* into French, introduced calculus into probability theory, worked on microscopy, tensile strength, cosmology amd geology, and the origin of life. His ideas were non-theological, rational, and ahead of their time if not always correct. From 1739 he was in charge of the Jardin du Roi, the natural history museum and botanical garden of Paris, which he much improved and enlarged. His vast and beautifully illustrated *Natural History* (44 vols., by 1804) attempted to provide a survey of the natural world and was much esteemed. In it he noted that animal species are not fixed but show variation, and he recognized vestigial features such as the pig's toes, a contribution to later theories of evolution, together with his view of 'common ancestors' for similar species. He devised some eccentric experiments: for example to check the legend that *Archimedes* fired the Roman fleet with mirrors and the Sun's rays when 'distant by a bowshot' he used 168 mirrors, and ignited timber at 50 m range.

BULLARD, (Sir) Edward Crisp
1907-1980

British geophysicist: made first measurement of geothermal heat flow through oceanic crust, and proposed dynamo theory for the Earth's magnetic field

Bullard served in naval research during World War II, afterwards working in Cambridge and North America before becoming director of the National Physical Laboratory, England. In 1964 he was appointed director of the Department of Geodesy and Geophysics at Cambridge.

Bullard made the first successful measurements of geothermal heat flow through the oceanic crust, establishing that it is similar in magnitude to that of continental crust, and not lower as had been thought.

In the late 1940s and 1950s, independently of *Elsasser*, he proposed the dynamo theory for the origin of the Earth's magnetic field, in which the field is generated by the motion of the Earth's liquid iron core undergoing convection. Providing that there is a small magnetic field to start with, the movement of the molten iron will set up electric currents which will in turn generate the observed magnetic field. In 1965 Bullard was also the first to use computer modelling techniques to study continental drift, finding an excellent fit between Africa and South America at the 500-fathom (close to 1000 m) contour.

R. W. Bunsen, G. Kirchhoff and H. E. Roscoe in 1862

BUNSEN, Robert Wilhelm
1811-1899

German chemist: wide-ranging experimenter, and pioneer of chemical spectroscopy

Bunsen's father was Librarian and Professor of Linguistics in Göttingen, and Robert studied chemistry there, before travelling and studying also in Paris, Berlin and Vienna. He became Professor at Heidelberg in 1852 and remained there until retirement, ten years before his death.

Bunsen was pre-eminently an experimentalist with little interest in theory. His first major research did much to support the radical theory, due largely to *Dumas* and *Liebig*, which held that organic groups ('compound radicals') correspond, in part, to the simple atoms of inorganic compounds. He prepared a series of compounds all containing the cacodyl group, $(CH_3)_2As$-; and did so despite their remarkably offensive character. They combine a repulsive and persistent odour, with toxicity and flammability. The pres-

ence in all of them of the same cacodyl group effectively established the theory. During this work Bunsen lost the sight of an eye, and nearly died of arsenic poisoning; he excluded organic chemistry from his laboratory thereafter.

With his fellow-professor *Kirchhoff* he discovered the use of spectroscopy in chemical analysis (1859) and within two years they had discovered the new elements caesium and rubidium with its aid. He devised the Bunsen cell, a zinc-carbon primary cell which he used to obtain metals (Cr and Mb) by electrodeposition from solution, and others (Mg, Al, Na, Ba, Ca, Li) by electrolysis of the fused chlorides. To find the relative atomic mass of these metals he measured their specific heat capacity (to apply *Dulong*'s law) and for this he designed an ice calorimeter. He was a master of gas analysis, and used it in many ways; e.g., his study of Icelandic volcanoes, and the improvement of English blast-furnaces. He was a pioneer, working with *Roscoe*, in photochemistry, and for this devised a photometer and an actinometer. His great interest in analysis led him to invent many laboratory devices, including the filter pump. The Bunsen gas burner was probably devised and sold by his technician, Peter Desdega, and based on one due to *Faraday*.

Bunsen was a great teacher and his lecture courses were famous; his researches continued until he was 80. Like *Dalton* he admitted that he never found time to marry. *Emil Fischer*'s wife said of Bunsen 'First, I would like to wash Bunsen, and then I would like to kiss him because he is such a charming man.'

BURKITT, Denis Parsons
1911-

Irish epidemiologist: discovered Burkitt's lymphoma, a cancer caused by a virus

Born and educated in Ulster, Burkitt entered Dublin to study engineering but changed to medicine and specialized in surgery. Working in Uganda in the 1950s, he discovered the type of cancer now known as Burkitt's lymphoma. This presents as swellings of the jaw, usually in children of 6-8 years. Burkitt toured Africa to examine its incidence, and found it mainly in areas where malaria is endemic; but no micro-organism linked with it could be detected initially, so a virus was clearly a possibility. However, attempts made in London to establish tissue cultures of the cancer cells were unsuccessful until 1964. Then the cells were grown in culture; and electron microscopy showed them to be infected with the Epstein-Barr virus. It seems likely that the lymphoma is caused by a conjunction of factors, including the virus (which is very common, worldwide) and exposure to malaria.

Burkitt is a protagonist for high-fibre diets, partly because some bowel diseases common in developed countries are rare in Africa, where such diets are usual.

BURNET, (Sir) Frank Macfarlane
1899-1985

Australian medical scientist: made studies of viruses and the immune system

A graduate in medicine from Melbourne, Burnet spent two year-long visits studying bacteriology in London, and the rest of his career in Melbourne. In the 1930s he worked on viruses, where his successes included studies on bacteriophages (viruses which attack bacteria), and a method for culturing some viruses in living chick embryo. This last work led him to the view that an animal's ability to produce antibody in response to an antigen is not inborn, but is developed during foetal life. (Evidence that this is correct was later found by *Medawar*.) Burnet also worked on the mode of action and the epidemiology of influenza virus, the cholera vibrio, polio and Q fever. His clonal selection theory (1951) offered a general scheme explaining how an immune system develops the ability to distinguish between 'self' and 'nonself' and initiated both controversy and further work by others. He shared a Nobel Prize with Medawar in 1960.

BURY, Charles
1890-1968

English physical chemist: little-known theorist on electronic structure of atoms

Bohr is usually credited with the feat of first giving a clear account of the arrangement of electrons in atoms and its relation to chemical behaviour. In fact the first rough suggestion of electron 'shells' is due to *J. J. Thomson* (1904), and *Langmuir* (1919) gave a more detailed shell model which is partly incorrect, which he linked with chemical behaviour. In 1921 Bohr gave a better version, but it was very brief and was only a limited account (he gives electronic structures only for the noble gases). Within a month, a concise, clear, and complete account was given by Bury (in the Journal of the American Chemical

Society), who had written his paper before he saw Bohr's. All later accounts use the Bury scheme.

Bury was an Oxford graduate in chemistry, who served five years in World War I. His classic paper written when he was 31 was his first, but he went on to study the relation of colour to structure in dyes, and the properties of micelles. Again, his work on dyes appears to have preceded better-known work by others: Bury was a modest man.

BUTENANDT, Adolf Frederick Johann

1903-

German organic chemist: developed chemistry of sex hormones

A student at Marburg and Göttingen, Butenandt later held posts in Danzig, Berlin and Tübingen. His work was mainly in the field of sex hormones. In 1929 he isolated the first pure sex hormone, oestrone, from pregnancy urine; his assistant Brika did the bioassays. They married in 1931. He also isolated the male hormone androsterone from male urine in 1931. He was awarded the Nobel Prize in 1939, but his government forbade his acceptance. He secured progesterone (20 mg from the ovaries of 50 000 sows) in 1934; and later worked on an insect hormone (ecdysone) and other insect pheromones. He showed the relation between the above compounds, which are all members of the steroid group, and did much to establish the chemistry of this interesting and valuable group.

BUYS BALLOT, Christoph Hendrik Diederik

1817-1890

Dutch meteorologist: described the direction of rotation of cyclones

Buys Ballot was appointed professor of mathematics at the University of Utrecht in 1847, and in 1854 founded the Netherlands Meteorological Institute. In 1857 he showed that, in the northern hemisphere, winds circulate counterclockwise around low-pressure areas and clockwise around high pressure ones, a fact now known as **Buys Ballot's law**; the situation is reversed in the southern hemisphere.

C

CAGNIARD DE LA TOUR, Charles
1777-1859

French physicist: discovered critical state of liquids

Cagniard studied at the École Polytechnique, Paris. He is primarily remembered for his discovery in 1822 of the critical state of liquids. For certain liquids, when heated in a sealed tube, the meniscus disappears and liquid and vapour become indistinguishable at a critical temperature. Cagniard was also an inventor, his best-known device being the disk siren (in which a note is produced by blowing air through holes in a spinning disk).

CAILLETET, Louis Paul
1832-1913

French physicist: pioneer of liquifaction of gases

Cailletet studied in Paris and then returned to Chatillon-sur-Seine to manage his father's ironworks. His first interest was metallurgy, which led him to study blast furnace gas and to interest himself in gas properties. At that time, attempts to liquify some gases (for example H_2, N_2 and O_2) had all failed and they were classed as 'permanent gases'. Cailletet learned of *T. Andrews*'s work on critical temperature, which suggested to him that more cooling was needed, as well as pressure, for success. He used the *Joule-Thomson* effect (the cooling which occurs when a gas expands through a nozzle) followed by pressure, and by 1878 had liquified these 'permanent' gases. He was interested in flying (even in advance of the development of the aeroplane) and the sundry devices he invented included a high-altitude breathing apparatus and an aircraft altimeter.

CALVIN, Melvin
1911-

American biochemist: elucidated biosynthetic paths in photosynthesis

Calvin studied at Michigan, Minnesota and Manchester and then began teaching at the University of California at Berkeley in 1937. Except for war work on the atomic bomb, he remained there for the rest of his career. His interest in photosynthesis began in Manchester and developed from 1946, when new and sensitive analytical methods (notably the use of

Melvin Calvin in 1961

radioisotope labelling, and chromatography) became available. **Photosynthesis** is the process whereby green plants absorb carbon dioxide from the air, and convert it by complex stages into starch and oxygen (which is discharged into the air, at the rate of about 10^{12} kg per year). This can be claimed as the most important of all biochemical processes, since animal life also depends on plant foods and on the oxygen-rich atmosphere which, over geological time, photosynthesis has provided.

Calvin allowed the single-celled green algae *Chlorella* to absorb radioactive CO_2 for seconds only, and then detected the early products of reaction. He identified a cycle of reactions (the reductive pentose phosphate or **Calvin cycle**) which form an important part of photosynthesis. He was awarded the Nobel Prize for chemistry in 1961.

Most recently his work involves the attempt to produce entirely synthetic sensitizers and catalysts which would permit the construction of a device to photochemically produce oxygen from water and reduce carbon dioxide to a useful chemical.

CAMERARIUS, Rudolf Jakob
1665-1721

German botanist: demonstrated sexual reproduction in plants

Camerarius followed his father as professor of medicine at Tübingen, and he was also director of the botanic garden there. *Ray* and others had suggested that plants can reproduce sexually, but it was Camerarius who first showed by experiment that this is so. In 1694 he separated some dioecious plants (i.e., plants in which the male and female flowers are borne on separate plants) and showed that although the pistillate plants gave fruit, they did not produce seed in the absence of staminate flowers. He identified the stamens as the male plant organs, and the carpels (consisting of the style, ovary and stigma) as the female apparatus of a flowering plant. He also described pollination.

CANDOLLE, Augustin-Pyramus de
1778-1841

Swiss botanist

Candolle studied in Geneva and Paris, and from 1806-1812 made a botanical survey of France as a government commission. His ideas on taxonomy, set out in his *Elementary Theory of Botany* (1813) developed from and replaced the schemes due to *Cuvier* and *Linnaeus* and were used for 50 years. He believed that morphology, rather than physiology, should be the basis of taxonomy; and that relationships between plants could be best seen by studying the symmetry of their sexual parts. From this he was led to the idea of homology. He also studied plant geography and the influence of soil type in his travels to Brazil and the Far East. He taught at Montpelier and, from 1816, at Geneva.

CANNIZZARO, Stanislao
1826-1910

Italian chemist: resolved confusions on atomic and molecular mass

Cannizzaro began his university life as a medical student, but attended a variety of courses and became attracted to chemistry, partly because he saw it as the basis of physiology. In 1847 he joined the rebel artillery in one of the frequent rebellions in his native Sicily, where his magistrate father was at the time Chief of the Police. The rebellion failed, and Cannizzaro wisely continued his chemistry in Paris, with *Chevreul*. Two years later he returned to Italy, teaching chemistry in three universities (all with poor equipment), and married an Englishwoman.

In 1853 he discovered the **Cannizzaro reaction**, in which an aldehyde (aromatic, or having no α-hydrogen) is treated with a strong base to give an acid and an alcohol:

$$2\,RCHO + NaOH \rightarrow RCO_2Na + RCH_2OH$$

However, his main work was done in 1858, when he cleared the way to a single system of relative atomic and molecular mass. He did this by seeing the value of the theory due to *Avogadro* (then dead) and using it to deduce that common gaseous elements exist as molecules (H_2, N_2, O_2) rather than as single atoms. With this in mind, Avogadro's law enables relative atomic and molecular mass to be deduced from the densities of gases and vapours. (Initially, as hydrogen gas was the lightest known, the hydrogen atom was assigned atomic mass = 1; we now use as a basis the common isotope of carbon = 12, which gives a very similar scale.) Cannizzaro's fervour as a speaker at a chemical conference in 1860, and a pamphlet he distributed there, convinced most chemists and removed basic ambiguities in chemical ideas, during the 1860s. The half-century of confusion on atomic mass which had followed *Dalton's* atomic theory had ended.

He became a Senator in 1871, and afterwards worked mainly on public health.

CANNON, Walter Bradford
1871-1945

American physiologist: introduced first radio-opaque agent

Cannon was very much a Harvard man; he was an arts student there, then a medical student, and professor of physiology from 1906-42. *Roentgen* discovered X-rays in 1896, and the next year Cannon, still a student, tried feeding a cat a meal containing a bismuth compound to give an X-ray 'shadow' of its alimentary tract. The method worked, and made the mechanics of digestion visible; and with a barium compound in place of bismuth, it has been used in diagnostic radiography ever since. Cannon went on to work on the effect of shock and emotion on the nervous system, and the transmission of nerve impulses. He developed *Bernard's* concept of the importance of a constant internal physiological environment (i.e., a narrow range of salt, sugar, oxygen and temperature in the living body) which he named **homeostasis**, and he studied the mechanism which achieves this essential equilibrium. Later he applied similar ideas to political and social organizations, but without the same success.

CARDANO, Girolamo
1501-1576

Italian mathematician and physician: gave general algebraic method for solving cubic equations

Cardano was the illegitimate son of a Milanese lawyer; a situation which caused difficulty for him both practically and emotionally. He was taught mathematics by his father when young and educated at Pavia and Padua where he studied medicine. He was unable to enter the college of physicians because of his birth, but eventually gained recognition through his work, and became professor of medicine

Girolamo Cardano

at Pavia in 1544 and at Bologna in 1562. His work in medicine is now eclipsed by his distinction as one of the greatest algebraists of his century. He recognized negative and complex roots for equations, found the relations between the roots of an equation and the coefficients of its terms, and gave a general algebraic method for solving cubic equations (**Cardano's solution**). He has been accused of pilfering parts of this method from *Tartaglia*, but the accusation has been contested.

His contribution to chemical thought is more substantial than is often recognized. He wrote an encyclopaedia of the sciences which discusses the major chemical theories of the time. He was credulous in many ways, but critical of alchemical claims. He recognized only three Aristotelian elements (earth, water and air), arguing ahead of his time, that fire is not a substance but a form of motion; and he distinguished between electrical and magnetic attraction. His writing includes a variety of chemical recipes, and his chemical and clinical interests are brought together in a text on toxicology.

Cardano's life was not easy, his childhood was marred by ill-health and harsh treatment while his talents emerged and were acknowledged late in life. His eldest son was convicted and beheaded for wife-murder, and his second son was exiled at Cardano's instigation as 'a youth of evil habits'. Cardano describes himself in his autobiography as '... timid of spirit, I am cold of heart, warm of brain, and given to never-ending meditation. I ponder over ideas ...'. He was a man who made more enemies than friends.

CARLSON, Chester

1906-1968

American physicist: inventor of xerography

Carlson worked for a printer before studying physics at the California Institute of Technology; he then worked for the Bell Telephone Company before taking a law degree and moving to the patent department of an electronics firm. During the Depression he decided that invention was a way to prosperity, and in his spare time he searched for a cheap, dry method of copying documents. After three years he focused on a scheme using electrostatic attraction to cause powder to adhere to plain paper, and got his first copies in 1938. It took another twelve years to develop a commercial xerographic copier; he died a very wealthy man.

CARNOT, (Nicolas Léonard) Sadi

1796-1832

French theoretical physicist: a founder of thermodynamics through his theoretical study of an idealized heat engine

Carnot's family was unusual. His father, Lasare Carnot, was the 'Organizer of Victory' for the Revolutionary Army in 1794, and became Napoleon's minister of war; unusually, he left politics for science in 1807 and did good work in pure and applied mathematics and in engineering. Sadi had one brother, Hippolyte, also a politician, whose son became President of France. Sadi was educated by his father and at the École Polytechnique, and served in the army as an engineer, leaving it as a captain in 1828. He was a cholera victim in the Paris epidemic of 1832.

His scientific work was highly original, and the single paper he published before his early death did much to create the new science of thermodynamics. His paper was *Reflections on the Motive Power of Fire* (1824) and it originated in Carnot's interest in steam engines, which had been developed by British engineers and as the nationalistic Carnot realized, were generating an industrial revolution in the UK. However, their theory was nonexistent and their efficiency very low. Carnot set out to deduce if the efficiency could be improved, and whether steam was the best 'working substance'. His paper is a brilliant success, despite the fact that he used the caloric theory of heat, which presumed it to be a 'subtle fluid'. (This did not affect the main answers; and incidentally, Carnot's notes show that long before his death he was converted to modern heat theory.) He also used the correct idea that perpetual motion is impossible, a fact of experience.

In his paper, Carnot considers an idealized steam engine, frictionless, with its working substance passing from heat source to heat sink through a series of equilibrium states, so that it is truly reversible. The pressure-volume changes in it constitute a **Carnot cycle**. He was able to show that the efficiency of such an engine depends only on the temperature (T_1) of the heat source and the temperature (T_2) of the heat sink; that the maximum fraction of the heat energy convertible into work is $(T_1 - T_2)/T_2$; and that it does not depend at all on the working substance (**Carnot's theorem**). These ideas, which were eventually to mean so much for both engineers and theoreticians, were too abstract to attract much interest in 1824. In 1849 when *W. Thomson* saw the paper he realized its importance, and he and *Clausius* made it widely known. The paper contains ideas linked with the laws of conservation of energy and the First Law of Thermodynamics, and led Thomson and Clausius towards the Second Law. Later still, *Gibbs* and others were to use thermodynamic ideas to forecast whether chemical reactions will occur.

CAROTHERS, Wallace Hume
1896-1937

American industrial chemist: discovered fibre-forming polyamides (nylons)

The son of a teacher, Carothers graduated from a small college and later both studied and taught chemistry at three universities, before moving in 1928, to the research department of the Du Pont Company at Wilmington. His object was 'to synthesize compounds of high molecular mass and known constitution'; an early success was

Neoprene, the first successful synthetic rubber, marketed from 1932. He then studied the linear polymers made by condensing a dibasic acid with a diamine. By heating adipic acid with hexamethylenediamine at 270° he obtained Nylon 6.6, which can be melt-spun into fibres:

$$HO_2C(CH_2)_4CO_2H + H_2N(CH_2)_6NH_2 \rightarrow$$
$$...CONH(CH_2)_6NHCO(CH_2)_4...$$

This polyamide has a relative molecular mass of $10-15 \times 10^3$, with useful properties as a textile fibre, and has had much commercial success. Carothers established useful principles in research on polymers. Despite his successes he suffered from depression, and soon after his marriage killed himself at the age of 41.

CARREL, Alexis
1873-1944

French-American surgeon: pioneer of vascular surgery, and perfusion methods

Carrel qualified in medicine at Lyons in 1900. He was a skilful surgeon, but lacked interest in routine surgery and in 1904 visited Canada, intending to become a cattle rancher. However, later in 1904 he moved to Chicago and in 1906 joined the Rockefeller Institute for Medical Research in New York. He remained there until retirement in 1939, except for an interlude as a French Army surgeon in World War I (when he shared the introduction of the Carrel-Dakin solution (mainly NaOCl) for the antiseptic treatment of deep wounds). Even before World War I he began to attack the problem of organ transplantation. One difficulty in this is the need to ensure a blood supply to the transplanted organ, without failure due to thrombosis or stenosis. Carrel developed methods for suturing blood vessels with minimum damage and risk of infection or thrombosis. These techniques greatly advanced vascular surgery.

He went on to study methods of keeping organs alive by perfusion (i.e., passage of blood or a blood substitute through the organ's blood vessels). With C. Lindbergh the aviator, he produced a perfusion pump ('artificial heart') in 1935. Major advances (e.g., in dealing with rejection of donor tissues) were needed before transplants of organs such as the kidney could be achieved by others after World War II, but Carrel's methods were essential for that later success.

CARRINGTON, Richard Christopher
1826-1875

English astronomer: discovered differential rotation of Sun with latitude

A wealthy amateur, Carrington made over five thousand observations of sunspots between 1853 and 1861, and showed that the Sun does not rotate as a solid body, but that its rotational period varies from 25 days at the equator to 27.5 days at latitude 45°. He also discovered solar flares in 1859.

CASIMIR, Hendrik Brugt Gerhard
1909-

Dutch physicist: originated the 'two-fluid' model of superconductivity

Casimir was educated at the universities of Leiden, Copenhagen and Zürich. He held a variety of research positions until, in 1942, he began a career with Philips. He became director of the Philips Research Laboratories in 1946.

Casimir's papers cover aspects of theoretical physics, particularly low-temperature physics and superconductivity. W. Meissner had examined some properties of superconductors, such as the expulsion of a magnetic field below the superconducting transition temperature (the **Meissner effect**). Casimir and C. Gorter proposed in 1934 that two sorts of electrons exist, normal and superconducting, and used this to explain the relation between thermal and magnetic properties in superconductors. When *Bardeen* and others produced the BCS theory it was clear that the two categories represented unpaired electrons and paired electrons (called Cooper pairs).

CASSINI, Giovanni Domenico
1625-1712

Italian-French astronomer: greatly enhanced knowledge of the planets

Born in Italy, Cassini became Director of the Paris Observatory in 1669 and never returned to Italy. He added greatly to our knowledge of the planets of the solar system. It was he who worked out the rotational periods of Jupiter, Mars and Venus, and tabulated the movement of the Jovian satellites discovered by *Galileo* (*Roemer* subsequently used his results to calculate the speed of light). Between 1671 and 1674 he discovered four new satellites of Saturn (Iapetus, Rhea, Dione and Tethys) and in 1675 observed the gap in Saturn's ring system first noted ten years before by William Balle, and now known as the Cassini division. Most importantly, he was able to calculate the first reasonably accurate figure (only 7% low) for the Earth's distance from the Sun (the astronomical unit). To do this he observed Mars from Paris at the same time as Richter observed it in French Guiana, 10 000 km away. The parallax gave the distance of Mars, and *Kepler's* third law then gave the distances of the other planets. In later life he attempted to measure the shape of the Earth, but concluded incorrectly that it was a prolate spheroid. Three generations of his descendants succeeded him as Director of the Paris Observatory; all were highly conservative astronomers, resisting major new theories.

CAUCHY, (Baron) Augustin Louis
1789-1857

French mathematician: founded complex analysis

The Terror of 1793-94 drove the Cauchy family to their country retreat at Arcueil, and there Augustin was educated by his father. He also became badly malnourished, which affected his health for the rest of his life. In 1805 he entered the École Polytechnique, and after moving to the École de Pont et Chaussés served as an engineer in Napoleon's army. In 1813 ill health caused his return to Paris; three years later he became a professor at the École Polytechnique. With the restoration of the Bourbons and departure of republicans such as *Monge* and others, Cauchy was elected to the Academy of Sciences. In the same year (1816) he published a paper on wave modulation which won him the Grand Prix of the Academy. His recognition and status increased (including a chair at the Collège de France), but all was lost with Charles X's abdication in 1830, following the July Revolution. Cauchy was extremely pious, and although sincere was 'a bigoted Catholic' even according to *Abel*. He refused to take a new oath of allegiance and went into exile.

A professorship at Turin followed, together with a tedious period as tutor to Charles X's son in Prague. Although Cauchy stuck to his principles, the Government fortunately turned a blind eye, and in 1838 he returned to a professorship at the École Polytechnique, and at the Sorbonne in 1848. He died of a fever at the age of 68, after a highly creative lifetime in mathematics, and mathematical physics, which included seven books and over 700 papers. His tally of sixteen named concepts and theorems compare with those of any other mathematician.

Cauchy played a large part in founding modern mathematics by his introduction of rigour into calculus and mathematical analysis. He published on convergence, limits and continuity and defined the integral as the limit of a sum. Together with *Gauss*, Cauchy created the theory of real and complex functions, including complex analysis and contour integration. He recognized the theory of determinants and initiated group theory by studying substitution groups.

Augustin Louis Cauchy

CAVENDISH, Henry
1731-1810

English chemist and physicist: studied chemistry of gases and of air, water, and nitric acid; made discoveries in heat and electricity and measured density of the Earth

As eldest son of Lord Charles Cavendish (FRS), and grandson of the 2nd Duke of Devonshire, Henry was wealthy and well educated. His mother died when he was two. He spent four years at Cambridge, took no degree, and studied in Paris for a year before making his homes in London. (For living, Gower Street; workshop and laboratory, Clapham; library, Dean Street, Soho). Thereafter he devoted his

Henry Cavendish. This is probably the only portrait of him, and was made without his knowledge.

synthesis of water in this way cast out the long-held idea that water is an element. These experiments also convinced Cavendish that heat was weightless. He examined air from different places, heights, and climates, and showed it to be of nearly constant composition. He showed that nitric acid is formed by passing sparks through air (when N_2 and O_2 combine, and the NO reacts with water). Cavendish, like *Priestley*, interpreted his results on the phlogiston theory, and Cavendish thought hydrogen was phlogiston. Cavendish, unlike Priestley, realised that *Lavoisier*'s theory would also explain his results. He noticed that a small residue ($\approx 1\%$) of air remained after long sparking; this was later found by *Ramsay* and *Rayleigh* to be argon, a noble gas and a new element.

In physics, Cavendish used a method devised by *Michell* to determine the gravitational constant (G), in 1798. *Bouguer* had earlier attempted to find the density of the Earth; Cavendish's value for G (from which the Earth's mass and density is easily calculated) gave a mean density of nearly 5.5 times that of water. (*Boys* obtained a slightly more accurate value, by the same method, a century later). Since most rock has a density in the range 3-4, a metal core for the Earth could be deduced.

Most of Cavendish's work on heat and electricity was not published by him, but was revealed from his notes after 1879 by *Maxwell*. He showed that Cavendish had distinguished between quantity and intensity of electricity; and that he had measured the electrical conductivity of salt solutions. He had proved that the inverse square law (*Coulomb*'s law) holds (within 2%) by showing that no charge exists inside a charged hollow spherical conductor, a result which is consistent only with that law. He worked on specific and latent heat (possibly knowing of *Black*'s work) and believed heat to stem from 'internal motion of the particles of bodies'. After 60 years of research, he chose (characteristically) to die alone. In his long lifetime this eccentric recluse

time and money to personal research in chemistry and physics. He had a most peculiar personality: although he enjoyed scientific friends and discussion, he otherwise avoided conversation to an extreme degree, especially with women. He was generous with money, but not to himself. He published only a part of his scientific work, although he was unperturbed by either jealousy or criticism. When he was 40 he inherited a large fortune, but he was not interested in it, although he did use part of it to form a library and apparatus collection. This was used by the public and by himself on the same terms, and characteristically was located well away from his house. He was described as 'the richest of the learned, and the most learned of the rich' and as having 'uttered fewer words in the course of his life than any man who lived to fourscore years'.

In 1766 he described methods for handling and weighing gases. He studied 'fixed air' (CO_2) showing that it was produced by fermentation or from acid and marble; and he re-studied 'inflammable air' (H_2, which had been studied by *Boyle*). He exploded mixtures of hydrogen and air with an electric spark, and found that no weight was lost, and that the product 'seemed pure water' (1784). The volume ratio he found to be 2:1; and the achieved most in chemistry; notably in showing that gases could be weighed, that air is a mixture, and that water is a compound– all fundamental matters if chemistry was to advance. His work in physics was equally remarkable, but was largely without influence because much was unpublished. The famous Cambridge physics laboratory named after him was funded by a talented mathematical kinsman, the 7th Duke of Devonshire, in 1871.

CAYLEY, Arthur

1821-1895

English mathematician: developed n-dimensional geometry, and the theory of matrices and algebraic invariants

Cayley, the son of an English merchant, spent his first eight years in Russia, where his father was then working. He was educated at King's College School, London and Trinity College, Cambridge. Reluctant to be ordained, which was a necessary condition to remain a Fellow of Trinity College, he became a barrister. For 14 years he practised law, and only accepted the Sadlerian Chair of Pure Mathematics in Cambridge in 1863 when the requirement over religious orders was dropped.

He managed to publish over 300 papers whilst a barrister, and by his death he had published over 900 covering all areas of pure mathematics, theoretical dynamics and astronomy. While they were both lawyers Cayley and his friend *Sylvester* established the theory of algebraic invariants.

Cayley also developed a theory of metrical geometry, linking together projective geometry and non-Euclidean geometry. Together with *Klein* he classified geometries as elliptic or hyperbolic depending on the curvature of space upon which the geometry was drawn (that is, whether a surface is saddle-like or dome-like).

Arthur Cayley

The theory of matrices was an invention of Cayley's and allowed compact manipulation of the many components of a geometrical system. The movement of a vector (directed line) when the space in which it is embedded is distorted can be described by this theory.

Cayley was a prolific mathematician with a strong and dependable character, much in demand both as a lawyer and administrator.

CELSIUS, Anders

1701-1744

Swedish astronomer: devised Celsius scale of temperature

Celsius devised a thermometric scale in 1742, taking the boiling point of water as 0° and the melting point as 100°. Five years later, colleagues at Uppsala observatory inverted the scale, to its present form.

In thermodynamics, temperatures are measured on the absolute or kelvin scale. However, the **Celsius scale** is often used for other purposes, and is now defined by the relation

$$(\text{temp in } °C)=(\text{temp in K})-273.15$$

CHADWICK, (Sir) James
1891-1974

English physicist: discoverer of the neutron

Chadwick graduated in physics in Manchester in 1911 and stayed there to do research under *Rutherford*. He won an award in 1913 to allow him to work with *Geiger* in Berlin, and when World War I began in 1914 he was interned. Although held in poor conditions in a racecourse stable for four years, he was able to do some useful research as a result of help from *Nernst* and others.

In 1919 he joined Rutherford again, who had moved to Cambridge, and for 16 years was to be his principal researcher. Chadwick's research with him was mainly with alpha particles (helium nuclei ^4_2He); from the way these were scattered by heavier nuclei he could work out the positive charge of the scattering nucleus and show it to be the same as the atomic number. They also used alpha particles to bombard light elements and induce artificial disintegration. Then, in 1932, he was able to re-interpret an experiment reported by the *Joliot-Curies*, which he saw as evidence for the existance of the neutron (charge 0, mass 1) which Rutherford had foreseen in 1920. Chadwick quickly did his own experiments to confirm his deduction; the neutron allowed a massive advance in knowledge of atomic nuclei, and was one of a series of major discoveries in atomic physics made in the 'marvellous year' of 1932, and largely in Rutherford's laboratory.

In 1935 Chadwick won the Nobel Prize for his discovery of the neutron, but soon afterwards friction with Rutherford began because Chadwick wanted to build a cyclotron and Rutherford opposed this. Chadwick went to Liverpool as professor and soon had his cyclotron (the first in the UK) and made the department there a leading centre for atomic physics. When World War II came, he was the natural leader of the UK's effort to secure an atomic bomb before the enemy succeeded in this. Clearly the work had to be done in the US, as the UK was exposed to German bombing. Chadwick made a masterly job of first propelling the work there into effectiveness, and then ensuring that collaboration proceeded smoothly.

Back in the UK after the war, advising government on nuclear matters and increasingly doubtful of the wisdom of its policies, he had an unsatisfying last phase in his career as Master of his old Cambridge college. *See photo p.219.*

CHAIN, (Sir) Ernst Boris
1906-1979

German-British biochemist: member of the team which isolated and introduced penicillin for therapeutic use

Having studied physiology and chemistry in his native Berlin, Chain left Germany in 1933 and worked in London and Cambridge. He joined *Florey*'s staff in Oxford in 1935 and from 1938 worked with him and N. G. Heatley on the production, isolation and testing of the mould product penicillin, which by 1941 was shown to be a dramatically valuable antibacterial. He shared a Nobel Prize in 1945, moved to Rome in 1948, and returned to Imperial College, London, in 1961. His work on penicillin led him to discover penicillinase, an enzyme which destroys penicillin; he later worked on variants of penicillin which were resistant to such destruction. Chain was a talented linguist and musician, with forceful but unpopular views on the organization of science.

CHAMBERLAIN, Owen
1920-

American physicist: discovered the antiproton

Chamberlain was educated at Dartmouth

College and the University of Chicago, and was appointed professor of physics at the University of California at Berkeley in 1958.

Like many physicists at the time, Chamberlain worked on the Manhattan atomic bomb project during the Second World War, studying spontaneous fission of heavy elements. After the war he conducted experiments with the bevatron particle accelerator at Berkeley, and in 1955, together with *Segrè* and others, discovered the antiproton, a new elementary particle with the same mass as the proton, but of opposite charge. Antiparticles had been predicted theoretically by *Dirac* in 1926. Chamberlain and Segrè shared the 1959 Nobel Prize for Physics for their discovery.

CHANDLER, Seth Carlo

1846-1913

American geophysicist: discovered variation in location of the geographic poles (Chandler wobble)

By occupation both a scientist and an actuary, Chandler became interested in the possible free nutation (oscillation) of the Earth's axis of rotation. By re-analysing repeated measurements of the latitudes of different observatories he discovered an annual variation in latitude (due to the motion of air masses) and also another variation with a period of roughly 14 months. Despite initially hostile reaction from the scientific establishment his conclusions were soon fully borne out. The cause of the secondary variation was subsequently explained, and it has since become known as the **Chandler wobble**: i.e. the apparent motion of the Earth's axis of rotation across the Earth's surface (detectable as a variation of latitude with time), with a period of approximately 14 months. It is caused by the precession (or free nutation) of the Earth's axis of symmetry about its axis of rotation. For a rigid planet the period would be exactly one year; the observed slightly longer period, and its broad spectral peak (428 ± 17 days), is due to elastic yielding of the Earth's interior.

CHANDRASEKHAR, Subrahmanyan

1910-

Indian-American astrophysicist: developed theory of white dwarf stars

Chandrasekhar studied in India and then in Cambridge before moving to the US in 1936. Chandrasekhar's interest has been the final stages of stellar evolution. He showed that when a star has exhausted its nuclear fuel, an inward gravitational collapse occurs, which will normally be eventually halted by the outward pressure of the star's highly compressed and ionized gas. At this stage the star will have shrunk to become an extremely dense white dwarf, which has the peculiar property that the greater its mass, the smaller its radius. This means that massive stars will be unable to evolve into white dwarves, and this limiting stellar mass is called the **Chandrasekhar limit**, and is about 1.4 solar masses. It has been shown that all known white dwarves conform with this limit.

CHAPMAN, Sydney

1888-1970

British applied mathematician: developed the kinetic theory of gases, and worked on gaseous thermal diffusion, geomagnetism, tidal theory, and the atmosphere

Chapman studied engineering at Manchester and mathematics at Cambridge, graduating in 1910. During his career he held professorships in Manchester, London, and Oxford, and from 1954 worked at the High Altitude Observatory, Boulder, Colorado, and the Geophysical Institute, Alaska.

Chapman's interests were broad. He made a notable contribution to the kinetic theory of gases, taking the theory beyond the earlier work of *Maxwell* and *Boltzmann*, to the **Chapman-Enskog theory of gases.**

Thermal diffusion refers to heat transfer between two parts of a solid, liquid, or gas, which are at different temperatures, in the absence of convection. He applied his theory of it to a variety of problems, notably in the upper atmosphere. (Later, isotopes for atomic fission were separated by use of gaseous thermal diffusion.) On geomagnetism, his other main interest, he investigated why the Earth's magnetic field varies with periods equal to the lunar day (27.3 days) and its submultiples; he showed this was due to a tidal movement in the Earth's atmosphere due to the Moon. The **Chapman-Ferraro theory of magnetic storms** predated modern plasma theory. He also studied the formation of ozone in the atmosphere, and the ionizing effect of solar ultraviolet light on the ionosphere (the **Chapman layer** being named for him). In his later years he developed with S. I. Akasosu the modern theory of geomagnetic storms, the ring current and the aurora.

CHARCOT, Jean-Martin
1825-1893

French neurologist: related many neurological disorders to physical causes

Charcot was born and studied medicine in Paris, and spent his career at its ancient and famous hospital, the Salpêtrière. Appointed there in 1862, he found it full of long-stay patients with diseases of the nervous system about which little was known. By careful clinical observation and later autopsy he was able to relate many of their conditions with specific lesions; for example the paralysis of polio with the destruction of motor cells in the spinal cord; the paralysis and lesions of cerebral haemorrhage; and a type of arthritis with neurosyphilis. He was the major figure in the Paris Medical School for many years, and his many pupils included Sigmund Freud, who developed

Charcot's special interest in hysteria. After his death his only son, Jean, gave up medicine and became the leading French polar explorer.

CHARGAFF, Erwin
1905-

Czech-American biochemist: discovered base-pairing rules in DNA

Chargaff studied at Vienna, Yale, Berlin and Paris, and worked in the US from 1935 at Columbia University, New York. His best-known work is on nucleic acids. By 1950 he had shown that a single organism contains many different kinds of RNA, but that its DNA is of essentially one kind, characteristic of the species and even of the organism. The nucleic acids contain nitrogenous bases of four types: adenine, thymine, guanine, and cytosine. Chargaff showed that the quantities of the bases are not equal, as some had thought; but that if we represent the number of the respective bases in a DNA by A, T, G and C respectively, then (very nearly) A=T, and C=G. These **Chargaff rules** were of great value as a clue to the double helix

Erwin Chargaff in 1970

structure for DNA put forward by J. Watson and *Crick* in 1953, in which the two helical nucleic acid strands are linked by bonds between complimentary bases, adenine linking with thymine, and cytosine linking with guanine, by hydrogen bonds.

CHARLES, Jacques Alexandre César
1746-1823

French physicist: established temperature-volume relationship for gases

Originally a clerk in the civil service, an interest in ballooning and the physics of gases together with a flare for public lecturing brought Charles fame, and ultimately a professorship of physics in Paris.

In 1783, together with his brother Robert, Charles made the first manned ascent in a hydrogen balloon, a feat which brought him considerable public acclaim. On a later flight he was to reach an altitude of 3000 metres. His interest in gases subsequently led him to formulate **Charles' law** in 1787, that the volume of a given amount of gas at constant pressure increases at a constant rate with rise in temperature. Further experimental work by *Gay-Lussac* and *Dalton* confirmed the relationship, which holds best at low pressures and high temperatures (i.e., it applies to ideal gases). Incidentally, *Amontons* had also discovered the relationship almost a century before but, failing to publicize the fact, did not receive the credit for it.

CHARNEY, Jule Gregory
1917-1981

American meteorologist: pioneer of numerical techniques in dynamic meteorology

Charney's work was principally concerned with dynamic meteorology. In 1947 he analysed the problem of the formation of mid-latitude depressions, in particular the dynamics of long waves in a baroclinic westerly current. He went on to work on numerical methods of weather prediction with *von Neumann*, developing a system of quasi-geostrophic prediction equations and the concept of the 'equivalent barotropic level'. Charney also tackled problems concerned with the flow of the Gulf Stream, the formation of hurricanes, and the large-scale vertical propagation of energy in the atmosphere.

CHERENKOV, Pavel (Alekseyevich)
1904-

Soviet physicist: discoverer of the Cherenkov effect

A graduate of Voronezh State University, Cherenkov worked at the Lebedev Institute of Physics from 1930. In 1934 he first saw the blue light emitted from water exposed to radioactivity from radium, which had been observed by many earlier workers who had assumed it to be fluorescence. Cherenkov soon found that this could not be the explanation because the glow is shown by other liquids; and he found it was caused by fast electrons (beta rays) from the radium, and that it was polarized. By 1937, working with I. M. Frank and I. E. Tamm, they were able to explain the effect. They showed that in general the effect arises when a charged particle traverses a medium (liquid or solid) when moving at a speed greater than the speed of light in that medium, and they were able to predict its direction and polarization. The effect is dramatically visible in the blue glow in a uranium reactor core containing heavy water; and it is used in a method for detecting high-energy charged particles. A counter of this type, using a photomultiplier, can detect single particles. The effect has some analogy with the shock wave and sonic boom produced when an aircraft exceeds the speed of sound in air. Cherenkov, Frank and Tamm shared a Nobel Prize in 1958.

CHEVREUL, Michel Eugène
1786-1889

French organic chemist: investigated fats and natural dyes

A surgeon's son, Chevreul learned chemistry as assistant to *Vauquelin*, and by 1824 became Director of Dyeing at the famed Gobelin tapestry factory. His best-known work is on animal fats, which he showed by 1823 could be separated into pure individual substances, which with acid or alkali broke down to give glycerol and a fatty acid. (The fatty acids were later shown to be long-chain monocarboxylic acids). Chevreul showed that soap-making (saponification) of animal fats by alkali could be understood and improved chemically, and that soaps are sodium salts of fatty acids. In 1825 Chevreul with *Guy-Lussac* patented a method of making candles using 'stearin' (crude stearic acid) in place of tallow, which was odorous, less luminous and unreliable; when developed, the improvement was of substantial importance. Chevreul showed that the urine of diabetic patients contained grape-sugar (i.e., glucose). He worked on organic analysis, and the chemistry of drying oils (used in paints), on waxes, and natural dyes; on theories of colour; on the use of divining rods, and (after he was 90) on the psychological effects of ageing. As a child of seven, he had watched the guillotine in action; after his centenary, he watched the construction of the Eiffel tower. He never retired.

CLAUSIUS, Rudolf
1822-1888

German theoretical physicist: a founder of thermodynamics, and especially linked with its Second Law

Clausius's father was a Prussian pastor and proprietor of a small school which the boy attended. Later he went to the University of Berlin to study history, but changed to science; his teachers included *Ohm* and *Dedekind*. He was short of money which delayed his graduation, but his ambition was to teach university physics and he did so at Zürich, Würzburg and Bonn. In the war of 1870 he and his students set up an ambulance service and he was badly wounded.

By the 1850s a major problem had arisen in heat theory: *Carnot*'s results were accepted, but while he believed correctly that when a heat engine produces work, a quantity of heat 'descends' from a higher to a lower temperature, he also believed that it passed through the engine intact. The first law of thermodynamics, largely due to *Joule*, visualizes some heat as being lost in a heat engine and converted into work. This apparent conflict was solved by Clausius, who showed in 1850 that these results could both be understood if it is also assumed that 'heat does not spontaneously pass from a colder to a hotter body' (the **Second Law of Thermodynamics**). The next year *W. Thomson* arrived at the same law, differently expressed; and there are now several other equivalent formulations of the same principle. Clausius developed this concept, of the tendency of energy to dissipate, and in 1865 used the term **entropy** *(S)* for a measure of the amount of heat lost or gained by a body, divided by its absolute temperature. One statement of the Second Law is that 'the entropy of any isolated system can only increase or remain constant'. Entropy was later seen (e.g., by *Boltzmann*) as a measure of a system's disorder. The Second Law generated much controversy, but Clausius, *Maxwell* and Thomson led a vigorous and successful defence, although we would not now fully accept Clausius's crisp summaries of 'the energy of the universe is constant' (First Law) and 'the entropy of the universe tends to a maximum' (Second Law), thereby predicting a 'heat-death' for the universe.

Clausius also did valuable work on the kinetic theory of gases, where he first used the ideas of 'mean free path' and 'effective molecular radius' which later proved so useful. In the field of electrolysis, Clausius was the first to suggest (in 1851) that a salt exists as ions in solution, before a current is applied. In each area he attacked, he showed outstanding intuition, and his work led to major developments by others; but Clausius was strangely little interested in these developments.

COCKCROFT, (Sir) John Douglas

1897-1967

British physicist: pioneered the transmutation of atomic nuclei by accelerated particles

Cockcroft had completed only his first year at Manchester University when World War I broke out, and he joined the Royal Field Artillery as a signaller. Remarkably he survived unscathed through three years and most of the later battles. Afterwards, he joined the Metropolitan Vickers Electrical Company and took his degree at Cambridge in mathematics (1924). He then became part of *Rutherford*'s research team at the Cavendish, and in 1932 made his reputation by a brilliant experiment with E. T. S. Walton, for which they received the 1951 Nobel Prize.

Cockcroft was methodical in his work, genial and decisive, and no waster of words. He soon became mainly interested in research management, and in 1940 was a member of the Tizard Mission to the US to negotiate wartime technological exchange. He then became head of the Air Defence Research and Development Establishment (1941-44). He was also Jacksonian Professor at Cambridge (1939-46). He became founding director of the Atomic Energy Research Establishment at Harwell (1946) and led the establishment of the Rutherford High-Energy Laboratory at Harwell (1959). In 1959 he became founding Master of Churchill College, Cambridge. Receiving many honours, Cockcroft became a leading statesman of science, combining research and administrative skills.

The experiment conducted by Cockcroft and Walton was triggered by *Gamow* mentioning (1928) to Cockcroft that bombarding particles may enter a nucleus by quantum mechanical 'tunnelling'. This could occur at much lower incident energies than those required to overcome Coulomb repulsion between the two. Using skilfully-built voltage-doublers, protons were accelerated to 0.8 MeV and directed at a lithium target. Alpha particles (helium nuclei) were found to be released; the first artificially induced nuclear reaction (transmutation) was occurring; and was later shown to be:

$$^{7}_{3}Li + ^{1}_{1}H \rightarrow ^{4}_{2}He + ^{4}_{2}He \ (+17.2 \ MeV)$$

(In his experiments on transmutation, Rutherford had used, as projectiles, particles from a natural radioactive source). With the publication of this exciting result the nuclear era began, and cyclotrons and linear accelerators were built to study nuclear physics. Rutherford, on seeing proof of the alpha particle generation, called it 'the most beautiful sight in the world'. When, later, Cockcroft suggested the generation of power by nuclear fission, Rutherford said the idea was 'all moonshine'.

COHN, Ferdinand Julius

1828-1898

German botanist and bacteriologist

Cohn was a precocious child and despite the difficulties caused by German anti-semitic rules, he was awarded a doctorate at Berlin for his work in botany when he was 19. He returned to his home city of Breslau (now in Poland) and became professor of botany there in 1872. A keen microscopist, he came to the important conclusion that the protoplasms (cell contents) of plant and animal cells are essentially similar. He was the first to devise a systematic classification for bacteria, and did much to define the conditions necessary for bacterial growth.

COHNHEIM, Julius
1839-1884

German pathologist: a pioneer of experimental pathology

A graduate in medicine from Berlin, Cohnheim became an assistant to *Virchow* and was probably his most famous pupil. He attracted many students himself, as a teacher of pathology at Kiel, Breslau and finally Leipzig. His early work was in histology, and soon after graduating he devised the freezing technique for sectioning fresh tissue, and later a method of staining sections with a·solution of gold. From 1867 he published a masterly series of studies on inflammation; he showed by experiments with frogs how the blood vessels responded in its early stages, and proved that the leucocytes (white cells) pass through the walls of capillaries at the site of inflammation and later degenerate to become pus corpuscles. *Mechnikov* and others were later to confirm and extend these studies.

Despite evidence, tuberculosis (then a major cause of death in Europe) was not easily accepted as infectious. Cohnheim provided new and convincing evidence by injecting tuberculous matter into the chamber of a rabbit's eye and then observing the tuberculous process through its cornea. He also studied heart disease, examining obstruction of the coronary artery and deducing correctly that the resulting lack of oxygen led to myocardial damage (infarction). This work was reviewed and the condition named as 'coronary thrombosis' by J. D. Herrick in 1912.

COLOMBO, Matteo Realdo
c.1516-1559

Italian anatomist: a discoverer of the lesser circulation of the blood

Son of an apothecary, Colombo was a student of anatomy, medicine and surgery under *Vesalius* and succeeded him at Padua and Pisa. In his book *On Anatomy* (1559) he gives more modern descriptions (without illustrations) than earlier anatomists. He describes the lens at the front of the eye (not in the middle, as earlier anatomists had believed) and the pleura and peritoneum. He describes clearly the lesser circulation through the lungs, and in a vivisection on a dog he cut the pulmonary vein and showed it contained blood and not air; and its bright red colour made him believe that the lungs had made it 'spiritous' (i.e., oxygenated) by air. He did not understand the general circulation, as *Harvey* did later.

COMPTON, Arthur Holly
1892-1962

American physicist: discovered the Compton effect concerning the wavelength of scattered photons

Compton was the son of a Presbyterian minister who was also a professor of philosophy, and inherited a deep religious faith from him. He obtained his doctorate at Princeton, and spent two years with Westinghouse Corporation. On travelling to Britain he spent a year doing research under *Rutherford* at Cambridge, before returning to America as head of the Physics Department at Washington University, St. Louis (1920). A professorship at Chicago followed in 1923. In 1945 he returned to Washington as Chancellor.

In 1923 Compton observed that X-rays scattered by passing through paraffin wax had their wavelength increased by this scattering. Compton and *Debye* explained this in detail, stating that photons (electromagnetic waves) behave as particles as well as waves; they lose energy E and momentum on making elastic collisions and as

$$E = hc/\lambda$$

where c is the speed of light, their wavelength λ increases. Here h is *Planck*'s constant. Compton found tracks in photographs taken in a Wilson cloud chamber, showing electrons recoiling from collisions with the invisible (because uncharged) photons of an X-ray beam. This work established *Einstein*'s belief that photons had energy and momentum, and also *de Broglie*'s assertion (1925) that in quantum mechanics, objects display both wave and particle properties. Compton and *C. T. R. Wilson* received the 1927 Nobel Physics Prize for their work, which is now part of the foundation of the new quantum theory (as opposed to *Bohr*'s old quantum theory).

Compton developed an ionization chamber for detecting cosmic rays, and in the 1930s used a world-wide survey to demonstrate that cosmic rays are deflected by the Earth's magnetic field and some are therefore charged particles (and not radiation). Variation of ray intensity with time of day, year and the Sun's rotation also indicated that the cosmic rays probably originate outside our galaxy (1938).

In 1941 Compton was asked to take part in feasibility studies and the development of plutonium production for the atomic bomb. His religious faith made him question what was happening, but he felt that only such a weapon would quickly end the massive slaughter of the war. He became director of a major part of the Manhattan Project at Chicago and built the first reactor with *Fermi* (1942), publishing an account in his book *Atomic Quest* (1958).

COOK, (Sir) James
1728-1779

British explorer: founder of modern hydrography and cartography; explored the Pacific, and showed that scurvy was preventable on a long voyage

The son of an agricultural labourer, Cook joined the Royal Navy in 1755, and was given his own command two years later. He is remembered for his voyages of discovery, which transformed knowledge of the Pacific, and which set the pattern for the great scientific expeditions of the

19th century. After much hydrographic work of the highest quality, Cook was charged with taking the *Endeavour* to Tahiti in 1768 with observers (including *Banks*) for the transit of Venus, on behalf of the Royal Society. At that time observations of transits of inner planets across the face of the Sun were one of the principal means of estimating the Earth-Sun distance. Cook went on to chart the east coast of Australia and the coast of New Zealand, showing it to consist of two main islands, and his voyage set an upper limit to the size of any possible southern continent. Both for this voyage and his second expedition, the Admiralty's secret orders to Cook required him to explore the South Pacific where they had 'reason to imagine that a continent, or land of great extent, may be found', and 'to take possession of it in the King's name'. These expeditions had both scientific and political objectives. Cook's second expedition in 1772-75 further delineated the possible extent of Antarctica, and also demonstrated that fresh fruit and vegetables were all that were needed to prevent scurvy, a major problem on long sea voyages at the time.

In 1776 he was made a Fellow of the Royal Society. His last expedition, begun in 1776, was intended to discover a northern route between the Atlantic and the Pacific, but ended in his tragic death when he was attacked by natives in Hawaii.

Improved sextants and other instruments, and especially Cook's talent and energy, ensured that more survey work and scientific research was done by him than by any previous expeditions. Modern maps of the Pacific with its coasts and islands owe much to him, and he set new standards of cartography and hydrography.

COOPER, Leon Neil
1930-

American physicist: contributed to BCS theory of superconductivity

Cooper was educated at Columbia University, obtaining his doctorate in 1954.

He collaborated with *Bardeen* and *Schrieffer* at Illinois on the BCS theory of superconductivity.

Soon after his doctoral work in quantum field theory, Cooper made a theoretical prediction of the existence of bound pairs of electrons at low temperature. Although two electrons repel each other, they may behave differently in a solid with a sea of electrons with an embedded lattice of positive ions. One electron distorts the lattice, pulling it in about it, and the other electron is attracted to the locally higher concentration of positive ions. This effect can be imagined from the similarity to two cannonballs on a mattress rolling together into the same depression. Thus at low temperature, when thermal vibrations do not disturb this process, bound pairs (called **Cooper pairs**) of electrons form. The **BCS theory** then accounts for superconductivity as being due to the fact that these pairs can move through a lattice with zero scattering by impurities because the pair is much larger than any impurity atom. For this work Bardeen, Cooper and Schrieffer shared the 1972 Nobel Prize for physics.

COPERNICUS, Nicolaus

1473-1543

Polish astronomer: proposed heliocentric cosmology

Copernicus was the nephew of a prince bishop. Having studied mathematics, law and medicine in Poland and in Italy, Copernicus was for most of his life a canon at Frauenburg Cathedral, his duties being largely administrative. Working mainly from the astronomical literature rather than from his own observations, he showed that a cosmology in which Earth and the planets rotate about the Sun offered a simpler explanation of planetary motions than the geocentric model of *Ptolemy*, which had been universally accepted for well over a thousand years. He circulated his preliminary ideas privately in a short manuscript in 1514, and

Nicolaus Copernicus

continued to develop the theory over the next thirty years. Among his suggestions was the idea that the fixed stars were much further away than had previously been thought, and that their apparent motion at night (and the Sun's motion by day) was due to Earth's daily rotation about its axis, but he retained the conventional idea that the planets moved in perfectly circular orbits. His ideas were first fully described in his book *De revolutionibus orbium coelestium* (The Revolution of the Heavenly Spheres), which although complete by 1530, was not published until 1543. Copernicus himself may only have seen the published book on the day he died.

Copernicus's ideas were immediately criticized by other astronomers, notably *Brahe*, who argued that if the Earth was moving then the fixed stars ought to show an apparent movement by parallax also. Copernicus's answer to this, that the stars were too far away for parallax to be apparent, was rejected on the grounds that it was inconsistent with the accepted size of the universe. The idea of a moving Earth was also hard to accept. The Church later officially banned *De revolutionibus* in 1616, and did not remove it from its Index of forbidden books until 1835.

His view that the Sun was the centre of the solar system gained credence from *Galileo*'s work on Jupiter's moons in 1609; but the parallax of a fixed star was not measured until 1838 by *Bessel*. However, the idea of a heliocentric (Sun-centred) system, with a moving Earth, had been accepted as a reality and not a mere mathematical device, long before that; and Copernicus's circular orbits for planets had been replaced by *Kepler*'s elliptical orbits by 1609. The 'Scientific Revolution' is often dated from Copernicus's work, reaching its climax with *Newton* about 150 years later. In the same year (1543) that Copernicus's *Revolution* appeared, *Versalius*'s book *On The Structure of the Human Body* was published; men's views of nature were changing fast.

CORI, Carl Ferdinand
1896-

Czech-American biochemist

Cori graduated in medicine in Prague in 1920, and in the same year married his classmate Gerty Radnitz. They formed a team until her death in 1951, moving to the US in 1922 and sharing a Nobel Prize in 1947 (the only other husband and wife pairs to do so being the Curies in 1903, and the Joliot-Curies in 1935). Their best-known joint research concerned the conversion of glucose to glycogen in the animal body and the reverse breakdown. *Bernard* had shown in 1850 that glycogen forms an energy reserve held in the liver and muscles, which is converted to the simpler sugar, glucose, when needed. The Coris discovered the precise steps involved in this essential biochemical process, and revealed the part played by sugar phosphates for the first time.

CORIOLIS, Gaspard Gustave de
1792-1843

French physicist: discovered the Coriolis inertial force

Coriolis was educated at the École Polytechnique in Paris, where he became assistant professor of analysis and mathematics, and eventually director of studies.

Coriolis was responsible for defining kinetic energy as $\frac{1}{2}mv^2$, and introducing 'work' as a technical term of precise meaning in mechanics. In 1835 Coriolis discovered the **Coriolis force**, an inertial force which acts on rotating surfaces at right-angles to their direction of motion, causing the elements of the surface to follow a curved, rather than straight, line of motion. Such effects are particularly important in oceanography and meteorology (e.g. the Ekman effect), and account for the movement of ocean currents near the Equator.

CORMACK, Allan Macleod
1924-

South African physicist: pioneer of X-ray tomography

Cormack studied at the University of Cape Town, and then worked on the medical applications of radioisotopes in Johannesburg, before moving to the US in 1956.

In 1963, independently of *Hounsfield*, Cormack developed the mathematical principles for the X-ray imaging of 'soft' biological tissue, and demonstrated its viability experimentally. Hitherto, X-rays had only been used for obtaining 'silhouettes', primarily of bone structure. Cormack showed that by effectively combining many X-ray images, taken in different directions through the human body, it was possible to build up a picture of a slice through the soft tissue. This technique, known as computer-assisted tomography (CAT), is the basis for the modern body scanners which have become an invaluable medical tool. Cor-

A. M. Cormack in 1987

mack and Hounsfield shared the Nobel Prize for medicine in 1979.

COULOMB, Charles Augustin de
1736-1806

French physicist: discovered inverse square law of electric and magnetic attraction

Coulomb trained as a military engineer, and served in Martinique for nine years. He eventually returned to France as an engineering consultant, but resigned from the Army altogether in 1791, and moved from engineering to physics. During the French Revolution he was obliged to leave Paris, but returned under Napoleon and became an Inspector-General of Public Instruction.

Not surprisingly in view of his military service, much of Coulomb's early work was concerned with engineering problems in statics and mechanics. He showed that friction is proportional to normal pressure (**Coulomb's Law of Friction**), and introduced the concept of the thrust line. However, he is primarily remembered for his work on electrical and magnetic attraction and repulsion. From 1784

onwards he conducted a series of very delicate experiments, using a torsion balance he had invented himself and capable of detecting forces equivalent to 10^{-5} g. He discovered that the force between two charged poles is inversely proportional to the square of the distance between them, and directly proportional to the product of their magnitude (**Coulomb's Law of Force**). This was a major result, paralleling *Newton's* law of gravitational attraction. He went on to show that a similar law applied to magnetic poles. The SI unit of electric charge, the **coulomb** (C), is named in his honour. It is the charge crossing any section of a conductor in which a steady current of 1 ampere flows for 1 second.

COULSON, Charles Alfred
1910-1974

English mathematician: a founder of modern theoretical chemistry

Coulson was unusual in holding professorships in theoretical physics (King's College, London 1947-52), applied mathematics (Oxford 1952-72) and theoretical chemistry (Oxford 1972-74). He also played a major role in creating the third of these subject areas, and wrote useful books on *Waves* and on *Electricity*. He also published on meteorology, biology and theology.

Coulson developed the application of quantum mechanics to the bonds between atoms in molecules. These bonds originate in the interaction between the outer electrons of the bonded atoms. He showed how to calculate those molecular bond-lengths and energies of interest to chemists. The method he used is called **molecular orbital** (MO) theory (1933). He also showed how bonds intermediate between single and double bonds could arise (1937). This then allowed him and H. C. Longuet-Higgins to explain the delocalised (i.e., multi-centre) bonding in such aromatic molecules as benzene. In 1952 he wrote his classic textbook *Valence* which proved valuable in the development of the subject. Later he studied bonding in molecules of biochemical importance.

Coulson influenced his generation not only as a theoretical chemist where his methods have proved of great value, but also as a leading Methodist and writer on science and Christianity. He was chairman of the charity Oxfam from 1965-71.

COUPER, Archibald Scott
1831-1892

Scottish organic chemist: pioneer of structural organic chemistry, and victim of misfortune

After leaving school Couper studied a variety of subjects; classics at Glasgow and philosophy at Edinburgh were separated by visits to Germany, where he learned German speedily. As the son of a wealthy manufacturer, he seems to have studied whatever interested him; he concentrated on chemistry somewhere between 1854 and 1856. By 1858 he had spent two years in Paris, researching on benzene compounds, and early in that year he completed a paper 'On a New Chemical Theory' and asked *Wurtz* to present it at the French Academy. However, Wurtz delayed and *Kekulé* published his theory of organic structure shortly before Couper's paper appeared. Couper's views were similar, but much more clearly expressed. He argued that carbon had a valence of two or four; and that its atoms could self-link to form chains. He showed chemical structures with broken lines to connect bonded atoms, and he saw these structures as representing chemical reality; in these respects his ideas were ahead of Kekulé's. However, the latter had priority of publication, and forcefully pressed his superiority. Couper quarrelled with Wurtz, returned to Edinburgh, and soon his depression led to illness. He never recovered, although he lived in mental frailty for another 33 years, ignored as a chemist.

Credit for the idea of a ring structure for benzene is rightly given to Kekulé (1865), but it is hardly known that the first ring structure for any compound was proposed seven years earlier by Couper, for a heterocyclic reaction product from salicylic acid and PCl_5.

Modern structural formulae were first widely used by A. C. Brown of Edinburgh from 1861, who included double and triple bonds between carbon atoms.

COUSTEAU, Jacques Yves
1910-

French oceanographer: pioneer of underwater exploration

Cousteau was in the French navy when World War II broke out, having graduated from the École Navale at Brest. Following distinguished service in the Resistance (during which time he designed and tested his first aqualung), he was awarded the Légion d'Honneur and the Croix de Guerre. After the war he became head of the Underwater Research Group of the French navy, and has since made many notable advances in the technology and techniques of underwater investigation, constructing a diving saucer capable of operating at 200 metres for long periods, and working with Auguste Piccard on the design of the first bathyscaphes. He set a world record for free diving in 1947, but is probably best known for pioneering underwater cinematography and for his studies of marine life.

CRICK, Francis (Harry Compton)
1916-

British molecular biologist: co-discoverer with J. D. Watson of double helix structure of DNA

The outstanding advance in the life sciences in this century has been the creation of a new branch of science: molecular biology. In this, Crick has been a central figure; and its key concept, that the self-replicating genetic material DNA has the form of a double helix with complementary strands, is due to him and J. D. Watson.

Crick graduated in physics in London, but his first research was interrupted by war service, working on naval mines. After the war he was attracted to Cambridge and to biology, and by 1949 was with the Cambridge Medical Research Council Unit, then housed in the Cavendish physics laboratory. His field of expertise was the use of X-ray crystal diffraction methods (originally devised by the *Braggs*) to examine the structure of biopolymers. The overall head of the Cavendish laboratory was then Sir Lawrence Bragg. In the 1950s and under his patronage, the team led by *Perutz*, and including J. Kendrew, Watson, *H. E. Huxley*, Crick and later *Brenner* were to have as dramatic an effect on molecular biology as *Rutherford*'s team had on particle physics in the 1930s, and in the same building.

In 1951 Watson joined the group. He was 23, a US zoologist with experience of bacterial viruses and an enthusiasm for

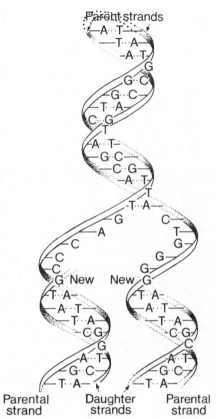

Crick and Watson model of the molecular structure of DNA. The helical strands consist of chains of alternating sugar and phosphate groups. They carry four types of base (A, C, G, T) which can link (by hydrogen bonds) only in the combinations A...T and C...G.

Francis Crick about 1954

genetics. He and Crick quickly became friends; they shared an optimistic enthusiasm that it should be possible to understand the nature of genes in molecular terms, and in under two years they were to succeed. Important background material was available for them. There was good evidence from *Avery*'s work that the DNA of genes formed the key genetic material. A. R. Todd had done much to show that DNA consists of chains of sugar residues (deoxyribose) linked by phosphate groups, and carrying base molecules (mainly of four types) attached to the sugar rings. *Chargaff* had shown that the number of these bases had a curious ratio relation. Helical structures

97

had been met with; *Pauling* had shown, as had Crick, that the protein keratin consists of chains of protein arranged in helical form; Pauling, like Crick, was an enthusiast for making molecular models as an aid to deducing possible structures.

Crick had devised a general theory which would show whether a given X-ray pattern was due to a helical structure; and his friendship with M. H. F. Wilkins at London gave him limited access to the X-ray pictures made there by Wilkins's colleague, Rosalind Franklin. With all this in mind, Crick and Watson built their models, and in 1953 focused on a model in the form of a double helix, with two DNA chains. It could accommodate all known features of DNA, with acceptable interatomic angles and distances, and would accord with Franklin's observed X-ray diffraction pattern. The helical shape had its sugar and phosphate chains on its outside, and the bases (linked in pairs, A with T, C with G) on the inside (see diagram). The model explains how DNA replicates, by the uncoiling of its double helical strands, with these strands then acting as templates. It also suggested how genetic information could be encoded, by the sequence of bases along the chains. Crick proposed as a **central dogma** the scheme DNA→RNA →protein, with the first arrow representing **transcription**, and the second, **translation**. (The conversion DNA→DNA, shown in the diagram, is known as **replication**).

Crick and Watson had found the broad answer to the question 'how do genes replicate and carry information?' and in the succeeding years most work on molecular biology has been directed to confirming, refining and extending these ideas. Crick himself has done much in this area, for example in work with Brenner demonstrating that the code is read in triplets of bases (codons), each defining one specific amino acid used to make a protein, and in showing that adjacent codons do not overlap. He has also studied the structure of small viruses and collagen, and the mechanism by which transcription and translation occurs; and he has offered novel ideas on the origin of life on Earth. He worked mainly in Cambridge until 1977 when he moved to the Salk Institute in San Diego, California. He shared the Nobel Prize for 1962 with Watson and Wilkins.

CRONIN, James Watson
1931-

American particle physicist: demonstrated the non-conservation of parity and charge conjugation in particle reactions

Cronin was educated at the University of Chicago, later working at Brookhaven National Laboratory and Princeton University before returning to Chicago as professor of physics in 1971.

Lee and *Yang* had shown in 1956 that parity was not conserved in weak interactions between subatomic particles. In 1964 Cronin, together with V. Fitch, J. Christensen and R. Turlay made a study of neutral kaons, and discovered the surprising fact that a combination of parity and charge conjugation was not conserved either. This was an important result since it was known that a combination of parity, charge conjugation and time *is* conserved, implying that the decay of kaons is not symmetrical with respect to time reversal.

CROOKES, (Sir) William
1832-1919

English chemist and physicist: discovered thallium; studied 'cathode rays'; predicted need for new nitrogenous fertilizers

Born the eldest of 16 children of a London tailor, little is known of Crookes's childhood. He was a student in the Royal College of Chemistry from 1848, and became *Hofmann*'s assistant. After two modest teaching jobs, he inherited some money, returned to London and set up a personal chemical research laboratory. He was also editor and proprietor of the influential *Chemical News* from 1859-1906.

In 1861 he examined the spectrum of crude selenium, and found a new bright green line. From this clue he was able to isolate a new element, thallium; he studied its rather strange chemistry, and measured its atomic mass. The accurate weighings for this (done in a vacuum) led to his invention of the **Crookes radiometer**, in which four light vanes, each with one face blackened, are pivoted in a glass container with gas at a low pressure. In light, the vanes rotate; the device helped to confirm the kinetic theory of gases. He also studied electrical discharges in vacuum tubes, already studied by J. Plücker and J. W. Hittorf. Crookes found that the 'cathode rays' travelled in straight lines, could cast shadows, heat obstacles, and be deflected by a magnet; he concluded they were negatively charged particles, but this found little support until *J. J. Thomson*'s studies (20 years later) firmly identified them as electrons. Crookes also invented the **spinthariscope** (1903; Greek for 'spark-viewer') to detect the α-particles (helium nuclei) emitted by radioactive elements. This consists of a screen coated with ZnS and viewed by a lens: each impacting particle causes a visible light flash. Crookes also studied a variety of problems in technical chemistry (sugar from beet; textile dyeing; electrical lighting; antiseptics; sanitation; diamond formation) and especially the need to produce fertilizer from atmospheric nitrogen if soil fertility was to be maintained (1898). He had much scientific imagination, and he also experimented in spiritualism, suggesting that telepathy resulted from wave communication between brains. His long, active life covered a most interesting period in science.

CROSS, Charles Frederick
1855-1935

English chemist: co-discoverer of viscose process

Cross studied chemistry at London, Zürich, and Manchester. With E. J. Bevan as partner, he worked on the chemistry of wood (which consists largely of cellulose and lignin). Their viscose process (1892) involves extracting cellulose from wood pulp (or other cheap source) by treating it with aqueous sodium hydroxide, followed by carbon disulphide. The cellulose solution can then be squirted through holes into dilute acid to regenerate the cellulose as fibre (rayon) or as film (cellophane).

CURIE, Marie
1867-1934

Polish-French physicist: discovered the radioelements polonium and radium

Marya Sklodowska grew up in Russian-dominated Poland; her family were intensely patriotic and the children took part in nationalistic activities furthering the Polish language and culture. Marya's father was a teacher of mathematics and physics and her mother the principal of a school for girls. She developed an interest in science, but her parents were becoming increasingly poor and their daughters had to support themselves; also, there was no provision for higher scientific education for women in Poland. She and her sister, Bronya, were very determined to gain their education. Marya took a post as a governess and helped Bronya go to Paris to study medicine, who in turn was to help her. In 1891 Marya went to Paris to study physics. She was extremely poor, but hardworking and very disciplined. By nature she was a perfectionist, incredibly tenacious, and independent. She graduated in physics in 1893 from the Sorbonne coming first in the order of merit. The following year, with a scholarship from Poland, she studied mathematics and graduated in second place. During this year she met Pierre Curie, then 35, and working on piezoelectricity at the School of Industrial Physics and Chemistry, and her plans to return to teach in

Poland changed; they married in July 1895.

In 1896 *Becquerel* had discovered radioactivity in a uranium salt. Marie Curie (as she was now known), looking for a research topic for a doctoral thesis, decided to study the 'new phenomena' discovered by Becquerel. Working in her husband's laboratory, she showed that radioactivity is an atomic property of uranium, and discovered that thorium emitted rays similar to uranium. In 1897 she gave birth to their daughter Irène (who also became a Nobel Prize winner in physics). When she examined the natural ores Marie discovered that the radioactivity of pitchblende and chalcolite was more intense than their uranium or thorium content implied, and correctly concluded that they must contain new radioactive elements. To find the new elements she began to separate the components of pitchblende to determine where the radioactivity lay, by a laborious process of fractional crystallization. Pierre Curie left his own research to join his wife in the work. No precaution against radioactivity were taken, as the harmful effects were not then known. Her notebooks were subsequently discovered to be highly radioactive and are still too dangerous to handle.

In July 1898 they announced the discovery of the existence of an element they named polonium, in honour of her native country, and in December, the even more radioactive radium. In order to isolate pure radium they obtained waste ore rich in uranium from mines in Bohemia, and working in an old shed, they purified and repurified the ore, work mostly undertaken by Marie. By 1902 they had obtained one tenth of a gram of radium chloride from several tonnes of ore. It was intensely radioactive, ionizing the surrounding air, decomposing water, evolving heat, and glowing in the dark.

In 1903 Marie Curie presented her doctoral thesis (and became the first woman to be awarded such a degree in France). In 1903 she was awarded the Nobel Prize for physics jointly with Pierre Curie and Henri Becquerel for their work on radioactivity. The following year their second daughter Eve was born, and the Curies appear to have begun to suffer from radiation sickness. Pierre Curie was named in 1904 as the new professor of physics at the Sorbonne and Marie was appointed 'chief of work' in the laboratory that was to be built for him; it was not opened until 1915. In 1906 Pierre was killed in a street accident and the professorship was offered to Marie; she became the first woman professor at the Sorbonne. She continued to work on radium chloride and attempted to isolate polonium, but most of her time was spent in supervizing the research of others and raising funds; along with caring for her two daughters.

In 1910 Marie was proposed for the decoration of the Légion d' Honneur, but turned it down in deference to her husband's refusal of a previous offer of the honour. At the same time she was a candidate for election to the Academy of Sciences in Paris (she would have been the first woman member), but was not elected.

In 1911 she was awarded a second Nobel Prize for chemistry for her discovery of polonium and radium. The original unit of measurement of the activity of a radioactive substance was named the **curie** (Ci); it is now defined as a decay rate of exactly 3.7×10^{10} disintegrations per second. Characteristically, she insisted on defining the unit herself. In 1914 she organized X-ray services for military hospitals; radiography had hardly begun, and there was as yet no provision for it. In 1921 the women of America, organized by Mrs W. B. Meloney, collected sufficient money to present Marie Curie with the gift of a gram of radium for her research work; it was an immense encouragement to her at a vital moment. She died at 67 from leukaemia; her exposure to radioactivity is suggestive in this.

Marie Curie was no theoretician, but she was a remarkably skilful radiochemist, and her discoveries did much to focus research on the new and major field of radioactivity: she was the first woman scientist of international distinction.

CURIE, Pierre
1859-1906

French physicist: discovered piezoelectric effect; pioneer in study of radioactivity

The son of a physician, Pierre Curie was educated at the Sorbonne where he became an assistant teacher in 1878. He was appointed laboratory chief at the School of Industrial Physics and Chemistry in 1882, and in 1904 was appointed to a new chair of physics at the Sorbonne. He and his brother Jacques first observed the phenomenon which they named **piezoelectricity**; this occurs when certain crystals (e.g., quartz) are mechanically deformed; they develop opposite charges on opposite faces, and conversely, when an electric charge is applied to a crystal, a deformation is produced. If a rapidly changing electric potential is applied, the faces of the crystal vibrate rapidly. This effect can be used to produce beams of ultrasound. Crystals with piezoelectric properties are used in microphones, pickups, pressure guages and quartz oscillators for time pieces. Jacques and Pierre Curie used the effect to construct an electrometer to measure small electric charges; this was later used by Pierre's wife in her investigation into radioactivity. For his doctorate (1895), Pierre Curie studied the effect of heat on ferromagnetism and showed that at a certain temperature, specific to a substance, it will lose its ferromagnetic properties and become paramagnetic; this is now known as the **Curie point** (e.g., 1043 K for iron). He had already shown that magnetic susceptibility for diamagnetic materials is generally independent of temperature, but for paramagnetic materials the susceptibility is inversely proportional to absolute temperature (**Curie's law**).

He married Marya Sklodowska and thereafter followed her into research on radioactivity. Together with *Becquerel* they were awarded the Nobel Prize for physics in 1903 for this work. Pierre Curie showed that one gram of radium gave out about 500 J per hour; the first indication of the energy available within the atom and the dangers of radioactivity.

CURTIUS, Theodor
1857-1928

German organic chemist

A pupil of *Kolbe*, he later held professorships at Kiel, Bonn and Heidelberg. He first made hydrazine N_2H_4 (1887) and hydrogen azide HN_3 (1890); and he studied organic azides and aliphatic diazo compounds. All these compounds are toxic or unstable (or both) but have proved of great value in organic synthesis. Hydrazine also has industrial uses, and methylhydrazines are used as rocket fuels (e.g., in the Apollo probes) with liquid oxygen as oxidant.

CUSHING, Harvey Williams
1869-1939

American physiologist and neurosurgeon: pioneering investigations of the physiology of the brain

A physician's son, Cushing studied medicine at Yale and Harvard, finally specializing in neurosurgery. He experimented on the effects of raised intracranial pressure in animals; his improved methods for diagnosis, localisation, and surgical removal of intracranial tumours stemmed from this work. For a long time his personal surgical skill in this work was unsurpassed. Measurement of blood pressure in his patients began in 1906, and knowledge of hypertension and its effects begins with his work. From 1908 he also studied the function and pathology of the pituitary gland at the base of the brain, again working first with dogs. He showed that acromegaly is linked with one type of pituitary overactivity in the growing animal, and dwarfism with its underactivity. **Cushing's syndrome**, which is associated with chronic wasting and other symptoms, he showed to be linked with a type of pituitary tumour; it is now known that other disorders which increase the production of corticosteroid hormones by the adrenal glands also lead to this syndrome.

CUVIER, (Baron) Georges (Léopold Chrétien Frédéric Dagobert)

1769-1832

French zoologist and anatomist: pioneer of comparative anatomy and vertebrate palaeontology

Georges Cuvier

Son of a Swiss soldier, Cuvier was educated in Stuttgart. He was a brilliant student, and from early childhood had been fascinated by natural history. From Stuttgart he went as tutor to a family in Normandy, and from 1785 taught in Paris, at the Museum of Natural History, then the largest scientific establishment in the world.

He did much to establish the modern classification of animals, extending that of *Linnaeus* by adding another broader level, the phylum. Thus he divided the invertebrates into three phyla. His work on molluscs and fish was particularly notable. In 1811, working with *Brongniart* on the Tertiary rocks of the Paris Basin, he became the first to classify fossil mammals and reptiles, thus founding vertebrate palaeontology.

Before this, he had developed comparative anatomy, and the technique of showing, from a few bones, a probable reconstruction of the entire animal of an extinct species. His emphasis was always on the facts, and he derided general theories. In long conflicts with *Lamarck* and E. Geoffroy St-Hilaire (both precursors of *Darwin*) he attacked theories of evolution: he believed in catastrophes, with the Biblical flood as the most recent. After each catastrophe, life was created anew. Cuvier became the world's most eminent biologist in his lifetime, with an authority akin to that of *Berzelius* in chemistry.

D

D'ALEMBERT, Jean Le Rond
1717-1783
French mathematician: discovered d'Alembert's Principle in mechanics

D'Alembert's forename comes from that of the church, St Jean le Rond, on whose steps he was found as a baby. He was probably the illegitimate son of a Parisian society hostess, Mme de Tenzin, and the chevalier Destouches, and the latter paid for his education while he was brought up by a glazier and his wife. He studied law and was called to the Bar in 1738, but then flirted briefly with medicine before choosing to study mathematics and to live on his father's annuity.

Early research by d'Alembert clarified the concept of a limit in the calculus, and introduced the idea of different orders of infinities. In 1741 he was admitted to the Académie des Sciences and two years later published his *Traité de dynamique* which includes **d'Alembert's Principle**, which is that *Newton*'s Third Law of motion holds not only for fixed bodies but also for those free to move. A wide variety of new problems could now be treated, such as the derivation of the planar motion of a fluid. He developed the theory of partial differential equations and solved such systems as a vibrating string and the general wave equation (1747). He joined *Euler*, Clairault, *Lagrange* and *Laplace* in applying calculus to celestial mechanics and determined the motion of three mutually gravitating bodies. This then allowed many of the celestial observations to be understood; for example, d'Alembert explained mathematically (1754) Newton's discovery of precession of the equinoxes, and also the perturbations in the orbits of the planets.

D'Alembert was then persuaded by a friend, Diderot, to participate in writing an encyclopedia, contributing on scientific topics. This project was denounced by the Church after one volume and d'Alembert turned instead to publishing eight volumes of abstruse mathematical studies. Shortly before his death J. H. Lambert wished to name his 'newly discovered moon of Venus' after d'Alembert, but the latter was still sufficiently acute to doubt (correctly) from calculations that it existed, and gently declined the offer.

DALE, (Sir) Henry Hallett
1875-1968
English physiologist and pharmacologist: worked on histamine and on acetylcholine

Educated in medicine in Cambridge, London and Frankfurt, Dale joined the Wellcome Laboratories in 1904, and at once began (at Sir H. Wellcome's suggestion) to study the physiological action of ergot (a potent extract from a fungal infection of rye) on test animals. This work led, through fortunate and shrewd observations, and the skill of his co-worker G. Barger, to the two research themes which are especially linked with their names. These are firstly the work on **histamine**, a compound released by injured cells or in reaction to foreign protein; and secondly the work on the neurotransmitter, **acetylcholine**. Both these areas have been fruitful for extended investigations, leading to fuller understanding of allergy and anaphylactic shock, and the nature of chemical transmission of nerve impulses. Dale directed the MRC from 1928 to 1942; in 1936 he shared a Nobel Prize. For many years he was a dominant spokesman for science in the UK, especially in the medical and allied sciences.

DALTON, John
1766-1844

English meteorologist and chemical theorist: proposed an atomic theory linked to quantitative chemistry

Dalton was the son of a weaver and a Quaker and grew up in an isolated village in Cumbria. He left his village when he was 15 for Kendal in central Cumbria and thereafter made his living as a teacher. In 1793 he moved to Manchester and taught science, and from 1799 he worked as a private tutor, giving short courses to groups of students for a modest fee. Throughout his life, from 1781, he kept daily meteorological records. This interest in weather and the atmosphere led to his work on gaseous mixtures generally.

In 1794 he wrote an excellent paper on colour vision (he was colour blind); in 1799 returning to his interest in the weather, he showed that springs arise from stored rainfall. This concern with rain and the water content of the atmosphere, which appears as the origin of all his work on gases and on atomic theory, arose through his life in the wet Lake District and the influence of a childhood teacher. He made his reputation in science in 1801 with his **Law of Partial Pressures**. This states that the pressure of a gas mixture is the sum of the pressures that each gas would exert if it were present alone, and occupied the same volume as the whole mixture. He also found the law of thermal expansion of gases, now known as *Charles's* law although Dalton published it first. In 1803, at the end of a paper on gas solubility, he noted rather casually his first table of relative atomic masses. The interest this aroused led him to develop his theory further, in lectures and in his book *A New System of Chemical Philosophy* (1808). Briefly, his **atomic**

theory proposed that every element consists of very small particles called atoms, which are indivisible and indestructable spheres. The atoms of one element were presumed to be identical in all respects, including mass, but to differ from atoms of other elements in their mass. Chemical compounds are formed by the union of atoms of different elements in simple ratios (i.e., elements A and B would form a compound AB; and possibly A_2B, AB_2, A_2B_3). This is known as the **Law of Simple Multiple Proportions**.

The theory was able to interpret the laws of chemical combination, and the conservation of mass; it gave a new basis for all quantitative chemistry. Each aspect of Dalton's theory has since been amended or refined, but its overall picture remains as the central basis of modern chemistry and physics.

Dalton assumed that when only one compound of two elements exists (for example water was the only compound of hydrogen and oxygen then known) it had the simplest formula; i.e., HO for water. On this basis, relative atomic masses ('atomic weights') could easily be found; the early lists were on the scale $H=1$, but now a scale on which the common isotope of carbon$=12$ is used. After *Avogadro's* work, corrections were needed (e.g. water is H_2O, not HO) and discussion by chemists on these changes, and improved analyses, greatly occupied 19th century chemists.

Dalton himself remains a strangely dull personality. His main work came after he was 30. He was a gruff lecturer, a poor experimenter, and his writing seems old-fashioned. Apart from the brilliant insight of his atomic theory, his other work seems pedestrian. He was independent, modest, and attributed his success to 'perseverance'.

DANIELL, John Frederic
1790-1845

English meteorologist and chemist: devised Daniell cell

Although his early research was in

meteorology (he devised a dew-point hygrometer, and theorized on the atmosphere and trade winds), Daniell is best-known for his work on primary cells. The earliest types quickly lost power. The **Daniell cell** (1836) uses amalgamated zinc as negative electrode and copper as positive electrode, and gives a nearly constant e.m.f. of ≈ 1.08 V. It proved a great asset in telegraphy and in the study of electrolysis. In 1831 Daniell became the first professor of chemistry at King's College, London. *See photo* p.138.

DART, Raymond Arthur

1893-1988

Australian anatomist and palaeoanthropologist: discovered Australopithecus africanus

After qualifying as a physician from the University of Sydney in 1917, Dart served in France before being appointed professor of anatomy at the newly-formed University of Witwatersrand, Johannesburg, in 1922. The work there he found to be a most depressing experience, until in 1924 one of his students showed him a fossil baboon skull that had been found in a lime quarry at Taung, Botswana. Dart arranged with the quarry managers for any other similar items to be preserved and sent to him, and soon afterwards the skull of a hitherto unknown hominid, named by Dart *Australopithecus africanus* ('southern ape of Africa'), was discovered. Dart's claim that *Australopithecus* was the 'missing link' between man and the apes was rejected by authorities of the day however, until *Broom* found further hominid remains in the Transvaal in 1936. It is now thought that *Australopithecus* lived about 1.2-2.5 million years ago, but it is still a matter of debate whether modern man is directly descended from him, or if he only represents an unsuccessful evolutionary branch from a much earlier common ancestor.

DARWIN, Charles (Robert)

1809-1882

English naturalist: developed a general theory of evolution and natural selection of species

Young Darwin must have been a disappointment to his talented family. His seven years at Shrewsbury School in his home town led to no career choice, and his two years at Edinburgh as a medical student he found 'intolerably dull'. His father, a successful physician, tried again, and sent him to Cambridge to study for the church; but although he made some good friends, his three years were 'sadly wasted there' and his main interests were still insect-collecting and bird-shooting. Then, when he was 22, he learned that Captain FitzRoy had been commissioned by the Admiralty to take the naval survey ship H.M.S. *Beagle* on a scientific expedition to circumnavigate the southern hemisphere, and was looking for an unpaid volunteer naturalist to join him. Darwin was attracted; his father was against it, but

Charles Darwin aged 29

his uncle Josiah Wedgwood approved and after some doubts, so did FitzRoy. Darwin's voyage on the *Beagle* began in 1831, and was to last five years and to stir a revolution in biology.

At that time, biologists in general believed either that species in natural conditions had continued without change since their original creation, or else (like *Lamarck*) they thought that a characteristic acquired in life could be simply inherited by the offspring. Darwin's experience on his voyage made him doubtful of both theories. For example, he studied the birds of the Galapagos Islands, off the western coast of South America. These ten rocky islands are typically about 80 km apart, with a similar climate, and are separated by deep and fast sea. They are free from gales, and their geology suggests they were never united and are geologically quite young. The few plants and animals resemble those in South America, but are different. Remarkably, each island has to a large extent its own set of plants and animals; there are tortoises, finches, thrushes and many plants which correspond in several islands but are detectably different, so that as the vice-governor Lawson told Darwin, speaking of tortoises, 'he could with certainty tell from which island any one was brought'.

Darwin published the *Journal* of his voyage in 1839, and from then on he gathered his notes on species and read extensively. He read T. R. Malthus's ideas of 1798 on human populations and their survival in the contest for food, and Darwin concluded that all plant and animal species undergo variation with time, and that some variations tend to be preserved and others destroyed, as a result of the inexorable contest for survival among all living things. Darwin's collection of material on this subject was made while he lived as a country gentleman in Kent, with his wife Emma Wedgwood (his first cousin) and their ten children. He discussed his views with his two close friends, the geologist *Lyell* and the bot-

anist *Hooker*, but he was in no hurry to publish them.

Then in 1858 he had a shock; *Wallace*, then in Malaya, sent him an essay offering the same essential idea, and inviting his opinion. As a result, he and Wallace published at the same time in 1858 by agreement. The next year Darwin's book *The Origin of Species by Means of Natural Selection . . .* appeared, giving his ideas in detail; it created excitement among biologists, and widespread discussion. Many churchmen were shocked by it, since Darwin's theory of evolution gave no special need for Divine intervention, and the theory implied also that man had evolved like other organisms and was not a product of a Biblical creation.

Darwin was modest and diffident, and the forceful arguments for his ideas were pressed by his friends, especially *T. H. Huxley*. Interestingly, Darwin had no understanding of mutation, or of heredity in the modern sense, and although *Mendel*'s work on heredity appeared in 1865 it was neglected then and effectively re-discovered only in 1900. The modern development of much of biology, anthropology and palaeontology is based on the idea of evolution of species, while discussion still continues on aspects of the subject such as whether the rate of evolutionary change is broadly uniform, or includes periods of both sluggish and rapid change.

Darwin was a very careful observer, and his theorizing showed both independence of mind, and a desire (combined with caution) to reach general theories in biology. His famous work is in his best-selling books, the *Voyage of the Beagle* and the *Origin of Species* (their short titles), but he also wrote on the evolution of man, on emotion in men and animals, and on climbing and insectivorous plants; he worked hard despite recurrent illnesses. He had ideas on the origin of life, and in a letter of 1871 to Hooker, wrote that 'if (and oh what a big if) we could conceive in some warm little pond, with all sorts of ammonia and phosphoric salts, light, heat, electricity, etc., present, that a protein compound was chemically formed ...' but he recognized that such speculation was then premature. In fact, ideas a century later were broadly in accord with his. Darwin also contributed to geology, but his valuable work on coral atolls and on land elevation has been overshadowed by his massive contribution to biology. He was never honoured by the Crown, a rather remarkable omission.

Other members of Darwin's family contributed to work on evolution. His grandfather Erasmus Darwin was a physician, biologist, engineer and poet, and the presiding genius of the Lunar Society; he had ideas on evolution which were ahead of their time. Erasmus's second wife was the grandmother of *Galton*, who examined the statistics of inherited talent, in his own and other families.

DAUSSET, Jean
1916-

French immunologist: made important investigations into blood transfusion reactions

From the time during World War II when

Jean Dausset

he served in a blood transfusion unit, Dausset was mainly interested in transfusion reactions. This led him in the early 1950s to discover that the belief that blood of group O can be used for all patients is false. If the donor has recently been given antidiphtheria or antitetanus vaccine, the resulting antibodies can produce shock reactions when the blood is transfused. Continuing his study of transfusion responses, Dausset found that patients who had many blood transfusions were prone to produce antibodies against the white cells. The antigen (human lymphocyte antigen, HLA) is, he suggested, related to the mouse H-2 system. The work led to 'tissue typing' by simple tests, and proved of great value in reducing rejection risks in organ transplant surgery. Dausset shared a Nobel Prize in 1980.

DAVIS, William Morris
1850-1934

American physical geographer: pioneer of geomorphology

After a period as a meteorologist in Argentina, Davis worked with the North Pacific Survey before being appointed to a lecturership at Harvard in 1877. He pioneered the study of landforms, conducting a classic study of the drainage system of the Pennsylvania and New Jersey area in 1889, in which he illustrated his idea of erosion cycles. He proposed that the erosive action of rivers causes first the cutting of steep V-shaped valleys, which mature into broader valleys and lead eventually to the formation of a rolling lowland landscape that he termed a 'peneplain'.

DAVISSON, Clinton Joseph
1881-1958

American physicist: discovered experimentally the diffraction of electrons by crystals

After graduating from the University of Chicago and taking his PhD at Princeton,

Davisson worked at Carnegie Institute of Technology (1911-1917). He then joined the Bell Telephone Laboratory (then Western Electric Co Laboratory) for wartime employment after being refused enlistment in 1917, and subsequently stayed until his retirement in 1945.

The Davisson and *Germer* experiment, which confirmed *de Broglie*'s hypothesis that particles could behave like waves (and thus fundamentally altered modern physics), was initially accidental and in part due to a patent suit. Western Electric were protecting their patent for *De Forest*'s three-element vacuum tube (with an oxide-coated filament) against *Langmuir*'s similar tube with a tungsten filament developed by him at General Electric Co. In order to help settle the suit (which dragged on for a decade), Davisson and Germer measured electron emission from oxide-coated platinum under ion bombardment. The purpose was to establish that the electron emission did not depend upon positive ion bombardment due to oxygen traces in the tube, and therefore that Langmuir's tube did not fundamentally differ from that already under patent. This they did, and the Supreme Court eventually ruled in Western Electric's favour. In the meantime Davisson and C. H. Kunsman investigated electron emission under electron bombardment as an easy extension to the work, and found a small number of primary electrons with the full energy of the incident beam deflected back alongside the many low energy secondary electrons. In 1925 an accidental explosion of a liquid-air bottle heavily oxidized a nickel surface which Davisson was investigating, and after heating to clean it (which also recrystallized it from polycrystalline into a few large crystals) it displayed a maximum scattering at a particular angle.

On visiting Oxford in 1926 and hearing of de Broglie's recent work, postulating wave behaviour for an electron, Davisson realised that he had seen diffraction maxima in the electron wave pattern. In 1927, Davisson with Germer obtained conclusive evidence that electron beams were diffracted on reflection by nickel crystals and had the wavelength predicted by de Broglie. For this he shared the 1937 Nobel Physics Prize with *G. P. Thomson*, who had observed similar electron diffraction, with high energy electrons passing through metal foil.

DAVY, (Sir) Humphry
1778-1829

English chemist: discoverer of sodium and potassium, exploiter of electrochemistry, and propagandist for science

Son of a Cornish woodcarver and small farmer, Davy became an apprentice pharmacist. However, in 1798 he was employed by *Beddoes* to work in his Medical Pneumatic Institution in Bristol, with the task of developing the medical uses of some newly-discovered gases. Davy made N_2O ('nitrous oxide' or 'laughing gas') in quantity, studied it fully, and through this work, and some useful friendships, was appointed as chemist by *Rumford* in the new Royal Institution in London, in 1801. He quickly became famous as a lecturer. His ideas on the uses of science appealed to the serious-minded, and demonstrations (especially of the inhibition-releasing effects of N_2O) attracted others. Davy made the Royal Institution a social and financial success; and thereby acquired the equipment (especially a large voltaic cell) to develop his interest in electrochemistry. In 1807 he made the reactive metals, potassium and sodium, by electrolysis; and soon he secured other new and reactive metals. These exciting discoveries were followed by experiments which showed that chlorine was probably an element (and not a compound); and further work related it to iodine (newly found by B. Courtois) and to fluorine.

In 1812 he was knighted, and three days later married Jane Apreece, a wealthy Scottish widow. He was now established

Humphry Davy

his younger brother John (also a chemist) says he was 'a little mad about it'. He was also an enthusiastic poet, and had friends with real literary talent, including Coleridge, Southey, and Wordsworth, who thought better of his poetry than do modern critics.

DE BARY, (Heinrich) Anton
1831-1888

German botanist: a founder of mycology

De Bary left medicine to teach botany in three German universities before settling in Strasbourg in 1872. His main work was in mycology, where he showed that fungi are the cause of rust and smut diseases of plants (and not a result, as others had thought). He went on to show that lichens consist of a fungus and an alga in intimate partnership, forming a remarkably hardy union with mutual benefits. De Bary named this **symbiosis**; the term now is used to cover three kinds of specialized association between individuals of different species, including **parasitism** (one organism gains, the other loses) as well as **commensalism** (one organism gains, the other neither loses nor gains) and **mutualism** (a mutually beneficial association, as in the lichens).

De Bary's excellent descriptions and classifications of fungi, algae, 'moulds and yeasts', established them as plants which happen to be small, and did much to create modern mycology.

DE BEER, (Sir) Gavin Rylands
1899-1972

English zoologist: refuted germ-layer theory in embryology, and theory of phylogenetic recapitulation

De Beer served in both world wars, in Normandy in 1944 with the Grenadier Guards as a Lieutenant Colonel; in the interval he graduated from Oxford and he afterwards taught there. After World War II he became professor of embryology in

as Britain's leading scientist, and he embarked on the first of many European tours. In 1813 he hired *Faraday* as an assistant (and also tried to use him as a valet on his travels). In 1815 he was asked to devise a safe lamp for use in gassy coalmines. This was the sort of problem which showed his talent well. In six months he had made the first thorough study of flame combustion and devised his safety lamp, which made mining of deep coal seams possible, even if firedamp (CH_4) was present.

Davy's reputation outstrips his chemical achievements, substantial though they were. He had great energy and talent, especially in attacking limited but important chemical problems. He was also snobbish, excitable, and ungenerous to other scientists; unskilled in quantitative work, and uneven in his knowledge or interest in theories (he doubted *Dalton*'s new atomic theory). His early death left 'brilliant fragments' (Berzelius); much interest in electrochemistry, and perhaps his finest 'discovery', Faraday. An important achievement was that he had sold science to the industrialists, especially through his success with the miner's safety lamp.

He had an intense interest in angling;

London, and from 1950 Director of the British Museum (Natural History) until he retired in 1960. In 1926 he much injured the germ-layer theory in embryology by showing that some bone cells develop from the outer (ectodermal) layer of the embryo (the theory had them form from the mesoderm). In 1940 he also refuted E. Haeckel's theory of phylogenetic recapitulation; according to this theory an organism in its embryonic stage repeats the adult stages of the organism's evolutionary ancestors. De Beer showed that in fact the situation is rather the converse; adult animals retain some juvenile features of their ancestors (**paedomorphism**). His many other researches included studies of the earliest known bird, *Archeopteryx*, and led him to propose a pattern of 'piecemeal' evolution to explain its possession of both reptilian and avian features (e.g., teeth and wings); and he worked on the origin of the Etruscans from blood group data, and on Hannibal's route over the Alps.

DE BROGLIE, (Prince) Louis-Victor Pierre Raymond

1892-1987

French physicist: discoverer of the wave nature of particles

Louis de Broglie was of a Piedmontese family; in 1740 Louis Soleil (Louis XIV) conferred on the head of the family the hereditary title of Duc, which de Broglie inherited in 1960 on the death of his brother Maurice (who was also a physicist). The German title Prinz dated in the family from service to the Austrians during the Seven Years War. De Broglie studied history at the Sorbonne, and acquired an interest in science by service at the Eiffel Tower radio station during World War I. He then took a doctorate at the Sorbonne (1924) and taught there, as the professor of theoretical physics at the newly founded Henri Poincaré Institute (1928-1962).

Our ideas concerning quanta stem from *Planck* (1900), and modern ideas on the interaction of matter and energy had begun with *Einstein* in 1905. De Broglie's work began with a derivation of *Wien*'s electromagnetic radiation law, based on light quanta with frequency ν, mass $h\nu/c^2$ and momentum $h\nu/c$ (1922). It then occurred to him to go beyond the idea of waves acting as particles and to suggest that particles can behave as waves. A particle such as an electron should move at the group velocity ν of a number of matter waves, which have wavelength $\lambda = h/m\nu$. This revolutionary idea appeared in de Broglie's doctoral thesis (1924), which was published as a paper of over 100 pages in *Annales de Physique* in 1925. The waves were detected and agreement with λ found through the wave interference, using the atoms of a crystal lattice as a diffraction grating. This was done by *Davisson* and *Germer* using slow electrons (59 eV) and *G. P. Thomson* using fast electrons in 1927. The wave-particle duality was used by *Schrödinger* in his formulation of quantum mechanics, and it also began the great debate as to whether there is determinacy in quantum mechanics. De Broglie received the Nobel Prize for physics in 1929.

DEBYE, Peter (Joseph William)

1884-1966

Dutch-American chemical physicist: developed ideas on dipole moments, and on solutions of electrolytes

Debye was educated in the Netherlands and in Germany, and then held posts in theoretical physics in several European countries in rapid succession. Despite these frequent moves, he produced in 1911-16 a theory of the change in specific heat capacity with temperature, and a method for X-ray diffraction analysis using powdered crystals (with P. Sherrer), and the idea of permanent molecular electric dipole moments. He showed how these moments can be measured, and how they can be used to find the shape of simple molecules, e.g. the molecule of water, H-O-H, is not linear but bent. He was also able to show that the benzene ring is flat. The unit of electric dipole moment, the debye (D) is the electronic charge $(e) \times 10^{-10}$ m. His work with *Hückel* led in 1923 to the **Debye-Hückel theory of electrolytes**, which deals with the behaviour of strong solutions of electrolytes, by taking account of the mutual interaction of the charged ions. (Previous theories had dealt only with very dilute solutions.) In 1934 he moved to Berlin, and in 1940 to the US, where he was professor of chemistry at Cornell until 1950. His work on light scattering in solutions, on polymers, and on magnetism is also important. He was awarded the Nobel Prize for chemistry in 1936, and in 1939 had the strange experience of seeing a bust of himself unveiled in his native city of Maastricht. He remained fit and youthful and clear-thinking, throughout his life.

DEDEKIND, Julius Wilhelm Richard
1831-1916

German mathematician: made far-reaching contributions to number theory

Dedekind studied at Brunswick and then formed a close association with *Riemann*, *Dirichlet* and *Gauss* at Göttingen, with each influencing the others. Dedekind learned about the method of least squares from Gauss, the theory of numbers, potential theory and partial differential equations from Dirichlet. After a short time he moved briefly to Zürich, and then returned to spend the rest of his long life as a professor at the Technische Hochschule, Brunswick. He lived long enough for much of his influential work (e.g., on irrational numbers) to become familiar to a generation of students in his later years, and he became a legend. Twelve years too soon, Teubner's Calendar for Mathematicians recorded him as having died on 4 September 1899. Much amused, Dedekind wrote to the editor: 'According to my own memorandum I passed this day in perfect health and enjoyed a very stimulating conversation ... with my ... friend Georg Cantor of Halle'.

Dedekind was one of the first to recognize the value of Cantor's work on infinite qualities. Dedekind himself made major steps towards modern standards of rigour, and was ahead of his time in his approach to number theory.

In 1858 he produced an arithmetic definition of continuity and clarified the concept of an irrational number (that is, roughly, a number that cannot be represented as a fraction). In the first of three great books he used **Dedekind cuts** (the categorization of irrational numbers by fractions) to rigorously examine the real number system.

Then in his second major work (1888) he established a logical foundation for arithmetic and described axioms that exactly represent the logical concept of whole numbers (these are now, incorrectly, called *Peano* axioms). Finally, Dedekind described the factorization of real numbers using modern algebra (1897-1900).

DE DUVE, Christian René
1917-

Belgian biochemist: discovered lysosomes

Born in England and educated in medicine in Louvain, de Duve worked in Sweden and the US before returning to Louvain in 1947, and later holding a dual post also at Rockefeller University, New York.

From 1949, de Duve obtained ingenious experimental evidence that some, at least, of a cell's digestive enzymes must be enclosed in small organelles within the cell. By 1955 these were positively identified with the aid of electron microscopy, and named **lysosomes**. These serve both to isolate the enzymes from attack on their own animal or plant cells, and to concentrate their attack when the lysosome fuses with a food vacuole. After digesting the macromolecules present in the food, the resulting small molecules of sugar or amino acid pass through the lysosome wall into the cell. Another function of lysosomes is to destroy worn-out cell organelles, or even cells. Some hereditary metabolic diseases (e.g., cystinosis) are due to absence of a lysosomal enzyme. De Duve shared a Nobel Prize in 1974.

DE FOREST, Lee
1873-1961

American physicist: inventor of the thermionic triode valve and pioneer of radio

De Forest studied at Yale University, writing his doctoral thesis on radio waves (probably the first thesis on the subject of radio in America). He went to work for the Western Electric Company, and in 1907 developed and patented the thermionic triode valve. This device, essentially a diode with an additional electrode between cathode and anode, could be used to amplify weak electrical signals, and was crucial to the development of radio communication, radar, television, and computers. The triode valve remained an essential component in all kinds of equipment for fifty years, before being superseded by the transistor. De Forest also worked on a film soundtrack system and a medical diathermy machine, the former being a commercial failure at the time, but later widely adopted.

DE LA BECHE, (Sir) Henry Thomas
1796-1855

British geologist: conducted first systematic geological survey of the British Isles

De la Beche entered military training school at the age of 14 and served in the Napoleonic Wars, but at their conclusion five years later gave up an army career and devoted himself to geology. He travelled widely, writing important descriptions of the Jurassic and Cretaceous rocks of the Devon and Dorset area, and also of the Pembrokeshire coast and of Jamaica. During the late 1820s he began his most significant work, the first systematic geological survey of Britain. Working at first as an amateur, his efforts led to the establishment of the Geological Survey of Great Britain in 1835, with himself as its first director.

DELBRÜCK, Max
1906-1981

German-American biophysicist: pioneer of molecular biology

Delbrück is unusual in 20th century science both for practising in three areas (physics, chemistry and biology) and for the fact that his place, although substantial as a discoverer, is largely that of an inspirer of others in the creation of molecular biology.

He began in physics, with a PhD from Göttingen in 1930, and spent two years on atomic physics with *Bohr*; then for a time worked in chemistry at the Kaiser Wilhelm Institute in Berlin; and from 1937 was at the California Institute of Technology where he moved into biology. *Morgan* and the '*Drosophila* geneticists' had gone to Pasadena from New York in 1928, taking with them the conviction that genetic problems should be solvable by chemistry and physics. Delbrück agreed, with the proviso that new concepts in these sciences would be needed, and his ideas were developed in the physicist *Schrödinger's* influential book *What is Life?* in 1945. Delbrück decided to work on viruses as the simplest life form. He did much to create bacterial and bacteriophage genetics, and in 1946 he showed that viruses can exchange (recombine) genetic material, the first evidence of recombination in primitive organisms. His firm belief in an 'informational basis' in molecular biology bore fruit in other hands, but with much help from his forceful catalytic ideas. He shared a Nobel Prize in 1969, which led to another of his famous parties.

DEMOCRITUS (of Abdera)

c.470-c.400 BC

Greek philosopher: pioneer of atomic theory

Almost nothing is firmly known of Democritus's life, and his ideas have survived through the writings of others, either supporting or attacking him. His idea of atoms seems to have begun with his teacher Leucippus, but Democritus much extended the theory. He proposed that the universe contains only a vacuum and atoms, and that these atoms are invisibly small and hard, eternal and are in ceaseless motion. On this adaptable, materialist view he explained taste, smell, sound, fire and death. He supposed that in their form and behaviour lay the natural god-less cause of all things and all events. Plato and *Aristotle* were not in favour of these ideas, which never formed a part of the mainstream of Greek philosophy, but they were adopted by the Greek philosopher Epicurus about 300 BC, and well recorded in a long poem ('On the Nature of Things') by the Roman, Lucretius. In the 17th century *Boyle* and *Newton* were aware of these ideas; it is doubtful if they contributed at all directly to modern atomic theory which began with *Dalton* about 1800.

DE MOIVRE, Abraham

1667-1754

French-British mathematician: founded analytical trigonometry and stated De Moivre's theorem

De Moivre had the misfortune to be a Huguenot (Protestant) at the time that Roman Catholic France revoked the Edict of Nantes and began to persecute them (1685). He was imprisoned in Paris for a year and moved to England on his release. Friendship with *Newton* and *Halley* aided his election to the Royal Society (1697). However, De Moivre remained poor, working as a tutor or consultant to gambling or insurance syndicates, and never obtained a university post. He died blind and disillusioned, with his work unrecognized.

His book *The Doctrine of Chances* (1718) is a masterpiece, and sets out the binomial probability or Gaussian distribution, the concept of statistical independence and the use of analytical techniques in probability. Deriving an expansion for $n! = n(n-1)(n-2) \ldots 3.2.1$, De Moivre summed terms of the binomial form. He established many of the elements of actuarial calculations. Above all he discovered the trigonometric relation

$$(\cos \theta + i\sin \theta)^n = \cos n\theta + i\sin n\theta$$

called **De Moivre's theorem** (1722), which is a powerful step in developing complex number theory.

DESCARTES, René

1596-1650

French philosopher and mathematician: creator of analytical geometry

Descartes has a dominant position in shaping modern philosophy, but this is not our concern here. With enough modest inherited wealth to live as he chose, he spent his life in travel, on his work in philosophy, mathematics, physics and physiology, and as a soldier serving in Holland, Bohemia and Hungary. In 1621 he left the army and in 1629 settled in Holland for some 20 years, before being persuaded to become tutor to Queen Christina of Sweden, a headstrong and athletic 19-year-old. From childhood Descartes had risen late and claimed to do his best thinking in a warm bed; the Queen's insistence on tutorials in philosophy at 5 a.m. in a freezing library either hastened or produced the lung disease which killed him within five months of arrival.

Although Descartes theorized extensively in physics and physiology, his lasting influence outside philosophy is in mathematics, where he created analytical or co-ordinate geometry, also named (after him) as **Cartesian geometry**. This translates geometrical problems into algebraic form, so that algebraic methods can be applied to their solution; conversely he applied (for the first time) geometry to algebra. His methods made a massive change in mathematical thought and remain familiar today, as in the equation of the straight line, $y = mx + c$ and the equations of familiar curves such as the conic sections. The thinker J. S. Mill claimed that Cartesian geometry 'constitutes the greatest single step ever made in the progress of the exact sciences.'

DE SITTER, Willem

1872-1934

Dutch cosmologist and mathematician: proposed expanding universe solution to equations of general relativity

De Sitter studied at the University of Groningen and, after a time at the Cape Town Observatory, was appointed professor of astronomy at Leiden in 1908, and director of the Leiden Observatory in 1919.

In 1916 *Einstein* published his theory of general relativity, and found a solution to the relativity equations that yielded a static universe. De Sitter showed soon afterwards that there was another solution, an expanding universe that contained no matter, the **de Sitter universe**. In 1927 *Lemaître* and *Friedmann* both found a further possible solution, an expanding universe containing matter. Soon afterwards it was shown that a transformation of the de Sitter universe yielded a similar, but mathematically much simpler, solution, now known as the **Einstein-de Sitter universe**.

DESMAREST, Nicolas

1725-1815

French geologist: demonstrated the igneous origin of basalts

Desmarest was by profession a trade and industry inspector for the department of commerce. In the 1760s he became interested in the large basalt deposits of central France (discovered by *Guettard* a decade before), and succeeded in tracing their origins to ancient volcanic activity in the Auvergne region. In 1768 he produced a detailed study of the geology and eruption history of the volcanoes responsible. His work was important because it demonstrated that basalts were igneous in origin, which led to the abandonment of the widely held belief that all rocks were sedimentary (the Neptunist theory of A. G. Werner).

DEVILLE, Henri Étienne Sainte-Claire

1818-1881

French chemist: developed methods for making light metals in quantity; studied high temperature reactions

Deville is one of the few major 19th century scientists to be born in the West Indies, where his family had been leading citizens for two centuries. With his older brother Charles he was educated in Paris. He chose medicine but was soon attracted to chemistry; in the 1840s he worked on essential oils and obtained methylbenzene and methyl benzoate from balsam of tolu, but his chemical fame began in 1849 when he made the crystalline and highly reactive dinitrogen pentoxide by treating warm silver nitrate with chlorine. From 1851 he held a post at the École Normale supérieure, with *Pasteur* as a colleague and close friend from 1857. The main work of the institution was to train senior school teachers, which Deville did for 30 years while maintaining a major research output. He was a masterly lecturer and experimentalist, uninvolved in disputes over theory. Realizing that sodium metal in quantity would be of great use, he developed a large-scale method for making it by reduction of sodium carbonate with carbon. One target was to use sodium to make aluminium by reduction of $AlCl_3$. In 1855 Deville was summoned to show aluminium, then rare, to the

Emperor; the latter was attracted by the idea of fitting his troops with helmets of the new metal, and a government grant to set up a pilot plant was arranged. Success followed; bars of aluminium were shown at the 1855 Exposition, and it quickly ceased to be mainly used for jewellery. Soon Deville made pure magnesium in quantity, and titanium, and crystalline boron and silicon, all by reduction of chlorides with sodium metal. He worked on the platinum metals and in 1872 was given the task of making the platinum-iridium (90-10) alloy for the standard kilogram and metre.

His interest in high temperature chemistry had begun in the 1850s and his oxy-hydrogen blowpipe method led to technical welding methods as well as studies of minerals and high-melting metals. From 1857 he also studied vapour densities, using porcelain bulbs and the vapour of boiling metal (Hg, Cd or Zn) to give a constant high temperature. He found that relative molecular mass could change with temperature; thus aluminium chloride is mainly Al_2Cl_6 at 500°, but $AlCl_3$ at 1000°C. Chemical changes due to heat which reverse on cooling were described as **dissociations** by Deville, who first fully examined such changes. He found that at high temperatures H_2O, CO_2, CO, HCl and SO_2 all dissociated.

de VRIES, Hugo
1848-1935

Dutch plant physiologist and geneticist: early investigator of plant genetics

De Vries, son of a Dutch prime minister of 1872, studied medicine in Holland and Germany and taught botany in both countries, and mainly in Amsterdam. As a pupil of *Sachs* at Würzburg he worked on turgor in plant cells, and used the term **plasmolysis** to describe shrinkage of protoplast from the plant cell wall, with loss of turgidity. He used these studies on water relations in plants both to advance knowledge of plant physiology and to

confirm *van't Hoff*'s views on osmotic pressure. In the 1880s he became interested in heredity, but he did not then know of *Mendel*'s work of the 1860s, and he began breeding plants in 1892. He got clear examples of the '3:1 ratio', and then came across Mendel's work in 1900, and did much to make the work widely known. His breeding experiments included some on the evening primrose, and the striking results led him to propose a bold general 'theory of mutation'; but we now use the word in a different sense, and de Vries's mutations resulted from changes in chromosome number (to which the evening primrose is prone; its genetic make-up is complex) and not to changes in genes. However, despite being wrongly based, de Vries's ideas on a rapid alternative to Darwinian evolution led to valuable debate and experimentation, which ultimately did much to establish the Darwinian view.

DEWAR, (Sir) James
1842-1923

Scottish chemist and physicist: pioneer of low temperature studies and of chemistry of metal carbonyls

Son of a wine-merchant, Dewar became attracted to chemistry at Edinburgh University and spent a summer in Ghent in *Kekulé*'s laboratory. In 1869 he went to teach chemistry at the Royal Veterinary College in Edinburgh. Although he was never interested in teaching students, he was a popular society lecturer on a wide range of scientific topics, and in 1875 became Jacksonian Professor at Cambridge. He was probably elected because of his work in physiological chemistry and was perhaps expected to do more of it; in fact he found the laboratory so poor that he was glad to be also appointed in 1877 to the Professorship of Chemistry at the Royal Institution, London. Thereafter he lived and worked in London, visiting Cambridge only briefly and infrequently in order to abuse his staff there for idleness and to visit G. D. Liveing, professor of chemistry; they collaborated in spectroscopic research for 25 years. Dewar had a strangely wide range of research interests, which he maintained with his own hands or with assistants, never having students or founding a 'school'. In the early 1870s he invented the Dewar flask (domestically a 'thermos' flask), a double-walled glass flask with the inner walls reflective and the space between them evacuated; heat is only slowly passed to or from the contents. From 1877 he worked on the liquifaction of gases, using the flasks for storage. He used *Cailletet*'s method for making oxygen, on a scale which allowed him to study low temperatures; and by 1898 he made liquid hydrogen in quantity and the solid in 1899, at a temperature below 14 K. At this temperature all known substances become solid, except helium. He tried to liquify helium, discovered on Earth in 1895, but did not succeed. With *F. A. Abel* he invented cordite. He worked on specific heat capacities, electrical effects at very low temperatures, metal carbonyls, diffusion, high vacua, coal tar bases, dissociation of molecules at high temperatures, emission and absorption spectra, soap films (he made them over 1 m in diameter) and the Sun's temperature. A small brusque Scot, he was unsurpassed in diversity and productivity as an experimentalist.

DICKE, Robert Henry

1916-

American physicist: predicted existence of cosmic microwave background

Dicke studied at Princeton University and at Rochester, and in 1957 was appointed professor of physics at Princeton, where he became Albert Einstein Professor of Science.

In 1964, Dicke made the prediction that, assuming the universe had been created by a cataclysmic explosion (the 'big bang'), there ought to be a remnant radiation, observable in the microwave region of the spectrum. At almost the same time, *Penzias* and *R. W. Wilson* did in fact observe this cosmic microwave background, although they were unaware of Dicke's theoretical work at the time. Together, their work established the big bang model of the origin of the universe as far more plausible than the rival steady-state theory. Interestingly, and unknown to Dicke at the time, *Gamow* and others had made a similar prediction in 1948.

Dicke is also interested in gravitation, and established that the gravitational mass and inertial mass of bodies are equivalent to an accuracy of at least one part in 10^{11}, an important result for general relativity. However, in 1961 the **Brans-Dicke theory** suggested that the gravitational constant (G) was not in fact constant, but varied slowly with time (by about 10^{-11} per year). Unfortunately the experimental observations required to verify this hypothesis are not yet sufficiently precise to prove it one way or the other.

DIELS, Otto (Paul Hermann)

1876-1954

German organic chemist: co-discoverer of Diels-Alder reaction

A member of an academically talented family, Diels studied chemistry in Berlin with *E. Fischer*. Most of his life was spent in the University of Kiel. In 1906 he discovered a new oxide of carbon (the monoxide and dioxide were long known); he made tricarbon dioxide (C_3O_2) by dehydrating malonic acid with P_2O_5:

$$CH_2(CO_2H)_2 - 2H_2O \rightarrow O=C=C=C=O$$

He showed in 1927 that cholesterol is dehydrogenated by heating with selenium, and that the hydrocarbon products include one of melting point 127° now known as **Diels's hydrocarbon**. The method can be applied generally to steroids, and many yield Diels's hydrocarbon; in this way and by interconversions, this biologically important steroid group was shown to all have the same carbon skeleton. By 1934 Diels's hydrocarbon had been synthesized by others and its structure was the critical clue which allowed other steroid structures to be assigned, all containing the four-ring skeleton of Diels's hydrocarbon: this skeleton became the defining feature of steroids.

In 1928, with his assistant K. Alder, Diels discovered the valuable general synthesis now known as the **Diels-Alder reaction**. In this, a conjugated diene reacts by 1,4-addition with one of a large group of unsaturated compounds (dienophiles) to give, usually, a six-membered ring compound as the product. The method has proved of great value in the synthesis of complex organic compounds. Diels and Alder shared a Nobel Prize in 1950.

DIESEL, Rudolph (Christian Karl)
1858-1913

German engineer: devised compression-ignition internal combustion engine

Born in Paris of German parents, Rudolph and his family left for London when the Franco-Prussian war of 1870 began, but he soon moved to Germany to continue his education, eventually studying at the Munich Polytechnic.

From 1880 to 1890 he worked on refrigeration plant, but his interest was in engines. He realised that on thermodynamic principles an internal combustion engine should desirably operate with a large temperature range, which implies a high pressure. His patent of 1893 and his engines produced in the late 1890s use a four-stroke cycle like the *Otto* engine (induction, compression, combustion, exhaust) but in the Diesel engine a higher-boiling petroleum fraction is used. In the induction stroke, air alone is drawn into the cylinder. On the compression stroke this air is compressed by up to 25:1 (unlike the 10:1 compression of the petrol:air mixture in a petrol engine) and this raises its temperature to near 600°C. Then an injector admits a fine spray of fuel into the heated air; it ignites spontaneously, and the combustion stroke provides power. An exhaust stroke to remove the burned gas completes the cycle. Diesel prospered, but in 1913 he vanished from the Antwerp-Harwich mail steamer and was presumed drowned; his body was never found.

Diesel engines are more efficient than petrol engines and were used in World War I in submarines, and later in ships and rail locomotives. The smaller units for buses, tractors, trucks and small electrical generators were developed in the 1930s, with important design contributions by two British engineers, C. B. Dicksee and H. Ricardo; by the 1980s larger commercial vehicles were normally powered by high-speed compression-ignition units.

DIOPHANTUS (of Alexandria)
Lived *c.* 250 AD

Greek mathematician: discoverer of the Diophantine equations

Although an outstanding mathematician of his time, very little is now known about Diophantus's life. His work is preserved in the six surviving volumes of his *Arithmetica* (a further seven volumes have been lost), which was probably the earliest systematic treatise on algebra. Diophantus was primarily interested in number theory and the solution of equations, and did much to advance algebra by his use of symbols for quantities, mathematical operations and relationships; previously such quantities had been described in words. He is perhaps best remembered as the discoverer of the **Diophantine equations**, indeterminate equations with rational coefficients for which a rational solution is required.

117

DIRAC, Paul Adrien Maurice

1902-1984

British theoretical physicist: major contributor to quantum mechanics; predicted existance of positron, and of other antiparticles

Dirac, the son of a Swiss father and English mother, studied electrical engineering at Bristol and mathematics at Cambridge. After teaching in America and visiting Japan and Siberia, Dirac was appointed in 1932 to the Lucasian Professorship in mathematics at Cambridge, where he remained until his retirement in 1969. He was then a visiting lecturer at four US universities before becoming professor of physics at Florida State University in 1971.

A uniquely gifted theoretician, Dirac contributed creatively to the rapid development of quantum mechanics. In 1926, just after *Born* and *Jordan*, he developed a general theoretical structure for quantum mechanics. In 1928 he produced the relativistic form of the theory describing the properties of the electron, and correcting the failure of *Schrödinger's* theory to explain electron spin discovered by *Uhlenbeck* and *Goudsmit* in 1925.

From the relativistic theory he proposed in 1930 that the theoretically possible negative energy solutions for the electron exist as states, but they are filled with particles of negative energy, so that other electrons cannot enter them. He predicted that a sufficiently energetic photon could create an electron-positron pair apparently from nowhere by knocking an electron out of one of these negative energy states. The positively charged hole left is the antiparticle to an electron, called a positron. Also, an electron meeting a positron can give mutual annihilation, releasing energy as a photon (light). All these predictions were verified experimentally by *C. D. Anderson* in 1932. Dirac's argument applies to all particles, not just electrons, so that all particles possess corresponding antiparticles.

In 1930 Dirac published *The Principles of Quantum Mechanics*, which is a classic work which confirmed his stature as a 20th century *Newton* in the minds of many physicists. The Nobel Physics Prize for 1933 was shared by Dirac and Schrödinger.

DIRICHLET, Peter Gustav Lejeune

1805-1859

German mathematician: contributed to analysis, partial differential equations in physics, and number theory

Dirichlet studied at Göttingen under *Gauss* and *Jacobi*, and also spent time in Paris where he gained an interest in *Fourier* series from their originator. He moved to a post at Breslau, but at 23 became a professor at Berlin, remaining for 27 years. He was shy and modest, but an excellent teacher; he was a close friend of Jacobi, and he spent 18 months in Italy with him when Jacobi was driven there by ill-health. On Gauss's death in 1855 Dirichlet accepted his prestigious chair at Göttingen, but died of a heart attack only three years later.

Dirichlet carried on Gauss's great work on number theory, publishing on Diophantine equations of the form $x^5 + y^5 = kz^5$, and developing a general algebraic number theory. Dirichlet's theorem (1837) states that any arithmetic series a, a+b, a+2b, a+3b, where a and b have no common divisors other than 1, must include an infinite series of primes. His book *Lectures on Number Theory* (1863), is a work of similar stature to Gauss's earlier *Disquisitiones*, and founded modern algebraic number theory.

Dirichlet also made advances in applied mathematics. In 1829 he stated the conditions sufficient for a Fourier series to converge (those conditions necessary for it to converge are still undiscovered). He worked on multiple integrals and the boundary-value problem (or Dirichlet problem), which is the effect of the conditions at the boundary on the solution of a heat flow or electrostatic equation.

It is not only Dirichlet's many specific contributions that give him greatness, but also his approach to formulating and analysing problems for which he founded modern techniques.

DÖBEREINER, Johann Wolfgang
1780-1849

German chemist: introduced Law of Triads, and studied catalysis

A coachman's son, Döbereiner was largely self-educated, but secured a teaching post at Jena, possibly through aristocratic influence. He held the teaching post worthily through his lifetime; one of his pupils was the philosopher, Goethe. He improved organic analysis, and made the first estimates of the abundance of elements in the Earth's crust. He used an earlier observation by *Davy* (that platinum caused organic vapours to react with air) to devise **Döbereiner's lamp**, a toy or demonstration device in which a jet of hydrogen was ignited by contact with platinum sponge. His main claim to fame is his observation of 'trias' (later, triads) of elements. These are groups such as Cl, Br, I; or Ca, Sr, Ba; or S, Se, Te in which the atomic mass of the middle element is close to the mean of the first and last elements in its group; and its physical and chemical properties likewise appear average. By 1829 this was developed as the **Law of Triads**. It then attracted little attention, but can now be seen as a step towards the Periodic Classification of the elements.

DOISY, Edward Adelbert
1893-1986

American biochemist: isolated vitamin K

Educated at Illinois and Harvard, Doisy spent most of his life at St Louis Univer-sity Medical School. In 1923 he devised a bioassay for the female sex hormone and secured potent extracts, but it was *Bute-nandt* who first isolated oestrone. Soon Doisy moved to the study of vitamin K, deficiency of which leads to the blood failing to coagulate. He was able to isolate a factor (K for koagulation) from alfalfa grass, and a related but different K factor from putrefied fish meal. These two potent antihaemorrhagic vitamins K_1 and K_2, were shown by Doisy to be derivatives of 1,4-naphthoquinone; such compounds are valuable in therapy, for example to reduce bleeding in patients with an obstructed bile duct. Doisy shared a Nobel Prize in 1943.

DOLLAND, John
1706-1761

English optician: introduced achromatic lenses for telescopes and microscopes

Dolland was for many years a silk-weaver; he was the son of a French Huguenot refugee. In 1752, however, he joined his son Peter in his business as an optician. They attacked the problem of chromatic aberration, i.e., the colour fringes in the images produced by a simple lens, which *Newton* had considered inherent in lenses. In fact C. M. Hall, a London lawyer, designed a compound lens of crown and flint glass which was largely achromatic (colour-free) and had telescopes made using them, from 1733. The Dollands almost certainly knew of this; however they did much experimental work, secured improved glass, and after John Dolland's patent of 1758 produced good quality achromats. This led to nearly colour-free refracting telescopes being made; although the reflecting type ulti-mately became dominant in astronomy, as a mirror is completely achromatic, requires only one flaw-free surface, and can be supported from the back. In microscopy Dolland-type lenses were of great value, as there is no easy alteration to a refracting system for obtaining optical magnification in the microscope.

DOMAGK, Gerhard
1895-1964

German biochemist: discoverer of sulphonamide antibacterial drugs

Ehrlich's success in treating some protozoal diseases by chemotherapy had led to high hopes of similar success in the treatment of bacterial diseases. Diseases due to protozoa are common in the tropics; in temperate regions, diseases due to the smaller bacteria are major problems. However, by 1930 hopes had faded; trial compounds usually failed to be effective in the presence of blood or pus. This was the position when Domagk began work on the problem. He had qualified in medicine at Kiel in 1921 and in 1927 began to direct research at the bacteriology laboratory of the I.G.Farbenindustrie at Wuppertal, while retaining a position at the University of Münster. His scheme was to test a series of new dyes made by I.G.Farben as drugs against streptococcal infections in mice, and in 1932 he found that the dye Prontosil Red was highly effective. Human trials soon followed, and included a dramatic cure of Domagk's daughter who had a serious sepsis following a needle prick. In 1936 a French group found that Prontosil is converted in the body into the rather simple compound sulphanilamide, which is the effective agent. It had been known since 1908, was cheap and unpatentable, and does not discolour the patient. Treatment of bacterial infections (for example pneumonia and streptococcal infections) was vastly improved by the use of sulphanilamide and related 'sulpha' drugs such as M.&B.693. After 1945 penicillin and other antibiotics became dominant, but sulpha drugs remain valuable. Domagk was awarded a Nobel Prize in 1939, but was not able to accept the medal until 1947 as his country was at war. The Nobel rules did not allow him to have the prize money after such a delay.

DOPPLER, Christian Johann
1803-1853

Austrian physicist: discovered the Doppler effect

Doppler was educated at the Vienna Polytechnic; and despite his ability, for some time he could only gain rather junior posts in tutoring or school-teaching. At 32 he decided to emigrate to America, but on the point of departure was offered a senior teaching post in a school in Prague. Six years later he became professor of mathematics at the State Technical Academy there, and in 1850 professor of experimental physics at Vienna.

His claim to fame rests on a single important discovery, the **Doppler effect** (1842). This proposed that the frequency of waves from a source moving towards an observer will be increased above that from a stationary source; and waves from a source moving away from an observer will be decreased in frequency. In 1845 a test was made at Utrecht, in which an open railway carriage carrying a group of trumpeters was taken at speed past a group of musicians with perfect pitch. It was one of the extraordinary occasions that made the 19th century approach to physics entertaining, and whilst unsubtle it demonstrated the correctness of Doppler's idea.

Doppler recognized that the effect applies not only to sound but also to light, and *Fizeau* (1848) pointed out that the spectral lines of stars should be shifted towards the red end of the spectrum according to the speed at which they are receding from us (the **Doppler shift**). *Huggins* observed this for the star Sirius (1868), and *Hubble* later used the red shift to infer the speed of recession of other galaxies from us: the 'expanding universe' of cosmology.

The Doppler effect has also been used to measure the speed of the Sun's rotation and Saturn's rings, and the rotation of double stars. It forms the basis of police radar speed traps for vehicles; and 'Doppler satellites' emitting a fixed radio frequency and whose position is known, are used by ships and aircraft to locate their position, and by mapmakers and surveyers to give precise locations using the global positioning system (GPS).

DOUGLASS, Andrew Ellicott
1867-1962

American astronomer and dendrochronologist: invented tree-ring dating technique (dendrochronology)

Douglass worked at the Lowell Observatory in Arizona. His interest in the Sun led to an interest in climate. While trying to construct an historical record of sunspot activity, Douglass realised that climatic conditions affected the width of the annual growth rings of trees, and that these distinctive patterns could often be recognized from tree to tree. (Fortunately in the dry climate of Arizona ancient wood is well preserved.) He developed this idea into an important dating technique, and succeeded in contructing a continuous dendrochronological time scale back to the first century (later workers extended this to about 5000 BC). Although the technique of radiocarbon dating has to a large extent superseded it, dendrochronology has proved vital in calibrating the radiocarbon time scale.

DRAPER, John William
1811-1882

English-American chemical physicist: a pioneer of scientific photography

Draper's life and his scientific interests were both oddly disperse. His father was an itinerant Methodist preacher, whose possession of a telescope attracted the boy to science. He began premedical studies in London in 1829, but emigrated to Virginia in 1832. Helped by his sister Dorothy's earnings as a teacher, he qualified in medicine by 1836, and then taught chemistry in New York. When Daguerre's process for fixing photographs was published in 1839, Draper took it up, and in 1840 he made what is probably the oldest surviving photographic portrait; it shows his sister Dorothy (exposure, 65 seconds). In the same year his photograph of the Moon began astronomical photography; and in 1850 he made the first microphotographs, to illustrate his book on physiology. In 1841 he proposed the principle that only absorbed radiation can produce chemical change (**Draper's law**; this principle was also known to C. J. D. Grotthus in 1817). He made early photographs in the infrared and ultraviolet regions; and he showed that all solids become incandescent at the same temperature, and when heated sufficiently, give a continuous spectrum. His later work was on the history of ideas.

DUBOIS, Marie Eugène Francois Thomas
1858-1940

Dutch anatomist and palaeoanthropologist: discovered Java man

After graduating in medicine from the University of Amsterdam in 1884, Dubois was appointed lecturer in anatomy, but resigned in 1887 after some disagreements with his professor. His great interest in the 'missing link' between apes and man prompted him to join the Dutch East Indian Army as a surgeon, this being a convenient way of getting to Java, where he believed that the remains of such a hominid might be found (on the grounds that it is the only place in which the orang-utan and gibbon are found). In 1891, having obtained support from the army in the form of a gang of convict labour, he eventually succeeded in finding the skullcap, femur and two teeth of Java man (*Homo erectus*), a hominid who lived approximately 0.5-1.5 million years ago. Dubois's belief that Java man represented the missing link was at first widely ridiculed, but was ultimately accepted after the announcement in 1926 of the discovery by Otto Zdansky of Peking man (also *Homo erectus*). Irritated by the lack of support for his theory, Dubois refused to allow study of his specimens until 1923, by which time he had convinced himself that they were merely the bones of a giant gibbon.

DU BOIS-REYMOND, Emil
1818-1896

German physiologist: pioneer electrophysiologist

Du Bois-Reymond's father was a Swiss teacher who moved to Berlin; he was an expert on linguistics, and authoritarian enough to 'arouse his son's spirit of resistance'. The family spoke French, and felt part of the French community in Berlin. Emil studied a range of subjects at Berlin for two years before he was fully attracted to medicine, which he studied under *J. P. Müller*. He graduated in 1843, and was then already working on animal electricity (discovered by *Galvani*) and especially on electric fishes. He introduced refined physical methods for measuring these effects, and by 1849 had a sensitive multiplier for measuring nerve currents; by then he had qualified as a university teacher. He found an electric current in intact, injured, and contracting muscles; he traced it correctly to individual fibres, and found that their interior is negative with respect to the surface. He showed the existence of a resting current in nerve, and suggested correctly that nerve impulses might be transmitted chemically. He was modest but also confident, and his ideas aroused vigorous debate; his experimental methods dominated electrophysiology for a century.

DUFAY, Charles
1698-1739

French chemist: discovered positive and negative charges of static electricity

Dufay came from an influential family, which secured an army career for him; he left as a captain to become a chemist at the Académie des Sciences when he was 25. He had no training in science, but he began to study electricity in 1733. He showed that there are two kinds of electricity (and only two) generated by friction; he called them vitreous and resinous because they were obtained by rubbing glass (or rock crystal, hair or wool) or resin (or amber, silk or paper) respectively; they are the positive and negative charges of today. Dufay showed that like types repelled, and unlike kinds attracted one another. The 'two fluid' theory of electricity was linked with these results in opposition to *Franklin*'s later one-fluid theory. Dufay's experiments included suspending a boy by silk cords, electrifying him by friction, and drawing sparks from him. *Gray* in London had done similarly, and had also distinguished conductors from insulators (e.g., silk from metal wire).

DULONG, Pierre Louis
1785-1838

French chemist: co-discoverer of law of constant atomic heat

Originally a physician, Dulong moved to chemistry as assistant to *Berthollet*. In 1811 he discovered NCl_3, which cost him an eye and two fingers. He was an early supporter of the hydrogen theory of acids. From 1815 he worked with A. T. Petit on thermometry; and in 1819 they published **Dulong and Petit's Law**. This stated that the specific heat capacity of a solid element when multiplied by its atomic weight, gives a constant which they called the atomic heat. The law is only approximately observed; and is best followed at or above room temperature (e.g., C, B and Si only have specific heat capacities in accord with it, at high temperature). It had some use, however, for easily giving rough atomic weights for new metals, at a time when this was valuable. In modern parlance we can express the law as: relative atomic mass (i.e. atomic weight)×specific heat capacity$\approx$25 JK^{-1} mol^{-1}=3R where R is the gas constant.

DUMAS, Jean Baptiste André
1800-1884

French organic chemist: classified organic compounds into types

Originally an apprentice apothecary, Dumas improved his knowledge of chemistry in Geneva and also attracted the notice of some eminent scientists, with the result that he was encouraged to go to Paris. There he got a post as assistant at the École Polytechnique, and by 1835 a senior post there. He initially worked on atomic weights, but his main distinction is that he was a leader in the group of mainly French chemists who partly rejected the authoritive views of *Berzelius* and offered new views on the relations between organic compounds, setting the stage for the major advances made later by *Kekulé*. Dumas's work in this began with his study of the choking fumes from candles used in the Tuileries. He found these had been bleached with chlorine, and from this clue examined the reaction of chlorine with other organic compounds. In some cases he showed that the reaction had replaced hydrogen by chlorine on an atom-for-atom basis, and yet gave a product of essentially the same type (e.g., acetic acid CH_3CO_2H gives a series of three chlorine-substituted acids CH_2ClCO_2H, $CHCl_2$-CO_2H, CCl_3CO_2H which are not greatly unlike their parent in their chemistry). This was in direct conflict with Berzelius's dualism theory, which did not allow for atoms of opposite electrical type replacing one another in this manner. Dumas pressed his theory of substitution, and his theory that organic compounds exist as 'types' (e.g., the alcohols) and argued that a type may contain a series of compounds whose formulae differ by a constant unit (e.g., CH_2). Somewhat similar views were developed by others (notably *Laurent, Gerhardt* and *Wurtz* in France, *Liebig* and *Hofmann* in Germany, and *Williamson* in England). During the period of debate many new and useful organic compounds were made, and theory was advanced, apparently with rejection of Berzelius's views. However, after 1930, it was seen that the Berzelius approach to organic reactions (in a much modified form) had an important part in understanding why organic reactions occur, while his opponents had also been right in their criticisms. Dumas, ambitious and energetic, followed a pattern more familiar in France than elsewhere, and moved from science to politics, holding various ministerial posts after 1848.

DUTROCHET, Henri
1776-1847

French plant physiologist: discovered some basic features of plant physiology

Born into a wealthy family, Dutrochet's early life was blighted by a club foot, ultimately fully corrected by a local healer (also the hangman) after medical men had failed. After the Revolution he became an army medical officer, but had to retire after catching typhoid in the Peninsular War.

After his resignation from the army in 1809 he seems to have spent his time researching in animal and especially plant physiology. He held the view that life processes are explicable in chemical and physical terms; and that cellular respiration is essentially similar in plants and animals. In 1832 he found the small openings (stomata) on the surface of leaves, later found to be the entry points for gas exchange in plants. *Ingen-Housz* had shown that plants absorb carbon dioxide and emit oxygen, and Dutrochet found that only those parts of plants containing the green pigment chlorophyll can do this. He was the first to study successfully the production of heat during plant growth. Although osmosis had been observed previously, it was he who first studied it fully, and proposed that it was the cause of sap movement in plants.

DU VIGNEAUD, Vincent

1901-1978

American biochemist: researcher on sulphur-containing vitamins and hormones

Originally a student of chemistry at Illinois, Du Vigneaud's postgraduate work in the US and in the UK became increasingly biochemical; from 1938 he was head of biochemistry in Cornell Medical School, and his research became 'a trail of sulphur research'. This began with studies on the hormone insulin in the 1920s. In the 1930s he worked on the sulphur-containing amino acid methionine, and showed that its function is particularly to transfer methyl ($-CH_3$) groups in biochemical reactions. In 1941 he isolated Vitamin H from liver, and showed it was identical with the growth factor biotin, which had been isolated in 1936 by F. Kögl (1 mg from 250 kg of dried duck egg yolk). Du Vigneaud deduced the complete (and rather complex) structure of biotin in 1942. He next studied two pituitary hormones, oxytocin and vasopressin, the first of which induces labour and milk flow. Both structures were determined, and in 1953 he synthesized oxytocin – the first synthesis of an active polypeptide hormone (it contains eight amino acids). For this work, in particular, he was awarded a Nobel Prize in chemistry in 1955.

DYSON, Freeman John

1923-

British-American theoretical physicist: unified the independent versions of quantum electrodynamics

Dyson, the son of a distinguished English

Freeman Dyson

musician, graduated from Cambridge and spent the war years at the headquarters of Bomber Command of the Royal Air Force. In 1947 he did research at Cornell and joined the staff at Princeton in 1953.

Shortly after the war several people began to apply quantum mechanics to systems in which particles (particularly electrons) interact with electromagnetic radiation (photons). In 1946 Willis Lamb observed a shift (the Lamb shift) in the lowest energy levels of the hydrogen atom, away from the previously predicted levels. *Schwinger, Tomonaga* and *Feynman* rapidly developed independent theories correctly describing how electrons behave when interacting with photons, and accounted for the Lamb shift. Dyson then showed how the formulations related to each other, and produced a single general theory of quantum electrodynamics.

Subsequently Dyson was involved in many areas of physics, in cosmology and even speculations on space travel.

E

EDDINGTON, (Sir) Arthur Stanley
1882-1944

British astrophysicist: pioneered the study of stellar structure; and discovered mass/luminosity relationship

Eddington was the son of the head of a school in Cumbria where, a century earlier, *Dalton* had taught. He was an outstanding student at Manchester and then at Cambridge, where he later became Director of the Observatory. The internal structure of stars is an area of study pioneered by Eddington. In 1926 he demonstrated that in order to remain in equilibrium, the inward gravitational pressure of a star must balance the outward radiation and gas pressure. He realised that there was consequently an upper limit on the mass of a star (of about 50 solar masses), because above this the balance between gravitation and radiation pressure could not be achieved. (Some stars, verging on instability, pulsate; these are the Cepheid variables). He discovered the mass-luminosity relationship, which shows that the more massive a star the greater its luminosity, and which allows the mass of star to be determined from its intrinsic brightness. Eddington provided some of the most powerful evidence for the theory of relativity by observing that light from stars near to the Sun's rim during the total solar eclipse of 1919 was slightly deflected by the Sun's gravitational field in accordance with *Einstein*'s predictions.

EDELMAN, Gerald (Maurice)
1929-

American biochemist: pioneer in study of molecular structure of antibodies

During his doctorate studies at Rocke-feller University Edelman investigated the immunoglobulins. He joined the staff there and continued his interest in these compounds; they are formed on the surface of B-lymphocytes, and when released into the body fluids are known as antibodies. They form a class of closely related proteins, each specific in its ability to bind with a particular antigen; the system forms a major part of the vertebrate animal's defence against infection. Edelman found that human immunoglobulin, a large protein molecule, is a combination of two kinds of protein chains ('light' and 'heavy') linked by sulphur bridges. He went on to study the sequence of amino acids in the chains of the immunoglobulin IgG and by 1969 had achieved this; the 1330 amino acids form a Y-shaped structure, in which the amino acids in the tips are very variable but the main part of the structure is constant. This result could be linked with *R. R. Porter*'s biochemical and immunological study of IgG to give a more detailed picture of this molecule, which is likely to be typical of antibodies. Edelman and Porter shared a Nobel Prize for 1972. *See photo p.23.*

EDISON, Thomas Alva
1847-1931

American physicist and prolific inventor

Edison received virtually no formal education, having been expelled from school as retarded, and was educated by his mother. During the American Civil War he worked as a telegraph operator, during which time he invented and patented an electric vote recorder. Three years later, in 1869, he invented the paper tape 'ticker', used for communicating stock exchange prices across the country, sold it for $30 000 and opened an industrial research laboratory. He was thereafter to apply himself full-time to inventing, filing a total of 1069 patents before his death. His more notable inventions include the carbon granule microphone, to improve *A. G. Bell's* telephone, the phonograph (a device for recording sound on a drum covered in tin foil, invented in 1877), and the electric light bulb. The bulb required an extraordinary amount of trial and error testing, using over 6000 substances until he found a carbonized bamboo fibre that remained lit for over 1000 hours in a vacuum. This led, in turn, to improved electricity generators (he increased their efficiency from 40 per cent to over 90 per cent), power cables, the electricity meter, and the revolutionizing of domestic lighting and public electricity supply. During his work on light bulbs he also discovered the **Edison effect**, that electricity flows from a heated filament to a nearby electrode, but not in the reverse direction, which was later to form the basis of the thermionic valve. Edison's impact on twentieth century life was immense, and his reputation as a prolific inventive genius unrivalled.

EHRLICH, Paul

1854-1915

German medical scientist: pioneer of chemotherapy, haematology and immunology

Ehrlich was born in eastern Germany, the son of an eccentric Jewish innkeeper and his talented wife. Her cousin Carl Weigert, a pathologist nine years older than Ehrlich, was an early friend and encouraged his interest in science. Undistinguished at school (where he hated examinations) he did well enough to enter university to study medicine, and qualified at Leipzig in 1878. With difficulty, partly because he was Jewish, he got a hospital post in Berlin. He spent his entire career there, except for a year in Egypt

using its dry air as a cure for his tuberculosis; at the time it was probably the best treatment.

While Ehrlich was a student the aniline dyes had recently been discovered, and Weigert had used them for microscopic staining. Ehrlich worked with him, and was impressed by the way in which some dyes would stain selectively. The study of this linked his interest in chemistry with his medical work, and was to form the basis of all his later research. He found how to stain and classify white blood cells; discovered the mast cells later found to be important in allergy; and he worked with *Behring* and *Kitasato* on antitoxins. His work on antibodies largely began modern immunology. It led him to think that although the search for vaccines against malaria and syphilis had failed, it might be possible to attack the parasites causing these diseases in another way, since they could be selectively stained. He also knew that when an animal died from lead poisoning, the lead was found concentrated in certain tissues. He hoped that he could find a synthetic chemical which would bind onto, and injure, the parasites. He was encouraged by his discovery that the dye Trypan Red was fairly effective against trypanosomes (the pathogens causing trypanosomiasis) in mice, although he also discovered that drug resistance soon developed. Both discoveries were important.

From 1905 he and his assistants began trials using compounds with molecules not unlike dyes, but which contained arsenic, as a part of his programme to find a 'magic bullet' which could locate and destroy the invading pathogenic cells. Their organoarsenical compound No. 606 (which had failed against trypanosomes) was eventually found by them in 1909 to be effective against the *Treponema pallidum* which causes syphilis, and it was soon used in patients as 'salvarsan'. The principles used by Ehrlich came to guide this new approach (chemotherapy) to disease, in which a compound is sought which will seek out and destroy the disease organisms, with only minor damage to the patient. In the event, it was over 20 years later before *Domagk* achieved the next major success.

Ehrlich inspired loyalty in some of his co-workers and high exasperation in others. He was dictatorial and impatient, and appeared to live largely on cigars and mineral water. He shared a Nobel Prize in 1909 for his work on immunity, which is only a part of his contribution to medical science.

EIJKMAN, Christiaan
1858-1930

Dutch physician: discovered cure for beriberi

Eijkman served as an army medical officer in the Dutch East Indies in the early 1880s, and he was sent back there in 1886 to study beriberi, then an epidemic disease in south Asia. This paralysing and often fatal disease is in reality a deficiency disease, whose rise was linked with increased use of polished (white) rice as the major diet in some 'closed' communities. When Eijkman began his work in Java, it was assumed to be an infection, but he noticed that some laboratory birds showed similar symptoms to beriberi victims; and they had been fed on left-over rice from a military hospital kitchen. Then a change occurred, and the birds recovered. Eijkman discovered that a new cook refused to give 'military rice' to civilian birds, and had changed to less refined rice. Eijkman went on to show that the disease could be cured by adding rice husks to the diet, and could be caused by feeding polished rice. He did not interpret his results correctly (he thought the bran contained a substance which protected against a poison) but his work was a valuable step towards the full recognition of vitamin deficiency diseases by *Hopkins* after 1900. Isolation and synthesis of vitamin B_1 (thiamin) was achieved by R. R. Williams in the 1930s;

deficiency of it in the diet causes beriberi. Eijkman and Hopkins shared a Nobel Prize in 1929.

EINSTEIN, Albert
1879-1955

German-Swiss-American theoretical physicist: conceived the theory of relativity

Einstein's father was an electrical engineer whose business difficulties caused the family to move rather frequently; Einstein was born whilst they were in Ulm. Despite a delay due to his poor mathematics he entered the Swiss Federal Institute of Technology in Zürich at the age of 17, and on graduating became a Swiss citizen and sought a post in a university, or even in a school. However, he had great difficulty in finding any job, and settled for serving in the Swiss Patent Office in Bern. It worked out well; he was a good patent examiner and the job gave him enough leisure for his research. In 1903 he married Mileva Maric, by whom he had two sons; this ended in divorce in 1919, and he then married his cousin Elsa who had two daughters by a previous marriage. It was whilst at the Patent Office that he produced the three papers published in 1905, each of which represented an enormous achievement, covering Brownian motion, the photoelectric effect and special relativity.

Einstein's first university post was secured in 1909 when he obtained a junior professorship at the University of Zürich, and a full professorship at Prague (1910) and Zürich (1912) followed. In 1913 he was made Director of the Institute of Physics at the Kaiser Wilhelm Institute in Berlin. The general theory of relativity was completed during World War I, and following its publication (1915) Einstein was awarded the 1921 Nobel Prize for physics for his work of 1905.

He began to undertake many lecture-tours abroad, and was in California when Hitler came to power in 1933. He never

A. A. Michelson, Albert Einstein and R. A. Millikan in 1931

returned to Germany, resigning his position and taking up a post at the Institute of Advanced Study, Princeton. Einstein put much effort into trying to unify gravitational, electromagnetic and nuclear forces into one set of field equations, but without success. He had some involvement in politics, in that he initiated the Allied efforts to make an atomic bomb (the Manhattan project) by warning Roosevelt, the American President, of the possibility that Germany would do so, in a letter in 1939. In 1952 Einstein was offered, and sensibly declined, the Presidency of Israel. He was also active in promoting nuclear disarmament after the Second World War. He led a simple life, full of kindness and shunning fame and power, with sailing and music as his main relaxations.

The first of his papers of 1905 considered the random movement of small suspended particles (Brownian motion,

discovered in 1828). The bombardment by surrounding molecules will make a tiny particle in a fluid dart around in an erratic movement, and Einstein's calculations provided the most direct evidence for the existence of molecules when confirmed experimentally by *Perrin* (1908).

The next paper by Einstein tackled the photoelectric effect by considering the nature of electromagnetic radiation, usually thought of as waves obeying *Maxwell*'s equations. Einstein assumed that light energy could only be transferred in packets, the quanta used by *Planck* to derive the black body radiation spectrum. Einstein then was able to explain fully the observations of *Lenard* (1902), in which the energy of electrons ejected from a metallic surface depended on the wavelength of light falling on it but not on the intensity. The result became a foundation for quantum theory, and clothed Planck's quanta with a physical interpretation.

Finally, Einstein set out the special theory of relativity (restricted to bodies moving with uniform velocity with respect to one another) in his third paper. *Maxwell*'s electromagnetic wave theory of light indicated that the velocity of a light wave did not depend on the speed of the source or observer and so contradicted classical mechanics. *Lorentz, FitzGerald* and *Poincaré* had found a transformation of Maxwell's equations for a region in uniform motion which left the speed of light unchanged, and not altered by the relative velocity of the space and observer (the Lorentz transformation).

Einstein correctly proposed that the speed of light is the same in all frames of reference moving relative to one another and, unknown to him, this had been established by the *Michelson-Morley* experiment (1881, 1887). He put forward the **principle of relativity**, that all physical laws are the same in all frames of reference in uniform motion with respect to one another. When applied it naturally gives rise to the Lorentz-FitzGerald transformation, with classical mechanics obeying this rather than simple addition of velocity between moving frames (the Galilean transformation). A further consequence derived by him was that if the energy of a body changes by an amount E then its mass must change by E/c^2 where c is the velocity of light.

From 1907 Einstein sought to extend relativity theory to frames of reference which are being accelerated with respect to one another. His guiding principle (the principle of equivalence) stated that gravitational acceleration and that due to motion viewed in an accelerating frame are completely equivalent. From this he predicted that light rays should be bent by gravitational attraction. In 1911 he reached a specific prediction: that starlight just grazing the Sun should be deflected by 1.7 seconds of arc. During a total eclipse of the Sun in 1919 *Eddington* measured this in observations made at Principe in West Africa, finding 1.61 seconds of arc. This dramatic confirm-ation immediately made Einstein famous world-wide, and made it clear that he had moved the foundation of physics.

In 1915 he had published the general theory of relativity in complete form, using Riemannian geometry and other mathematical ideas due to Minkowski (1907), *Riemann* (1854) and Ricci (1887). Mass was taken to distort the 'flatness' of space-time, and so give rise to bodies in space moving along curved paths about one another. Whilst the resulting 'gravitational' attraction is very close to that predicted by *Newton*'s law, there are small corrections. Einstein and C. Grossmann estimated that the ellipse traced out by Mercury around the Sun should rotate by 43 seconds of arc per century more than that given by Newtonian theory. The observed value is indeed 43 seconds of arc larger and Einstein reported: 'I was beside myself with ecstasy for days'.

General relativity produced many other startling predictions, such as that light passing from one part of a gravitational field to another would be shifted in wavelength (the **Einstein redshift**). This was observed astronomically in 1925, and terrestially with a 23 m tower on Earth using the *Mossbauer* effect by R. Pound and G. Rebka in 1959. Gamma rays moving from the bottom to top of the tower were found to have a longer wavelength.

Cosmological models of the universe were also completely changed by general relativity, and *Friedmann* (1922) put forward a model which represented an expanding universe obeying Einstein's equations.

During the 1920s and 1930s Einstein engaged in debate over quantum theory, rejecting *Born*'s introduction of probability ('God may be subtle, but He is not malicious'). He also sought to find a unified theory of electromagnetic and gravitational fields, without success. By 1921 he had been prepared to say 'Discovery in the grand manner is for young people...and hence for me a thing of the past'.

EINTHOVEN, Willem

1860-1927

Dutch physiologist: introduced clinical electrocardiography

Einthoven's father was a physician in Java, where the family lived until he was ten, afterwards settling in Utrecht. He studied medicine there and was appointed professor of physiology at Leyden in 1886. The next year A. D. Waller in England showed that a current was generated by the heart, but his recording device was cumbersome and insensitive. Einthoven was interested in physics, and he devised a sensitive string galvanometer. It used a fine wire stretched between the poles of a magnet. When a current passed through the wire it was deflected, and an optical system magnified this for recording. Einthoven made electrocardiograms (ECGs) from the chest wall and from contacts on the arms and legs, and described his results from 1903. Soon afterwards, cardiologists gave full accounts of coronary artery disease, and Einthoven and others (especially Sir T. Lewis in London) related the ECG tracings to clinical data for this and other heart diseases. This became an important diagnostic method, and Einthoven won a Nobel Prize for 1924.

EKMAN, Vagn Walfrid

1874-1954

Swedish oceanographer: explained the variation in direction of ocean currents with depth

After graduation, Ekman worked at the International Laboratory for Oceanographic Research in Oslo for several years before returning to Sweden in 1908. He was appointed professor of mathematical physics at Lund in 1910. In the 1890s the Norwegian arctic explorer *Nansen* had noted that the path of drifting sea ice did not follow the prevailing wind direction, but deviated about 45 degrees to the right. In 1905 Ekman was able to explain this as an effect of the Coriolis force, caused by the Earth's rotation. He went on to describe the general motion of near-surface water as the result of the interaction between surface wind force, the Coriolis force, and frictional effects between different water layers. **Ekman flow** thus accounts for situations in which near-surface water moves in the opposite direction to that at the surface, and with the net water transport at right angles to the wind direction. The resulting variation of water velocity with depth is known as the **Ekman spiral**. An analogous situation exists in atmospheric flow.

ELSASSER, Walter Maurice

1904-

German-American theoretical physicist: developed theory of Earth's magnetic field

Elsasser was born and educated in Germany; he left that country in 1933 and spent three years in Paris where he worked on the theory of atomic nuclei. In 1936 he settled in the US, and began to specialize in geophysics. During the 1940s he developed the dynamo model of the Earth's magnetic field, which attributes the field to the action of electric currents flowing in the Earth's fluid metallic outer

Walter M. Elsasser in the 1960s

core. These currents are amplified through mechanical motions in the same way in which currents are maintained in power station generators. The analysis of past magnetic fields, frozen in rocks, has since turned out a very powerful tool for the study of geological processes.

EMELÉUS, Harry Julius
1903-

British inorganic chemist: revitaliser of experimental inorganic chemistry

A student at London, Karlsruhe and Princeton, Emeléus was professor of inorganic chemistry at Cambridge from 1945-70. He worked on a wide variety of topics, and his experimental work did much to dispel the pre-1945 view that rather little of interest remained to be done in inorganic chemistry. His early work was on phosphorescent flames and on photochemistry. In the 1940s he made novel silicon compounds; and after 1950 many new halogen compounds, especially trifluoromethyl (CF_3^-) derivatives of metals and non-metals.

Harry Emeléus in the 1950s

EMILIANI, Cesare
1922-

Italian-American geologist: demonstrated the cyclic nature of ice ages, and established the climatic history of the Quaternary period

Emiliani emigrated to America in 1948, graduating from the University of Chicago in 1950, where he remained until moving to the University of Miami in 1956. Following the suggestion of *Urey* that the isotopic ratio of oxygen ($^{18}O/^{16}O$) in sea water depends upon the prevailing temperature (due to isotopic fractionation), Emiliani pioneered a technique for determining the past temperature of the oceans by measuring the $^{18}O/^{16}O$ ratio in the carbonate remains of micro-organisms in ocean sediments. By selecting only pelagic species for study (i.e., those that live near the ocean surface) he was able to establish, in 1955, that there had been seven glacial cycles during the Quaternary period, almost double the number of ice ages that were formerly thought to have occurred. Oxygen isotope methods are now an established technique in palaeoclimatic studies.

EMPEDOCLES (of Acragas)
c.490-c.430 BC

Greek philosopher: proposed early view on nature of matter

Active in politics, poetry, medicine and mysticism, Empedocles is credited with the suggestion that all substances are derived from four 'roots' or elemental principles: fire, air, water and earth. These are joined or separated by two forces, attraction and repulsion (or love and strife). This view, especially as developed later by *Aristotle*, was influential for 2000 years, until *Boyle*'s work. Empedocles is said to have ended his life by jumping into the volcanic crater on Mount Etna, possibly in an attempt to prove his divinity.

ENDERS, John Franklin

1897-1985

American virologist: developed improved method for culturing viruses

Enders had several early career changes. He left Yale in 1917 to become a flying instructor in World War I; began a career as an estate agent and left it to study languages at Harvard; and then changed to microbiology, thereafter staying at the Harvard Medical School through a long career. Before his work, few laboratory cultures of viruses were available and these were inconvenient (e.g., cultures in a living chick embryo). Enders argued that living cells should be adequate, without the whole animal, if bacterial growth was prevented by adding penicillin. In 1948 together with F. C. Robbins and T. H. Weller he cultured the mumps virus using a homogenate of chick embryo cells and ox serum with added penicillin. The next year a similar method was used for the polio virus, and in the 1950s for the measles virus. For measles they were able to develop a vaccine by 1951, which came into widespread use in 1963. The trio shared a Nobel Prize in 1954, and their methods of culturing viruses allowed virology to advance with successes such as the Salk and the Sabin polio vaccines.

ERATOSTHENES (of Cyrene)

c.270-c.190 BC

Greek astronomer and polymath: gave first accurate measurement of the Earth's circumference

Eratosthenes was educated in Athens, and became chief librarian of the Alexandrian Museum. He devised an ingeniously simple way of measuring the circumference of the Earth. Eratosthenes knew that on a certain day the Sun at its highest point (mid-day), at Cyrene (now Aswan), was exactly overhead (it was known to shine down a deep well). He determined that on the same day at Alexandria, when the Sun was at its highest point, it was at an angle corresponding to 1/50th of a circle south of its zenith. Knowing the distance between the two places he therefore calculated that the Earth's circumference was fifty times that length. His result was probably fairly accurate, perhaps within fifty miles of the correct value.

Among his other discoveries Eratosthenes suggested a method of separating primes from composite numbers (known as the **Sieve of Eratosthenes**); he obtained an improved value for the obliquity of the ecliptic (the tilt of the Earth's axis), and he produced the first map of the world based on meridians of longitude and parallels of latitude. In later life he became blind and, no longer able to read, committed suicide.

ESAKI, Leo

1925-

Japanese physicist: discovered the tunnel (Esaki) diode

Whilst working for his doctorate on semiconductors at the University of Tokyo (1959), Esaki was also leading a small research group at the Sony Corporation. He chose, in 1957, to investigate conduction by quantum mechanical 'tunnelling' of electrons through the potential energy barrier of a germanium p-n diode. Such conduction is in the reverse direction to the normal electron drift, and using narrow junctions (only 100 Å wide) with heavy impurity doping of the p-n junction, Esaki observed the effect. He realised that with narrower junctions the effect would become so strong that the total current would actually fall with increasing bias (negative resistance), and succeeded in making such devices (tunnel or **Esaki diodes**) in 1960. These devices have very fast speeds of operation, small size, low noise and low power consumption; they have widespread electronic applications in computers and microwave devices. In 1960 Esaki joined IBM's

Thomas J. Watson Research Centre, and in 1973 was awarded a Nobel Prize with *Josephson* and I. Giaever for work on tunnelling effects.

ESKOLA, Pentti Elias

1883-1964

Finnish geologist

Eskola graduated in chemistry in Helsinki in 1906, but then turned to petrology, especially the mineral facies of rocks. He believed that in metamorphic rocks, the mineral composition (when equilibrium is reached) is controlled only by the chemical composition (1914). His lifework was the close study of the metamorphic rocks of Scandinavia.

EUCLID

Lived c. 300 BC

Greek mathematician: recorded, collated, and extended mathematics of the ancient world

Euclid offers strange contrasts; although his work dominated mathematics for over 2000 years, almost nothing is known of his life and personality. One alleged remark survives, his reply to Ptolemy Soter, King of Egypt, who hoped for an easy course of tuition: 'in geometry there is no straight path for kings'. Working in Alexandria, then a new city but a centre of learning, Euclid brought together previous work in mathematics and his own results and recorded the whole in a systematic way in 13 books, entitled *Elements of Geometry*.

The system attempted to be fully rigorous in proving each theorem on the basis of its predecessors, back to a set of self-evident axioms. It does not entirely succeed, but it was a noble attempt, and even the study of its deficiencies proved profitable for mathematicians. His work was translated into Arabic, then into Latin, and from that into all European languages. Its style became a model for mathematicians and even for other fields

of study. Six of the books deal with plane geometry, four with the theory of numbers (including a proof that the number of primes is infinite) and three with solid geometry, including the five Platonic solids (the tetrahedron, octahedron, cube, icosahedron and dodecahedron; Euclid finally notes that no other regular polyhedrons are possible).

Only in the 19th century was it realised that other kinds of geometry exist. This arose from the fact that while most of the Euclidean postulates are indeed self-evident (e.g., 'the whole is greater than the part'), the fifth postulate ('axiom XI') is certainly not so. It states that, 'if a point lies outside a straight line, then one (and only one) straight line can be drawn in their plane which passes through the point and which never meets the line'. Then in the 19th century it was accepted that this certainly cannot be deduced from the other axioms, and *Lobachevsky* and others explored geometries in which this 'parallel axiom' is false. In the 20th century, *Einstein* found that his relativity theory required that the space of the universe be considered as a non-Euclidean space; it needed the type of geometry devised by *Riemann*. For all everyday purposes, Euclidean space serves us well and the practical differences are too small to be significant.

Euclid's achievement was immense. He was less talented than *Archimedes*, but for long-lived authority and influence he has no peer. Within the limits of his time (with its inadequate concepts of infinity, little algebra, and no convenient arithmetic) his attempt at an unflawed, logical treatment of geometry is remarkable.

EULER, Leonhard

1707-1783

Swiss mathematician: the most prolific mathematician in history

Euler was the son of a Calvinist pastor, who gave him much of his early education including mathematics. Later he studied at the University of Basle, where he became close friends with members of the Bernoulli family, and *Daniel Bernoulli* in particular. Because he was still rather young (he graduated at 16), Euler could not obtain a post at the university. However, Daniel persuaded Euler to join him at Catherine I's Academy of Science at St Petersburg (now Leningrad) in 1727. The Empress died the day Euler arrived in Russia, and the future of the academy became uncertain. After an unhappy period working in the Naval College and medical section of the Academy he became professor of physics in 1730. When Bernoulli returned to Switzerland in 1733 Euler succeeded him as professor of mathematics.

The repressive reign of a boy Tsar led Euler, now married, to retreat into reclusive mathematical work, and this solitariness increased during the reign of Anna Ivanovna (1730-40) which was one of the bloodiest in Russian history. During this time Euler lost the sight of his right eye, perhaps due to looking at the Sun accidently during his astronomical studies. Although conditions eased in Russia after Anna's death, Euler departed to join Frederick the Great's Berlin Academy of Science in 1741. Despite great authority in mathematics Euler frequently engaged ineptly in philosophical discussions, and Frederick sought a replacement. In 1766 Euler took up Catherine the Great's offer of the Directorship of the St Petersburg Academy, accompanied by his family and servants (18 people in all). He became totally blind soon after his arrival, but due to his remarkable ability to calculate in his head his productivity did not diminish and he successfully carried out his work for another 15 years. He remained in Russia for the rest of his life.

Euler was the most prolific mathematician in history, and contributed to all areas of pure and applied mathematics. In analysis he lacked *Gauss*'s or *Cauchy*'s rigour but he had a gift for deducing important results by intuition or by new ways of calculating quantities. He systematized much of analysis, he cast calculus and trigonometry in its modern form, and showed the important role of e (**Euler's number**, 2.718 28...). Euler developed the use of series solutions, paying due regard to convergence; he solved linear differential equations and developed partial differential calculus. He applied these analytical tools to great effect in problems in mechanics and celestial mechanics and introduced the principle of virtual work. The formidable three-body problem of the Earth, Sun and Moon system was solved approximately by him (1753, 1772), leading to an award of £300 by the British Government for the resulting improvement in navigational tables. In the course of this he developed much of classical perturbation theory.

He worked on number theory, fluid flow, geometry, and acoustics. A large number of theorems are named after this extraordinarily creative and productive man. One of the best-known is **Euler's rule**, which shows that for a polyhedron with v vertices, f faces, and e edges, then $v + f - e = 2$.

He was active in mathematics to the moment of his death, on a day spent partly in calculating the laws of ascent of the recently invented hot-air balloons.

EULER, Ulf Svante von

1905-1983

Swedish physiologist: discovered biochemical function of noradrenalin

Son of a physiologist who won a Nobel Prize in chemistry, Euler was a student and later a professor at the Royal Caroline Institute in Stockholm. In 1903 T. R. Elliott of Cambridge made the novel suggestion, based on experiments, that nerve transmission is at least partly chemical. For a time this idea was largely ignored but it led to later successes by *Dale* and by O. Loewi; and in 1946 Euler isolated a neurotransmitter of the sympathetic nervous system and showed it to be noradrenalin, and not adrenalin as had been believed. Already, in 1935, he had initiated work in another area by showing that human semen contained a potent chemical which lowered blood pressure and contracted muscle, which he named prostaglandin. (*Bergstrom* later isolated two prostaglandins; more are now known and they form an important biochemical group.) Euler shared a Nobel Prize in 1970.

EWING, William Maurice
1906-

American marine geologist: made first measurements of the thickness of the oceanic crust, and discovered the global extent of mid-ocean ridges

Ewing joined the Lamont-Doherty Geological Observatory, New York, in 1944, and was instrumental in making it one of the world's leading geophysical research institutes. Using marine seismic techniques he discovered that the oceanic crust is much thinner (5-8 km thick) than the continental crust (c.40 km thick). He also demonstrated the global extent of mid-ocean ridges, and in 1957 discovered the presence of a deep central rift in them. His studies of the ocean sediment showed that its thickness increases with distance from the mid-ocean ridge, which added support for the sea-floor spreading hypothesis proposed by *H. H. Hess* in 1962.

EYRING, Henry
1901-1981

American physical chemist: developed the theory of reaction rates

Trained as a mining engineer, Eyring changed to chemistry for his PhD and worked thereafter on chemical kinetics and the theory of liquids; his career was spent in Princeton and Utah.

In a chemical reaction, some chemical bonds are broken, and new bonds are formed. Eyring developed methods based on quantum mechanics for calculating the energies involved from which the rate of the chemical reaction can be calculated (in selected cases) and also the effect of temperature on the rate.

F

FABRE, Jean Henri

1823-1915

French entomologist

Always poor, Fabre spent his working life as a science teacher and was aged 50 before he could spend all his time as a field entomologist. Five years later, in 1878, he bought a small plot of land in Serignan, Provence, to make an open-air laboratory. There he observed and wrote about the insect world in a way which revitalized interest in it by others, and which made him the best-known of all entomologists. His early research was on parasitic wasps, but his close studies of a variety of groups led him to write a ten-volume survey of insects which remains a classic.

FABRICIUS, David

1564-1617

German astronomer: discovered first variable star

A clergyman and an amateur astronomer, Fabricius discovered that the brightness of the star *o* Ceti regularly varied from magnitude 9 to magnitude 3 over a period of about eleven months. This was the first variable star to be found, causing him to name it Mira (the marvellous). In fact, Mira's change in luminosity is the result of a true change in surface temperature, rather than the eclipsing effect of a binary companion (e.g., Algol).

FABRIZIO, Girolamo (Fabricus ab Aquapendente)

*c.*1533-1619

Italian anatomist: pioneer of scientific embryology

Fabrizio is often named in Latin, coupled with the Tuscan village of Aquapendente where he was born. He was a student in Padua, and later taught there for 50 years. He first studied the classics, and then medicine; his teacher of anatomy and surgery was *Fallopius*, whom he succeeded as professor in 1565. He researched and wrote on the larynx, the eye, muscular action, and respiration. He supervized the building of the anatomy theatre in Padua, which was the first of its kind and which still exists. It was there that he demonstrated the valves in the veins to his students, including *Harvey* who became interested in the problem of blood circulation; Fabrizio did not understand the function of the valves, which were to be a key in Harvey's work.

Fabrizio's most original research was in embryology. In 1600 he wrote a comparative study of the late foetus in various animals, and in 1604 he described the formation of the chick in the hen's egg from the sixth day. His well-illustrated descriptions mark the beginning of embryology as a new branch of biology.

After he officially retired in 1613 he continued as an active researcher until his death, aged about 86.

FAHRENHEIT, Gabriel Daniel

1686-1736

German physicist: developed the mercury thermometer and the Fahrenheit temperature scale

Fahrenheit worked as a glassblower in Holland, specialising in the construction of meteorological instruments. He succeeded in improving the reliability and accuracy of the alcohol thermometers of the day, and in 1714 constructed the first successful mercury thermometer, following *Amontons*'s work on the thermal expansion of the metal. Using these instruments he discovered that different liquids each have their own characteristic boiling point, which varies with atmospheric pressure. He also discovered the phenomenon of supercooling of water, whereby water may be chilled a few degrees below its freezing point without solidification.

He is best remembered, however, for devising the **Fahrenheit scale of temperature**, which used as its reference points the melting temperature of a mixture of ice and salt (the lowest temperature he could obtain), and the temperature of the human body. This range was subdivided into 96 equal parts, with the freezing point of water falling at 32°F and the boiling point at 212°F.

FAJANS, Kasimir
1887-1975

Polish-American physical chemist: devised rules for chemical bonding

Born in Warsaw, Fajans studied in Germany and in England, and worked in Munich from 1917 to 1935, when he emigrated to Chicago. His early research was in radiochemistry, where he had ideas on isotopes, and the displacement law, simultaneously with others. Although he worked in several areas of physical chemistry, he is best known for **Fajans's Rules** on bonding between atoms. The first rule is that as highly charged ions are difficult or impossible to form, so covalent bonds are more likely to result as the number of electrons to be removed or donated increases; the second rule is that ionic bonding is favoured by large cations and small anions. Both rules follow from simple electrostatic energy requirements; and they lead to the 'diagonal similarities' shown by elements in adjacent Periodic groups (e.g., Li and Mg; Be and Al; B and Si).

FALLOPIUS (Falloppio, Gabriello)
1523-1562

Italian anatomist

Fallopius first studied to become a priest, but changed to medicine and was taught anatomy by *Vesalius*. From 1551 he taught in Padua, and ten years later his textbook extended and corrected Vesalius's work. His discoveries included structures in the human ear and skull, and in the female genitalia. He first described the tubes from the ovary to the uterus; he did not know their function. It was almost 300 years later that the ovum was discovered; ova are formed in the ovary and pass down these Fallopian tubes to the uterus; if they are fertilized on their way, the embryo develops in the uterus.

FARADAY, Michael
1791-1867

English chemist and physicist: discovered benzene and the laws of electrolysis; invented an electric motor, dynamo and transformer; creator of classical field theory

Faraday was an extraordinary man, with an exceptional talent for intuitive grasp of the way physical nature may work, combined with a genius for experiment and great energy. He is usually regarded as the greatest of all experimental physicists. *Einstein* had the view that physical science has two couples of equal magnitude; *Galileo* and *Newton*, and Faraday and *Maxwell*: an interesting equation.

Faraday's talents ripened late (he was at his best in his 40s; many scientists have their major ideas behind them at 30) but he began his education late. His father was an ailing blacksmith, and the boy became a bookseller's errand boy at 13. He learned bookbinding, read some of the books, and was captivated by an article on elasticity in an encyclopaedia he had to rebind, and by Mrs Marcet's *Chemistry*. These books were to shape his life, and he soon joined a club of young men who met weekly to learn elementary science. He

J. F. Daniell (*left*) and Michael Faraday

was given tickets to attend *Davy*'s last course of lectures at the Royal Institution, and he wrote elegant notes of these and bound them. These notes he sent to Davy, and applied for a job with him. Davy firmly recommended him to stay with bookbinding, but he had injured an eye (making NCl_3) and took Faraday as a temporary helper. After a few weeks he gave him a permanent job as assistant; Faraday was later to become his co-worker, then his successor at the Royal Institution, and in time his superior as a scientist. Faraday learned quickly and he was lucky, because Davy decided to make a grand European tour, taking Faraday with him as helper and valet. The young man was to meet most of the leading scientists during a one-and-a-half year tour, made despite the Anglo-French war by special permission; it was a strange education, but it gave him an awareness of most of the physical and chemical science of the time and he became a skilful chemical analyst. The main omission was mathematics, a shortcoming which he never repaired. His first solo research, made when he was 29, was the synthesis of the first known chlorocarbons (C_2Cl_6 and C_2Cl_4) and until 1830 he was mainly a chemist. In 1825 he discovered benzene, which was later to be so important in both theoretical and technical chemistry. He worked on alloy steels, and he liquified chlorine and a range of other gases by pressure and cooling. He was established at the Royal Institution, became an excellent lecturer, and never left until retirement; he could have become rich from consultant work, but he belonged to a fervent religious group and he declined both wealth and public honours.

From about 1830 he increasingly studied electricity. An early venture was the study of electrolysis, and in 1832 and 1833 he reported the fundamental **laws of electrolysis**: (1) the mass of a substance produced by a cathode or anode reaction in electrolysis is directly proportional to the quantity of electricity passed through the cell, and (2) the masses of different substances produced by the same quantity of electricity are proportional to the equivalent masses of the substances (by equivalent mass is meant the relative atomic mass divided by the valence). Faraday had an excellent set of new words devised for him by W. Whewell for work in this area: electrolysis, electrolyte, electrode, anode, cathode, ion. It follows from the laws of electrolysis that an important quantity of electricity is that which will liberate one mole of singly-charged ions. This amount, the **Faraday constant** F, is defined by $F=N_Ae$ where N_A is the Avogadro constant and e is the charge on an electron. F can be measured accurately (e.g., by electrolysis of a silver solution) and has the value 9.648×10^4 C mol^{-1}. Also named for Faraday is the unit of capacitance, the **farad** (F). It is the capacitance of a capacitor (condenser) having a charge of one coulomb (C) when the potential difference across the plates is one volt. This is a large unit and the more practical unit is the **microfarad**, equal to 10^{-6} F.

Faraday's work on electricity in the 1830s largely developed the subject. *Oersted* had shown that a current could produce a magnetic field; Faraday argued that a magnetic field should produce a current. He found this to be so, provided that 'a conductor cut the lines of magnetic force'. He had discovered electromagnetic

induction (independently discovered by *J. Henry*) and to do it he used his idea of lines and fields of force producing a strain in materials, an idea which was to be highly productive. With it he was able to devise primitive motors, a transformer, and a dynamo: and he cast off the old idea of electricity as a fluid (or two fluids), and moved to solve some basic problems. For example, he showed that current from an electrostatic machine, a voltaic cell, and a dynamo is the same, and devised methods to measure its quantity. He examined capacitors, and the properties of dielectrics; and he discovered diamagnetism. In the early 1840s he was unwell for five years with 'ill health connected with my head'. It may have been mercury poisoning.

Back at work in 1845, he worked on his idea that the forces of electricity, magnetism, light and gravity are connected, and was able to show that polarized light is affected by a magnetic field. He failed to get a similar result with an electric field (*Kerr* succeeded in 1875) and the general theme of the 'unity of natural forces' has been pursued to the present day. In 1846 *Wheatstone* was due to speak at the Royal Institution, but at the last moment panicked and Faraday had to improvise a lecture. He included his 'Thoughts on Ray Vibrations', which Maxwell claimed were the basis of the electromagnetic theory of light which Maxwell, with new data and more mathematical skill, devised 18 years later.

Faraday had a very strange mind, but it well fitted the needs of physics at the time. His personality offers curious contrasts; he had much personal charm, but no social life after 1830. He had great influence on later physicists, but no students, and worked with his own hands helped only by a long-suffering ex-soldier, Sergeant Anderson. He had highly abstract ideas in science, but he was a most effective popularizer; his Christmas lectures begun in 1826 are still continued. In quality and in quantity, he remains the supreme experimentalist.

FEHLING, Hermann Christian von
1812-1885

German organic chemist

A pupil of *Liebig*, Fehling taught in Stuttgart. He is best known for the test reagent **Fehling's solution**, which contains a deep blue copper(II) complex in aqueous alkaline solution. If the organic test sample on boiling with this removes the blue colour and reduces the copper to brick-red copper(I) oxide, it is likely to be an organic aldehyde or reducing sugar. However, formates, lactates, haloforms, and some esters and phenols also give a positive test.

FERMAT, Pierre de
1601-1665

French mathematician: 'the prince of amateurs'

As a senior Government law officer (a job he did not do very well) it is remarkable that Fermat found time to maintain his skills as a linguist, amateur poet and, most notably, as an amateur mathematician. After 1652, when he nearly died of plague, he did give most of his time to mathematics, but he still did not publish his work in the usual sense, and his results are

Pierre de Fermat

known through his letters to friends, notes in book margins, and challenges to other mathematicians to find proofs for theorems he had devised.

His successes included work on probability, in which he corresponded with *Pascal* and reached agreement with him on some of its basic ideas; on analytical geometry, where again he achieved parallel results with another talented researcher, *Descartes*, and went further in extending the method from two dimensions to three; and on the maxima and minima of curves and tangents to them, where his work was seen by *Newton* as a starting point for the calculus. In optics he devised **Fermat's principle** and used it to deduce the laws of reflection and refraction and to argue that light passes more slowly through a dense medium. He worked on the theory of equations, and especially on the theory of numbers. Here he was highly inventive, and some of his results are well known, but as he usually did not give proofs, they teased other mathematicians in seeking proofs for a long time, with much advantage to the subject. Proofs were eventually found, but not in every case. **Fermat's Last Theorem,** noted in one of his library books, states that the equation $x^n+y^n=z^n$ where n is an integer greater than 2, can have no solutions for x, y and z, and records 'I have discovered a truly marvellous demonstration which this margin is too narrow to contain'. Since he wrote this, in about 1637, generations of mathematicians have attempted to find a proof. By 1960 it had been shown to be true for all values of n less than 125 000; and it was hoped that work by Y. Miyaoka in Tokyo in 1988 would yield a full proof, but it was quickly found to contain a flaw.

FERMI, ENRICO
1901-1954

Italian-American nuclear physicist: built first atomic reactor

Enrico Fermi was the greatest Italian scientist of modern times and was highly creative both as a theoretical and experimental physicist. The son of a railway official, he showed ability from an early age, and earned his PhD at Pisa, researching on X-rays. Fermi then worked with *Born* at Göttingen and with P. Ehrenfest at Leiden, before returning to a professorship at Rome in 1927. He had already published over 30 papers, including some on quantum statistics (**Fermi-Dirac statistics**) followed by work on spin-½ particles (now called fermions) such as the electron.

Fermi worked hard to build up Italian physics, supported by O. M. Corbino, but the circle of talent around him was dispersed by the growth of Fascism, and Fermi and his wife, who was Jewish, left for Columbia University New York in 1938. While in Rome, Fermi worked on the *Raman* effect, hyperfine structure, cosmic rays and virtual quanta. In 1933 he produced the theory of radioactive beta-decay, whereby a neutron emits an electron (β-particle) and an anti-neutrino and becomes a proton. The following year he showed that rather as the *Joliot-Curies* had used helium nuclei (α-particles) to induce nuclear transmutations, neutrons were even more effective. This led to his rapid discovery of over 40 new radioactive isotopes. He then, by chance, discovered that paraffin wax could be used to slow down the neutrons, and make them more effective, by a factor of hundreds, in causing transmutations of nuclei (they remain close to the target nucleus longer and are thus more likely to be absorbed). For all this work he received the 1938 Nobel Prize in physics.

Fermi had misinterpreted the transmutation of uranium with neutrons, but the ideas of *Frisch* and *Meitner* in 1938 corrected this, and proposed that nuclear fission with production of additional neutrons was occurring. Hahn and Strassmann in Berlin had also exposed uranium to neutrons, and both parties realised that vast amounts of energy could be released in such a chain reaction. Fermi, *Szilard* and *Einstein* moved quickly to warn Roosevelt and urge him to develop a nuclear weapon before Germany did so. The Manhattan project was set up (at a final cost of $2 billion) and Fermi's group at Chicago obtained the first controlled self-sustaining nuclear reaction (in a graphite-moderated reactor or 'pile' at Stagg Field stadium) on 2 December, 1942. An historic telephone call was made by *Compton* to the managing committee at Harvard stating that 'the Italian navigator has just landed in the New World'.

Fermi continued to work on the project and attended the first test explosion of the fission bomb (A-bomb) in the New Mexico desert. While approving of its use against Japan, he, like *Oppenheimer*, opposed the development of the fusion bomb (H-bomb). He defended Oppenheimer, the director of Los Alamos Laboratory, where the work was done, against charges of disloyalty and of being a security risk.

Fermi took a professorship at Chicago after the war, but died young of cancer. He was much liked as an inspiring teacher and warm and vivacious character, enjoying sports and displaying clarity as a lecturer and research leader. Element number 100 was named Fermium after him.

FERNEL, Jean François
*c.*1497-1558

French physician: made systematic survey of physiology and pathology

Fernel did not begin to study medicine until he was 27, after he had studied philosophy and the classics. He was an innkeeper's son, and his life was spent in Paris. He was very successful in medicine, and became personal physician to Henry II of France. His main contribution to medical science was his textbook (1554) which was a standard work for over a century, with about 30 editions, reprintings, and translations. Its first part deals systematically with physiology; the second part with pathology, giving an account of human organs in a diseased state – a method which, like the word pathology, was new. The final part dealt with treatment. Fernel was an excellent observer who rejected the use of astrology and his influence, through his book, was extensive and useful.

FESSENDEN, Reginald Aubrey
1866-1932

Canadian-American physicist: devised amplitude modulation for radio transmission

Born and educated in Canada, Fessenden's first job was in Bermuda but in 1886 he joined *Edison*'s laboratory in New Jersey. Then he moved in 1890 to Edison's great rival, Westinghouse, for two years and then to academic life at Purdue and later at Pittsburgh; and in 1900 to the US Weather Bureau, and then back to industry.

Before 1900 he began to work on radio, which *Marconi* and others were using to transmit messages by sending signals mimicking Morse code. Fessenden sent out a continuous signal or 'carrier wave' at a steady high frequency, and varied the amplitude of the waves to correspond to the sound waves of voices or music. At the receiver, these **amplitude modulations** could be reconverted to reproduce the sound. By Christmas Eve 1906 he was able to broadcast what was probably the first sound programme in the US. He also devised the 'heterodyne effect' to improve amplification, and established two-way radio communication between the US and Scotland. He was second only to Edison in the number and variety of his patents (over 500) and like him he was involved in many lawsuits. Modern radio is largely based on the work of Marconi, Fessenden and *De Forest* (who devised the triode).

FEYNMAN, Richard Phillips
1918-1988

American theoretical physicist: developer of mathematical theory of particle physics

Feynman's father, a New York maker of uniforms, developed the boy's interest in scientific ideas and logical observation. The young man graduated from Massachusetts Institute of Technology and Princeton, worked on the atomic bomb (the Manhattan project), and later joined the staff of the California Institute of Technology.

During the late 1940s Feynman developed new techniques for considering electromagnetic interactions within quantum theory, contributing methods on field theory which have been used widely. He showed that the interaction between electrons (or between positrons, the positively charged antiparticle to an electron, see *Dirac*) could be considered by regarding them as exchanging virtual photons (electromagnetic radiation). This electron-electron scattering can be described quantitatively as a sum of terms, with each term coming from a matrix element describing a topologically distinct way in which a photon can be exchanged. Each term can be written as a **Feynman diagram** consisting of lines called Feynman propagators which describe the exchange of particles. This work contributed greatly to a new theory of quantum electrodynamics (QED) which deals with nuclear particle interactions and which is in excellent agreement with experiment. Feynman received the 1965 Nobel Physics Prize for fundamental work on QED, together with *Schwinger* and *Tomonaga*.

Feynman was a colourful character in modern physics, whose originality and showmanship made him a highly-regarded lecturer (Feynman's *Lectures in Physics* are a delight to students). He enthused over any kind of puzzle, and enjoyed the company of a wide variety of people; he was renowned as a story-teller and practical joker. His recreations he listed as 'Mayan hieroglyphics, opening safes, playing bongo drums, drawing, biology experiments and computer science.' One of his few antagonisms was pomposity. When authority tried to close a topless restaurant in Pasadena, he went to court to defend it, and claimed to use it frequently to work on physics.

FIBONACCI, Leonardo

*c.*1170-*c.*1250

Italian mathematician: introduced the Arabian numeral system to Europe

Fibonacci's father was an Italian consul in Algeria, where Fibonacci himself was educated from the age of twelve by an Arabian mathematician. No doubt because of this he learned of the Arabian (originally Hindu) system of numerals, and through his *Book of the Abacus* (1202) he demonstrated how they could be used to simplify calculations. This resulted in the widespread adoption of the system in Europe.

Fibonacci was primarily interested in the determination of roots of equations, his greatest work, in 1225, dealing with second order Diophantine equations (indeterminate equations with rational coefficients for which a rational solution is required), and was unsurpassed for 400 years. He also discovered the **Fibonacci sequence** (1, 1, 2, 3, 5, 8 . . .), a series in which each successive number is the sum of the preceding two. This series has many curious properties, its appearance in leaf growth patterns being one biological example.

FISCHER, Emil Hermann

1852-1919

German organic chemist: the unsurpassed master of natural product chemistry

Fischer was born near Cologne, to a grocer who acquired a wool-spinning mill and a brewery hoping his son would follow him in business, or failing that, become a chemist. The father, a Rhinelander, passed to his son his cheery temperament and an appreciation of wine. Fischer did so well at school that he passed the leaving examination too young to enter the university, and so he joined his

uncle's timber trade. To the sorrow of his relatives, he then set up a private laboratory to work in during the day and spent the evenings playing the piano and drinking. In the family judgment 'he was too stupid for a business-man and therefore he must become a student'. This he did and read physics and botany, and a little chemistry under *Kekulé*, in 1871 in Bonn. In the following year he moved to Strasbourg to study under *Baeyer*, and in 1875 he went to Munich following Baeyer. He had already discovered phenylhydrazine, which was to become so useful to him ten years later. It also gave him chronic eczema.

He had become a single-minded and successful organic researcher. However, since he 'could not give up smoking and did more wine-drinking than was good for him' he had to recuperate every year. Nevertheless, his researches went well, on purines, sugars, dyes and indoles. But the dreadful odour of skatole so adhered to him and his students that they encountered difficulties in hotels when travelling. In 1885 he moved to Würzburg as professor, and in 1892 succeeded *Hofmann* as professor in Berlin. The chair carried much work in administration and he complained bitterly about the loss of time and energy during his twelve years in Berlin.

His work on natural products was superb. As well as bringing order to carbohydrate chemistry, partly by use of phenylhydrazine, and synthesizing a range of sugars including glucose, his studies on glycosides, tannins and depsides are outstanding: especially those on the peptides and proteins, begun in 1899. These compounds are fundamental to biochemistry. It was he who clearly grasped their essential nature as linear polypeptides derived from amino acids; he laid down general principles for their synthesis and made an octadecapeptide (having 15 glycine and 3(−)-leucine residues, relative molecular mass 1213) in 1907. He had much personal charm, and wrote with great clarity and brevity. For his contributions to natural product chemistry, he received the second Nobel Prize awarded in chemistry, in 1902.

FISCHER, Hans
1881-1945

German organic chemist: synthesized porphyrins

Fischer graduated in Marburg in chemistry and in Munich in medicine, where he was professor of organic chemistry from 1921. In the last stage of World War II his laboratory was destroyed by bombing, and Fischer killed himself. His work from 1921 was almost entirely on the porphyrin group of compounds, which contain four pyrrole rings linked together. His first major success with these difficult but important compounds was with haemin, the red non-protein part of haemoglobin, which carries oxygen from the lungs to the tissues. In it the four pyrrole rings are linked together to form a larger (macrocyclic) ring, with an iron atom at the centre. Fischer found the detailed structure, and synthesized it in 1929. He went on to study the chlorophylls, the green pigments of plants which are key compounds in photosynthesis. He showed that they are porphyrins related in structure to haemin, with magnesium in place of iron. For this porphyrin work he was awarded the Nobel Prize for 1930. He went on to find the structure of bilirubin (the pigment of bile, and related to haemin) and synthesized it in 1944.

FISHER (Sir) Ronald Aylmer
1890-1962

English statistician and geneticist: pioneer of modern statistical methods

Fisher's father was a successful auctioneer, and the boy was one of eight children; he also had eight children, 'a personal expression of his genetic and evolutionary convictions', although he and his wife later separated. He was small, forceful, eloquent, and eccentric.

Fisher graduated in Cambridge in 1912 in mathematics and physics, and spent from 1913-19 in a variety of jobs (his poor eyesight excluded him from service in World War I). Then he was appointed as the only statistician at the Rothamsted Experimental Station, with 66 years of data on agricultural field trials to examine. He was there for 14 years before moving to London, and to a Cambridge chair of genetics in 1943. When he was 69 he joined the Commonwealth Scientific and Industrial Research Organization (CSIRO) staff in Australia. Before he went to Rothamsted he worked on the statistics of human inheritance, showing that *Mendel*'s laws must lead to the correlations observed. He went on to show that Mendel's work on genetics and *Darwin*'s on natural selection are in good accord, rather than in conflict as some had believed. His work on the Rothamsted field data led him to major advances on the design of experiments, and on the best use of small samples of data. He unravelled the genetics of the rhesus blood factor. A smoker himself, he argued to the end that smoking should not be causally related to disease. In nearly all other matters his views and methods have been adopted and extended, and used in all the many areas where statistical analysis is possible.

FITZGERALD, George Francis
1851-1901

Irish physicist: suggested the Lorentz-FitzGerald contraction to explain the failure of the Michelson-Morley experiment to detect the 'ether'

FitzGerald was educated at Trinity College, Dublin, remaining there as a professor for the rest of his life. Although he did not publish much original work himself, he was influential in 19th century physics through his informal suggestions and discussions with others, tending to pass on ideas to experimenters, rather than publish them himself. He is chiefly remembered for his hypothesis that, in order to explain the failure of the *Michelson-Morley* experiment to detect the 'ether', bodies moving through an electromagnetic field contracted slightly in their direction of motion, in proportion to their velocity. This accounted for light appearing to move at the same speed in all directions. The same idea was also developed by *Lorentz*, becoming known as the **Lorentz-FitzGerald contraction**, and was an important stepping stone towards *Einstein*'s theory of relativity. FitzGerald also proposed that the tails of comets are made up of small rock particles, and that solar radiation pressure is responsible for the fact that their tails always point away from the Sun.

FIZEAU, Armand Hippolyte Louis
1819-1896

French physicist: determined the velocity of light experimentally

Born into a wealthy family, Fizeau turned from studying medicine to research in optics. With *Foucault* he improved the early photographic process introduced by Daguerre and obtained the first detailed pictures of the Sun (1845).

Fizeau made the first accurate determination of the speed of light (1849). In an experiment using an 8 km light path between the hill-tops of Suresnes and Montmartre, he sent a light-beam through a rotating toothed wheel, and reflected it from the far hilltop so that it returned through the wheel. At a certain speed of the wheel the return signal was blocked by a tooth of the wheel, enabling the speed of light to be calculated.

The following year, Fizeau working with L. F. C. Brequet, showed that light travels more slowly in water than in air: *Foucault* simultaneously made the same discovery. This was strong evidence against *Newton*'s particle theory of light and for *Huygens*'s and *Fresnel*'s wave theory. In 1851 Fizeau measured the effect on light when it is passed through a moving medium (water); the result was in excellent agreement with Fresnel's prediction. Fizeau was the first to apply *Doppler*'s results on moving wave sources and observers to light as well as sound. Other experiments by Fizeau included using the wavelength of light for measurement of length by interferometry, and using interference to find the apparent diameter of stars.

Many honours were given to Fizeau for his work, including membership of the Academie des Sciences (1860) and Foreign Membership of the Royal Society (1875).

FLAMSTEED, John
1646-1719

English astronomer: constructed first comprehensive telescopic star catalogue

Flamsteed's poor health, which was to hinder his work, led to frequent absence from school and he was largely self-educated until he entered Cambridge in 1670. Some youthful publications impressed Lord Brouncker (first President of the Royal Society), with his knowledge of navigational astronomy.

Charles II appointed Flamsteed as the first Astronomer Royal in 1675, charging him with the construction of accurate lunar and stellar tables, needed to enable seafarers to determine longitude at sea, a major problem in the 17th century. The Royal Greenwich Observatory was created for the purpose, and the task was to occupy Flamsteed for the rest of his life. His desire not to publish anything until his work was complete led to bitter disputes with other scientists; he irritated *Newton* in particular (then President of the Royal Society), and this led in 1712 to the virtual seizure of his papers by the Royal Society. Flamsteed did eventually finish the work, which contained the positions of nearly 3000 stars to an accuracy of 10 seconds of arc, but it was not published until six years after his death.

FLEMING, (Sir) Alexander

1881-1955

Scottish bacteriologist: discoverer of penicillin

An Ayrshire farmer's son, Fleming spent four years as a clerk in a London shipping office before a small legacy allowed him to study medicine at St Mary's. His later career was spent there, except for service in the Royal Army Medical Corps in World War I. In that war he saw many fatal cases of wound infection, and the experience motivated his later interest in a non-toxic antibacterial; his first result in the search was lysozyme, an enzyme present in nasal mucus, tears and saliva. It pointed to the possibility of success, but could not be got in concentrated form and was inactive against some common pathogens.

Then in 1928 he made the observations which were eventually to make him famous, and which are often claimed as the major discovery in medical science in this century. Fleming had left a culture dish of staphylococci uncovered, and by accident it became contaminated with an airborne mould. He noticed that the bacteria were killed in areas surrounding the mould, which he identified as *Penicillium notatum*. He cultured the mould in broth, and confirmed that a chemical from it (which he named penicillin) was bactericidal, and did not injure white blood cells (a pointer to its lack of toxicity). He saw it as a possibly useful local antiseptic. However, the chemical methods of the time were inadequate to allow concentrated penicillin to be obtained; it is easily destroyed and present only in traces in a culture broth. Later success came though work in World War II by a team led by *Florey*, and Fleming had no real part in the later work and was cool in his attitude to it.

The widespread use of penicillin from the 1940s onwards made a vast change in the treatment of many infections; it also led to a successful search for other antibiotics, and it made Fleming a near-legendary figure, partly because of a wartime need for national heroes. The legend portrayed him as lucky and diffident; both were exaggerations, since his discovery was a part of his systematic work and good observation, and he fully enjoyed his retrospective fame.

FLEMING, (Sir) John Ambrose

1849-1945

British physicist and electrical engineer: inventor of the thermionic valve

Fleming had a mixed education, studying at times at University College and at the Royal College of Chemistry, London, and at Cambridge under *Maxwell*. After intermittent periods of teaching and study, he was appointed professor of electrical technology at University College, London.

Although he worked on a number of electrical engineering problems, including radio telegraphy and telephony, Fleming's outstanding contribution was the invention of the thermionic valve, in 1900. This was based on an effect noticed by *Edison* (to whose company Fleming had been a consultant), and consisted of a vacuum tube containing a cathode heated to incandescence by an electric current, and an anode. When the anode was maintained at a positive potential with respect to the cathode, an electric current could flow from cathode to anode, but not in the opposite direction. This electric 'valve', or diode, was to form an essential component in electronic devices such as radios, television sets and computers, for half a century, until eventually superseded by the cheaper and more robust transistor. The right-hand rule, a useful mnemonic, is due to Fleming.

FLEMMING, Walther

1843-1905

German cytologist: pioneer of cytology and discoverer of mitosis

Flemming studied medicine in five

German universities, and later became professor of anatomy at Kiel. Using the new aniline dyes as microscopic stains, and the improved microscopes of the 1860s, he found that scattered fragments in an animal cell nucleus became strongly coloured; he named this substance chromatin. In cell division, the chromatin granules coalesce to form larger threads (named chromosomes in 1888 by *Waldeyer*). He went on to show that simple nuclear division as described by *Remak* is not the rule, and the more common type of cell division he named '**mitosis**'. In this, the chromosomes split lengthwise, and the identical halves move to opposite sides of the cell, entangled in the fine threads of the starlike aster (in animal cells only). The cell then divides, giving two daughter cells with as much chromatin as the original. Flemming gave a fine account of the process in 1882, and it has been intensively studied ever since. He did not know of *Mendel*'s work, and so he could not relate his work to genetic studies; that realisation did not come for 20 years.

FLOREY, Howard Walter (Baron Florey of Adelaide)

1898-1968

Australian pathologist: central figure in introduction of penicillin as useful antibiotic

Born and educated in Adelaide, Florey studied physiology in Oxford and pathology in Cambridge; in 1931 he became professor of pathology in Sheffield and in 1934 at Oxford. In the early 1930s he began to study lysozyme, an antibacterial enzyme present in mucus and discovered by *Fleming* in 1922. In 1935 *Chain* joined the department and in 1936 N. G. Heatley; both were chemists, and so the group had the skills to begin a study of the antibacterials formed in small amounts by certain moulds.

Fleming in 1928 had discovered a good candidate, penicillin, which he had been unable to isolate because of its instability, and this came early on the group's programme. By 1941 they had isolated enough penicillin to try on nine human patients and the results were good. The war was at a critical stage and large-scale production was begun in the US out of range of enemy bombers, as a result of Florey's discussions with US drug companies. By 1944 enough was available to treat casualties in the Normandy battles, as well as severe civilian infections, with impressive results. Fleming, Florey and Chain shared a Nobel Prize in 1945 for their work on penicillin.

Florey went to work on other antibiotics, but he was always involved in other areas of experimental pathology, especially on the lymphatic and vascular systems. Although he lived in the UK from 1922 and in Oxford from 1935 he retained his Australian outlook and accent, and did much to found the Australian National University at Canberra.

FLOURENS, (Marie Jean) Pierre

1794-1867

French anatomist and physiologist: early experimental physiologist

Flourens qualified in medicine in 1813 at Montpellier, and then went to Paris where *Cuvier* befriended him, secured teaching and research posts for him and ensured that after his own death his appointments would pass to Flourens.

From 1820 Flourens began to work on the central nervous system, using pigeons and later dogs, whose sacrifice yielded fundamental information. He found that vision depends on the integrity of the cerebral cortex, and removal of part of it produces blindness on the opposite side. Removal of the cerebellum causes loss of co-ordination of movement; he also found that loss of the semi-circular canals of the ear causes loss of balance, while respiration is controlled by a centre in the medulla oblongata. He did not attempt to remove or to stimulate small centres of the cerebellum, and it was *Hitzig* in 1870 who established cerebral localization. Flourens attacked the pseudo-science of phrenology, and largely demolished it. In 1847 he showed that trichloromethane ($CHCl_3$) is an effective anaesthetic for small animals, and later in the year the Scottish obstetrician J. Y. Simpson first used it for human patients in childbirth. In his old age Flourens mounted a forceful attack on *Darwin*'s theory of evolution, describing his ideas as 'childish and out of date'.

FOCK, Vladimir Alexandrovich

1898-

Soviet theoretical physicist: advanced the quantum mechanics of many-electron systems

Fock received his training at Petrograd (1922), and then moved to the Institute of Physics. He was appointed professor at Leningrad in 1961.

Simultaneously with R. Hartree, Fock first developed a means of solving quantum mechanical problems for atoms in which more than a single electron is present (i.e., atoms other than hydrogen). The possible energy levels of an electron in a hydrogen atom had been solved by *Schrödinger* in 1926, and the Hartree-Fock approximation for other atoms appeared in 1932.

Other important research by Fock includes work on general relativity.

FORBES, Edward

1815-1854

British naturalist: showed that marine life existed at great depths

Forbes studied medicine at Edinburgh, but soon became more interested in natural history. He became curator and later palaeontologist to the Geological Society, and subsequently professor of natural history at Edinburgh and at the Royal School of Mines.

Travelling widely in Europe and in the region bordering the Eastern Mediterranean (he joined a naval expedition as naturalist in 1841), Forbes collected much fauna and flora, particularly molluscs (which he classified systematically), studying their migration habits, and the inter-relationships between animals. He divided British plants into five groups, and proposed that Britain had once been joined by land to the continent, from whence the plants had migrated in three distinct periods. He also discounted the contemporary belief that marine life existed only near the sea surface, by dredging a starfish from a depth of 400 m in the Mediterranean. His *Natural History of European Seas* (1859) was the first general study of oceanography.

FOUCAULT, Leon

1819-1868

French physicist: measured the speed of light; and demonstrated rotation of the Earth

Foucault was the son of an impoverished bookseller, and he studied first medicine and then physics. He became editor of the *Journal de Débats* (1845) and a physicist at the Paris Observatory (1855). He was a brilliantly gifted experimentalist with great originality and instinct, but died of paralysis at 48, having been elected a member of the Académie des Sciences (1865) and the Royal Society (1864).

Foucault collaborated with Fizeau on the toothed-wheel experiment which first measured the speed of light terrestrially. In 1850 he took over *Arago*'s experimental equipment and first measured the speed of light in water, showing that it was slower than in air. This was important evidence in favour of the wave-theory of light and contrary to the prediction of *Newton*'s particle theory of light. Foucault then constructed a rotating mirror experiment for measuring the speed of light and used it to obtain a more accurate value (1862).

The simplicity and imaginativeness of Foucalt's measurement in 1850 of the rotation of the Earth by a swinging pendulum (**Foucault's pendulum**) make it an outstanding achievement. The effect occurs because the Earth rotates leaving the plane of the swinging pendulum fixed with respect to the stars. In 1852 Foucault demonstrated this with a 67 m pendulum with a 28 kg ball hung from the dome of the Panthéon in Paris. The experiment was carried out there with the help of Napoleon III, before an admiring crowd who watched a needle attached to the ball inscribe a mark in sand; the mark moved as the Earth rotated about the plane of the pendulum's swing. This was the first direct (i.e., non-deductive) demonstration of the Earth's rotation.

Other important work by Foucault included invention of the gyroscope in 1852, and improvements to reflecting telescopes. He discovered the yellow (sodium D) lines in emission spectra corresponding to the dark lines seen in absorption spectra by *Fraunhofer*; the value of this, however, was only realised later by *Kirchhoff*.

FOURIER, (Baron) (Jean Baptiste) Joseph

1768-1830

French mathematician: discovered Fourier series and the Fourier Integral Theorem

Fourier, the son of a tailor, was orphaned at age eight. He had a mixed education, at military school, an abbey, and later (after a narrow escape from the guillotine during the French Revolution in 1794) at the École Normale. He joined the staff of the École Normale, newly-formed to train senior teachers, and the École Polytechnique in Paris. When Napoleon invaded Egypt in 1798 Fourier accompanied him, but it is unlikely that he became governor of Lower Egypt as often stated. He became the Prefect of the département of Grenoble for 14 years but resigned during Napoleon's Hundred Days campaign.

Fourier died in 1830 of a disease contracted whilst in Egypt.

Fourier established linear partial differential equations as a powerful tool in mathematical physics, particularly in boundary-value problems. For example, to find the conduction of heat through a body of a given shape when its boundaries are at particular temperatures the heat diffusion equation can be solved as a sum of simpler trigonometric components (**Fourier series**). This way of solving the linear differential equations which often occur in physics has led to much use of the method on many new problems to the present day. Importantly, any arbitrary repeating function may be represented by a Fourier series; for instance, a complex musical waveform can always be represented as the sum of many individual frequencies. At a different level, the understanding of Fourier series and integrals has contributed greatly to the development of pure analysis, particularly of functional analysis. On the problem of heat conduction through a uniform solid, **Fourier's law** states that the heat flux is given by the product of the thermal conductivity and the temperature gradient.

FRACASTORO, Girolamo

*c.*1478-1553

Italian logician and physician: proposed early theory of germ origin of disease

Having studied a variety of subjects at Padua, Fracastoro became Lecturer in Logic there in 1501. After moves due to war and plague, he settled in Verona from 1516, practising as a physician until 1534. Thereafter he spent his retirement in research. His major medical book, *On Contagion and Contagious Diseases* (1546), gave the first logical explanation of the long-known facts that some diseases can be passed from person to person, or passed by infected articles. Fracastoro had in 1530 described and named syphilis (previously 'the French disease') which

Girolamo Fracastoro

was epidemic in Europe from about 1500. He proposed that infection is due to minute self-multiplying bodies which can infect by direct contact, or indirectly through infected articles, or which can be passed at a distance. His ideas were not widely adopted, many preferring the notion of miasmata, exhalations from earth or air which caused disease. Only much later did *Pasteur* and others show the essential correctness of Fracastoro's proposals.

FRANCK, James

1882-1964

German-American physicist: gave first experimental demonstration of the quantized nature of molecular electronic transitions

Franck studied law at Heidelberg, but left after only a year in order to study physics at Berlin instead. After service in the First World War (he was awarded the Iron Cross), he became professor of experimental physics at Göttingen. In 1933,

being a Jew, he felt obliged to leave Germany, settling eventually in the United States, where he became professor of physical chemistry at the University of Chicago. During the Second World War he worked on the American atomic bomb project, proposing in the Franck Report that the bomb be demonstrated to the Japanese on uninhabited territory, before being used on a city.

Franck's major work concerned the quantized nature of energy absorption by molecules. In 1914, together with Gustav Hertz (1887-1975), he demonstrated that gaseous mercury atoms, when bombarded with electrons, absorb energy in discrete units (or quanta). For mercury atoms this unit of energy is 4.9 eV. Following the absorption, which leaves the mercury atom in an energetically excited state, the atom returns to its original (or ground) state by emitting a photon of light. This experiment constituted the first experimental proof of *Bohr*'s ideas on energy levels in atoms, and Franck and Hertz were awarded the 1925 Nobel Prize in physics for their work.

Later, in conjunction with E. Condon, he also studied the energy requirements for vibration and rotation of diatomic molecules, showing that these were also quantized, and that dissociation energies (the energy required to break the chemical bond between the two atoms), could be extrapolated from them. The **Franck-Condon Principle** states that the most probable electronic transitions are those in which the vibrational quantum number is preserved, since electronic transitions take place on a much shorter time-scale than vibrational ones.

FRANKLAND, (Sir) Edward

1825-1899

British organic chemist: originator of the theory of valence

Frankland was apprenticed to a druggist in Lancaster for six years in an ill-advised attempt to enter the medical profession.

Guidance from a local doctor led him to study chemistry under Lyon Playfair at the Royal School of Mines in London (1845). He later studied with *Bunsen* at Marburg and *Liebig* at Giessen. At 28 Frankland became the founding professor of chemistry at the new Owens College (1851-7) which became the University of Manchester. He moved to St Bartholomew's Hospital, London (1857); the Royal Institution (1863) and the Royal School of Mines (1865).

He prepared and examined the first recognized organometallics, the zinc dialkyls. In his view, their reaction with water gave the free alkyl radicals (in fact, the corresponding dimeric alkanes). Vastly more significant was his later recognition, after thinking about a range of compounds, of numerical, integral limitations in atomic combining power: the theory of valence – this being the number of chemical bonds that a given atom or group can make with other atoms or groups in forming a compound. He used the word 'bond' and modern graphic formulae (Frankland's notation) and through these ideas did much to prepare foundations for modern structural chemistry. He also made major contributions to applied chemistry, notably in the areas of water and sewage purification – paramount requirements for good public health.

FRANKLIN, Benjamin
1706-1790

American statesman: classic experimenter and theorist on static electricity

Franklin had an unusually wide range of careers: he was successful as a printer, publisher, journalist, politician, diplomat and physicist. Trained as a printer, and working in New England and for nearly two years in London (England), Franklin found he also had talents as a journalist; and when he was 27 he published *Poor Richard's Almanac*. In this, he 'filled all the little spaces that occurred between the remarkable days in the calendar with proverbial sentences...' which he concocted. Most are trite platitudes of the 'honesty is the best policy' kind, but some show the sly irony of his journalism (of which the best-known sample is probably his advice to young men to take older mistresses, 'because they are so *grateful*'). The almanac made him both famous and prosperous, and by franchises in printing shops and other businesses in which he provided a third of the capital and took a third of the profit, he made himself wealthy.

When he was nearly 40 he became interested in electricity, which at that time provided only amusing tricks, but at least the dry air of Philadelphia made these more reproducible than in damper climates. Franklin's experiments and ideas turned electrical tricks into a science; made him the best-known scientist of his day; and perhaps for the first time showed that what we would now call pure research, could have important practical uses.

Franklin proposed that electrical effects resulted from the transfer or movement of an electrical 'fluid', made of particles of electricity (we would now call them electrons) which can permeate materials (even metals) and which repel each other but are attracted by the particles of ordinary matter. A charged body on this theory is one that has either lost or gained electrical fluid, and is in a state he called positive or negative (or plus or minus). Linked with this 'one fluid' idea was the principle or **law of conservation of charge**: the charge lost by one body must be gained by others, so that plus and minus charges appear, or neutralize one another, in equal amounts and simultaneously. Franklin's logic had its defects, but it was a major advance; and he continued to experiment, and worked on insulation and grounding. He examined the glow which surrounds electrified bodies in the dark, and it may have been this which caused a friend to show that a grounded metallic point could quietly 'draw off' the charge from a nearby charged object. This led Franklin to his idea that it should be possible to prove whether clouds are electrified (as others had suggested) and also to propose that 'would not these pointed rods probably draw the electrical fire silently out of a cloud before it came nigh enough to strike, and thereby secure us from that most sudden and terrible mischief?'. He planned in 1750 an experiment using a metal rod passing into a sentry box mounted on the steeple of a new church; but delay in building it led him to try using a kite instead, and he found that the wet string did indeed conduct electricity from the thundercloud and charge a large capacitor. The electrical nature of such storms was proved; lightning conductors became widely used; Franklin became famous; and others trying such experiments were killed.

He was in London for most of the years 1757-75 representing the American colonies and trying to prevent the rising conflict. When despite his efforts war began, he was active in support of the revolution and was one of the five men who drafted the Declaration of Independence in 1776. In the same year he went as ambassador to France, and largely through his fame as a scientist and his popularity, secured an alliance in 1778. Afterwards he continued to be active in American politics; despite being an Anglophile, a womanizer and a tippler, he was increasingly seen as the virtuous home-spun true American sage. His work in physics amused him but was always directed to practical use; he devised the Franklin stove with an efficient underfloor air-supply for heating, invented and used bifocal spectacles, used a flume for testing ships by using models, and his work on the Gulf Stream was a pioneering study in oceanography. By having ship's captains record its temperature at various depths and its velocity, he mapped the Gulf Stream and studied its effects on weather.

In the 1780s he was present at the first ascents by hydrogen balloons made by *Charles* at Versailles and he enthused over the possibility of studying the atmosphere and of aerial travel; and he foresaw aerial warfare. His book *Experiments and Observations on Electricity, made at Philadelphia in America* (1751) not only founded a new science, but had the incidental result of interesting *Priestley* in science, with momentous results for chemistry.

FRASCH, Herman
1851-1914

German-American industrial chemist: devised process for extraction of sulphur from underground deposits

Frasch was the son of a prosperous pharmacist in Württemberg, and began his training in pharmacy when he emigrated to the US in 1868 at age 17. Industry was expanding after the Civil War, and he soon interested himself in the new petroleum industry. One of its problems was that some wells yielded a 'sour' oil (nicknamed skunk oil) containing sulphur and organic sulphides. Frasch found a method for removing these by reaction with metal oxides. His interest in sulphur changed direction in 1891, when he began work on the problem of obtaining sulphur from deposits overlain by a limestone caprock and by quicksand. His method (the **Frasch process**) was to sink a trio of concentric pipes into the deposit; superheated water was pumped down one to melt the sulphur (m.p. 119° C) and air down another, to bring up a froth of molten sulphur through the remaining pipe. The process gave an abundant supply of 99.5% pure sulphur, and broke the Sicilian supply monopoly after about 1900.

FRAUNHOFER, Josef von
1787-1826

German physicist and optician: described atomic absorption bands in the solar spectrum

Fraunhofer was apprenticed as a mirror-maker and lens-polisher in Munich, rising

Josef von Fraunhofer

be due to atomic absorption in the Sun's outer atmosphere, and tell us a great deal about its chemistry. Similar lines are observed for other stars and have been equally informative. Fraunhofer's work was also important in establishing the spectroscope as a serious instrument, rather than merely a scientific curiosity.

to become a director of his company in 1811. His miserable time as an apprentice was relieved when he was buried under the collapsed workshop, and the Elector celebrated his survival with a gift of money which gave him independence. His interest in the theory of optics, and his scientific discoveries, led him eventually to become director of the Physics Museum of the Bavarian Academy of Sciences in 1823, but he died of tuberculosis three years later.

Fraunhofer's main interest, and the motivation behind his experiments, was in producing a good quality achromatic lens. During the course of his investigations into the refractive properties of different glasses he used a prism and slit to provide a monochromatic source of light. In doing so, he noticed that the Sun's spectrum was crossed by many dark lines, and he proceeded carefully to measure the wavelengths of almost six hundred of them. Later, he used a diffraction grating to prove that the lines were not due to the glass of the prism, but were inherent in the Sun's light. These **Fraunhofer lines** were subsequently shown by *Kirchhoff* to

FREDHOLM, Erik Ivar
1866-1927

Swedish mathematician: founded the theory of integral equations

Fredholm studied at Uppsala, and subsequently worked as an actuary until gaining his doctorate ten years later. He then became a lecturer in mathematical physics at Stockholm (1898), and moved from studying partial differential equations to their inverse, integral equations. In the next five years he rapidly established the field that was later extended by *Hilbert* in his work on eigenfunctions and infinite-dimensional spaces. In 1906 Fredholm became a professor at Stockholm.

Fredholm built upon earlier research by G. Hill and V. Volterra. He studied two integral equations (denoted, of the first and second kind) named after him: and later found a complete algebraic analogue to his theory of integral equations in linear matrix equations.

FRESNEL, Augustin Jean
1788-1827

French physicist: established and developed the wave-theory of light

When the French Revolution arrived Fresnel's father took his family to a small estate near Caen. After showing great practical skills Fresnel entered the École Polytechnique and despite ill-health gained distinction. He qualified as an engineer at the École des Ponts et Chaussées, but was removed from his post during 1815 for supporting the Royalists. He spent the Hundred Days of Napoleon's return at leisure in Normandy, and began his great work on the wave-theory of light.

He performed some new experiments on interference and polarization effects. *Huygens* and *Young* had suggested that light consisted of longitudinal waves; in order to explain polarisation effects Fresnel replaced this with a theory of light as transverse waves. He steadily established his theory as able to account for light's observed behaviour.

Fresnel also applied his skills to the development of more effective lighthouses. The old optical system for them consisted of metal reflectors and he introduced stepped lenses (**Fresnel lenses**). This work still forms the basis of modern lighthouse design. Fresnel was made a member of the Academie des Sciences (1823) and of the Royal Society (1827).

FRIEDEL, Charles

1832-1899

French mineralogist and organic chemist: co-discoverer of Friedel-Crafts reaction

Friedel was born in Strasbourg, and as a student there was taught by *Pasteur*. Later he studied under *Wurtz* in Paris, before becoming Curator at the École des Mines, and professor of mineralogy there in 1876. His early work was on the synthesis of minerals, but then he moved to organic chemistry and succeeded Wurtz at the Sorbonne in 1884.

His famous work was done in 1877 with an American, J. M. Crafts. The **Friedel-Crafts reaction** is of great value in organic synthesis. An aromatic hydrocarbon is heated with an alkyl halide and a Lewis acid (typically $AlCl_3$), and alkylation of the hydrocarbon is the result, e.g.,

$$C_6H_6 + C_2H_5Cl \rightarrow C_2H_5C_6H_5$$
$$\text{(ethylbenzene)}$$
$$+ HCl$$

In modified forms, such reactions are used in the petrochemical industry. Also useful is the acylation reaction, in which the hydrocarbon reacts with an acyl chloride and $AlCl_3$, e.g,.

$$C_6H_6 + CH_3COCl \rightarrow CH_3COC_6H_5$$
$$\text{(methylphenyl ketone)}$$
$$+ HCl$$

FRIEDMAN, Herbert

1916-

American astronomer: pioneered X-ray astronomy

From the 1940s onwards Friedman and his colleagues used rockets to launch X-ray devices above the Earth's absorbing atmosphere to observe the Sun, studying solar X-ray and ultraviolet activity through a complete 11-year solar cycle, and producing the first X-ray and ultraviolet photographs of the Sun in 1960. In 1962 the first non-solar X-ray source was discovered by a team led by *Rossi*, and two years later Friedman made the first attempt to identify accurately such a source with an optical object, making use of the occultation of Tau X-1 by the Moon. He was able to show that this X-ray source coincided with the Crab nebula, a supernova remnant.

FRIEDMANN, Aleksandr Alexandrovich

1888-1925

Soviet cosmologist: developed mathematical model of expanding universe

Friedmann applied *Einstein's* field equations to cosmology, and showed that general relativity did permit solutions in which the universe is expanding. He did this work in 1917, during the Siege of Petrograd. At the time Einstein preferred static solutions; he and *de Sitter* had to introduce arbitrary terms into their solutions. The Friedmann solution gave model universes that are more physically reasonable, and lay the foundations for the 'big bang' theory of modern cosmology. Friedmann also made significant contributions to fluid mechanics.

FRISCH, Karl von

1886-1982

Austrian ethologist: observer of the dancing bees

Frisch studied zoology at Munich and Trieste, and later taught zoology at four universities, spending the longest period in Munich. For over 40 years he made a close study of the behaviour of the honey bee. His results showed that bees can use polarized light to navigate back to the hive; that they cannot distinguish between certain shapes; and that they can see some colours, including ultraviolet (invisible to man) but not red. He also concluded that a forager bee can inform other workers of the direction and distance of a food source by means of a coded dance, a circular or figure-of-eight movement performed at the hive. He believed that information on food was also communicated by scent.

In the 1960s, A.M.Wenner claimed that sound as well as scent is used; bees emit a range of sounds audible to other bees. Later still, the problem was further examined by J. L. Gould, who used ingenious ways to test if false information could be transmitted by bees. By the 1980s it seemed that dance, scent and sound are all used in bee communication, at least by foragers reporting on a food source. Frisch is regarded as a key figure in developing ethology, by combining field observation with experiment. He shared a Nobel Prize in 1973 with *Lorenz* and *Tinbergen*.

FRISCH, Otto Robert

1904-1979

Austrian-British physicist: early investigator of nuclear fission of uranium

Frisch studied physics in his home city, Vienna, and then took a job at the national physical laboratory in Berlin. In 1930 he went to Hamburg to work with *Stern*, but he was sacked in 1933 as a result of the Nazi anti-Jewish laws, and worked for a year in London and then in Copenhagen (with *Bohr*) until World War II. At Christmas 1938 he visited his aunt, *Lise Meitner*, then a refugee in Stockholm and a former co-worker with O. Hahn in Berlin. She had a letter from Hahn reporting that uranium nuclei bombarded with neutrons gave barium. Frisch and Meitner walked in the snow and talked about it 'and gradually the idea took shape that this was no chipping or cracking of the nucleus but rather a process to be explained by Bohr's idea that the nucleus was like a liquid drop; such a drop might elongate and divide itself'. This division would give lighter elements such as barium, and more neutrons, so a chain reaction should occur. Frisch worked out that this should be easiest for heavy nuclei such as uranium; and Meitner calculated that it would release much energy (about 200 MeV). Back in Copenhagen, Frisch confirmed the energy of the fragments in experiments in an ionization chamber. He named the effect 'nuclear fission'. Working in Birmingham from 1939, he and *Peierls* confirmed Bohr's view that a chain reaction should occur more readily with the rare isotope of uranium, ^{235}U, rather than the common ^{238}U. They also calculated that the chain reaction would proceed with huge explosive force even with a few kilograms of uranium. If an atomic bomb based on this was made in Germany it would clearly decide the war, and they wrote to the British scientific adviser on this; their letter probably spurred government to action, and soon Frisch was working at Los Alamos on the A-bomb project, which reached success in 1945.

G

GABOR, Dennis
1900-1979

Hungarian-British physicist: invented holography

The son of a businessman, Gabor studied electrical engineering in Budapest and Berlin. He worked as a research engineer with the firm of Siemens and Halske, but in 1933 he had to flee from the Nazis and spent the rest of his life in Britain. He was initially with the British Thomson-Houston Co at Rugby and from 1948 at Imperial College, London.

In 1947-48 Gabor conceived the idea of using the phase (or position in the wave's cycle) as well as the intensity of received waves to build up a fuller image of the object in an electron microscope. In this way he hoped to extract better electron images so that atoms in a solid might be resolved, but soon he developed the method for use in an optical microscope also. The phase of the electron or light waves was obtained by mixing them with coherent waves directly from the wave source, and the waves then form a standing wave that is larger or smaller according to whether the two are in phase or out of phase. This interference pattern is recorded on a photographic plate. The waves from different parts of the object travel a varying number of wavelengths to the plate, and so the interference pattern and phase of the waves gives information on the three-dimensional shape of the object.

When the plate (**hologram**, from the Greek *holos*, whole) is placed in a beam of coherent waves a three-dimensional image of the object is seen, and as the observer moves a different perspective appears. (A coherent wave is one in which the wave train consists of waves exactly in phase; not several waves with different phases and intensities). For light Gabor achieved this crudely, using a pinhole in a screen in front of a mercury lamp. In 1960 lasers were invented and these powerful coherent sources allowed high quality holograms to be made by E. Leith and J. Upatnieks (1961). Gabor was awarded the Nobel Prize in 1971.

GAJDUSEK, Daniel Carleton
1923-

American virologist: pioneer in study of slow virus infections

Educated in physics at Rochester and in medicine at Harvard, Gajdusek later worked with *Pauling* at the California Institute of Technology, and in Iran and Papua New Guinea before returning to the US. It was in New Guinea in the 1950s that he studied the Fore people, who frequently die from a disease they call 'kuru'. He found that it could be passed to other primates (e.g., chimpanzees) but that it took twelve months or more to develop after infection. Since then other diseases have been shown, or suspected, to be due to slow and persistent virus infections (one example is the herpes 'cold sore'). Kuru was the first to be observed and identified in humans, and is possibly transmitted among the Fore by their cannibal rituals in which the brains of the dead are eaten by their relatives. Gajdusek shared a Nobel Prize in 1976.

GALEN

AD 129-199

Roman physician, anatomist and physiologist: his ideas on human anatomy and physiology were taught for 15 centuries

Born in Pergamon (now in Western Turkey) Galen began studying medicine early; at 21 he went to Smyrna to study anatomy, and later to Asia Minor to study drugs; later still he visited Alexandria where he examined a human skeleton. In his time human dissection was no longer carried out (although Galen may have done some) and his practical anatomy and physiology was based in part on his work on animals, including the Rhesus monkey. His lifetime coincided with a high point in the success of the Roman Empire, and the army had its medical service; but science did not flourish in Rome and Galen's interest in medical sciences was unusual. He had a large practice in Rome and was physician to four successive emperors. His extensive writing was partly based on the ideas of *Hippocrates* and *Aristotle*, and he added his own results and theories. His descriptions of the anatomy of the muscular system are excellent, and his studies on the physiology of the spinal cord and the effects of injury at various levels were a major advance. In his mind, every organ and all its parts have been formed for a purpose,

and he theorizes at length on this. However, most of his physiological theories were erroneous, and like others of his time, he had no knowledge of the circulation of the blood. He was fully aware of the existing medical experience and theory, he was highly industrious, and his authority was very long-lived.

GALILEI, Galileo

1564-1642

Italian astronomer and physicist: discovered Jupiter's moons, and laws governing falling bodies

Usually known by his first name, Galileo was born in Pisa; he was the son of a musician and became a medical student, but his interest moved to mathematics and physics. He became the ill-paid professor of mathematics at Pisa when he was 25, moved to Padua in 1591, and later to Florence. Galileo never married, but when he was 35, Marina Gamba (a Venetian girl) came to live with him, and they had two daughters and a son. When he moved to Florence in 1610 he left Marina behind, and she married soon after.

Galileo's fame rests partly on the discoveries he made with the telescope, an instrument which he did not invent, but

Galileo's own drawings of phases of the moon, showing its craters and mountains. His telescope magnified about thirty times.

was certainly the first to exploit successfully. His design used a convex object glass and a concave eyepiece, and gave an erect image. In 1610 he observed for the first time mountains on the Moon, four satellites around Jupiter, and numerous stars too faint to be seen with the naked eye. These observations he described in his book *Sidereal Messenger* (1610) which made him famous. He also discovered the phases of Venus, the composite structure of Saturn (although he was unable to resolve the rings as such; it looked to him like a triple planet), and sunspots. His discovery of heavenly bodies that were so demonstrably not circling Earth, together with his open public support for the Copernican heliocentric cosmology, was to bring him into conflict with the Church. He wrote his *Dialogue on the Two Chief World Systems, Ptolemaic and Copernican* in 1632. He tried in the book to make his support for the Copernican view diplomatic, and he seems to have believed that the Church authorities would be sympathetic, but he misjudged their resistance to such novel ideas. The next year he was before the Inquisition, and was shown the torture chamber and forced to recant. He was sentenced to house arrest for life, at the age of 69.

Among his notable non-astronomical findings were the isochronism (constant time of swing, if swings are small) of a pendulum, which he timed with his pulse when he was a medical student. (He designed a clock with its escapement controlled by a pendulum, and his son constructed it after his death.) He also found that the speed at which bodies fall is independent of their weight. The latter was the result of experiments rolling balls down inclined planes, and not by dropping weights from the leaning tower of Pisa, as was once widely believed. His work on mechanics is in his *Discourses Concerning Two New Sciences* (1638), which completes the claim to regard him as the Father of Mathematical Physics. (The two 'new sciences' which he created are now known as 'strength of materials'

and 'dynamics'). He died in the year in which *Newton* was born. His work sets the modern style; observation, experiment, and the full use of mathematics as the preferred way to handle results.

The **gal**, named after him, is a unit of acceleration, 10^{-2} m s^{-2}. The **milligal** is used in geophysics as a measure of change in the regional acceleration due to gravity (g).

Galileo was an able musician, artist and writer; a true man of the Renaissance. His massive contribution to physics makes him one of the small group of the greatest scientists of all time; and his startling discoveries, his forceful personality and his conflict with the church help to make him the most romantic figure in science.

GALOIS, Évariste

1811-1832

French mathematician: founded modern group theory

Galois was born with a revolutionary spirit, politically and mathematically, and at an early age discovered his untameable genius for original work in mathematics. He was taught by his mother until the age of twelve, and at school found interest only in exploring books by creative mathematicians such as A-M. Legendre, *Lagrange* and later *Abel*. Twice (in 1827 and 1829) Galois took the entrance examinations for the École Polytechnique (which was already one of the foremost colleges for science and mathematics) but failed on each occasion. At 17 he submitted a paper to the French Academy of Sciences via *Cauchy*, but this was lost. Following his father's suicide Galois entered the École Normale Supérieure to train as a teacher. During 1830 he wrote three papers breaking new ground in the theory of algebraic equations and submitted them to the Academy; they too were lost.

In the political turmoil following the 1830 revolution and Charles X's abdication Galois chided the staff and students of the École for their lack of backbone, and was expelled. A paper on the general solution of equations (now called **Galois theory**) was sent via *Poisson* to the Academy, but was described as 'incomprehensible'. In 1831 he was arrested twice, for a speech against the king and for wearing an illegal uniform and carrying arms, and received six months' imprisonment. Released on parole, Galois was soon challenged to a duel by political opponents. He spent the night feverishly sketching out in a letter as many of his mathematical discoveries as he could, occasionally breaking off to scribble in the margin 'I have not time'. At dawn he received a pistol shot through the stomach, and having been left where he fell was found by a passing peasant. Following his death from peritonitis eight days later he was buried in the common ditch of South Cemetery, aged 20.

The letter and some unpublished papers were discovered by *Liouville* 14 years later, and are regarded as having founded (together with Abel's work) modern group theory. It outlines his work on elliptic integrals and sets out a theory of the solutions (roots) of equations by considering the properties of permutations of the roots. If the roots obey the same relations after permutation they form what is now called a **Galois group**, and this gives information as to the solvability of the equations.

GALTON, Francis

1822-1911

English geographer and anthropologist: invented the statistical measure of correlation

Galton was born near Birmingham. His family included prosperous manufacturers and bankers as well as scientists and, from an early age, he developed a life-long passion for scientific investigation. In 1844 he graduated from Cambridge and, in that same year, his father's death left him with the independence of a financial fortune. Galton wanted to undertake scientific geographical exploration and a cousin (Douglas Galton) introduced him to the Royal Geographical Society in London. With the Society's advice, Galton financed and led a two-year expedition to an uncharted region of Africa. On his return to England in 1852, his geographical work brought him recognition in scientific circles. He was made a Fellow of the Royal Society in 1856 and took up the life of a London-based scientist-at-large. He never held, or sought, paid employment but was an active officer in the Royal Geographical Society, the Royal Society, the Anthropological Institute, and the British Association for the Advancement of Science. These societies gave him contact with leading scientists and also the opportunity to report his own investigations.

Galton's investigations were many and varied but consistently stressed the value of quantitative evidence. His motto was: whenever you can, measure and count. For example, in order to construct large-scale weather maps, he sent a questionaire to several weather stations around Europe asking for specified measurements on specified dates. When he received and mapped these data, in 1863, he discovered and named the now familiar 'anticyclone'. In 1875 he published, in *The Times*, the first newspaper weather map.

Throughout his life, Galton energetically pursued a variety of investigations. However, in 1859, a book appeared which stimulated him to concentrate more and more on the measurement of human individual differences. This book was *The Origin of Species* by *Darwin*, who was another of Galton's cousins.

People obviously differ greatly in their physical and mental characteristics, and the question that intrigued Galton was: to what extent do these characteristics depend on heredity or on environmental conditions? He pursued this question by various investigations, e.g., selectively breeding plants and animals, and collecting the medical histories of human twins who are genetically identical. In his human investigations, he faced the challenge that there was, at that time, no reliable body of measurements across generations. For example, how do the heights of parents relate to the adult heights of their children? He assembled large amounts of inter-generational data about height and other characteristics. Then he faced the further problem that there was, at that time, no mathematical way of expressing compactly the extent to which, say, the heights of offspring vary as a function of the heights of parents. By working over his accumulated measurements Galton solved this problem and, in 1888, he presented to the Royal Society his technique for calculating the **correlation coefficient**.

Galton's technique of 1888 was basically sound but crude by modern standards. It was much improved by later workers. It provided a powerful new tool which, nowadays, is widely used, for example, in medical science. Galton was a pioneer in several areas, for example he invented the term 'eugenics' to describe the science of production of superior offspring and was largely responsible for the introduction of fingerprinting as a means of identifying individuals in criminal investigations. But his most enduring contribution is perhaps his invention of the correlation coefficient.

GALVANI, Luigi

1737-1798

Italian anatomist: discoverer of 'animal electricity'

Galvani taught anatomy at Bologna, where he had graduated. His best-known work concerns his study of the effects of electricity on frogs. Among his systematic studies, a chance observation was important; this was that dead frogs being dried by fixing by brass skewers to an iron fence showed convulsions. He then showed that convulsions followed if a frog was part of a circuit involving metals. He believed that electricity of a new kind (animal electricity, or **galvanism**) was produced in the animal, but in 1800 *Volta* devised the voltaic pile and resolved the problem: the current originated in the metals, not the frog. Galvani's name lives on in the word 'galvanized' (meaning stimulated as if by electricity; also used for the zinc-coating of steel) and in the 'galvanometer' used from 1820 to detect electric current.

GAMOW, George

1904-1968

Soviet-American physicist: explained helium abundance in universe; suggested DNA code of protein synthesis

Born in Odessa and a student in Leningrad, Gamov worked in the US from 1934. He made important advances in both cosmology and molecular biology. In 1948, together with *Alpher* and *Bethe*, he suggested a means by which the abundances of chemical elements observed in the universe (helium in particular) might be explained (see Alpher for an account of α-β-γ theory). Gamow also showed, in 1956, that the heavier elements could only have been formed in the hot interiors of stars. He showed that our Sun is not cooling down, but is slowly heating up; and was a major expounder of the 'big bang' theory of the origin of the universe.

In molecular biology Gamow made a major contribution to the problem of how the order of the four different kinds of nucleic acid bases in DNA chains could govern the synthesis of proteins from amino acids. He realised that short sequences of the bases could form a 'code' capable of carrying information for the synthesis of proteins; and that since there are twenty amino acids making up proteins, the code must consist of blocks of three nucleic acid bases in order to have a sufficient vocabulary of instructions. Some details were wrong, but this central idea was known by 1960 to be correct.

GARROD, (Sir) Archibald Edward
1857-1936

English physician: discovered nature of congenital metabolic disorders

Whilst studying four human disorders (alcaptonuria, albinism, cystinuria and pentosuria) Garrod discovered that in each case a chemical substance derived from the diet was not being completely metabolized by the body, with the result that a product which is normally only an intermediate was excreted in the urine. He deduced that this metabolic failure was due to the absence of an enzyme (in 1958 this was proved to be correct). The family histories of patients also showed that the disorders were not due to infection or some random malfunction, but were inherited on a Mendelian recessive pattern. Garrod's results thus showed that Mendelian genetics applied to man, and were the first to suggest a connection between an altered gene (mutation) and a block in a metabolic pathway. This major concept, the biochemical basis of genetics, was surprisingly ignored (as *Mendel*'s original work on genetics had been) for thirty years.

His daughter Dorothy, an archaeologist, was the first woman to hold a Cambridge professorship.

GAUSS, Karl Friedrich
1777-1855

German mathematician: one of the greatest of all mathematicians

Gauss was of the stature of *Archimedes* and *Newton* and in range of interests he exceeded both. He contributed to all areas of mathematics and to number theory (higher arithmetic) in particular. His father was a gardener and merchant's assistant; the boy showed early talent, teaching himself to count and read, correcting an error in his father's arithmetic at age three, and deducing the sum of an arithmetic series $(a, a+b, a+2b \ldots)$ at the age of ten. Throughout his life he had an extraordinary ability to do mental calculations. His mother encouraged him to choose a profession rather than a trade, and fortunately friends of his schoolteacher presented him to the Duke of Brunswick when he was 14; the Duke thereafter paid for his education and later for a research grant. Gauss was grateful, and was deeply upset when the Duke was mortally wounded fighting Napoleon at Jena in 1806. Gauss attended the Collegium Carolinum in Brunswick and the University of Göttingen (1795-98). He devised much mathematical theory between the ages 14-17; at 22 he was making substantial and frequent mathematical discoveries, usually without publishing them. After the Duke's death he became Director of the Observatory at Göttingen, and was able to do research with little teaching as he preferred.

Up to the age of 20 Gauss had a keen interest in languages and nearly became a philologist; thereafter foreign literature and reading about politics were his hobbies (in both he had conservative tastes). When at 28 he was financially comfortable he married Johanne Osthof; unbelievably happy, Gauss wrote to his friend W. Bolyai: 'Life stands before me like an eternal spring with new and brilliant colours'. Johanne died after the birth of their third child in 1809, leaving her young husband desolate, and although he married again and had three more children, his life was never the same, and he turned towards reclusive mathematical research. This was done for his own curiosity, and not published unless complete and perfect (his motto was 'Few, but ripe') and he often remained silent when others announced results that he had found decades before. The degree to which he anticipated a century of mathematics has become clear only since his death, although he won fame for his work in mathematical astronomy in his lifetime. Of the many items named after him, the **Gaussian error curve** is perhaps best known.

During his years at the Collegium Carolinum, Gauss discovered the method of least squares for obtaining the equation for the best curve through a group of points and the law of quadratic reciprocity. While studying at Göttingen he prepared his book *Researches in Arithmetic (Disquisitiones Arithmeticae)* published in 1801, which developed number theory in a rigorous and unified manner; it is a book which as Gauss put it 'has passed into history' and virtually founded modern number theory as an independent discipline. Gauss gave the first genuine proof of the fundamental theorem of algebra: that every algebraic equation with complex coefficients has at least one root that is a complex number. He also proved that every natural number can be represented as the product of prime numbers in just one way (the fundamental theorem of arithmetic). The *Disquisitiones* discusses the binomial congruences $x^n \equiv A \pmod p$ for integer n, A and p prime; x is an unknown integer. The algebraic analogue of this problem is $x^n = A$. The final section of the book discusses $x^n = 1$ and weaves together arithmetic, algebra and geometry into a perfect pattern, and the result is a work of art.

Gauss kept a notebook of his discoveries, which includes such entries as

$$\text{E}\gamma\text{PHKA! num} = \triangle + \triangle + \triangle$$

which means that any number can be written as a sum of three triangular numbers (i.e. $\triangle = \frac{1}{2}n(n+1)$ for n integral). Other entries such as 'Vicimus GEGAN' or 'REV. GALEN' inscribed in a rectangle have never been understood but may well describe important mathematical results, possibly still unknown.

The notebook and Gauss's papers show that he anticipated non-Euclidean geometry as a boy, 30 years before J. Bolyai (son of Wolfgang) and *Lobachevsky*; that he found *Cauchy*'s fundamental theorem of complex analysis 14 years earlier, that he discovered quaternions before *Hamilton* and anticipated Legendre, *Abel* and

Jacobi in much of their important work. If he had published, Gauss would have set mathematics half a century further along its line of progress.

From 1801 to 1820 Gauss advanced mathematical astronomy by determining the orbits of small planets such as Ceres (1801) from their observed positions; after it was first found and then lost by *Piazzi*, it was rediscovered a year later in the position predicted by Gauss.

During 1820 to 1830 the problems of geodesy, terrestrial mapping, the theories of surfaces, and conformal mapping of one domain to another aroused his interest. Later, up to about 1840, he made discoveries in mathematical physics, electromagnetism, gravitation between ellipsoids, and optics. He believed that physical units should be assembled from a few absolute units (mainly length, mass and time); an idea basic to the SI system. Gauss was a skilled experimentalist and invented the heliotrope, for trigonometric determination of the Earth's shape, and with Weber the electromagnetic telegraph (1833). From 1841 until his death Gauss worked on topology and the geometry associated with functions of a complex variable. He transformed virtually all areas of mathematics.

GAY-LUSSAC, Joseph Louis
1778-1850

French chemist: established law of combining volumes of gases; discovered a variety of new chemical compounds, including cyanogen, and developed volumetric analysis

An adventurous child and a brilliant student, Gay-Lussac grew up during and after the French Revolution. *Lavoisier* had done much to create modern chemistry in the 1780s, but he had been guillotined in 1794. From then on the time was ripe for the subject to develop. Gay-Lussac studied engineering before becoming interested in physics and chemistry. He became well known through his hot-air balloon ascents in 1804. These were intended to find if magnetism persisted at height, and if the composition of air changed. The first ascent was with *Biot*; in the second (alone) he rose to 7 km (23 000 ft) the highest then achieved. (The composition of air, and magnetism, appeared to be unchanged). The next year he made a tour of Europe, visiting scientists and scientific centres, and had the luck of observing a major eruption of Vesuvius.

In 1808 he published the **law of combining volumes**; this states that the volumes of gases that react with one another, or are produced in a chemical reaction, are in the ratios of small integers. This law clearly gave support to *Dalton*'s atomic theory which had so recently appeared, although Dalton failed to grasp this, or even to accept Gay-Lussac's experimental results which led to the law. Earlier Gay-Lussac had found that all gases expand equally with rise of temperature, a result discovered by *Charles*, but not published by him. These two laws regarding gases formed the basis for *Avogadro*'s law of 1811.

By 1808 Gay-Lussac had an established reputation as a scientist; and Paris was then the world's centre for science. It proved an eventful year for him; he married Joséphine Rogeot, then a 17-year-old shop assistant, who he had seen reading a chemistry book between serving customers. He also began to work with his friend L. J. Thenard, a collaboration which was very fruitful. With Thenard, in 1808, Gay-Lussac made sodium and potassium in quantity (by reduction of the hydroxides with hot iron), discovered the amides and oxides of these metals, and isolated the element boron (nine days ahead of *Davy*). In 1809 they made the dangerously reactive fluorides HF and BF_3. Gay-Lussac was temporarily blinded by a potassium explosion which demolished his laboratory, but he never lost his enthusiasm for experimentation. In 1814 he published his research on the new

element iodine (discovered by B. Courtois) which was a model study. In 1815 he first made cyanogen (C_2N_2), and showed it to resemble the halogens, and to be the parent of a series of compounds, the cyanides. He developed volumetric analysis as an accurate method; and devised new industrial methods in chemistry.

He usually worked with his own hands, which at that time some thought inappropriate for such an eminent scientist. Davy described him in 1813 as 'lively, ingenious, and profound, with ... great facility of manipulation ... the head of the living chemists of France'. He remains one of chemistry's immortals, like Lavoisier, *Berzelius*, Davy, and his own pupil *Liebig*.

GEBER (Jabir ibn Hayyan)
c.721-c.815

Arabic alchemist

Son of a druggist, and orphaned young, Geber became the best-known of Arab alchemists. One result of his fame is that later writers used his name (perhaps to provide authority, or as a mark of respect). He was the resident physician and alchemist in the court of the Caliph Haroun al-Rashid (of *Arabian Nights* fame). His writings give detailed (but mystical) accounts of the principles whereby base metals could possibly be transmuted into gold; and he was familiar with a range of chemical substances and methods including distillation, sublimation and crystallization.

GEIGER, Hans Wilhelm
1882-1945

German physicist: invented a counter for charged nuclear particles

Having studied electrical discharges through gases for his doctorate, Geiger moved from Erlangen in Germany to

Manchester, where soon he began work under *Rutherford*. Together they devised a counter for α-particles (1908) which consisted of a wire at high electric potential passing down the centre of a gas-filled tube. The charged α-particles cause the gas to ionize, and the gas briefly conducts a pulse of current which can be measured. They showed that α-particles have two units of charge, and Rutherford later established that they are helium nuclei. In 1909 Geiger and E. Marsden demonstrated that gold atoms in a gold leaf occasionally deflect α-particles through very large angles, and even directly back from the leaf. This observation led directly to Rutherford's nuclear theory of the atom as like a small solar system rather than a solid sphere (1913). In 1910 Geiger and Rutherford found that two α-particles are emitted when uranium disintegrates. Work by Geiger and J. M. Nuttall showed that there is a linear relation between the logarithm of the range of α-radiation and the radioactive time constant of the emitting atoms (the **Geiger-Nuttall** rule). Geiger took part in the identification of actinium-A (1910) and thorium-A (1911). Both are isotopes of element number 84, polonium.

Geiger served in the German artillery during World War I. Following this he was Head of the Physikalisch-Technische Reichsanstalt in Berlin and in 1925 used his counter to confirm the *Compton* effect by observing the scattered radiation and the recoil electron. Geiger became a professor at Kiel later that year and in 1928, together with W. Müller, produced the modern form of the **Geiger-Müller** counter. In this, a metal tube acts as the negative cathode, and contains argon at low pressure and a central wire anode. A window of thin mica or metal admits radiation, which ionizes the gas. The current pulse is amplified to operate a counter and produce an audible click. From 1936 he worked on cosmic rays, artificial radioactivity and nuclear fission. Geiger was ill during World War II, and

died soon after losing his home and possessions in the Allied advance into Germany.

GELL-MANN, Murray

1929-

American theoretical physicist: applied group theory to understanding of elementary particles

Gell-Mann was educated at Yale University and Massachusetts Institute of Technology, gaining his PhD at 22. Work with *Fermi* followed, and he then moved to California Institute of Technology where he became professor of theoretical physics in 1956.

At 24, Gell-Mann made a major contribution to the theory of elementary particles by introducing the concept of **'strangeness'**, a new quantum number which must be conserved in any so-called 'strong' nuclear interaction event. Using strangeness Gell-Mann and Y. Ne'eman (independently) neatly classified elementary particles into multiplets of 1, 8, 10 or 27 members. The members of the multiplets are then related by symmetry operations, specifically unitary symmetry of dimensions 3 or SU(3). The omega-minus particle was predicted by this theory, and was observed in 1964, to considerable acclaim. Their book on this work was entitled *The Eightfold Way*, a pun on the Buddhist eightfold route to nirvana (loosely, heaven).

Gell-Mann and G. Zweig introduced the concept of quarks which have one-third integral charge and baryon number. From these the other nuclear particles (hadrons) can be made. The name is an invented word, associated with a line in Joyce's *Finnegan's Wake*: 'Three quarks for Muster Mark!'

Another major contribution was Gell-Mann's introduction (with *Feynman*) of currents for understanding the weak interaction. For all this work he was awarded the Nobel Prize for physics in 1969.

GERHARDT, Charles Frédéric

1816-1856

French chemist: classified organic compounds according to type

Gerhardt studied chemistry in Germany, but after quarrelling with his father he became a soldier. He was 'bought out' by an unknown friend, and returned to chemistry with *Liebig*, and later with *Dumas* in Paris, where he met *Laurent*. Together they did much to advance organic chemical ideas. The **Theory of Types** reached a high point in their hands. This was a formal system of classifying organic compounds, by referring them all to one (or more) of four types (hydrogen, hydrogen chloride, water and ammonia) by formal replacement of hydrogen by organic radicals. Examples based on the water type would be

H
  O, water
H C_2H_5
       O, ethanol
    H_5 C_2H_5
           O, diethyl ether
        C_2H_5

Combined with the idea of homologous series (compounds differing by CH_2 units) this gave a general system of classification, with some predictive power. Type formula (such as those above) were not thought to represent structures, but were formal representations of relationships and reactions. The theory rejected *Berzelius*'s idea of 'dualism' (opposed charges within two parts of a molecule); and this combined with Gerhardt's anti-authoritarian and quarrelsome personality ensured controversy (which was fruitful in leading to new results).

GERMER, Lester Halbert

1896-1971

American physicist: demonstrated experimentally the wave-like nature of electrons

After starting his career at Western Electric and Bell Telephone Laboratories, Germer moved to Cornell University. His career was spent studying thermionics, erosion of metals and contact physics. Germer, with *Davisson*, carried out one of the crucial experiments in physics in 1927. This demonstrated that particles, in their case electrons, also display wave-like properties.

GIAUQUE, William Francis

1895-1982

American physical chemist: pioneer of low temperature techniques

Giauque hoped to become an electrical engineer when he left school at Niagara Falls, but he failed to find a job in a power plant and for two years worked in a laboratory at a chemical plant, which moved his interest to chemistry. This became his main study at the University of California, Berkeley, where he subsequently remained for all his professional life.

In 1925 he proposed a method known as **adiabatic demagnetization** for achieving temperatures below 1 K, which had hitherto been unattainable. The method consists of placing a sample of a paramagnetic substance, at as low temperature as possible, in a very strong magnetic field; this causes the elementary magnetic ions in the substance to become aligned. When the magnetic field is switched off the elementary magnetic ions tend to increase their entropy by becoming randomly aligned, but since this requires energy the temperature of the sample will drop. Despite considerable practical difficulties, Giauque himself achieved a temperature of 0.1 K by this technique in 1933, and soon afterwards temperatures of a few thousands of a kelvin had been reached. The method remains the basis for reaching very low temperatures today. Giauque was awarded the Nobel Prize for chemistry in 1949 for his discovery. He was also the first to discover, in 1929, that atmospheric oxygen contains the isotopes ^{17}O and ^{18}O.

GIBBS, Josiah Willard

1839-1903

American physical chemist: founder of chemical thermodynamics

Before 1850, the Americas had produced few physical scientists of renown, with only *Franklin* and *Rumford* in the pre-revolutionary US; but the next 30 years saw the work of *J. Henry*, H. A. Rowland, and Gibbs, who was perhaps the most original of all of them and the only theorist. From youth he maintained the family tradition of skill in classical languages, but also won prizes in mathematics, and in 1863 he gained the first Yale PhD in engineering, and the second PhD awarded in the US.

The next three years he spent at Yale as a tutor (two years in Latin, and one in physics) before spending two years in France and Germany, with the two survivors of his four sisters, attending lectures by leading chemists, mathematicians and physicists. In 1871 he was appointed professor of mathematical physics at Yale. He held the job until his death, despite being unsalaried for the first nine years on the curious grounds that he was not in need of money. He was not a good teacher and few understood his work. He never married, and lived with his sisters in New Haven, close to the college. His ideas, which founded chemical thermodynamics and statistical mechanics, were expressed in elegantly austere mathematical form, in lesser-known journals, so few chemists understood them; some of his results were later re-discovered by *Planck* and *Einstein* (among others) to their disappointment, and even *Poincaré* found reading his papers 'difficult'.

His ideas were of permanent use, and were also still giving new insights a century after their appearance. In the 1870s he derived the **Gibbs phase rule** which deals elegantly with heterogeneous equilibria, and devised the concept now known as the **Gibbs function** which enables prediction of the feasibility and

direction of a hypothetical chemical change in advance of direct trial. His later work covered chemical potential (an idea invented by him), surface adsorption, and the deduction of thermodynamic laws from statistical mechanics. It could be said that his fellow-American Rumford began to solve the problem of heat, and Gibbs completed the solution. In the 1890s his work was translated into French and German, and recognition and public honours followed. He remains probably the greatest theoretical scientist born in the US.

GILBERT, Walter

1932-

American molecular biologist: isolated the first gene repressor

Gilbert made a remarkable transition: from a basis of physics and mathematics at Harvard and Cambridge, and a post at Harvard as a theoretical physicist, he changed in 1960 to biochemistry and molecular biology and became professor of biophysics at Harvard in 1964 and of molecular biology in 1968.

Monod and F. Jacob in 1961 had proposed that gene action is controlled by a 'repressor substance' whose function is to 'turn off' the gene when it is not needed. In 1966 Gilbert and B. Muller-Hill devised and successfully used an ingenious method for isolating one of these hypothetical substances, which are present only in traces in cells. They purified their sample of the lac-repressor (i.e., the repressor which represses the action of the gene which forms an enzyme which acts on lactose) and showed it to be a protein.

Later he worked on the problem of finding the sequence of bases in DNA, and devised an elegant method, broadly similar to *Sanger*'s but suitable for either single- or double-stranded DNA; the two methods are complementary and each is best suited to particular cases. Gilbert shared a Nobel Prize for chemistry in 1980.

GILBERT, William
1544-1603

English physician and physicist: pioneer of the study of magnetism and the Earth's magnetic field

Gilbert was a physician by profession, being royal physician to both Elizabeth I and James I, but is remembered for his extensive work on magnetism. He discovered how to make magnets by stroking pieces of iron with naturally magnetic lodestones, or by hammering iron whilst aligned in the Earth's magnetic field, and also found that the effect was lost on heating. From his investigations of magnetic dip he concluded that the Earth acted as a giant bar magnet, and he introduced the term 'magnetic pole'. His book *De magnete* (1600) is a classic of experimental science and was widely read throughout Europe. It is often considered to be the first great scientific work written in England.

William Gilbert

GLASER, Donald Arthur
1926-

American physicist: invented the bubble chamber for observing elementary particles

Graduating in 1946 from the Case Institute of Technology in his home town of Cleveland, Ohio, Glaser then did cosmic ray research at California Institute of Technology for his doctorate (1950). For ten years he worked at the University of Michigan, and from 1959 at the University of California at Berkeley. In 1964 he turned to molecular biology.

By the early 1950s the *Wilson* cloud chamber was failing to detect the fastest high-energy particles available. Glaser realised that particles passing through a superheated liquid will leave tracks of small gas bubbles nucleated along the trajectory. In 1952 he produced a prototype bubble chamber a few centimetres across, filled with diethyl ether. The tracks were observed and recorded with a high-speed camera. Bubble-chambers up to several meters across and filled with liquid hydrogen were developed by *Alvarez,* and used in many of the major discoveries of the 1960s and 1970s in particle physics. Glaser received the 1960 Nobel Prize for physics. He had calculated which liquids would be suitable for use in a bubble chamber, but as he 'wanted to be sure not to omit simple experimental possibilities' he also tried beer, ginger beer and soda water. None worked; water is most unsuitable because it has a high surface tension and a high critical pressure.

GLASHOW, Sheldon Lee
1932-

American physicist: produced a unified theory (QCD) of electromagnetism and the weak nuclear interaction

After Cornell and Harvard Glashow spent a few years in postdoctoral work at the Bohr Institute, at the European Organization for Nuclear Research (CERN) in

Geneva, and in the US, and in 1967 returned to Harvard as professor of physics.

Glashow produced one of the earliest models explaining the electromagnetic and weak nuclear forces. The *Weinberg-Salam* theory then developed this further and was a coherent theory for particles called leptons (electrons and neutrinos). Glashow extended their theory to other particles such as baryons and mesons by introducing a particle property called 'charm'. He used *Gell-Mann*'s theory that particles were made up of smaller particles called quarks, and postulated that a fourth 'charmed' quark was necessary, giving a group of particles described by SU4 (Unitary Symmetry of Dimension 4). The dramatic discovery of the J (or psi) particle which confirmed this approach was made by *Ting* and *Richter* in 1974. They found other predicted particles during the next two years. Since then the quark theory has been extended to include a 'coloured' quark, and the theory (which is known as quantum chromodynamics, QCD) is now discussed on the basis of Glashow's approach. He shared a Nobel Prize in 1979.

GLAUBER, Johann Rudolph
1604-1668

German chemist: understood formation of salts from bases and acids

Glauber developed an interest in chemistry after having apparently been cured of typhus through drinking mineral waters. He was one of the first to have clear ideas about the formation of salts from bases by the action of acids, and prepared a wide range of chemicals. He is credited with the discovery that sulphuric acid and common salt react to form hydrochloric acid and sodium sulphate (**Glauber's salt**). Something of a charlatan, the latter was soon on sale as a cure for a wide range of ailments (and is used as a laxative). He wrote several useful treatises on industrial chemistry, and noticed the peculiar precipitates known as 'chemical gardens'.

GODDARD, Robert Hutchings
1882-1945

American physicist: pioneered the liquid-fuel rocket

Goddard was born and educated in Worcester, Massachusetts, USA, attending the Polytechnic Institute and Clark University. He held the position of professor of physics at Clark University for most of his life.

Goddard was interested in the practical aspects of space travel from an early age, and in 1919 published a classic paper outlining many of the basic ideas of modern rocketry. Unlike some other pioneers of the space age, he was not content merely to test his ideas on paper, and in 1926 built and tested a rocket propelled by gasoline and liquid oxygen. In 1929 he established a research station in New Mexico, backed by the Guggenheim Foundation, and had soon sent up instrumented rockets, the forerunners of those used for atmospheric research, and developed a gyroscopic guidance system. By 1935 his rockets had broken the sound barrier, and demonstrated that they could function in the near-vacuum of space. His pioneering work was, however, not publicly acknowledged by the US Government until 15 years after his death, when it awarded his widow a million dollars for its numerous infringements of his 214 patents, incurred during its space and defence programmes.

GÖDEL, Kurt
1906-1978

Austrian-American mathematician: showed that mathematics could not be totally complete and totally consistent

Growing up Gödel was frequently ill and

had a life-long concern with his health. He studied mathematics at Vienna and saw much of the development of the positivist school of philosophy, and was apparently unconvinced. In 1930 he received his PhD, proving in his thesis that first-order logic is complete – so that in first-order logic every statement is provable or disprovable within the system. He then investigated the larger logical system put forward by B. Russell and A. N. Whitehead in their *Principia Mathematica*, and his resulting paper of 1931 may well be the most significant event in 20th century mathematics.

The paper was titled 'On Formally Undecidable Propositions of *Principia Mathematica* and Related Systems', and showed that arithmetic was incomplete. In any consistent formal system able to describe simple arithmetic there are propositions that can be neither proved nor disproved on the basis of the system. Gödel also showed that the consistency of a mathematical system, such as arithmetic, cannot necessarily be proved within that system. Thus a larger system may have to be used to prove consistency, and its consistency assumed; all pretty unsatisfactory. The programme for developing mathematical logic suggested by *Hilbert*, G. Frege and Russell therefore was untenable, and it is now clear that there is not a set of logical statements from which all mathematics can be derived.

Between 1938 and 1940 Gödel showed that restricted set theory cannot be used to disprove the axioms of choice or the continuum hypothesis; this was extended in 1963 when P. Cohen showed that they are independent of set theory. Gödel also contributed to general relativity theory and cosmology, and was a close friend of *Einstein* at Princeton. Gödel had married and emigrated there in 1938 when the Nazis took Austria, and was a professor there from 1953 to 1976. He was a quiet and unassuming man with a variety of interests.

GOEPPERT MAYER, Maria
1906-1972

German-American mathematical physicist: discovered and explained the 'magic numbers' of nucleons in some atomic nuclei

Maria Goeppert succeeded in making major contributions to science despite many obstacles. She first studied mathematics at Göttingen, perhaps because *Hilbert* was a family friend, but in 1927, attracted by *Born*'s lectures, she switched to physics. She worked on electronic spectra, and in 1930 married an American chemist, Joseph Mayer. They went to Johns Hopkins where she had a lowly job with one of the 'only two people there who would work with a woman' – her husband. Her work on molecular spectra by quantum methods gained the respect of *Urey* and *Fermi* who invited the couple to Columbia, but they could find a paid job only for 'Joe'. However, she continued to research, especially on the newly discovered elements heavier than uranium; so when World War II began and the atom bomb project developed, she was much in demand and soon ran a team of 15 people. It was she who calculated the properties of UF_6, the basis of a separation method for the 'fission isotope' ^{235}U.

After the war both Mayers went to Chicago, and it was there in 1948 that she found the pattern of 'magic numbers': atomic nuclei with 2, 8, 20, 28, 50, 82 or 126 neutrons or protons are particularly stable. (The seven include helium, oxygen, calcium and tin). At first Mayer offered no theory to account for this, although she saw the analogy with electron shell structures. However, by 1950 and aided by a clue from her friend Fermi, Mayer worked out a complete shell model for atomic nuclei, in which spin orbit coupling predicted precisely the 'magic number' stable nuclei actually observed. In this model, the magic numbers describe nuclei in which certain key neucleon shells are complete. For this work she shared a Nobel Prize in 1963 with J. H. D. Jensen of Heidelberg who had arrived independently at rather similar conclusions on nuclear shell structure.

GOLD, Thomas

1920-

Austrian-American astronomer: proponent of steady-state theory; contributor to the theory of pulsars

An Austrian emigré, Gold studied at Cambridge, subsequently working there and at the Royal Greenwich Observatory before moving to the US in 1956, where he later became director of the Center for Radiophysics and Space Research at Cornell University.

Gold, a leading proponent of the steady-state theory for the origin of the universe, published in 1948 the 'perfect cosmological principle' with *Bondi* and *Hoyle*, according to which the universe looks the same from every direction, and at all times in its history. It is considered to have no beginning and no end, with matter being spontaneously created from empty space as the universe expands, in order to maintain a uniform density. Although the theory enjoyed support for a number of years, the discovery of the cosmic microwave background in 1964 by *Penzias* and *R. W. Wilson* gave conclusive support to the rival 'big bang' theory.

Pulsars, discovered by *Bell* and *Hewish* in 1968, are another area of interest to Gold, who was quick to propose an explanation for their strange radio signatures: he suggested that they were rapidly rotating neutron stars, sweeping out a beam of radio energy like a lighthouse. His hypothesis was verified when the gradual slowing down of their rate of spin, a phenomenon that he had predicted, was detected.

More recently, Gold has been involved with a Swedish project to drill deep into the Earth's mantle to find commercial amounts of methane. He believes that significant amounts of hydrogen and helium remain within the Earth's interior from the time of the planet's formation, and rejects the conventional organic theo-

ries of hydrocarbon formation, believing that oil fields are formed by the outward migration of this primordial gas.

GOLDSCHMIDT, Hans

1861-1923

German chemist

Goldschmidt invented the alumino-thermic or thermite process named after him, which consists of the reduction of metallic oxides, using finely divided aluminium powder fired by magnesium ribbon. A similar mixture was much used in magnesium-cased incendiary bombs in World War II.

GOLDSCHMIDT, Victor Moritz

1888-1947

Swiss-Norwegian chemist: pioneer of geochemistry and crystal chemistry

Born in Zürich, Goldschmidt graduated from the University of Christiania (now Oslo) in 1911, becoming director of the Mineralogical Institute there when he was 26. He had already had great success in applying physical chemistry to mineralogy. In 1929 he moved to Göttingen, but returned to Norway in 1935 when the Nazis came to power. As a Jew he was fortunate that although imprisoned he was temporarily released; he escaped to Sweden in a haycart, and moved to England in 1943.

Goldschmidt is regarded as the founder of modern geochemistry. Using X-ray techniques he established the crystal structures of over 200 compounds and of 75 elements and made the first tables of ionic radii. In 1929, on the basis of these results, he postulated a fundamental law relating chemical composition to crystal structure: that the structure of a crystal is determined by the ratio of the numbers of ions, the ratio of their sizes, and their polarization properties; this is often known as **Goldschmidt's law**. It enabled Goldschmidt to predict in which minerals various elements could or could not be found. He also showed that the Earth's crust is made up largely of oxy-anions (90% by volume) with silicon and the common metals filling the remaining space.

GOLGI, Camillo
1844-1926

Italian histologist: classified nerve cells and discovered synapses

Golgi followed his father in pursuing a medical career, and studied at Padua and Pavia; he was later a physician in Pavia for seven years, and in 1875 became a professor there. He was interested in the use of organic dyes for histological staining (much used by *Koch*, *Ehrlich* and others) and in 1873 he made his own major discovery: the use of silver compounds for staining. Using this method with nerve tissue he was able to see new details under the microscope, allowing him to classify nerve cells, and to follow individual nerve cells (which appeared black under the microscope when treated with silver) and he showed that their fibres did not join but were separated by small gaps (synapses). In the 1880s he studied the asexual cycle of the malaria parasite (a protozoon) in the red blood cells, and related its stages to the observed stages of the various forms of malaria. In 1898 he described a peculiar formation in the cytoplasm of many types of cell ('the Golgi body') which has been much studied since, especially by electron microscopy; it appears to be a secretory apparatus, producing glycoproteins and other essential cell materials. Golgi shared a Nobel Prize in 1906.

GOODRICKE, John
1764-1786

English astronomer: explained nature of variable stars

After careful observation of the variable star Algol, Goodricke suggested that its rapidly varying brightness was caused by a dark body orbiting a brighter one and partially eclipsing it. This was the first plausible explanation to be made for the nature of variable stars. He received the Copley Medal for his work, the Royal Society's highest honour, and was made an FRS. Goodricke was a deaf mute and died when he was only 21.

GOUDSMIT, Samuel Abraham
1902-1978

Dutch-American physicist: first suggested that electrons possess spin

After attending university at Amsterdam and Leiden, Goudsmit obtained his PhD in 1927 and emigrated to the US, holding a post at Brookhaven National Laboratory from 1948 to 1970.

At the age of 23, with fellow-student *Uhlenbeck*, he developed the idea that electrons possess spin (i.e., they have intrinsic quantized angular momentum), with an associated magnetic moment, and used this to explain many features of atomic spectra. Spin later emerged as a natural consequence of relativistic quantum mechanics in *Dirac*'s theory of the electron (1928), and was found to be a property of most elementary particles, including the proton and neutron.

After first working on radar during World War II, Goudsmit was appointed head of the Alsos mission in 1944. This was to accompany and even to precede front-line Allied troops, seeking indications of the development of a German atomic bomb. He found that there was little danger of the Germans possessing such a weapon before the war ended. He was awarded the Medal of Freedom for this work, and later published an account in his book *Alsos* (1947).

GRAHAM, Thomas
1805-1869

Scottish physical chemist: studied passage of gases, and dissolved substances in solution, through porous barriers

Son of a Glasgow manufacturer, Graham studied science in Glasgow and Edinburgh, despite his forceful father's desire that he should enter the church. He held professorships in Glasgow and London, and became a founder of physical chemistry, and first president of the Chemical Society of London (the first national chemical society). One part of his work deals with the mixing of gases separated by a porous barrier (diffusion), or allowed to mix by passing through a small hole (effusion). **Graham's Law** (1833) states that the rate of diffusion (or effusion) of a gas is inversely proportional to the square root of its density.

The density of a gas is directly proportional to its relative molecular mass, M. So if the rate of diffusion of one gas is k_A and its density d_A, and that of a second gas k_B and d_B, it follows that:

$$k_A/k_B = d_B^{1/2}/d_A^{1/2} = M_B^{1/2}/M_A^{1/2}$$

Diffusion methods were used in 1868 to show that ozone must have the formula O_3; and more recently were used to separate gaseous isotopes.

Graham studied phosphorus and its oxyacids (which led to the recognition of polybasic acids, in which more than one hydrogen atom can be replaced by a metal); and he examined the behaviour of hydrogen gas with metals of the iron group. He found that H_2 will pass readily through hot palladium metal and that large volumes of the gas can be held by the cold metal.

His work on dialysis began the effective study of colloid chemistry. He found that easily crystallizable compounds when dissolved would readily pass through membranes such as parchment, whereas compounds of a kind which at that time had never been crystallized (in fact, of high relative molecular mass, such as proteins) would not dialyse in this way. This gives a method (today using polymers such as cellophane rather than parchment) for separating large, colloidal molecules from similar compounds; this is useful in biochemistry, and in renal dialysis, where the blood of a patient with kidney failure is purified in this way.

GRAM, Hans Christian Joachim
1853-1938

Danish physician and microbiologist

Gram's life and work was based in Copenhagen; but during a visit to Berlin in 1884, he devised his famous microbiological staining method. He showed that bacteria can be divided into two classes; some (e.g., pneumococci) will retain aniline-gentian violet after treatment with iodine solution by his method; others (the Gram-negative group) do not.

Gray's method of demonstrating the electrical conductivity of the human body.

GRAY, Stephen

c. 1666-1736

English physicist: distinguished between electrical conductors and insulators

Gray was a dyer's son who began to follow the same trade but after meeting *Flamsteed* (the Astronomer Royal) was attracted to astronomy and obtained a job as an observer at Cambridge for a year. Back in London, he experimented with electrical devices, and in 1729 (when he was over 60) he made a major discovery. He had electrified a glass tube by friction, and found by chance that the electricity was conducted along a stick or thread mounted in a cork inserted in one end of the tube. Led by this, he found that a string resting on silk threads would conduct for over 100 m, but if the string was supported by brass wires the transmission failed. Based on this, he distinguished conductors (such as the common metals) from insulators (such as silk and other dry organic materials). In the 18th century, experiments with electricity were difficult; primitive electrostatic machines, changes in humidity, and induction effects easily led to confusion. Gray also observed that two spheres of the same size, one solid and one hollow, had the same capacity for storing electric charge.

GREEN, George

1793-1841

English mathematician: established potential theory in mathematical physics

Green left school early to work in the family corn mill and bakery and studied mathematics on his own. When his father died the mill was sold and he became financially independent. At age 40 he began to study at Cambridge; he graduated in 1837 and received a Fellowship, but became ill and died soon afterwards.

In 1828 he published a paper in a local journal of which only a few copies were issued. It was discovered by *W. Thomson* after Green's death, and shown to leading physicists including *Maxwell*; both realised its great value. In it Green uses the term 'potential' and developed this mathematical approach to electromagnetism. He also included his famous theorem, which gives a way of solving partial differential equations by reducing a volume integral to a surface integral over the boundary (**Green's theorem**).

GREGORY, James

1638-1675

Scottish mathematician: contributed to discovery of calculus

A graduate of Aberdeen, Gregory went on to study at Padua, and became the first professor of mathematics at St Andrews when he was 30. Six years later he moved to Edinburgh, and died a year later. While in Italy he published a book in which he discovered convergent and divergent series (terms he used for the first time), the distinction between algebraic and transcendental functions, and circular, elliptic and hyperbolic functions. He found series expressions for the trigonometric functions, and gave a proof of the fundamental theorem of calculus (in

James Gregory

1667) although he does not note its significance. In letters of 1670 he used the binomial series and *Newton*'s interpolation formula (both independently of Newton) and the series named after B. Taylor.

He also contributed to astronomy; when he was 25 he suggested that transits of Venus (or Mercury) could be used to find the distance of the Sun from the Earth, and the method was later used. He proposed in the same book that telescopes could be made using mirrors in place of lenses, avoiding the optical aberration inevitably introduced by a lens. Five years later Newton made such a reflecting telescope, and large telescopes have usually been reflectors ever since.

GRIGNARD, (Francois Auguste) Victor

1871-1935

French organic chemist: discovered use of organomagnesium compounds in synthesis

Grignard, a sailmaker's son, studied at Lyons to become a teacher of mathematics. Later he moved to chemistry, and to research in organic chemistry under P. A. Barbier, who gave him a research project 'as one throws a bone to a dog'. He found that magnesium would combine with reactive organic halogen compounds in dry diethyl ether solution, to give an organomagnesium compound. Such compounds could be used (without isolating them) in reactions with a variety of carbonyl and other compounds to give organic alcohols, organometallics and other useful products. These **Grignard reactions** became the most useful of organic synthetic methods, were greatly used in research, and led also to increased interest in other organometallic compounds.

In World War I Grignard (who had done military service in 1892 and become a corporal) began by guarding a railway bridge, but was soon transferred to chemical warfare; he worked on the detection of mustard gas, and the making of phosgene ($COCl_2$). In 1919 he succeeded Barbier at Lyons, and remained there, largely working on extensions of his major discovery. He shared a Nobel Prize in 1912.

GROVE, (Sir) William Robert

1811-1896

English lawyer and physicist: devised first fuel cell

It is rare for anyone to practice law and science together, as Grove did. He became a barrister, but poor health was thought to point to a less active life, and he turned to electrochemistry. He invented the Grove Zn-Pt cell which was popular, and survived in a form modified by *Bunsen*. Then to improve his income, Grove returned to legal work. He defended Palmer, the 'Rugeley poisoner' in a famous murder trial in 1856; and became a judge in 1871, meanwhile continuing his scientific interests. He devised in 1842 what he called a 'gas battery'; in fact the first fuel cell, not to be confused with the Grove cell described above. The fuel cell had two platinum strips, both half-immersed in dilute H_2SO_4; one strip was half in H_2 gas, the other in O_2 gas. When a wire connected the ends, a current flowed. Other pairs of gases (e.g. H_2 and Cl_2) also gave a current. Grove realised that the current came from a chemical reaction.

In 1845 he made the first electric filament lamp; and in 1846 showed that steam is dissociated (to H_2 and O_2) on hot platinum. He also studied lighting in mines, and discharge tubes, and offered early ideas on energy conservation.

In 1891, at the jubilee of the Chemical Society of which he was a founder, he said 'for my part, I must say that science to me generally ceases to be interesting as it becomes useful'.

GUERICKE, Otto von

1602-1686

German engineer and physicist: inventor of the air pump; created and investigated properties of a 'vacuum'

After a wide-ranging education, Guericke became one of the four burgomasters of Magdeburg in 1646, in acknowledgement of his service to the town as an engineer and diplomat during its siege in the Thirty Years War. His interest in the possibility of a vacuum (which *Aristotle* had denied) led him to modify and improve a water pump so that it would remove most of the air from a container. He showed that in the resulting 'vacuum' a bell was muffled, and a flame was extinguished. Most dramatically, at Regensburg in 1654 he showed that when two large metal hemispheres were placed together and the air within was pumped out, they could not be separated by two teams of eight horses.

He also built the first recorded electrostatic machine, consisting of a globe of

Otto von Guericke

crude sulphur which could be rotated by a crank and which was electrified by friction.

GUETTARD, Jean Etienne

1715-1786

French geologist: proposed the igneous origin of basalts

Guettard was the keeper of the natural history collection of the Duc d'Orleans. In 1751 he proposed, whilst travelling in the Auvergne region of France, that a number of the peaks in the area were former volcanoes, on the basis of the basalt deposits he found nearby. Although he later withdrew this hypothesis, his suggestion led *Desmarest* to investigate and map the area in detail. His findings were, in turn, to lead to the abandonment of the Neptunist theory of *A. G. Werner*, which had stated that all volcanic activity was recent and all rocks were sedimentary in origin. His geological map of France was constructed with the help of his young friend *Lavoisier*, and probably began the latter's interest in science.

GULDBERG, Cato Maximilian

1836-1902

Norwegian physical chemist: deduced law of mass action for chemical reactions

Guldberg spent his career in Oslo, where he was professor of applied mathematics from 1869. He and P. Waage (his friend and brother-in-law, and professor of chemistry) were interested in *Berthelot's* work on the rates of chemical reactions, and this led them in 1864 to deduce the **law of mass action**. This states that for a homogeneous system, the rate of a chemical reaction is proportional to the active masses of the reactants. The molecular concentration of a substance in solution or in the gas phase is usually taken as a measure of the active mass. The theory did not become known until the 1870s, largely because it was published in Norwegian, as also happened with his other work in physical chemistry.

GUTENBERG, Beno

1889-1960

German-American geophysicist:
demonstrated that the Earth's outer core is
liquid

Gutenberg studied at Darmstadt and at Göttingen before being appointed professor of geophysics at Freiberg in 1926. In 1930 he moved to America to join the California Institute of Technology, becoming director of its seismological laboratory in 1947.

By 1913 it was known that, on the opposite side of the Earth to an earthquake, there is a shadow zone in which compressional P waves arrive later than expected and with reduced amplitude, and in which shear S waves are absent; *Oldham* had previously interpreted the delayed arrival of P waves as evidence for the existence of a core. Gutenberg realized that the absence of shear waves also meant that the core was liquid. He showed that the boundary between the solid mantle and the liquid core occurs at a depth of 2900 km; this interface is known as the **Gutenberg discontinuity**. It is now believed that there is an additional solid inner core, at a depth of about 5150 km (see *Lehmann*).

H

HABER, Fritz
1868-1934

German physical chemist: devised nitrogen 'fixation' process

Haber's father was a dye manufacturer, and so he studied organic chemistry to prepare him for the family firm. However, physical chemistry interested him more, and he worked on flames and on electrochemistry. By 1911 he was well known, and was made Director of the new Kaiser Wilhelm Institute for Physical Chemistry at Berlin-Dahlem. From about 1900 he worked on the problem of ammonia synthesis. *Crookes* had shown that if the world continued to rely on Chile nitrate deposits to provide nitrogenous fertilizer for agriculture, famine was inevitable. Haber solved the problem by 1908, showing that nitrogen from air could be used to make ammonia; the reaction $N_2+3H_2\rightarrow 2NH_3$ could be used at $c.400°C$ under pressure with a modified iron catalyst. With C. Bosch to develop the process to an industrial scale, production was established by 1913; the **Haber-Bosch process** made about 10^8 t of ammonia annually by the 1980s. About 80% of this is used to make fertilizers. In World War I it solved also the problem of making explosives for Germany, since nitric acid (essential for their production) can be made by oxidizing ammonia. Haber was also in scientific control of Germany's chemical warfare, and devised gas masks and other defence against the Allies' gas warfare. The Nobel Prize for 1918 was awarded to him for the ammonia synthesis.

In 1933 he resigned his post and emigrated in protest against anti-Semitism, but he did not re-settle well and worked only briefly in Cambridge. He died while on his way to a post in Israel.

HADAMARD, Jacques
1865-1963

French mathematician: developed theory of functionals

Hadamard's parents recognized his mathematical ability and he attended the École Normale Supérieure in Paris. His doctoral thesis was on function theory; he taught at the Lycée Buffon, and then at Bordeaux. At 44 Hadamard became professor of mathematics at the Collège de France in Paris, and later at the École Polytechnique and École Centrale. In 1941, aged 76, he left occupied France for the US and then joined the team in London using operational research for the RAF. Returning to France after the war, he retired to his interests in music, ferns and fungi.

Hadamard produced new insights in most areas of mathematics and influenced the development of the subject in many directions. He published over 300 papers containing novel and highly creative work. In the mid-1890s he studied analytic functions, that is those arising from a power series which converges. He proved the *Cauchy* test for convergence of a power series. In 1896 he proved the prime number theorem (first put forward by *Gauss* and *Riemann*) that the number of prime numbers less than x tends to $x/\log_e x$ as x becomes large. This is the most important result so far discovered in number theory; it was independently proved by C. J. Poussin in the same year.

Hadamard investigated geodesics (or shortest paths) on surfaces of negative curvature (1888) and stimulated work in probability theory and ergodic theory. He then considered functions $f(c)$ that depend on the path c, and defined a 'functional' y as $y=f(c)$. The definitions of continuity, derivative and differential become generalizations of those for an ordinary function $y=f(x)$ where x is just a variable. A new branch of mathematics, functional analysis, with relevance to physics and particularly quantum field theory grew out of this.

Hadamard also analysed functions of a complex variable and defined a singularity as a point at which the function is no longer regular. A set of singular points may still allow the function to be continuous – and such regions are called 'lacunary space', the subject of much modern mathematics. Finally he initiated the concept of a 'well-posed problem' as one in which a solution exists that is unique for the given data, but depends continuously on those data. A typical example is the solution of a differential equation written as a convergent power series. This has proved to be a powerful and fruitful concept and since then the neighbourhood and continuity of function spaces have been studied.

Hadamard published books on the psychology of the mathematical mind (on *Poincaré* in particular), and was an inspiring lecturer who influenced several generations of mathematicians.

HADFIELD, (Sir) Robert Abbot

1858-1940

English metallurgist: discovered several new steel alloys

After a local schooling and training as a chemist, Hadfield started work in his father's small steel foundry in Sheffield. Due to his father's ill-health he took over the firm when he was 24 and inherited it six years later. Hadfield continued the research he had begun in the early 1880s into steel alloys, publishing 150 scientific papers.

Improving the *Bessemer* process of steel-making which relied on the use of phosphorus-free iron ore, R. F. Mushet had added spiegeleisen (Fe-C-Mn), but this resulted in a metal which although hard was too brittle. Hadfield found that by adding large amounts of manganese (12-14%) and subsequent heating (to 1000°) and quenching in water, he produced a steel alloy both hard and strong and suitable for metal-working and railway-points. His firm took out the patent on this in 1883. Continuing his work on steel alloys he produced silicon steels and showed that they have valuable magnetic properties and were suitable for use in transformers.

His firm also produced armour-piercing and heat-resisting steels. He was knighted in 1908 and created a baronet in 1917.

HADLEY, George

1685-1768

English meteorologist: explained nature of the trade winds

Initially trained as a barrister, Hadley became more interested in science, and took over responsibility for the Royal Society's meteorological observations. *Halley* had proposed in 1686 that the trade winds were due to hot equatorial air rising, and pulling in colder air from the tropics, but was unable to account for their direction. In 1735 Hadley suggested that the reason that these winds blew from the north-east in the northern hemisphere, and from the south-east in the south, was the Earth's rotation from west to east. This form of circulation is now known as a **Hadley cell**. His brother, John, was a skilled instrument maker, developing the reflecting telescope, and inventing the forerunner of the sextant.

HALDANE, John Burdon Sanderson
1892-1964

Scottish physiologist and geneticist: showed that enzyme reactions obey laws of thermodynamics

Haldane is one of the most eccentric figures in modern science. If his life has a theme, it is of bringing talents in one field of work to the solution of problems in quite a different area. He was self-confident, unpredictable, and difficult to work with. His family was wealthy and talented, and his father was Britain's leading physiologist.

The latter (John Scott Haldane, 1860-1936) was led to study death in coalmine disasters and from this to discover how poisoning by carbon monoxide arose; and then to discover the part played by carbon dioxide in controlling breathing. His work on deep sea diving and mountain ascents added to his work on respiration, and with his Oxford pupils he laid the basis of modern respiratory physiology.

His son J. B. S. Haldane went to Eton, where he began to conflict with authority; service in World War I made him an atheist. He went to Oxford to study mathematics and biology, but graduated in classics and philosophy. In 1910 his interest moved to genetics as a result of studying his sister's 300 guinea pigs. He began to teach physiology; he knew a good deal about respiration through helping his father, and he had also worked on defence against poison gas in the war, but otherwise he had 'about six weeks start on my future pupils'. He researched on respiration and the effect on it of CO_2 in the blood. For this he used himself as an experimental animal, changing his blood acidity by consuming $NaHCO_3$, and by drinking solutions of NH_4Cl to get hydrochloric acid into his blood. Later he turned to biochemistry, applying his mathematical ability to calculate the rates of enzyme reactions and giving the first proof that they obey the laws of thermodynamics. Then he turned to genetics, and the mathematics of natural selection,

and of genetic disease and mutation in man. In 1938 he began work on deaths in submarine disasters, and regularly risked his life in experiments on underwater escape.

He wrote on popular science; including over 300 articles in the *Daily Worker* (he was a Communist, as well as the nephew of a viscount). In 1957 he emigrated to India, claiming this was a protest against the Suez affair, but probably because of the opportunity to work on genetics there; as usual, he quarrelled with his colleagues. Dying of cancer, he wrote comic poems about the disease, which produced praise and offence to their readers in about equal numbers.

HALE, George Ellery
1868-1938

American astronomer: discovered sunspots to be associated with strong magnetic fields

Son of a wealthy engineer, Hale had an early interest in astronomy and studied physics at Massachusetts Institute of Technology. Whilst still an undergraduate he invented the spectroheliograph, an instrument capable of photographing the Sun at precise wavelengths, and now a basic tool of solar astronomy. In 1908 he discovered that some lines in the spectra of sunspots are split, and correctly interpreted this as being due to the presence of strong magnetic fields (the *Zeeman* effect). Together with *Adams* he later discovered that the polarity of the magnetic fields of sunspots reverses on a 23-year cycle.

Hale realised that larger telescopes were essential in order for astronomy to advance, and put much of his energy and organizational ability into providing them. In 1892 he persuaded Charles Yerkes, a Chicago businessman, to fund a 40-inch refracting telescope for the University of Chicago, still the largest refractor ever built. Hale followed this by arranging for the Carnegie Institute to fund a 60-inch reflector for the Mount

Wilson Observatory, and for a 100-inch reflector financed by John D. Hooker that was to remain the largest in the world for 30 years. His greatest achievement however, was to persuade the Rockefeller Foundation to provide the money for a telescope that would be the ultimate in size for Earth-based observations – the 200-inch (5 m) Mount Palomar reflector. Construction began in 1930 and was to take 20 years. It remains perhaps the most famous telescope in the world, although it now comes second in size to the 236-inch (6 m) telescope at the Soviet Special Astrophysical Observatory in the Caucasus.

HALES, Stephen
1677-1761

English chemist and physiologist: developed gas-handling methods; classic experimenter on plant physiology and on blood pressure

Hales studied theology at Cambridge, and in 1709 became Perpetual Curate of Teddington. There he stayed, refusing preferment, so that he could maintain his work in chemistry and biology. He seems to have been much influenced by *Newton's* work, and his own is marked by careful measurement and the early use of physics in biology.

His book *Vegetable Staticks* (1727) describes 124 experiments on gases, which he made in several ways and collected using a pneumatic trough. This device was a major advance in gas manipulation. Oddly, he assumed all the gases he made were air; it was *Priestley*, using and improving Hales's methods, who examined their different properties. In the same book, Hales describes his experiments showing that plants take in a part of the air (actually CO_2) and that this is used in their nutrition. He measured growth rates, and showed that light is needed, and that water loss (by transpiration) is through the leaves, and causes an upward flow of sap, whose pressure he measured. Later he examined blood pressure, inserting and tying a vertical tube 11 feet long into an artery of a horse to measure the height to which the blood rose, and calculating also the output from the heart and the flow-rate in arteries, veins and capillaries. He showed that capillaries are liable to constriction and dilation, which later was seen to be of great significance.

His inventiveness was wide-ranging; he worked on the preservation of foods, water purification, the ventilation of buildings and ships, and the best way to support pie crusts. His theme was usually the application of physics to problems in biology.

HALL, Asaph
1829-1907

American astronomer: discovered the moons of Mars

Hall discovered two Martian satellites in 1877, naming them Phobos and Deimos (after the sons of Mars, meaning 'fear' and 'terror'). By a curious coincidence Jonathan Swift in *Gulliver's Travels* 15 years earlier had suggested that Mars had two satellites, whose size and orbital period accurately matched those of Phobos and Deimos. Hall was also the first to measure accurately the period of rotation of Saturn.

HALLER, Albrecht von
1708-1777

Swiss anatomist and physiologist: pioneer of neurology

A child prodigy, he is claimed to have written a Greek dictionary at age ten. Haller's working life was divided into a period spent founding the medical school at Göttingen, and his last 24 years spent back in his native Berne. A man of wide-ranging talents, Haller was the first to offer views on the nervous system of a modern kind. He recognized the tendency of muscle-fibres (which had been discovered by *Leeuwenhoek*) to contract when stimulated, or when the attached nerve is stimulated, and he named this 'irritability'. He showed that only the nerves can transmit sensation, and that they are gathered into the brain. His work in neurology was extended by *C. Bell* and by *Magendie*. He wrote the first textbook of physiology and worked on the circulation, respiration, and digestion; always with an emphasis on experiment. He was also a poet, a bibliographer, a botanist, and a writer on politics.

HALLEY, Edmond
1656-1742

English astronomer and physicist: made numerous contributions to astronomy and geophysics

Son of a wealthy businessman, Halley was an experienced observer as a schoolboy, before he entered Oxford in 1673. He became a most remarkable and prolific scientist who made important discoveries in many fields. He was also highly likeable and even good looking. He made his name as an astronomer by travelling at the age of 20 to St Helena, where he remained for two years to produce the first accurate catalogue of stars in the southern sky (also the first telescopically-determined star survey), which was published in 1679. His interest in comets was kindled by the great comet of 1680, which prompted him to compute the orbits of 24 known comets; noting that orbits of comets seen in 1531, 1607 and 1682 were very similar, he deduced that they were the same body, and predicted its return in 1758. (It is now known by his name). It was the first correct prediction of its kind, and demonstrated conclusively that comets were celestial bodies and not a meteorological phenomenon, as had sometimes been believed.

His other astronomical discoveries were numerous: in 1695 he proposed the secular acceleration of the Moon; in 1718

Edmond Halley

he observed the proper motion of the stars after observing Sirius, Procyon and Arcturus; he was the first to suggest that nebulae were clouds of interstellar gas in which formation processes were occurring. He succeeded *Flamsteed* as Astronomer Royal in 1720 at the age of 63, and commenced a programme of observation of the 19-year lunar cycle, a task that he completed successfully and which confirmed the secular acceleration of the Moon. Halley's celebrated friendship with *Newton* enabled him to persuade Newton to publish his *Principia* through the Royal Society, of which Halley was Clerk and Editor. When the Society was unable to finance the book Halley paid for its printing himself.

If his interests within astronomy were broad, so were his achievements in other branches of science. In 1686 he published the first map of the winds on the Earth's surface, and formulated a relationship between height and air pressure; between 1687 and 1694 he studied the evaporation and salinity of lakes, and drew conclusions about the age of the Earth; between

181

1698 and 1702 he conducted surveys of terrestrial magnetism and of the tides and coasts of the English Channel; in 1715 he correctly proposed that the salt in the sea came from river-borne land deposits. He realised that the aurora borealis was magnetic in origin, constructed the first mortality tables, improved understanding of the optics of rainbows, and estimated the size of the atom. If Halley was fortunate in his talents, wealth and personality, he certainly made good use of his assets.

HAMILTON, (Sir) William Rowan
1805-1865

Irish mathematician: a brilliant mathematician who invented quaternions and a new theory of dynamics

Hamilton was born in Dublin. His father, a solicitor, sent him to Trim to be raised by his aunt and an eccentric clergyman-linguist uncle when he was three. He showed an early and astonishing ability at languages (he had mastered 13 by age 13), and later also wrote rather bad poetry and corresponded with Wordsworth, Coleridge and Southey. At ten he developed an interest in the mathematical classics, including those by *Newton* and *Laplace*, and later went to Trinity College, Dublin. There he did original research on caustics (patterns produced by reflected light).

At Trinity College Hamilton was one of the very few people to have obtained the highest grade (optime) in two subjects: Greek and mathematical physics.

His work on caustics led to his discovery of the **law of least action**: for a light path the action is a simple function of its length, and the light travels along a line minimizing this. Such least action principles dependent on a function of the path taken can powerfully express many laws of physics previously given in more clumsy differential equation form.

At age 22 and before he graduated, Hamilton was appointed professor of astronomy at Dublin (1827) and made

Astronomer Royal of Ireland, so that he would be free to do research. He was not a good practical astronomer, despite engaging three of his many sisters to live at the Dunsink observatory to help him.

The field of complex numbers interested him, and he invented **quaternions**. From 1833 he had considered a+*i*b as an ordered pair (a,b) and considered how rotations in a plane were described by the algebra of such couples. The quaternion refers to a triple and describes rotations in three dimensions. This was an algebra in which (for the first time) the commutative principle that *ij=ji* broke down. For a quaternion

$a+bi+cj+dk$, $i^2=j^2=k^2=ijk=-1$ and $ij=-ji$.

Whilst important for the way that the concepts of algebra were generalized, the subject never had major uses in physics, which was better served by vector and tensor analysis.

In his later years Hamilton became a recluse, working and drinking excessively. His name remains familiar in the Hamiltonian operators of quantum mechanics.

HARDEN, (Sir) Arthur
1865-1940

English biochemist

Educated at Manchester and Erlangen, Harden worked at the Lister Institute throughout his career. He is best known for his work on the alcoholic fermentation of sugars which *Buchner* had shown could be brought about by a cell-free extract of yeast, which was thought to contain an enzyme 'zymase'. Harden showed that zymase is actually a mixture of enzymes, each a protein which catalyses one step in the multi-step conversion of sugar to ethanol; and that non-protein co-enzymes are also present in zymase and are essential for the process. He found that sugar phosphates are essential intermediates in fermentation; and that conversion of carbohydrate to lactic acid in muscle is intimately related to fermentation. These are both key matters in the development of biochemistry. Harden shared a Nobel Prize in 1929.

HARDY, Godfrey Harold
1877-1947

English mathematician: developed new work in analysis and number theory

Hardy was the son of an art teacher; he was a precocious child, whose tricks included factorizing hymn-numbers during sermons. His early mathematical ability won him a scholarship to Winchester School, and then another to Trinity College, Cambridge where he was elected a Fellow. In 1919 he became Savilian Professor of Geometry at Oxford, but returned in 1931 as professor of Pure Mathematics at Cambridge.

Hardy's early research was on particularly difficult integrals, and he also produced a new proof of the **prime number theorem**: that the number of primes not exceeding x approaches $x/\log_e x$ when x approaches infinity. He began to collaborate with his close friend J. E. Littlewood on research into the partitioning of numbers, on the Goldbach conjecture (that every even number is the sum of two prime numbers, still unproved) and later the *Riemann* zeta-function. Together they wrote nearly 100 papers during 35 years.

In 1908 Hardy and W. Weinberg discovered independently a law fundamental to population genetics. It describes the genetic equilibrium of a large random-mating population, and shows that the ratio of dominant to recessive genes does not vary down the generations. This was strong support for *Darwin's* theory of evolution by natural selection. It was Hardy's only venture into applied mathematics.

Hardy was an excellent teacher, and he introduced a modern rigorous approach to analysis. He encouraged the young Indian genius Srinivasa Ramanujan, bringing

him to Cambridge to do research. Hardy was a staunch anti-Christian, a firm friend of Bertrand Russell, and a passionate and talented cricketer and 'real tennis' player.

HARTMANN, Johannes Franz
1865-1936

German astronomer: discovered interstellar gas

In 1904 Hartmann discovered the first strong evidence for interstellar matter. While observing the spectrum of δ Orionis, a binary star, he noticed that the calcium lines were not Doppler-shifted like the other lines in its spectrum (as would be expected for an orbiting pair of stars). This must mean that the calcium lines must come from other gaseous matter between δ Orionis and Earth.

HARVEY, William
1578-1637

English physician: founded modern physiology by discovering circulation of the blood

Harvey was the eldest of seven sons in the close family of a yeoman farmer. After Cambridge he went to the greatest medical school of the time, at Padua, and studied there in 1600 under *Fabrizio*, who discovered but did not understand the valves in the veins. Back in London from 1602, Harvey was soon successful and was physician to James I (and later to Charles I) but his main interest was in research. By 1615 he had a clear idea of the circulation, but he continued to experiment on this. He did not publish his results until 1628 in the poorly printed slim book *On the Motions of the Heart and Blood*, usually known as *De motu cordis*, a short form of its Latin title. It is one of the great scientific classics. By dissection and experiment he had shown the valves in the heart, arteries and veins are one-way; that in systole the heart contracts as a muscular pump, expelling blood; that the right ventricle supplies the lungs and the left ventricle the rest of the arterial system; that blood flows through the veins towards the heart; these facts, and the quantity of blood pumped, led to his conclusion that 'therefore the blood must circulate'. This idea refuted the earlier views of *Galen* and others, and Harvey was ridiculed; but his work was accepted within his lifetime. He was not able to show how blood passed from the arterial to the venous system, as there are no connections visible to the eye. He supposed correctly that the connections must be too small to see; *Malpighi* observed them with a microscope soon after Harvey's death. Modern animal physiology begins with Harvey's work, which was as fundamental as *Newton*'s work on the solar system.

Harvey was an enthusiastic, cautious and skilful experimenter. Another area of his work was embryology; his book *On the Generation of Animals* (1651) describes his work on this, which was soon superseded by microscopic studies. His work on animal locomotion was not found until 1959.

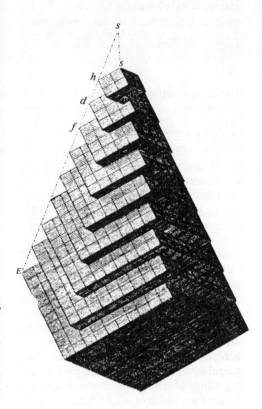

Haüy's drawing of a crystal built up of rhomboidal units

HAÜY, René Just
1743-1822

French mineralogist: founder of crystallography

Although Haüy's father was an impoverished clothworker, the boy's interest in church music secured an education for himself through the help of the church. He became a priest; and professor of mineralogy in Paris, in 1802. *Steno* had shown in 1670 that the angle between corresponding faces in the crystals of one substance is constant (irrespective of crystal size or habit), but he had not studied crystal cleavage. *Hooke* and also *Huygens* proposed that a crystal must be built of identical particles piled regularly 'like shot', or as *Newton* phrased it, 'in rank and file'. Haüy developed these ideas; he accidentally broke a calcite crystal and noted that the pieces were all rhombohedral, which implied a common underlying structure. He showed in 1784 that the faces of a calcite crystal might be formed by stacking cleavage rhombs regularly, if the rhombs are assumed to be so small that the face appears smooth (see diagram). Similar principles would lead to other crystal shapes built from appropriate structural units. In developed form, this is still the modern view.

As a priest, Haüy was in some danger in the French Revolution, but friends protected him; and Napoleon (the first world leader with a scientific or engineering training) appointed him to a post, and directed him to write a textbook of physics for general use.

HAWKING, Stephen William

1942-

English theoretical physicist: advanced understanding of space-time and space-time singularities

Hawking graduated from Oxford in physics and after a doctorate at Cambridge on relativity theory, remained there to become a Fellow of the Royal Society (1974) and Lucasian Professor of Mathematics (1979). He developed a highly disabling and progressive neuromotor disease whilst a student, limiting movement and speech. His mathematical work is carried out mentally and communicated when in a developed form. His life and work is an extraordinary conquest over severe physical disability.

Hawking began research on general relativity, recognizing that *Einstein*'s theory takes no account of the quantum mechanical nature of physics and is not adequately able to describe gravitational singularities such as 'black holes' or the big bang. In *The Large Scale Structure of Space-Time* (with G. F. R. Ellis, 1973) he

Stephen Hawking

showed that a space-time singularity must have occurred at the beginning of the universe and space-time itself, and this was the big bang (a point of indefinitely high density and space-time curvature). The universe has been expanding from this point ever since.

Hawking has greatly advanced our knowledge of black holes – these are singularities in space-time caused by sufficient mass to curve space-time enough to prevent the escape of light waves (photons). The boundary within which light cannot escape is called the event horizon and is given by the *Schwarzschild* radius. Hawking established that the event horizon can only increase or remain constant with time, so that if two black holes merge the new surface area is greater that the sum of that of the components. He showed that black hole mechanics have parallels with thermodynamic laws (in which entropy must increase with time). He also showed that black holes result not only from the collapse of stars, but also from the collapse of other highly compressed regions of space.

During 1970-74 Hawking and his associates proved J. Wheeler's conjecture (known as the **'no-hair theorem'**) that only mass, angular momentum and electric charge is conserved once matter enters a black hole.

In 1974 Hawking deduced the extraordinary result that black holes can emit thermal radiation. For example if a particle-antiparticle pair are created close to an event horizon, and only one falls inside, then the black hole has effectively emitted thermal radiation. A finite temperature can therefore be associated with a black hole, and the analogy between black hole mechanics and thermodynamics is real.

More recently Hawking has sought to produce a consistent quantum mechanical theory of gravity, which would also link it with the other three basic types of force (weak nuclear, strong nuclear, and electromagnetic interaction).

HEAVISIDE, Oliver

1850-1925

British physicist: developed theoretical basis of cable telegraphy

Lacking a university education, Heaviside worked initially as a telegraph operator until deafness forced him to stop. Unmarried, he lived with his parents, never obtained an academic position (although he received several honours), and eventually died in poverty.

Working alone, Heaviside developed much of the mathematics behind the theory of telegraphy and electric circuits, formulating the now familiar concepts of impedance, self-inductance and conductance, and using complex numbers in the analysis of alternating current networks many years before others did so. He showed how audio signals could be transmitted along cables without distortion, and proposed a method of using a single telephone line to carry several conversations simultaneously (multiplexing). Following *Marconi*'s success in transmitting radio signals across the Atlantic, he suggested (independently of A. E. Kennelly 1861-1939) that there had to be a reflecting layer in the upper atmosphere, otherwise the curvature of the Earth would have prohibited the signals from being received. The existence of the **Heaviside layer** was demonstrated experimentally over 20 years later by *Appleton*.

Although most of Heaviside's earlier work was ignored, leading him to become embittered and a recluse, his valuable contributions were later acknowledged, and he was elected an FRS in 1891. The last, unpublished, volume of his *Electromagnetic Theory* was torn up by burglars a few days after his death, but is known to have described a unified field theory combining electromagnetism and gravitation.

HEEZEN, Bruce Charles

1924-1977

American oceanographer: demonstrated existence of turbidity currents

Educated at Iowa State University and Columbia University, New York, Heezen worked at the Lamont-Doherty Geological Observatory at Columbia from 1948 until his death. In 1952 he used records of the times of the breakage of underwater communications cables off the Grand Banks, Newfoundland, during the 1929 Grand Banks earthquake to demonstrate that a sediment 'slump', or turbidity current, travelling at up to 85 km per hour, had taken place. Such turbidity currents transporting large amounts of sediment down the continental slope had previously been proposed as the cause of submarine canyons, but not observed. In 1957 Heezen and *Ewing* demonstrated the existence of a central rift in mid-ocean ridges.

HEISENBERG, Werner Karl

1901-1976

German physicist: developed quantum mechanics, and discovered the uncertainty principle

Heisenberg, son of a professor of Greek at the University of Munich, was educated at Munich and Göttingen. He worked with *Born* in Göttingen, and *Bohr* in Copenhagen. In 1927 he returned to a professorship in Germany at Leipzig.

Heisenberg was a major creative figure amongst those who revolutionized physics by quantum mechanics. At 24 he formulated a non-relativistic form of the theory of quantum mechanics, producing the **matrix mechanics** version, and received the 1932 Nobel Physics prize for this work. An equivalent theory called **wave mechanics** was produced independently by *Schrödinger* in 1925 and they were shown to be equivalent by *von Neumann*.

Heisenberg broke away from the visual concept of the atom, and avoided problems such as the apparent wave-particle duality, by considering only observable quantities of the atom as 'real'. He separated in the theory the system of interest, and operations on that system, to produce an observable quantity. Respectively these were expressed as a matrix, and a mathematical operation on the matrix to give a value. He used the theory to predict successfully the observed frequencies and intensities of atomic and molecular spectral lines. He concluded that two forms of molecular hydrogen, called ortho- and para-hydrogen, exist with their nuclear spins aligned in the former and opposed in the latter.

In 1927 Heisenberg discovered a further aspect of quantum mechanics, the **principle of uncertainty**; that it is impossible to determine exactly both the position and momentum of a particle simultaneously. The uncertainty in position $\triangle x$ and in momentum $\triangle p$ obey $\triangle x \triangle p \geqslant h/4\pi$ where h is the Planck constant. This relation removed absolute determinacy, or cause and effect, from physics for the first time and replaced it with a statistical probability. This deeply troubled *Einstein* and some others, but is now generally accepted. *Laplace*'s claim that the future of the Universe could in principle be deduced from the position and velocity of all particles if given at one instant was rejected. For example: to try to locate the accurate position of an electron, radiation of short wavelength (such as gamma rays) might be bounced off it. However, such energetic rays will radically alter the electron's momentum on collision, so that certainty in its position is attempted at the expense of that in momentum. In 1932, after *Chadwick* had discovered the neutron, Heisenberg proposed that a nucleus of protons and neutrons was a more satisfactory model than one of protons and electrons, as had been assumed. The components of the nucleus should be held together by quantum mechanical exchange forces, which was later confirmed by *Yukawa's* theory of the strong nuclear interaction by which pi-mesons were exchanged. Later Heisenberg put forward a unified field theory of elementary particles (1966) which received little general support.

During the Nazi period, Heisenberg chose to remain and preserve the German scientific tradition, though he was not a Nazi supporter. He was attacked by the Nazis for refusing to reject in any way Einstein's physics. As a consequence he lost the chance of the professorship at Munich in 1935 as *Sommerfeld*'s successor. During the war Heisenberg was called to lead the atomic energy and weapons programme, becoming director of the Kaiser Wilhelm Institute, Berlin in 1941. After the war he helped establish the Max Planck Institute at Göttingen, and moved with it to Munich in 1955 as its director.

Heisenberg's wartime role is controversial. He claimed to have had no intention of allowing an atomic bomb to reach Hitler's hands, and stated that in such a key role he could have diverted the programme if it ever neared success. He claimed to have revealed this to *Bohr* in 1941, but Bohr has said that he failed to understand Heisenberg's guarded comments. The weapon was not produced by Germany probably because of a higher priority for planes and flying bombs.

HELMHOLTZ, Hermann (Ludwig Ferdinand von)

1821-1894

German physicist and physiologist: a discoverer of the law of conservation of energy; achieved major results in theories of electricity and magnetism, and on the physiology of vision and hearing

Helmholtz must be the most versatile scientist of his century; he did first-class work in physics and physiology, both theoretical and experimental, and he was no mean mathematician. He has been claimed to be the last scholar whose work ranged over the sciences, philosophy, and the arts. He believed that his diversity of interests was helpful to him in giving novel viewpoints in his researches.

As a child he was 'delicate' and often ill, but his parents did their best to amuse him. At school he found he did badly at memory work and rote-learning, but he enjoyed the logic of geometry and was delighted by physics. However, his father knew of no way of studying physics except as a medical student, for which he could get a university grant, provided he followed it by some service as an army surgeon. He must have done well as a medical student at Berlin, because after a short time as an army surgeon he became professor of physiology at Königsberg and later at Bonn and Heidelberg, and of physics at Berlin.

He was 26 and working in medicine when he published his pamphlet 'On the Conservation of Force' in 1847; his ideas in it on the Law of Conservation of Energy were much more precise than the ideas on the law given by J. R. Mayer, and more wide-ranging than those of *Joule*; Helmholtz gave examples of the law in mechanics, heat, electricity and chemistry, with numerical values.

By 1850 he had moved to physiological optics and colour vision. An early success for him in this area was his invention of the **ophthalmoscope** for viewing the human retina. (*Babbage* had invented a

Hermann von Helmholtz aged about 26

similar device three years earlier, but his medical friends failed to use it). Helmholtz was more successful, and his device not only revolutionized the study of diseases of the eye but also was of value to physicians generally, in giving the only direct view of the circulatory system. His study of the sense organs was continued in work on the ear and the mechanism of hearing, where he argued that the cochlea resonates for different frequencies and analyses complex sounds; and he developed a theory on the nature of harmony and musical sound (he was a skilful musician).

Earlier he had worked on the speed of nerve impulses and showed that this was of the order of a tenth of the speed of sound. He was a masterly experimenter, but in later life he gave up physiology for physics and became more interested in theoretical work, including *Maxwell*'s on electromagnetic radiation. He encouraged his pupil and friend *Hertz* to work in this area, with important results; Hertz discovered radio waves in 1888. Other pupils included *Boltzmann* and *Michelson*; he had a great many pupils, his fame as a physicist compared with that of his friend *Kelvin* in England, and in Germany he was said to be 'the most illustrious man next to Bismarck and the old Emperor'.

HELMONT, Jan Baptista van

*c.*1579-1644

Belgian alchemist, chemist and physiologist: made early studies of conservation of matter

A member of a noble and wealthy family, Helmont studied the classics, theology and medicine before turning 'for seven years to chemistry and the relief of the poor'. He believed in alchemy, but his own work represents a transition to chemistry proper. He used a chemical balance, and understood clearly the law of indestructibility of matter (e.g., that metals, dissolved in acid, can be recovered). He knew a fair range of inorganic

J. B. van Helmont

salts, and the acids H_2SO_4 and HNO_3. He believed that all matter was based on two elements or principles, air and water. In an experiment on this, he grew a willow tree for five years, when its weight increased from 5 to 169 pounds; the earth it had grown in had hardly lost weight, and he had given the tree only rainwater. So in his view the tree (and presumably all vegetation) was made of water. He was half-correct (willow is about 50% water); but he failed to realise that the plant had taken in CO_2 from the air. He studied gases (he was the first to use the word gas, based on the Greek *chaos*) but he had no method of collecting them; and better distinctions between different gases had to wait for *Priestley*'s work. He had rather confused ideas on animal digestion, but in directing thought to animal chemistry his views were valuable.

HENDERSON, Thomas
1798-1844

Scottish astronomer: first measured stellar parallax

Henderson was a legal clerk and amateur astronomer who became director of the Cape of Good Hope Observatory in 1831. He was the first to detect and measure the parallax of a star, α Centauri, in 1832. (α Centauri is actually three stars, and at four light years distance, is still the closest star system to us). Unfortunately, his hesitation in publishing his discovery before he had thoroughly checked his result meant that *Bessel*, who in 1838 made similar measurements on 61 Cygni, received most of the credit for the first determination of a stellar distance.

HENRY, Joseph
1797-1878

American physicist: pioneer of electromagnetism

Strangely, no American after *Franklin* did much for the study of electricity for 75 years, when Henry did a great deal. In many ways Henry is the traditional American of folklore; tall, handsome and healthy, he was still a strenuous researcher at 80. Growing up in Albany in New York State with a widowed mother, he was not fond of schoolwork, and at 15 was apprenticed to a watchmaker but the business soon failed. For a year he wrote plays and acted in them, and then by chance read a book on science which reshaped his life. He attended the Albany Academy, did well, and spent a period as a road engineer before taking a job as teacher of mathematics at the Academy, researching on electricity in his spare time. His research gave him enough reputation to secure a post at the College of New Jersey (which became Princeton) in 1832, teaching a full range of sciences.

In 1825 *Sturgeon*, a London bootmaker and itinerant science lecturer, devised an electromagnet, with a varnished soft iron core wrapped by separate strands of uninsulated wire. Henry in 1829 much improved this by using many turns of thin, insulated, wire. (He supervised the making of one at Yale in 1831 which would lift a tonne.) Also in 1831 he made the first reciprocating electric motor, as 'a philosophic toy'. Like his magnets it was powered by batteries, his only source of current. He had wire in plenty, from an unknown source, and used miles of it. In 1830 he discovered electromagnetic induction, 'the conversion of magnetism into electricity'. *Faraday* also discovered it independently soon after, and published first. However, Henry in 1832 was the first to discover and to publish on self-induction, and the unit is named after him. A coil has a self-inductance of one **henry** (H) if the back EMF in it is one volt when the current through it is changing at one ampere per second. In 1835 he introduced the relay which made long-distance electric telegraphy practical, an important step in North America.

When he was 49, Henry became first director of the Smithsonian Institution. This had a curious history. James Smithson was an unrecognized bastard son of the Duke of Northumberland. Resentful of his position, he was determined that 'my name shall live in the memory of man when the Northumberlands . . . are extinct and forgotten' and he therefore left a large fortune to go to the US (with which he had no links of any kind) to found 'an Establishment for the increase and diffusion of knowledge'. Henry shaped it well; it became 'the incubator of American science' and he was the model administrator. A strict Calvinist, he resisted patents or wealth for himself and refused for 32 years to increase his salary of $3500.

HENRY, William
1774-1836

English chemist: discovered law of gas solubility

Henry was the third and most successful son of Thomas Henry, whose profitable ventures in chemistry had included the early use of chlorine for bleaching textiles, the preparation and use of bleaching powder (Cl_2 absorbed in lime) as a useful alternative to the gas, and the making of

'calcined magnesia' (i.e., $Mg(OH)_2$) for medicinal use. Young William was injured by a falling beam at the age of ten; the injuries gave him ill health and pain throughout his life, and he finally killed himself. He qualified in medicine in 1807, but his research was mainly in chemistry. He is now best known for **Henry's law**, which states that the mass of a gas dissolved by a given volume of a solvent, at a constant temperature, is directly proportional to the pressure of gas with which the solvent is in equilibrium. The law holds well only for slightly soluble gases at low pressures.

Henry was a close friend of *Dalton*, but despite superior skill and range as an experimenter, lacked his friend's boldness as a theorist, and never committed himself to the atomic theory whose birth he had assisted.

HERMITE, Charles
1822-1901

French mathematician: developed theory of hyperelliptic functions and solved the general quintic equation

Hermite had an inability to pass examinations, and congenital lameness, but he greatly influenced his generation of mathematicians. Having entered and then been dismissed from the École Polytechnique, Hermite finally, but only just, graduated at 25; by then he was clearly an innovative mathematician. He gained a teaching post at the Collège de France, was elected to the Paris Academy of Sciences (1856) and immediately caught smallpox. Recovering, he eventually received a professorship at the École Normale (1869) and the Sorbonne (1870).

Hermite's creative work included extending *Abel*'s theorem on elliptic functions to hyperelliptic functions, and using elliptic functions to give a solution of the general equation of the fifth degree, the quintic (1878). He proved that the number e is transcendental (that is, not a solution of any algebraic equation with rational coefficients) and used the techniques of analysis in number theory. He set out the theory of **Hermite polynomials** (1873) which are polynomial functions now much used in quantum mechanics, and of **Hermitian forms**, which are a complex generalization of quadratic forms.

Hermite was kindly, encouraging and appreciative towards colleagues and students; he was an idealist who possessed a 'serene beauty of spirit'.

HERO (of Alexandria)
lived *c*.62 AD

Greek physicist: invented steam powered engine

Apart from writings ascribed to him, nothing is known of Hero. Some have argued that he had little scientific knowledge, and was simply a recorder of ingenious devices, but recent study shows him to have grasped all the mathematics of his time. His books *Pneumatics* and *Mechanics* make it clear that he was a teacher of physics, and these and other books survey the knowledge and devices known in his day, including pumps, siphons, a turbine, a coin-operated machine, and surveying instruments. He devised **Hero's engine** in which steam emitted by two nozzles facing in opposite directions caused rotation.

HERSCHEL, (Sir) (Frederick) William
1738-1822

German-British astronomer: discovered Uranus, the Sun's intrinsic motion through space, and the true nature of the Milky Way

Herschel followed his father in becoming a musician in the Hanoverian Guards, entering as an oboist at 14. At 19 he went to England, working as a freelance musician before appointment as an organist in Bath. He was a keen amateur telescope maker and observer. His sister Caroline joined him in Bath in 1772.

Herschel's first important discovery was the planet Uranus in 1781. This achieve-ment, helped by his desire to name it after George III, resulted in his appointment the following year as Court Astronomer. This enabled him to finance the construction of a reflecting telescope 20 feet in length and with an aperture of 20 inches, with which he was to make many further discoveries. In 1787 he found two satellites of Uranus, Titania and Oberon, and soon afterwards two of Saturn, Mimas and Enceladus. In 1783 he discovered the intrinsic motion of the Sun through space by careful analysis of the proper motions of seven bright stars, showing them to converge towards a point. He had a special interest in double stars, cataloguing 800 of them and discovering in 1793 that many were in relative orbital motion. In 1820 he published a catalogue of over 5000 nebulae (a task that his son, John, was to continue in the southern hemisphere). He was the first to recognize the true nature of the Milky Way as a galaxy by counting the number of stars visible in different directions, finding that the greatest number lie in the galactic plane, and the least toward the celestial poles. Investigating the effect of parts of the Sun's spectrum on a thermometer, he discovered infra-red radiation, outside the visible range.

Caroline Herschel (1750-1848) trained as a concert singer before joining her brother in England. She began as his housekeeper, and became his astronomical assistant and co-worker. When not in these roles she was an enthusiastic observer on her own account, with a particular interest in comets (she discovered eight new comets).

HERSCHEL, (Sir) John (Frederick William)
1792-1871

British astronomer and physicist: surveyor of the southern sky

Although Herschel's father Sir William, the 'gauger of the heavens' did much notable scientific work, his only child John did more and ranged outside his father's astronomical interests. His famous father was rather overwhelming, but his close friendship with his Aunt Caroline ended only with her death at 98.

He graduated from Cambridge in mathematics in 1813 with the highest distinction, and then promptly began to study law, but physics soon attracted him and his home experiments with polarized light gave some valuable results; he also deduced that polarized light should be rotated by an electric field, as was later confirmed experimentally by *Faraday*. From 1816 he assisted his father in the study of double stars and nebulae and then decided to extend their survey of the sky to the Southern Hemisphere. He arrived at the Cape in 1834, accompanied by his young and glamorous wife, two large telescopes, a mechanic and a children's nurse, and in four years of energetic work did much to map the southern sky. He worked in meteorology and in geophysics and planned *Sir J. Ross's* geomagnetic survey of the Antarctic. He was an expert chemist, and major contributions to early work on photography are due to him; he devised a sensitized paper, introduced 'hypo' as a fixing agent, and was a pioneer in astronomical photography. In 1839 he made the first photograph on a glass plate, prepared the first coloured photographs of the Sun's spectrum, and introduced the words 'negative' and 'positive' into photography. In 1850 he became Master of the Mint, a strange move dictated either by financial need or because of *Newton's* example; he did the job well but without enjoyment for five years. At his death he was 'mourned by the whole nation, as a great scientist and one of the last of the universalists'.

HERSHEY, Alfred Day

1908-

American biologist: demonstrated information-carrying capability of bacteriophage DNA

A graduate of Michigan State College,

Hershey taught at Washington University, St Louis, until 1950, and then worked at the Carnegie Institution of Washington. His best-known work was done in the early 1950s with Martha Chase, when they proved that DNA is the genetic material of bacteriophage (the virus which infects bacteria). They used phage in which the DNA core had been labelled with radioactive phosphorus, and the protein coat of the phage was labelled with radioactive sulphur. The work showed that when phage attacks a bacterial cell it injects the DNA into it, leaving the protein coat on the outside; but the injected DNA causes production of new phage, complete with protein. The DNA must carry the information leading to the formation of the entire phage particle. *Avery* had been cautious on the status of DNA as an information-carrier; Hershey proved it. Hershey was a phage expert already, having shown that spontaneous mutations occurred in it in 1945. He shared a Nobel Prize in 1969.

HERTZ, Heinrich Rudolph

1857-1894

German physicist: discovered radio waves

Hertz studied at the universities of Munich and Berlin, the latter under *Helmholtz*, whom he served as an assistant. In 1885 he was appointed professor of physics at Karlsruhe Technical College, and later held a professorship at the University of Bonn.

Influenced by Helmholtz and by *Maxwell's* electromagnetic theory, he was the first to demonstrate the existence of radio waves, generated by an electric spark. In 1888 he showed that electromagnetic waves were emitted by the spark, and could be detected by a tuned electric circuit up to 20 m away. Further experiments demonstrated that the waves, which had a wavelength of about a foot, could be reflected (from the laboratory walls), refracted (through a huge prism of pitch), polarized (by a wire mesh) and diffracted (by a screen with a hole in it) in the same way as light, and travelled at the same speed. This was an important verification of Maxwell's ideas. Hertz also discovered in 1887 that an electric spark occurs more readily when the electrodes are irradiated with ultraviolet light (the **Hertz effect**), a consequence of the photoelectric effect. Hertz died at 36 (from blood poisoning), and did not live long enough to see *Marconi* turn radio transmission into a means of worldwide communication. The SI unit of frequency, the **hertz** (one cycle per second), is named in his honour.

HERTZSPRUNG, Ejnar
1873-1967

Danish astronomer: discovered stellar spectral type/luminosity relationship

Trained as a chemical engineer, Hertzsprung did research in photochemistry before appointment as an astronomer at the Potsdam Observatory in 1909. His work on photography led to his success in classifying stars. Hertzsprung was the first to realise that there was a relationship between the spectral colour of stars and their luminosity; for most stars the more blue the colour, the brighter the star. He also found that a small proportion of stars did not fit this pattern, being far brighter than might be expected for their colour. These two groups are now called main sequence stars (the numerous faint dwarfs), and red giants (fewer, more luminous), respectively. His results were published in 1905 and 1907 in obscure journals. Independently, in 1913, *Russell* came to the same conclusions, the usual representation of their results being known as the **Hertzsprung-Russell diagram**. This discovery had a great effect on ideas about stellar evolution.

His second important achievement was to utilize the period-luminosity relationship of Cepheid variable stars, discovered by *Henrietta Leavitt* in 1912, as a means of calculating stellar distances. In 1913 Hertzsprung was able to determine the distance of some nearby Cepheids from their proper motion (the only method available for measuring stellar distance up to that time), and using Leavitt's results he began to calibrate the Cepheid variable technique. These first measurements of distances outside our galaxy were developed by *Shapley*. Hertzsprung was an active researcher until he was over 90.

HERZBERG, Gerhard
1904-

German-Canadian physical chemist: devised methods of analysing electronic spectra to detect new molecules and to find molecular dimensions

Born and educated in Germany, Herzberg taught at Darmstadt from 1930 until 1935 when he emigrated to Canada. For 20 years until 1969 he was head of the physics division for the National Research Council in Ottawa, which he made into a centre of international renown in spectroscopy. He developed and used spectroscopic methods for a variety of purposes; including the measurement of energy levels in simple atoms and molecules for use in testing theories of their structure: and for the detection of unusual molecules and radicals, some of which could be detected by flash photolysis in the laboratory, and others by astrophysical methods (for example CH and CH$^+$ in interstellar space, and the flexible C_3 in comets). For his work on the electronic structure and geometry of molecules, particularly free radicals, he was awarded the Nobel Prize for chemistry in 1971.

HESS, Germain Henri
1802-1850

Swiss-Russian chemist: pioneer of thermochemistry

When Hess was three years old his father, a Swiss artist, became tutor to a rich

Moscow family, and the boy moved from his birthplace (Geneva) to Russia. He was there for the rest of his life, taking a medical degree at Tartu in 1825, and then visiting *Berzelius* in Stockholm. The visit was only for a month, but its influence was permanent. From 1830 he studied the heat evolved in chemical reactions, as a route to the understanding of 'chemical affinity'. Rather little had been done in thermochemistry since the work by *Lavoisier* and *Laplace*. **Hess's law (the law of constant heat summation)** of 1840 states that the heat change accompanying a chemical reaction depends only on the final and initial states of the system, and is independent of all intermediate states. The law enables the heat of reaction to be calculated in a case where direct measurement is impractical. Hess's law follows from the law of conservation of energy, but the latter was not clearly understood in 1840.

Hess researched in other areas, and did much for the development of chemistry in Russia, where he taught in St Petersburg.

HESS, Harry Hammond

1906-1969

American geologist and geophysicist: proposed sea-floor spreading hypothesis

Hess spent most of his academic life at Princeton University, moving there in 1934. During World War II he distinguished himself in the US Navy by conducting echo-sounding work in the Pacific, during which he discovered a large number of strikingly flat-topped seamounts, which he interpreted as sunken islands, naming them guyots (after Arnold Guyot (1807-1884), an earlier Princeton geologist).

Following the war there was a great increase in knowledge about the sea bed, and it became apparent that parts of the ocean floor were anomalously young. In 1962, following the discovery of the global

extent of the mid-ocean ridges and their central rift valleys by *Ewing*, Hess proposed his **sea-floor spreading hypothesis** to account for these facts. He suggested that material was continuously rising from the Earth's mantle to create the mid-ocean ridges, which then spread out horizontally to form new oceanic crust; the further from the mid-ocean ridge, therefore, the older the crust would be. He envisaged that this process would continue as far as the continental margin, where the oceanic crust would sink beneath the lighter continental crust into a subduction zone, the whole process thus forming a kind of giant conveyor belt. Palaeomagnetic and oceanographic work, notably by *Matthews* and *Vine*, have subsequently confirmed the hypothesis. Later, as chairman of the Space Science Board of the National Academy of Sciences, Hess also had an influential effect on the American space programme.

HESS, Victor Francis

1883-1964

Austrian-American physicist: discovered cosmic rays

Son of a forester, Hess was educated at Graz, receiving his doctorate in 1906. He worked on radioactivity at Vienna until 1920, and afterwards at Graz, New Jersey and Innsbruck. In 1931 he set up a cosmic ray observatory on the Hafelekar mountain. When the Nazis occupied Austria in 1938 Hess was dismissed, as his wife was Jewish, and he became professor of physics at Fordham University, New York City.

In 1910 T. Wulf measured the background radioactivity of the atmosphere at the top of the 300 m Eiffel Tower with a simple electroscope, and showed that it was greater than at ground level, indicating that it came from an extraterrestrial source; but the results were not conclusive. A. Gockel in 1912 also used the rate of discharge of a gold-leaf electroscope to measure the radioactive ionization of the air, this time from a balloon; again the results were inconclusive. However in 1911-12 Hess made ten balloon flights and showed that the ionization is four times greater at 5000 m than at ground level. Night ascents and an ascent during an eclipse of the Sun in 1912 showed that the radiation could not be from the Sun. *Millikan* in 1925 named these high-energy particles 'cosmic rays'. Their study led to *Anderson*'s discoveries of the positron and muon, and *Powell*'s discovery of the pi-meson. Hess shared the 1936 Nobel Prize for physics with Anderson.

HESS, Walter Rudolf
1881-1973

Swiss neurophysiologist: showed that localized areas in the brain control specific functions

Hess studied medicine at five universities in Switzerland and Germany and became a specialist ophthalmologist, but gave up this career to work in physiology, and from 1917-51 headed physiology in the university of Zürich. The precision surgery he had learned as an ophthalmologist was to prove useful; in the 1920s he began his study of the autonomic nervous system, which controls involuntary functions such as breathing, blood pressure, temperature, and digestion.

It was already known roughly which parts of the brain are involved in this control; but Hess made this knowledge much more precise. He used cats into which, under anaesthetic, a fine insulated wire with a bare end was inserted so that the end was located at a defined point in the midbrain. When the animal was again conscious, a very small current was passed into the wire. Hess found that by this stimulation of small groups of cells in the midbrain he could induce a variety of reactions, including sleep, rage, evacuation, and changes in blood pressure and respiration. Similarly, in the hypotha-

lamus he located centres which appeared to control other parts of the sympathetic and parasympathetic components of the autonomic system. This influential work led to detailed mapping of the brain and began to relate physiology to psychiatry. He shared a Nobel Prize in 1949.

HEVESY, György
1885-1966

Hungarian-Swedish radiochemist: introduced use of radioactive 'tracers' in analysis

Hevesy was a highly mobile chemist; he worked in at least nine research centres in seven countries. His visit to work with *Rutherford* in Manchester (1911-13) established his interest in radiochemistry. While there he found that ordinary lead and radioactive 'radium-D' are chemically inseparable; later it was realised that radium-D is an isotope of lead, with relative atomic mass 210 and which happens to be radioactive. So very small amounts of lead can be 'traced' by mixing into the lead some radium-D and then taking advantage of the fact that minute levels of radioactive material are easily located by using a counter, or by photography. In this way Hevesy and F. A. Paneth in 1913 were able to find the solubility in water of lead sulphide and lead chromate; both are insufficiently soluble for traditional methods to measure their solubility accurately. In 1934 he used a stable but trackable isotope (deuterium) in heavy water, D_2O, to measure the water-exchange between goldfish and their surroundings. Also in 1934 he used radiophosphorus to locate phosphate absorption in human tissue. The technique has since been much used, and suitable '**marker**' isotopes for use as tracers are now widely available. In 1935 he devised a variant of this, activation analysis.

In 1922 *Bohr* predicted the existance of a new element, and suggested Hevesy should look for it in zirconium ore. Working with D. Coster who had experience of *Moseley*'s X-ray method, Hevesy found the new element (atomic number 72) and it was named hafnium (Hf). He was awarded a Nobel Prize in 1943 for his work on tracers.

HEWISH, Antony

1924-

British radio astronomer: identified first pulsar

Hewish studied physics at Cambridge and worked with *Ryle* on radio telescopes. He became particularly interested in the scintillation of quasars, the radio equivalent of twinkling stars, and used this to examine the solar wind and clouds in interplanetary space.

In 1967 he completed a radio telescope of unusual design for further work on scintillation. Together with his student *Bell*, he discovered remarkably regular pulsed signals coming from a tiny star within our galaxy; they had found the first pulsar. Many other pulsars have since been found, and are believed to be rapidly rotating neutron stars, typically only ten miles in diameter, which emit beamed radiation like a lighthouse. Hewish was awarded the Nobel Prize for physics for this discovery in 1974.

Antony Hewish (*left*) and Martin Ryle

HEYROVSKY, Jaroslav

1890-1967

Czech physical chemist: inventor of polarography

Heyrovsky studied physical science at Prague, and in 1910 came to London as a research student in physical chemistry. It was then that he began work on polarography, but this was interrupted by World War I and the method was perfected by him in Prague in the 1920s. It is an electrochemical method of analysis, applicable to ions or molecules which can be electrolytically oxidized or reduced in solution using mercury electrodes. By plotting the voltage as current curve (a polarogram) as the voltage between the electrodes is increased, different species are revealed as steps in the curve. The method is able to analyse several substances in one solution, and is capable of high sensitivity. He won a Nobel Prize in 1959.

HILBERT, David

1862-1943

German mathematician: originated the concept of Hilbert space

Hilbert was educated at the universities of Königsberg and Heidelberg, spending short periods also in Paris and Leipzig. After six years as a privatdozent (unsalaried lecturer) at Königsberg he became a professor there in 1892. In 1895 he was given the prestigious chair in mathematics at Göttingen, which he retained until 1930. He was a talented, lucid, teacher and the university became a major focus of mathematical research. Hilbert contributed to analysis, topology, geometry, philosophy and mathematical physics and became recognized as one of the greatest mathematicians in history.

His earliest research was on algebraic invariants, and he both created a general theory and completed it by solving the central problems. This work led to a new and fruitful approach to algebraic number theory, and this was the subject of his masterly book *Der Zahlbericht* (Number Information) (1897). He gathered and reorganized number theory, and included many new and fundamental results; this became the basis for the later development of class-field theory.

Abandoning number theory whilst many problems remained, Hilbert wrote another classic, *Grundlagen der Geometrie* (Foundations of Geometry) in 1899. It contains fewer innovations, but describes the geometry of the 19th century, using algebra to build a system of abstract but rigorous axiomatic principles. Later Hilbert developed work on logic and consistency proofs from this. Most important of all he developed within topology (using his theory of invariants) the concept of an infinite-dimensional space where distance is preserved by making the sum of squares of co-ordinates a convergent series. This is now called **Hilbert space**, and is much used in pure mathematics, and in classical and quantum field theory. His ideas on operators in Hilbert space prepared the way for *Weyl, Schrödinger, Heisenberg* and *Dirac*.

Hilbert's book also gave rise to the **'Hilbert programme'** of building mathematics axiomatically and using algebraic models rather than intuition. Whilst a productive controversy arose greatly influencing mathematical philosophy and logic, this formalistic approach was later displaced by *Gödel's* work. Hilbert's views on proof theory were later developed by G. Gentzen. In 1900 Hilbert proposed 23 unsolved problems to the International Congress of Mathematicians in Paris. The mathematics created in the solution of many of these problems has shown Hilbert's profound insight into the subject.

HINSHELWOOD, (Sir) Cyril (Norman)

1897-1967

English physical chemist: applied kinetic studies to a variety of problems

Hinshelwood's career, except for war service from 1916 working on explosives in an ordnance factory, was spent almost entirely in Oxford. His early research, developed from his war work, was on the explosion of solids, but he soon turned his interest to explosive gas reactions. In the 1920s he made a close study of the reaction of hydrogen with oxygen, which was a model for such research, and led to a shared Nobel prize in 1956. He also studied the rates and catalytic effects in other gas reactions, and reactions in the liquid phase. His later work applied the ideas of chemical kinetics to the growth of bacterial cells. In 1950 he made the suggestion, little noticed at the time, that in the synthesis of protein in living cells it is nucleic acid which guides the order in which amino acids are linked to form protein. The suggestion was correct.

Hinshelwood was an expert linguist and classical scholar, and was simultaneously president of both the Royal Society and the Classical Association; the only man, to date, to hold both offices. His own paintings were given a London exhibition a year after his death; and he was an expert collector of Chinese ceramics.

HIPPARCHUS (of Rhodes)

*c.*170-*c.*125 BC

Greek astronomer and geographer: discovered precession of the equinoxes, constructed the first star catalogue, and invented trigonometry

Stimulated by the observation of a new star in 134 BC, Hipparchus constructed a catalogue of about 850 stars, and was the first to assign a scale of 'magnitudes' to indicate their apparent luminosity, the brightest being first magnitude and the faintest visible to the naked eye being sixth magnitude. His scale, much refined, is still used. Comparison with earlier records of star positions led him to the realization that the equinoxes grew progressively earlier in relation to the sidereal year. (The equinoxes are the twice-yearly

197

times when day and night are of equal length; they are the points where the ecliptic, the Sun's path, crosses the celestial equator). He evaluated the amount of precession as 45 seconds of arc per year, and determined the length of the sidereal and tropical years, the latter accurate to within six minutes. Hipparchus suggested improved methods of determining latitude and longitude on the Earth's surface, following the work of *Eratosthenes*. He constructed a table of chords, a precursor of the sine, and is therefore credited with the invention of trigonometry. All his major writing is lost, but his work was preserved and developed by *Ptolemy*.

HIPPOCRATES (of Cos)

c. 460-370 BC

Greek physician: traditional founder of clinical medicine

Little is known of his life with any certainty, except that he taught at Cos, travelled widely, and had exceptional fame in his lifetime. The many writings under his name must include work by others, since over 100 years separate the earliest and the latest books in the 'collection'. The best of them represent a stage where medicine was emerging from a magical and religious basis, and was seeking to become rational and scientific in its approach to diagnosis, prognosis and treatment. Success in this attempt was limited, but for nearly 2000 years no better work was done; like *Aristotle*'s work, Hippocratic ideas were to dominate their field and become sanctified by time. Many diseases listed in the Hippocratic Collection were ascribed to imbalance of the four 'humours' of the body; and treatment was largely restricted to rest, diet and exercise, rather than drugs. His case histories are admirably concise, and many of his descriptions and comments are still valid.

HIS, Wilhelm

1831-1904

Swiss anatomist and physiologist: introduced the microtome

His qualified in medicine in 1855, and became professor of anatomy at Basle and later at Leipzig. His great practical innovation was the microtome for cutting very thin serial sections for microscopy (1866). He used it especially in his study of embryos; he gave the first accurate description of the human embryo. His son, also Wilhelm, first described the specialized bundles of fibres in the heart, 'the bundles of His', which are part of its electrical conducting mechanism.

HITCHINGS, George Herbert

1905-

American pharmacologist: deviser of new drugs

Educated at Washington and Harvard, Hitchings worked in universities for nine years before he joined the Wellcome company in 1942 and spent his main career there. He has been notably successful in devising new drugs; in 1942 he began a programme of pharmacological study of the long-known group of purine compounds, which had first been made from uric acid and whose chemistry had been intensively examined by *Baeyer* and *E. Fischer*. Hitchings argued that the place of the purines in cell metabolism could lead to their use in the control of disease, and his approach was well rewarded. In 1951 his group made and tested 6-mercaptopurine (6MP) and found it to inhibit DNA synthesis, and therefore cell division; it proved useful in the treatment of some types of cancer, especially leukaemia. Further work on it showed in 1959 that it inhibited production of antibodies in the rabbit; and a related compound (Imuran) was used from 1960 to control rejection in kidney transplantation, where the normal body processes would treat the transplant as a foreign protein and form antibodies against it. The work on 6MP also led Hitchings to the discovery of allopurinol, which blocks uric acid production in the body and which therefore forms an effective treatment for gout (which is due to uric acid deposition in the joints). Other drugs introduced by Hitchings include the antimalarial Daraprim and the antibacterial Trimethoprim.

HITZIG, Eduard
1838-1907

German psychiatrist and physiologist

Although *Flourens* had shown in 1824 that removal of parts of the brain in animals led to loss of functions such as sight, he did not experiment on the effect of electrical stimulation of the brain, and it was not seen as a source of muscular action. Hitzig, working as a psychiatrist in Zürich, reported in 1870 that electrical stimulation of points in the cerebral cortex of a dog produced specific movements in the opposite side of its body. With G. T. Fritsch he identified five such centres in the region now called the motor-area, and such studies to relate movement to a map of the brain were continued by him and others into the 20th century. Hitzig was less successful in his attempts to identify the site of abstract intelligence in the frontal lobes of the brain.

HODGKIN, (Sir) Alan Lloyd
1914-

English neuro-physiologist: major contributor to understanding of nerve impulses

As a student of biology and chemistry in Cambridge, Hodgkin became interested in the basis of nervous conduction, and he found by accident that it was easy to obtain single nerve fibres from a shore crab and these could be used in experiments despite their small size (diameter about 1/30 mm). In the US in 1938 he was impressed by the possibility of using larger nerve fibres from the squid. Some squids (the genus *Loligo*) are half a metre long and highly active, and have giant nerve fibres up to one mm in diameter.

It had long been known that a nerve impulse is electrical and that a major nerve fibre (axon) acts as a cable, but detailed knowledge was much advanced by the work of Hodgkin and his colleagues, especially A. F. Huxley. Their study of the squid axon began in 1939, was interrupted by their war service, and continued after 1945. They were able to insert a fine micro-electrode into an axon, and place a second electrode on the outer surface of its surrounding membrane. Even in a resting state there is a potential difference between the electrodes; the negative 'inside' has a resting potential compared with the positive exterior surface. When an impulse passes, this is reversed by the action potential for about a millisecond; the nerve impulse is a wave of depolarization passing along the axon. Hodgkin developed a detailed theory of the origin of this membrane potential, relating it to the presence of sodium and potassium ions and their distribution across the membrane. This knowledge of the biophysics of nervous conduction is basic to further understanding of the nervous system, and Hodgkin and Huxley shared a Nobel Prize in 1963 with J. C. Eccles, who also worked on nerve transmission. Hodgkin became President of the Royal Society in 1970, and Master of Trinity College, Cambridge, in 1978.

HODGKIN, Dorothy Crowfoot
1910-

British X-ray crystallographer: applied X-ray crystal analysis to complex biochemical molecules

Dorothy Crowfoot was born in Cairo, where her father worked in the Education Service. Soon he moved to the Sudan, to become Director of both Education and Antiquities; she retained always an interest in the region and in archaeology. From

Dorothy Crowfoot Hodgkin

age ten her interest in chemistry was strong, and after school life in England she went to Oxford where in her final year she specialized in X-ray crystallography, and then went to Cambridge to work with J. D. Bernal: after two years there she returned to an Oxford post in 1934 and remained there. She married the historian Thomas Hodgkin in 1937.

Dorothy Hodgkin developed the X-ray diffraction method of finding the exact structure of a molecule (originally devised by the *Braggs*) and applied it to complex organic molecules. Among her most striking successes were the antibiotic, penicillin, whose structure she deduced in 1945 (before it had been deduced by purely chemical methods); and vitamin B_{12}, lack of which leads to pernicious anaemia. This vitamin has over 90 atoms in a complex structure, and her analysis in 1956 (after eight years work) was a high-point for X-ray methods. Until then, computing aid for X-ray crystallographers was primitive, and Hodgkin used remarkable chemical intuition combined with massive computation. When modern computers became available, she was able to complete a study of insulin (with over

800 atoms) which she had begun in the 1930s, and in 1972 described its detailed structure. She won the Nobel Prize for chemistry in 1964.

HOFMANN, August Wilhelm von
1818-1892

German organic chemist: major discoverer of new organic compounds of nitrogen

Hofmann began his studies in Giessen as a law student, but attendance at some of *Liebig*'s chemistry lectures changed his interests; and Liebig welcomed this, perhaps because Hofmann's father, an architect, was overseeing the building of the new chemical laboratory. Young Hofmann's first research was on coal tar aniline ($C_6H_5NH_2$) and began the interest in organic amines which was to prove so important. He won prizes, became engaged to Liebig's wife's niece, and came to London as the young head of the new Royal College of Chemistry in Oxford Street in 1845. He stayed for 20 years, and he and his students created organic chemistry in England. One of these students, *Perkin*, made the first synthetic dye produced on any scale (mauve from aniline) and founded the British organic chemical industry. Other students, and Hofmann himself, made a variety of new organic dyes. From them, in turn, medicinal chemicals were developed.

In 1850 Hofmann showed that ammonia can be progressively alkylated by a reactive alkyl halide to give a mixture of amines. Thus ethyl iodide with ammonia in a sealed container (he was a large-scale user of champagne bottles from Windsor) gives the ethylamines, which he represented as follows, in a way which advanced the 'Type Theory':

H	C_2H_5	C_2H_5	C_2H_5
HN	HN	C_2H_5N	C_2H_5N
H	H	H	C_2H_5

He made similar compounds from phosphine (PH_3) in 1855. He moved to a professorship in chemistry in Berlin in 1865. Hofmann was not a theorist, but he had excellent instincts as an experimentalist, and this, combined with his use of the theory available to him, led to his high output of new results. The **Hofmann rearrangement** (1881) gives a primary amine as the organic product (via an isocyanate) when an amide is heated with bromine (or chlorine) and alkali: $RCONH_2 \rightarrow [RNCO] \rightarrow RNH_2$. Also named after him is the **Hofmann exhaustive methylation** reaction, which allows a complex nitrogen-containing organic compound to be degraded to simpler, identifiable, products; its early use was to determine structures, but later it became a subject for the study of reaction mechanism. Hofmann produced hundreds of research papers; he had many assistants, and a large number of friends; he was married four times, and had eleven children.

HOFMEISTER, Wilhelm (Friedrich Benedict)

1824-1877

German botanist

Hofmeister followed his father into his prosperous music and bookselling business in Leipzig and in his interest in plants, and by age 27 became well known as a botanist through his work on mosses and ferns (cryptogams). He went on to show that this group is related to the higher seed-bearing plants (phanerogams), and that the gymnosperms (conifers) lie between the cryptogams and the angiosperms (flowering plants); this prepared the way for a unified view of the plant kingdom. This work was linked with his discovery of the alternation of generations between sporophyte and gametophyte in lower plants. He was appointed professor at Heidelberg in 1863, and at Tübingen in 1872.

HOFSTADTER, Robert

1915-

American physicist: used electron scattering by nuclei to give details of nuclear structure

Graduating from New York and Princeton, Hofstadter afterwards worked at the Norden Laboratory Corporation (1943-46), Princeton and Stanford (1950) with a full professorship at 39; he was director of the Stanford high-energy physics laboratory from 1967 to 1974.

In 1948 Hofstadter invented an improved scintillation counter using sodium iodide, activated by thallium. At Stanford he used linearly accelerated electrons scattered by nuclei to study nuclear structure. The charge density in the nucleus was revealed to be constant, but falling sharply at the nuclear surface, with a radial distribution related to the nuclear mass. Neutrons and protons were shown to have size and shape (i.e., were not 'points') and could be regarded as made up of charged shells of mesons, with the total charge cancelling out in a neutron. Hofstadter was led to predict the rho-meson and omega-meson, both of which were later observed experimentally. He shared a Nobel Prize in 1961.

Robert Hofstadter

HOLLERITH, Herman
1860-1929

American computer scientist: introduced the modern punched card for data processing

A graduate of the Columbia University School of Mines in New York City, Hollerith did some teaching at MIT and worked on air brakes and for the US Patent Office before joining one of his former teachers to assist with the processing of the US Census of 1880. By 1887 he had developed his machine-readable cards and a 'census machine' which could handle up to 80 cards per minute, enabling the 1890 census to be processed in three years. Punched cards had been used by Jacquard before 1800 to mechanically control looms, but Hollerith introduced electromechanical handling and used the cards for computation: the **Hollerith code** relates alphanumeric characters to the positions of holes in the punched card. After the 1890 census, Hollerith adapted his device for commercial use and set up freight statistics systems for two railroads, founding the Tabulating Machine Company in 1896 to make and sell his equipment; by later mergers this became the International Business Machines Corporation (IBM). Hollerith's ideas were initially more used in Europe than in the US, but from the 1930s punched card methods became widespread.

HOLMES, Arthur
1890-1965

English geologist and geophysicist: devised modern geological time-scales

Holmes pioneered the use of radioactive decay methods for dating rocks, whereby careful analysis of the proportions of elements formed by radioactive decay, combined with a knowledge of the rates of decay of their parent elements, yields an absolute age. He was the first to use the technique, in 1913, to systematically date fossils whose stratigraphic (i.e. relative) ages were established, and was thus able to put absolute dates to the geological time scale for the first time.

In 1928 he suggested that convection currents within the Earth's mantle, driven by radiogenic heat, might provide the driving mechanism for the theory of continental drift, which had been advanced by *Wegener* some years earlier. He also proposed that new oceanic rocks were forming throughout the ocean basins, although predominantly at ocean ridges. Little attention was given to his ideas until the 1950s, when palaeomagnetic studies established continental drift as a fact.

He wrote several influential textbooks on geology, in particular *The Principles of Geology* (1944).

HOOKE, Robert
1635-1703

English physicist: brilliant inventor of devices, and producer of ideas then developed by others

Born in the Isle of Wight, Hooke was intended for the church and went to Oxford as a chorister. However, his poor health was thought to make him unsuited to the church and he turned to science, becoming assistant to *Boyle* in Oxford and making an improved air pump for him. From childhood on, Hooke was an ingenious and expert mechanic. In 1660 he moved to London, and was one of the founders of the Royal Society in 1662. He was made Curator; one of his tasks was to demonstrate 'three or four considerable experiments' for each weekly meeting. He later added other posts (one of these, as a Surveyor of London after the Great Fire, made him rich), but the Royal Society work helped to shape Hooke's life as a prolific experimenter whose ideas were usually fully explored by others. As he was combative, this led to many disputes on priority, notably with *Newton*.

In the 1660s he found **Hooke's law:** this is now often given in the form that, provided the elastic limit is not exceeded, the deformation of a material is proportional to the force applied to it. He did not publish this until 1676 (as a Latin anagram) and in intelligible form in 1678. Also in the 1660s he realised that a spiral spring can be used to control the balance-wheel of a time-piece, but *Huygens* made the first working model in 1674. He was fascinated by microscopy, and in his book *Micrographia* (1665) Hooke describes the use of the compound microscope which he had devised. He used the word 'cell' to describe the angular spaces he saw in a thin section of cork, and since then the word has come to be used for the membrane-bounded units of plant and animal life. The book includes also the idea that light might consist of waves; but further work on this was mainly by Huygens. Also in the book is his theory of combustion, which is good enough to make it very likely that he would have discovered oxygen if he had continued with chemistry. In the 1660s Hooke had ideas on gravity, as did many others, and he even suggested (in 1679) that its force obeys an inverse square law. These ideas may have been useful to Newton; what is certain is that Newton's toil and his mathematical genius succeeded in developing the idea brilliantly, and that Newton forcefully resisted Hooke's claims of priority.

Hooke had no rival as a deviser of instruments; the microscope, telescope and barometer were all much improved by him, and his other inventions include a revolving drum recorder for pressure and temperature, and a universal joint. His contribution to science is unusual; he did much, but his devices and ideas were largely developed by others. He certainly did more than anyone else to change the Royal Society from a club of virtuosi to a professional body. He was respected, but was too cynical and miserly to be much liked.

HOOKER, (Sir) Joseph Dalton
1817-1911

English botanist: plant taxonomist, phytogeographer and explorer

Educated at Glasgow in medicine, Hooker became Assistant Surgeon and Naturalist on *Ross*'s Antarctic expedition of 1839-43 on board HMS *Erebus* and *Terror*. His books *Flora Antarctica*, *Flora Novae-Zelandiae* and *Flora Tasmaniae* were a result. He travelled widely in India, Palestine and the United States, where he spent three years collecting plants. There followed his *Himalayan Journals* (1854), the *Rhododendrons of the Sikkim Himalaya* (1849) and his seven volume *Flora of British India* (1872-97). He undertook further expeditions to Syria and Palestine, and to the Atlas Mountains in Morocco. He became director of Kew Gardens, succeeding his father, Sir William J. Hooker, who had created the gardens.

His friendship with *Darwin* led to his being instrumental, with *Lyell*, in presenting the joint communication of Darwin and *Wallace* on the origin of species to the Linnean Society, and in persuading Darwin to publish *On the Origin of Species*. He joined with *Bentham* in producing the magisterial *Genera Plantarum* (7 vols., 1862-83) giving their important system of classification; and was an authority on Antarctic flora. He became president of the Royal Society in 1873.

HOPKINS, (Sir) Frederick Gowland
1861-1947

English biochemist: made first general scientific study of vitamins

Hopkins believed firmly that chemical reactions in living cells, although complex, are understandable in normal chemical and physical terms. This faith, and his amiable forcefulness, made him 'the father of British biochemistry'. His beginnings were not indicative of his future fame. His widowed mother chose a career for him at 17, in an insurance office. Later he worked as an analyst, especially on forensic cases. When he was 27 he inherited some money and entered the medical school at Guy's Hospital, and after qualifying worked with *Garrod*, founder of biochemical genetics. At 37 he went to Cambridge, but his teaching load was so great that his health broke down in 1910. He recovered fully, and his college (Trinity) then gave him a research post. Recovered in health, and almost 50, he began the work for which he is famous: on 'accessory food factors' (vitamins), and in 1914 became the first professor of biochemistry in Cambridge. His classic studies on nutrition showed that young rats failed to grow on a diet of pure protein, carbohydrate, fat, salts and water; but the addition of small amounts of milk (2-3 cm^3 rat^{-1} day^{-1}) caused them to thrive. The 'vitamin hypothesis' followed, as did much work on vitamins in Cambridge and elsewhere. Hopkins worked also on the biochemistry of muscle, on enzymes, on $-SH$ groups, and on glutathione. He shared the Nobel Prize for 1929 with *Eijkmann*.

HOPPE-SEYLER, Ernst Felix

1825-1895

German biochemist: first to isolate nucleic acid

Orphaned early, Hoppe-Seyler was brought up by his brother-in-law, and followed him by studying medicine. He only practised briefly however, and after some research training with *Virchow* he worked in Tübingen and later Strasbourg, mainly on the use of chemical and physical methods in physiology. He isolated haemoglobin, the red pigment of blood, and studied its reaction with carbon monoxide; he was also the first to obtain pure lecithin, and he studied oxidation in animal tissues and enzyme action. His Swiss pupil F. Miescher first isolated a nucleic acid, in 1869, and later Hoppe-Seyler extended this work. He

founded in 1877 a journal for physiological chemistry, editing it in a characteristically autocratic way, and was a major figure in establishing classical biochemistry as a separate branch of science.

HORROCKS, Jeremiah

1618-1641

English astronomer

Educated at Cambridge University, but self-taught in astronomy, Horrocks became a curate at Hoole, in Lancashire; a brilliant amateur astronomer, he achieved a great deal in his short life. He is particularly remembered as the first observer (1639) of a transit of Venus across the face of the Sun, which he had predicted using *Kepler*'s Rudolphine tables. From the transit the value of planetary distances can be calculated by Kepler's laws; hence its importance. In the two years before his death, Horrocks achieved a remarkable range of accurate measurements, especially in the solar system.

HOUNSFIELD, Godfrey Newbold

1919-

British physicist: developed first X-ray tomographic body scanner

Hounsfield received no formal university education, but studied at the City and Guilds College and at the Faraday House College for Electrical Engineering in London. In 1951 he joined Electrical and Musical Industries (EMI), becoming head of the medical research division.

Independently of *Cormack*, Hounsfield developed the technique of X-ray computer-assisted tomography (CAT), whereby high-resolution images of the soft body tissues (which are normally almost transparent to X-rays) are built up by computer from many measurements of the absorption of X-ray beams in different directions through the body. In the early 1970s he developed the first commercial

G. N. Hounsfield

CAT body scanner at EMI; such machines are now an invaluable medical tool. Hounsfield has continued to lead research into medical imaging, pursuing in particular the use of nuclear magnetic resonance (NMR) techniques. In 1979 Hounsfield shared the Nobel Prize for physiology or medicine with Cormack.

HOYLE, (Sir) Fred

1915-

British cosmologist and astrophysicist: jointly proposed the steady-state theory of the universe

Even as a small boy in a Yorkshire village, Hoyle was 'at war with the system', and became a long-term truant. Later he had problems in entering Cambridge. In 1973 he resigned his chair there after disputes with the university authorities.

Together with *Gold* and *Bondi*, Hoyle proposed the **steady-state theory** for the origin of the universe in the 1950s. This theory assumes that the universe is not only homogeneous and isotropic in space, but also unchanging with time. The known expansion of the universe is explained by the continuous and spon-

taneous creation of matter to maintain the mean mass density at a constant value. Newer evidence has left that theory with few supporters. Hoyle also suggested (in 1957, with W. A. Fowler and G. and E. M. Burbidge) how elements heavier than helium and hydrogen might have been created by nuclear synthesis in the interior of stars, eventually being ejected into space and incorporated into new stars formed from clouds of interstellar matter. All this work has led to fruitful advances, directly or through their effect on others. He is also a believer in an extraterrestrial origin for life, suggesting that biological molecules such as amino acids are synthesized in space on dust particles. His view that infective agents such as viruses can arrive from space has found little support. He has, however, been notably successful as a theorist, and as a writer both of popular science and of science fiction.

HUBBLE, Edwin Powell

1889-1953

American astronomer and cosmologist: discovered expansion of universe, and measured its size and age

Hubble was trained in Chicago and Oxford in law; he was also a distinguished athlete and boxer. After a short career in law he turned to astronomy, working for most of his life at Mount Wilson Observatory. Using the 100-inch telescope at Mount Wilson, Hubble was able in 1923 to resolve the nebulous outer part of the Andromeda galaxy into individual stars, obtaining a distance of 900 000 light years for several Cepheid variable stars he found there. Together with further work this proved for the first time that what were then thought of as 'spiral nebulae' were in fact spiral galaxies, and lay well beyond our own galaxy. In 1929 he was able to measure the recessional velocities of 18 galaxies, and discovered that these velocities increased in proportion to their distance from Earth. This relationship (v=Hd) is now known as **Hubble's law**, the constant of proportionality being **Hubble's constant** (H). This work gave the first direct evidence supporting the idea of an expanding universe, a concept that had been proposed a few years earlier by the cosmologists *Friedmann* and *Lemaître*, and now fundamental to our understanding of the universe. Hubble's observations meant that two fundamental quantities of the universe could be calculated for the first time: its 'knowable' size, or the distance at which the recession velocity reaches the speed of light, which is about 18 billion light years; and the age of the universe, which Hubble himself estimated as 2 billion years, but modern values range between 12 and 20 billion years. Hubble also introduced a widely used system of classification for the shape of galaxies.

David H. Hubel

HUBEL, David Hunter

1926-

Canadian-American neurophysiologist: investigator of the basis of visual perception

Hubel qualified in medicine at McGill University, Montreal, and since 1959 has worked at Harvard. With T. Wiesel he has done much to aid understanding of the mechanism of visual perception at the cortical level, using microelectrodes and modern electronics to detect the activity of individual neurons, especially in area 17 of the visual cortex. The cells of this striate cortex lie in several layers arranged in columns, which run through the thickness of the cortex (a few mm). Hubel and Weisel found that stimulation of cells on the retina by light causes excitation of particular cells in the striate cortex. The cell activation in the cortex by visual stimulation is very specific; some cells respond to spots of light, others to a line whose tilt is critical, so that a change of 10° in its angle greatly alters the response. Still others respond only to specific directions of movement or to specific colours. The visual cortex has become the

best-known part of the brain through studies of this kind. Hubel and Wiesel in addition established that many of the connections responsible for these specific response patterns are present already at birth but may be modified or even destroyed if the young animal is visually deprived. These results have had an important influence on treatment of congenital cataracts and strabismus (squint). Hubel and Wiesel shared a Nobel Prize in 1981.

HÜCKEL, Erich

1896-1980

German physicist and theoretical chemist: developed molecular orbital theory of bonding in organic molecules

Hückel's study of physics at Göttingen was interrupted by World War I, when he spent two years on aerodynamics before returning to finish his course. He worked as assistant first to the mathematician *Hilbert*, and then to *Born*; but he did not like the work, and he also wished to travel. He joined his former teacher *Debye* at Zürich, and began working on what is now known as the **Debye-Hückel theory** of electrolyte solutions. This assumes that strong electrolytes are fully dissociated into ions in solution, and calculates properties (such as electrical conductivity) for dilute solutions on this basis. Then, after a major illness, he worked on colloid chemistry first with his father-in-law R. Zsigmondy and then with F. G. Donnan in London, and then moved to Copenhagen to work on quantum theory with *Bohr*. The latter suggested that Hückel should try to calculate properties of the CC double bond by wave mechanics. Hückel classified the electrons making up such bonds as σ (sigma) and π (pi) types on a symmetry basis, and was able to make useful calculations of bond properties. **Hückel molecular orbital (HMO) theory** has been widely applied to organic molecules. One result is **Hückel's rule**, which proposes that aromatic stability will be shown by planar monocyclic molecules in which all the cyclic atoms are part of the π-system, only if the number of such π-electrons is $4n+2$, where n is an integer. The rule has provoked much fruitful study of molecules predicted by the rule to show 'aromaticity'. Hückel's work on such compounds probably began with a suggestion from his elder brother Walter, an organic chemist. From 1937 Erich was professor of theoretical physics at Marburg.

HUGGINS, (Sir) William
1824-1910

British astronomer and astrophysicist: pioneered stellar spectroscopy, and discovered stellar red shifts

Huggins was a wealthy amateur, who used his private observatory in South London to study a full range of celestial objects. Like *Lockyer*, he was attracted by spectrum analysis and its possible use in astronomy; Huggins pioneered the study of the spectra of stars, finding them to contain elements already known on Earth and in the Sun. He went on to investigate nebulae, making the important discovery that they were composed of luminous gas; he later showed that a comet contained hydrocarbon molecules. In 1868 he made perhaps his most profound discovery, observing that the spectrum of Sirius is shifted towards the red end of the spectrum. He correctly interpreted this as being due to the Doppler effect, obtaining a recessional velocity of about 40 km s^{-1} (25 miles per second), and proceeded to measure the red shifts of many other stars. With the advent of the gelatine dry plate he pioneered the technique of spectroscopic photography, from 1875. (The particular advantage of photography over the eye is that a faint image can be 'accumulated'.)

HUMBOLDT, (Baron) Alexander von
1769-1859

German explorer: pioneer of geophysics and meteorology

Humboldt had wide scientific interests and a passion for travel, and was wealthy enough to indulge both his enthusiasms. His father, a Prussian soldier, wished him to enter politics, but the boy preferred to study engineering; while doing so he was attracted to botany, and moved to Göttingen to study science. He seems to have been happiest with geology, and spent two years at a school of mining before working as a mining engineer, when he devised and tested safety lamps and rescue apparatus. Then in 1796 he inherited enough money to travel, but the Napoleonic Wars frustrated him until 1799, when he began an epic exploration of central and south America. He covered over 6000 often dangerous miles with his friend the botanist A. Bonpland, before returning to Europe with a large collection of scientific specimens and observations after five years of absence. Analysis of his results, along with some diplomatic missions, kept him busy for the next 20 years. His wide-ranging interests were largely in geophysics, meteorology, and geography. He studied the Pacific coastal currents, and was the first to propose a Panama canal. He introduced isobars and isotherms on weather maps, made a general study of global temperature and pressure, and eventually organized a world-wide scheme for collecting magnetic and weather observations. He studied American volcanoes and showed that they followed geological faults, and deduced that volcanic action had been important in geological history and that many rocks are of igneous origin. He set a world record by climbing the Chimorazo volcano (5876 m) and was the first to link mountain sickness with lack of oxygen, to study the fall of mean temperature with rising altitude, and to relate geographical conditions to the animal life and vegetation. In 1804 he discovered that the Earth's magnetic field decreases from the poles to the equator. His writing has been said 'to combine the large and vague ideas, typical of the 18th century thought, with the exact and positive science of the 19th'.

HUME-ROTHERY, William

1899-1968

English metallurgist

Soon after beginning a military career Hume-Rothery had meningitis and was left totally deaf; so he entered Oxford to study chemistry, graduated well, spent three years researching in metallurgy in London, and then returned to Oxford, which was his base thereafter. He brought together a range of ideas and techniques for the understanding of alloys; his first researches were on intermetallic compounds, and he went on to study alloy phases, compositions and crystal structures, using modern electronic theory, *Goldschmidt*'s findings on the importance of atomic size, and both microscopy and X-ray methods of examination. His books set out the empirical rules governing alloy formation and behaviour very fully and did much to advance the subject and to convert it from an art to a science.

HUTTON, James

1726-1797

British geologist: proposed the uniformitarian principle in geology

Hutton had a disorganized start to his career. After leaving school he was apprenticed in a lawyer's office, but left for the continent to train as a doctor, and qualified as MD at Leyden. However, it was a profession that he failed to take up, turning instead to farming; after studying agriculture in England and abroad, he returned to Scotland and a family farm near Edinburgh. After 14 years the success of a business extracting NH_4Cl from soot gave him an independent income, and in 1768 he returned to Edinburgh to pursue science.

Hutton is widely regarded as the founder of geology as a modern science. He rejected the scriptural time scales hitherto accepted, which dated the Earth as only a few thousand years old, and argued that it was immeasurably ancient, with 'no vestige of a beginning, no prospect of an end'. He considered the erosive action of rivers to be a major agent in creating continental topography, and believed that sediments washed into the sea by rivers accumulated and were metamorphosed via geothermal heat to form new rocks, which would eventually be uplifted and form new land masses. Such ideas ran contrary to previous ideas of a 'catastrophic' origin of the continents, at a fixed point in time corresponding to the biblical Creation. Hutton's concept of a cyclic process of denudation, transport, sedimentation, lithification, uplift and renewed denudation is often referred to as the **Plutonic theory**, due to the crucial part played in it by terrestrial heat; or as **uniformitarianism**, since it assumes that geological processes act in a continuous manner over a long time.

HUXLEY, Hugh (Esmor)

1924-

British physiologist: devised sliding filament theory of muscle contraction

Huxley studied physics at Cambridge,

worked on radar in World War II, and afterwards was attracted to biophysics, working at the Massachusetts Institute of Technology and in London and in Cambridge from 1961. From the 1950s he has been especially associated with the **sliding filament model of muscle contraction** and with the development of methods in X-ray diffraction and in electron microscopy designed for this work, but also applicable in other studies.

Skeletal muscle is a very abundant animal tissue; it makes up some 40% of the human body mass. Its main purpose is to convert chemical energy into mechanical work, under neural control. Skeletal muscle tissue is a parallel array of myofibres, each consisting of some hundreds of myofibrils which form long cylinders. The myofibril is divided into sarcomeres arranged end to end, and since the myofibrils are arranged with the sarcomeres in register, this gives to skeletal muscle its striated appearance. (The fibres of smooth muscle are not arranged in sarcomeres.) Within each sarcomere are the filaments which form the contractile apparatus; it can shorten by some ten per cent. These filaments are of two kinds: the thicker myosin filaments interdigitate with the slender actin filaments. With Jean Hanson, Huxley developed the theory that these thick and thin protein filaments slide past each other in muscle contraction. The process has a complex system of regulation through changes in calcium ion concentration, and uses ATP as the energy source. When the muscle relaxes, the crossbridges which project from the thick filaments and which have drawn the structure together are detached, and the whole structure regains its original length.

HUXLEY, Thomas Henry

1825-1895

English biologist: forceful supporter of theory of evolution

Despite having a schoolmaster father,

young Huxley had only two years of regular schooling and was mainly self-taught. He was attracted to medicine and attended a post-mortem at 14, but he may have contracted an infection there which recurred throughout his life. He became an apprentice to a medical brother-in-law, did well, studied medicine and surgery in London and joined the Royal Navy.

Although his duties on HMS *Rattlesnake* on a four-year voyage around Australia were as surgeon and he had only a microscope and makeshift net as equipment for natural history, he did useful new work on plankton and after a discouraging interval this established him on the scientific scene in London. However, these interests exasperated the Admiralty and he became a self-employed writer on science in 1850, and a lecturer on natural history from 1854 at the School of Mines. This gave him an income to marry his Australian girlfriend of eight years before; they eventually had seven children. Their son Leonard was the father of Julian (biologist), Aldous (writer) and Andrew Fielding Huxley (physiologist). For 30 years, while waiting for a job in physiology, Huxley worked in zoology and palaeontology.

These interests led him to his best-known place in science, that of advocate for his friend *Darwin*'s ideas on evolution. In famous debates and essays on this Huxley showed his forceful expertise, notably in a debate with Bishop Wilberforce at the British Association meeting in Oxford in 1860, when his reply to the Bishop's query on whether Huxley's ancestry was from an ape on his grandfather's or his grandmother's side made it clear that Darwin's theory was not to be crushed by the church. Huxley replied, in summary, that he would rather be descended from an ape than a bishop; and he earned the name of 'Darwin's bulldog'. He was a clear and elegant writer and a charming man. His careful study of the primates established man as one of them, and made evolution a matter of public debate in terms of science rather than emotion.

Aside from all this, Huxley did much excellent work of his own in zoology and palaeontology and in shaping biological education.

HUYGENS, Christiaan
1629-1695

Dutch physicist and astronomer: proposed wave theory of light; discovered Saturn's rings; introduced the pendulum clock; worked on the theory of dynamics, and the compound pendulums

Well educated as a member of a wealthy family in The Hague, Huygens studied law before turning to science and mathematics. He was, after *Newton*, the most influential physical scientist of the late 17th century. In 1655, using an improved home-made telescope, he was the first to describe correctly Saturn's ring system, also discovering Titan, its largest moon. He announced the discovery and observation of Saturn's rings in the form of a cypher. The following year he obtained the first solution to the problem of the dynamics of colliding elastic bodies. *Galileo* had discovered the constancy of a simple pendulum's period; and Huygens showed that for small swings $T = 2\pi(l/g)^{1/2}$ where T = period, l = length, g = acceleration due to gravity. He designed a pendulum clock; and later invented the more accurate compound pendulum (which moves in a cycloidal arc). Physics could not have moved on without accurate time measurement.

Huygens's greatest achievment, however, was his wave theory of light, first expounded in 1678. He described light as a vibration spreading through an all-pervading 'ether' which consisted of microscopic particles, and he considered every point on the wave-front to be the source of a series of secondary spherical wavelets, the envelope of which defined the wave-front at the next instant (known as **Huygens's Construction**). He was thus able to give a simple explanation for the laws of reflection and refraction of light, and for the double refraction of some minerals. He correctly predicted that light travelled slower in denser media. Newton preferred a particle theory of light. The present view that each concept can be appropriate, depending on the experimental situation, came only in the 20th century.

I

INGEN-HOUSZ, Jan
1730-1799

Dutch plant physiologist: early student of photosynthesis

Ingen-Housz studied physics, chemistry and medicine and researched in all three; his early career was guided by a British army surgeon who met the family when encamped near his home at Breda in the Netherlands. He travelled widely in Europe, as a popular and expert user of the pre-Jenner inoculation method (a risky affair using live virus) against smallpox. He spent his last 20 years in London, where he published his work on gas exchange in plants. He showed that the green parts of plants absorb carbon dioxide and give off oxygen only in the light; in darkness they release carbon dioxide. This process, **photosynthesis**, is perhaps the most fundamental reaction of living systems, since it is the source of much plant substance, and animal life depends on the life of plants. Ingen-Housz made a number of curious inventions and discoveries. They include a device for giving oxygen to a patient with chest disease; a pistol which used an explosive mixture of air and diethylether vapour and which was fired electrically; a hydrogen-fuelled lighter to replace the tinderbox; and thin glass microscope cover plates.

INGOLD, (Sir) Christopher Kelk
1893-1970

English physical organic chemist: developed electronic theory of organic chemistry

A student of chemistry at Southampton and London, Ingold spent two years in industry before returning to Imperial College London as a lecturer. In 1924 he became professor at Leeds, and in 1930 at London, where he stayed. At Leeds he developed ideas on the electronics of organic reactions, somewhat parallel to those of *Robinson*, and much controversy followed. Ingold thereafter worked on reaction rates and the details of reaction mechanism, usually with E. D. Hughes. Much physical organic research has followed on this line; and the terminology, at least, has followed Ingold's preference rather than Robinson's.

IPATIEFF, Vladimir Nikolayevich
1867-1952

Russian-American chemist: pioneer of catalytic and isomerization reactions of hydrocarbons

Ipatieff trained for a military career in Czarist Russia, as was usual for those, like him, from an aristocratic family. However, he became interested in chemistry through the influence of an uncle, and initially was self-taught, with the help of *Mendelayev*'s book *The Fundamentals of Chemistry*. He attended a military school, became an officer of the Imperial Russian Army in 1887 and entered the Mikhail Artillery Academy (1889-92) studying chemistry and mathematics. After graduation, he became an instructor and, eventually, professor of chemistry at the Academy. He studied in Munich under *Baeyer* (1896) and there synthesized isoprene, so beginning his interest in hydrocarbons. This led to further work at the Academy on high-pressure catalytic and hydrogenation reactions. He developed the Ipatieff 'bomb' for this work.

During World War I Ipatieff co-ordinated Russia's chemical industries; he was a Lieutenant-General by 1916. The Revolution of 1917 interrupted Ipatieff's work (it was within his brother's house that the Czar and his family were murdered), and he was fortunate to survive when officers of the Imperial Army were at risk. His skills were needed by the Bolsheviks and after a difficult period he worked for Soviet Russia, helping to re-build its chemical industry.

By 1929 he began to worry about his own safety in Soviet Russia and in 1930 left Russia for America. At the age of 64 he remade his life and career, learned English, was appointed professor of chemistry at Northwestern University (Illinois) and acted as consultant to the Universal Oil Products Company of Chicago, who established the Ipatieff High Pressure Laboratory at Northwestern University, which he directed. In the US he continued his work on hydrocarbons; he studied their formation, hydrogenation and dehydrogenation, cyclization and isomerization, with the emphasis on high-pressure catalysed reactions. Such processes are of great importance in the petroleum industry.

When aged 40, Ipatieff had the unusual experience of meeting his formerly unknown half-brother Lev Chugaeff, also an organic chemist, and they remained good friends.

ISAACS, Alick
1921-1967

Scottish virologist: discoverer of interferon

A graduate of Glasgow, Isaacs studied at Sheffield and Melbourne before returning to London and the Virology Division of the National Institute for Medical Research in 1950. He was much concerned with the way viruses apparently interact with each other, and in 1957 he reported on the substance interferon which he found to be released from cells in response to viral infection, and which inhibits the replication of viruses. Interferon is now known to consist of a group of related proteins, able to block the action of viral m-RNA. Fuller understanding of this action will clearly be of value in virology and interferons have been used in clinical trials as anticancer agents; their difficult availability has delayed assessment of their value in therapy.

J

JACOBI, Karl Gustav Jacob
1804-1851

German mathematician: contributed to the theory of elliptic functions, analysis, number theory, geometry and mechanics

Jacobi was the son of a Jewish banker, and showed wide-ranging talent from childhood. He became a lecturer at Königsberg in 1826; and in 1832 he became a professor there. He encouraged students to do original work before they had read all the previous work on a topic. As he said to one student: 'Your father would never have married, and you wouldn't be here now, if he had insisted on knowing all the girls in the world before marrying one'. In 1848 he made a brief but disastrous foray into politics and lost for a time the royal pension on which he, his wife and seven children lived; in 1851 he died of smallpox.

Jacobi, together with *Abel*, created the theory of elliptic functions, and Jacobi also applied them to number theory and developed hyperelliptic functions. He did research on differential equations and determinants, and Jacobian determinants are now used in dynamics and quantum mechanics.

JANSKY, Karl Guthe
1905-1950

American radio engineer: discovered first astronomical radio source

Jansky studied physics at Wisconsin, and joined the Bell Telephone Co in 1928. While working for them in 1931 Jansky was given the task of investigating sources of interference to shortwave radio communications. ('Static'; causes include thunderstorms, and nearby electrical equipment.) Using a rotatable directional antenna he detected a weak static emission that appeared at approximately the same time every day. He soon demonstrated that it was coming from the direction of the centre of the galaxy, and suggested in 1932 that it was caused by interstellar ionized gas rather than from the stars. His discovery did not receive much attention at the time, despite its potential value (e.g., radio waves penetrate dust clouds which obscure the galactic centre for optical astronomy), but it was to lead to the development of radio astronomy after the Second World War. The unit of radio emission strength is named after him (1 jansky$=1$ W m^{-2} Hz^{-1}). Jansky did not continue in radio astronomy, which was kept alive by *Reber* until its post-radar expansion after World War II.

JEANS, (Sir) James Hopwood
1877-1946

British astrophysicist: suggested 'tidal' theory for formation of solar system

Beginning as a mathematician, Jeans applied his talents to problems in astrophysics. Jeans advanced understanding of the stability of rotating masses, of particular application to stellar dynamics. Together with *Jeffreys*, Jeans proposed the 'tidal' or 'passing star' theory for the formation of the solar system, whereby the gravitational pull of a star passing close to the Sun extracted a filament of material from which the planets subsequently condensed. The theory has since been abandoned in favour of a revised version of *Laplace*'s nebular hypothesis.

213

JEFFREYS, (Sir) Harold

1891-

British geophysicist and astronomer: theoretical seismologist, and co-author of 'tidal' theory of formation of solar system

After graduating in mathematics in 1913, Jeffreys spent his entire academic career at Cambridge. He is best known for his work on the internal structure of the Earth, and in particular on theoretical seismology, his earthquake travel time tables (worked out with K. E. Bullen in the 1930s) still being standard. Together with *Jeans*, Jeffreys proposed the 'tidal' theory of the formation of the solar system, in which it was suggested that a passing star might have drawn a filament of material out of the Sun, from which the planets subsequently condensed. The theory has since been abandoned in favour of revised versions of *Laplace*'s nebular theory. Jeffreys also worked on a variety of planetary problems, and was a notable opponent of the theory of continental drift, favouring instead a hypothesis in which the Earth contracts.

JENNER, Edward

1749-1823

English physician and naturalist: pioneer of vaccination

Jenner, a vicar's son, was apprenticed to a surgeon at 13, and at 21 became a pupil of J. Hunter for three years. They had similar interests and became life-long friends; Jenner did well and could have continued in London, but chose to return to his native village (Berkeley, Gloucestershire) to practise medicine. At that time smallpox was a long-known and feared disease; epidemics were frequent, mortality was high (typically 20% of those infected) and survivors were disfigured. It was known that survivors are immune to reinfection; and that inoculation from a patient with a mild attack of the disease protected against it, but this carried the risk of severe or fatal illness.

Jenner was told by a patient that country people who had cowpox (vaccinia; a rather rare disease of the udders of cows, transmittable to humans and not severe) did not afterwards become smallpox victims. Jenner found ten such cases. In 1796 he took lymph from a cowpox vesicle on a dairymaid's finger and inoculated this into a healthy boy; six weeks later he inoculated him with smallpox matter, but the boy did not develop smallpox. He went on to show that matter from the boy (fluid from a vesicle) could be used to inoculate other individuals, and passed by inoculation from person to person indefinitely without losing its protective effect. He used a thorn for inoculations.

The new procedure ('vaccination') was widely but not universally welcomed, and by 1800 was much used. In the UK it was made compulsory in 1853, and this was enforced by 1872. Smallpox became the first major disease to be fully overcome, at least in civilized communities; by 1980 it was officially extinct, as there were no recorded cases. It is now known that smallpox (variola) is one of a group of related pox diseases, whose causal agent is a rather large virus of high virulence. Inoculation of the cowpox virus causes production of antibodies effective against smallpox, for a period of up to about two years.

Jenner was a keen and skilful naturalist, with a special interest in birds. He did major work on the cuckoo and other migratory birds; and he arranged the plants from *Cook*'s first expedition. The British government awarded him £30 000 for his discovery of vaccination.

JOHANSON, Donald

1943-

American palaeoanthropologist: discovered Australopithecus afarensis, *the oldest hominid yet found*

After graduating in anthropology from the University of Chicago in 1966,

Johanson conducted research in Chicago and Alaska before joining an archaeological expedition to the Omo River, southern Ethiopia, from 1970-72. He then turned his attention to Afar, in north-eastern Ethiopia, where he and Maurice Taieb had found fossil-bearing beds of considerable age. In 1973 he discovered the remains of a knee joint of a previously unknown hominid in deposits over 3 million years old, at that time the earliest conclusive evidence of man's bipedalism. A partial skeleton of *Australopithecus afarensis* was found by Johanson the following year, a female of about 20 years of age and four feet in height which he nicknamed 'Lucy', and which remains the earliest known ancestor of man, almost a million years more ancient than any other known hominid.

JOLIOT, Frédéric
1900-1958

French nuclear physicist: co-discoverer of artificially-induced radioactivity

Trained in science in Paris, Joliot became assistant to *Marie Curie* in 1925 and soon proved his skill as an experimenter. Mme Curie's elder daughter Irène was already her assistant in the Radium Institute, and she and Joliot married in 1926. Their personalities were very different, he an extrovert, she very diffident. Only in 1931 did they begin to collaborate in research, with notable success. They also perpetuated a family tradition; their daughter Hélène (b.1927) became a nuclear physicist and married a physicist grandson of *Langevin*.

Foreseeing the consequences of the nuclear fission of uranium discovered by others in 1939, Joliot secured from Norway the world's major stock (less than 200 kg) of heavy water (^2H_2O; used as a moderator in early atomic piles) and when France was invaded in 1940, he arranged for it to be sent to the UK. After the war, as their leading nuclear physicist, he directed work on France's first atomic pile, which operated in 1948; but his successes became confused by his showmanship, his need for adulation, and his communist sympathies, and he was removed from his post as High Commissioner for Atomic Energy in 1950.

JOLIOT-CURIE, Irène
1897-1956

French nuclear physicist: co-discoverer of artificially-induced radioactivity

Irène, daughter of Pierre and Marie *Curie*, had a unique education; she was taught at home, in physics by her mother, in maths by *Langevin* and in chemistry by *Perrin*. In World War I she served as a radiographer; inadequately protected against radiation then and later, she became a victim like her mother of leukaemia, fairly certainly because of exposure to radiation, and which eventually killed them both.

In the 1930s she did notable work on artificial radioactivity with her husband *F. Joliot* for which they shared the Nobel Prize for physics in 1935. In World War II she escaped to Switzerland, and in 1946 became director of the Radium Institute and a director of the French Atomic Energy Commission. Her work in the 1930s with Joliot led them in late 1933 to make the first artificial radioelement by bombarding aluminium with alpha-particles (helium nuclei, ^4_2He) which gave a novel radioisotope of phosphorus. Similar methods then led them and others to make a range of novel radioisotopes some of which have proved of great value in research, in medicine and in industry.

JORDAN, Ernst Pascual
1902-

German theoretical physicist: one of the founders of quantum mechanics

Jordan grew up and did his first degree in Hannover, moving to Göttingen for his doctorate. After gaining a post at the University of Rostock (1929) he became professor of physics there in 1935. Chairs of physics at Berlin (1944) and Hamburg (1951) followed.

At 23 Jordan collaborated with *Born*, and then *Heisenberg*, to set out the theory of quantum mechanics, using matrix methods (1926). Later he contributed to the quantum mechanics of electron-photon interactions, called quantum elec-trodynamics, whilst it was in its early stages of development. Another area that he published significant research in was that of gravitation.

JORDAN, (Marie-Ennemond) Camille
1838-1922

French mathematician: major contributor to group theory

Jordan trained as an engineer at the École Polytechnique, and worked as one whilst pursuing mathematics in his spare time. At 35 he joined the mathematical staff of the École Polytechnique, and also taught at the Collège de France.

Jordan absorbed the ideas of the ill-fated *Galois* and developed a rigorous theory of finite, and then infinite, groups. He linked permutation groups and Galois's study of permuting the roots (solutions) of equa-tions to the problem of solving polynomial equations. Jordan published a classic on group theory (1870). He advanced sym-metrical groups, and reduced the linear differential equations of order n to a group theoretic problem. Finally he generalized *Hermite*'s work on the theory of quadratic forms with integral coefficients. Jordan inspired *Klein* and *Lie* to pursue novel research on group theory. Topology also interested Jordan and he devised homolo-gical or combinatorial topology by investi-gating symmetries in polyhedra.

JOSEPHSON, Brian David
1940-

English theoretical physicist: discovered tunnelling between superconductors

Josephson studied at Cambridge, and

B. D. Josephson

remained to become a professor of physics (1974). He discovered the **Josephson effect** while still a research student (1962), by considering two supercon-ducting regions separated by a thin region of insulator (perhaps 1-2 nm thick). He showed theoretically that a current can flow between the two with no applied voltage, and that when a DC voltage is applied an AC current of frequency proportional to the voltage is produced. Experimental verification of this effect by J. M. Rowell and *P. W. Anderson* at Bell Telephone Laboratories supported the **BCS theory** which Josephson had used. The application of a steady magnetic field across the junction alters the current. Such **Josephson junctions** have been used to measure accurately h/e, voltage and magnetic fields, and in fast switching devices for computers. He shared a Nobel Prize in 1973.

JOULE, James Prescott
1818-1889

English physicist: established the mechanical theory of heat

Joule grew up in a wealthy Manchester brewing family, a shy and delicate child;

he received home tuition from *Dalton* in elementary science and mathematics. He was early attracted to physics and especially to the problems of heat and began experimental work in a laboratory near the brewery. Joule's skill enabled him to measure heat and temperature changes accurately, and he was later encouraged to pursue his work by *W. Thomson*.

When he was 18, Joule began his study of the heat developed by an electric current; and by 1840 he had deduced the law connecting the current and resistance of a wire to the heat generated (**Joule's law**). Between 1837 and 1847 his work established the principle of conservation of energy and the equivalence of heat and other forms of energy. J. R. Meyer arrived at the idea of conservation in the 1840s but in an unclear form; and W. Thomson and *Helmholtz* also were major contributors, but Joule made it a precise and explicit concept. The amount of mechanical work required to produce a given amount of heat was determined by Joule in 1843; he measured the small amount of heat produced in water by the rotation of paddles driven by falling weights.

Thomson and Joule collaborated for seven years from 1852 in a series of experiments, mainly on the **Joule-Thomson effect**, whereby an expanding gas is cooled as work is done to separate the molecules. Joule also produced a paper on the kinetic theory of gases which included the first estimation of the speed of gas molecules (1848). He was over-modest and made himself into an assistant to Thomson rather than follow his own lines of thought; and he became unwell when he was 55 and did little more afterwards.

Joule remains one of the foremost experimentalists of his century; his main work was done before he was 30, on one problem of great importance, the mechanical equivalent of heat. He attacked this with ingenuity, made precise measurements and tenaciously located sources of error. The SI unit of energy, the **joule** (J) is the energy expended when the point of application of a force of 1 newton moves through 1 metre in the direction of the force, so $1\,J = 1\,Nm = 1\,kg\,m^2\,s^{-2}$. Heat and work are measured in the same units.

K

KAMERLINGH-ONNES, Heike
1853-1926

Dutch physicist: first liquified helium, and discovered superconductivity

Kamerlingh-Onnes studied physics at Groningen and then spent two years in Heidelberg studying under *Bunsen* and *Kirchhoff*; his special interest was then in finding new proofs of the Earth's rotation, but after he became professor at Leyden in 1882 he concentrated on the properties of matter at low temperatures. *Dewar* had liquified nitrogen, and by cooling hydrogen with this and using the Joule-Thomson effect he had obtained liquid hydrogen. Kamerlingh-Onnes used an improved apparatus and similar principles; in 1908 by cooling helium with liquid hydrogen to about 18 K and then using the Joule-Thomson effect (the cooling of a gas when it expands through a nozzle) he obtained liquid helium, which he found to boil at 4.25 K. If it was boiled rapidly by pressure reduction the temperature fell to just below 1 K, but it did not solidify. In 1911 he found that metals such as mercury, tin and lead at very low temperatures become **superconductors**, with near-zero electrical resistance. He won the Nobel Prize for 1913 for his work in low temperature physics, which he dominated until he retired in 1923. A theoretical explanation of superconductivity had to wait until the work of *Bardeen* and others in 1957.

KANT, Immanuel
1724-1804

German philosopher: had influential ideas on cosmology

Although primarily known for his work in philosophy, in 1755 Kant proposed the nebular hypothesis for the formation of the solar system, which was later to be developed and made famous by *Laplace*. More influential was Kant's work on gravitation, in which he argued that forces could act at a distance without the necessity for a transmitting medium. He also suggested (correctly) that the Milky Way is a lens-shaped collection of stars: and that tidal friction slowed Earth's rotation.

KAPITSA, Piotr Leonidovitch
1894-1984

Russian physicist: experimenter on high magnetic fields and low temperatures

Son of one general (an engineer) and grandson of another, Kapitsa studied electrical engineering at the Petrograd Polytechnic, graduated in 1918, and continued there as a lecturer for three years. In 1919 his first wife and two children died in the famine following the revolution, and in 1921 the unhappy young man visited England and secured a place in *Rutherford*'s Cambridge laboratory. Both were energetic, outspoken, and talented experimentalists, who formed a high regard for each other. Kapitsa became a popular figure, adventurous, ingenious and with wide-ranging interests.

After completing his PhD he began to work independently, on the problem of obtaining very high magnetic fields. For this he designed and built circuits which passed currents of 10 000 A or more through a small coil for 0.01 s or less, a time shorter than it would take the coil to burn out. By 1924 he could in this way obtain field strengths of up to 50 T, which

Piotr Kapitsa (*left*) as best man at the wedding of James Chadwick (*right*)

he used in studies on the properties of materials in high fields. The electrical resistance of metals increases in high fields, and this effect increases at low temperatures, so Kapitsa turned his ingenuity to the design of an improved liquifier for helium. His work went so well that a new laboratory building (the Mond) was built for his work and opened in 1933. (He had the sculptor Eric Gill carve a crocodile over its entrance; it was not until 1966, revisiting his laboratory, that he admitted that this represented Rutherford.) By 1934 his new method for making liquid helium allowed him to study its strange properties; he discovered that it conducts heat better than copper, and it shows **superfluidity**, that is apparent complete loss of viscosity, below 2.2 K. (Later, his friend *Landau* was able to explain these properties of helium II.)

Also in 1934 he returned to the USSR to visit his mother; and he was not allowed to leave, despite protests from the West. Soon, he learned (from reading *Pravda*) that he had been made head of a new and luxurious Institute for Physical Problems near Moscow. His equipment was sent to him from Cambridge, and his wife (he had remarried) was allowed to return to the UK for their children. One of his col-

leagues was Landau, who was arrested in the 1930s and accused of being 'an enemy of the state'. Kapitsa protested forcefully, and successfully; Landau, unusually, survived.

From 1939 Kapitsa worked on liquid air and oxygen, which aided Soviet steel production. He did not work on atomic weapons, and wrote to Stalin in 1946 criticizing the competence of the notorious Beria, head of the NKVD (secret police) as director of the programme. For this he was exiled to house arrest in the country, where he worked on high temperature physics and on ball lightning (a type of plasma) aided by his sons; after eight years Stalin was dead and Beria executed, and Kapitsa was restored to his post and worked on plasmas. Soon he was permitted visitors, and in his seventies was allowed to travel. In 1929 he had been elected an FRS (the first foreigner for many years) and in 1978 he shared a Nobel Prize for his work in low temperature physics.

KARRER, Paul
1889-1971
Swiss organic chemist: best known for work on carotenoids and vitamins

Karrer's father was a Swiss dentist; Paul was born in Moscow, but returned with his parents to the Swiss countryside when he was three, and in 1908 began to study chemistry at Zürich under *A. Werner*. His D.Phil work with him was in inorganic chemistry, and afterwards he worked with *Ehrlich* in Frankfurt on organo-arsenic compounds for use in chemotherapy.

In 1919 he succeeded Werner, and remained in Zürich thereafter, working on organic natural products of several kinds.

In 1926 he began work on natural pigments, concentrating on the carotenoids, complex molecules containing many C=C bonds and including lycopene ($C_{40}H_{56}$, from tomatoes), the carotenes, the vitamins A_1 and A_2, and retinene the light-sensitive pigment of the eye. In the

Kekulé

1930s his masterly studies of these closely-related compounds revealed their structures, which he confirmed in many cases by synthesis (e.g., of vitamin A_1, $C_{20}H_{29}OH$, in 1931). He also worked on other vitamins (B_2 and E), on alkaloids, and on coenzymes. He shared a Nobel Prize in 1937.

KEKULÉ, Friedrich August
1829-1896

German organic chemist: founder of structural organic chemistry, and proposer of ring structure for benzenoid compounds

Kekulé began his student career in archi-tecture at Giessen, but he heard *Liebig* give evidence in a murder trial and was attracted to his chemistry lectures. Later he studied in Paris and London. He claimed that the key idea of organic molecular structure came to him in a daydream, on the upper deck of a London bus. His theory (1858) adopted *Frankland*'s idea of valence; that each type of atom can combine with some fixed number of other atoms or groups. Kekulé proposed that this 'valence' for carbon atoms is four. He also proposed that carbon atoms could be linked together to form stable chains, which was a new and vital idea.

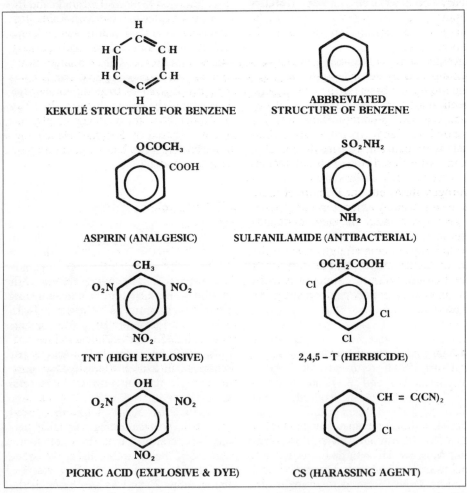

KEKULÉ STRUCTURE FOR BENZENE

ABBREVIATED STRUCTURE OF BENZENE

ASPIRIN (ANALGESIC)

SULFANILAMIDE (ANTIBACTERIAL)

TNT (HIGH EXPLOSIVE)

2,4,5 – T (HERBICIDE)

PICRIC ACID (EXPLOSIVE & DYE)

CS (HARASSING AGENT)

Structure diagrams for benzene and some derivatives

It only needed the further idea, gradually developed by many chemists, that these structural formulae based on carbon chains represented molecular reality, for organic chemical theory to make the largest step in its history: for these structure diagrams, as the formulae became, could be deduced from the chemical and physical properties of the compound. From the diagram, in turn, new properties could be predicted; and so these molecular structures became the fruitful focus of every organic chemist's thinking. In the hands of *Baeyer* especially, experimental work on this basis pushed ahead. The ideas of structural theory became well known through Kekulé's lectures in Ghent (from 1858) and then at Bonn (from 1867) and from his textbook (1859).

Kekulé contributed little as an experimentalist, but his second gift to theory did much to form a basis for the new organic chemical industry making dyes and drugs from coal tar products. This was his proposal of 1865, that the six-carbon nucleus of benzene consisted, not of a chain, but a closed ring of carbon atoms. In benzene each carbon atom carries a hydrogen atom, but one or more of these can be replaced by other atoms or groups, to give a vast range of compounds (see diagram). As with his structure theory, Kekulé was anticipated by *Couper* in the idea of a cyclic molecule, but the latter's illness ensured Kekulé's superior place in developing the theory and securing his reputation.

KENDALL, Edward Calvin

1886-1972

American biochemist: pioneer of corticosteroid biochemistry

Kendall studied chemistry at Columbia University, New York, and afterwards worked mainly at the Mayo Foundation in Rochester, Minnesota. During World War I he isolated from the thyroid gland a new amino acid, thyroxin. This contains iodine, and it is a component of the thyroid hormone (thyroglobulin) which partly controls the rate of the body's metabolism. Kendall went on to study the hormones of the cortex (outer part) of the adrenal glands. In the 1930s he isolated a series of steroids from this source; one of them (Kendall's compound E, later named cortisone) was shown by his co-worker P. S. Hench to relieve the symptoms of rheumatoid arthritis. During World War II there was a belief that the Germans were buying adrenal glands from Argentine slaughterhouses and using extracts from them to help their pilots fly at great heights. The rumour was false, but it led to intensified study and by 1943 no less than 23 corticosteroids had been isolated in the US or in Switzerland, and Kendall and others had devised synthetic routes to make related compounds. Since then, corticosteroids have been much used to treat inflammatory, allergic and rheumatic diseases. In 1950 the Nobel Prize for medicine or physiology was shared by Kendall, Hench and T. Reichstein, who had worked on these compounds at Zürich.

KEPLER, Johannes

1571-1630

German astronomer and physicist: discovered laws of planetary motion

The son of a mercenary, Kepler had smallpox at the age of three, damaging his eyesight and the use of his hands, which makes his achievements the more remarkable. Kepler became a follower of *Copernicus* whilst studying theology at Tübingen, intending originally to go into the church. He became a teacher of mathematics in the Protestant Seminary at Graz in Austria. In 1600, having been forced to leave his teaching post due to the religious persecution of Protestants, he was invited to join *Brahe* in Prague, who assigned him the task of working out the orbit of Mars. Two years later Brahe died, leaving Kepler his 20-year archive of astronomical observations. In 1609, having failed to fit Brahe's observations of Mars into the perfectly circular orbits of the Copernican cosmology, he formulated **Kepler's first two laws of planetary motion**: that planets follow elliptical orbits with the Sun at one focus; and that the line joining a planet to the Sun, as it moves, sweeps through equal areas in equal times. At last understanding the principles of planetary motion, Kepler then proceeded with the more onerous but valuable task of completing the 'Rudolphine Tables', the tabulation of Brahe's results for his sponsor Emperor Rudolph, a job which he did not complete until 1627. A fine scientist, he was also a mystic and astrologer, cast horoscopes, and believed in the 'music of the spheres' (from the planets).

In 1611 civil war broke out, Rudolph was deposed, and Kepler's wife and child died. He moved to Linz, where he propounded his **third law of planetary motion**: that the squares of the planetary periods are proportional to the cubes of their mean distances from the Sun. He also wrote a book on the problems of measuring the volumes of liquids in wine casks that was to be influential in the evolution of infinitesimal calculus.

Johannes Kepler

KERR, John
1824-1907

British physicist: discovered the electro-optical and magneto-optical Kerr effects

Kerr was educated at the University of Glasgow, becoming a research student with Lord Kelvin (*W. Thomson*), and working with him in the converted wine cellar known as 'the coal hole'. He later became a lecturer in mathematics at the Free Church Training College for Teachers in Glasgow, continuing his research in his free time.

Kerr is best remembered for the effect that bears his name. In 1875 he showed that birefringence (double refraction) occurs in some materials such as glass when subjected to a high electric field. With great experimental skill he showed that the size of the effect is proportional to the square of the field strength; the **electro-optical Kerr effect** is used today as the basis for ultra fast optical shutters (*c.* 10^{-10} s), using a **Kerr cell** in which a liquid (e.g., nitrobenzene) undergoes birefringence. He also discovered the **magneto-optical Kerr effect**, in which plane-polarized light reflected from the polished pole of an electromagnet becomes elliptically polarized: the effect has been used in the study of domain structure and other magnetic properties of ferromagnetic materials.

KETTLEWELL, Henry Bernard Davis
1907-1979

English lepidopterist and geneticist: experimented to confirm Darwin's theory of natural selection

A medical graduate who practised in England and worked on locust control in South Africa, Kettlewell's best-known work was done as an Oxford geneticist in the 1950s. He noted that many species of peppered moths which in the mid-19th century were light in colour had became dark by the 1950s. He deduced that the darkening (melanism) was related to the darkening of the tree stems on which the moths remained by day, by industrial smoke. This would cause dark forms to survive predation by birds more successfully. To test his idea, he released light and dark forms of one moth (*Biston betularia*) in large numbers in both a polluted wood near Birmingham, and in an unpolluted wood. Recapture of many of the moths after an interval confirmed that the light form survived best in the unpolluted wood, and the converse in the Birmingham wood. The result provides some experimental confirmation of *Darwin's* theory of natural selection.

KHORANA, Har Gobind
1922-

Indian-American molecular biologist: co-discoverer of genetic code and first synthesizer of a gene

Educated at universities in the Punjab, at Liverpool, Zürich and Cambridge, Khorana moved to Vancouver in 1952 and extended his work in the area he had studied in Cambridge; the synthesis of nucleotide coenzymes. From 1960-70 he was at Wisconsin, and while there he carried out valuable syntheses of polynucleotides with known base sequences. These were of great value in establishing the 'genetic code word dictionary'. This refers to the fact that the four bases (A, C, G and T) present in DNA chains are 'read' in linear groups of three (codons), as was known by the late 1950s. It was also known that the sequence is non-overlapping and 'commaless'. Since four bases in groups of three allow $4^3=64$ combinations, but these code for only 20 amino acids which make up proteins, it would appear that some codons are 'nonsense codons' and/or some amino acids are coded by more than one codon.

Khorana had a major part in the work which established the dictionary, by his synthesis of all the 64 codons. This was an essential step in the further development of molecular biology. It turns out that the

H. Gobind Khorana

first two bases in a codon triplet are the main determinants of its specificity. Khorana's continued work on RNA and DNA has included the synthesis of a DNA from *E. coli*, a gene with 126 nucleotide base pairs. He has been at the Massachusetts Institute of Technology since 1970 and shared a Nobel Prize in 1968 with M. W. Nirenberg and R. W. Holley, who also made major contributions in this area.

KIPPING, Frederick Stanley
1863-1949

English chemist: discoverer of silicones

A student at Manchester and Munich, Kipping became a co-worker and friend of W. H. Perkin Jnr., and a professor at Nottingham from 1897 to 1936. Early in his research career he attempted to make compounds of silicon analogous to some of the familiar organic compounds based on carbon; specifically he sought ketone analogues. His actual product was a polymer mixture, soon named 'silicone', and over a period of years he published extensively on compounds of this type. He foresaw no practical use for them as

223

late as 1937, but wartime needs for new materials linked with his methods led to their production in the 1940s for use eventually as specialist lubricants, elastomers, hydraulic fluids, sealing compounds, insulators and surgical implants; specialist uses include the soles of moon boots for astronauts. This family of polymeric organosilicon compounds contain chains of Si-O-Si links, and are inert and water-repellent. A key step was the discovery in 1940 by E. G. Rochow of an easy route to methyl silicones.

KIRCHHOFF, Gustav Robert

1824-1887

German physicist: pioneer of spectroscopy; devised theory of electrical networks

Kirchhoff was educated at the University of Königsberg (now Kaliningrad, USSR), and spent his professional life at the universities of Breslau, Berlin and Heidelberg. An early accident made him a wheelchair user, but did not alter his cheerfulness.

Kirchhoff was still a student when in 1845 he made his first important contribution to physics, formulating **Kirchhoff's laws**, which enable the current and potential at any point in a network of conductors to be determined. The two laws are extensions of Ohm's law, and state that: (i) the sums of the currents in a network must be zero at circuit junctions, $\Sigma\ I=0$, and (ii) $\Sigma\ IR=\Sigma\ V$, when applied to a closed loop in the network. Kirchhoff's other contributions to the study of electricity include demonstrating that oscillating current in a conductor of zero resistance propagates at the speed of light, and the unification of static and current electricity.

Kirchhoff was a life-long friend and collaborator of the chemist *Bunsen*, and it was with him that much of his work on spectroscopy was done. They established atomic flame spectroscopy as an analytical technique, using the nearly colourless flame of the gas burner invented by Bunsen, and a prism designed by Kirchhoff. In 1860 they demonstrated that when metal compounds are heated in a flame they emit spectral lines which are characteristic of the metal concerned, a fact which led Bunsen to discover the elements caesium and rubidium shortly afterward. Kirchhoff discovered that the dark *Fraunhofer* spectral lines in the Sun's rays were intensified when sunlight passed through the burner flame containing certain salts, leading him to the realisation that they were absorption lines

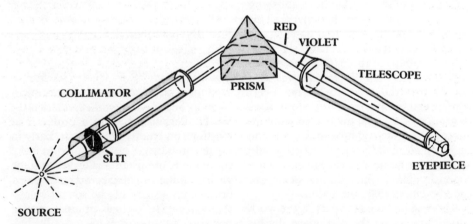

Basic components of a prism spectrometer. Light from the source passes through an adjustable slit, and the collimator lens forms a parallel beam. This is refracted and dispersed by a prism, and the resulting spectrum is observed through a telescope, fitted with cross hairs and mounted to rotate horizontally so that line positions in the emission spectrum can be measured.

corresponding to elements found in the Sun's atmosphere. He also showed that the ratio of the emission and absorption powers of radiation of a given wavelength from all bodies is the same at the same temperature (**Kirchhoff's law of emission**), from which he later developed the concept of the black body. The study of black body radiation was the key in the development of quantum theory. *See photo p.73.*

KIRKWOOD, Daniel

1814-1895

American astronomer: discovered and explained the gaps in asteroid belt

Kirkwood observed that the orbits of the asteroids are not evenly distributed within the asteroid belt, there being a number of bands in which no asteroids are found (the **Kirkwood gaps**). He demonstrated that these bands correspond to orbital periods that are simple fractions of Jupiter's orbital period, and that any asteroids lying within the 'gaps' would eventually be gravitationally perturbed into other orbits. Kirkwood was similarly able to explain the *Cassini* division in the rings of Saturn as being due to the effect of its satellite Mimas.

KITASATO, Shibasaburo

1852-1931

Japanese bacteriologist: co-discoverer of antitoxic immunity, and of the plague bacillus

Kitasato grew up in an isolated mountain village, where his father was mayor. He studied medicine at Tokyo, and in 1886 was sent by his government to study bacteriology with *Koch* in Berlin. He proved an exceptionally good student and became a close friend; and in 1889 he grew the first pure culture of the tetanus bacillus, which A. Nicolaier had described in 1884. In 1890, working with *Behring*, they showed that animals injected with small doses of tetanus toxin developed in their blood the power of neutralizing the toxin; and that their blood serum could protect other animals for a time. This discovery (**antitoxic immunity**) quickly led to the use of serum (made in horses) for treating tetanus, and a similar antitoxin was developed for treating diphtheria, and for protection against the diseases. The theory of these immunological reactions was developed especially by *Ehrlich*.

In 1892 Kitasato returned to Japan, and in 1894 he was sent to Hong Kong to study the bubonic plague epidemic there. He succeeded in identifying the plague bacillus, at nearly the same time as A. Yersin from Paris.

KLAPROTH, Martin Heinrich

1743-1817

German chemist: a founder of analytical chemistry, and discoverer of new elements

Klaproth came into chemistry from an apprenticeship as an apothecary, as did a number of chemists of his time. By 1810 his fame was such that he had left his pharmacy and was appointed the first professor of chemistry in the new university of Berlin. Before then he had done much to develop analytical chemistry, and the standard methods of gravimetric analysis (e.g., heating precipitates to constant weight) owe much to him. His analyses led him to deduce that new elements must be present in various minerals; e.g., uranium in pitchblende (1789; named in honour of the new planet, Uranus) zirconium in zircon (1779), strontium in strontianite (1793), and titanium in rutile (1795). In each case, the free element was later isolated by others. He began the study of the rare earth metals, and he showed that nickel is present in meteorites. He was an early supporter of *Lavoisier*'s ideas, and did much to ensure that they were taught in Germany.

KLEIN, Christian Felix
1849-1925

German mathematician: the founder of modern geometry unifying Euclidean and non-Euclidean geometry

Klein studied at Bonn, Göttingen, Berlin and Paris, and began research in geometry, although he had at first wished to do physics. Work on transformation groups with *Lie* followed in 1870, and he became professor of mathematics at Erlangen at 23, having just finished service as a medical orderly in the Franco-Prussian war. In his inaugural lecture of 1872 at Erlangen he put forward the audacious 'Erlanger programm', a unification of mathematics to be achieved by considering each branch of geometry as the theory of invariants of a particular tranformation group. This was well received and influenced his colleagues to unify geometry. During most of his career he held a professorship at Göttingen, and helped to make it a centre for all the exact sciences, as well as mathematics.

Euclidean geometry comes from the metrical transformation, projective geometry from linear transformations, topology from continuous transformations and non-Euclidean geometries from their particular metrics.

Klein developed projective geometry, taking it from three to *n* dimensions and applied group theory widely, for example to the symmetries of regular solids (1884).

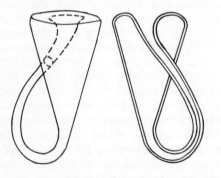

The Klein bottle, a one-sided closed surface with no 'inside'

He invented the **Klein bottle** in topology, which is a one-sided closed surface with no boundaries (it has no 'inside').

Klein also added to number theory and the theory of differential equations, and recast *Riemannian* geometry as a part of function theory. In the 1890s Klein and *Sommerfeld* worked out the theory of the gyroscope and produced a standard textbook on it; he was against the tendency of mathematics to become highly abstract, and liked engineering applications. He was also uninterested in detailed calculations, which he gladly left to his students.

KOCH, Robert
1843-1910

German bacteriologist: a founder of medical bacteriology

Koch was one of 13 children of a mine official; he studied medicine at Göttingen, served in the Franco-Prussian war of 1870, and became a district medical officer in a small town in east Germany. He became interested in anthrax, and worked on the disease in a room in his house, using a microscope given to him by his wife. Anthrax is a deadly disease of cattle, which caused huge losses in France at that time. It is highly contagious, can be passed to man, and can infect animals in fields from which cattle have been excluded for years. It was known to be caused by a bacterium. Koch found by 1876 that the anthrax bacilli can form spores (if the temperature is not too low, and if oxygen is present) and these are resistant to heat and to drying. These spores can re-form the bacillus. Koch was able to isolate the anthrax bacillus from the blood of infected cows and he produced pure cultures, able to cause the disease. For the first time, a laboratory culture was shown to cause disease. (*Pasteur* was working competitively on similar lines, and in 1882 made an anthrax vaccine which protected against the infection).

Koch much improved techniques in bacteriology. He used dyes to stain bacteria and so make them more visible under the microscope; he used a solid medium (agar gel) to grow them conveniently and separately on plates, or in the flat glass dishes designed by his assistant J. R. Petri; and he aided surgery by showing that steam kills bacteria more effectively than dry heat. From 1879 he worked in the Health Office in Berlin, where in 1882 he identified the tubercle bacillus. This was difficult work; the bacillus is small and slow-growing, but human tuberculosis ('TB') was responsible for one in seven of all European deaths at that time. In 1890 Koch was persuaded to announce a vaccine against it, but the claim was premature and his 'cure' survived only as a test method to show whether a patient had experienced tuberculosis.

From the 1880s he travelled widely, much enjoying his position as one of the first of the 'international experts'. He did major work on cholera in Egypt, in India on bubonic plague, in Java on malaria, in East Africa on sleeping sickness, and in South Africa on rinderpest. Although not as wide-ranging a biological genius as Pasteur, he is the greatest figure in medical bacteriology, and many of its leaders after him were his pupils. His Nobel Prize in 1905 was for his work on tuberculosis. His criteria that an organism causes a disease (**Koch's postulates**) remain as critical tests: they require (a) the presence of the organism in every case of the disease examined; (b) the preparation of a pure culture; (c) the re-production of the disease by a pure culture, removed by several generations from the organisms first isolated. Use of these principles of 1890 established modern medical bacteriology.

KOLBE, (Adolf Wilhelm) Hermann
1818-1884

German organic chemist: developed useful routes in organic synthesis

Kolbe was the eldest of 15 children of a Lutheran pastor. He studied chemistry under *Wöhler* and *Bunsen*, and with L. Playfair in London. He succeeded Bunsen at Marburg in 1851, and moved to Leipzig in 1865. He was an inspiring teacher and a talented researcher, despite holding firmly to outdated theories (mainly *Berzelius*'s) and his intemperate criticism of newer ideas (he vigorously abused *Kekulé*'s structure theory, for example).

His many successes in synthesis include the **Kolbe reaction**, in which a hydrocarbon is made by electrolysis of an alkali metal salt of an organic acid (this was the first use of electrolysis in organic synthesis):

$$2RCO_2K + 2H_2O \rightarrow R-R + 2CO_2 + 2KOH + H_2$$
$$\text{At anode} \quad \text{At cathode}$$

For example:

$$2Br(CH_2)_{11}CO_2K \rightarrow Br(CH_2)_{22}Br$$

Also named after him is the Kolbe or **Kolbe-Schmitt reaction**, in which an alkali metal phenoxide is heated with carbon dioxide under pressure; a carboxyl group enters the ring, and the product is a phenolic acid; e.g., a synthesis of salicyclic acid:

$$C_6H_5ONa + CO_2 \rightarrow o-(NaO)C_6H_4CO_2H$$

KOLMOGOROV, Andrei Nikolaievich
1903-

Soviet mathematician: advanced the foundations of probability theory

Kolmogorov graduated from Moscow in 1925 and in 1933 became director of the Institute of Mathematics. In 1933 his book *Foundations of the Theory of Probability* became the first rigorous treatment of the subject. The 'additivity assumption' basic to probability is set out (due originally to Jakob Bernoulli): that if an event can occur in an infinite number of ways its probability is the sum of the probabilities of each of these ways. Kolmogorov then explored **Markov processes** – those where a probability of a variable depends on its previous value but not its values before that. He constructed such processes by analytic means.

Another of his interests was the theory of algorithms (or mathematical operations, such as division), and he showed its relationship to computing and with cybernetics, which is concerned with communication and control, and 'feedback'. Kolmogorov produced a theory of programmed instructions and of how information is conveyed along communication channels.

KORNBERG, Arthur
1918-

American biochemist: devised artificial synthesis of DNA using enzymes

Kornberg graduated in chemistry and biology at City College New York in 1937, and in medicine at Rochester in 1941. For the next ten years he worked at the National Institutes of Health at Bethesda; he was also a lieutenant in the US Coast Guard. From 1959 he was professor of biochemistry at Stanford. His main concern was always with enzymes, and in 1956 he made an outstanding discovery. This was his isolation of an enzyme from *E. coli*, now called DNA polymerase I, which he showed was able to synthesize

Arthur Kornberg in 1987

DNA from nucleotide molecules (which can themselves be made synthetically) in the absence of living cells, provided that the reaction mixture included some natural DNA to act as a template and primer. This last idea was both novel and of great importance in later work on DNA. Kornberg shared a 1959 Nobel Prize with S. Ochoa for this work.

KREBS, (Sir) Hans Adolf
1900-1981

German-British biochemist: discovered energy-generating cycle in living cells

Krebs followed his father in studying medicine, and in the German practice of the time did so at five universities; and then spent four years working in Berlin on biochemical problems with *Warburg*. The latter had developed a method for studying metabolic reactions by using thin tissue slices and measuring their gas exchange manometrically, and Krebs used and improved this technique in 1932 to show how, in the liver of most animals, amino acids lose nitrogen to give urea in a process now known as the **ornithine cycle**.

The next year he escaped from Germany to England and after a short period in Cambridge, settled in Sheffield for 20 years; here most of his work was done, and notably his work on the **Krebs cycle** (also known as the citric acid or tricarboxylic acid cycle). This cycle is the central energy-generating process in cells of most kinds; occurs in their mitochondria; and generates energy for the entire organism. It was already known that foods in general are broken down to glucose and then to pyruvic acid; but those stages yield little energy. Krebs showed how the glucose is broken down in a full cycle of changes to carbon dioxide, water and energy. For this fundamental study of metabolism, Krebs shared a Nobel Prize in 1953 with F. Lipmann, who worked out important details of the cycle.

KROGH, (Schack) August
1874-1949

Danish physiologist: studied physiology of respiration

A shipbuilder's son, young Krogh was always an enthusiast for experiment, and soon after beginning medicine at Copenhagen he moved to zoology and to medical physiology. He spent his life in Copenhagen, as a zoophysiologist. As a student he worked in his room on the hydrostatic mechanism of *Corethra* larvae, devising methods for analysing gas in their air bladders and showing that they 'function like the diving tanks of a submarine'. He went on to study gas exchange in the animal lung, and the whole problem of how an animal responds to a 'call for oxygen', both in vertebrates and in insects. In this, the behaviour of the capillaries is critical, and Krogh studied their movement and expansion in the frog's tongue, and from this developed a general picture of the behaviour and response of the capillary system and its regulatory mechanism, which involves both nerves and hormones. He won a Nobel Prize in 1920.

KRONECKER, Leopold
1823-1891

German mathematician: developed algebraic number theory and invented the Kronecker delta

Kronecker was born into a rich Jewish family, and was taught at school by E. E. Kummer, who became a lifelong friend. From this time sprang his interest in number theory and arithmetic, and he went on to take his degree at Berlin (1843), receiving his doctorate in 1845 for research on complex units. Kronecker spent the next ten years managing the family estate and an uncle's banking business: he prospered and married well. When he returned to Berlin to do mathematics he was financially independent, and only lectured at the Berlin Academy

from 1861 for his own pleasure. He declined the chair at Göttingen (1868) but accepted Kummer's old chair at Berlin, holding it until his death. Kronecker was a man of wide culture, supporting the arts and interested in philosophy and Christian theology, becoming a Christian shortly before his death.

In his early mathematical research on complex units Kronecker nearly anticipated Kummer's famous concept of ideal numbers, and his work on number theory, algebra and elliptic functions unified much previous research. On algebraic numbers he rederived much of existing theory without referring to what he (incorrectly) claimed were the ill-defined complex and irrational numbers. He once made the comment in an after-dinner speech: 'God made the integers, all else is the work of man'. He was often in debate with *Weierstrass* and G. Cantor, and this gave rise to his system of axioms (1870) to support a formalist viewpoint. In linear algebra Kronecker invented the **Kronecker delta** ($\delta_{mn}=1$ if m=n and $\delta_{mn}=0$ otherwise), and established its use when evaluating determinants. It is famous as the first example of a tensor quantity being used.

KÜHNE, Wilhelm
1837-1900

German physiologist: discovered reversible photosensitivity of animal eye pigment

Although Kühne was a medical man, taught by *Virchow* and *Bernard*, and he was a professor of physiology (mainly at Heidelberg) his selection and approach to problems was rather that of a chemist. He worked on trypsin from pancreatic juice, and coined the name **enzyme** (Greek, 'in yeast') for the class of 'ferments' which activate chemical change in living cells. Other compounds which interested him were also proteins; he studied post-mortem change in muscle and found the protein myosin to be the cause of rigor mortis. In the 1860s he separated various types of egg albumen; and when in 1876 F. Boll discovered a photosensitive protein pigment in the retina of a frog's eye, Kühne took up the study of this 'visual purple' (now known as rhodopsin) and showed that it is bleached by light and regenerated in the dark. The retina works, he showed, like a renewable photographic plate; and he obtained a pattern of crossbars of a window on the retina of a rabbit, which had been kept in the dark, exposed to a window, and killed. It needed new techniques, in the 1930s, for G. Wald and others to advance knowledge of the mode of action of rhodopsin.

KUIPER, Gerard Peter

1905-1973

Dutch-American astronomer: discovered Miranda and Nereid

Educated in Leyden, Kuiper moved to the US in 1933. He discovered two new satellites: Miranda, the fifth satellite of Uranus; and Nereid, the second satellite of Neptune, in 1948 and 1949. He also studied the planetary atmospheres, detecting carbon dioxide on Mars and methane on Titan, the largest Saturnian satellite. Kuiper was involved with the early American space flights, including the Ranger and Mariner missions.

L

LAËNNEC, René Théophile Hyacinthe
1781-1826

French physician: invented the stethoscope

Laënnec studied at the Charité Hospital in Paris and qualified as a doctor in 1804. Despite ill-health he did much to advance clinical diagnosis, and his writing on disease is modern in approach. It was well known that listening to chest sounds (auscultation) was useful in diagnosis, and tapping the chest (percussion) had been shown by J. L. Auenbrugger in 1761 to be informative also.

In 1816 Laënnec met a difficulty in hearing the heart action of a plump and shy young woman, and solved it by connecting his ear to her chest with a paper tube. He was surprised to find that the heart sounds were then louder and clearer. He soon replaced his paper tube with a wooden tube, 30 cm long: the first stethoscope. It was not until the end of the century that the binaural stethoscope, with rubber tubes to both ears, replaced the simple tube in general use, and became the physician's most readily identifiable instrument. Laënnec was able to link chest sounds with a range of diseases, mainly of the heart and lungs, and described his results in his book *On Mediate Auscultation* (1819). He was an outstanding clinician.

LAGRANGE, (Comte) Joseph Louis
1736-1813

French mathematician: revolutionized mechanics

Born of a French father and Italian mother in Turin, Lagrange saw the family wealth frittered away when he was a teenager. He took to mathematics early and became a professor at the Royal Artillery School in Turin at 19. He moved in 1766 to succeed *Euler* as Director of the Berlin Academy of Sciences. In 1797 he moved to Paris as professor of mathematics at the École Polytechnique. His first wife died young; when he was 56 he married a teenage girl, remaining happily married until his death. He was a highly productive mathematician but his health broke down due to overwork, and he suffered periodically from intense spells of depression; he virtually gave up mathematics by his late 40s. He was modest and widely liked.

The great book for which he is known, the *Analytical Mechanics*, was started when he was 19, but despite early progress was only finished and published when he was 52. It developed mechanics, and used a powerful combination of the calculus of variations and the calculus of four-dimensional space to treat mechanical problems generally. The book does not use geometric methods as *Newton* did (there are no diagrams!).

Lagrange made contributions to the gravitational three-body problem and to number theory; he proved some of *Fermat's* unproven theorems, and solved the ancient problem of finding an integer x such that (nx^2+1) is a square where n is another integer (not a square).

Lagrange worked with *Lavoisier* on weights and measures, and in effect was the father of the metric system. Napoleon thought very highly of him.

LAMARCK, Jean (Baptiste Pierre Antoine de Monet)
1744-1829

French naturalist: proposed early ideas on variation and on evolution

Lamarck's fame is peculiar. Part of his

work, on classification and on variation, was widely approved in his own time and later; but some of his ideas on evolution were strongly attacked then and since, and partly so through misunderstanding of his emphasis and meaning. The eleventh and youngest child of poor aristocrats, he joined the army at 16, served in the Seven Years War, and then (for health reasons) gave up the army and, after working in a bank, began to study medicine.

His interest first focused on botany, and his writing on this (and, especially, his introduction of an easy key for classification) impressed the famous naturalist *Buffon*, and he became botanist to the King in 1781, and after the revolution, a professor of zoology in Paris in 1793. After that he worked mainly in zoology, especially on the invertebrates (a term he introduced; he was also a very early user of the word 'biology'). After 1800 he put forward general ideas on plant and animal species, which he began to believe are not 'fixed'. One reason for his view is that domesticated animals vary greatly from their wild originals. He proposed that in Nature it is the environment which produces change; his most quoted example is the giraffe's neck which he thought was a result, over generations, of the animal reaching up for food. A facet of his views was that such a change could be inherited; and this attracted ridicule, and was largely abandoned after the work of *Darwin* and *Mendel*. Somewhat unfairly, 'Lamarckism' is linked with the idea of inheritance of a characteristic acquired in life. In this form Lamarck has few supporters (the Soviet botanist T. Lysenko was one), although recent claims have been made that acquired immunological tolerance in mice can be inherited. More broadly, Lamarck and Buffon can now be seen as having views on common descent, a 'chain of being' for living things, which formed a precursor to the theory of evolution offered by Darwin and *Wallace*.

LAND, Edwin Herbert
1909-

American inventor: invented Polaroid, and a fast photographic process

To obtain polarized light (i.e., light in which the electromagnetic vibrations are all in one plane) the early method was the use of a *Nicol* prism. Later it was realised that passing light through some organic crystals gave polarized light (i.e., the crystals are dichroic) but the crystals could not be grown to large size. While Land was a Harvard student, he realised that very small crystals would serve the purpose if they were all aligned together and not randomly orientated; and he found a way of doing this, with the aligned crystals (of quinine iodosulphate) embedded in a clear plastic sheet of any required size. The result was given the trade name Polaroid, and it is widely used in scientific instruments requiring polarized light; and in sunglasses, where it is useful because reflected sunlight is partly polarized. Land abandoned his degree course to develop his inventions; the best-known is an ingenious camera in which a multi-layered film is used with developing chemicals included, which are released to process the film in seconds, to give an acceptable colour print. He never graduated in the usual sense; but Harvard awarded him an honorary doctorate in 1957 to add to his exceptionally large collection of honorary degrees.

LANDAU, Lev Davidovitch
1908-1968

Soviet theoretical physicist: explained remarkable properties of liquid helium

Landau was the son of a petroleum engineer and a doctor, and attended the universities of Baku and Leningrad. In 1929 he met *Bohr* in Copenhagen, forming a long-lasting and productive working friendship. In 1932 he moved to Kharkov, becoming professor of physics in 1935. In 1937 *Kapitsa*, setting up the Institute of

Physical Problems in Moscow, asked Landau to be director of theoretical physics. A professorship at Moscow State University followed in 1943. As a great teacher and personality Landau (known as Dau) created the strong school of theoretical physics in Moscow, contributing to statistical physics, thermodynamics, low-temperature physics, atomic and nuclear physics, astrophysics, quantum mechanics, particle physics and quantum electrodynamics. He published from 1938 (with E. M. Lifshitz) a famous series of textbooks. Landau explained the superfluidity and high thermal conductivity properties of helium II using the concepts of a phonon (quantized vibrational excitation) and a roton (quantized rotational excitation). He was awarded a Nobel Prize in 1962 for this work and other contributions to condensed matter physics.

Sadly, he was critically injured in a road accident in 1962, and never recovered, dying six years later.

LANDSTEINER, Karl

1868-1943

Austrian-American immunologist: discoverer of human blood groups

Born and educated in Vienna, Landsteiner graduated there in medicine in 1891, and spent the next five years in university research in chemistry partly with E. Fischer in Würzburg. He held posts in pathology in Vienna until 1919, then moved to the Netherlands and finally, in 1922, to the Rockefeller Institute in New York. 'His work in medical science was wide-ranging, but his results in immunology and especially on blood groups outshine the rest.

Before 1900, blood transfusion had an unpredictable outcome. In that year Landsteiner showed that the blood serum from one patient would often cause the red blood cells of another to 'clump' (agglutinate). He went on to show that all

human blood can be grouped, in terms of the presence or absence of antigens (A and B) in the red cells, and the corresponding antibodies in the serum. Either antigen may be present (blood groups A and B) or both (AB) or neither (O), giving four groups of this kind. Using this idea, with simple tests for grouping blood samples, R. Lewisohn's discovery in 1914 that sodium citrate prevents clotting – and helped also by refrigeration – blood banks and blood transfusion were widely used by the time of World War II. Other blood antigens were later found, for example the MNP system (in 1927) and the Rhesus factor (1940) both discovered by Landsteiner and his co-workers, and both (like the A, B, AB and O types) inheritable. Other blood group systems have since been found. The complexity of blood types now known leads to millions of blood type combinations.

Landsteiner's work won him a Nobel Prize in 1930, and has been valuable not only for safe transfusion, but also in paternity cases, forensic work, and in anthropology for tracing race migration.

LANGEVIN, Paul

1872-1946

French physicist: established modern theory of magnetism, and invented sonar

Langevin was a student of *Perrin* in Paris and later worked there with *Pierre Curie*; in between he spent nearly a year with *J. J. Thomson* in Cambridge. His interests in physics were wide-ranging and he became the leading French physicist of his time.

Work on ionized gases led him to study the magnetic properties of gases; most are feebly diamagnetic (repelled by a magnetic field) but ozone (O_3) is paramagnetic (weakly attracted into the field). Langevin showed in 1905 that magnetic behaviour could be understood in terms of the electrons present in atoms; electrons had recently (1895) been discovered by Thomson.

In World War I, he worked on a method for detecting U-boats by echo-sounding, using the reflection of ultrasonic waves (i.e., sound waves of very high frequency, and not audible). Curie had studied the piezoelectric effect—the small change in the size of some crystals produced by an electric field. Langevin used radio circuitry to produce rapid changes in electric potential in a crystal, so that it vibrated and formed an ultrasonic generator. Reflection of the waves for submarine detection was developed too late for World War I, but was used in World War II as 'sonar'. It is used also to survey the seabed, to detect fish shoals, and in medical scanning.

Shortly before World War II, Langevin worked out how to slow down fast neutrons, a method essential for the later work by others on atomic reactors. After France fell to the Germans in 1940, he was outspoken in his anti-fascist views and was soon under house arrest; his daughter was sent to Auschwitz and his son-in-law was executed. Langevin escaped to Switzerland and survived to return to his Paris job, as director of a research group.

LANGLEY, Samuel Pierpont
1834-1906

American astronomer and aviation pioneer: invented the bolometer and pioneered infrared astronomy

Langley was mainly self-educated as an engineer and astronomer. His most important contribution to astronomy was the invention of the bolometer, a device consisting of a thin blackened platinum wire which, when used in conjunction with a spectrometer and a galvanometer, allows very precise measurement of the energy of radiation at different wavelengths. This enabled him to study the solar spectrum at wavelengths of up to 5.3 μm in the far infrared, to measure variations in the solar flux, and also to quantify the selective absorption of energy by the Earth's atmosphere.

Being interested in the possibility of manned flight, Langley constructed a steam-powered model aircraft in 1896 which achieved flights of up to 1200 m in length, and which was the first heavier-than-air powered machine to fly. Unfortunately a full-sized version failed to leave the ground.

LANGMUIR, Irving
1881-1957

American chemical physicist: inventor of ideas and devices, often related to surfaces

Langmuir was the third of four sons, and was only 17 when his father died; but the latter worked in insurance and the family was financially secure. The young man attended the School of Mines at Columbia (New York) and then studied at Göttingen with *Nernst*. His work there, on the dissociation of gases by a hot platinum wire, began an interest in surface chemistry which he never lost. In 1901 he joined the General Electric Company research centre at Schenectady, New York, and worked there for 41 years. An early success for him was the improvement of tungsten filament lamps, by filling them with inert gas (argon) at low pressure to reduce evaporation; and by using a coiled-coil filament. Further work on hot filaments led to the discovery of atomic hydrogen and the invention of a welding torch using its recombination to H_2 to achieve a temperature of 6000°C.

In 1919-21 he worked on ideas of atomic structure, developing the ideas of *Lewis* to form the **Lewis-Langmuir octet theory of valence** which was simple and useful in explaining a range of chemical phenomena. The words electrovalence and covalence were first used by him. His interest in hot surfaces moved to thermionic emission, where his work advanced both theory and practice. His study of surface films on liquids allowed some deductions on molecular size and shape; and his work on gas films on solids led to the **Langmuir adsorption isotherm**, the first important theory of the adsorption of gases on solid surfaces.

His ideas on surface adsorption advanced understanding of heterogeneous catalysis. He was awarded the Nobel Prize for chemistry in 1932 largely for this, becoming the first scientist fully employed in industry to receive a Nobel Prize. He went on to work on electric discharges in gases, and made the first full studies of plasmas (a word he coined). He was a keen sailor and flyer, and his studies of atmospheric physics led to trials in weather control (e.g. rain-making by seeding clouds with solid CO_2). He had a wide range of interests, including music, conservation, and Scouting; and his distinctions include having Mount Langmuir in Alaska named after him.

Pierre Simon de Laplace

LAPLACE, (Marquis) Pierre Simon de
1749-1827

French mathematician, astronomer and mathematical physicist: developed celestial mechanics; suggested hypothesis for origin of the solar system

Although from a poor family, Laplace's talent led him to become an assistant to *Lavoisier* in thermochemistry. Later he moved to astronomy, and became a minister and senator, skilfully contriving to hold a state office despite violent political changes. Laplace's most important work was on celestial mechanics. In 1773 he showed that gravitational perturbations of one planet by another would not lead to instabilities in their orbits (*Newton* had believed that such small irregularities would, without divine intervention, eventually lead to the end of the world). He later proved two theorems involving the mean distances and eccentricities of the planetary orbits, and showed that the solar system has long-term stability. In 1796 Laplace proposed in a note that the Sun and planets were formed from a rotating disk of gas; he did not know that *Kant* had made a similar

suggestion; modified forms of this nebular hypothesis are still accepted. Between 1799 and 1825 he published his five-volume opus *Mécanique Céleste* (Celestial Mechanics), which incorporated developments in celestial mechanics since Newton as well as his own important contributions. (The book has its oddity; frequently the phrase 'it is obvious that' occurs, in mathematical equations, when it is far from obvious. And Napoleon is said to have remarked, critically, that it had no mention of God.) Laplace is also remembered for putting probability theory on a firm foundation, and for developing the concept of a 'potential', and its description by the Laplace equation. In the fields in which Laplace worked and where Newton had worked previously, he is seen as second only to Newton in his talent.

LARMOR, (Sir) Joseph
1857-1942

Irish physicist: worked out the electrodynamics of electrons

Larmor was educated at Queen's University Belfast and Cambridge and took posts at Queen's College Galway and Cambridge. In 1903 he became Lucasian Professor of Mathematics there. He was also a member of parliament for eleven years.

Larmor was active in the final phase of classical physics that laid the ground for the breakthroughs in relativity and quantum mechanics. He incorrectly believed in the ether (i.e., an absolute space-time frame) and that it was involved in all wave propagation. He contributed to electromagnetic theory, optics, mechanics and the dynamics of the Earth. In electrodynamics he showed (1897) that the plane of an orbiting electron in an atom wobbles (or precesses) when in a magnetic field (**Larmor precession**). The expression for the power radiated by an accelerated electron (proportional to the square of its charge and the square of its acceleration) is also due to him.

LARTET, Edouard Armand Isidore Hippolyte
1801-1871

French palaeontologist: demonstrated that man had lived in Europe during the Ice Age, and discovered Cro-Magnon man

The son of a wealthy landowner, Lartet studied law at Toulouse before taking over the management of the family estates. He became interested in fossils and discovered two early primates, *Pliopithecus* in 1836 (an ancestor of the gibbon) and *Dryopithecus* in 1856 (an early ape). In 1863 he discovered the first evidence that man had been living in Europe during the Ice Age when he found, in a cave at La Madeleine near Toulouse in southern France, a piece of ivory with the figure of a woolly mammoth carved on it. Five years later, at Cro-Magnon in the Dordogne, he found several skeletons of Cro-Magnon man, the earliest known predecessor of man in Europe (although a relatively recent ancestor by hominid standards).

LAURENT, Auguste
1807(or 8)-1853

French organic chemist: classifier of organic compounds

Laurent was an organic chemist of much talent and energy, who studied under *Dumas*. Thereafter his life was fraught with misfortune to an operatic extent; employers swindled him, posts he hoped for were unavailable or were found to lack facilities, a business venture failed, and his contributions to theory brought him abuse until almost the end of his life. His last post, as underpaid Assayer to the Mint, provided a damp cellar as laboratory and he died of lung disease just before his book *Methods of Chemistry* (1854) was published, leaving a near-destitute family. He was a skilful experimenter with a passion for classification; in particular, he developed Dumas's ideas on organic substitution. He recognized that organic compounds could be classed in 'types', and he used this, and his idea of a nucleus of carbon atoms within an organic compound, to organize much of the organic chemistry of his time. This led to vigorous debate, from which a clearer view of organic compounds emerged by 1860. Laurent also did valuable work in benzene and related chemistry. His work in organic chemical theory is interwoven with *Gerhardt*'s work.

LAVOISIER, Antoine Laurent
1743-1794

French chemist and social reformer: creator of the Chemical Revolution and victim of the French Revolution

Lavoisier's father was a prosperous lawyer in Paris, and the boy studied law after leaving school. However, he had been interested in science at school, and later a family friend *Guettard*, the geologist, took him on field trips. Lavoisier worked on the first geological map of France; this work, and his competition essay on a method of street-lighting, was so good

A. L. Lavoisier

that he was elected to the Royal Academy of Sciences in 1768, when he was only 25. In the same year he bought a part-share as a 'tax-farmer', to give him an income while he followed his new interest, chemistry. The tax-collecting company had leased from the Government the right to collect some indirect taxes for six years. The investment proved reasonable; he worked hard on company business; and at 28 he met and married the 14-year old daughter of a fellow tax-farmer. She became the expert assistant in his chemical work. Later, involvement in the tax-farm was to prove unfortunate.

Lavoisier worked on a scheme for improving the water supply to Paris, and on methods of purifying water. He showed in 1770 that water cannot be converted into earth, as was then widely believed. In this, as in all his work, he used the **law of conservation of matter**, that in chemical operations, matter is neither created nor destroyed. He went on to show that air is a mixture of two gases; oxygen, which combines with reactive metals on heating, and which supports combustion and respiration; and the unreactive nitrogen. He found that metals combine with oxygen to give oxides which

are basic ('alkaline'), whereas the non-metals (S, P, C) give acidic oxides. In this work he used the sort of logic he admired in *Black*'s studies on lime; and he was helped by information from *Priestley*; but he used his own work, and that of others, to form a general theory of combustion, oxidation and the composition of the air, in an original way. His new theory soon displaced 'phlogiston' from chemist's minds, and directed chemistry onto new and valuable paths. He showed that water was a compound of hydrogen and oxygen; *Cavendish*'s work on this was skilful, but it was Lavoisier who first explained the results. (Similarly, *Scheele* and Priestley had made oxygen before him, but failed to understand its significance).

From 1776 he lived and worked happily at the Royal Arsenal, in effective charge of gunpowder production and research. It was there, with *Laplace* as Lavoisier's co-worker, that Black's early work on calorimetry was extended; an ingenious ice calorimeter was made for this, and heats of combustion and respiration were measured; this was the beginning of thermochemistry. (A young assistant to Lavoisier at the Arsenal, E. I. du Pont, emigrated to America and in 1802 began making gunpowder on the banks of the Brandywine River at Delaware. The venture prospered, and founded a major US chemical industry.) In 1787, with three other French chemists, Lavoisier introduced the method of naming chemical compounds which has been used ever since. His main contributions to chemistry were elegantly set out in his *Elementary Treatise on Chemistry* (1789) with fine plates by his wife. In it he gave his definition of a chemical element, as 'the last point which analysis can reach'; this was *Boyle*'s view, but Lavoisier used it experimentally and gave a working list of elements. The book had enormous influence on chemistry, comparable with *Newton's Principia* in physics a century earlier.

Lavoisier had remarkable energy: from 1778 he ran an experimental farm near Blois to improve the poor level of French agriculture; he developed schemes for improving public education, equitable taxation, savings banks, old age insurance, and other welfare schemes. His liberal and generous views found too few imitators, however, and by 1789 revolution had begun. All might have gone well for Lavoisier, for although the tax-collecting firm was a natural target, its affairs were in good order and charges against the tax-farmers could be refuted. But revolution followed its usual pattern of moving to extremism, and Marat, a leading figure in the Terror, had early in his career pursued scientific ambitions but his worthless pamphlet 'Physical Researches on Fire' had been condemned by Lavoisier. A new charge of 'counter-revolutionary activity' was speedily contrived which ensured a guilty verdict, and France's greatest scientist was guillotined the next day.

LAWES, (Sir) John Bennet
1814-1900

English agriculturalist: founder of Rothamsted Experimental Station

Lawes had an amateur interest in chemistry, but after inheriting a farm estate at Rothamsted in 1834 he became an enthusiast for agricultural chemistry. He found that ground bones ('mineral phosphates') were effective in some fields but not in others; and soon discovered that acid treatment of bones made a universally effective fertilizer (it converts the insoluble tricalcium phosphate into soluble monocalcium phosphate, a conversion which acidic soils perform naturally). Despite bitter opposition from his mother (who was against 'trade') he began to make and sell 'superphosphate' prepared from bone or mineral phosphate and sulphuric acid, and used the profits to finance further experiments at Rothamsted. Aided by a chemist, J. H. Gilbert, much valuable work was done there, including the demonstration by 1851 that as well as minerals, plant growth generally

requires nitrogenous manure (in conflict with *Liebig*'s views). In 1889 Lawes put Rothamsted under control of a trust, and its scientific studies of agriculture continued.

LAWRENCE, Ernest Orlando
1901-1958

American physicist: invented the cyclotron and produced new radioactive elements

Lawrence's father was head of a teacher's college and his mother had taught mathematics. The boy grew up in South Dakota; he was tall, energetic, fond of tennis and physics, and impatient of 'culture' and of inactivity throughout his life. He studied at South Dakota, Minnesota and Yale and in 1928 moved to a post at the University of California at Berkeley, becoming director of the Radiation Laboratory in 1936.

From 1929 Lawrence worked to produce sufficiently energetic particles for nuclear reactions, having noted *Eddington*'s suggestion that stars may be 'powered' by nuclear reactions. Linear accelerators for making high-energy particles were awkwardly long and used high voltages. Lawrence decided to accelerate

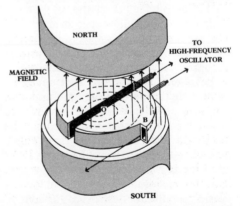

Lawrence's cyclotron. The oscillator reverses the PD between the dees several million times per second. Positive ions (e.g. protons, H^+) are released at the centre, and are accelerated into nearly circular paths until they emerge with a high energy. The spiral path is actually many km long, i.e. the spiral is 'tightly wound'.

particles on a spiral path within a pair of semi-cylinders ('dees') mounted in a vacuum between the poles of an electro-magnet. An AC voltage at high frequency applied to the dees gave the particles their impetus. The first small cyclotron (using a 10 cm magnet) operated in 1931. Later and larger cyclotrons achieved proton beams of 8×10^4 eV, and converted lithium nuclei to helium nuclei to confirm *Cockcroft* and Walton's first nuclear transformation (1932). Hundreds of new radioactive isotopes were eventually pro-duced, including most of the tran-suranium elements; Lawrence investi-gated their use in medicine. Mesons and antiparticles were generated and studied, with Lawrence coordinating the efforts of a team. Lawrencium (Lw, atomic number 103) was named after him, and he received the 1939 Nobel Prize for physics. In 1940 his team isolated plu-tonium and neptunium, and he contri-buted to the development of the atomic bomb.

LEAKEY, Louis Seymour Bazett

1895-1972

British-Kenyan archaeologist and palaeoanthropologist: discovered several hominids

The son of a British missionary working in British East Africa (now Kenya), Leakey became interested in Stone Age man while he was young. He studied anthropology at Cambridge, reading French and Kikuyu (the tongue of the natives amongst whom he had been brought up), and taking part in a British Museum expedition to Tanga-nyika in his second year. Between 1926 and 1935 he organized a series of archaeo-logical and palaeontological expeditions to East Africa, the later ones visiting Olduvai Gorge, Tanzania, where a German lepidopterist had found fossils in 1911. During expeditions there he found hominid skulls and stone tools which he believed to represent an early ancestor of man. In 1959 his wife *Mary Leakey* found

the remains of another hominid which Leakey named *Zinjanthropus boisei*, and which was dated by the newly-developed K/Ar technique at 1.75 million years old. Further discoveries followed, including in 1960 the remains of *Homo habilis*, a tool-making hominid with a relatively large brain. Leakey's findings established East Africa as the possible birthplace of man, and traced his ancestry further back than had been possible previously. His son Richard is also a noted East African palaeoanthropologist.

LEAKEY, Mary

1913-

British palaeoanthropologist: discovered several hominids

Mary Leakey had a somewhat unconven-tional upbringing, travelling a good deal and lacking a regular formal education. Her father was a landscape painter. Interested in archaeology and early man, she attended lectures at University College, London, and between 1930 and 1933 worked on several archaeological digs in England. Her ability as an illustra-tor brought her into contact with *Louis Leakey*, whom she joined in 1935 on an archaeological expedition to Olduvai Gorge, East Africa, and married the following year. She spent much of her life searching for hominids in East Africa, and made many of the discoveries for which she and her husband became well-known. In 1959 she found the skull of *Zinjanth-ropus boisei*, a species of *Australopithecus* and a possible ancestor of man. It is notable as the first hominid to be reliably dated, by the K/Ar method, at 1.75 million years. In 1976 Mary Leakey led an expedition to Laetoli, Tanzania, on which the earliest evidence of man's ancestors yet found was discovered: two sets of hominid footprints in a layer of volcanic ash provided indisputable evidence that man's predecessors walked upright 3.75 million years ago.

LEAVITT, Henrietta Swan

1868-1921

American astronomer: discovered period-luminosity relationship of Cepheid variable stars

Originally an amateur astronomer and volunteer assistant at Harvard Observatory, Leavitt joined the staff there in 1902. Whilst studying Cepheid variable stars she noticed that the brighter they were the longer their period of light variation. By 1912 she had succeeded in showing that the apparent magnitude decreased linearly with the logarithm of the period. This simple relationship proved invaluable as the basis for a method of measuring the distance of stars. Prior to this discovery only distances of up to about a hundred light-years could be determined, by measurement of stellar parallax.

LEBESQUE, Henri Leon

1875-1941

French mathematician: introduced the modern definition of the integral

Lebesque was a product of the École Normale Supérieure, and from 1921 taught at the Collège de France. His main contributions were to set theory, the calculus of variations and function theory. He and E. Borel built the modern theory of functions of a real variable, and Lebesque in particular produced a new general definition of the integral (1902), developed beyond the Riemannian definition. This led to important advances in calculus, curve rectification, and trigonometric series and initiated measure theory.

LE CHATELIER, Henri Louis

1850-1936

French physical chemist and metallurgist: devised a much-used but doubtful principle

As a young man, Le Chatelier was much influenced by his father Louis, an engineer who was Inspector General of Mines for France. Tuition from his father and family friends such as *Deville* aided him and shaped his interests, and he became a professor in the École de Mines in 1877. His early research was on cement (his grandfather operated lime kilns); he worked also on the structure of alloys, on flames and on thermometry. In the 1880s he developed the idea known as **Le Chatelier's principle**: this states that if the conditions (temperature, pressure, or volume) of a chemical system initially at equilibrium are changed, then the equilibrium will shift in the direction which will tend to annul the change, if possible. The principle has been much criticised, and it is best replaced by two laws due to *van't Hoff*; they are (a) increase in pressure favours the system having the smaller volume, and (b) rise in temperature favours the system formed with absorption of heat. Thus for the equilibrium $N_2+3H_2\rightleftharpoons2NH_3$ in which the volume diminishes when the reaction proceeds to the right, an increase of pressure will shift the equilibrium in favour of ammonia formation. Also, as ammonia formation is exothermic, rise in temperature favours the reactants.

LECLANCHÉ, Georges

1839-1882

French engineer: devised carbon-zinc electrical cell

Educated in Paris, Leclanché was employed as a railway engineer from 1860. By 1866 he had devised his carbon-zinc electrical cell, which was soon adopted by the Belgian telegraphic service. Modified to the non-spillable form of the familiar dry cell, it has been greatly used: this has a carbon rod as the positive pole, surrounded by a wet paste of carbon black, manganese dioxide and ammonium chloride, with a thickener such as sawdust, inside a zinc container which is the negative pole.

LEDERBERG, Joshua

1925-

American geneticist: pioneer of bacterial genetics

A New Yorker almost from birth, Lederberg graduated in biological science at Columbia University, and then enrolled there in 1944 as a medical student during his service in the US Naval Reserve. At that time bacteria were not thought to have genes, or sex. During his course on medical bacteriology, Lederberg began experiments to test this and in 1946 went to Yale to work on it with the experienced microbiologist E. L. Tatum. They were skilful and lucky in the choice of the intestinal bacterium *E. coli* strain K-12 for their work, and within weeks showed that mutants of this strain crossed; in a large colony, a few reproduced by sexual mating ('conjugation'). Lederberg went on to show that this is not uncommon and can be used to map bacterial genes; bacterial genetics had begun and its methods became valuable to geneticists, as had earlier use of the fruit fly *Drosophila* and the fungus *Neurospora*.

His next major discovery, made with *Zinder* in 1952, was that bacteriophage (a bacteria-infecting virus) could transfer genetic material between strains of bacteria ('transduction') to produce recombinant types. For the first time genes had been deliberately inserted into cells, a basis for 'genetic engineering'. In 1957, with G. Nossal, he showed that immune cells produce single types of antibody, a result which was basic to the development of monoclonal antibodies by others. With his first wife, Lederberg obtained the first firm evidence that adaptive mutations in bacteria can occur spontaneously; this had been an unproved assumption in the theory of evolution. After Yale, Lederberg taught genetics at Wisconsin and at Stanford and became President of Rockefeller University in 1978. At age 33, he had shared a Nobel Prize with *Beadle* and Tatum in 1958. Aside from his work on bacterial genetics,

Joshua Lederberg in 1945

he researched on artificial intelligence, and the specific problem of computerizing some of the work of organic chemists by devising a linear notation for organic molecular structures. In collaboration with E. A. Feigenbaum, these studies pioneered the development of 'expert systems'.

LEE, Tsung Dao

1926-

Chinese-American theoretical physicist: demonstrated that parity is not conserved in the weak nuclear interaction

Lee studied for his degree in China, having his work interrupted by the Japanese invasion during World War II; he fled to another province. In 1946 he won a grant to Chicago, studying astrophysics under *Teller*; work at Princeton (1951-53) and Columbia followed. He became a professor at Columbia in 1956.

Whilst the electromagnetic and strong nuclear interactions conserve parity (that is, are identical in a mirror-image of the physical system) Lee and *Yang* showed in 1956 that this is not so for the weak nuclear interaction. They demonstrated this extraordinary result, with far-reaching implications, by considering nuclear β-decay (electron emission). They suggested a number of experiments, and in the ensuing months their conclusion was verified. Lee and Yang also argued (1960) that the very light neutral particle called the neutrino (see *Pauli*) produced in electron emission was different from the neutrino associated with muon emission. This was verified by experiment in 1961. In the same paper they predicted the existence of the **W**-boson as the heavy particle conveying the weak nuclear force, and this has since been shown experimentally. They also indicated the existence of neutral weak currents, first observed in 1973. Lee and Yang became the first Chinese to win a Nobel Prize, in 1957.

LEEUWENHOEK, Antony van
1632-1723

Dutch microscopist: observed blood corpuscles, protozoa, bacteria and spermatozoa

Leeuwenhoek had no formal training in science, and rather limited schooling. Apprenticed to a draper, he later had his own shop in Delft and a paid post in local government. He became an enthusiastic user of microscopes. The compound microscope was in use before 1650 but was optically poor, and Leeuwenhoek preferred to use a small single lens, doubly convex and of very short focus. He ground these himself and mounted them between metal plates; in all he made some hundreds of these magnifiers. He was a passionate microscopist, ingenious, secretive and with the advantage of having very unusual eyesight, so that he could use magnifications of 50× to 200× with his ultra-small lenses. He also used 'a secret method' which may have been dark-ground illumination; or the enclosure of

his specimens in a drop of liquid in some cases. His results were mostly sent to the Royal Society in illustrated letters (375 of them); unsystematic, enthusiastic, and written in Nether-Dutch, and his fame attracted visits by other microscopists and even royalty.

He was the discoverer or an early observer of blood capillaries, red blood cells, protozoa, bacteria (in 1683), Rotifers, Hydra, Volvox, and spermatozoa (of dog). He was opposed to the idea of spontaneous generation, which was not disproved until *Pasteur*'s work a century and a half later. He ground 419 lenses and lived, actively researching, to age 90.

LEHMANN, Inge
1888-

Danish seismologist: discovered solid inner core within Earth's outer liquid core

Lehmann observed in 1936 that compressional P waves travelling through the Earth's core undergo a marked increase in velocity at a depth of about 5150 km. She argued from this that there is a solid inner core within the outer liquid core already shown to exist by *Gutenberg*. It is believed that this inner core consists of solid iron and nickel.

LEIBNIZ, Gottfried Wilhelm
1646-1716

German mathematician: one of the greatest polymaths in history

The son of a Lutheran professor of moral philosophy, Leibniz developed an interest in a wide range of subjects from his father's library. He attended the universities of Leipzig, Jena and Altdorf, where he received his doctorate in law in 1666. Leibniz was to show talent in law, theology, statecraft, history, literature, and philosophy as well as mathematics.

He took up a career as a somewhat shady lawyer and diplomat working initially for the Elector of Mainz. During two trips to London in 1673 and 1676 *Huygens* and *Boyle* interested him in current work in mathematics, and in his spare moments Leibniz proceeded to make the immense discoveries of both the calculus (independently from *Newton*) and combinatorial analysis. Leibniz was at the same time much involved with establishing the legal rights of the legitimate and many illegitimate members of the household of the three electors whom he was to serve. Frequently on the move, and prolifically noting his brilliant thoughts on many subjects, he was involved in diplomacy and in making plans for a French invasion of Egypt. His talents were dissipated in the sordid tasks of his master's power-broking. He also became involved in an unsuccessful attempt to unite the Catholic and Protestant churches in 1683, and the founding of the Berlin Academy of Sciences (1700). When his last employer, the Elector of Hanover, had been steered into becoming George I of England, Leibniz was discarded and left behind to write the Brunswick family history. He died neglected, dogged by illness and in the midst of controversy over his invention of the calculus.

In mathematics Leibniz had tremendous flair. He invented a calculating machine (1672) far beyond *Pascal*'s which could only add and subtract; it could also multiply, divide and find square roots. When a young man, he conceived of a universal language for logic and began the study of symbolic logic. Later came his construction of the differential and integral calculus, and a fierce priority dispute on this with Newton; Leibniz did his work following him (after 1665) but independently. The notation now used in calculus is that due to Leibniz. A minor part of his work was on infinite series, where he discovered in 1674 a curious relation between π and all the odd numbers: $\pi/4 = 1 - 1/3 + 1/5 - 1/7 + 1/9 \ldots$ which had earlier been found by *Gregory*.

LEMAÎTRE, (Abbé) Georges Edouard 1894-1966

Belgian astronomer and cosmologist: originator of the big bang theory for the origin of the universe

Lemaître studied at the University of Louvain, and afterwards trained and was ordained as a Catholic priest. He then spent some time at Cambridge and in America before accepting the position of professor of astronomy at Louvain in 1927, where he remained for the rest of his career.

Lemaître was an originator of the big bang theory for the origin of the universe. In 1927 he found a solution to *Einstein*'s equations of relativity that resulted in an expanding universe (Einstein's own solution was a static one), and two years later *Hubble* showed observationally that this was indeed the case. Independently, the Russian *Friedmann* came to similar conclusions. However, Lemaître further suggested that, by backward extrapolation, the universe must at one time have been small and highly compressed, which he referred to as the 'primal atom'. He conjectured that radioactive decay had resulted in an explosion, the 'big bang'. Although the importance of Lemaître's work was not fully appreciated at the time, the big bang theory is now accepted as the best model for the origin of the universe.

LENARD, Phillipp Eduard Anton 1862-1947

German physicist: investigated the photoelectric effect and cathode rays

Lenard, the son of a wine-merchant, was educated at Budapest and in Germany where he became professor at Heidelberg in 1907.

Before 1914 Lenard made a series of fundamental contributions to physics. He took the known fact that ultraviolet light falling on some metals causes electron emission (the photoelectric effect) and showed that this occurred only with light below a critical wavelength; that the electron velocity increases with falling wavelength and is independent of light intensity; and finally that increasing the light intensity produces a larger number of emitted electrons (1902). *Einstein* explained all these observations in 1905 and with *Planck* introduced light quanta (photons) into physics, preparing the way for the development of quantum theory.

Lenard showed that cathode rays are an electron beam and received the 1905 Nobel Prize for physics for this work. The cathode rays would penetrate air and thin metal sheets, and he deduced that atoms contained much empty space and both positive and negative charge (1903). *Rutherford*'s work confirmed and extended this picture of the atom (1911).

Lenard had disputes over priority with *Roentgen* (Lenard having narrowly failed to discover X-rays) and with *J. J. Thomson*, but his case does not appear strong. Lenard's book *Great Men of Science* (1934) is marred by his omission of contemporaries with whom he had quarrelled. He was distressed that Germany lost World War I, and afterwards by the death of his son and the loss of his savings by massive inflation. He developed an extreme dislike of the increasing mathematical sophistication of physics through the influence of Einstein and others. From 1919 Lenard argued for the establishment of 'German physics' untainted by Jewish theories, attacking Einstein as a socialist, pacifist and a Jew, but above all for being a theoretician. As the only leading scientist who was a Nazi supporter, Lenard acquired increasing power, and in the 1930s a generation of scientists left Germany, with most of Germany's capacity to achieve creative physical science departing with them.

LENZ, Heinrich Friedrich Emil

1804-1865

Russian physicist: discovered Lenz's law

Lenz studied chemistry and physics at the University of Dorpat (now Tartu), served as geophysicist on a voyage around the world when he was 19, and on his return was appointed to the staff of St Petersburg Academy of Science, eventually becoming Dean of Mathematics and Physics.

On his voyage around the world Lenz made some important investigations of barometric pressure and of sea temperature and salinity, establishing (and explaining) the difference in salt content between the Atlantic and Pacific Oceans and the Indian Ocean. However, he is best remembered for his work on electromagnetism; **Lenz's law** states that the current induced by an electromagnetic force always flows in the direction to oppose the force producing it. This is a special case of the more general law of conservation of energy. He also showed that the resistance of eight metals increases with temperature, and discovered (independently from *Joule*) the proportionality between the production of heat and the square of the current flowing in a wire.

LEVERRIER, Urbain Jean Joseph

1811-1877

French astronomer: predicted position of Neptune, and discovered advance of perihelion of Mercury

Leverrier was a student and then a teacher at the École Polytechnique, initially in chemistry and later in astronomy. Realising that the irregularity of the orbit of Uranus was due to the influence of an undiscovered planet further out, Leverrier succeeded in computing the mass and orbit of the perturbing body. He sent his prediction of the missing planet's position to Johann Galle in Berlin, who discovered Neptune on his first night of looking, 23 September 1846. Although Leverrier initially received the credit for the discovery, it soon became clear that *J. C. Adams* had made the same prediction a year earlier; this led to a celebrated dispute, not made easier by Leverrier's arrogance and violent temper.

Leverrier was the first to appreciate the advance of the perihelion (the point of its orbit nearest the Sun) of Mercury, and predicted the existence of a planet between Mercury and the Sun to explain it, even going so far as to name it Vulcan. No such planet has ever been found, and the advance of the perihelion was subsequently explained using *Einstein*'s theory of general relativity.

LEVI-MONTALCINI, Rita
1909-

Italian neurophysiologist: discovered nerve growth factor

Montalcini's training was difficult; her Italian-Jewish family long opposed her entry to medical school, and when she graduated World War II began, and as a non-Aryan she had to go into hiding. Her early research was done in her bedroom with G. Levi on the neuroembryology of the chick; eggs were easy to secure and could be eaten after experimentation. In 1947 she went to Washington University in St Louis, and in 1949 with V. Hamburger showed that the embryonic nervous system produces many more nerve cells than are needed; the number of survivors depends on the volume of tissue they need to serve. From this clue, she went on to discover the nerve growth factor (NGF), which appears to be critically involved in the growth of nerves of all kinds, including those of the central nervous system.

With the biochemist S. Cohen she showed that male mouse saliva is a good source of NGF; and he went on to discover the related epidermal growth factor (EGF). In 1979 Levi-Montalcini retired from directing the Laboratory for Cell Biology in Rome, and in 1986 she shared a Nobel Prize with Cohen; she was then 77. Her work may well prove fundamental to the understanding and treatment of senile dementia.

LEWIS, Gilbert Newton
1875-1946

American physical chemist: major contributor to the theory of chemical bonding

A Harvard graduate, Lewis studied in Germany for two years and then went to the Philippines as a government chemist. From 1905-12 he was at the Massachusetts Institute of Technology, and then spent the rest of his career at the University of California. He died at Berkeley while experimenting on fluorescence.

Lewis developed *Gibbs*'s ideas on chemical thermodynamics, and made the experimental measurements which allowed the outcome of a range of chemical reactions to be predicted by calculation. He was also a pioneer in taking ideas concerning electrons from physics and applying them in chemistry. From 1902 he shaped his ideas on this subject and published them in 1916; they were then publicized and expanded by *Langmuir* and later by *Sidgwick*. In developed form (as in his work of 1923) Lewis's ideas focused on the arrangement of electrons around atomic nuclei. He assumed that elements heavier than the lightest two (H and He) had a pair of electrons surrounding the nucleus, with further electrons (in number to balance the nuclear charge) in groups, with a group of eight as especially stable. Bonding between atoms of the lighter elements occurred in such a way that atoms gained or lost outer electrons to create octets, either by transfer (electrovalence) or by sharing (covalence). Noting that nearly all chemical compounds contain an even number of electrons, he concluded that the **electron pair** is especially important, and a shared pair can be equated with a covalent bond. The familiar 'dot diagrams' showing the electronic structure of many simple compounds are devised on this simple theory.

Lewis also saw the importance of electron pairs in another context. He defined a base as a substance which has a pair which can be used to complete the stable shell of another atom; and an acid as a substance able to accept a pair from another atom, to form a stable group of electrons. This very general concept of **Lewis acids and bases** has proved valuable.

Probably no man has done more to advance chemical theory in this century, but he was always a diffident as well as an attractive and engaging person, with an unorthodox mind.

LIBBY, Willard Frank
1908-1980

American chemist: developed radiocarbon dating technique

Libby taught at the University of California at Berkeley until 1941, when he joined the Manhattan Project developing the atom bomb. After the war he moved to the Institute of Nuclear Studies at the University of Chicago, returning to California in 1959.

In 1939 Serge Korff discovered ^{14}C, a radioactive isotope of carbon with a half-life of 5730 years, and showed that it is produced in the upper atmosphere by the action of cosmic rays on nitrogen atoms. In 1947 Libby and his colleagues utilized this discovery to develop their radiocarbon dating technique, which has proved to be invaluable in archaeology and Quaternary geology. The technique is based on the fact that living biological material contains ^{14}C and ^{12}C in equilibrium with the atmosphere (which contains a very small but approximately constant proportion of ^{14}C to ^{12}C). However, when the organism dies it stops taking up carbon dioxide from the atmosphere, and so the proportion of ^{14}C to ^{12}C starts to diminish as the ^{14}C undergoes radioactive decay. By measuring the proportion of ^{14}C to ^{12}C, therefore, the time since death may be determined. The technique is applicable with reasonable accuracy in dating organic objects up to about 40 000 years old, but greater

accuracy can be achieved by calibrating the technique with objects of known age, and this has been done back to about 5000 years ago. This calibration is desirable because the rate of production of ^{14}C in the atmosphere varies slightly with time. Libby was awarded the 1960 Nobel Prize for chemistry for his work.

LIE, Marius Sophus
1842-1899

Norwegian mathematician: discovered the theory of continuous transformation groups

Lie was inspired to study mathematics by reading *Poncelet* and J. Plücker on geometry, and spent his life fruitfully developing the latter's idea of creating geometries from shapes as elements of space rather than points. Research in Berlin (with *Klein*) and in Paris was somewhat marred by being arrested as a spy (1870), but this false charge was soon dropped, and he left Paris just before the Germans besieged it. A year in a mental hospital interrupted later work at Leipzig, and he then returned to a post created for him at Christiania in Norway (now Oslo University).

Lie, along with his close friend Klein, introduced group theory into geometry, using it to classify geometries. Lie discovered the contact transformation which maps curves into surfaces (1870). Work on transformation groups followed (1873) and he invented **Lie groups** which use continuous or infinitesimal transformations. Lie used these groups to classify partial differential equations, making the traditional methods of solution all reduce to a single principle. The Lie group also gave the basis for the growth of modern topology.

LIEBIG, (Baron) Justus von
1803-1873

German organic chemist: the greatest chemical educator of his time

As a druggist's son, Liebig was attracted early to chemistry. In 1822 he went to

Justus von Liebig

study in Paris (then the centre for chemistry) and became assistant to *Gay-Lussac*. By 1825 he became professor in the very small university at Giessen, near Frankfurt. He stayed there for nearly 30 years, and set up his famous laboratory for students of practical chemistry. It was not the first, as he claimed; but, like his research group of graduate students, it was the model on which systematic training in chemistry was afterwards based elsewhere. His university is now the Justus von Liebig University. In 1826 his work showed that the fulminates, and the very different cyanates (made by *Wöhler*) had the same molecular formulae. This sort of phenomenon (isomerism) could not then be explained, but it showed that a molecule was not merely a collection of atoms; they were arranged in particular ways, with each arrangement corresponding to one compound and one set of properties. The work led also to his friendship with Wöhler, and their valuable work on the benzoyl group. The friendship survived when Liebig's combative nature had eventually spoiled all his other chemical friendships.

By 1830, Liebig had developed a method for the analysis of organic compounds which was quick and accurate, by burning them in a stream of air, and oxidizing the products fully to CO_2 and H_2O; collecting and weighing this CO_2 and H_2O gave a direct way to find the percentages of carbon and hydrogen in the organic compound. Liebig and his students used this method to analyse hundreds of organic compounds, and the results were basic for the great advances to be made (notably by *Kekulé*) in organic chemistry after about 1850.

In his middle age, from 1840, Liebig worked on what we would now call biochemistry. He argued (correctly) that carbohydrates and fats are the fuel of the animal body; and (incorrectly) that fermentation did not involve living cells. In agriculture, he argued (rightly) for the use of potassium and phosphorus-containing fertilizers, but underrated the importance of nitrogen, and of soil structure, in fertility. He always played a vigorous – sometimes ferocious – part in debates on chemical theory; his pupils dominated organic chemical teaching; and his views moved agriculture towards chemistry. He made a good deal of money out of his scientific work, and attracted criticism for it.

LIND, James
1716-1794

Scottish physician: treated scurvy after making first controlled experiment in clinical nutrition

A surgeon's apprentice at 15, Lind later became a Naval surgeon. He was interested in scurvy ('the plague of the sea') first seen in sailors at the end of the Middle Ages when, for the first time, sea voyages lasted some months. Vasco de Gama had noted in 1498 that oranges were temporarily curative. In 1747, Lind made his excellent nutritional experiments, dividing a crew of scorbutic sailors into small groups given different dietary supplements for 14 days. He found that citrus fruit with the diet gave much improvement in six days; and in 1754 he published *A Treatise on the Scurvy*. Adoption of the treatment and use of fruit to prevent the disease was slow, although *Cook* used the method in his great southern explorations of the 1770s, losing only one man (out of 118) to scurvy in three and a half years. Only by 1795 was lime juice given regularly to sailors; even so, cases were still reported in the following century, from prisons, the Crimean War, and polar expeditions (possibly including Scott's). By 1907, Norwegian workers had induced scurvy experimentally in guinea pigs; *Hopkins*'s classic work on vitamins had begun; and in 1928 *Szent-Gyorgy* isolated vitamin C (ascorbic acid), present in citrus fruit, and deficiency of which leads to scurvy.

LINDBLAD, Bertil
1895-1965

Swedish astronomer: proposed rotation of our galaxy

Jacobus Kapteyn had discovered from a survey of stellar motion in 1904 that most stars fell into two groups, or streams, moving in opposite directions in the sky. In 1924 Lindblad was the first to propose the rotation of our galaxy as an explanation for this phenomenon, an idea that was soon confirmed by *Oort*.

LINNAEUS, Carl
1707-1778

Swedish botanist: the great classifier of plants; popularized binomial nomenclature

Carl von Linné, (Linnaeus is the Latinized form), began his training in medicine at the University of Lund in 1727, but his father, a pastor and enthusiastic gardener, was unable to maintain his education. Linnaeus became interested in plants, and moved to the university at Uppsala with the help of a benefactor. Here he investigated the newly proposed theory that plants exhibit sexuality. O. Rudbeck (of *Rudbeckia*) arranged that Linnaeus should take over his unwanted

Carl Linnaeus

lectures on botany, and attendance rose from 80 to 400. He began to form a taxonomic system based on the plant sex organs, stamens and pistils. In 1732, Linnaeus undertook a visit to Lapland, and to mainland Europe (1733-35), in order to examine its flora and animal life.

Deciding to earn his living as a physician (out of necessity), he went to Holland to qualify (1735). While there he published *Systema Naturae* in which he divided flowering plants into classes depending on their stamens, and subdivided them into orders dependent on the number of their pistils. This system, though useful for ordering of the many new species being discovered, only partly showed the relationship between plants.

Linneaus returned to Sweden as a practising physician in 1738, gaining patients in court circles. In 1741 he was appointed . professor of medicine and botany at Uppsala and was able to extend his teaching, and his collection and investigation of plants. Linnaeus's passion for classification led him to list the species and gather them into related groups (genera), to gather related genera into classes, and classes into orders (*Cuvier* later grouped related orders into phyla).

Linnaeus's lasting service to taxonomy was his introduction in 1749 of binomial nomenclature; he gave each plant a latinesque generic noun followed by a specific adjective. This became the basis for modern nomenclature. Until that time plants had been given a name and short Latin description of their distinguishing features, unsatisfactory both as a name and description, and leading to a tangled overgrowth, strangling further development. The Linnaean system helped pave the way towards notions of evolution, an idea Linneaus rejected emphatically; he insisted no new species had been formed since Creation, and that none had become extinct.

Linneaus was an excellent teacher and his students travelled widely, imbued with his enthusiasm, in search of new forms of life; it is estimated that one in three died in the search.

He was a complex, self-conscious personality. He had a tidy mind and absolute belief in the value of his system. His contemporaries accepted his belief that he had brought about a revolution and he was skilful in getting others to accept his system, even though that meant setting aside much of their own work. He cleared the way for development in biology without taking part in it. The Linnaean system based solely on the sexual organs was completely artificial, but convenient. By his success he stifled botanical development for a century.

After Linnaeus's death his collection was bought by Sir James Smith. The London-based Linnaean Society, founded by Smith in 1788, purchased the books and herbarium specimens in 1828.

LIOUVILLE, Joseph
1809-1882

French mathematician: developed the theory of linear differential equations

Liouville held a professorship at the École Polytechnique for many years (1838-51), then moved to the Collège de France (1851-79). He was briefly elected to the constituent assembly in 1848, but his political career only lasted one year.

He is famous for developing **Sturm-Liouville theory**, which is part of the theory of linear differential equations and important in physics; he worked also on boundary-value problems. He made further contributions in differential geometry, conformal transformation theory and complex analysis, influencing developments in measure theory and statistical mechanics. He was the first to prove the existence of transcendental numbers (and an infinite number of them) and he suggested that e is transcendental (1844); this was proved by *Hermite*. Liouville was also editor of the influential *Journal de mathématiques pures et appliquées* from 1836 to 1874.

LIPSCOMB, William Nunn
1919-

American inorganic chemist: developed low temperature X-ray crystallography, and devised structures for boron hydrides

Educated at Kentucky and California, Lipscomb became a professor at Harvard in 1959. The boron hydrides had first been made by *Stock*, but their structures had proved mysterious; in terms of established theory they appeared to be electron-deficient. Lipscomb deduced their structures in the 1950s by X-ray diffraction analysis of their crystals at low temperatures, a technique which he and others were to use later on a variety of chemical problems. He went on to theorize on the bonding in the boron hydrides, and to extend his ideas to the related carboranes, and to use nuclear magnetic resonance methods to examine molecules. His approaches to these problems have proved highly fruitful in chemistry; he was awarded a Nobel Prize in 1976.

LISTER, (Baron) Joseph
1827-1912

English surgeon: introduced antiseptic surgery

Lister was the son of a Quaker wine merchant who was also a skilful microscopist; his achromatic microscope design (1830) marks the beginning of modern microscopy. As an arts student in London, young Lister attended as a spectator the first surgical operation under a general anaesthetic, in 1846. He then turned to medicine, qualified as a surgeon in 1852, and worked in Edinburgh, Glasgow and later in London. His main work on antisepsis was done in Glasgow. At that time, surgery was usually followed by inflammation and 'putrefaction'; of limb amputations, about half were fatal from this sepsis, and abdominal surgery was largely avoided because of it. It was widely (but erroneously) thought that sepsis was due to air reaching moist tissues, and awkward but ineffectual attempts had been made to exclude air from surgical sites. The work of *Semmelweis* in Vienna, where he showed in 1846 that sepsis after childbirth in hospital could be avoided by cleaning the hands of surgical operators, had been ignored.

In 1865 Lister read *Pasteur*'s work on fermentation. Lister concluded that sepsis was akin to fermentation, and was initiated by infectious agents, some airborne. By 1867 he had shown that antiseptic procedures are very successful; his methods were quickly adopted in Germany (e.g. in the war of 1870), and more slowly in the UK. Lister used crude phenol solution as his preferred antiseptic for dressings and instruments, and as a spray in the air of the operating theatre. Later (from 1887) he gave up the spray, and increasingly used aseptic methods, with steam as a sterilizing agent. His work enormously reduced the incidence of fatal post-surgical infection, and encouraged surgeons to develop abdominal and bone surgery. Lister's scientific work was largely related to his 'antiseptic system'; he published on inflammation, bacteriology (he was probably the first to grow a micro-organism in pure culture) and on surgical ligatures and their sterilization (his preference was catgut). He revolutionized general surgery by making it safe and was widely honoured for his work.

Joseph Lister

LOBACHEVSKI, Nikolai Ivanovich
1793-1856

Russian mathematician: discovered one of the first non-Euclidean geometries

Lobachevsky's father died when he was about six, and after his mother had moved the family to Kazan he attended the new university there in 1807. He joined its staff in 1814 and in 1827 became its Rector. He was honoured by his government, but in 1846 fell into disfavour for reasons which are unclear; he had done much for his university and his country.

From 1827 onwards Lobachevski developed the first non-Euclidean geometry to be published, although J. Bolyai was doing similar work at the same time and *Gauss* had done so decades before, but without publication. *Euclid*'s fifth postulate ('axiom XI') could not be proved. The fifth postulate is: that given a straight line and a point, just one straight line can be drawn in their plane passing through the point and never meeting the other line. Euclidean geometry was widely thought adequate to describe the world and the universe. Lobachevskian geometry accepts Euclidean postulates except the fifth, and occurs on a curved surface with two lines always meeting in one direction and diverging in the other. The angles of a triangle no longer add up to two right angles but sum to less than that. Lobachevsky's work was only widely accepted as important when *Einstein*'s general theory of relativity showed that the geometry of space-time is non-Euclidean; it also prepared the way for the systematic exploitation of non-Euclidean geometry by *Riemann* and *Klein*. Euclidean geometry is now seen as a special case, adequate for all everyday purposes, within a more general system.

LOCKYER, (Sir) Joseph Norman

1836-1920

British astronomer: discovered helium in Sun

As a young civil servant at the War Office, Lockyer developed an interest in astronomy and made it his career. He was particularly interested in the Sun, and in the use of the recently-introduced methods of spectral analysis. Following the eclipse of 1868 Lockyer discovered, independently of the French astronomer P. Janssen, that solar prominences could be seen with a spectroscope at any time, not merely during eclipses, and that the forms of the prominences slowly changed with time. He identified an unknown element in the Sun's spectrum which he named helium, and which was subsequently isolated in the laboratory by *Ramsay* in 1895. In 1873 he proposed that some unfamiliar solar spectral lines were caused by the dissociation of atoms into

simpler substances with their own spectra (the electron was not to be discovered until 20 years later; we now recognize the dissociation as loss of electrons). Lockyer was also interested in archaeology, pioneering the study of possible astronomical alignments with ancient structures. He founded the Science Museum in London and also the science journal *Nature*, of which he was Editor for fifty years.

He was a fearless fellow, in debate and as an expedition leader in pursuit of solar eclipses, and he was a founder of solar astrophysics.

LODGE, (Sir) Oliver Joseph

1851-1940

British physicist: pioneer of radiotelegraphy

Lodge's father was a supplier of pottery materials and he grew up in the Potteries, in Staffordshire. The family was prolific; Lodge had twelve children, he was the eldest of nine, and his thrice-married grandfather had 25 children.

After working for his father for seven years, he studied physics at the Royal College of Science and at University College, London. In 1881 he was appointed professor of physics at Liverpool, and in 1900 became the first Principal of the University of Birmingham.

Lodge performed early experiments into radio, showing in 1888 that radio-frequency waves could be transmitted along electric wires. Simultaneously, however, *Hertz* demonstrated that such waves could be transmitted through air, establishing the basis for radio communication and somewhat overshadowing Lodge's work. Lodge went on, however, to make some useful technical advances, designing an improved radio detector (based on the drop in resistance of some metallic powders when exposed to electromagnetic radiation), and demonstrating a form of radio telegraphy in 1894. He was the first person to attempt to detect radio waves from celestial objects. In the 1880s the

Michelson-Morley experiments had shown that the 'ether' did not exist unless it moved with the Earth, but in 1893 Lodge devised an ingenious experiment which demonstrated that even such a stationary ether did not exist. In later years he devoted much effort to the scientific investigation of extrasensory perception and psychic phenomena.

LOEFFLER, Friedrich August

1852-1915

German bacteriologist

Educated in medicine in Würzburg and Berlin, Loeffler became an assistant to *Koch* in the 1880s. Bacteriology was then a young science; pure cultures were difficult to secure and new techniques were needed. In 1884 Loeffler devised a new medium (thickened serum) in which he was able to culture the bacillus of diphtheria, then a major killing disease especially of children. He had previously discovered the organism responsible for glanders (a contagious disease, mainly of horses).

In 1898 with P. Frosch he showed that foot-and-mouth disease could be passed from one cow to another by inoculation with a cell-free extract. This demonstration that a disease of animals is due to a virus was a basic step in the founding of virology; it followed the discovery, by others, of viral diseases of plants. Soon after Leoffler's work, *Reed* showed that yellow fever is a viral disease, transmitted by mosquitoes.

LONDON, Fritz Wolfgang

1900-1954

German-American physicist: discovered the London equations in superconductivity

Fritz and Heinz (b.1907) London were the sons of a professor of mathematics at Bonn and became famous for contributions to superconductivity published together. Fritz studied classics, and did research in philosophy leading to a doctorate at Bonn. Later he was attracted by theoretical physics and worked with *Schrödinger* at Zürich in 1927, and published on the quantum theory of the chemical bond with W. Heitler. In 1930 he calculated the non-polar component of forces between molecules, now called van der Waals or **London forces**. Having fled from Germany in 1933 the brothers did research in F. E. Simon's group at Oxford. They soon published major papers on superconductivity giving the London equations (1935). Fritz moved to Duke University in the US and continued to work on superconductivity, and on the superfluidity of ^{3}He (see *Kapitsa*).

LONSDALE, (Dame) Kathleen

1903-1971

British crystallographer: applied X-ray diffraction analysis to organic crystals

The tenth and last child of an Irish postmaster, Kathleen Yardley came to London when she was five and graduated there in physics when she was 19. For 20 years she worked at the Royal Institution, and for the next 20 at University College, London, developing methods pioneered by the *Braggs* for finding molecular structure by X-ray diffraction of crystals. In 1929 she worked out her first structure of great interest to organic chemists: it was that of hexamethylbenzene, and her work showed that its benzenoid ring is a flat and regular hexagon of carbon atoms, whose carbon-carbon bond lengths she measured. Two years later she worked out the structure of hexachlorobenzene using (for the first time) *Fourier* analysis to solve the structure; the method was to become the major technique used by her and others. When she began her work on organic structures, she 'knew no organic chemistry and very little of any other kind'; but this work was of very great value to organic chemists, as was her work on the physics of crystals, which gave reality to the concept of molecular orbitals.

A passionate pacifist, Lonsdale refused in 1939 to register for civil defence or any other national service, and in 1943 she was fined £2 for the omission; refusing to pay, she spent a month in prison. In 1945 the Royal Society agreed to elect women Fellows, and she became the first female FRS.

LORENTZ, Hendrik Antoon
1853-1928

Dutch theoretical physicist: contributed greatly to the theory of the electron and of electromagnetism

Lorentz completed his studies early at Arnhem and Leyden; a thesis on light reflection and refraction won him the first Chair of Theoretical Physics in Holland at Leyden when he was 24. In 1912 he became director of the Teyler Institute, Haarlem. He did a great deal to found theoretical physics as an academic discipline in Europe.

Lorentz's thesis showed how to solve *Maxwell*'s equation when an interface between two materials is present. He was then able to predict the *Fresnel* formula for the behaviour of light in a moving medium. In 1892 his 'electron theory' was published; it regarded electrons as embedded in the ether which transmitted Maxwell's electromagnetic fields, and obeyed an additional relation for the force of the field on the electron (1895), now known as the **Lorentz force**. The Lorentz force was proposed independently by *Heaviside* (1889). Lorentz showed, by averaging microscopic forces on electrons to give macroscopic forces on materials, how Maxwell's 'displacement current' arises and why an additional term is needed. These results were later confirmed by experiment. Lorentz coined the word 'electron' in 1899, and identified electrons with cathode rays. He showed how vibrating electrons give rise to Maxwell's electromagnetic waves, and with

Zeeman explained the Zeeman effect whereby atomic spectral lines are split in the presence of magnetic fields (1896). For this research Lorentz and Zeeman were awarded the 1902 Nobel Prize for physics. So successful was the 'electron theory' that its failure to explain the photoelectric effect (see *Lenard*, and *Einstein*) was a major clue to the need for quantum theory.

Lorentz studied the result of the *Michelson-Morley* experiment, which gave no indication that the Earth was moving through the ether. He showed that if moving bodies contracted very slightly in the direction of motion, the observed results could occur. Derived independently by *FitzGerald*, this is known as the **Lorentz-FitzGerald contraction**. In 1904 Lorentz developed a firm mathematical description of this, the **Lorentz transformation**, and this was later shown by Einstein to emerge naturally out of his special relativity theory (1905).

LORENZ, Konrad (Zacharias)
1903-1989

Austrian ethologist: a founder of modern ethology

A surgeon's son, Lorenz studied medicine in Vienna in the US and graduated in 1928. Afterwards he taught anatomy in Vienna but by the mid-1930s his interest had moved to animal psychology; in fact he had collected animals and recorded their habits from childhood. In the late 1930s he made close studies of bird colonies, and in 1935 described 'imprinting'. An example of this is the way a young bird regards the first fair-sized moving object it sees as a representative of its species. This is usually a parent, but Lorenz showed it could be a model, a balloon, a tractor or a human being. In Lorenz's view, much behaviour is genetically fixed or innate; this was in conflict with the ideas of most psychologists of the 1930s who saw behaviour as entirely flexible or learned. Their emphasis was on laboratory experimentation on animal learning, while Lorentz valued studies of species-specific behaviour in the wild. In 1942 he joined the German army, was captured and spent four years as a prisoner in the USSR. Later, working in Austria, he continued his studies on birds and other animals, and his generalisations did much to found ethology as a particular branch of animal behaviour study. Lorenz has been criticized for his emphasis on innate patterns, and for his extrapolations from animals to man. His views on human agressiveness, population expansion and environmental deterioration are pessimistic. He shared a Nobel Prize in 1973 with *Tinbergen* and *Frisch*.

LOSCHMIDT, Johann Joseph

1821-1895

German physical chemist: early worker on valence theory and on molecular size

Born into a peasant family in what is now Czechoslovakia, Loschmidt studied in Prague and Vienna. In the 1840s he tried to establish himself in business but the times were difficult and in 1854 he became bankrupt. He taught science in Vienna, and became a friend of *Stefan*. His book *Chemical Studies, I* (1861) (there was never a Part II) included some novel and correct ideas: that sugar is an ether-like compound, that ozone is O_3, that benzene is cyclic, and that double and triple bonds can usefully be shown as connecting lines. He assumed variable valences for some atoms (e.g., 2, 4 or 6 for sulphur) but fixed values for C (4), O (2) and H (1). His book had little influence, and Loschmidt moved to work on the kinetic theory of gases; he calculated the first accurate value for the size of air molecules. From this he calculated in 1867 the number of molecules of gas per cm^3, but his value is about 30 times too small. However, for this pioneer attempt to obtain a value for the *Avogadro* constant N_A, the constant is sometimes named as the Loschmidt number (L); Avogadro never gave any pertinent numerical calculations on this.

LOWELL, Percival

1855-1916

American astronomer: predicted existence and position of Pluto

Son of a wealthy Boston family, Lowell travelled extensively after graduating from Harvard. His sister Amy was a major poet, and his brother became president of Harvard. Lowell's interest in astronomy was first stimulated by *Schiaparelli*'s report in 1877 of 'canali' on Mars. He became convinced that Mars was inhabited by an intelligent race and wrote books on the subject. At the beginning of this century such views were not so ridiculous as they appear today, and the excellent observatory he built in Arizona in 1894 at a height of 2200 m became an important centre for planetary studies. However, Lowell's most important contribution was the prediction (based on its gravitational influence on Uranus), of a ninth planet beyond Neptune. Although he himself searched for it from 1905 until 1914, Pluto was not detected until 1930 by *Tombaugh*, working at Lowell's own observatory. It was named after the Greek god of outer darkness.

LOWER, Richard

1631-1691

English physiologist: made first successful direct blood transfusion

Lower qualified in medicine at Oxford, when he assisted his teacher *Willis* with dissections, and then moved to London to practise; he was an early Fellow of the Royal Society, and had belonged to the Oxford group who founded it. In Oxford in 1665 he demonstrated transfusion of blood from the artery of one dog to the vein of another. Later attempts by others to transfuse from animals to humans led to some deaths, and only after *Landsteiner*'s work from 1900 on blood groups did human transfusion become useful. Lower's *Treatise on the Heart* (1669) gives a good account of the structures of the heart. He recognized that it is not 'inflated by spirits' but acts as a muscular pump, with systole as the active phase and diastole a 'return movement'. He studied the colour change between dark venous blood and red arterial blood, experimented with dogs, and deduced that the red colour results from mixing the dark blood with inspired air in the lungs; he realised that the purpose of respiration is to add something to the blood. After the 1670s he concentrated on his medical practice, and the great advance in physiology was made by *Harvey* in his discovery of the circulation of the blood.

LUBBOCK, John (Baron Avebury)

1834-1913

English biologist: contributor to archaeology, entomology, and politics

Lubbock's father was a successful banker and amateur mathematician, and the boy was placed in the family bank at 15. He was successful enough, but his main interest was in biology, in which he was self-taught. Fortunately he could concentrate fully on different matters at short intervals, and in his adult life banking, biology, politics and education all engaged him. He was lucky that *Darwin* lived near the family home, made a friend of the boy, and developed and used his talent for drawing. Lubbock early became an enthusiast for Darwin's ideas and helped to expound them, and he was one of the few men whose opinions mattered to Darwin.

In 1855 he found the first fossil musk-ox in Britain, which gave early evidence of an ice age. In the 1850s and 1860s he began to link ideas on evolution with studies in archaeology and human prehistory, and he travelled widely in Europe to study lake village sites and tumuli there. He coined 'neolithic' and 'palaeolithic' for the New and Old Stone Ages. His books on prehistory were pioneers in the field, but his work here did not obstruct another of his pursuits, entomology. He worked especially on the social insects, and devised the '**Lubbock nest**' in which he could examine colonies in a movable glass-sided container. His methods (including the first use of paint marking of insects for their identification, and obstacles and mazes to test intelligence) led to much new knowledge of their habits, instincts, and intelligence. With a device designed for him by *Galton* he showed that ants can distinguish colours, and see ultraviolet light; and he found bee's colour preferences.

He became well-known as an MP by introducing bills, on Bank Holidays ('St Lubbock's Days' in 1871), Wild Bird Protection, Open Spaces, Ancient Monuments, and a dozen more. He belongs to the rare group, including *Franklin*, distinguished in science, politics, and commerce. Few later amateur scientists can compete with that distinction.

LUDWIG, Karl Friedrich Wilhelm

1816-1895

German physiologist: pioneer of modern physiology

Ludwig enrolled as a medical student in Marburg in 1834, but he had a stormy student career. He soon had a heavily scarred lip through duelling, and conflict with the university authorities sent him to study elsewhere; but he returned to Marburg in 1840 and was teaching there by 1846. Later he taught in Zürich, Vienna and Leipzig. His work helped to create modern physiology; in this he saw no place for 'vital force', and he sought explanations of living processes in terms of physics and chemistry. In this, he was much influenced by his friend the chemist *Bunsen*. When Ludwig began, physiology had few experimental instruments. He developed the kymograph (1846) and used it to discover much about respiration and the circulation; he devised the mercurial blood pump (1859), the stream gauge (1867) and a method of maintaining circulation in an isolated organ, perfusion, (1865). His blood pump allowed the study of blood gases and respiratory exchange. Later he worked on the action of the kidneys and the heart, on salivary secretion, and on the lymphatic system. During 30 years he and his students did much to create modern physiology, and when he died almost every leading physiologist had at some time studied with him.

LUMMER, Otto

1860-1925

German physicist: experimentalist on black body radiation

After a period as assistant to *Helmholtz*, in 1904 Lummer became professor at Breslau. His early work was on photometry, and later he worked on spectrometry, but his best-known work is on radiant heat. Since a black body approximates to a perfect absorber, it follows that a black body should form an ideal radiator; but this at first seemed to be an abstract concept. However, in the 1890s Lummer and *Wien* realised that a small aperture in a hollow sphere, heated to the required temperature, should be equivalent to a black body at the same temperature. Experimental work on this basis was carried out with Wien and later with *E. Pringsheim* on the distribution of energy in black body radiation, and was important in leading to *Planck*'s quantum theory of 1900.

LYELL, (Sir) Charles

1797-1875

British geologist: established principle of uniformitarianism in geology

Lyell at first embarked on a legal career, but his interest in geology led in 1823 to his appointment as secretary of the Geological Society. During the first part of the 19th century geology had made great advances in the collection of information, but most geologists still believed in one or more world-wide 'catastrophes' to account for the creation of what they found. Lyell was responsible for the general acceptance of the **principle of uniformitarianism**, the idea that rocks and geological formations

Charles Lyell

are the result of the ordinary processes that go on every day, but acting over very long periods of time. This principle was first advocated in a general way by *Hutton*, but was much more convincingly illustrated and argued by Lyell. In 1830 he published his popular *Principles of Geology*, in which he applied his ideas in explaining many of the geological features that he had discovered on his extensive travels through Europe and America. This classic work greatly influenced *Darwin* in developing his theory of evolution, a concept which Lyell, strangely enough, never accepted.

LYOT, Bernard Ferdinand

1897-1952

French astronomer: invented the coronagraph

Lyot worked at the Paris Observatory at Meudon from 1920. He invented the coronagraph, a device which allows the Sun's corona to be observed without the necessity for a total solar eclipse, in 1930. This is achieved by creating an artificial eclipse inside a telescope with very precisely aligned optics. Lyot also pioneered the study of the polarization of light reflected from the surface of the Moon and of the planets, allowing him to infer something of their surface conditions.

M

MACARTHUR, Robert Helmer
1930-1972

Canadian-American ecologist: developed theories of population biology

Born in Canada, MacArthur moved to the US when he was 17 and studied mathematics at university, moving to Yale for his doctorate. However, in the second year of his PhD work he changed to zoology. After two years military service he returned to Yale and then concentrated on ecology. From 1965 until his early death from cancer he was professor of biology at Princeton. His first research was on five closely similar species of warbler which co-exist in the New England spruce forest, and which were thought to violate the **competitive exclusion principle**, i.e., that in 'equilibrium communities' no two species of the same animal occupy the same niche. He found that the birds tend to occupy different parts of the trees, and that the principle was followed. From then on, he studied population biology, and the strategies used to form multi-species communities. He devised ways to quantify ecological factors, and to predict mathematically the level of diversity of bird species in a given habitat. His ideas have proved influential, including his division of animals into r and K species. The r species are opportunistic, with high reproductive rates, heavy mortality, short lives, and rapid development. The K-strategists are larger, develop more slowly, and are more stable; and he was able in 1962 to show that natural selection principles apply to both groups.

MACEWEN, (Sir) William
1848-1924

Scottish surgeon: pioneer of aseptic surgery, neurosurgery and orthopaedic surgery

Macewen was very much a Glaswegian, graduating there in 1869 and afterwards working there until his death. He was a student under *Lister* at the time antiseptic methods were started in the Glasgow Royal Infirmary, but he soon modified these methods and became a pioneer of aseptic techniques, giving up the carbolic spray by 1879 and using boiling water or steam to sterilize gowns, dressings and surgical instruments. A full surgeon by age 28, his forceful personality allowed him to impose rigorous aseptic routines, and his surgery was bold and effective. In the 1880s he operated on abseses and tumours of the brain with success; surgery of the skull was ancient, but work on the brain was novel and called for skilful diagnosis and localization and precise surgery. In 1893 he reported on 74 brain operations; 63 succeeded. At the same period he developed successful bone surgery, including bone grafts. His interest in bone growth led to his work on the growth of deer antlers, published when he was over 70; he devised methods and instruments for corrective bone surgery on acute deformaties such as those resulting from rickets, then common in Glasgow children.

MACH, Ernst
1838-1916

Austrian theoretical physicist: fundamentally reappraised the philosophy of science; 'the father of logical positivism'

Mach was mainly educated at home until

age 15, but later studied at Vienna. There he became interested in the psychology of perception as well as in physics. An appointment as professor of mathematics at Graz followed (1864), and he later moved to Prague (1867) as professor of experimental physics, and to Vienna in 1895 as a professor of philosophy. A slight stroke in 1897 caused partial paralysis and he had to retire from the university in 1901. Thereafter, for twelve years he was a member of the upper chamber of the Austrian parliament.

The theme of Mach's work was his belief that science, partly for historical reasons, contained abstract and untestable models and concepts, and that science should discard anything that was not observable. Mach argued that all information about the world comes through sensations, and that the world consists of data; that which may not be sensed is meaningless. An historical view of science also convinced Mach that discoveries are made in many ways, not particularly related to the scientific method, and that accidents and intuition play a role. Mach influenced the authors of quantum mechanics, particularly the 'Copenhagen' school of *Bohr*, and the theory sharply distinguishes between observable quantities and the abstract mathematical wavefunction from which it is derived and which has a higher information content. Mach and his book *Mechanics* (1863), greatly influenced *Einstein*. What is now known as **Mach's principle** states that a body has no inertial mass in a universe in which no other mass or bodies are present, as inertia depends on the relationship of one body to another. Einstein's efforts to put this on a sound footing led to his theory of relativity. This result was not to Mach's liking and he rejected it.

Mach also did some experimental work, and investigated vision, hearing, optics and wave phenomena. In 1887 he published photographs of projectiles in flight showing the accompanying shock waves. In supersonic flow, the **Mach angle** is that between the direction of motion of a body and the shock wave. In 1929 the **Mach number** was named as the ratio of the projectile speed to the speed of sound in the same medium. At Mach 1, speed is sonic; below Mach 1, it is subsonic; above Mach 1, it is supersonic.

MACKENZIE, (Sir) James
1853-1925
Scottish cardiologist: developed instrumental methods for study of heart disease

Mackenzie was an Edinburgh medical graduate who did most of his work in Burnley. Following the unexpected death of a pregnant girl from a heart attack, he began to keep regular detailed records of heart action. For this he devised improved instruments to record ink-tracings on paper of the pulses in arteries and veins, which he correlated with heart action. He soon found that some irregularities of rate and rhythm were common and appeared unrelated to disease (previously all such disorders were thought to be signs of disease), while other arrhythmias did point to disease. His book *Diseases of the Heart* (1908) described his polygraph and its use, and was a milestone in cardiology. His recognition that advanced mitral valve disease leads to auricular fibrillation was a step towards its later treatment. He did much to reintroduce digitalis as a heart drug; it had been used by *Withering* but had fallen into disfavour because the dose needs careful regulation. The chemically pure digoxin gives much better control and is widely used.

MAGENDIE, Francois
1783-1855
French physiologist: pioneer of experimental pharmacology

Magendie graduated in medicine in Paris in 1808, and afterwards practised and taught medicine in Paris. In 1809 he described his experiments on plant poisons, using animals to find the precise physiological effect and then testing out the compounds on himself. In this way he introduced into medicine a range of the compounds from plants now known as alkaloids and which contain one or more nitrogen atoms within ring structures; many have striking pharmacological properties, and Magendie showed some of the medicinal uses of strychnine (from the Indian vomit-nut), morphine and codeine (from opium) and quinine (from cinchona bark). Magendie's studies were remarkably wide-ranging. He showed in 1816 that protein is essential in the diet, and that not all kinds of protein will suffice. He studied emetic action; the absorption of drugs; olfaction; and the white blood cells. In 1822 he showed that spinal nerves have separate paths controlling movement and sensation, confirming and extending *C. Bell's* work. His enthusiasm for vivesection sacrificed hundreds of animals, mainly dogs, which was much disapproved in England (but not in France); he pursued data, avoided theory, and did much to found the French school of experimental physiology.

MAIMAN, Theodore Harold
1927-

American physicist: constructed the first laser

Maiman was the son of an electrical engineer, and after military service in the US Navy, he studied engineering physics at Colorado University. Later he did his doctorate in electrical engineering at Stanford and joined the Hughes Research Laboratories in Miami in 1955. The maser (producing coherent microwave radiation) had been devised and induced to work by *Townes* in 1953, and Maiman improved the design of the solid-state version. He then constructed the first working **laser** (Light Amplification by Stimulated Emission of Radiation) in the Hughes Laboratories in 1960, although Townes and *Schawlow* had published a theoretical description. A ruby crystal with mirror-coated cut ends was used and this resonant cavity was stimulated by flashes of light to produce a coherent, highly monochromatic, pulsed laser beam. The first continuous wave (CW) laser was constructed by A. Javan of Bell Telephone Laboratories in 1961.

Since then, lasers have found use in a variety of applications, including spectroscopy, repair of retinal detachment in the eye, and in compact disc (CD) players. Maiman left Hughes to found Korad Corporation in 1962 which became a leading developer and manufacturer of lasers; he also founded Maiman Associates in 1968 and Laser Video Corporation in 1972. In 1977 he joined TRW Electronics of California.

MALPIGHI, Marcello
1628-1694

Italian biologist: discovered capillary blood vessels

Born in the year in which *Harvey* published his *De motu cordis* describing the circulation of blood in mammals, Malpighi graduated first at Bologna in philosophy, and then in medicine in 1653. From 1666 he was professor of medicine there, and the Royal Society of London began to publish his work, largely based on his microscopy and carried out in the 1660s and 1670s. In 1660 he began his studies of lung tissue, and the next year used frog lung. This was well suited to the early microscope, which had developed in *Galileo*'s time after 1600, but was optically poor; much of the best work in the 1650s was done using a single lens rather than a compound system. Frog lung is almost transparent, with a simple and conspicuous capillary system. Malpighi was able to observe the latter for the first time and to see that it was linked to the venous system on one side and to the arterial system on the other, thereby vindicating and completing Harvey's work on the

Marcello Malpighi

MANTELL, Gideon Algernon

1790-1852

English geologist: discovered first fossil dinosaurs

Son of a shoemaker in Lewes, Mantell studied medicine in London. In 1811 he began work as a surgeon in Lewes, but his interest in geology increased and after moving to Brighton in 1833, the interest became obsessive; his fossil-filled house became a public museum and his wife and children were displaced. He wrote much on the small fossils of the Downs, but his major discovery is that of the first dinosaur; aquatic saurian remains had been described previously, but great land saurians (dinosaurs) were unsuspected until Mantell's discoveries in 1822 at Tilgate Forest in the Cretaceous rocks of the English Weald. Mrs Mantell first noticed the teeth, with some bones, and Mantell named the large herbivorous reptile *Iguanodon*, because of its relation to the much smaller modern lizard, iguana. In 1932 Mantell discovered the armoured dinosaurs. He was essentially an enthusiastic and expert amateur, aided in vertebrate palaeontology by his surgeon's knowledge of anatomy. A full-scale model iguanodon

animal circulation. Later he studied the skin, nerves, brain, liver, kidney and spleen, identifying new structures. In 1669 he gave the first full account of an insect (the silkworm moth) and then began his work on the chick embryo. In the 1670s he turned to plant anatomy, discovering stomata in leaves and describing the development of the plant embryo.

MANSON, (Sir) Patrick

1844-1922

Scottish physician: pioneer of tropical medicine

Manson qualified in medicine at Aberdeen in 1865, and then worked in China for 23 years. He virtually founded the specialty of tropical medicine, in part by his studies of tropical parasitic infection. He studied the life-cycle of the parasite causing filariasis, and deduced that it is passed to man by a common brown (*Culex*) mosquito. In 1894 he suggested that malaria was also spread by a mosquito, and he helped *R. Ross* in the work which proved this. He also studied flukes, ringworms and guinea worms; and he effectively founded the London School of Tropical Medicine.

Gideon Mantell

was shown at the Crystal Palace in 1854. Public interest in the massive Mesozoic creatures (up to 35 m long) has remained high ever since.

MARCONI, (Marquis) Guglielmo
1874-1937

Italian physicist and engineer: pioneer of radiotelegraphy

Of mixed Italian and Irish parentage, Marconi was privately educated, and later studied at the Technical Institute of Livorno.

At the age of 21, intrigued by *Hertz*'s 'electric waves', Marconi developed radio equipment capable of transmitting for a range of over a mile (the length of the family estate). In 1896 he succeeded in interesting the British government in his invention, and three years later transmitted Morse code across the English Channel. This attracted considerable attention, particularly from the Admiralty, who began to install his equipment on Royal Navy ships. In 1901 he transmitted across the Atlantic from Cornwall to a kite-borne antenna in Newfoundland, and became a household name overnight, at the age of 27. In 1909 he shared the Nobel Prize for physics.

Although Marconi did not discover radio waves, and may be thought of as primarily an electrical engineer and businessman, he developed much of the technology necessary for its practical use, such as the directional aerial and the magnetic detector. During World War I he developed short-wave radio equipment capable of directional transmission over long distances, and by 1927 had established a worldwide radio telegraph network on behalf of the British government. He spent most of his life improving and extending radio as a practical means of communication, and building a company to commercialize it; from 1921 he used his steam yacht *Elettra* as his home, laboratory, and mobile receiving station.

MAREY, Etienne-Jules
1830-1904

French physiologist: ingenious inventor of physiological instruments

Marey's work as a physiologist gave him scope for his passion for novel mechanical devices. The arterial system of the animal body is a complex arrangement of muscular and elastic tubes; in 1860 Marey devised a portable sphygmograph which amplified the pulse movement and drew a trace of the pulse wave on smoked paper, and so gave some basic physiological information. He also began in 1876 to study irregularities of heart action, using his polygraph which recorded the venous pulse and heartbeat simultaneously; these had not been much noticed previously and he found one type in which at varying intervals there are two heartbeats which follow abnormally rapidly (extrasystoles). In the 1890s *Mackenzie* improved the polygraph and studied heart irregularities further, and both related them to disease and showed that some are non-pathological.

In 1868 Marey showed that insect wings follow a basic figure-of-eight movement, by observing a fragment of gold leaf fixed to the wing tip of a fly held under a spotlight, and also by having the wingtip brush against the smoked surface of a rotating cylinder. He saw the value of scientific photography and in 1881 devised the first useful cine camera, which used a ribbon of sensitized paper with 'stopped motion' synchronized with a rotating shutter which cut off light as the paper moved forward. By 1890 he was using this to analyse human and animal movements, by high-speed photography to slow down rapid movements; and he also invented its converse, time-lapse photography to speed up slow changes such as plant growth. From 1868 he was professor of natural history at the Collège de France, succeeding *Flourens*.

MARKOV, Andrei Andrevich
1856-1922
Russian mathematician: originator of Markov chains

A graduate of St Petersburg, Markov taught there for 25 years until his political activism led him in 1917 to a self-imposed exile in the small town of Zaraisk. His early work was on number theory, and on probability theory which he worked on from the 1890s. This led him to discover the sequence of random variables now known as **Markov chains**. A Markov chain is a chance process which has the unusual feature that its future path can be predicted from its present state as accurately as if its entire earlier history was known. Markov appears to have thought that literary texts were the only firm examples of such chains, and applied the idea to an analysis of vowels and consonants in a text by Pushkin, but his method has since been applied in quantum theory, particle physics and genetics.

MARRIOTTE, Edmé
1620-1684
French experimental physicist

The Abbé Marriotte lived in the same period as *Boyle*, and in 1676 he announced his discovery of the same law for gases which Boyle had discovered in 1662. (In France Boyle's law is named after Marriotte.) Marriotte noted also the effect of a rise in temperature in expanding a gas; and he attempted to calculate the height of the atmosphere. He also studied elastic collisions, colour and the eye (he discovered the 'blind spot' in 1660). He was a founder member of the French Academy of Sciences.

MARSH, Orthniel Charles
1831-1899
American palaeontologist

A student at Yale followed by three years' study in Europe, Marsh became in 1882 the first vertebrate palaeontologist of the US Geological Survey, as well as teaching at Yale. He established his subject in the US, and his four major expeditions to the western US with his students (and William 'Buffalo Bill' Cody as scout) in the 1870s produced startling fossil discoveries. They included fossil mammals which showed the evolution of the horse, early primates, dinosaurs, winged reptiles and toothed birds, and he traced the enlargement of the vertebrate brain from the Palaeozoic era.

MARTIN, Archer (John Porter)
1910-
English biochemist: co-discoverer of paper chromatography

Martin graduated in Cambridge in 1932 and took his PhD there in biochemistry in 1938, working on vitamins (this included looking after 30 pigs, unaided, in work on pellagra). Then he joined the staff of the Wool Industries Research Association at Leeds. There, working with R. L. M.

Archer Martin in 1975

Synge on the problem of separating complex mixtures of amino acids into their components, they developed the technique of partition chromatography. By 1944 the most familiar form had been devised by Martin; it combined with brilliant simplicity both the partition and adsorption methods. This is paper chromatography, in which a small amount of sample applied as a spot to a piece of paper is caused to move and to separate into its components by allowing a solvent front to move across the paper. The method is simple and has been of great value to chemists in analysing a variety of complex non-volatile mixtures, and is especially useful in biochemistry.

From 1948 Martin was on the staff of the Medical Research Council and from 1953 he worked particularly on gas-liquid chromatography. This separates volatile mixtures, by use of a column of absorbent (such as silicone oil) on an inert support. Again, the method has proved a hugely successful analytical technique. Martin and Synge shared the 1952 Nobel Prize.

MATTHEWS, Drummond Hoyle

1931-

British geologist: co-discoverer of magnetic anomalies across mid-ocean ridges

Together with his student *Vine*, Matthews showed in 1963 that the oceanic crust on either side of mid-ocean ridges is remanently magnetized in alternately normal and reversed polarity, in bands running parallel to the ridge. This, they argued, was consistent with the sea-floor spreading hypothesis proposed by *H. H. Hess* the year before, and was seen as powerful support for Hess's hypothesis. Newly-formed crust would become magnetized in the prevailing direction of the Earth's magnetic field at the time of its emergence, but since this field undergoes periodic reversals, the oceanic crust would be expected to be magnetized alternately in opposite directions. Vine and Matthews showed that this was

D. H. Matthews

indeed the case, and also showed that the magnetic patterns were symmetrical about the mid-ocean ridges, and that the same patterns were found for ridges in different oceans.

Matthews has since turned his attention to the continental crust, using deep seismic reflection techniques to study the lithosphere to depths of 80 km, an order of magnitude deeper than can be reached by drilling.

MATUYAMA, Motonori

1884-1956

Japanese geologist: discovered reversals in Earth's magnetic field

The son of a Zen abbot, Matuyama taught at the Imperial University in Kyoto and studied at the University of Chicago, before being appointed professor of theoretical geology at Kyoto. In 1929, whilst studying the remanent magnetization of basalts, Matuyama discovered that the direction of the Earth's magnetic field appeared to have changed its polarity since early Pleistocene times. Further investigations, notably by A. Cox and R. Doell in the 1960s, have revealed that the

263

Earth's field has abruptly reversed over 20 times during the past five million years, in an apparently random fashion. Reversals are now believed to be in some way caused by fluctuations in the convection currents within the Earth's liquid core that is the source of the field. The predominantly reversed period between 0.7 to 2.4 million years ago is known as the **Matuyama reversed epoch**.

MAUNDER, Edward Walter
1851-1928

British astronomer: discovered long-term variations in solar activity

In 1893, whilst checking historical records of sunspot activity, Maunder realised that between 1645 and 1715 there had been little activity, and that in 32 years not a single sunspot had been seen. This event, which coincides with a pronounced period of cooling in the Earth's climate (the Little Ice Age), is now known as the **Maunder minimum**. He also discovered that the solar latitude at which sunspots appear varies in a systematic way during the solar cycle.

MAURY, Matthew Fontaine
1806-1873

American oceanographer: conducted first systematic survey of ocean winds and currents

Sometimes referred to as the 'father of physical oceanography', Maury was a US naval officer who was forced to retire due to a leg injury. In 1842 he became director of the US Naval Observatory and Hydrographic Office, and organized the first systematic collection of information on winds and currents from merchant ships, greatly improving knowledge about oceanic and atmospheric circulation. In 1847 he began to publish pilot charts, which enabled sailing voyages to be dramatically shortened, cutting as much as a month from the New York to California voyage. Maury also produced the first bathymetric profile across the Atlantic (from Yucatan to Cape Verde), with a view to the laying of a submarine cable. At the outbreak of the American Civil War in 1861 he became commander of the Confederate Navy, a move which later led to a period of exile in Mexico and England.

MAXWELL, James Clerk
1831-1879

Scottish physicist: produced the unified theory of electromagnetism, and the kinetic theory of gases

Maxwell went to school at the Edinburgh Academy, where his country accent, home-designed clothes and sense of humour gained him the undeserved nickname of 'Dafty', and possibly caused his shyness; he was happier at Edinburgh University which he entered at 16. The previous year he had invented the now-familiar (but strangely undiscovered) method of drawing an ellipse using pins and thread.

In 1850 he entered Trinity College, Cambridge and graduated as Second Wrangler, winning the Smith's Prize (1854). Two years later he secured a professorship at Marischal College, Aberdeen, where he married the Principal's daughter, and in 1860 he moved to King's College, London. After the death of his father (1865), who had cared for him since his mother died when he was eight and of whom he was very fond, he remained at the family home in Scotland as a gentleman-farmer doing research. However, he was persuaded to become the first Cavendish Professor of Experimental Physics in Cambridge, setting up the laboratory in 1874. He contracted cancer five years later and died soon afterwards, aged 48. In setting up the Cavendish Laboratory, he formed an institution unique in physics, to be headed by a

James Clerk Maxwell at Cambridge aged 24; he is holding the colour top used in colour vision demonstrations

succession of men of genius, and producing graduates who dominated the subject for generations.

Maxwell was the most able theoretician of the 19th century, perfectly complementing *Faraday*, who was its most outstanding experimentalist. He began research on colour vision in 1849, showing how all colours could be derived from the primary colours red, green and blue. This led, in 1861, to his producing the first colour photograph using a three-colour process; the photograph was of a tartan. Other early work (1855-59) showed that Saturn's rings must consist of many small bodies in orbit rather than a solid or fluid ring which he showed would be unstable. He casually referred to this as 'the flight of the brickbats'.

His monumental research on electromagnetism had small beginnings. Fara-

day viewed electric and magnetic effects as stemming from fields of lines of force about conductors or magnets, and Maxwell showed that the flow of an incompressible fluid would behave in the same way as the fields (1856). Then, in 1861-2, he developed a model of electromagnetic phenomena using the field concept, and analogous vortices in the fluid which represented magnetic intensity, with cells representing electric current. Having explained all known electromagnetic phenomena, Maxwell introduced elasticity into the model and showed that transverse waves would be propagated in terms of known fundamental electromagnetic constants. He calculated that the waves would move at a speed very close to the measured speed of light. He unhesitatingly inferred that light consists of transverse electromagnetic waves in a hypothetical medium (the 'ether').

To study electromagnetic waves further, the fluid analogy was taken over into a purely mathematical description of electromagnetic fields. In 1864 he developed the fundamental equations of electromagnetism (**Maxwell's equations**) and could then show how electromagnetic waves possess two coupled disturbances, in the electric and magnetic fields, oscillating at right angles to one another and to the direction in which the light is moving. The original mechanical model was now rightly cast off.

Furthermore, Maxwell stated that light represented only a small range of the spectrum of electromagnetic waves available. *Hertz* confirmed this in 1888 by discovering another part of the spectrum, radio waves, but by this time Maxwell was dead. Maxwell also suggested the *Michelson-Morley* experiment (1881, 1887) to search for an absolute electromagnetic medium (the ether). Its proven absence prompted *Einstein*'s research on relativity (1905) and the era of modern physics.

Maxwell also contributed to the kinetic theory of gases, building on the existing picture of a gas as consisting of molecules in constant motion, colliding with their container and with each other; this picture was due to *Bernoulli* and to two little-known men, J. Herapath and J. J. Waterston. As gases diffuse into each other rather slowly, *Clausius* deduced that although they travel fast, the molecules must have a very small 'mean free path' between collisions.

From 1860 Maxwell (and independently *Boltzmann*) used statistical methods to allow for the wide variation in the velocities of the various molecules in the gas, deriving the **Maxwell-Boltzmann distribution** of velocities. Maxwell showed how this depends on temperature, and that heat is stored in a gas in the motion of the gas molecules. The theory was then used to explain the viscosity, diffusion and thermal conductivity of gases.

Maxwell and his wife found experimentally (1865) that gas viscosity is independent of pressure; and that it is roughly proportional to the temperature, and rises with it (the reverse of the behaviour of liquids). This did not agree with Maxwell's theory, and he could only gain agreement by assuming that molecules do not collide elastically but repel one another with a force proportional to their separation raised to the fifth power. This and further work by Boltzmann from 1868 allowed the full development of the kinetic theory of gases.

Maxwell was a shy man, who was deeply religious, with a strong sense of humour and no trace of pomposity. Like Einstein, and in contrast to *Newton* or Faraday, Maxwell made his enormous advances in physics without excessive mental strain. He excelled in his sure intuition in physics, in applying visual models or mathematical methods without being tied to them, and above all in freeing himself from preconceptions, and in exercising his creative imagination. Maxwell's summary of electromagnetism in his field equations is an achievement equalled only by that of Newton and Einstein in mechanics.

MAYOW, John
1641-1679

English physician: early experimenter on combustion

Mayow studied law and medicine at Oxford, practised medicine in Bath, and experimented in Oxford where he perhaps worked with *Hooke* and *Boyle*. In a book published in 1674 he gives a theory of combustion similar to Hooke's but supported by new experiments. He burned candles in air in a closed space over water, and found that the reduced volume of gas which remained would not support combustion; he got similar results using a mouse in place of a burning candle to consume part of the air. He concluded that air consists of at least two parts; one ('the nitro-aerial spirit') supports combustion or respiration, which are in this way related processes; the other part of air is inert. Ignited gunpowder continued to burn under water, so its 'nitre' contained the nitro-aerial spirit; it is surprising he did not try heating nitre (KNO_3) alone and so discover oxygen, and this may be because he visualized his 'spirit' as a philosophical principle rather than as a gaseous substance. In experiments with an air-pump (probably Boyle's) he found that venous blood under the pump effervesced only gently, but arterial blood bubbled freely if fresh. He had sensible, if primitive, views on chemical affinity. In many ways Mayow was ingenious both as an experimenter and in ideas, but it can be said also that few of the ideas were new and his theory of combustion was hopelessly confused in comparison with *Lavoisier*'s clear-mindedness a century later.

McCLINTOCK, Barbara
1902-

American plant geneticist: discoverer of jumping genes

Educated at Cornell, McClintock spent time at Caltech and at Freiburg, then taught at Missouri, and later returned to teach at Cornell. From the 1940s she worked at the Cold Spring Harbor Laboratory, where she discovered and studied a class of mutant genes in maize. It was in maize genetics that she made her major discoveries which were, strangely, to be neglected by most other geneticists for many years before late recognition and the award to her of the first unshared Nobel Prize for physiology or medicine to be given to a woman, in 1983.

Her results with maize led her to the very novel idea that the function of some genes is to control other genes; and that some of them are able to move on the chromosome and control a number of other genes. This concept of **'jumping genes'** is now familiar and accepted, even though it is far from fully understood; as she demonstrated, it must involve physical movement of DNA from site to site. One aspect of McClintock's work, on promotor and suppressor genes, was to be much extended by *Monod* in the 1960s.

Edwin M. McMillan in 1952

McMILLAN, Edwin Mattison
1907-

American physicist: discoverer of neptunium

Educated at Caltech and Princeton, McMillan joined the University of California at Berkeley in 1935 and was there for the rest of his career. In the late 1930s he was mainly concerned with nuclear reactions, and the design of cyclotrons.

In 1940 with P. Abelson he showed that when uranium is bombarded with neutrons, one nuclear reaction which occurs leads to formation of a new element, the first discovered to be heavier than uranium; it was named neptunium.

The nuclear reactions are:

$$^{238}_{92}U + n \rightarrow ^{239}_{92}U + \gamma \text{ (gamma radiation) (an instantaneous reaction)}$$

and

$$^{239}_{92}U \rightarrow ^{239}_{93}Np + e^- \text{ (beta radiation) (half-life of } ^{239}_{92}U, 23m)$$

McMillan obtained evidence that the radioactive neptunium decayed to form a new element plutonium (number 94) but in 1940 he moved to defence work on radar and sonar, and the new transuranic elements were studied by *Seaborg*, with continuing success. For their work on this Seaborg and McMillan shared the 1951 Nobel Prize for chemistry.

Lawrence's cyclotron had met a limit to its performance in the early 1940s; particles accelerated in it above a certain speed increased in mass in accord with *Einstein*'s theory of relativity, and this put them out of phase with the electric impulses. McMillan in 1945 devised a solution to this, by use of a variable frequency for the impulses, adjusted to keep in phase with the particles. This machine, the **synchrocyclotron**, could be designed to give results up to 40 times more powerful than the best cyclotrons.

MECHNIKOV, Ilya Ilich (in French, Elie Metchnikof)

1845-1916

Russian-French biologist: discoverer of phagocytosis

Educated in Russia and Germany, Mechnikov taught zoology in Odessa from 1872. Ten years later he inherited modest wealth, and went to Messina in Italy on a research visit. There he studied the conveniently transparent larvae of starfish, and noticed that some of their cells could engulf and digest foreign particles; he called these amoeba-like cells 'phagocytes' (cell eaters). In 1888 he moved to Paris to the Pasteur Institute, and continued his search for phagocytic action. He found that in human blood a large proportion of the white cells (leucocytes) are phagocytic and will attack invading bacteria. Infection leads to an increase in the number of white cells, and phagocytosis at the site of a local infection leads to inflammation and a hot, red, swollen and painful region with dead phagocytes forming pus. From 1898 Mechnikov studied human ageing; he believed that phagocytes eventually began to digest the cells of the host (an early idea of auto-immune disease) aided by the effects of intestinal bacteria. If these effects could be resisted, he argued, the normal human life-span would be 120-130 years. For his work on phagocytosis he shared a Nobel Prize in 1908.

MEDAWAR, (Sir) Peter Brian

1915-1987

British immunologist: pioneer in study of immunological tolerance

Born in Brazil, the son of a Lebanese-British businessman, Medawar was educated in England at Marlborough (which he much disliked) and then at Oxford, studying zoology under J. Z. Young from 1932. In the 1940s he began to study skin grafts in connection with wartime burn victims, and when he moved in 1947 to Birmingham he continued this interest. He was a keen and skilful experimenter; he was aware that grafts are successful between certain types of twins; and he knew of *Burnet*'s work suggesting that an animal's ability to produce antibodies against foreign cells (and hence rejection of a transplanted tissue) is not inherited but is developed in foetal life, and so he believed that 'immunological tolerance' should be achievable. Medawar's ingenious work with mouse skin grafts supported Burnet's idea. From this stemmed the successful human organ transplants achieved by surgeons from the 1960s, using tissue-typing to secure a partial matching between the donor organ and the patient, and using also immuno-suppressive drugs to inhibit the normal immune response which would cause rejection. Medawar moved to London in 1951, and shared a Nobel Prize with Burnet in 1960. He did not allow the strokes he had in his last 18 years to much limit his work, and his seven popular books were written in this period.

MEITNER, Lise

1878-1968

Austrian-Swedish physicist and radiochemist: co-discoverer of nuclear fission

Meitner studied physics in Vienna under *Boltzmann* and in Berlin with *Planck*. Soon she was attracted into radiochemistry, and worked with O. Hahn in Berlin in this field for 30 years.

Despite her talents she was a victim of more than one prejudice, being both a female and a Jewish Protestant. In academic Vienna she was regarded as a freak; she was only the second woman to obtain a doctorate in science there. In Berlin, the normally sensible *E. Fischer* 'did not allow women in the laboratory', although he welcomed her two years later when the State regulations changed. In 1912 she began working with Hahn at

Berlin-Dahlem, but the war soon interrupted their work. His leaves from the German Army sometimes coincided with hers from nursing duty in the Austrian Army; however, some radiochemistry involves long gaps between measurements; and so they were able to continue some of their work and announce a new radioelement, radioactinium, at the war's end. In 1918 she became head of physics in the Institute, and continued her work on radioactivity.

In the 1930s she and Hahn worked on uranium bombarded with neutrons, initially not realising that fission was occurring. By the late 1930s her Jewishness was a threat to her safety, and friends (including Hahn and *Debye*) helped her escape through Holland to Denmark and then to Sweden. In Stockholm a cyclotron was being built; although aged 60 she learned Swedish and built up her research group again. Hahn sent her the results of his work on neutron bombardment of uranium, which she discussed with her nephew *Frisch* who was visiting her. They shaped their joint ideas on 'nuclear fission' into a paper, which was actually composed over a telephone line since he had then returned to Copenhagen.

She declined to work on the atomic bomb, hoping that the project would prove impossible, and did no more work on fission. In 1960 she retired to live in England, after 22 years in Sweden.

MENDEL, Gregor (Johann)

1822-1884

Austrian botanist: discovered basic statistical laws of heredity

In the long term Mendel was certainly successful; he laid a foundation for the science of genetics. In another sense he was a failure; he did not succeed in examinations, and his research was largely ignored until 16 years after his death.

A peasant farmer's son, he entered the Augustinian monastery in Brno (now in Czechoslovakia) when he was 21 and was ordained four years later. He became a junior teacher, and during the 1850s twice tried to pass the teachers' qualifying examination. From 1851 he was sent by his order to study science for two years in Vienna, and afterwards he began his plant-breeding experiments in the monastery garden. He was elected Abbot in 1868 which left him little time to continue this work; in any event his modest personality and reputation were unsuited to publicize his scientific ideas, and most biological interest was directed elsewhere. Mendel's work had to await rediscovery by *de Vries* and others to become appreciated, in 1900. Even then it needed the vigorous advocacy of *Bateson*, and many plant and animal breeders, to be accepted.

Mendel's famous work on the inheritance of characters was done on the edible pea (*Pisum* spp.), where he studied seven characters, such as stem height, seed shape, and flower colour. The plants were self-pollinated, individually wrapped (to prevent pollination by insects) and the seeds collected and their offspring studied. The characters were shown not to blend on crossing, but to retain their identity. Mendel had a gardener's skill and his experiments were excellently organized. He found that the characters were inherited in a ratio always close to 3:1; he theorized that hereditary elements or factors (now called genes) exist which determine the characters, and that these segregate from each other in the formation of the germ cells (gametes).

His results of 1856 are summarized in two laws, expressed in modern terms as follows. The characters of a diploid organism are controlled by alleles occurring in pairs. Of a pair of such alleles, only one can be carried in a single gamete. This is **Mendel's First Law**, or the **Law of Segregation**. We now know, although Mendel did not, that this law follows from the process of meiosis and the physical existence of alleles as genes. He also found that each of the two alleles (i.e., the two forms) of one gene can combine randomly with either of the alleles of another gene

(**Mendel's Second Law**, or the **Law of Independent Assortment**). Genetics has both confirmed and refined Mendel's laws; *Morgan*'s work showed how linkage and crossing-over modify the second law.

Mendel was disappointed that his work aroused little interest, and he sent his paper to *Naegeli*, the leading German botanist, who advised him to experiment with more plants; Mendel had already studied 21 000. Curiously when *Fisher* in 1936 studied his results, he found they are statistically too ideal; possibly because a few intermediate plants occur, which Mendel classified to accord with his expectations. Or, perhaps, an assistant tried too hard to be helpful.

MENDELAYEV, Dmitri Ivanovich

1834-1907

Russian chemist: devised Periodic Table of chemical elements

Mendelayev grew up in Siberia, the last-born of a family of 14 children. His father, a teacher, became blind at this time, but his mother was a forceful woman and she re-opened and ran a nearby glass factory to give an income. When Dmitri was 14 his father died, and the factory was destroyed by fire; but the boy had done well at school and his mother decided that he deserved more education. They made the long trip to St. Petersburg (Leningrad) and he began to study chemistry, and was so successful (despite much illness) that he was given an award to study with *Bunsen* in Germany. Back in St. Petersburg from 1861, he began his career as a teacher and researcher in the university.

His career was not smooth; he was irascible and outspoken, supported the students' political ideas, and quarrelled with two successive ministers of education. He and his wife divorced and he remarried, without waiting the seven years then required by Russian law. Officially a bigamist, he was not penalised for this, but the priest was. Mendelayev

was more honoured outside Russia than within it, and he was never admitted to the Imperial Academy of Sciences, despite his work for the Russian chemical industry and his great scheme which brought order and prediction to inorganic chemistry; this was his **periodic table** (or periodic law or classification).

Mendelayev saw the need for a new textbook of chemistry in the 1860s, and in shaping his ideas for this book he prepared a series of cards, each listing the main properties of one chemical element; he liked playing patience as a relaxation. In arranging these, he was struck by the fact that if the 60 cards were placed in rows, with most of the elements in order of increasing relative atomic mass, then elements with similar chemical features were found to lie in the vertical groups (the periodic law). Mendelayev did not know of *Newlands*'s primitive work on similar lines, and his went much further. In his table of 1868-9, he boldly transposed some pairs of elements on the basis that their claimed atomic masses must be in error if they were to fit the scheme; likewise he left spaces for three yet undiscovered elements. For the latter, he predicted their properties from those of their known neighbours. By 1886 the predicted elements were discovered by other chemists, and their real properties were found to be in good accord with prediction. Later still, the noble gases and the transuranium elements were fitted into the table. The whole scheme brought order into chemistry by allowing a great range of known facts to be arranged and classified. It stands like *Newton*'s work in physics or *Darwin*'s in biology as one of the great intellectual advances in science. It was devised on an entirely empirical basis, and it was half a century later that *Moseley's* work, and that of *Bohr*, provided an explanation for it in terms of atomic structure.

Mendelayev produced his table when he was 34. It made him famous, and he worked on it for a few years, but then moved to a variety of other matters. It has framed and shaped ideas in inorganic chemistry ever since. In 1955 a new element, atomic number 101, was named mendelevium (Md) in his honour.

MERCATOR, Gerardus (Gerhard Kremer)

1512-1594

Dutch cartographer and geographer: invented Mercator map projection

Educated at the University of Louvain under G. Frisius (1508-1555), Mercator set up a centre for the study of geography at Louvain in 1534, issuing a number of maps, and also making surveying instruments and globes. Persecuted as a Protestant he moved to Duisberg in 1552, from where in 1569 he issued a map of the world in the new projection which now bears his name. The **Mercator projection** was a great advance because it allowed navigators to plot their course as a straight line of constant heading, corresponding to a great circle on the globe. To achieve this meridians of longitude were made parallel, instead of converging at the Poles. Mercator is also credited with coining the term 'atlas' to describe a set of maps.

Gerardus Mercator

Matthew Meselson in 1964

MESELSON, Matthew (Stanley)

1930-

American molecular biologist: showed how DNA double helix replicates

Born in Colorado, Meselson first studied liberal arts at Chicago and then physical chemistry at Caltech where he remained to teach physical chemistry. In 1961 he moved to Harvard.

When *Crick* and J. Watson in 1953 proposed that genes were constructed of a double helix of DNA, they also suggested that when this duplicated, each new double helix in the daughter cells would contain just one DNA strand from the original helix ('semiconservative replication'). The alternative would be for one daughter cell to contain both the old strands, and the other daughter to receive both new strands ('conservative replication'). In 1957 Meselson and F. W. Stahl showed by ingenious experiments using the bacterium *E. coli* labelled with nitrogen-15 that replication is indeed semiconservative; an important result, verifying Crick and Watson's ideas, and using intact dividing cells without the use of injurious agents.

Meselson has also worked on ribosomes, the cell organelles which are the site of protein synthesis. The ribosomes are 'instructed' on protein construction by m-RNA, and if given abnormal instructions will produce abnormal protein. When a virus invades a bacterial cell, the viral DNA releases its m-RNA which acts on the bacterial ribosomes, causing them to make viral protein rather than bacterial protein.

MEYER, Victor
1848-1897

German chemist: wide-ranging chemical experimenter

Meyer's father, a dye merchant, wished his sons to become chemists; Victor wanted to be an actor. The family persuaded him to attend some lectures in Heidelberg, and *Bunsen*'s lectures on chemistry duly converted him. He became an enthusiastic and successful chemistry student, and later a strikingly effective lecturer perhaps because of his acting skills. After working as assistant to Bunsen and to *Baeyer* he became professor at Zürich at the early age of 24. Later he succeeded Bunsen at Heidelberg, but in the 1880s he became ill and depressed and later killed himself with cyanide, a fate too common among famous chemists.

His early work on benzene compounds established the orientation of many substituted acids; but his main fame in the 1870s was due to his work on nitroparaffins; he was also the first to prepare oximes, by the reaction of hydroxylamine H_2NOH with an aldehyde or ketone. His name is much linked with a method for finding relative molecular mass by measuring vapour density; he used this first for organic compounds and then (at temperatures up to 3000°C) for inorganic compounds and elements. In 1883 he discovered (through a lecture demonstration which failed) the novel sulphur ring-compound thiophene, parent of a series of sulphur compounds. He also did valuable work in stereochemistry (he invented this word, usefully shorter than *van't Hoff*'s 'chemistry in space') and he discovered '**steric hindrance**' which he first observed in ortho-substituted benzoic acids. He made a novel range of aromatic iodine compounds, and he studied what later came to be seen as electronic effects on acidity in organic molecules.

MEYERHOF, Otto Fritz
1884-1951

German-American biochemist: elucidated mechanism of lactic acid formation in muscle tissue

Meyerhof studied medicine at Heidelberg, and began to specialize in psychiatry. However, he became attracted to biochemistry and in 1909 worked with *Warburg* and studied his methods; afterwards in Kiel, Berlin and Heidelberg, he used similar techniques to examine the chemical changes linked with muscular action. *Hopkins* had shown that lactic acid is formed in a working muscle, and Meyerhof showed how this is formed, and how it is removed when the muscle rests. He became increasingly unhappy in Nazi Germany and moved to France in 1938, and when France fell in 1940 he escaped to the US, and worked in Philadelphia until his death. He shared a Nobel Prize in 1922 with A. V. Hill, who had worked in Cambridge and Manchester on the heat evolved in muscle action. Hill was able to measure this with delicate thermocouples, and to deduce from his results that oxygen is taken up only after (and not during) the action of muscle.

MICHAELIS, Leonor
1875-1949

German-American biochemist: made early deductions on enzyme action

Educated in Germany, Michaelis worked in Berlin until 1922 when he went to Japan; in 1926 he moved to the US, first to

Johns Hopkins and then to the Rockefeller Institute. He showed in 1913 that an expression (the **Michaelis-Menten** equation) will describe the change in the rate of an enzyme-catalysed reaction when the concentration of substrate is changed; and from this and other studies he deduced that reaction between an enzyme and its substrate was preceded by their combination to form a complex. It was 50 years before this was confirmed by direct experiments. Rate studies on enzymes, and on the transport of substances through cell membranes, are now normally based on these ideas.

MICHELL, John

c. 1724-1793

English astronomer: discovered double stars, and estimated stellar distances

A Cambridge graduate in divinity, Michell was professor of geology there for two years before becoming a village rector near Leeds, a post he held for life. His scientific work was mainly in astronomy, where he had two major achievements. First, he discovered the existence of physical double stars; he deduced this from the observation that there is a large number of apparent close pairs, which he argued could not be due only to stars being near the same line of sight. *Herschel* in 1803 gave observational proof. Secondly, he was the first to make a realistic estimate of a stellar distance, by a neat argument based on the apparent brightness of the star Vega. By this means he estimated Vega to be about 460 000 AU distant, about a quarter of the correct value.

MICHELSON, Albert Abraham

1852-1931

American physicist: devised optical measurement methods of great accuracy; and showed that the hypothetical ether probably did not exist

Born in Strelno (now in Poland), Michelson emigrated with his parents to the US as a child of four. At 17 he entered the Annapolis Naval Academy (after an entry appeal in which he saw President Grant) and following graduation and a tour of duty at sea, was appointed as Instructor in Physics and Chemistry there.

His interest in science was apparently much increased from this time; and when he needed to demonstrate to the midshipmen how the speed of light can be measured, he applied himself to improving the accuracy of the measurement. It is certainly of fundamental importance for physics (and for navigation) and Michelson was to measure it with increasing accuracy throughout his life. The optical devices he used for this, based on his interferometer, were useful for a variety of purposes in physics.

In the early 1880s he visited Europe for two years on study leave, and his first interferometer was built in *Helmholtz*'s laboratory and paid for by *A. G. Bell*. It allowed the speed of light to be compared in two pencils of light split from a single beam. One result of this work concerned the so-called ether. Since waves such as sound waves or water waves require a substance or 'medium' for their transmission, it had been widely presumed that light and other electromagnetic waves must likewise require a medium, and a hypothetical ether, invisible, universal and weightless, had been invented for the purpose. However, Michelson's refined results would show the effect on light of the Earth's motion through the ether; but there was no effect, and physicists were forced to doubt if the ether really existed.

In 1881 Michelson left the Navy, and next year became professor of physics in Cleveland, Ohio. There he continued and improved his optical measurements, and with *Morley* (the professor of chemistry) confirmed the null result on the ether in 1887. This classical **Michelson-Morley experiment**, a major result in physics, won him a national prize in 1888, 'not only for what he has established, but also for what he has unsettled'. In a sense the problem was not 'settled' until 1905 when *Einstein*'s theory of relativity dispensed with the need for ether.

Michelson went on to apply his ingenuity and skill in optics to measure the metre in terms of the wavelength of light; and to solve some astronomical problems (he was the first to measure the angular diameter of a star; it was Betelgeuse, and the margin of error was equivalent to a pinhead's width at a distance of 1000 miles) and to refine his value for the velocity of light (close to 3×10^8 m s^{-1} in air). He also discovered new features of spectra; and he used his interferometer to measure tidal movement due to the Moon's effect not on the seas, but on the solid Earth. From 1890 until his death he worked at Chicago; in 1907 he became the first American to be awarded a Nobel Prize. *See photo* p.128.

MIDGLEY, Thomas
1889-1944

American engineer and inventor: introduced tetra-ethyl lead (TEL) antiknock and Freon refrigerant

Midgley was the son of one inventor and the nephew of another. He studied engineering at Cornell, finishing with a PhD in 1911. Working for Delco in World War I, he led a team working on the problem of 'knocking' in petrol engines. (Knocking or pinking is the metallic noise due to pre-ignition.) After finding some antiknock additives as a result of random trials, Midgley realized that their effectiveness can be related to the position of the heaviest atom in the compound, within the Periodic Table. On this basis in 1921 he tried tetra-ethyl lead, $Pb(C_2H_5)_4$, and found it to be very effective, used with some 1,2-dibromo-ethane to reduce lead oxide deposits in the engine. The mixture has been extensively used although there has been rising concern since 1980 that the lead in vehicle exhausts is a health hazard. Midgley also devised the octane number method of rating petrol quality.

In 1930 Midgley introduced Freon 12 (CF_2Cl_2) as a non-toxic non-flammable agent for domestic refrigerators; again, he used the Periodic Table as a guide to select a suitable compound with the required properties. In the 1980s there has been rising concern that chlorofluorocarbons (CFCs) such as Freon cause destruction of the ozone layer of the upper atmosphere, with potentially damaging climatic and other effects as a result of the increased passage of ultraviolet radiation following ozone loss.

MILANKOVICH, Milutin
1879-1958

Yugoslav climatologist: developed astronomical theory of climatic change

Milankovich was educated in Vienna, but in 1904 moved to the University of Belgrade, where he spent the rest of his academic career. He is remembered for his work on the cause for long-term changes in the Earth's climate. Following earlier proposals by J. Herschel and J. Croll, he recognized that the major influence on the Earth's climate is the amount of heat received from the Sun. Three astronomical factors can affect this: the eccentricity of the Earth's orbit (which varies on a time scale of about 100 000 years), the tilt of the Earth's axis (time scale of 40 000 years), and a precessional change which determines whether the northern or southern hemisphere receives most radiation (time scale of 20 000 years). Milankovich spent 30 years computing the amount of radiation received at different latitudes for the past 650 000 years, and was able to demonstrate that changes in insolation corresponded with the known ice ages. Although the **Milankovich hypothesis** has always been controversial, increasingly astronomical factors are now recognized as an explanation for the series of Quaternary ice ages.

MILLER, Jacques (Francis Albert Pierre)

1931-

French-Australian immunologist: discovered function of the thymus gland

Educated in Sydney and London, Miller worked from 1966 at the Hall Institute, Melbourne. Until his work in 1961, the function of the thymus gland was not known. The gland is in the chest of mammals, close to the heart, and becomes relatively smaller from infancy to adulthood. To discover the function of such an organ, one general method is to remove it from a mature experimental animal and to examine the resulting changes; but in the case of the thymus, no significant change could be observed. Likewise its removal in human adults in cases where it had become cancerous produced no obvious physiological change. Miller pointed to an answer by removing the thymus from one-day old mice (which weigh only about a gram). Then, thymectomy produced much change; normal growth failed and death followed in 8-12 weeks. Suggestively, the lymph nodes shrink, the lymphocyte blood count falls, and immune responses fail, so that skin grafts from unrelated mice (or even rats) are not rejected. From this basis, later work showed that T-lymphocytes are formed in the foetal thymus, and fulfil a critical role in the complex cell-mediated immune response.

MILLER, Stanley Lloyd

1930-

American chemist: experimented to simulate production of pre-biotic biochemicals from simple gas mixtures

A graduate of California and Chicago, Miller worked at the University of California at San Diego from 1960. His most familiar work was done when he was a research student with *Urey* in Chicago in 1953. Interested in the possible origin of life on Earth, he devised an experiment using an early planetary reducing atmosphere as proposed by Urey in 1952; it contained water vapour, methane, ammonia and hydrogen. This simple gas mixture (H_2O, CH_4, NH_3, H_2) was passed for some days through an electric spark discharge (to simulate a thunderstorm's energy input) and Miller then analysed it. He found traces of hydrogen cyanide, methanal, methanoic, ethanoic and other acids, urea, and a mixture of amino acids. The result is certainly suggestive, bearing in mind the short period of the experiment in comparison with 'prebiotic time'. Since Miller's work, others using similar methods and other intense energy sources (e.g., ultraviolet light, and gamma radiation) have produced more complex organic molecules (including the nucleic acid base, adenine) but it remains very unclear how a mixture of organic compounds might have evolved into something like a living system as we now know it.

MILLIKAN, Robert Andrews

1868-1953

American physicist: determined e and h accurately for the first time

Millikan was the son of a Congregational minister and small farmer and grew up in the still romantic age of the American midwest. His talent at school was mainly in classics, and he did little physics; but in his second year at Oberlin college he was invited to teach elementary physics, and was told 'anyone who can do well in Greek can teach physics'. He learned quickly, and was soon immersed in the subject, which was not then much developed in the US. Then he went to Columbia, where he was the sole graduate student in physics there in 1893-5. Later he studied in Germany, and in 1896 was offered a job in Chicago with *Michelson*. He took it, and was there until he went to the California Institute of Technology in 1921.

Between 1909 and 1913 Millikan determined the charge on an electron with considerable accuracy, not surpassed until 1928. Between two horizontal plates a cloud of fine oil droplets was introduced and irradiated with X-rays so as to introduce varying amounts of charge on some of them. By adjusting the voltage on the plates, electric force and buoyancy could be made to just counterbalance gravity for an oil-drop viewed by a microscope. Calculation then revealed its charge; a long series of measurements showed that the measured charge always occurred in multiples of a single value, the charge (e) on a single electron. Millikan was lucky to use a field strength (about 6000 volts cm^{-1}) within the narrow range in which the experiment is possible.

He then studied the photoelectric effect (1912-16) confirming *Einstein*'s deduction of 1905, that the energy E of an electron is given by $E=h\nu-E_o$ where μ is the frequency of the incident radiation and E_o is the energy required to leave the metal (the work function), and h is *Planck*'s constant. For his accurate measurements of e and h Millikan was awarded the 1923 Nobel Prize for physics.

During the 1920s Millikan did research into cosmic rays, showing in 1925 that they come from space. Millikan argued that they are uncharged and consist of electromagnetic radiation, but *Compton* showed them to consist of particles. However, Millikan was responsible for directing *C. D. Anderson* to view cosmic rays in a Wilson cloud chamber, which led to Anderson's discovery of the positron. *See photo* p.128.

MILNE, Edward Arthur
1896-1950

British astrophysicist and mathematician: proposed the cosmological principle

Milne was educated at Cambridge, where he later became assistant director of the Solar Physics Observatory. In 1929 he was appointed professor of mathematics at Oxford, and stayed there for life, except during World War II when he worked on ballistics, rockets and sound ranging for the Ordnance Board.

Milne's early work was on stellar atmospheres, in particular the relationship between stellar class and temperature. In 1932 he turned to cosmology, proposing the **cosmological principle** – that the universe appears (on the macroscopic scale) the same from whatever point it is viewed. This remains a basic axiom of much modern cosmological thought. Milne later attempted to deduce a complete model of the universe from somewhat philosophical 'first principles', but was not successful.

MILSTEIN, Cesar
1927-

Argentinian-British molecular biologist: co-discoverer of monoclonal antibodies

Born and educated in Argentina, Milstein was a chemistry student, research student and staff member in Buenos Aires before his first stay in Cambridge from 1958. Back in Buenos Aires in 1961, he returned to Cambridge in 1963 to join *Sanger* on the Medical Research Council staff. There he worked on the structure of an immunoglobulin (an antibody) and then on a corresponding m-RNA, which led him towards **monoclonal antibodies** (MCAs). An MCA is a single specific and chemically pure antibody, produced in cloned cells, that is cells which are genetically identical, by a method devised in 1975 by Milstein and G. Köhler. Such MCAs are of great value in diagnosis and testing, for example they are now routinely used in the UK for typing of blood before transfusion; and they are potentially valuable in therapy, e.g., an MCA against rhesus-D antigen can now be used for mothers who are Rh-negative but are pregnant with Rh-positive children.

To make an MCA, formation of the required antibody is first induced in an experimental animal by injection of an antigen. After a few weeks, antibody-rich B-lymphocytes are taken from its spleen.

Cesar Milstein

These cells are then fused with a malignant cell line (such as a myeloma cell). In some cases the resulting cell, a hybridoma, combines the lymphocyte's ability to produce a pure antibody with the cancerous cell's immortality, so that after selection and cloning it can be grown in culture indefinitely in laboratory conditions; in this way the antibody (which is normally present in serum only in trace amounts and mixed with other antibodies) can be produced in quantity.

The discovery of MCAs promises a revolution in biological research and in clinical diagnosis, and possibly in treatment for a variety of diseases including some cancers. Milstein, Köhler and N. Jerne shared a Nobel Prize in 1984. Jerne, an immunological theorist, had proposed in 1955 the first selection theory of antibody formation, which was then expanded by *Burnet* who proposed the **clonal selection theory**. This states that each antibody is produced by a lymphocyte, and that the effect of antigen is just to increase the number of cells

producing specific antibodies. Later G. Nossal showed that as predicted, individual lymphocytes produce only one kind of antibody, a necessary result for the success in producing useful hybridomas.

MINKOWSKI, Rudolph Leo
1895-1976

German-American astronomer: made first optical identification of radio galaxy

In 1954 Minkowski, with *Baade*, made the first definite optical identification of a radio source beyond our galaxy, Cygnus A. This object was found to be a very distant galaxy emitting an immense amount of radio energy, about ten million times that generated by a normal galaxy, and it is thought to be undergoing a violent explosion.

MITSCHERLICH, Eilhardt
1794-1863

German chemist and mineralogist: discovered law of isomorphism

Mitscherlich's youthful enthusiasm was the Persian language, which he studied at Heidelberg and Paris with the hope of visiting Persia as a diplomat. When this appeared impossible he decided to study medicine, with the intention of travelling as a physician. To begin, he studied science in Göttingen; and was soon so attracted by chemistry that he gave up the idea of visiting Persia. He moved to Berlin in 1818 to study chemistry, and soon noticed that potassium phosphate and potassium arsenate form nearly identical crystals. He went to Stockholm to work with *Berzelius* for two years, continuing to measure crystal angles and forms; where these were closely similar in different compounds, he described them as isomorphous. His **law of isomorphism** states that isomorphous crystals have similar chemical formulas. For example, he showed that the manganates, chromates, sulphates and selenates are isomorphous;

from this the formula of the newly-discovered selenates could be deduced (as the formulas of the first three were known), and from the formula the relative atomic mass of selenium was found by analysis.

Berzelius and others found the law useful in deducing formulas, and therefore atomic masses, for several elements, and for correcting earlier erroneous formulas. Mitscherlich continued his work on crystallography; he found that some substances (e.g., S) can crystallize in two forms (dimorphism) or even more (polymorphism). From 1825 Mitscherlich was professor in Berlin. As well as crystallography, he worked on organic chemistry, microbiology, geology and catalysis. He first made benzene (and named it) by heating calcium benzoate; and also nitrobenzene, azobenzene, and benzenesulphonic acid. He helped his youngest son develop an important industrial process for obtaining cellulose from wood pulp by treatment with hot aqueous calcium hydrogen sulphite solution.

MÖBIUS, August Ferdinand
1790-1868

German mathematician and astronomer: inventor of barycentric calculus, and of the Möbius strip

Möbius studied law at the University of Leipzig, before abandoning it in favour of mathematics and astronomy. In 1816 he was appointed professor of astronomy at Leipzig, and in 1848 became Director of its observatory.

Although in astronomy Möbius developed barycentric calculus, which simplifies a number of geometric and mechanical problems, he is better known for his work on topology. In this field he invented the single-sided object known as the **Möbius strip**. This can be formed by taking a strip of paper, rotating one end through 180° and connecting the ends together. Interestingly, Möbius's description of it was only discovered in his papers

after his death. Möbius is also remembered for posing the five-colour problem (the problem is to find a map for which not less than five colours are required to adequately identify all the countries). To date no one has succeeded in finding a solution, four colours always appears sufficient.

MOHOROVICIC, Andrija
1857-1936

Yugoslavian geophysicist: discovered the boundary between the Earth's crust and the mantle

Mohorovicic was educated at the University of Prague, being appointed professor at the Zagreb Technical School in 1891, and later at Zagreb University. In 1909, whilst observing a distant earthquake, Mohorovicic discovered that some seismic waves from the earthquake had travelled through deep higher-velocity rocks and arrived before waves travelling through the Earth's crust. He realised that the Earth's crust must therefore overlay a denser mantle, and measured the depth to this transition (the **Mohorovicic discontinuity**, or 'Moho') to be about 30 km. This corresponds to the thickness of the continental crust. The depth of the Moho has now been extensively mapped using reflection seismic techniques, and is known to vary between only 10 km under the oceans, to about 50 km at some places beneath the continents.

MOHS, Friedrich
1773-1839

German-Austrian mineralogist: devised scale of mineral hardness

Born appropriately at Gernrode in the Hartz mountains (which are rich in minerals), Mohs became professor of mineralogy at Graz in 1812 and at Vienna in 1826. He is now remembered for the scale of relative hardness named after him. This runs from talc (1) to diamond

(10); the mineral with the higher number scratches anything beneath it or equal to it in hardness. The scale is not linear (the true hardness differences do not coincide with the simple intervals of Mohs's scale); and the hardness of crystals is usually different in different crystal directions. The scale is useful in field mineralogy.

MOISSAN, (Ferdinand Frederic) Henri
1852-1907

French inorganic chemist: first isolated fluorine; pioneer of high-temperature chemistry

Coming from a poor family, Moissan's pursuit of education and his enthusiasm for chemistry proved difficult, until marriage and a generous father-in-law eased his financial position. After his first successes in chemistry, he held posts in Paris in the university. In the early 1880s he began to experiment on ways to isolate the element fluorine from its compounds. Earlier attempts by *Davy* and others had shown only that fluorine must be highly reactive, and some attempts had fatal results. Moissan succeeded in 1886 by electrolysis of a solution of KF in HF, at $-50°$ in an apparatus made of platinum and calcium fluoride. Fluorine was isolated at the anode as a yellow gas, and as the most chemically reactive of all elements, afforded Moissan a rich seam of new chemistry.

Later he explored boron chemistry (he was the first to make pure boron) and he attempted the synthesis of diamond by crystallizing carbon from molten iron under pressure. He was the first to make a range of metal hydrides, which proved to be highly reactive. His interest in high temperature chemistry led him to devise electric furnaces, in which a carbon arc gave temperatures up to 3500°. In this way another new area of chemistry was opened up, and Moissan was able to make synthetic gems such as ruby, and silicides, borides and carbides of metals, as well as metals such as Mb, Ta, Nb, V, Ti, W and U which were then little known. He was awarded a Nobel Prize in 1906.

MOND, Ludwig
1839-1909

German-British industrial chemist

Son of a prosperous Jewish merchant, Mond studied chemistry under *Kolbe* and *Bunsen*. From 1858 he had jobs in chemical industry, and devised a rather unsatisfactory process for recovering sulphur from the offensive 'alkali-waste' of the Leblanc soda-making process. He operated this in Widnes in the 1860s. In 1872, with J. T. Brunner, he began to use the new Solvay process in his own works at Winnington, Cheshire. This made soda (Na_2CO_3) from common salt, ammonia and carbon dioxide, and displaced the Leblanc process.

In 1889 the corrosion of warm nickel by CO was noted, and found to be due to the formation of volatile $Ni(CO)_4$. Mond saw this as a novel way of purifying nickel, by forming and purifying the tetracarbonyl, and then decomposing it by heat; and he set up the Mond Nickel Company to do this. Mond became very wealthy, and his benefactions included the re-equipping of the Royal Institution's laboratory, and the gift of his valuable art collection to the National Gallery. Brunner, Mond and Company in 1926 became a major component in the merger which formed ICI.

MONGE, Gaspard
1746-1818

French mathematician: founder of descriptive geometry

Monge was educated at the Collège de la Trinité in Lyons, and later at the military academy at Mézières, subsequently becoming professor of mathematics there. He was an active supporter of Napoleon, becoming Minister of the Navy in 1792, and seeing active service in Egypt in 1798.

He helped found the École Polytechnique in 1795, becoming its Director.

Monge is remembered as the founder of descriptive geometry, the basis of modern engineering drawing, and for his work on the curvature of surfaces. The theory of the class of **Monge equations** (equations of the type $Ar+Bs+Ct+D=0$), was developed by him. He was wide-ranging in his interests, tackling problems as diverse as partial differential equations, the composition of nitrous acid, and capillary phenomena. His interest in chemistry led him to synthesize water from hydrogen and oxygen in 1783 independently of *Lavoisier*, although the two later collaborated on the same problem.

MONOD, Jacques (Lucien)
1910-1976

French molecular biologist: devised schemes for control of gene action

A graduate of Paris, Monod taught zoology there from 1934, served in the French Resistance in World War II, and joined the Pasteur Institute in 1945, becoming its director in 1971. He worked particularly with F. Jacob on the problem of how gene action is switched 'on' and 'off' especially in the enzyme syntheses they control in mutant bacteria, and which in turn control the bacterial metabolism. In this area he introduced the idea of **operons**, groups of genes with related functions which are clustered together on a chromosome, and are controlled by a small end-region of the operon called an **operator**. This in turn can be made inactive by a **repressor**, which combines with and switches off the operator. The scheme was developed in 1961 to include the idea of messenger RNA (mRNA) which carries genetic information from the DNA of the chromosomes (the operon) to the surface of the ribosomes, where protein synthesis occurs. These ideas found much support in experiments on micro-organisms; their

extension to more complex plants and animals is less firmly established. Monod and Jacob with A. Lwoff shared a Nobel Prize in 1965. Monod was talented in science and active as a sportsman, musician and philosopher. His work on the origin of life led him to argue that it arose by chance and evolved by Darwinian selection through necessity, with no overall plan.

MONRO, Alexander
(*primus*, 1697-1767; *secundus*, 1733-1817; *tertius*, 1773-1859)

Scottish anatomists: an anatomical dynasty

This dynasty dominated the teaching of medicine and surgery in Edinburgh for 126 years, and did much to create and then to increase the fame of the 'Edinburgh School'. The first of the Alexanders, himself the son of a surgeon, was the first professor of anatomy (or any medical subject) there, and under him the number of students increased four-fold; his son (*'secundus'*) was the most able of the three, and wrote on the distinction between the lymphatic and circulatory systems and on the physiology of fishes; when he retired he had taught 13 404 students, including 5831 from outside Scotland. *Tertius* wrote much but made no real anatomical discoveries.

MONTGOLFIER, Joseph-Michel de
(1740-1810) and **Jacques-Etienne de** (1745-99)

French inventors: inventors of the hot air balloon

These brothers who both worked in the family paper-making business, became interested in the possibility of balloon flight about 1782. Their earliest paper models were hydrogen-filled but the gas soon escaped. Their first large model, which reached 25 m, had an envelope of silk taffeta and was lifted by hot air, heated by burning a mix of chopped hay and wool. In 1783 they made a much larger balloon of canvas covered with paper and used it to raise a sheep, a cock and a duck in a wicker cage, and later in the year two friends ascended, with a brazier to maintain the heat. They remained air-borne for half an hour, reaching about 100 m and travelling across Paris; this was the first human flight. Etienne never ascended in a balloon, and Joseph only once, under a huge balloon more than 30 m in diameter in which he flew with six friends. Lighter-than-air dirigibles soon began to use hydrogen, and in this century helium, but hot air balloons have again become popular since World War II. Joseph also designed a parachute and tested it with a sheep dropped from a tower in 1784, but afterwards did no more in aeronautics. The 'ballooning craze' he had begun spread rapidly to the US, and the English Channel was crossed in 1785.

MOORE, Stanford
1913-1982

American biochemist: co-inventor of method for analysing amino acids

Moore spent his career at the Rockefeller Institute, having graduated in chemistry from Vanderbilt University in 1935 and followed this with a PhD from Wisconsin. A central problem in protein chemistry is to determine which amino acids are present in a protein chain, and in what amount. Only when this is known can work begin on the sequence of the amino acids in the chain. With W. Stein, Moore devised in the early 1950s a general method of analysis. First, the protein is hydrolysed completely (e.g., by warm acid) to give a mixture of amino acids. These are then separated from one another by applying the mixture to the top of a column of ion exchange resin, and then eluting the column with a series of buffer solutions of progressively changing acidity. The amino acids emerge separately from the column, can be identified

by their rate of emergence, and the quantity of each is measured by the intensity of the blue colour it gives on reaction with ninhydrin. By 1958 Moore and Stein had devised an ingenious automated analyser to carry out all these steps on a small sample. The problem of finding the sequence of amino acid groups in the chain can then be attacked by methods such as those used by *Sanger* in his work on insulin (1950). The Moore-Stein analytical method was soon used for cases varying from the simple heptapeptide evolidine (seven amino acid groups) to the enzyme ribonuclease (124 amino acid groups). Moore, Stein and *Anfinsen* shared the Nobel Prize for chemistry in 1972.

MORGAGNI, Giovanni Battista
1682-1771

Italian anatomist: pioneer of pathology

Graduating in Bologna, Morgagni taught anatomy there and later in Padua. Although active in anatomical research throughout his life, his great work was not published until he was 80. This was a survey of about 700 cases, written in the form of 70 letters to an unknown medical friend. For each case, he describes first the clinical features of the illness in life, and then the post mortem findings. His object is always to relate the illness to the lesions found at autopsy. He did not use a microscope. After Morgagni's book, physicians increasingly related symptoms to 'a suffering organ' rather than to an 'imbalance of the four humours' and developed methods such as percussion (Auenbrugger, 1761) ausculation (*Läennec*, 1819) and X-radiography (*Roentgen*, 1896) to locate lesions causing disease. Morgagni was the first to describe syphilitic tumours of the brain and tuberculosis of the kidney, and to recognise that where paralysis affects one side of the body only, the lesion is on the other side of the brain. The modern science of morbid anatomy, central to pathology, begins with him. He and his wife Paola had 15 children.

MORGAN, Thomas Hunt

1866-1945

American geneticist: established chromosome theory of heredity

Morgan was a product of two prominent American family lines (including his great-grandfather F. S. Key, who composed the national anthem) and he grew up in rural Kentucky with an interest in natural history. He studied zoology there at the State College and then at Johns Hopkins University. His later career was at Columbia, and then at the California Institute of Technology from 1928.

A quick, humorous and generous man, he is linked especially with the use in genetics of the fruit fly, *Drosophila melanogaster*, and with establishing the **chromosome theory of heredity**, and the idea that genes are located in a linear array on chromosomes. When he began his work on genetics he was doubtful of the truth of *Mendel*'s views, but his studies with *Drosophila* soon convinced him and he became a vigorous supporter. W. Sutton in 1902 had suggested that Mendel's 'factors' might be the chromosomes; Morgan proved him right, and showed that the units of heredity (the genes) are carried on the chromosomes. With his co-workers he established sex-linkage initially through the observation that the mutant variety, white-eye, occurs almost exclusively in fruit flies which are male; he also discovered cross-over (the exchange of genes between chromosomes) and he and his team devised the first **chromosome map**, in 1911 (it showed the relative position of five sex-linked genes; by 1922 they had a map showing the relative positions of over 2000 genes on the four chromosomes of *Drosophila*). He won a Nobel Prize in 1933.

MORLEY, Edward Williams

1838-1923

American chemist and physicist

Morley's work in science is marked by his passion for precise and accurate measurements. Like his father he was a Congregational minister, but from 1882 he taught science in the college which became Western Reserve University in Ohio. His early research was on the oxygen content of air; his purpose was to test a meteorologist's theory of the atmosphere. From this he moved to a study of the relative atomic mass of oxygen, which he measured to within 1 in 10 000. (Only after his retirement was it known that such measurements represent the weighted average of the stable isotopes of the element concerned.) Lastly, he worked with *Michelson* in their famous experiments to detect the 'ether-drift'.

MOSELEY, Henry Gwyn Jeffreys

1887-1915

English experimental physicist: showed identity of atomic number and nuclear charge of a chemical element

Moseley came from a family of scientists, and graduated from Oxford in physics in 1910. At once he joined *Rutherford* in Manchester, but in 1913 he returned to Oxford to work. In 1914 he visited Australia, and on the outbreak of World War I he joined the Royal Engineers and later fought at Gallipoli. He was shot through the head by a Turkish sniper during the battle of Suvla Bay.

Moseley's major work was on the characteristic X-rays which *W. H. Bragg* and others had shown to be produced from metals used as targets in an X-ray tube. *Von Laue*'s work had shown that X-ray frequencies could be measured by crystal diffraction, and Moseley was instructed in this by *W. L. Bragg*. In 1913, using a crystal of potassium hexacyanoferrate(II) to measure the X-rays, he used over 30 metals (from Al to Au) as targets, and found that the X-ray lines changed regularly in position from element to element, in the order of their position in the Periodic Table. He suggested that this regular change must mean that the nuclear charge can be equated with what he called the 'atomic number'. His work allowed prediction that six elements were missing from the Table, and from their position, their properties and likely association could be predicted. As a result, these new elements were soon sought and found. The relation between an element's X-ray frequency and its atomic number is known as **Moseley's law**. He was also able to resolve confusion over the identity of the rare earth metals; but his major achievement was to link chemical behaviour (as shown by an element's place in the Periodic Table) with the physics of atomic constitution. Rutherford called him 'a born experimenter' who, as *Soddy* described it 'called the roll of the elements'.

MÖSSBAUER, Rudolph Ludwig
1929-

German physicist: discovered the Mössbauer effect, which he used to verify Einstein's general relativity theory

Mössbauer was taking his doctorate at the Max Planck Institute for Medical Research in Heidelberg (1955-57) when he discovered what is now called the **Mössbauer effect**. When an atom absorbs a gamma ray it recoils, and by energy conservation the wavelength of the re-emitted gamma ray is altered. However, Mössbauer found that at low temperatures one can avoid (for a certain fraction of gamma ray processes) the excitation of vibrational motions in a solid. In such processes, the lattice recoils as a whole and recoil shifts of the energy are absent in the associated gamma-lines; in effect recoilless nuclear resonance provides very high precision (1 in 10^{12}) in the absorbed and re-emitted gamma ray wavelength. This precision allows detection of different electronic environments surrounding particular nuclei (**Mössbauer spectroscopy**). Thus Fe^{2+} and Fe^{3+} can be separately detected in Fe_3O_4. Also, *Einstein*'s general relativity theory

R. L. Mössbauer

was verified by measuring the change in wavelength of a gamma ray due to its moving from one point of gravitational potential to another (1960). Mössbauer shared the 1961 Nobel Prize for physics, and has since held professorships at the California Institute of Technology (until 1965) and at Munich.

MOTT, (Sir) Nevill Francis
1905-

English physicist: discovered aspects of the electronic structure of disordered materials

Mott's parents both worked at the Cavendish Laboratory, and he studied mathematics at Cambridge. He became a lecturer and Fellow there, working with *Rutherford*, and later with *Bohr* in Copenhagen. With H. Massey he applied the new quantum mechanics to the scattering of particles in atomic physics, and established this field. At 28 Mott moved to a professorship at Bristol, and, influenced by H. Jones, became interested in solid-state physics. Close collaboration between theoreticians and experimentalists led to rapid progress. Metal and alloy behaviour (with Jones), and ionic crystals (with R. W. Gurney) formed the subject of books by Mott. Work during the war led to research on dislocation, defects and material strengths. In 1954 he moved to the Cavendish Professorship and started research on the transition between metallic and insulating behaviour (the **Mott transition**). He decisively shaped the Cavendish Laboratory's research activities, and 'retired' in 1965.

Then at 60 he returned to full-time research, choosing to work on the new area of noncrystalline semiconductors, and immediately recognizing the significance of *P. W. Anderson*'s papers on electronic localization. Once again he published a classic text on his interest (with E. A. Davis) which established a complex but rapidly growing area of research. Mott was knighted in 1962; and shared the 1977 Nobel Prize for physics for his work on the electronic properties of disordered materials.

Mott is one of the major theoretical physicists of this century, opening new and difficult areas of solid-state physics and materials science. He has influenced a generation in showing how to model the complexity of physical problems such as fracture of metals or electronic processes in disordered semiconductors.

MUELLER, Erwin Wilhelm

1911-1977

German-American physicist: invented field-ion microscope

A graduate in engineering from Berlin, Mueller worked for industrial laboratories in Berlin and for the Fritz Haber Institute until 1952 when he joined Pennsylvania State University. In 1936 he invented the **field-emission microscope**, in which a high negative voltage is applied to a fine metal tip, held in a vacuum near a phosphorescent screen. Electrons emitted from the tip travel to the screen and form a highly magnified image of the tip's surface, allowing study of conditions at that point of atoms and molecules provided they are stable enough to survive the conditions at the tip. In 1951 he devised a **field-ion microscope**, in which the metal tip is held positive in gas at a low pressure. Gas adsorbed on the tip becomes ionized, and the resulting positive ions are repelled from the tip and form the image. The resolution is improved by cooling the tip with liquid helium, and in this way in 1956 Mueller was able to obtain well-resolved images from atoms for the first time.

MULLER, Hermann Joseph

1890-1967

American geneticist: discoverer of use of X-rays to induce genetic mutation

Muller became an enthusiast for genetics at 16; he had already founded the first science club at his Harlem school, and won a scholarship to college. By 1915 he began his experiments on spontaneous gene mutation, a key effect in the study of genetics, under the guidance of *T. H. Morgan*, the leading American geneticist. Muller already saw natural mutations as not only rare, but usually as both detrimental (often lethal) and recessive; and he saw the gene itself as the true basis of both evolution and of life itself, as its ability to reproduce itself was the central property of living matter. In 1926 he achieved the abundant and easy production of mutations by use of X-rays, which hugely increased the scope of genetic studies. He concluded, correctly, that mutation is in essence no more than a chemical reaction. He used the fruitfly *Drosophila* for much of his work, but the method can be applied to reproductive cells of any kind. Since then, chemicals (such as colchicine, and mustard gas) have been used in place of X-rays or other high-energy radiation to induce mutations.

Muller moved to Germany in 1932 but in 1934 he moved on to the USSR, only to find its political climate even more unhappy for him; Edinburgh was his home from 1937-40 and thereafter the US. His influence in genetics was very great and his X-ray work won him the Nobel Prize in 1946. He was much concerned both that environmental radiation from many sources can injure human genes, and that modern medicine tends to preserve mutants in the population, and he advocated sperm banks to maintain and improve the human gene pool.

MÜLLER, Johannes Peter
1801-1858

German physiologist: made wide ranging discoveries, contributing to anatomy, zoology, and neurology

The Müller family were Moselle winegrowers, but Johannes's father was a prosperous shoemaker in Coblenz. The boy entered the newly-founded university at Bonn in 1819, and his combination of talent and great ambition soon attracted attention. In 1826 he became a professor there. When a post became vacant in Berlin, he took the remarkable step of proposing himself for the job, and got it. He was a frequent victim of depression, and his death was probably due to suicide, but this is uncertain because he had forbidden an autopsy. When well, he was intensely productive as a physiologist. His first work covered problems of locomotion in animals. Then, in 1820, he attacked the Bonn prize question: does the foetus breathe in the womb? Experiments on a ewe showed that the blood-colour entering and leaving the foetus indicated that it did respire. (Afterwards Müller was antagonistic to vivisection on warm-blooded animals, although he was a great user of frogs.) His later work was wide-ranging; he studied electrophysiology, the sensory system of the eye, the glandular system, the human embryo, and the nervous system. He showed the

value of microscopy in pathology, developing procedures now used in daily clinical work, especially on tumours. He worked on classification in zoology, especially on marine animals. He proposed the **law of specific nerve energies** in 1840. This states that each sensory system will respond to a stimulus (whether this is mechanical, chemical, thermal, or electrical) in the same way, specific to itself. Thus the eye always responds with a sensation of light, however it is stimulated; the ear with a sensation of sound, and so on. Man does not perceive the external world directly, but only the effects on his sensory systems. 'In intercourse with the external world we continually sense ourselves' – an important statement for philosophy.

His many pupils include *Schwann, Du Bois-Reymond, Helmholtz*, J. Henle, and *Virchow*. He is widely regarded as the greatest of all physiologists.

MÜLLER, Paul Hermann
1899-1965

Swiss chemist: developed DDT as an insecticide

Educated in Basle, Müller spent his career from 1925 with the Swiss chemical company of J. R. Geigy. From 1935 he attempted to find an insecticide which would be rapid and persistent, but harmless to plants and to warm-blooded animals. By 1940 he had patented as an insecticide a chemical first made in 1873; it was dichlorodiphenyltrichloromethane ('DDT') which is cheaply and easily produced. This was highly effective, e.g., in killing lice (the carriers of typhus fever) and so preventing epidemics at the end of World War II. For 20 years it was much used, but fell into disfavour when the emergence of resistant insect species limited its effectiveness, while it was also found to have a damaging effect on other animals; its persistence in food chains was then seen as a disadvantage, and by the

1970s its use was banned or limited in some advanced countries. Müller was awarded a Nobel Prize in 1948.

MULLIKEN, Robert (Sanderson)
1896-1986

American chemical physicist: developed molecular orbital theory, and investigated molecular spectroscopy

An organic chemist's son, Mulliken graduated in chemistry at MIT in 1917 and went on to study poison gases, and then in 1919 began work in Chicago on a problem in chemical physics (isotope separation). Except for some research visits he was to spend the rest of his long career at Chicago, working on a variety of topics in chemical physics involving molecular spectra and quantum theory. By 1932 *Bohr*, F. Hund and others had done much to show how energy levels in atoms could be understood in theory, and be related experimentally to atomic spectra. Mulliken extended these ideas to molecules. His central idea was that in a molecule, the electrons which bind the nuclei together move in the field produced by two or more nuclei; the atomic orbitals (a word he devised) become molecular orbitals extending over these nuclei. He showed how the energies of these orbitals could be found from the spectra of the molecules. These ideas formed the basis of **molecular orbital** (MO) theory and were developed by Mulliken and by *Coulson*, *Hückel* and others in Europe to become the major approach to understanding the bonds between atoms in molecules. He was awarded the Nobel Prize for chemistry in 1966.

MUNK, Walter Heinrich
1917-

American oceanographer and geophysicist: improved understanding of the Earth's rotation

Born in Vienna, Munk emigrated to America when he was 16. He was

Walter H. Munk

educated at the California Institute of Technology and the University of California, and has held positions at Scripps Institution of Oceanography of the University of California.

Munk's special interest is the rotation of the Earth, and its variability. In 1961, together with G. MacDonald, he showed how a variety of geophysical factors – including tides, air circulation, and glaciation – all have measurable effects on the length of the day, which varies by roughly 0.002 seconds between summer and winter.

MURCHISON, (Sir) Roderick Impey
1792-1871

British geologist: first identified the Silurian, Devonian and Permian periods

Murchison entered the army at 15, served briefly in the Peninsular War and then married and settled near Durham to follow his interest in foxhunting. At 32 he became friendly with *Davy* and his enthusiasm moved to science and particularly to geology, where he had a flair for stratigraphy. He made a series of arduous geological field explorations, at times with *Sedgwick* or *Lyell*, and in 1839 he produced his major book *The Silurian System* based on his study of the greywackes of South Wales. With Sedgwick he established the Devonian system in southwest England, and an expedition to Russia in 1841 led him to define another world-wide system, the Permian, based on rock stratification in the Perm area.

After about 1840 he became arrogant and intolerant, and in disputes with Sedgwick and others he treated the Silurian as personal property. He was always totally opposed to *Darwin*'s theory of evolution. In 1855 he succeeded *de la Beche* as Director-General of the Geological Survey.

MUYBRIDGE, Eadweard James

1830-1904

British-American photographer: pioneered use of photography to study animal locomotion

Born Edward James Muggeridge, Muybridge believed the adopted spelling was the Anglo-Saxon form of his name. Muybridge emigrated to California when he was 22 and became a professional photographer. His 'composite' landscapes were impressive, and by about 1870 he was the official photographer to the US Government.

In 1872 ex-Governor Leland of California commissioned Muybridge to photograph his horses in motion, to resolve an argument about the horse's gait, but his first efforts failed to give decisive results. Muybridge was interrupted in this work by his trial for the murder of his wife's lover. He was acquitted, and after a prudent absence he returned to the problem in the late 1870s and soon proved that a trotting horse has all its feet off the ground at times (as Leland had claimed). He used a battery of up to 24 small cameras with shutters speeded to 1/500 second and released by clockwork or by threads successively broken by the horse.

His books and lectures on animal locomotion broke new ground and attracted both scientific and popular audiences. By the 1880s, sponsored by the University of Pennsylvania, he was using up to 36 cameras and the new faster dry plates to study running and jumping men, as well as animals; his book *Animal Locomotion* (1887) contains over 20 000 figures. Despite its high price the book sold well; probably because the largest category of photographs showed nude women engaged in such actions as falling, jumping and throwing water at one another. He devised projection equipment for sequential pictures (the Zoopraxiscope, 1879) and his Zoopraxographical Hall in Chicago in 1893 has been claimed as 'the world's first motion picture theatre'. However, a cinema as we now know it was first opened by the Lumière brothers in Paris in late 1895.

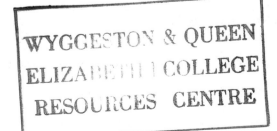

N

NAEGELI, Carl Wilhelm von
1817-1891

German botanist: made early studies of cell division and plant growth

Educated in Zürich, Naegeli gave up medicine to study botany under *Candolle* and then *Schleiden*. From 1857 he was professor at Munich. In 1842 he had studied pollen formation with great care, accurately describing cell division including division of the nucleus. He saw the chromosomes but regarded them as unimportant; and when *Mendel* sent him a copy of his classic paper on peas, Naegeli disregarded it. Naegeli's views on evolution were broadly Darwinian, but he supported *Lamarck* in believing that evolution ocurs in jumps rather than by gradual variation. Oddly, he also believed in spontaneous generation of a rather special sort. In plant taxonomy he did good work, but his best work was on plant growth: he recognized the distinction between meristematic tissue and structural tissue, and he worked on cell ultrastructure.

NANSEN, Fridtjof
1861-1930

Norwegian explorer and biologist: pioneer of Arctic exploration

Nansen graduated in zoology from the University of Christiania (now Oslo), later being appointed professor of zoology and then of oceanography at the Royal Frederick University, Christiania. Nansen is known as a pioneer of Arctic exploration. In 1888 he crossed the Greenland ice sheet for the first time, demonstrating that it covered the entire island. Between 1893 and 1896 he made an epic voyage in the *Fram,* a specially strengthened ship which he allowed to freeze into the ice pack, and to be carried by the currents around the Arctic Ocean, reaching 87°57′N, further north than anyone had been before. He later.did further oceanographic work in the Barents and Kara Seas, and in the north-east Atlantic. An ardent nationalist, Nansen played an important part in the separation of Norway from Sweden in 1905, becoming the first ambassador to Britain of the newly-independent State. In 1922 he was awarded the Nobel Peace Prize in recognition of his humanitarian work for famine relief and refugee aid after World War I.

NAPIER, John
1550-1617

Scottish mathematician: inventor of logarithms

Napier was educated in France and at the University of St Andrews. He came from a landed family and pursued mathematics as a hobby, his other interests being religious controversy and the invention of machines of war.

His studies of imaginary roots led him to develop the principle of the logarithm, and he then spent 20 years computing tables of them (in the course of which he also developed modern decimal notation), publishing his results in 1614. His work was enthusiastically received, but the base that he had chosen was not always convenient (he used the base $e=2.717...$), leading *Briggs* to calculate, in 1617, a table of logarithms to base 10. In the same year Napier also described a system of rods ('Napier's bones') designed for practical multiplication and division. *Kepler*, then involved in the tedious process of calculating planetary orbits, was largely responsible for the introduction of logarithms outside the UK. Napier also made a number of contributions to spherical trigonometry.

NATTA, Giulio
1903-1979

Italian polymer chemist: developed theory and technology of stereospecific polymerization

Natta graduated in chemical engineering at Milan Polytechnic, and after short periods at three Italian universities returned to Milan in 1938 as professor of industrial chemistry. From 1938 his work was directed to new polymers, initially synthetic rubbers. In 1953 he began work with the catalysts shown by K. Ziegler to polymerize alkenes under mild conditions. By 1954 he had shown that these catalysts can give polymers which are stereoregular, that is the repeating unit in the polymer chains has a recurring and regular space-arrangement (stereochemistry). This feature (named as 'tacticity' by Natta's wife) is important because a suitable stereoregular form has commercially useful properties of high strength and melting-point. He found that propene could be made to give an isotactic polypropylene well-suited for moulded products. Both the ideas and the products devised by Natta have been much used; with Ziegler, he shared a Nobel Prize in 1963.

NÉEL, Louis Eugène Félix
1904-

French physicist: discovered antiferromagnetism

Néel graduated from the École Normale Supérieure and worked under P. Weiss at the University of Strasbourg. In 1940 he moved to Grenoble and became the driving force in making it one of the most important scientific centres in France, becoming director of the Centre for Nuclear Studies there in 1956.

Néel's research has been concerned with magnetism in solids. He predicted in 1936 that a special type of magnetic ordering called 'antiferromagnetism' should exist. Whereas unpaired electron spins align in a ferromagnet (e.g., Fe), they are arranged up-down-up-down from site to site in an antiferromagnetic lattice (e.g., in FeO). Above a critical temperature, the **Néel temperature**, the antiferromagnetic substance then becomes paramagnetic. This was experimentally confirmed in 1938, with full neutron diffraction confirmation in 1949. Néel also first suggested (1947) that antiferromagnetism could occur with unequal up-and-down moments (ferrimagnetism) as in some ferrites (ceramics important in electronics; lodestone is an ancient example). Néel was awarded the Nobel Prize for physics in 1970. Néel has also studied the past history of the Earth's magnetic field.

NERNST, (Hermann) Walther
1864-1941

German physical chemist: pioneer of chemical thermodynamics, and discoverer of Third Law of Thermodynamics

Nernst studied physics in four German universities and worked in two more, becoming increasingly concerned with the application of physics to chemical problems. He was appointed to a professorship in Berlin in 1905. He was small and an apparently unimpressive person, and at one time wished to become an actor. In his chosen career he had remarkable success. His early researches on electrochemistry, and on thermodynamics, established his fame. In 1904 he devised an electric lamp which he sold for a million marks. The lamp was soon superseded for lighting by *Edison's*, but it had made Nernst rich. He acquired a country estate and indulged his passion for the new enthusiasm, the motor car.

Of his many contributions to chemical thermodynamics, the best-known is his 'heat theorem' which became the **Third Law of Thermodynamics**: all perfect crystals have the same entropy at absolute zero. He argued that it was the last law of thermodynamics; because the First Law had three discoverers, the Second two, and the Third, one (Nernst). In fact the Zeroth Law was yet to be formally enunciated, and has no single discoverer.

Nernst's widespread research in physical chemistry included much electrochemistry; the concept of **solution pressure** is due to him, and much of the thermodynamic treatment of electrochemistry, as well as contributions to the theory of indicators and buffer action. In photochemistry he proposed the now familiar path for the fast reaction between hydrogen and chlorine, involving a chain reaction based on atomic chlorine.

Nernst was kindly but immodest, and he and his family were known as the most hospitable academic family in Berlin. In World War I he saw early that Germany must lose, and tried to persuade the Kaiser and others to seek peace, without success. Both his sons were killed in the war. Afterwards he declined an offer to become ambassador to the US. He was awarded a Nobel Prize in 1920. From the beginning he opposed Hitler's policies; unsuccessful, he retired to his country estate. He told his wife shortly before he died, 'I've already been to Heaven. It was quite nice, but I told them they could have it even better'. Anecdotes about him, from his many distinguished pupils, are legion. No-one in his time held a wider or deeper grasp of physical chemistry, or did more to advance it.

NEWLANDS, John Alexander Reina

1837-1898

English chemist: devised primitive form of periodic classification of chemical elements

Newlands studied chemistry in London

under *Hofmann*, and later became an analytical chemist, specializing in sugar chemistry. In 1860 he spent a period in Italy as a volunteer in Garibaldi's army; his mother Mary Reina was of Italian descent.

In 1864 and during the next two years, Newlands showed that if the chemical elements are numbered in the order of their atomic weight, and tabulated, then 'the eighth element starting from a given one is a kind of repetition of the first, like the eighth note in an octave of music'. Thus his **Law of Octaves** (as he called it) showed the halogens grouped together, and the alkali metals in another group. He did not leave gaps for undiscovered elements, and his rigid scheme had some unacceptable features and was much criticized; one critic asked him derisively if he had tried an alphabetical arrangement. In 1869 *Mendelayev* published a table which is essentially modern; Newlands then tried to claim priority, and was so persistent that the Royal Society awarded him its Davy Medal in 1887. Newlands certainly had a part of the periodic classification in mind, but he did not develop the idea as effectively as did Mendelayev or J. L. Meyer.

NEWTON, (Sir) Isaac

1642-1727

English physicist and mathematician: discovered the binomial theorem; invented calculus; and produced theories of mechanics, optics and gravitation

Newton was born prematurely in the year *Galileo* died, three months after the death of his father, the owner of Woolsthorpe Manor in Lincolnshire. He was left in the care of his grandmother at Woolsthorpe when his mother remarried, and came under the influence of his uncle, who recognized his talents. Newton went to the grammar school in Grantham, and after farming at Woolsthorpe for two years was sent to Trinity College, Cambridge, in 1661. He remained there for nearly 40 years.

Isaac Newton's earliest portrait,
made when he was 46

As a student Newton attended Isaac Barrow's lectures on mathematics. In 1665 the Great Plague caused him to return to his isolated home at Woolsthorpe. Here he worked on many of the ideas for which he is famous, during what became known as his 'miraculous year'. Later (c.1716) Newton wrote in his notebooks:
'In the beginning of the year 1665 I found the method for approximating series and the rule for reducing any dignity [power] of any binomial to such a series [i.e., the binomial theorem]. The same year in May I found the method of tangents of Gregory and Sulzius, and in November had the direct method of Fluxions [i.e., the elements of the differential calculus], and in the next year in January had the Theory of Colours, and in May following I had entrance into the inverse method of Fluxions [i.e., integral calculus], and in the same year I began to think of gravity extending to the orb of the Moon . . . and . . . compared the force requisite to keep the Moon in her orb with the force of gravity at the surface of the Earth. . . . All this was in the two years of 1665 and 1666, for in those years I was in the prime of my age for invention, and minded Mathematics and Philosophy more than at any time since.'

On returning to Trinity College, he was elected a Fellow (1667) and succeeded Isaac Barrow as Lucasian Professor in 1669 at the age of 26. He was made a Fellow of the Royal Society in 1672. During 1669-76 Newton presented many of his results in optics and became engaged in controversies concerning them. In 1679 he began to correspond with *Hooke*, renewing his interest in dynamics and solving the problem of elliptical planetary motion discovered by *Kepler*. *Halley* visited Newton in 1684 and persuaded him to write a work on dynamics, which was written within 18 months; his *The Mathematical Principles of Natural Philosophy* (the 'Principia'). It is the most important and influential scientific book ever written.

From that point Newton's mathematical interests waned, giving place to theology (ironically, bearing in mind his college, he seems to have been anti-Trinitarian) and involvement in political life. He also spent much time and effort on alchemy, without result. In 1687 he courageously accompanied the Vice-Chancellor to London to defend the University against illegal encroachments by James II. In 1692 Newton 'lost his reason' as he phrased it; probably he suffered a period of severe depression.

Then his interests turned to London and via his friendship with Charles Montague, first earl of Halifax, Newton became Warden and then Master of the Mint in 1696 and 1698, skilfully reforming the currency. He was knighted for this in 1705. In London, a young niece became his housekeeper.

In 1701 he resigned the Lucasian Professorship and his Fellowship at Trinity, although he remained President of the Royal Society from 1703 until his death. He was elected a Whig member of parliament for the University, but was not very active politically.

Much of Newton's last 20 years were spent in acrimonious debate over priority in scientific discoveries with *Flamsteed* and *Leibniz*, and in this Newton showed some ruthlessness and obsessiveness. Following a painful illness (due to a gallstone), Newton died in 1727, and is buried in Westminster Abbey. He had been remarkably fit, even in old age, and reasonably wealthy.

Newton's researches on mechanics display great mastery and established a uniform system based on the **three laws of motion**: (i) a body at rest or in uniform motion will continue in that state unless a force is applied, (ii) the applied force equals the rate of change of momentum of the body, (iii) if a body exerts a force on another body there is an equal but opposite force on the first body. From these Newton explained the collision of particles, Galileo's results on falling bodies, Kepler's three laws of planetary motion and the motion of the Moon, Earth and tides. The deductions were made using calculus, but were proved geometrically in the *Principia* to clarify it for contemporary readers. The **general theory of gravitation**, that any two bodies of mass m_1, m_2 at a distance d apart, attract each other with a force F:

$$F = G\ m_1 m_2 / d^2$$

where G is a universal constant, was developed by Newton from his original work on the Moon's motion of 1665. It may well be correct (as Newton's niece maintained) that the idea stemmed from seeing an apple fall from a tree beside his Woolsthorpe home. Three centuries ahead of the technology he showed that the escape speed s of an artificial satellite from a planet of mass m and radius r is given by $s = (2Gm/r)^{1/2}$. At speeds less than this, the projected satellite will return to the planetary surface.

Newton published another celebrated treatise, the *Opticks* of 1704, which was an organized and coherent account of the behaviour of light. Based on ingenious experimental work it proposed a corpuscular theory of light, but added ideas of periodicity (which were missing even in Hooke's and *Huygens*'s wave theory). Such phenomena as refraction of light by a prism (with the production of colours by dispersion) and **Newton's rings** of coloured light, about the point of contact between a lens and mirror, were considered. Also named after him is the **Newtonian telescope**, which used mirrors rather than lenses to gather light and achieve magnification.

Newton's name is linked with a variety of matters in physics, in addition to those already noted (e.g. the laws of motion). Thus the SI unit of force, the **newton (N)**, is based on the second law, in the form which defines the force F which produces a constant acceleration a in a body of mass m, by the relation $F = ma$. The newton is the force which produces an acceleration of 1 m s^{-2} when it acts on a mass of 1 kg.

In fluid mechanics, **Newtonian fluids** are those whose viscosity is independent of the rate of shear or the velocity gradient. Colloids and some other solutions form non-Newtonian fluids. Newton's **law of cooling** states that the rate at which a body loses heat to its surroundings is proportional to the temperature difference between the body and its surroundings. It is empirical, and applies only to small differences of temperature, and to forced convection.

Newton exerted a unique and profound influence on science and thought. As a mathematician he discovered the **binomial theorem** (1676) and the **calculus**; the latter, together with his **law of universal gravitation** are the peaks of his achievement, and the basis of his colossal stature. His work established the scientific method and placed physics on a new course, giving mathematical expression to physical phenomena, and permanently altering modern thought.

Einstein wrote of him: 'Nature was to him an open book, whose letters he could read without effort ... In one person he combined the experimenter, the theorist, the mechanic and, not least the artist in exposition. He stands before us strong, certain, and alone: his joy in creation and his minute precision are evident in every word and every figure.'

Interestingly Newton's view of himself at the end of his life has a different emphasis: 'I do not know what I may appear to the world; but to myself I seem to have been only like a boy playing on the seashore, and diverting myself in now and then finding a smoother pebble or a prettier shell than ordinary, whilst the great ocean of truth lay all undiscovered before me.'

NICHOLSON, William
1753-1815

British chemist: discovered phenomenon of electrolysis

Nicholson had a wide-ranging career, being variously an agent for the East India Company and for Josiah Wedgwood, the pottery manufacturer, a schoolmaster, a patent agent, and a waterworks engineer.

Within months of *Volta*'s invention of the first electric battery, Nicholson had built the first one in Britain. Soon afterwards he discovered that if the leads from it were immersed in water, bubbles of hydrogen and oxygen were produced. His discovery of the phenomenon of electrolysis was followed up by *Davy*, who was to become a pioneer of the new field of electrochemistry. Nicholson also invented a hydrometer, and both wrote and translated a number of well-respected chemical textbooks.

NICOL, William
1768-1851

British geologist and physicist: inventor of the Nicol prism

Nicol lectured in natural philosophy at the University of Edinburgh. In 1828 he invented the **Nicol prism**, which utilizes the doubly refracting property of Iceland spar, and proved invaluable in the investigation of polarized light. Unfortunately his failure to publish this discovery meant that his work was not widely appreciated until *Sorby* recognized its potential some 40 years later.

NICOLLE, Charles (Jules Henri)
1866-1936

French microbiologist: identified the louse as the vector of typhus

Nicolle became director of the Pasteur Institute in Tunis in 1902, and soon began to study the epidemic typhus fever there. The typhus fevers are a group of related diseases, long-known and world-wide, with a mortality of 10-70%; their causal pathogens are the rickettsia, which lie between bacteria and viruses in size and type. Nicolle's success in combating typhus began when he noted that the victims infected others before they entered hospital, but did not infect others when in hospital. He deduced that the path of infection was broken when they were separated from their clothing and cleaned, and guessed that the body louse was the vector. Experiments with monkeys proved his guess to be correct, and showed that the louse is only infective after taking blood from a victim, and that it spread infection through its faeces. After this work (1909) vigorous attack on the lice has led to effective control. His later work on typhus showed that antibodies exist in recovered patients; and also after influenza and measles. He also discovered the 'carrier' state, important in immunology. Other rickettsial diseases (e.g., Rocky Mountain fever) are carried by ticks and by mites. Nicolle was awarded a Nobel Prize in 1928.

NOBEL, Alfred Bernhard
1833-1896

Swedish chemist: inventor of dynamite

Nobel's father was an inventive engineer who travelled widely. The family moved to Russia in 1842 (where Nobel's father was supervising the manufacture of a submarine mine he had devised) and Alfred was educated there by tutors; his studies included chemistry and five modern languages. He went in 1850 to study chemistry in Paris, and then travelled widely in Europe before visiting the US to work with J. Ericsson, the Swedish-American inventor of the marine screw propeller. He returned to Russia and then to Sweden in 1859. He was much interested, like his father, in the use of explosives in civil engineering, especially in the developing US market. In 1865 he began to manufacture glyceryl trinitrate ('nitroglycerin', discovered in 1847 by A. Sobrero), but the dangerously explosive liquid caused accidents in handling; his factory blew up the same year with five deaths (including that of his brother Emil). In 1866 he found that it was a safe high explosive if absorbed in kieselguhr; the mixture was sold in waxed card tubes as 'dynamite'. In 1875 he invented blasting gelatin or gelignite (nitroglycerin in nitrocellulose), an even better blasting agent; and he profited from oil wells he owned in Russia. His inventions were wide-ranging, and covered by 355 patents. His fortune was large and much of it was left to endow the Nobel Prizes. Element 102 is named nobelium after him.

NODDACK, Ida Eva Tacke
1896-

German inorganic chemist: co-discoverer of rhenium

Ida Tacke was educated in Berlin and then worked in the Physico-Chemical Testing Laboratory there with W. Noddack, whom she married. With O. Berg they searched for the missing element 75, predicted by *Moseley*'s results. They found it in 1925 in traces in the mineral columbite and named it rhenium after the Rhine. They also claimed to have found element 43, but were mistaken in this claim.

In 1934 *Fermi* had obtained unclear results by bombarding uranium with slow neutrons. Ida Noddack suggested that nuclear fission had occurred, but Fermi and others were unconvinced, and her idea was rather passed over. Five years later, in World War II, the same idea offered by *Frisch* was speedily examined and accepted, and dramatic results soon followed.

NORTHROP, John Howard
1891-1987

American biochemist: obtained a range of crystalline enzymes

Educated at Columbia University, New York, Northrop worked throughout his career at the Rockefeller Institute in the same city, starting in 1916. In 1926 J. B. Sumner had for the first time crystallized an enzyme (a biochemical catalyst) and showed it to be a protein. However, the value of this work, on the enzyme urease, was insufficiently grasped by most researchers. Northrop saw its importance, and used similar methods to obtain pure crystalline samples of other enzymes; he did this in the early 1930s. His pure enzymes included the digestive enzymes trypsin and pepsin, and also ribonuclease and deoxyribonuclease. They were found to be proteins (as, in fact, all enzymes appear to be). This work changed both attitudes and techniques; enzymes were no longer regarded as mysterious, and the availability of pure enzymes was of great value in laboratory work. Later, in 1938, Northrop isolated a bacterial virus, and showed this also to be a type of protein (a nucleoprotein). He shared the 1946 Nobel Prize for chemistry with Sumner and *W. M. Stanley*, who had first crystallized a plant virus.

O

OERSTED, Hans Christian
1777-1851

Danish physicist: discovered that an electric current produces a magnetic field

Oersted studied physical science and pharmacy at the University of Copenhagen, and after a period of travel journalism and public lecturing he was appointed professor of physics there in 1806, later becoming Director of the Polytechnic Institute in Copenhagen.

Oersted is remembered for his discovery that an electric current flowing through a wire induces a magnetic field around it, something that he felt ought to be true on intuitive grounds. In a famous experiment first performed in front of his students in 1820, he placed a magnetic compass needle directly below a wire; when the current was switched on the needle moved slightly. His discovery led to a surge of activity by other physicists interested in electricity and magnetism. He also obtained the first accurate value for the compressibility of water, in 1822.

OHM, Georg Simon
1789-1854

German physicist: discovered relationship between current and voltage in a conductor

Ohm was educated at the University of Erlangen. He held rather indifferent academic posts in Cologne, Berlin and Nuremberg, before being appointed professor of physics at Munich in 1849.

Ohm formulated the law for which he is now best known early in his career, in 1827, but received little recognition for 20 years. **Ohm's law** states that the current flowing in a conductor is directly propor-tional to the potential difference across it, provided there is no change in the physical conditions (e.g., temperature) of the conductor; the constant of proportionality is known as the conductance of the conductor, the reciprocal of the resistance. Ohm came to this conclusion by an analogy with *Fourier*'s work on heat flow along a metal rod. He also discovered that the human ear is capable of breaking down complex musical sounds into their component frequencies, an important conclusion, but again one that was ignored at the time. The SI unit of electrical resistivity, the **ohm** (Ω), is named in his honour. It is defined as being the resistance of a conductor through which a current of one ampere is flowing when the potential difference across it is one volt, i.e., $1\,\Omega = 1\,VA^{-1}$. (The unit of conductivity, the inverse of resistivity, was formerly known as the mho; now, the siemens).

OLBERS, Heinrich
1758-1840

German astronomer: discovered Pallas and Vesta, and presented Olbers' Paradox

Olbers, a physician and amateur astronomer, discovered two asteroids, Pallas and Vesta, and rediscovered the asteroid Ceres (discovered by *Piazzi*, but lost again). He suggested that the asteroids originated in a small planet in the same orbit which had exploded. He also found five comets, one of which is named after him, and devised an accurate method of calculating their orbits.

He is now best known, however, for his phrasing in 1823 of a deceptively simple, but important question: 'why is the sky dark at night?' This quandary, raised in the 18th century, became known as **Olbers' paradox**. He assumed that the stars are evenly distributed and infinite in number (as *Newton* proposed) and presented the thought that in whatever direction we look in the night sky, it would be expected that the line of sight will end on the surface of a star. In which case, he argued, the entire night sky ought to have a brightness comparable to that of the Sun.

In modern cosmology the problem has been re-examined and the present answer seems to be that the expansion of the universe has the effect that at a certain distance objects are receding from Earth at the speed of light. This limits the seeable size of the universe, and within this limited radius there are not sufficient stars in all directions to yield a bright night sky.

OLDHAM, Richard Dixon

1858-1936

British seismologist and geologist: first observed P and S waves, and discovered the Earth's core

Oldham was educated at the Royal School of Mines, in 1879 joining the Geological Survey of India (of which his father was director). Upon retirement in 1903 he became director of the Indian Museum in Calcutta. Following the Assam earthquake of 1897, Oldham was able clearly to distinguish in the seismograph record for the first time between the P (*p*rimary, or compressional) and S (*s*econdary, or shear) waves (predicted theoretically by *Poisson*). In 1906 he discovered that at points on the Earth's surface opposite to the epicentre of an earthquake the P waves arrive later than expected, when compared with their arrival times at other places on the globe. He correctly recognized this as clear evidence for the existence of the Earth's core, through which P waves travel more slowly than in the mantle.

OORT, Jan Hendrik

1900-

Dutch astronomer: detected galactic rotation, and proposed theory for origin of comets

Oort worked mainly in Leiden, as director of the Observatory from 1945-70. In 1927 he proved, by extensive observation of the proper motion of stars, that our galaxy is rotating, with the nearer stars to the centre having higher angular velocities than more distant ones. (Recalling that the inner planets of the Solar System move more rapidly than the outer ones.) He established that the Sun is about 30 000 light years from the centre of the galaxy, and that it completes an orbit in about 225 million years, moving at 220 km s^{-1}. The galaxy has a mass about 10^{10} that of the Sun. He was influential in the discovery in 1951 of the 21-centimetre radio emission from interstellar hydrogen, which has allowed the distribution of interstellar gas clouds to be mapped. This technique has also revealed a large 'hidden' mass of stars at the centre of the galaxy. In 1956 Oort observed that light from the Crab supernova remnant was strongly polarized, implying that it was synchrotron radiation produced by electrons moving at relativistic velocities through a magnetic field.

In 1950 Oort suggested the existence of a sphere of incipient cometary material surrounding the solar system, at a distance of about 50 000 A.U., and with a total mass of perhaps 10-100 times that of the Earth. He proposed that comets occasionally detached themselves from this **Oort cloud** and went into orbits about the Sun. Because the cloud is spherical comets can approach the Sun at any angle, and not just in the plane of the ecliptic.

OPARIN, Alexandr Ivanovich

1894-1980

Russian biochemist: pioneered chemical approach to the origin of life

Although his training and his work was in

plant physiology in Moscow, Oparin's name is most familiar through his initiation of modern ideas on the 'origin of life', a phrase now much linked with him. He emphasized that early in the Earth's history its atmosphere did not contain oxygen (which was generated later, by plant photosynthesis); that simple organic substances could have been present in a 'primeval soup' before life began; and that the first organisms were probably heterotrophic, i.e., used organic substances as food and were not capable, as present-day autotrophs are, of feeding on simple inorganic substances. Oparin believed that the key characteristics of life are its organization and integration, and that the processes which led to it should be susceptible to reasonable speculation and experiment; and he did much to make these attitudes respectable.

OPPENHEIMER, (Julius) Robert

1904-1967

American theoretical physicist: contributed to quantum mechanics and the development of the atomic bomb

Oppenheimer was born into a wealthy New York family and was educated at Harvard and Göttingen. In 1929 he took up posts at both the University of California at Berkeley and California Institute of Technology, having studied under *Rutherford, Heisenberg* and *Dirac* whilst travelling in Europe. When the Manhattan Project to develop an atomic bomb was set up in 1942, Oppenheimer was asked to become Director of the Los Alamos laboratories where much of the work was done. Having carried out this role with great skill, leading to the rapid development of the bomb, he attempted to remain a Government adviser on nuclear weapons, but was forced to resign in 1953. He became Director of the Institute for Advanced Study at Princeton in 1947 and remained there as a professor after his retirement in 1966.

Oppenheimer's early success in research began in 1930 when he analysed *Dirac*'s relativistic quantum mechanics and theory of the electron (1928). He showed that a positively charged anti-particle with the same mass as the electron should exist, and this positron was first seen by *C. D. Anderson* in 1932. During the 1930s Oppenheimer built up a formidable team of young theoretical physicists around him, the first time that the subject had been studied intensely outside Europe. Once made Director of Los Alamos he concentrated on gathering the finest scientists and generating an atmosphere of urgency, skilfully handling the interface between his military superior, General Groves, and the unorthodox research scientists under him.

Oppenheimer's wife and brother were left-wing sympathizers and possibly communists, and he ran into difficulties in 1943 when Groves demanded the name of a communist agent who had approached Oppenheimer; after much delay he finally gave it. The first atomic test explosion took place in July 1945, and two atomic bombs ended the war with Japan a month later.

After the war Oppenheimer initially continued his important role in atomic energy, but he opposed the development of the hydrogen (fusion) bomb. In 1953 his political background and his support for the Super program (the hydrogen bomb project) were questioned, and President Eisenhower removed his security clearance, ending his Government service. However, the Fermi Award was conferred on him by President Johnson in 1963.

OSTWALD, Friedrich Wilhelm

1853-1932

German physical chemist: pioneer of modern physical chemistry

Modern physical chemistry was largely created by three men; *van't Hoff, Arrhenius,* and Ostwald. His parents were German but they had settled in Latvia, then (as now) under Russian domination. He had a happy childhood, with some hobbies of a fairly chemical kind; painting (he ground his own colours), photography (he made his own wet plates) and firework-making. He had to repeat one school year, and he had problems with the compulsory Russian language. He studied chemistry at Dorpat (now Tartu) University, did well, and became professor at the Riga Poly-technic in 1881. His fame spread, and in 1887 he was called to Leipzig University, where he remained. His work in physical chemistry was wide-ranging; he studied the rates of hydrolysis of salts and esters, the conductivity of solutions, viscosities, the ionization of water and catalysis; he was awarded the Nobel Prize in 1909. He took up new ideas in physical chemistry with enthusiasm, did much to unify and expand the subject, and saw the study of the energetics of chemical reaction as central to the subject.

For a long time Ostwald believed that atoms were only a convenient hypothesis and had no real existence; but in the 20th century direct evidence for them had arrived, and by 1908 he was a late convert to 'atomism'.

OTTO, Nikolaus August

1832-1891

German engineer: effectively devised the four-stroke internal combustion engine

Although he lacked conventional engi-neering experience, Otto became fasci-nated by the gas engine devised by E. Lenoir; this was a double-acting low compression engine, and the first internal combustion engine to be made on any scale. Otto and two friends began to make similar engines; and then in 1876 he described the system usually called the **Otto cycle**, in which an explodable mixture of air and gas is drawn into the cylinder by the piston (the induction stroke), compressed on a second (com-pression) stroke, ignited near the top dead centre piston position (the combus-tion stroke, in which the hot expanding gases provide the power to drive the piston) and the burned gases are then driven out of the cylinder on a fourth (exhaust) stroke. The new engine was quiet and fairly efficient and sold well. However, in 1886 his competitors showed that A. B. de Rochas had suggested the principle in an obscure pamphlet, although he had not developed the idea, and this invalidated Otto's patent. Soon Otto's gas engine, mainly used in small factories, was developed for use with gasoline (petrol) vapour and air, using a carburettor to control the mix-ture, and improved ignition systems; the resulting engine was well suited for the motor car. In these developments K. Benz, G. Daimler, W. Maybach and F. W. Lanchester all played important parts, and the result is still dominant for this purpose.

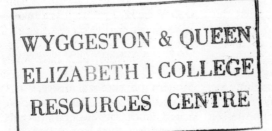

P

PALADE, George Emil
1912-

Romanian-American cell biologist: discoverer of ribosomes

Palade qualified in medicine at Bucharest, and became professor of anatomy there. When Soviet forces entered Romania in 1945 he moved to the US, working first at the Rockefeller Institute and from 1972 at Yale. His work was particularly on the fine structure of cells as revealed by electron microscopy. He showed beyond doubt that one type of organelle, the mitochondrion (typically a thousand of these small sausage-shaped structures are present in each animal cell) form the sites where energy (in the form of adenosine triphosphate, ATP) is generated by enzymic oxidation, to meet the energy needs of the cell. In 1956 he discovered smaller

George E. Palade in the 1970s

organelles (now called ribosomes) found to be rich in ribonucleic acid (RNA) and showed that they are the sites of protein synthesis. Subsequently he worked out in detail the pathway followed by secretory proteins in glandular cells. He shared a Nobel Prize in 1974.

PAPPUS (of Alexandria)
lived *c*. 300 AD

Greek mathematician: made major contributions to geometry

The name of a son is the only detail known of Pappus's personal life; but his books are the main source of knowledge of Greek mathematics before his time, and his own contributions to geometry are substantial. Theorems named after him deal with the volume and surface generated by a plane figure rotating about an axis in its own plane. His work was the high point in the field of Greek geometry.

PARACELSUS (Theophrastus Bombastus von Hohenheim)
1493-1541

Swiss alchemist and physician: pioneer of medical chemistry

Paracelsus's father was a physician working near Zürich, who gave his son his early medical training. The young man travelled very widely, before settling in Strasbourg. There he achieved cures of some influential people, and as a result was appointed City Physician in Basle. In lectures and books he pressed the view that alchemy should be directed not only to transmuting base metal into gold, but principally should aim to prepare effective

Paracelsus

medicines. His ideas found support, but he used such offensive language in abusing opponents that, following a legal case which he lost, he had to leave Basle, and he died in Salzburg. He was certainly a loud-mouthed and often drunk and boastful mystic; but he probably did much to deflect alchemy towards improving medical chemistry.

PARSONS, (Sir) Charles Algernon
1854-1931

British engineer and inventor: designed first effective steam turbine

Some of Parsons's talents can be seen in his parents; his mother was a talented modeller and photographer, and his father (the Earl of Rosse) was an astronomer who made and used some outstanding telescopes (his 1.65 m reflector at Parsonstown in Ireland was without rival, and he used it to discover much about nebulae) and was President of the Royal Society.

Charles studied in Dublin and Cambridge, did well, and then became an engineering apprentice. His firm had interests in electric lighting, and he saw the need for a high-speed engine to drive

dynamos. For this he devised the multi-stage steam turbine, which he patented in 1884; it used high pressure steam and ran at up to 20 000 rpm. Parsons set up his own company to make turbo-generators, and from the early 1890s developed his turbines also for marine use. For this he devised reduction gearing, and he also studied the cavitation due to propellor blades and improved their design. At the 1897 Naval Review on the Solent to celebrate the Queen's Jubilee, his 48 m *Turbinia* with Parsons at the wheel created a sensation; its 2000 hp moved it at an unheard-of 34½ knots. By 1906 his turbines were fitted in the warship *Dreadnought*, and soon the great Cunarders followed suit; some of his turbines generated 70 000 hp.

He went on to design searchlights for naval use, and large telescopes. The company of Grubb Parsons have retained their special position in this field. Parsons used his scientific and mathematical skill to stride ahead of existing engineering practice and to become a leading engineer of his time, the first to join the Order of Merit, and the most original British engineer since *Watt*. Power generation and marine propulsion were never to be the same after his work.

PASCAL, Blaise
1623-1662

French mathematician, physicist and philosopher: pioneer of theory of probability

Educated by his father, Pascal showed early intellectual ability, proving one of the most important theorems of projective geometry by the age of 16. He was fervently religious, belonging to the rigorous Jansenist sect of the Roman Catholic church.

Much of Pascal's early work was on projective geometry, including a treatise on conic sections in 1640 in which he deduced 400 propositions, deriving most of those put forward by *Apollonius*. The most notable was **Pascal's theorem** (for

Blaise Pascal

any hexagon inscribed in a conic, the intersections of opposite pairs of sides are collinear), also known as the problem of *Pappus*, which had been used by *Descartes* as a test case for the power of his own analytical geometry. At the age of 19 Pascal invented a calculating machine that could add and subtract, in order to help his father with his business; one of the first computers. Later, his interest moved towards physics, demonstrating with the help of his brother-in-law that air pressure decreased with altitude as *Torricelli* had predicted, by taking a mercury barometer to the summit of Puy de Dôme (a height of 1200 m, near Clermont Ferrand) in 1646. His interest in hydrostatics also led him to demonstrate that pressure exerted on a confined fluid is constant in all directions (**Pascal's law**). Together with *Fermat*, he also developed the mathematics of probability and combinatorial analysis, using the familiar **Pascal triangle** to obtain the coefficients of the successive integral powers of the binomial $(p+q)^n$. In 1655, after a profound religious experience, Pascal entered the Jansenist retreat at Port

Royal, where his sister was already a nun, and did little further mathematical work. His philosophical work *Pensées* was published in 1670.

The SI unit of pressure (or stress), the **pascal** (Pa), defined as a force of one newton per square metre, commemorates his work on hydrostatics, and the modern programming language, Pascal, marks his contribution to computing.

PASTEUR, Louis
1822-1895

French chemist and microbiologist: founder of stereochemistry and developer of microbiology and immunology; exponent of germ theory of disease

Pasteur is one of the greatest figures in science, who made major changes in all the fields in which he worked. He was enormously talented, with great powers of scientific intuition; he was also ambitious, arrogant, combative, and nationalistic.

His father served in the Peninsular War, and then returned to the family tanning business in Dôle, near the Swiss border. Louis was the only son, with three sisters. His school record was only moderate, but just good enough for him to go to Paris and to hope for entry at the teacher training college, the École Normale. In preparing for this for a second time (the first time his physics was classed as 'passable' and chemistry 'mediocre'), he went to lectures on chemistry by *Dumas*, along with 700 other students. The subject captured him, he became a 'late developer', and all his future work showed a chemical approach even to biological problems.

His first major research, done at the École Normale, concerned tartaric acid (a by-product in wine making). *Biot* had shown that one form of the acid is optically active (i.e., it rotates polarized light when in solution). Pasteur examined a salt of the optically inactive form of tartaric acid, and showed that the crystals were of two kinds, which were non-super-posable mirror-images of each other (i.e., were dissymmetric). He separated these and showed they were both active, with equal and opposite rotation. He deduced, correctly, that the molecules themselves must therefore be dissymmetric, a fundamental idea and one that was more fully explored by *van't Hoff*. It was the beginning of stereochemistry.

This work had interested Pasteur in fermentation, and when he became professor of chemistry at Lille in 1854 he found this useful, because alcohol-making was its main industry. Back at the École Normale from 1857 he continued this interest, which was to carry him from chemistry to biology and from there to medicine. In becoming a microbiologist and improving wine and beer making technology in his early middle-age, Pasteur became convinced that spontaneous generation did not occur. Work by *Spallanzani* and by *Schwann* should have established the view expressed by *Virchow*: 'all cells come from cells'. But the experimentation is not easy and the debate continued. However, Pasteur's now-classic studies showed in the early 1860s that putrifaction of broth and fermentation of sugar did not occur spontaneously, in sterile conditions, but could be readily initiated by air-borne micro-organisms. He put his view with typical force, and it has been generally accepted since. He introduced **pasteurization** (brief, moderate, heating) to kill pathogens in wine, milk and other foods. Since fermentation, putrefaction and suppuration of wounds were fairly widely regarded as kindred processes, it was reasonable for *Lister* to use Pasteur's principles to revolutionize surgery, but Pasteur himself was not involved in this. However, in 1860 he said he planned to work in medicine, and he eventually achieved his own revolution there.

His first experience with animal diseases was with silkworms, then a major French industry, but much threatened by infections. Pasteur, helped by a microscope and

Louis Pasteur aged 18

his fermentation experience and with wife, daughter and several assistants acting with him as novice silk-growers, fairly soon established procedures to deal with the two infections then rife. Then, in 1868 when he was 46, he had a stroke; he was fully paralysed for two months, and partly paralysed thereafter. His work habits were unchanged, but his irritability increased. Most experiments now had to be performed under his direction but not with his own hands. In one way this suited him; he disliked vivesection, but saw it as essential for some of his research, and preferred others to perform the work.

Only in the late 1870s did Pasteur achieve success against a disease in a larger animal. In 1879 by a fortunate chance he noted that if a chicken-cholera bacillus culture was 'aged' or 'attenuated' by storage, it failed to produce the disease in chickens on injection; but the injected chickens (after an interval) were resistant even to infection by a fresh culture. He deduced that the change in virulence of the culture on attenuation, so that it protected but did not infect, could be compared with the use of the mild cowpox vaccine against the virulent smallpox, studied by *Jenner* before 1800. Pasteur used the idea to make a vaccine against anthrax (a major disease of cattle, and sometimes found in man). The scheme worked well, and Pasteur staged a demonstration for agriculturists in May 1881 on a farm. Fifty sheep, cows and goats were divided into two equal groups, and one group of 25 was inoculated with 'attenuated' vaccine. After two weeks all 50 were given an injection of a strong anthrax culture. Two days later, a crowd formed to see the dramatic result: the protected 25 were all healthy; of the others, 22 were dead, 2 dying, 1 sickening.

In 1880 he began to study rabies. The work was dangerous, and difficult because the first step he wished to take – isolation of the pathogen – was not then possible; it is now known to be a virus. However, he could inject dogs, guinea pigs and rabbits with rabid saliva and thereby infect them; and he found that spinal cord from a rabid rabbit, if kept in dry air for a few days, formed an attenuated vaccine which could be used to protect and to treat other animals. However, he was understandably fearful of human trials. Then in 1885 he was brought nine-year old Joseph Meister, who had been bitten 14 times by a rabid dog. The child was treated with the vaccine, survived, and later became a caretaker at Pasteur's institute. In 1886, 2671 patients were treated, and only 25 died. This success made Pasteur world-famous, and an Institute was built for his research, by public subscription; it was opened in 1888. But by then he was old and ill, and rabies was his last success.

Medicine was never the same after his work; infectious disease could now be combatted by established techniques, and research guided by a general theory. Vaccines were sought against most major diseases, but only in some cases could a vaccine be made. Pasteur had all the marks of genius, including an intuition on when to continue with a study of details until success followed, and when to leave a field for other workers to explore. He had a number of distinguished co-workers; the best was his wife. He was buried in the chapel of the Pasteur Institute in Paris. In 1940 the invading Nazis ordered Meister to open the ornate crypt for inspection, but the gatekeeper chose to kill himself rather than do so.

PAULI, Wolfgang
1900-1958

Austrian-Swiss-American physicist: discovered the Pauli exclusion principle in quantum mechanics

The son of a professor of physical chemistry at the University of Vienna, Pauli obtained his PhD at Munich in 1921. Encouraged by *Sommerfeld*, Pauli wrote an article, subsequently published as a small book, on relativity which was admired by *Einstein* for its 'deep physical insight'. Pauli studied further with *Bohr* in Copenhagen and *Born* in Göttingen. He then taught at Hamberg and gained a professorship in 1928 at the Federal Institute of Technology, Zürich, remaining there until his death in 1958, except for five war years spent at Princeton (when he became a US citizen).

Working on quantum mechanics, he contributed the **Pauli exclusion principle** (1924), which explained much about atomic structure. The principle requires that no two electrons in an atom can be in the same quantum state. The original Bohr-Sommerfeld model of the atom (1915) specified for each electron in an atom three quantum numbers (n, l, m) and Pauli additionally required the electron to have another, called the spin quantum number $s = \pm \frac{1}{2}$. Pauli's principle that no more than one electron is able to occupy a state described by n, l, m and s then gave the correct formation of electronic shells in atoms, gave a theoretical basis for the Periodic Classification, and explained the *Zeeman* effect of atomic spectra. This concept of spin, able to have one of two values, was verified experimentally by *Goudsmit* and *Uhlenbeck* in 1926. For his idea of the exclusion principle Pauli was awarded the Nobel Prize for physics in 1945. It was much overdue.

Pauli also studied the relation between the spin of a particle and the statistics of energy level occupancy (quantum statistics); the paramagnetic properties of gases and metals (including electrons in metals); the extension of quantum mechanics from one to a large number of particles; the explanation of the meson, and the nuclear binding force.

Furthermore, Pauli solved a major problem concerning beta decay, in which atomic nuclei eject electrons and apparently contravened the conservation of energy principle. The energies of emitted electrons cover a continuous range up to a maximum value, and it was unclear what happened to the 'missing' energy if an electron had less than the maximum. Pauli realised that this energy could be carried off by an undetected, very light neutral particle (named the neutrino, Italian for little neutral one, by *Fermi*) emitted at the same time as the electron. This was correct and the neutrino was first observed more directly by F. Reines in 1956.

Pauli had a caustic wit, he was not a good lecturer, and he was notoriously bad as an experimentalist; but he is one of the giants of 20th century theoretical physics.

PAULING, Linus (Carl)

1901-

American chemist: the outstanding chemist of the 20th century

Pauling's chemical beginnings were very ordinary. He grew up in a country area in Oregon, and his father (a pharmacist) died when he was nine; the boy began experimenting with chemicals when he was eleven and continued at school. By 15 he had decided to become a chemical engineer. He attended the small Oregon Agricultural College, and did well enough (especially in chemical analysis) to be paid to teach first-year students. He went on to the California Institute of Technology, working for his PhD on X-ray studies of inorganic crystals. He read intensively and his memory was remarkable. He began to develop a scheme to assign sizes to atoms in crystals, and used these dimensions to work out the structures of a wide range of minerals, including eventually the silicates and some other major groups which had previously been seen as a structural mystery. After his PhD in 1925, he spent two years studying in Europe, mainly in Germany with *Sommerfeld*. This led him to an extensive study of the use of quantum theory in understanding chemical bonds. By the early 1930s he had largely developed the valence-bond (VB) approach to bonds, using concepts such as 'hybridization' of bonds and 'resonance' for calculating bond energies, lengths and shapes and magnetic properties. He also devised an electronegativity scale, valuable in predicting bond strength. From his return to CIT in 1927 he held a position there for 35 years, together with others in California.

In the 1930s he began to work on biochemical problems, beginning with X-ray studies on the precise shape of amino acids and peptides. From this he went on to deduce two model structures for proteins: these are the 'pleated sheet' and 'α-helix' types, both found in important biological structures. Other ventures in biochemistry included theories of the chemical basis of anaesthesia and of memory; and with *Delbrück* he studied the structure and action of antibodies. Here he used the new idea of 'complimentary structures in juxtaposition'. This last idea, together with his ideas on helical structures in biomolecules and on hydrogen-bonding as an important determiner of their shape, form the key aspects of J. Watson and *Crick*'s model of DNA as a self-replicating double helix. Also in the

1940s he proposed that sickle-cell disease (a genetic anaemia) results from a change in the normal amino acid content of haemoglobin; proof of this gave the earliest example of a disease being traced to its precise origin at the molecular level.

Pauling's work has generated some controversy; his view on the value of a high vitamin C level in the diet in combatting a range of ills from the common cold to old age are not universally accepted; and his political views in pursuit of world peace led to problems (his passport was withheld for a time). He won two Nobel Prizes; for chemistry in 1954, and for peace in 1962. His elementary texts remain among the best available.

His work in science is exceptional in its range, covering inorganic and organic chemistry, theoretical chemistry and practical devices, work on minerals and in biology. His work in chemistry is without peer in the 20th century in its vitality, vision and significance. His contributions to novel chemical theory continued in his eighties.

PAVLOV, Ivan Petrovich
1849-1936

Russian physiologist: discoverer of the conditioned reflex

When Pavlov graduated in medicine at St Petersburg in 1875 he had already done useful research in physiology, and his interest was mainly in this field rather than in practical medicine. In the 1880s he studied in Germany and from 1890 he held research posts in St Petersburg (now Leningrad), finally building up a very large research centre.

In the 1890s Pavlov studied digestion, using great surgical skill to modify dogs so that, for example, part of the stomach (a 'Pavlov pouch') could be separated from the rest and its gastric juice collected. He discovered the secretory nerves to the pancreas, and he studied the nerves and action of the salivary glands. During this work he noted the way in which dogs salivate when stimulated by the routine of feeding, even before the arrival of food; this led him to the study of reflexes which became his life-long and best-known work, although his Nobel Prize of 1904 was for his work on digestion. He knew food in a dog's mouth causes gastric juice to flow; this is an example of an unconditioned reflex. If a bell is always rung before food appears, the dog will soon salivate when the bell is rung even without the food. Such conditioned or trained reflexes are easily induced in dogs, but can be established in other animals; they can be linked with stimuli other than sound, and depend on a response in the cerebral cortex. Pavlov did extensive and ingenious work on such reflexes, and since then others have studied conditioning both in the laboratory and in the wild, and in vertebrates and invertebrates. Pavlov was a critic of Soviet communism and tried to move abroad in 1922 but failed. Despite this his work was well funded, and it remains more highly regarded in the USSR than outside it, where it has certainly given a psychological dimension to physiology but even more has contributed to behaviorist approaches to psychology.

PEANO, Giuseppe
1858-1932

Italian mathematician: introduced the Peano axioms into mathematical logic

Peano grew up on a farm and from the age of twelve was taught privately in Turin. On winning a scholarship to Turin University his talent was fully revealed, and by 32 he held a professorship there. The lack of rigour in mathematics provoked him (like *Dedekind*) to try to unravel the areas where intuition had concealed the logic of analysis. During the 1880s he looked at the integrability of functions; he proved that first order differential equations $y'=f(x,y)$ are always solvable if the function f is continuous. In 1890 this was

305

generalized to the first statement of the axiom of choice. In the same year he demonstrated a curve that is continuous but filled space, indicating that graphical methods are limited in the analysis of continuous functions.

Peano worked on the application of logic to mathematics from 1888, producing a new notation. He also wrote down a set of axioms that covered the logical concept of natural numbers (**Peano axioms**), later acknowledging that Dedekind had anticipated him in this. Peano's work in this area was probably more important than that of the other great figures—*Boole*, G. Frege and B. Russell.

Peano also initiated geometrical calculus by applying the axiomatic method to geometry. However after 1900 his interests shifted and he did no more creative mathematics, working on a general European language (Interlingua) and on the history of mathematics.

PEARSON, Karl
1857-1936

English statistician: pioneer of statistics applied to biology

Pearson's father was a barrister and Karl also qualified in law but never practised; but he did well in Cambridge in mathematics and afterwards studied physics and biology in Germany. At his Cambridge college he successfully rebelled against compulsory chapel attendance, and then infuriated the authorities by occasional appearances there. In 1884 he became a professor of mathematics at University College, London and was soon influenced by two colleagues there, *Galton* and W. Weldon – both enthusiasts for the application of arithmetic to the study of evolution and heredity. In the 1890s Pearson developed statistical methods for a range of biological problems, largely published in a journal he did much to found, *Biometrika*. His forceful and effective work led him to define standard deviation (an idea

already well established) and to break new ground on graphical methods, probability theory, theories of correlation, and the theory of random walk. In 1900 he devised the **chi square test**, a measure of how well a theoretical probability distribution fits a set of data, and valuable in showing for example whether two hereditary features (e.g., height and eye colour) are inherited independently, or in showing whether one drug is more effective than another. His productivity was enormous, right up to his death, and his work largely founded 20th century statistics.

PEIERLS, (Sir) Rudolf Ernest
1907-

German-British theoretical physicist: contributed to solid-state physics, quantum mechanics and nuclear physics

Peierls was educated at Berlin, and then studied under *Sommerfeld* in Munich, *Heisenberg* in Leipzig and as *Pauli*'s assistant in Zürich. Research in Rome, Cambridge and Manchester followed and in 1937 he was appointed professor at Birmingham. In 1963 he moved to Oxford and from 1974-77 to the University of Washington, Seattle.

Peierls began research in physics during the dawn of quantum mechanics in 1928; the basic theory was complete but its applications to almost every physical system hardly begun. Peierls studied the theory of solids, and analysed how electrons move in them, concentrating on the effect of magnetic fields (notably the Hall effect). In 1929 he explained heat conduction in non-metals, predicting an exponential growth of their thermal conductivity at low temperatures, as was verified in 1951. He also developed the theory of diamagnetism in metals. Turning to nuclear physics he began to work out how protons and neutrons interact, and in 1938 showed how resonances (or dramatic increases in interaction) occur at particular beam energies

Rudolf Peierls about 1956

in nuclear collisions. After World War II had begun, Peierls and *Frisch* studied uranium fission and the neutron emission that accompanies it with a release of energy. In an influential report (1940) they showed that a chain reaction could be generated in quite a small mass of enriched uranium, giving an atomic bomb of extraordinary ferocity. The British Government took this up, and Peierls led a theoretical group developing ways of separating uranium isotopes and also calculating the efficiency of the chain reaction. The work was moved to the US as part of the combined Manhattan Project (1943), and by 1945 yielded the first atomic weapons and quickly brought the war with Japan to an end.

PELLETIER, Pierre-Joseph

1788-1842

French chemist: founder of alkaloid chemistry

Pelletier followed the family profession of pharmacy and studied at the École de Pharmacie in Paris, and afterwards taught there. From about 1809 he began to examine natural products using mild methods of separation (mainly solvent extraction) rather than the older methods such as destructive distillation. An early success was his isolation of chlorophyll from green leaves; and in 1817 with *Magendie* he isolated the emetic substance from ipecacuanha root, and named it emetine. In the next few years he isolated a series of 'vegetable bases' from plants; they are the cyclic nitrogenous bases now known as **alkaloids**, which often show potent physiological properties. With his friend J. Caventou he isolated strychnine, brucine, colchicine, veratrine, and cinchonine, and (later) piperine and caffeine. Their most valuable discovery was quinine from cinchona bark (1820), which for a century was the only effective treatment for malaria, and almost the earliest chemotherapeutic agent in the modern sense.

PENROSE, Roger

1931-

English theoretical physicist: major contributor to theories on black holes

Son of a distinguished geneticist and expert on mental defects, Penrose studied at University College London, and Cambridge. After posts in London, Cambridge and the US he became professor of applied mathematics at Birkbeck College London (1966), and Rouse Ball Professor of Mathematics in Oxford (1973).

Like *Hawking*, Penrose has revealed many of the properties of black holes by his research. **Black holes** occur when large stars collapse and reach a density such that even light (photons) cannot escape from the intense gravitational attraction. The 'event horizon' marks the region within which light cannot escape. Hawking and Penrose proved that a space-time singularity arises at the centre of a black hole, and Penrose established that event horizons always prevent us from observing these singularities from the outside.

However, if a black hole is rotating but uncharged, (a **Kerr black hole**) it possesses a region around it in which matter will always be broken into one mass that falls inside the hole and the remainder which is ejected. Curiously, the ejected mass-energy must exceed that of the original matter, so that the Kerr black hole has lost mass-energy on accreting matter. Overall, Penrose's research has added much to our knowledge of gravitation, and he has added to the efforts to formulate a satisfactory quantum theory of gravity, which are as yet unsuccessful.

PENZIAS, Arno Allan
1933-

American astrophysicist: co-discoverer of the 3 K microwave background radiation

A refugee from Nazi Germany, Penzias was educated in New York, and joined Bell Telephones in 1961.

In 1948 *Gamow, Alpher* and R. Herman hypothesized that the radiation released during the 'big bang' at the creation of the universe ought to have permeated the universe and progressively cooled, to a present day temperature of about 5 K above absolute zero. In 1964 *Dicke* and P. J. Peebles at Princeton repeated and extended this theoretical work. At the same time, but unknown to them, Penzias and his colleague *R. W. Wilson* were exploring the Milky Way with a radio-telescope at the Bell Telephone Laboratories in New Jersey, a mile or two away. Working at a wavelength of 7 cm they found more radio noise than they had expected, or could account for from any known terrestrial source (they even excluded the effect of pigeon droppings on the radio-telescope's surface). The signal was equally strong from all directions, and corresponded to that emitted by a black body at 3.5 K. Their discovery has provided some of the strongest evidence for the big bang theory for the origin of the universe, and is arguably the most important discovery, bearing on cosmology, made in this century. Penzias and Wilson were awarded the Nobel Prize for physics in 1978.

Arno Penzias

PERKIN, (Sir) William Henry
1838-1907

English chemist: made first synthetic dye and founded organic chemical industry

Young Perkin's interest in chemistry began in a familiar way. He records that when he was about twelve, 'a young friend showed me some chemical experiments and the wonderful power of substances to crystallize in definite forms especially struck me . . . and the possibility also of making new discoveries impressed me very much . . . I immediately commenced to accumulate bottles of chemicals and make experiments.' Despite his father's opposition Perkin entered the Royal College of Science to study chemistry at 15. At 17 he was assisting *Hofmann* there, and also doing some research at home. Hofmann had mentioned the desirability of synthesizing quinine. Perkin, at home for Easter in 1856, tried to make quinine by oxidizing aniline. The idea was quite unsound, but Perkin noticed that the dark product contained a purple substance, later named mauve, which dyed silk. At age 18, helped by his father, he set up a small factory to make his 'mauve' and, later, other synthetic dyes based on coal tar products. Remarkably, they dealt successfully with the novel problems of chemical manufacture and marketing, although little commercial equipment or material was available (they even had to make nitric acid, and re-purify coal tar benzene) and their skills were those of the 18-year-old boy and his retired builder father. Young Perkin even maintained his academic research, solving by 1860 some important problems on organic acids and synthesizing the amino acid glycine. Mauve manufacture went on for ten years; it was used for textiles and the Victorian one-penny lilac postage stamp. Later Perkin manufactured magenta and alizarin dyes. By age 36, he was able to retire as a dyemaker and pursue his research exclusively. He developed a general synthesis of aromatic acids (the **Perkin reaction**) and studied magnetic rotatory power.

Chemical interests seem to run in the family; a grandfather had a laboratory in his Yorkshire farmhouse, and Perkin's three sons were all distinguished organic chemists. His own venture began the synthetic organic chemical industry, in which leadership soon passed to Germany. Academic organic chemistry was maintained in Britain especially by Professor W. H. Perkin Jnr. (1860-1929), and his pupils at Edinburgh, Manchester and Oxford.

PERRIN, Jean Baptiste
1870-1942

French physical chemist: gave first definitive demonstration of the existence of atoms

Perrin studied in Lyons and Paris, and in 1910 became professor of physical chemistry at the Sorbonne, but fled to America in 1941.

While studying for his doctorate, Perrin investigated cathode rays, showing them to be negatively charged, and obtaining a rough value of their charge/mass ratio by measuring the negative charge required to stop them illuminating a fluorescent screen. *J. J. Thomson* was soon to improve upon his results. Perrin is better known, however, for his classic studies of Brownian motion in 1908, in which he measured the distribution of particles of gamboge (a yellow gum resin from a Cambodian tree) suspended in water. His results confirmed a mathematical analysis of the problem by *Einstein*, and enabled Perrin to give accurate values for *Avogadro's* constant and for the size of the water molecule. His work was widely accepted as final proof of the existence of atoms, and he was awarded the Nobel Prize for physics in 1926.

PERUTZ, Max (Ferdinand)
1914-

Austrian-British molecular biologist: showed structure of haemoglobin

Both sides of Perutz's family were textile manufacturers. After studying chemistry in Vienna he came to Cambridge in 1936 to work for a PhD in crystallography with J. D. Bernal. The latter had shown in 1934 with Dorothy Crowfoot (*Hodgkin*) that a wet crystal of a protein (pepsin) would give an X-ray diffraction pattern, thereby implying that it might be possible to use the X-ray method that the *Braggs* had used for inorganic compounds to deduce the structure of proteins. However, Bernal gave Perutz some dull work on minerals and it was 1937 before Perutz secured some crystals of haemoglobin and found them to give excellent X-ray patterns. Haemoglobin is the protein of red blood cells, which carries oxygen to the tissues and CO_2 to the lungs.

M. F. Perutz

The invasion of Austria in 1938, and World War II, diverted Perutz from protein work for a time; but from 1947 he directed a Medical Research Council Unit in Cambridge, consisting at first only of himself and his student J. C. Kendrew. In 1953 Perutz showed that the haemoglobin structure could be solved by comparison of two or more X-ray diffraction patterns, one from the pure protein and the others from the same protein with heavy atoms such as mercury attached to it at specific positions. This method led to the solution of the first two protein structures; Perutz and his colleagues solved haemoglobin (relative molecular mass 64 500) and Kendrew and his colleagues solved the related (but simpler) myoglobin from sperm whale muscle. Their methods have been adopted and extended to several hundred other proteins, including enzymes, antibodies and viruses.

The Unit became the MRC Laboratory of Molecular Biology, chaired for many years by Perutz, and a focus of world talent in its field, attracting *Brenner, Crick, H. E. Huxley, Milstein* and *Sanger* among others. Perutz and Kendrew shared a Nobel Prize in 1962. Perutz went on to study the structural changes in haemoglobin which occur when it takes up oxygen; and its mutant forms, characteristic of some inherited diseases. Before 1950 Perutz also did research on the crystallography and mechanism of flow of glaciers. He joined the Order of Merit in 1988.

PHILLIPS, Peregrine
c. 1800-?

English vinegar manufacturer: devised contact process for sulphuric acid

Phillips's position in science is curious; almost nothing is known about him, and the process he patented in 1831 was not used by him on any scale. The old method of making sulphuric acid was by burning sulphur in a lead chamber and then oxidizing the resulting SO_2 with nitrogen oxides, and absorbing the resulting SO_3 in water. The Phillips patent proposed to pass SO_2 and oxygen over a platinum catalyst to make SO_3 and offered great advantages, but initial difficulties delayed its use until 1876 when R. Messel used it. Now, the process makes over 90% of the world's sulphuric acid.

PIAZZI, Guiseppe
1746-1826

Italian astronomer: discovered the first asteroid, Ceres

Piazzi was a monk whose interest in astronomy came in early middle age. In 1814 he published a catalogue of 7646 stars visible from Sicily, and established that proper motion was a common property of stars, and not only of a few nearby ones. He discovered the first asteroid, Ceres, in 1801, but after only three fixes of its position lost it, being temporarily prevented from observing due to illness. However it was soon recovered (by *Olbers*) following a remarkable calculation of its orbit by *Gauss*, based on the three observations. The thousandth asteroid was named Piazzia in his honour.

PICARD, Charles Emile
1856-1941

French mathematician: advanced analysis and analytical geometry

Soon after entering the École Normale Supérieur in 1874 Picard made some useful discoveries in algebra, and earned his doctorate. At 23 he became a professor at Toulouse, and from 25 taught at the Sorbonne and at the École Normale Supérieur.

Picard proved two theorems (known as his 'little theorem' and 'big theorem') which show that an integral function of a complex variable takes every finite value, except for possibly one exception. Picard also developed a theory of linear differential equations which paralleled *Galois*'s theory of algebraic equations using group theory. By studying integrals associated with algebraic surfaces he created areas of algebraic geometry with applications in topology and function theory.

PINCUS, Gregory Goodwin
1903-1967

American biologist: introduced the oral contraceptive pill

Pincus followed in his father's footsteps by graduating in agriculture at Cornell; his father was a lecturer in the subject. Then he studied genetics and physiology at Cambridge, Berlin and Harvard, and later founded his own consultancy in experimental biology. In 1951 he was influenced by the birth control campaigner Margaret Sanger to concentrate on reproductive physiology. With M. C. Chang he studied the antifertility effect of steroid hormones (notably progesterone) in mammals, which act by inhibiting ovulation. In this way, re-fertilization is prevented during pregnancy. Synthetic hormones similar in their effects to progesterone became available in the 1950s, and Pincus saw that they could be used to control fertility. He organized field trials of suitable compounds in Haiti and Puerto Rico in 1954 which were very successful, and oral contraceptives (the 'pill') have been widely used ever since. His success is a pharmaceutical rarity – a synthetic chemical agent which is nearly 100% effective, and one which has had remarkable social results.

PLANCK, Max (Karl Ernst Ludwig)
1858-1947

German physicist: originated quantum theory, making 1900 the transition between classical and modern physics

The son of a professor of civil law, Planck attended university at Berlin and Munich, finishing his doctorate in 1880. He then went to Kiel, becoming a professor there in 1885. A move to Berlin in 1888 followed. In 1930 he became President of the Kaiser Wilhelm Institute; he resigned in 1937 in protest at the behaviour of the Nazis towards Jewish scientists. At the end of World War II the Institute was moved to Göttingen and renamed the Max Planck Institute and Planck was reappointed President.

In 1900 Planck published a paper which, together with *Einstein*'s paper of 1905, initiated quantum theory. *Kirchhoff, Stefan, Wien,* and *Rayleigh* had studied the distribution of radiation emitted by a black body as a function of frequency and temperature. Wien found a formula that would agree with experiments at high frequencies, whilst Rayleigh and *Jeans* found one for low frequencies. Planck discovered one that worked at all frequencies ν, but this needed the assumption that radiation is emitted or received in energy packets (called quanta): these have an energy $E = h\nu$ where h is the **Planck constant** $(6.626 \times 10^{-34} \text{ J Hz}^{-1})$. This assumption is counter to classical physics and its adoption began the modern age of using quantum theory in physics. The conservative Planck immediately recognized how revolutionary the result was, and on a New Year's day walk in 1900 with his small son told him how the age of classical physics had just passed away. Rapid acceptance of the idea came with its use in Einstein's prediction of the photoelectric effect (1905) and in *Bohr*'s successful theory of the electronic structure of atoms (1913). A full quantum theory arrived in the 1920s, when Planck and others had shown how to express all the new concepts consistently. Planck was awarded the Nobel Prize in 1919 for his discovery of the energy quanta.

Planck bore the tragedies of his second son dying in World War I, his twin daughters both dying in childbirth and finally his first son Erwin being executed for his part in the plot against Hitler of July 1944. He was always anti-Nazi, but the other founder of 20th century physics, his friend Einstein, never forgave Planck for not showing firmer opposition; it is not clear that he could have achieved more. Planck is one of the very few scientists to be immortalised on a coin (the German 2 DM piece of 1958).

PLINY (Gaius Plinius Secundus)

c. 23-79

Roman writer on natural history: the first encyclopaedist

Pliny was a child of a wealthy Roman family and so was well educated; at 23 he began an official career as a member of the second great Roman order, the equestrian order. His early duties as was usual were in the army: he served in the cavalry on the Rhine frontier, and his first writing was on the use of javelins by cavalry.

In about 57 AD he left the army and wrote on grammar and on Roman history, and travelled in the Roman empire as a financial controller. He must then have begun his most famous work, the 37 books of his *Natural History*. His last post was as commander of the fleet at Misenum near Naples. He probably never married, but adopted a nephew (Pliny the Younger) as his heir. His energy as a writer was remarkable; he needed little sleep, and his motto was 'to live is to be awake'. He saw the eruption of Vesuvius in 79 AD, and was killed near Pompeii by its fumes.

He was a passionate gatherer of the scientific and technical knowledge of his time, ever-anxious to record the facts for posterity. He writes that 'it is god-like for man to help man'; and his curiosity was boundless. His *Natural History* covers astronomy, geology, geography, zoology, botany, agriculture and pharmacology; and the extraction of metals and stone and their uses, especially in art. His emphasis is on facts, and his theorizing is spasmodic. His fact-gathering was uncritical and myth and legend are mingled with observation. Pliny has a unique place as a source of information on the science and technology of his time.

POINCARÉ, Jules Henri

1854-1912

French mathematician: discovered automorphic functions and contributed independently to relativity theory

Poincaré was the son of a physician and was educated at the École Polytechnique and École des Mines. After teaching at the University of Caen he spent his life from 1881 as a professor at the University of Paris. He became a member of the Académie des Sciences (1887) and also of the Académie Française (1909). Poincaré earned a colossal reputation as 'the last universalist' producing about 500 papers and 30 books which contributed to a wide variety of branches of mathematics and allied subjects, finding a wide readership.

In pure mathematics Poincaré discovered automorphic functions, which are a generalization of periodic functions in being invariant under an infinite group of linear fractional transformations. This led to work on parameterization of curves, the solution of linear differential equations with rational algebraic coefficients and topology. He also did significant work on the theory of numbers, on probability theory and ergodicity.

In mathematical physics Poincaré published a paper on the dynamics of the electron (1906) which independently obtained within electromagnetic theory several of the results of *Einstein*'s theory of special relativity (1905). In celestial mechanics he made important contributions to the theory of orbits, the shape of rotating fluids, the gravitational three- and n-body problems and the origination of topological dynamics. In the course of this work Poincaré developed powerful new techniques such as asymptotic expansions and integral invariants.

POISSON, Siméon-Denis
1781-1840

French mathematician: contributed to electrostatics, magnetostatics, probability theory and complex analysis

Poisson's talent in creative mathematics was recognized by *Lagrange* whilst he was at the École Polytechnique. He had begun training as a surgeon, but found he had neither taste nor talent for the work. In 1800 he was appointed to a post at the École. Poisson's mathematical contributions were to mathematical physics, and he added to this by conducting experiments in sound and heat. He developed the theory of heat and elasticity (**Poisson's ratio** is the ratio between the lateral and longitudinal strain in a wire).

In 1812 Poisson adopted an early 'two-fluid' theory of electricity which was later superseded. He used *Lagrange's* potential function, originally applied in gravitation, and showed that it could be used for electrostatic problems. Using a suggestion by *Laplace* he used the technique to prove the formula for the force at the surface of a charged conductor, and to

solve for the first time the charge distribution on two spherical conductors a given distance apart. *Coulomb*'s experimental results were in close accord with Poisson's formula.

His paper of 1824 constructed a 'two-fluid' theory of magnetism, and expressed the magnetic potential at any point as a sum of volume and surface integrals of magnetic contributions (magnetostatics).

Poisson built upon Laplace's work in probability theory. Poisson's formula gives the probability of a given number of events if its probability is low, and it has wide applicability. The Poisson distribution which is related to this was later shown to be a special case of the general binomial distribution. Poisson also wrote an important memoir in 1833 on the Moon's motion.

In pure mathematics he advanced complex analysis, being the first person to integrate complex functions along paths or contours in the complex plane (now called contour integration).

PONCELET, Jean-Victor
1788-1867

French mathematician: substantially advanced projective geometry

On 18 November 1812 the bedraggled remnant of the French Grand Army under Marshal Ney was overwhelmed at Krasnoi on the frozen Steppes of Russia; Poncelet, a young engineer, was left for dead on the battlefield. A search party who found him took him for questioning, as he was an officer, and so he survived to be marched through a Russian winter for five months before entering a prison at Saratov in March 1813.

He passed what turned out to be two years of captivity recalling all the mathematics he could from his three years at the École Polytechnique (1807-10); and he went on to contribute new mathematics to projective geometry. After he was released his sense of duty led him to put his creative urge on one side and to do routine military engineering tasks, and later to work on water-power. However, in the notes that he produced under such difficult conditions are the principle of duality (the equivalence of various geometric theorems), and the first use of imaginary points in projective geometry.

PORTER, (Sir) George
1920-

British physical chemist: developed flash photolysis for detection of short-lived photochemical entities

Porter took his first degree in Leeds, and in his final year took a course in radio physics; and in World War II as a naval officer he worked with radar. In Cambridge from 1945, he worked with R. G. W. Norrish on the detection and study of the short-lived radical intermediates involved in photochemical gas reactions. Porter developed the idea of using a flash technique to produce the radicals, by discharging a large bank of capacitors to produce a short, high-energy flash (the principle of the photographic flash gun) and using this flash (lasting 10^{-3} s or less) to break up the gas to form radicals and excited molecules. A second flash, after a brief delay, served to give a spectrum of the contents of the reaction tube, so that the radicals could be detected and their lifetimes calculated. Porter developed these ideas in ingenious ways; by 1975 he could detect molecules with a life of only a picosecond (10^{-12} s); he extended the method to liquids; he showed that radicals can be trapped in a supercooled liquid (a glass); and he applied laser beams to photochemical studies. His work has done much to develop photochemistry, including its application to biochemical problems. In 1966 he became Director of the Royal Institution; he shared a Nobel Prize in 1967 with Norrish and M. Eigen.

PORTER, Rodney (Robert)
1917-1985

English biochemist and immunologist: deduced general structure of antibodies

Born and educated in Liverpool, Porter had just graduated there when his career was diverted by military service from 1940 to 1946; afterwards he worked on proteins with *Sanger* in Cambridge. Then, in London from 1949, he developed his interest in antibodies. He showed in 1950 that some could be partly broken down without total loss of their antigen-binding ability; and by the early 1960s he was able to show that antibodies contain both 'heavy' and 'light' protein chains; and that they have three distinct regions, of which two are alike and serve to bind antigens, leading to 'clumping' (agglutination). Aware also of *Edelman*'s results, and of data from electron microscopy, Porter made a brilliant guess at the overall molecular architecture of antibodies. His scheme could incorporate the facts then known, and it inspired further work by *Milstein* and others which have refined it further. Ideas on antibodies which had begun with *Ehrlich* and had developed with *Landsteiner* and *Pauling* at last took on a firm outline which fruitfully linked their biochemistry with their immunology. Porter became professor of biochemistry at Oxford in 1967, shared a Nobel Prize with Edelman in 1972, and was killed in a road accident in 1985.

POWELL, Cecil Frank
1903-1969

English physicist: used photographic emulsion to detect new elementary particles

The son of a gunsmith, Powell studied at Cambridge and obtained his PhD there in 1927 for work with *C. T. R. Wilson*, on condensation in cloud chambers. In that year he went to Bristol, and spent his career there. In the 1930s he began to use photographic plates (later, films) to record the tracks of fast nuclear particles. These tracks (due to ionization which leaves blackened silver grains) can be studied under a microscope and Powell showed that the mass, charge and energy of a particle can be estimated from the tracks it produces. In this way he discovered a new particle in 1947; this was the pi-meson or pion, with mass 273 times that of an electron, and which had been predicted by *Yukawa* in 1935. Since 1947 other unstable particles have been discovered by the same method, and Powell's work marks the start of modern high-energy particle physics. He used the photographic method with 'stacks' of plates, both at mountain height with cosmic rays as the source of particles (as in his pion work) and carried by free balloons above the atmosphere. He won the Nobel Prize in 1950.

POYNTING, John Henry
1852-1914

English physicist: demonstrated existence of radiation pressure

Poynting gained his qualifications from Manchester and Trinity College, Cambridge, becoming professor of physics at Birmingham in 1880. He held this post until his death.

He researched on electromagnetic waves, and **Poynting's vector** (1884, based on *Maxwell*'s theory) gives the direction and magnitude of energy flow from the electric and magnetic fields at a point. He showed that radiation has momentum and exerts a pressure (1904), which can be large under astronomical conditions. He also (from 1878) used a balance to measure *Newton*'s gravitational constant, essentially by *Cavendish*'s method, and by 1891 had a result close to the modern value.

PRATT, John Henry
1809-1871

British cleric and geophysicist: proposed isostatic principle to account for gravity anomalies

Pratt went to India in 1833 as a chaplain with the East India Company, and in 1850 became Archdeacon of Calcutta. As an amateur scientist, he recognized that the cause of some surveying errors found by George Everest near the Himalayas was that the mountains were failing to exert as great a gravitational attraction as Everest had allowed for. In 1854 he suggested his **isostatic principle** in which the higher a mountain range the lower its density, so that the effective pressure in the lithosphere beneath the crust remains constant. *Airy* suggested a similar idea soon afterwards, and their principle of isostasy has since been found to account for gravity anomalies in a wide range of situations.

PRIESTLEY, Joseph
1733-1804

English-American chemist: discoverer of gases, including oxygen

After a difficult Yorkshire childhood during which he was orphaned, and often ill, Priestley began training as a nonconformist minister, and three years later (in 1755) was appointed Unitarian minister in a Suffolk village. Later he taught in schools, and was librarian-companion to Lord Shelburne, afterwards Prime Minister. His stutter and his radical views in theology and in particular in politics made him unpopular as a preacher. As a vociferous supporter of the French Revolutionary idea he became very unpopular and after his house had been burned in 1791 by a Birmingham mob, he felt forced to seek refuge in the more liberal US in 1794.

He had a simple character, much personal charm and exceptional intelligence, and wrote on theology, education, history, philosophy, politics, physics, chemistry and physiology and knew at least nine languages. He was an amateur in science, with little use for theory, but he was the greatest English-speaking experimental chemist of the 18th century, even though his interpretation of his results was usually unsound.

He met *Franklin* in London in 1766, and suggested that he would write a 'History of Electricity' if Franklin would lend him some books; he had earlier done some reading in science, and shown his school pupils in Nantwich some experiments in electricity and optics. It was a good book, published in 1767 and included new experiments; Priestley became FRS in 1766. After this his interest in science turned to chemistry; but theology was always more important to him than science.

His work as a minister in Leeds in 1767 was near a brewery, and he became interested in the 'fixed air' (CO_2) generated by fermentation; and then in other gases, although only three were then known; air, CO_2 (studied by Black) and H_2 (studied by *Cavendish*). All these formulae and modern names came much later, of course. Priestley used the pneumatic trough invented by *Hales* to collect gases, filling it with mercury if the gas was water-soluble. He used a large lens and the sun to provide a clean heat. Within a few years he had discovered and examined the gases we now know as HCl, NO, N_2O, NO_2, NH_3, N_2, CO, SO_2, SiF_4, and O_2; as *Davy* said, 'no single person ever discovered so many new and curious substances'. His results were described in papers and books, notably *Experiments and Observations on Different Kinds of Air and other Branches of Natural Philosophy* (1790).

His most famous experiment was carried out on 1 August 1774 at Bowood (Shelburne's house near Calne, Wiltshire). He had been given a large (12 inch) lens, and used it to try to make gases by heating various chemicals given by his friend Warltire. When he heated mercury oxide (HgO) he was surprised to find that it gave a colourless gas which was not very soluble in water, and in which a candle burned with a dazzling light. A few months later he wrote that 'two mice and myself have had the privilege of breathing it' and recommended its use in medicine. In October 1774 in Paris he talked with *Lavoisier* about this; later Lavoisier repeated and improved the experiment, and saw (as Priestley had not) the full significance of the discovery. *Scheele* had in fact made oxygen earlier, in this and other ways, but did not publish until 1777, after Priestley. However, Priestley showed that O_2 is given off by plants, and that it is essential for animals. He also studied H_2 and used it to reduce metals, noticing that water is formed in this reaction; and that water is also formed by exploding H_2 with O_2.

Priestley had exceptional energy and skill; but he remained always a firm believer in the erroneous phlogiston theory in chemistry, although his own results did much to refute that theory.

He also studied the densities of gases, their thermal conductivity, and electrical discharges in gases. After he joined his sons in the US he continued to work in chemistry until 1803, although he declined the professorship of chemistry at Philadelphia.

PRIGOGINE, Ilya

1917-

Russian-Belgian theoretical chemist: developed irreversible thermodynamics

Living in Belgium from age twelve, Prigogine was educated in Brussels and has been a professor there from 1951; he also has posts in the US.

Classical thermodynamics is concerned with reversible processes and, in chemistry, with equilibrium states. In fact such situations are rare in the real world; e.g., the Earth's atmosphere receives energy continuously from the Sun, and living cells are also not in equilibrium with their surroundings. Inanimate systems tend in general to a state of increasing disorder (i.e., their entropy increases) whereas living systems achieve an organized and ordered state, from relatively disorganized materials. Prigogine developed mathematical models of these non-equilibrium systems, and was able to show in

observations encouraged *Planck* to formulate his quantum theory in order to account for his results.

Ilya Prigogine

general terms how such dissipative structures (as he named them) are created and sustained. His ideas have application in studies on the origin of life and its evolution, and on ecosystems in general. He was awarded the Nobel Prize in 1977.

PRINGSHEIM, Ernst
1859-1917

German physicist: measured the wavelength of thermal radiation as function of temperature

Pringsheim studied at the universities of Heidelberg, Breslau and Berlin, holding the position of professor of physics at Berlin, before eventually returning to Breslau in 1905 as professor of experimental physics.

Pringsheim developed the first accurate infrared spectrometer in 1881. His subsequent work with *Lummer*, on black body radiation in the infrared region, enabled him to confirm experimentally the *Stefan-Boltzmann* law relating radiated energy of a body to its temperature, and *Wien*'s displacement laws, which describe the wavelength at which maximum energy is emitted at a given temperature. His

PRINGSHEIM, Nathanael
1823-1894

German botanist: made important studies of algae and cell reproduction

Pringsheim's father wished him to become an industrialist like himself, but the boy was attracted to science. A course in medicine was a compromise, but on graduation he escaped to research in botany. He did little teaching, and inherited enough money to follow his interests in his home laboratory in Berlin and his Silesian estate.

Pringsheim contributed to the revival of scientific botany in the later 18th century, mainly by his work on lower plants. He was an early observer of sexual reproduction in algae, and of the alternation of generations between the two sexual forms of zoospores and the asexual spore resulting from their fusion. His work on marine algae led him to the view that natural selection is unimportant in evolution; he thought (like *Naegeli*) that variations are spontaneous, without survival value, and tend always to greater complexity of form. His studies supported the view that cells result from the division of pre-existing cells, and not from a process of free-cell formation as claimed by *Schleiden*. With J. von Sachs he first described the plastids, granules found only in plant cells and containing either starch or chlorophyll.

PROUST, Louis Joseph
1754-1826

French analytical chemist: defender of law of constant proportions

Proust followed his father in becoming an apothecary in Paris, but in his thirties he

Louis Proust

moved to Spain. From 1789 he taught in Madrid, but his well-equipped laboratory was pillaged by Napoleon's troops during the seige of Madrid in 1808 and he returned to France.

Proust was a skilled and prolific analyst. He opposed *Berthollet*'s view that chemical compounds could vary in composition over a wide range. Proust's extensive work led him by 1797 to the **Law of Constant Proportions**: that different samples of a pure substance contain its elementary constituents (elements) in the same proportions. Thus malachite $Cu_2CO_3(OH)_2$, whether from nature or synthesized in various ways, had the same composition. In a courteous conflict of views, Proust showed that Berthollet's samples were in fact mixtures. By 1805 Proust's view prevailed, and soon after, the law was seen to relate directly to *Dalton*'s atomic theory. However, 130 years later it was found that some compounds (e.g., some intermetallic compounds, and some sulphides) can have slightly variable compositions, and are sometimes called berthollides.

PROUT, William

1785-1850

English physician and chemist: proposed that the hydrogen atom is 'primary matter'

Like many chemists of his time, Prout was trained in medicine; and like most English physicians of his century, he studied in Scotland, qualifying at Edinburgh in 1811. He began his medical practice in London, and from 1813 he also researched and gave lectures on 'animal chemistry'. He is best known for **Prout's hypothesis**, which appeared anonymously in 1815. This suggested that (i) the relative atomic masses of all elements are exact multiples of that of hydrogen; and (ii) that hydrogen is a primary substance or 'first matter'.

The idea stimulated analytical work, which showed that Prout was wrong; for example chlorine has an atomic mass close to 35.5 times that of hydrogen. Nevertheless, over a century later, *Aston*'s work on isotopes revealed a real basis for Prout's idea; and in modern terms the hydrogen nucleus (the proton) is a kind of primary substance.

PTOLEMY (of Alexandria)

c. 90-170

Egyptian-Greek astronomer: wrote classic summary of Greek astronomy, geography and optics

Little is known of Ptolemy's life or original work. He was probably born in Egypt, and became Hellenized; his name should not be confused with the Kings of Egypt. His fame lies in his four books which summarize five hundred years of Greek astronomical ideas, and which dominated western thought on astronomy until the time of *Copernicus*, fourteen centuries later. His *Almagest* (Arabic for 'The Greatest'; he called it 'The Mathematical Collection') described the motions of the heavens on a geocentric basis, making use of various devices such as epicycles (80 in all) to obtain a plausible match with observations (the Ptolemaic system; it owed much to

Ptolemy

work by *Hipparchus*, now lost). He gave distances and sizes for the Sun and the Moon, a catalogue of 1028 stars, descriptions of astronomical instruments, and computed π to be 377/120 (3.1417). In the *Geography* he described a system of determining latitude and longitude, and a map of the world (based largely on the travels of merchants and Roman officials). Ptolemy's world did not include the Americas, or extend below the Equator (which he placed too far north); but his view that the Earth was spherical, and his exaggeration of Asia eastward, encouraged Columbus in his famous attempt to reach Asia by sailing to the west. Ptolemy's *Optics* dealt with the basics of reflection and refraction, and the *Tetrabiblios* is the origin of much modern astrology. Many of his accounts are due to Hipparchus including the trigonometry, whose basis remains today.

PURCELL, Edward Mills

1912-

American physicist: developed nuclear magnetic resonance; and first detected the interstellar 21 cm microwave emission

Purcell graduated from Purdue in elec-

trical engineering and then studied physics at Karlsruhe and at Harvard, where he taught from 1938. During 1941-45 he worked on the development of microwave radar at Massachusetts Institute of Technology, returning to Harvard as professor of physics.

Purcell was instrumental in the late 1940s in developing nuclear magnetic resonance (nmr) methods for measuring the magnetic moments of atomic nuclei, in solids and liquids. Any atomic nucleus with spin (such as hydrogen or fluorine) will, if held in a powerful magnetic field, absorb radiation in the radio-frequency range by a resonance effect, and measurement of this has given valuable information on features of the absorbing nuclei and their molecular environment. This nmr method has since become a dominant method in chemistry for a variety of analytical purposes. For his work on nmr, Purcell shared the 1952 Nobel Prize for physics with *Bloch*.

In radioastronomy Purcell was in 1951 the first to report observation of the 21 cm wavelength microwave radiation emitted

Edward M. Purcell in 1953

by interstellar neutral hydrogen. This was predicted theoretically by *van de Hulst* and has been used in the mapping of much of our galaxy, and in deducing the temperature and motion of the interstellar gas.

PURKINJE, Johannes Evangelista

1787-1869

Czech histologist and physiologist: advanced cell theory and observed cellular division

Educated by monks, Purkinje first trained for priesthood; then he studied philosophy, and lastly medicine. He graduated in 1818, with a famous thesis on vision which gained him the friendship of Goethe, the poet-philosopher. Helped by this, he became professor at Breslau, and later in Prague. In 1825 he first observed the nucleus in bird's eggs; in 1832 he began to use a compound microscope, and soon made many new observations. In 1835 he described ciliary motion; in 1837 he outlined the key features of the cell theory, which was to be fully propounded by *Schwann* in 1839. Also in 1837 he described nerve cells with their nuclei and dendrites and the flask-like cells (**Purkinje cells**) in the cerebellar cortex. In 1838 he observed cell division, and the following year he was the first to use the word 'protoplasm' in the modern sense. His improvements in histology included early use of a mechanical microtome in place of a razor, to obtain thin tissue slices.

PYTHAGORAS (of Samos)

c. 560-480 BC

Greek mathematician, astronomer and mystic: founder of a cult united by the belief that 'the essence of all things is number'

Although his name is so familiar, rather little is known of Pythagoras's personal life. Born on the Greek island of Samos in the eastern Mediterranean, he travelled widely before settling about 530 BC at Croton, then a Greek colony, in south-east Italy. There he founded the sect which survived for a century after his death. With Pythagoras as their cult leader, the sect was devoted to a life of political and religious mysticism, in which astronomy, and especially geometry and the theory of numbers, was central. Number was seen as pure, magical, and the key to religion and philosophy. This secret society became powerful and aroused hostility, which eventually destroyed it.

Pythagoras himself is said to have discovered the theorem on right-angled triangles named after him; and to have begun the science of acoustics with his work on the tones produced from a stretched string, which are perceived as harmonious to the ear provided that the lengths of string for the two tones have a simple number relation (for example a length ratio of 2:1 corresponds to a musical octave). This was probably the first mathematical expression of a physical law, and the beginning of mathematical physics. A variety of arithmetical and geometrical relations were discovered by members of the sect, which inspired their belief in number as a basis for astronomy and even for morality. In their view the Earth was a sphere, and it and the stars moved in circles in a spherical universe, because these were 'perfect' forms in a mystical sense. They were dismayed by the discovery that the square root of two is irrational (i.e., is not expressible as a perfect fraction) and are reputed to have put to death a member of the sect who revealed this secret to others. The political ambitions of the sect led to its persecution and Pythagoras was exiled to Metapontum about 500 BC. At an unknown date later in the century, the Pythagoreans were involved in a democratic rising in which many were killed, and the rest dispersed.

Although Pythagoras's ideas on the significance of numbers were erroneous, his contributions were important in mathematics: few ideas are more fundamental than that of irrational numbers.

R

RABI, Isidor Isaac
1898-1988

Austrian-American physicist: developed molecular beam experiments

Rabi grew up in the Yiddish community of New York, studying at Cornell and Columbia Universities. He obtained a professorship there in 1937 and remained until retirement.

During a brief period (1927-29) working with *Stern*, Rabi was greatly impressed by the recent Stern-Gerlach experiment. Starting a research programme at Columbia, Rabi invented the atomic- and molecular-beam magnetic resonance methods of observing spectra. In this a constant magnetic field excites the molecules into a set of states and a radio wave signal of the right frequency can resonantly flip the molecule from one magnetic state to another. The magnetic properties of the molecule or atomic nucleus may then be found accurately. The magnetic moment of the electron was measured in this way to nine significant figures, thereby testing the theory of quantum electrodynamics (QED). The technique was also a precursor of the nmr (nuclear magnetic resonance) method developed by *Purcell* and by *Bloch*, and has also been applied to an atomic clock, nmr spectrometry, the maser and the laser. Rabi won the 1944 Nobel Prize for physics for this work.

During the war Rabi worked on microwave radar and afterwards was concerned with administration and scientific policy-making, serving as Chairman of the General Advisory Committee of the Atomic Energy Commission and as a member of the delegation to UNESCO which founded CERN (laboratory in Geneva for high-energy physics).

RAINWATER, Leo James
1917-

American physicist: unified two theoretical models of the atomic nucleus

After studying at the California Insitute of Technology, Rainwater went to Columbia University, and remained there to become professor of physics in 1952. During the war he contributed to the Manhattan (atomic bomb) Project.

In 1950, two theories were available to describe the atomic nucleus, and each was in accord with some experimental results. In one model the nuclear particles were arranged in concentric shells; the other model described the nucleus as analogous to a liquid drop. Rainwater in 1950 produced a collective model, in which the two ideas were combined. In association with Aage Bohr (son of *Niels Bohr*) and B. R. Mottelson, Rainwater developed this theory and they secured experimental evidence in its support. The three shared a Nobel Prize in 1975.

RAMAN, (Sir) Chandrasekhara Venkata
1888-1970

Indian physicist: showed that light scattered by molecules will show lower and higher frequency components (the Raman effect)

Raman gained a distinguished first class honours degree from Madras, but the lack of scientific opportunities in India prevented him then starting a career as a physicist. Instead he worked as an auditor in the Indian Civil Service for ten years, continuing his research in his leisure time. The work he produced in sound and on diffraction secured him the professorship of physics at Calcutta. During his time there (1917-33) he discovered the Raman effect (1928), established the *Indian Journal of Physics* (1926), became President of the Indian Science Congress, was knighted (1929) and received the 1930 Nobel Prize for physics (the first awarded to an Asian). He had an important influence in building up the study of physics in India.

Viewing the blue colour of the Mediterranean in 1921 he concluded that *Rayleigh*'s explanation of the colour in terms of light scattering from suspended particles was inadequate. Raman realized that the scattering and frequency shift of the light is due to the water molecules themselves. Light is generally scattered by molecules in solids, liquids or gases, lower and higher frequency components being added as the molecular bonds absorb or impart energy to the deflected photons (**the Raman effect**).

Raman's discovery led to one of the earliest confirmations of quantum theory, and also gave a powerful method of analysing molecular structure (**Raman spectroscopy**).

RAMÓN Y CAJAL, Santiago
1852-1934
Spanish neurohistologist: a founder of modern neurology

Cajal was not bright at school; he was apprenticed to a barber, then to a shoemaker, and lastly followed his father (at the latter's insistence) in studying medicine. He began to practice in 1873, and then served in the army in Cuba. From 1884 he was a professor in Spain, at Madrid from 1892-1922. He was often unwell, having contracted malaria in Cuba, and then tuberculosis in Spain. About 1885 he was shown a microscope section of brain tissue, stained with silver by *Golgi*'s method. Cajal was fascinated by it, and proceeded to improve the method. Within a few years he had added greatly to knowledge of the nervous system, and his work on it filled the rest of his life. He worked on the connections of the cells in the brain and spinal cord and showed the great complexity of the system. (The human brain contains about 10^{10} nerve cells, each connected with about 50 others, giving a total of 5×10^{11} synapses.) In opposition to Golgi, he argued that the nervous system consisted only of discrete nerve cells and their processes, with the axons ending in the grey matter of the brain, and not joining other axons or the cell bodies of other nerve cells (the neuron theory). He worked also on the difficult problem of the degeneration and regeneration of nerve cells, on the neurologia, and on the retina. He shared a Nobel Prize with Golgi in 1906.

RAMSAY, (Sir) William
1852-1916
Scottish chemist: discovered the noble gases, a new group of elements

Ramsay was proud of the fact that his ancestors included several scientists, and he moved easily into science at Glasgow, and then into chemistry with *Bunsen* at Heidelberg. In 1880, at Bristol, he began to make exact measurements of gas densities, and became an expert glassblower. In 1887 he moved to London and in 1894 began the work that made him famous. *Rayleigh* had shown that nitrogen from the air is 0.5% denser than nitrogen made chemically. Ramsay thought that this might be due to a previously unknown heavier gas in the air, and he set to work to find it. He sparked dry air to remove oxygen, and then passed the nitrogen repeatedly over hot magnesium, when most of the gas was slowly absorbed: $3Mg + N_2 \rightarrow Mg_3N_2$. He was left with a denser, monatomic gas; an inert new element which was named argon, and which makes up less than 1% of the air. Looking for it elsewhere, Ramsay found another new gas in the mineral cleveite, whose spectrum showed *Crookes* that it was helium, previously observed only in the Sun. Ramsay went on to examine air for traces of other new inert gases, and by distilling liquid air he discovered three more: krypton, xenon, and neon. Ramsay proposed that the five new gases formed a new group of 'zero-valent' elements in the Periodic Table. In 1910 he found the sixth of these gases, radon, which is formed with helium by the radioactive decay of the metal, radium. The group are now known as the noble gases. All are very rare (except argon, A), and chemically unreactive, although in 1962 *Bartlett* found some reactivity for Xe and Kr. This inertness was important in early theories of chemical bonding. They all show striking spectra: except for the ultra-rare Rn, they are used in discharge and fluorescent tubes, and for work requiring an inert atmosphere. Liquid He is used as a cryogen (an extreme refrigerant); it has the lowest boiling point known $(-269°C)$. Although uncommon on Earth, helium is the second most common element (23%) in the universe as a whole. Ramsay was awarded the Nobel Prize for chemistry in 1904. He is the only man to have discovered an entire Periodic Group of elements. He was much liked; and all his best work was done with a co-worker.

RAOULT, Francois Marie

1830-1901

French physical chemist: pioneer of solution chemistry

Little is known of Raoult's early life; but his family was poor and although he began to study in Paris he could not afford to complete his course. He worked as a teacher, and began his research in physical chemistry in difficult circumstances, but this allowed him to gain a degree from Paris, in 1863. From 1867 he taught in the university at Grenoble. In the 1870s he tried to devise a new method for finding the alcohol content of wine, and this led him to study the freezing points of solutions of organic substances. He found that the depression of freezing point of a solution (compared with that of a pure solvent) was simply related to the quantity of dissolved solute and to its relative molecular mass (**Raoult's law**, 1882). Five years later he showed a similar relation for the effect of a dissolved solute on the vapour pressure of a solution, and therefore on the elevation of its boiling point. In 1889 *Beckmann* showed that this elevation of boiling point, for a measured amount of substance in a suitable solvent, is a very convenient method for measuring the relative molecular mass of the substance; the method has been in routine use ever since.

RAY, John

1627-1705

English naturalist: pioneer of plant taxonomy

Ray's father was the village blacksmith and his mother a herbalist at Black Notley in Essex; the boy went to Cambridge at 16 and taught classics there after his graduation. His university career was ended after the Civil War when he refused to conform to new laws on religious observance. He was already a keen naturalist, and from 1662 he was supported by his wealthy ex-pupil and fellow-naturalist, F. Willughby. They toured Europe as well as England to study both flora and fauna. Ray used a taxonomic system which emphasizes the division of plants into cryptogams (flowerless plants), monocotyledons and dicotyledons, the basic scheme used today. His major work on botany covers some 18 600 species with much information on each. He saw the species as the fundamental unit of taxonomy, although he eventually realised that species are not immutable. His taxonomy was not surpassed until the work of *Linnaeus*. Ray was ahead of his time in his view that fossils are petrified remains of plants and animals, an idea not accepted until a century later. Willughby died in 1672, and Ray lived on in his house but eventually quarrelled with his widow, and returned to Black Notley to write on a variety of matters including travel, proverbs, and natural history.

RAYLEIGH (Baron) (John William Strutt)

1842-1919

English physicist: did classic work on sound, light and electricity

Rayleigh had high ability as a mathematician, which he found useful in the unusually wide range of problems in physics which attracted him, and he was a skilful experimenter. When his father died in 1873 Rayleigh inherited the title, and continued to work in his laboratory in the family mansion, Terling Place, in Essex. He agreed to succeed *Maxwell* in Cambridge, but only for five years; in that time his physics students increased from six to 70. His first researches were on waves, both in optics and in acoustics; his book *The Theory of Sound*, written in part in a houseboat on the Nile, is a masterpiece of classical physics. His enthusiasm for precise measurement led him, in Cambridge, to work on the standardization of the ohm and ampere. Interest in *Prout*'s hypothesis caused his work on gas densities, and led *Ramsay* to the discovery of argon. His interest in radiation and spectra led him to study black body (isothermal) radiation, and the **Rayleigh-Jeans formula** for this represented the best that classical theory could achieve in this area. However, although the formula agrees well with experiment for long wavelength radiation, it fails entirely for shorter wavelengths (see diagram). The problem was solved by *Planck*'s novel idea that energy is emitted in small packets or quanta; this concept was to revolutionize physics, but it was never fully accepted by Rayleigh. He won the Nobel Prize for physics in 1904, for his work on gas densities and on argon. He was married to the sister of Britain's most intellectual prime minister, A. J. Balfour.

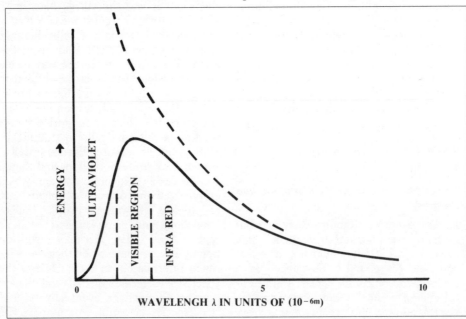

Diagram of energy distribution for a black body emitting at 6000 K (e.g. the sun). The broken curve shows values predicted by the Rayleigh-Jeans formula at 6000 K

RÉAUMUR, René-Antoine Ferchault de

1683-1757

French technologist and naturalist: pioneer entomologist

A member of the lesser nobility, Réaumur was probably educated by the Jesuits before studying law; but soon he was attracted to mathematics, and then to metallurgy and biology. From 1713, he had the huge task of compiling an encyclopaedia of technology, commissioned by Colbert (Louis XIV's finance minister) and intended to aid French industry. Soon he was engaged in studying iron and steel making, porcelain and thermometry. His researches in these areas were of value to his successors, rather than to his contemporaries.

His lasting fame rests on his work as a naturalist, where he worked on molluscs and especially on insects. His work on bees was particularly detailed. He also wrote on regeneration in hydra and in marine animals, and he showed that digestion is a chemical process. In all these matters, his work did much to spur research by others. He inherited a castle in 1755, but two years later had a fatal fall from his horse.

REBER, Grote

1911-

American radio astronomer: discovered first discrete radio sources in Milky Way

Stimulated by the discovery by *Jansky* of radio emission from the Milky Way, Reber built a steerable parabolic radio antenna in 1937 and began to investigate in more detail. An amateur, he was for many years the world's only radio astronomer, since no professionals had followed up Jansky's reports. His discovery of strong, discrete sources in Cygnus, Taurus and Cassiopeia persuaded them of the value of observations at radio frequencies, and led to the development of radio astronomy.

REED, Walter

1851-1902

American epidemiologist: established the cause of yellow fever

Reed trained in medicine in the University of Virginia and in New York, joined the US Army Medical Corps in 1875 and served in a series of frontier posts before specializing in bacteriology in the 1890s. Then in 1900 he was appointed to lead a small commission to study yellow fever, based in Cuba.

Yellow fever has a dramatic history; it has frequently proved a devastating epidemic disease, especially when non-immune groups (usually Europeans or North Americans) entered new areas (as in central Africa or the Caribbean) and became exposed. It is now known to occur in two forms; the long-known type is urban yellow fever; largely by Reed's work, this is known to be due to a virus carried only by the female *Aëdes aegypti* mosquito. Reed's group tested theories on the transmission of yellow fever using army volunteers, and fairly soon were able to prove a theory (due to C. Finlay) that the mosquito was the transmitting vector. By 1901 Reed had shown that the pathogen was a non-filterable microorganism, again using army volunteers; for the first time a virus was deduced as the cause of a specific human disease. (*Loeffler* had already shown that foot-and-mouth disease in cattle is a viral disease). Reed's work was quickly followed by vigorous attacks, by drainage or addition of kerosene, on the mosquito's breeding places; one notable success, that of W. C. Gorgas in Panama, proved to be a major factor in the completion of the Canal there. Since 1937 a vaccine has been available, and a large measure of control has been achieved; but in Africa especially, jungle yellow fever (a strain transmitted by a variety of mosquito vectors) remains a major problem, with mass vaccination as the preferred public health strategy.

REGNAULT, Henri Victor
1810-1878

French physical chemist: made experimental contributions to study of thermal properties of gases

Regnault's father was an officer in Napoleon's army, and died in 1812 in the Russian campaign; the boy was soon orphaned, but a friend of his father found him a job in a Paris shop. He worked hard for entrance to the École Polytechnique, graduated there, and became first *Gay-Lussac*'s assistant and then his successor there in 1810. From 1854 he was director of the famous Sèvres porcelain factory, until his laboratory was destroyed by the Prussians in the war of 1870. Regnault had no clear plan of research, but he did valuable work in several areas. He discovered a series of organo-chlorine compounds, including the chlorinated ethenes and CCl_4. He worked on specific heat capacities, and measured deviations from *Dulong* and Petit's law; he measured the thermal expansion coefficient of gases accurately, and found it varied slightly with the nature of the gas; and he studied the deviations from *Boyle*'s law. He was cautious and no theorist; but his careful measurements made over 30 years were used by physical chemists and engineers for a generation.

REID, Harry Fielding
1859-1944

American geophysicist: proposed elastic rebound theory of earthquakes

Reid has been claimed to be the first American geophysicist. His mother was the grandniece of George Washington, and his prosperous parents took him as a child to Switzerland. There began his love for mountains and glaciers. He graduated from Johns Hopkins University in 1876 in physics and mathematics, and returned there in 1894 to teach until his retirement. His major work was his 'elastic rebound'

theory of the source of the earthquake waves. The theory proposed that strain developed in the Earth's crust due to forces acting from below, of unknown origin. The strain leads eventually to breaks (faults) in the crust. The sudden release of strain energy by faulting, when the fracture strength is exceeded, can lead to an offset across the fault of up to 15 m. The rupture travels as a wave at about 3.5 $km s^{-1}$, for a distance up to 1000 km. The theory was soon accepted ($\approx$1911) in the US, but more slowly (up to 50 years later) elsewhere.

REMAK, Robert
1815-1865

Polish-German physician: advanced understanding of structure of nerves

A student of *J. P. Müller* at Berlin, Remak remained there to work in general practice and in the university, although he was denied a senior teaching post because he was Jewish. In his early twenties he did notable work on the microscopy of nerve; he discovered the myelin sheath of the main nerves in 1838, and also showed that the axis-cylinder (axon) arises in the spinal cord and runs continuously. In this and his further work he saw that nerves have a flattened solid structure, and are not merely structureless hollow tubes as they had been viewed for centuries. He was also a pioneer embryologist, and one of the first to fully describe cell division and to argue that all animal cells came from pre-existing cells.

REYNOLDS, Osborne
1842-1912

British engineer and physicist: gave definitive analysis of turbulent flow

Reynolds studied mathematics at Cambridge, before being appointed as the first professor of engineering at Owens College (now Manchester University).

Reynolds was one of the outstanding theoretical engineers of the 19th century. Most of his work concerned fluid dynamics, problems such as the flow around ship's propellors, vortex production by moving bodies, and the scaling up of test results from models. He is remembered particularly for his work on the turbulent and laminar flow of liquids, and for defining (in 1883) the dimensionless quantity **Reynolds' number** to determine the type of flow regime. Reynolds' number depends upon the viscosity, velocity, density and linear dimensions of the flow. He also carried out definitive work on lubrication, explained why radiometers rotate, and performed a classic determination of the mechanical equivalent of heat.

RICHARDS, Theodore William

1868-1928

American analytical chemist: famed for his accurate determination of relative atomic mass by quantitative chemical analysis

From age 14 Richards was keenly interested in astronomy, but poor eyesight caused him to change his college studies to chemistry. After doing well at Harvard he visited Europe to learn the latest chemical methods; despite an offer at Göttingen he returned to a professorship at Harvard and stayed there. His particular interest became the exact determination of 'atomic weights' (i.e., relative atomic masses) and he carried classical gravimetric analysis to a level of high refinement in this work. He obtained accurate values for 25 elements, and his co-workers secured atomic weights for another 40, so giving a firm basis for quantitative analytical chemistry. He showed in 1913 that the atomic weight of ordinary lead differs from that of lead derived from uranium by radioactive decay: this work confirmed ideas on radioactive decay series, and *Soddy's* prediction of the existence of isotopes. Richard's values for relative atomic mass were the best available until the widespread use of physical methods based on mass spectrometry gave even greater accuracy and precision, after World War II.

RICHTER, Burton

1931-

American particle physicist: experimentally demonstrated existence of charmed quarks

Richter studied at the Massachusetts Institute of Technology, then joined the high-energy physics laboratory at Stanford University, becoming a professor in 1967.

Richter was largely responsible for the Stanford Positron-Electron Accelerating Ring (SPEAR), a machine designed to collide positrons and electrons at high energies, and to study the resulting elementary particles. In 1974 a team led by him discovered the J/psi hadron, a new heavy elementary particle whose unusual properties supported *Glashow's* hypothesis of charmed quarks. Many related particles were subsequently discovered, and stimulated a new look at the theoretical basis of particle physics. Richter shared the 1976 Nobel Prize for physics with *Ting*, who had discovered the J/psi almost simultaneously. Richter has been a strong proponent of the current trend in particle physics towards building larger and larger particle accelerator rings.

RICHTER, Charles Francis

1900-

American seismologist: devised Richter scale of earthquake strength

Richter worked at the Carnegie Institute before moving to the California Institute of Technology in 1936, becoming professor of seismology there in 1952. In 1935 he devised the scale of earthquake strength which bears his name. Unlike earlier, qualitative, scales, the Richter scale is an absolute scale based on the logarithm of the maximum amplitude of the earthquake waves observed on a seismograph, adjusted for the distance from the epicentre of the earthquake. Generally speaking earthquakes of magnitude 5.5 or greater cause significant damage. The largest earthquakes observed this century registered magnitude 8.9 on the Richter scale, and the earthquake which destroyed San Francisco in 1906 registered magnitude 8.25.

RIEMANN, Georg Friedrich Bernhard
1826-1866

German mathematician: originated Riemannian geometry

Riemann, the son of a Lutheran pastor, studied theology to please his father, and then studied mathematics under *Gauss* at Göttingen to please himself. In 1859 he became professor of mathematics there. At the age of 39 he died of tuberculosis. His friend *Dedekind* said of Riemann 'The gentle mind which had been implanted in him in his father's house remained with him all his life, and he served his God faithfully, as his father had, but in a different way.'

Riemann's papers were few but perfect, even in Gauss's eyes, producing profound consequences and new areas of mathematics and physics. Riemann's earliest publication was a new approach to the theory of complex functions using potential theory (from theoretical physics) and geometry to develop **Riemann surfaces**, which represent the branching behaviour of a complex algebraic function. These ideas were extended by introducing topological concepts into the theory of functions; this work was developed by *Poincaré* to advance algebraic geometry. In another paper Riemann defined a function $f(s)$, the Riemann zeta function, where

$$f(s) = 1 + \frac{1}{2^s} + \frac{1}{3^s} + \frac{1}{4^s} + \ldots$$

where $s = u + iv$ is complex, and conjectured that $f(s) = 0$ only if $u = \frac{1}{2}$ for $0 < u < 1$.

No-one has proved Riemenn's hypothesis, and it remains one of the important unsolved problems in number theory and analysis. Another of Riemann's contributions to analysis was the introduction of the **Riemann integral**, defined in terms of the limit of a summation of an infinity of ever smaller elements.

In 1854 Riemann gave his inaugural lecture 'Concerning the Hypotheses which underlie Geometry': a mathematical classic. The content was so fruitful that it altered mathematics and physics for a century afterwards. Riemann considered how concepts like distance and curvature could be defined generally in n-dimensional space, extending Gauss's work (1827) on non-Euclidian geometries. He foresaw how important this was for physics and provided some of the mathematical tools for *Einstein* to construct his general theory of relativity (1915).

ROBINSON, (Sir) Robert
1886-1975

English organic chemist: master of organic synthesis and pioneer of electronic theory of organic chemistry

His family had a prosperous business making surgical goods, but young Robinson hoped to become a mathematician. However, his father wished to construct a bleach works (on the information supplied by Chambers *Cyclopaedia*) and so pressed him to study chemistry. He was sent to Manchester, did well, and was afterwards successively professor at Sydney, Liverpool, St Andrews, Manchester, London and Oxford. He also had links with ICI and Shell. He was highly productive; his name is on more than 700 papers (20 after his 80th birthday) and 32 patents. One area of his talent was the chemistry of natural products; he worked on natural dyes such as brazilin, on the anthocyanins (plant petal pigments) and on alkaloids (he established the structure of the complex plant alkaloids strychnine and morphine) and steroids and antibiotics. His work carried organic chemistry to its highest points of achievement in the period before complex equipment came in, from 1960. Typically he would both show the structure of a natural product and devise elegant methods for its laboratory synthesis. In some cases he devised a method which neatly imitates a natural biosynthetic route.

In Manchester, Robinson took up the ideas of his teacher Arthur Lapworth on the electronic mechanism of organic reactions, and at first with him and later alone, he offered an electronic theory which helps to explain and predict the course of reactions of organic molecules. However, his interests moved on and he left others (such as *Ingold*) to expand the subject. Similarly his seminal work on the biogenesis of organic compounds in plants was largely developed by others.

Robinson had a keen intuition in chemistry, as well as a highly analytical mind displayed both in his synthetic schemes and in chess (he was a powerful player). He was also a mountaineer, a keen traveller, and an alarming motorist. In personality he was forceful and abrasive, and an irascible defender of his priorities. He was awarded a Nobel Prize in 1947; and received most of the other honours open to him, including the Order of Merit.

ROCHE, Edouard Albert
1820-1883

French mathematician: proposed limits on the stability of planetary satellites

Roche studied at Montpelier and Paris, subsequently being appointed professor of pure mathematics at Montpelier, a post he held through his entire working life.

In 1850 Roche calculated that a satellite orbiting a planet of equal density would break up under the influence of gravity, if it were to approach closer than 2.44 times the radius of the planet. This limit is now known as the **Roche limit**, and is thought to be the reason why the particles in the rings of Saturn, which extend out to 2.3 times Saturn's radius, do not aggregate into a moon.

ROEMER, Ole Christensen
1644-1710

Danish astronomer: discovered finite velocity of light

In 1675, whilst working with *Cassini* on tables of the eclipses of Jupiter's moons, Roemer noticed that the moons reached their predicted eclipse positions later than expected when Earth was moving away from Jupiter, and earlier when it was moving towards it. He realised that this discrepancy must be due to the finite time that light took to reach Earth. Using Cassini's recent determination of Jupiter's distance he was thus able to calculate the speed of light to be 140 000 miles per second (2.25×10^8 m s^{-1}), about 75% of the correct value. Although this was the first proof of the finite speed of light, it was not until *Bradley* confirmed Roemer's result in 1729 by the measurement of stellar abberation that it became widely accepted. Roemer became Astronomer Royal in Copenhagen, and its mayor in 1705.

ROENTGEN, Wilhelm Konrad
1845-1923

German experimental physicist: discoverer of X-rays

Originally a student of engineering at Zürich Polytechnic, Roentgen was attracted to physics, which he studied and later taught in several German universities. He was professor of physics in Würzburg when he made his famous discovery, in 1895. While using a discharge tube (in which an electric discharge is passed through a gas at low pressure) in a darkened room, he noticed that a card coated with $BaPt(CN)_4$ glowed when the tube was switched on. Roentgen soon found that the radiation causing this was emitted from the discharge tube at the region where the cathode rays (now known to be a stream of electrons) struck the glass end of the discharge tube. The new rays were found to have a much greater range in air than cathode rays; they travelled in straight lines, and were not deflected by electric or magnetic fields; they passed through card and even through thin metal sheet, and could be detected by a fluorescent screen or photographic plate. He named them X-rays. If passed through a human hand onto a photographic plate, the bones were seen as shadowed areas against the lighter flesh, and metal objects (for example a ring) gave opaque shadows. Roentgen suggested that the new rays were an electromagnetic radiation akin to light but of shorter wavelength, and this was proved by *von Laue* in 1912.

Roentgen was awarded the first Nobel Prize in physics, in 1901, 'for the discovery of the remarkable rays subsequently named after him'; in fact they are still known as X-rays. Their study added much to physics, gave a new technique for use in medicine, and after the work of the *Braggs* in 1915 led to X-ray crystallography as a new and immensely valuable method for the study of crystal and

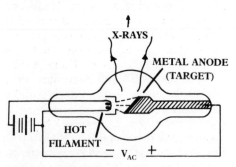

Diagram of an X-ray tube. A current heats the tungsten filament to a temperature high enough for it to emit a stream of electrons. The potential difference V_{AC} is large (>20 000 volts) so the electrons are strongly attracted to it and strike the metal anode target at high speed, emitting X-rays. Ancillary equipment to evacuate the tube, to water-cool the anode, and to protect the operator from X-rays is not shown.

molecular structure. A modern X-ray tube uses a hot wire to generate electrons, which are accelerated by a high voltage and then strike a metal target, emitting X-rays (see diagram). Roentgen did excellent work on other areas of experimental physics. He took out no patents on his work, and died in some poverty in the period of high inflation in Germany.

ROHRER, Heinrich
1933-

Swiss physicist: invented the scanning tunnelling microscope

Rohrer joined IBM at Zürich in 1963, and later began to collaborate with Gerd Binnig who joined in 1978. Together they took up work that Russell Young at the National Bureau of Standards in Washington had initiated; to build a scanning tunnelling microscope. A tungsten electron field emitter tip was moved across a surface by precision piezoelectric transducers and the tip raised or lowered to keep the tip the same distance above the surface. The result could be plotted as a contour map of the surface. Binnig and Rohrer achieved a working microscope by reducing the tip to a single atom and bringing it within a couple of atomic diameters of the surface; as a result by 1981 they could even produce images of single atoms. By reducing vibration a horizontal resolution of ≈ 2 Å and a vertical resolution of ≈ 0.1 Å was possible. Application of the technique to the study of semiconductor surfaces, microelectronics, chemical reactions on surfaces and biochemistry have occurred rapidly. As a result Rohrer and Binnig shared the 1986 Nobel Prize for physics with *Ruska* (a key figure in the invention of the electron microscope).

ROSCOE, (Sir) Henry Enfield
1833-1915

English chemist: pioneer in photochemistry, vanadium chemistry, and chemical education

Son of a Liverpool lawyer, Roscoe's

enthusiasm for chemistry began at school. As a Dissenter, he went to University College, London and studied under *Graham* and *Williamson*, and then in Heidelberg with *Bunsen*. Back in London in 1855, he juggled several modest chemical jobs in teaching and consultancy to make a living; but in 1857 he became professor in Owens College in Manchester which gave him great scope. The college was unpopular in 1857, but Roscoe soon attracted students and convinced manufacturers of their value. His Manchester school of chemistry, then the best in Britain, did much to convert Owens College into the Victoria University. In 1885 he became an MP for Manchester for ten years, and then Vice-Chancellor of London University.

His research with Bunsen was on the chemical action of light, using particularly the reaction: $H_2 + Cl_2 \rightarrow 2HCl$. This was the first research in quantitative photochemistry. In 1865 he heard that vanadium ores had been found in a Cheshire copper mine, and this led him to explore vanadium chemistry. He was the first to make the metal, by reduction of VCl_2. He always had an interest in industrial chemistry, and in technical education. *See photo p.73.*

ROSS, (Sir) James Clark
1800-1862

English polar explorer: located north magnetic pole, and explored Antarctic Ocean

Entering the Royal Navy when he was twelve, James Ross served under his uncle John Ross in surveys of the White Sea and the Arctic, and later with W. E. Parry in four attempts in the 1820s to reach the North Pole over the ice. From 1829-33 he was with his uncle on a private expedition (financed by the distiller F. Booth) to explore the Arctic, and in 1831 he located the north magnetic pole. Back in the Navy as a captain from 1834, his expertise in magnetic measurements led to him being employed by the Admiralty in 1838 to make a magnetic survey (declination and dip) of the UK, and the next year to command an expedition to the Antarctic. This voyage lasted four years; he discovered Victoria Land, the 12 000 ft volcano he named Mount Erebus, and 'the marvellous range of ice cliffs barring the approach to the Pole'. When he returned he had made the greatest survey of its kind, covering magnetic, geological and meteorological observations and studies of marine life at great depths; and only one man had been lost through illness, largely because Ross ensured good supplies of a mixed diet. In 1848 he commanded his last expedition searching for the arctic explorer Sir J. Franklin who had disappeared looking for the North-west passage; this was not achieved, but new observations were made. He left the Navy with the rank of rear admiral.

ROSS, (Sir) Ronald
1857-1932

British physician: discovered major steps in life-cycle of malarial parasite

Ross was born in India, where his father was a British army officer; he came to the UK to school when he was eight, studied medicine in London, and joined the Indian Medical Service in 1881. His interest in medicine increased from that time; but his interest in poetry, fiction and mathematics was lifelong and he published in all these fields. From 1890 he studied malaria, and when on study-leave in London in 1894 he was shown the malarial parasite by *Manson*, who suggested that it was transmitted by mosquitoes. Malaria was a long-known disease, and in the 1880s had been shown by C. L. A. Laveran and others to be due to a protozoon (a single-celled animal parasite) which invaded the red blood cells. The life-cycle of the protozoon (the genus *Plasmodium*) is complex, with several stages in human blood and liver, and other stages in the stomach and salivary gland of a species of mosquito. Ross, back in

London in 1895, dissected over 100 infected mosquitos before he saw, in 1897, the same stages that Laveran had seen in human blood, and which Ross found in the *Anopheles* mosquito. By 1900 he and others had shown that human malaria is passed by the bite of the *Anopheles*. Although still a major problem, control of malaria in many areas followed this knowledge of its transmission.

Ross worked in England after retiring from the Indian Medical Service in 1899, first in Liverpool and then in London; he was awarded a Nobel Prize in 1902.

ROSSBY, Carl-Gustaf Arvid

1898-1957

Swedish-American meteorologist: discovered large-scale waves in the upper atmosphere, and the jet stream

Rossby was educated at the University of Stockholm and at the Bergen Geophysical Institute. In 1926 he emigrated to America, where he subsequently held professorships at the Massachusetts Institute of Technology and at the University of Chicago. In 1940 Rossby demonstrated that large-scale undulatory disturbances exist in the uniform flow of the westerly winds in the upper atmosphere, developing in the zone of contact between cold polar air and warm tropical air; such waves are inherent features of a rotating fluid with a thermal gradient. There are usually 3-5 such **Rossby waves** in each hemisphere, with wavelengths of up to 2000 km. Rossby also showed that the strength of the westerly winds has an important influence on global weather, either allowing the normal sequence of cyclones and anticyclones to develop when the westerlies are strong, or allowing cold polar air to sweep south when they are weak. He is further credited with the discovery of the jet stream, the broad ribbon of upper westerly winds travelling at about 45 m s^{-1} in the mid-latitudes.

ROSSI, Bruno Benedetti

1905-

Italian-American physicist: discovered cosmic rays to be positively charged particles, and found the first astronomical X-ray source

In 1934 Rossi demonstrated that many cosmic rays were positively charged particles by an experiment in the Eritrean mountains, using two sets of Geiger counters pointing east and west. A 26 per cent excess of particles travelling in an eastward direction was found, indicating that these cosmic rays were positively charged particles and were deflected eastwards by the Earth's magnetic field. Rossi also contributed to the birth of X-ray astronomy in 1962; he led a team which discovered the isotropic flux of X-rays incident on the Earth, and the first astronomical discrete X-ray source, Scorpio X-1, by use of a rocket-borne probe.

ROUS, Francis Peyton

1879-1970

American pathologist and oncologist: showed that some cancers are caused by a virus

During his second year as a medical student at Johns Hopkins University in Baltimore, Rous scraped his finger on a tuberculous bone while doing an autopsy and became infected. After surgery he spent a year working as a cowboy, before returning to medicine and graduating in 1905. He spent a long career of over 60 years at the Rockefeller Institute in New York, working mainly on cancer. In 1911 he showed that a spontaneous cancerous tumour in a fowl could be transplanted by cell grafts, and (remarkably) that even cell-free extracts from it would convey the tumour. This pointed to the cause being a virus, and by the 1930s several types of animal cancer were shown to be due to a virus. The Rous chicken sarcoma remains the best-known example. Initially the idea of a virus causing cancer was hard to believe, as the pattern of the disease is so different from that of typical viral infections. Rous developed methods for culturing viruses and cells; and he proposed that cancer-formation (carcinogenesis) typically involves two processes, initiation and promotion, which can require two different agents, which may be chemical, viral, radiological, or even mechanical. He shared a Nobel Prize in 1966. He was an active researcher until he was 90.

ROUX, Pierre Paul Émile
1853-1933

French bacteriologist: co-discoverer of first bacterial toxin

Even before he graduated in medicine in Paris, Roux assisted *Pasteur*, working with him on anthrax and rabies, and in 1904 he succeeded him as director of the Pasteur Institute. With A. Yersin he cultured the diphtheria bacillus in broth, and in 1888 showed that if this was filtered through unglazed porcelain, the cell-free extract produced the symptoms of the disease when injected into test animals. For the first time it was shown that, at least in this case, the effects of a bacterial infection are largely due to a potent toxin produced by the bacteria; he wrote, 'snake venoms themselves are not as deadly'. *Behring* and *Kitasato* went on to show that blood serum from infected guinea pigs contained a counter-poison, an **antitoxin**; Roux used horses in place of guinea pigs, which gave enough serum to use on human patients, from 1894.

RUBNER, Max
1854-1932

German physiologist: made important investigations of animal metabolism and energy balance

Rubner was professor of physiology at Marburg and later at Berlin. Before 1800 *Lavoisier* had shown by experiments using a guinea-pig in a calorimeter that its heat production was the same as that given by burning a quantity of carbon, equal to that in the CO_2 it expired, and so he concluded that metabolism is equivalent to burning at body temperature. Rubner developed such experiments on mammalian heat production, and proposed his **surface law**: that the rate of metabolism is proportional to the superficial area of the mammal, and not to its weight. He also found that recently fed animals lost heat more quickly than fasting animals, pointing to a cellular regulatory system. He confirmed the results obtained by Lavoisier and others that metabolic energy production is equal to ordinary combustion despite the temperature difference; this implies that the law of conservation of energy applies to animate as well as inanimate objects. Rubner compared the energy available from various foods, showed that carbohydrates, fats and proteins were broken down equally readily, and that a mammal's energy useage for growth purposes is a constant fraction of its total energy output.

RUMFORD, (Count), (Sir) Benjamin Thompson
1753-1814

American adventurer, social reformer, inventor and physicist: measured relation between work and heat; founded Royal Institution

It would be hard to name a scientist who had a more extraordinary life than Rumford. He was a store apprentice, then a part-time teacher, gymnast and medical student with an interest in electrical machines. At 18 he married a rich young widow of 30, and decided to become a gentleman-soldier and farmer; he so impressed his seniors that at 19 he had become a Major in the militia and Squire of Concord.

However, excitement was on the way: New England was the centre of the American Revolution. His family had

Benjamin Thompson (Count Rumford)

been there since 1630 and he had good prospects if he cast in his lot with the revolutionaries, but Thompson supported the 'loyalist' view and did so by acting as a secret agent for the British Army. There is no good evidence that he was a double agent, but by 1776 he was prudent to leave America for England, where he took up his scientific interests again (on projectiles, appropriately), was elected FRS in 1779, and next year became Undersecretary of State in the Colonial Office at 27. In 1782, seeking active service, he went back to America, did well as a soldier, and was shocked when peace was declared the following year.

This left him with no clear future, and he had no wish to 'vegetate in England'; but soon through carefully nurtured contacts he was appointed adviser to the Elector of Bavaria, being knighted, rather surprisingly, by King George of England as a preface to his new career. He was highly effective in Bavaria, reforming the conditions of the army, setting up welfare schemes for the poor which were well ahead of their time, and creating a large park in Munich still treasured as the English Garden. He became a wealthy and respected public figure, with the title of

Count, and Minister for War. He was there for 14 years before moving to London in 1798, where he was welcomed as a great philanthropist and an expert on new methods for heating and feeding the poor.

Scientific work was always a part of Rumford's life and in Munich he made his greatest contribution to physics. He visited the arsenal and 'was struck by the very considerable degree of heat which a brass cannon acquires in a short time in being bored. . .' Now at the time, heat was thought to consist of a subtle fluid, 'caloric', which was squeezed out of the metal on boring. But Rumford showed by using a blunt borer that an apparently limitless amount of heat could be got from one piece of metal; and that the supposed 'caloric' seemed to be weightless. He concluded that caloric was non-existant, and that heat was the 'motion of the particles of a body'. He went on to measure the relation between work and heat, getting a result within 30% of the modern value. This concept was fundamental to modern physics, and the quantitative relation between heat and work was soon studied with great care by *Joule*.

Rumford was always an enthusiast for the application of science, himself designing improved stoves, lamps and carriages; and in London in 1800 he planned and largely created the Royal Institution, which has been so valuable in British science ever since. Rumford's appointment in 1801 of *Davy*, aged 22, to work at the Royal Institution was a happy and fruitful choice. Soon Rumford was travelling again, partly in exasperation as a result of disputes with the Royal Institution's managers. He settled in Paris, and in 1805 married Anne Lavoisier, widow of the great chemist and reformer. The marriage quickly proved unfortunate; their quarrels were dramatic, and Rumford spent much time in his laboratory, studying the heat generated in combustion and using for this an improved Lavoisier calorimeter. He separated from

Anne, but he had friends, money, a resident mistress, visits from his American daughter Sally, and a substantial reputation. F. D. Roosevelt rated him with *Franklin* and Thomas Jefferson, as 'the greatest mind America has produced'. He may well be the most colourful character in 19th century science.

RUSKA, Ernst August Friedrich
1906-1988

German physicist: pioneer in development of transmission electron microscope

The electron microscope has had such a revolutionary effect in science (especially biology) that it must rank with the telescope, optical microscope and spectroscope as an outstanding device. Like these devices it has no universally agreed single discoverer; claims and counterclaims have been made, but the award of a Nobel Prize to Ruska in 1986 for the discovery makes him a central figure.

He studied high voltage and vacuum methods in Munich and Berlin, the appropriate background for his pioneer work on electron optics. By the mid-1920s it was known that electrons could not only behave as particles, but in appropriate experiments could behave as waves; and H. Busch found that a magnetic coil could focus a beam of electrons, rather as a convex lens could focus a light beam. In 1928 M. Kroll and Ruska (then a research student in Berlin) made a microscope giving 17× magnification using these methods of electron optics, and by 1933 Ruska made an instrument giving 12 000×, and commercial models were in use by 1938. However, G. R. Rüdenberg secured the first patent, which was upheld in a law suit in the US (but not in Germany). Ruska's work, supported by the Siemens and Halske company, was continued in a converted bakery in Berlin during World War II, until Soviet troops looted the laboratory. His transmission electron microscope eventually achieved up to $10^6×$, compared with 2000× for an optical microscope. Ruska shared his Nobel Prize with G. Binnig and *Rohrer* of IBM who from 1978 worked in Zürich on a complementary device, the scanning tunnelling microscope, using an ultrasharp tip at high voltage to explore conducting surfaces and valuable for the study of metal surfaces, and giving resolution down to atomic size.

RUSSELL, Henry Norris
1877-1957

American astronomer: inferred stellar evolution from spectral type/luminosity relationship

Apart from a period in Cambridge, Russell spent his working life in Princeton. In 1913 he discovered that the absolute magnitude (intrinsic brightness) of stars correlates well with their spectral types, which are indicative of surface temperature, and related to their colour. He displayed his findings on a diagram of stellar magnitude *vs.* spectral type, now known as the **Hertzsprung-Russell** (or **H-R**) **diagram**, after *Hertzsprung* who had obtained the same results a few years earlier, but his publication in an obscure journal had received little attention. Russell went on to suggest that the diagram represented an evolutionary path, with stars evolving into hot, bright blue-white giants and ending as cold red dwarfs. Although this theory was soon abandoned, the diagram has remained a valuable tool in astrophysics.

Russell also studied chemical abundances in the Sun (a yellow dwarf) from the solar spectrum, concluding in 1929 that hydrogen makes up 60% of the Sun's volume, at the time a surprisingly large figure, but now known to be an underestimate.

RUTHERFORD, (Sir) Ernest (Lord Rutherford of Nelson)
1871-1937

New Zealand-British physicist: founded nuclear physics

Born near Nelson in New Zealand into a

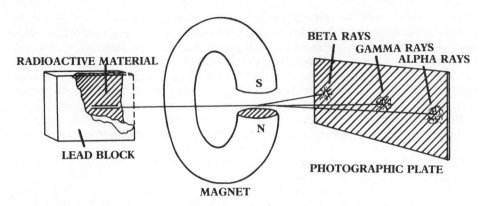

When radiation from a radioactive source such as radium passes through a magnetic field, it is split into three types. The gamma radiation (short X-rays) is undeflected; and the alpha rays (helium nuclei) and beta rays (electrons) are deflected in opposing directions.

wheelwright's large family, Rutherford showed wide-ranging ability at school, won a scholarship to Canterbury College, Christchurch, and in his final years there concentrated on mathematics and physics. In his last year there he invented a sensitive radio-wave detector, just six years after *Hertz* had discovered radio waves and in the same year that *Marconi* began to use radio for practical purposes.

In 1895 he won a scholarship to Cambridge to work under *J. J. Thomson*; he borrowed money for his passage to England, and soon began research on the conductivity produced in air by X-rays, recently discovered by *Roentgen*. He was J. J. Thomson's first research student. Three years later Rutherford became a professor at McGill University, Montreal. Within a short period he greatly extended the foundations of nuclear physics, taking advantage of collaboration with the chemist *Soddy* and a good supply of the costly radium bromide. They produced nine papers in 18 months.

Radioactivity had been discovered in uranium in 1896 by *Becquerel*, and in thorium by G. C. Schmidt; Pierre and Marie *Curie* had discovered two more radioactive elements, radium and polonium. Rutherford's studies revealed (1898) that the radioactive emission consisted of at least two kinds of rays; those

which were less penetrating he called alpha rays (helium nuclei), and the others beta rays (electrons). Two years later he discovered a third, and even more penetrating kind, the gamma rays (electromagnetic waves). Together with Soddy he proposed in 1903 that radioactive decay occurs by successive transformations, with different and random amounts of time spent between ejection of each of the successive rays, sometimes years and sometimes fractions of a second. Whilst the process is random it is governed by an average time in which half the atoms of a large sample would be expected to decay. This idea that atoms of some elements are not permanent, but can disintegrate, was then revolutionary.

A skilful set of experiments was then designed with T. Royds to examine alpha rays; having found that the mass and charge were correct for helium nuclei, this was finally proved by sending the rays into an evacuated thin glass vessel and observing the build-up of helium gas inside.

In 1907 Rutherford returned to Britain, and in Manchester he extended his study of alpha particles, working with *Geiger* on the detector named after him, and inventing the scintillation screen for observing them. Geiger and E. Marsden made the surprising discovery that about one in 8000 particles striking a platinum foil was deflected back from it. As Rutherford put it '. . . quite the most incredible event that has ever happened to me in my life . . . It was almost as if you fired a 15-inch shell at a piece of tissue paper and it came back and hit you.' Knowing that collision with a comparatively light electron could not produce such a large deflection, he deduced (1911) that atoms possess a very small but massive nucleus at their centre, holding all the positive charge to balance that of all the electrons about them. This was the first correct model of the atom, and *Bohr* developed it during a three-month visit by showing which electronic orbits would be allowed by the 'old' quantum theory (which *Planck* had introduced in 1900).

The first World War caused Rutherford to work on sonic methods for detecting submarines, but in 1919 he returned to his research on succeeding J. J. Thomson as Cavendish professor of physics at Cambridge. Another major discovery occurred within months; he observed that nuclei could be made to disintegrate by artificial means, rather than waiting for their natural disintegration. This work he did himself, as young men were not yet back from the war. Alpha particles striking atomic nuclei, such as nitrogen, would knock out a proton to leave a different and lighter nucleus. Between 1920 and 1924 Rutherford and *Chadwick* showed that most light atoms could be broken up by using alpha particles. Chadwick's later discovery of the neutron, and the nuclear disintegrations of heavier atoms achieved by *Cockcroft* and E. T. S. Walton using a linear accelerator, owed much to discussions with Rutherford. These and other major discoveries in his laboratory made 1932 a 'marvellous year' for nuclear physics. He also was involved, together with M. Oliphant and P. Harteck, in the first nuclear fusion reaction (1934) by bombarding deuterium with deuterium nuclei to produce tritium.

Rutherford initiated and directed the beginnings of nuclear physics. He received the Nobel Prize for chemistry in 1908, and the simplicity and power of his work gives him a place as one of the greatest experimental physicists of all time. In personality he was forceful, exuberant and enormously likeable, with physicist friends world-wide, many of them former students of his. He was not, of course, always right; his response to a suggestion that nuclear energy might one day be useful was that the idea was 'all moonshine'.

RUZICKA, Leopold
1887-1976
Croatian-Swiss organic chemist: devised isoprene rule

Ruzicka grew up in Croatia (now in Yugoslavia) when it was part of Austria-Hungary, and after an education in Germany and Switzerland he finally became professor in Zürich. In 1916 he began work on perfumes; one famous study concerned the costly perfume fixatives in musk (from a Himalayan deer) and civet (from an African wildcat). He found that the key compounds, muscone and civetone, are cyclic ketones. What was remarkable is that both contain large rings of carbon atoms (16- and 17-membered, respectively). It had been thought that such large rings could not exist. In fact, Ruzicka's work showed them to be stable, and he devised methods of synthesis. He also worked on steroids, specially the male sex hormones; his synthesis of testosterone made him rich and he became a major collector of early Dutch paintings. His work on terpenes led to the **isoprene rule**, which proposes that terpenes have structures based on units of the five-carbon isoprene molecule, joined head-to-tail (1920). In this form, or in its later version (which proposes the biogenesis of these compounds from isopentenyl pyrophosphate) the rule has proved a valuable guide to structure. Ruzicka shared a Nobel Prize in 1939.

RYDBERG, Johannes (Robert)
1854-1919

Swedish spectroscopist: early theorist on atomic number

Educated at Lund, Rydberg stayed there for his entire career, as professor of physics from 1901. He was fascinated by *Mendelayev*'s periodic table of the elements, and he had the brilliant and valuable intuition that the periodicity was related to atomic spectra and atomic structure. Working on atomic emission spectra in 1890, he found a simple general formula for the frequency of some of the spectral lines. He introduced the useful idea of **wave numbers** ($1/\lambda$, where λ is the wavelength); and showed that *Balmer*'s equation giving the frequencies of many lines in the hydrogen spectrum could be generalized in the form $1/\lambda = R(1/m^2 - 1/n^2)$. Within 30 years successive spectral series were found fitting this formula, with simple integral values for n and m; the Balmer series is that having $m = 2$. The constant R is known as the **Rydberg constant**. Rydberg himself never reached his goal of relating spectra to atomic structure, but his view that a relation between structure and spectra must exist was valuable and reached fruition with *Bohr*'s work on atomic structure in 1913 from which Rydberg's formula emerges, with a value of R calculated in excellent agreement with experiment.

Rydberg's study of the periodic table led him in 1897 to see the importance of atomic number (rather than atomic weight), a view confirmed by *Moseley* in 1913; and in 1906 he stated for the first time that 2, 8 and 18 (i.e., $2n^2$ where $n = 1$, 2, 3) are the numbers of elements in the early periods. He also corrected the number of lanthanides to 32.

RYLE, (Sir) Martin
1918-1984

British astronomer: produced first detailed map of the radio sky

Ryle was largely responsible for the development of radio astronomy after World War II, following the pioneering discoveries of *Jansky* and *Reber*. He began a series of surveys at Cambridge in the 1950s, culminating in 1959 in a definitive catalogue of the strengths and positions of 500 radio sources (increased to 5000 in 1965). By using radio dishes separated by up to 5 km, Ryle was able to obtain a large effective aperture, and to produce detailed radio maps of areas of sky. In this way interstellar clouds, quasars and radio galaxies could be studied. In showing that the distant parts of the universe appear different from the nearer parts, Ryle's results supported the 'big bang' view of its origin (rather than a 'steady state' theory) and led to major public disputes with *Hoyle*. *See photo p.196.*

S

SABINE, Wallace Clement
1868-1919
American physicist: the founder of architectural acoustics

A midwesterner from a farming family, Sabine did well as a physics student at Harvard and became an instructor there in 1890. Except for war work in World War I (he was in effect the first chief scientist for the US Air Force, in 1917-18) he never left Harvard. Five years later Harvard President C. W. Eliot asked for his help; the acoustics of a major new lecture theatre were so bad as to make it useless. Little was then known of architectural acoustics, but Sabine saw that such problems must arise from the size, shape, and materials of a room, which affect the reverberation time. In the disastrous new theatre this time was 5½ s, so that a speaker had the first and last words of a sentence mingled. For speech this time should be 1 to 2 s; and for music, about 25% longer. Since size and shape are not easily much altered, Sabine worked on the materials; he and two helpers spent many nights (after midnight, when the street was quiet) moving cushions from another large theatre to the disaster area, making tests, and returning them before dawn. Authority was dismayed by the delay and after two years demanded action; Sabine prescribed 22 hair-felt blankets, and the place was rendered usable for the next 75 years.

He had devised an electrically-blown organ pipe and drum recorder to measure reverberation time at 512 Hz, and he now worked hard to develop a formula which would allow calculation of the acoustics of an unbuilt hall. With the aid of more massive cushion moving experiments, he derived, in 1898, the **Sabine formula**: $T=KV/Sa$, where T is the time in seconds for a sound to decay 60 decibels in the hall; K is a near-constant, inversely proportional to the speed of sound; V the volume of the room; S is the total area of all the room surfaces; and a is the average sound absorption coefficient of these surfaces (it varies from about 0.01 for plaster to 1.0 for an open window). With its aid, he was able to advise on a projected new Boston Symphony Hall, opened in 1900. However, musicians were critical of the result; this was probably because an orchestra of 90 sounded thin in such a large hall; today with 104 players the sound is fuller. From 1904 he was much in demand to advise on architectural acoustics, and his methods have been in use ever since.

SACHS, Julius von
1832-1897
German botanist: pioneer of plant physiology

Sachs was an assistant to *Purkinje* at Prague, and after various posts in Germany became professor at Würzburg from 1868. During nearly half a century he made massive contributions to plant physiology, which before him was largely neglected. Much apparatus and technique now familiar is due to him, and his many pupils continued to develop the subject. His early work was on stored nutrients in seeds and on the culture of plants in nutrient solutions (hydroponics). He studied the uptake of minerals by plants, and the influence of temperature on plant growth, and discovered the 'law of cardinal points'. In 1861 he showed that photosynthesis actually occurs in chloroplasts and that the first 'visible' product of carbon dioxide uptake is starch, deposited in the chloroplasts. He studied etiolation and the formation of flowers and roots; and geotropism, phototropism, and hydrotropism. When, after about 1880, he moved more towards theory, he was less successful; and his authority held back new views and delayed new discoveries. In his last years he strongly attacked *Darwin*'s views on evolution.

SAHA, Meghnad

1894-1956

Indian astrophysicist: demonstrated that elements in stars are ionized in proportion to their temperature

The son of a small shopkeeper in Dacca, Saha was educated at Presidency College, Calcutta, and afterwards visited Europe. He taught at the University of Allahabad, and in 1938 he was appointed professor of physics at Calcutta.

The absorption lines in the spectra of stars vary widely in their elemental abundances with some showing only hydrogen and helium lines, and others showing numerous metal lines. In 1920 Saha demonstrated that this did not necessarily represent a true variation in elemental composition, but a different degree of ionization of the metal atoms, which was related to temperature by **Saha's equation** for a monatomic gas. At higher temperatures the metal atoms exist only in ionized form, and the absorption lines of neutral metal atoms become very weak. The proportions of the various ions of the same metal can be used to estimate stellar temperature. *Russell* used Saha's results to estimate the amount of hydrogen in the Sun.

SALAM, Abdus

1926-

Pakistani theoretical physicist: developed unified theory of the weak nuclear force and electromagnetism

Salam's early career shifted between Punjab University, Cambridge University and Lahore, where he became a professor at the Government College and Punjab University. He then lectured at Cambridge (1954-56) and in 1957 became professor of theoretical physics at Imperial College of Science and Technology, London. Salam's concern for his subject in developing countries led to his setting up the International Centre of Theoretical Physics in Trieste in 1964.

Physicists recognize four basic forces in nature: gravity, electromagnetism, and the 'strong' and 'weak' nuclear forces, which are active only within nuclear range. In 1979 Salam won the Nobel Prize for physics together with *Weinberg* and *Glashow*. Independently each had produced a theory explaining both the 'weak' nuclear force and 'electromagnetic' interactions. This led to the prediction of neutral currents, later found by experiments at CERN (European Organisation for Nuclear Research) in 1973, and 'intermediate vector bosons' first seen in 1983.

SANDAGE, Allan Rex

1926-

American astronomer: made first identification of an optical object with a quasar

Sandage studied at the University of Illinois and the California Institute of Technology, before joining the Hale Observatories, initially as an assistant to *Hubble*. In 1960 Sandage made the first optical identification of a quasar, objects originally seen only as discrete radio sources. Together with T. Matthews he found a faint optical object at the same location as the quasar 3C 48, and showed that it had a very unusual spectrum. The strange spectrum was soon shown by *M. Schmidt* to be the result of a massive red shift. Sandage went on to identify many more quasars via this peculiarity of their spectra, and he also showed that most quasars are not radio emitters.

SANGER, Frederick

1918-

English biochemist: pioneer of chemical studies on the structure of proteins and nucleic acids

Sanger, a physician's son, graduated in Cambridge in 1939 and has researched there ever since; he has been on the staff of the Medical Research Council laboratories from 1951.

In the early 1940s he devised a method using 2,4-dinitrofluorobenzene (**Sanger's reagent**) to label the amino acid at the 'free amino' end of the protein chain. By combining this method with the acid or enzymic break-up of the longer protein chains to give shorter, identifiable fragments, Sanger was able to deduce the sequence of amino acids in the chains of the protein hormone, insulin; by the early 1950s he had worked out the sequence of the 51 amino acids in its two-chain molecule, and found the small differences in this sequence in insulins from pig, sheep, horse and whale.

After he was awarded a Nobel Prize for this, in 1958, he moved on to the bigger problem of the structure of nucleic acids.

Frederick Sanger

These biological macromolecules have double helical chains of nucleotides whose base sequence determines the information carried by the genes. He worked first on RNA, whose chains are of modest length, and then moved to DNA which has very long chains, with up to 10^8 units in a chain. Sanger used a highly ingenious combination of radioactive labelling, gel electrophoresis, and selective enzymes which can split or grow DNA chains at specific points.

By 1977 he and his group were able to deduce the full sequence of bases in the DNA of the virus Phi X 174, with over 5400 bases. Mitochondrial DNA, with 17 000 bases, soon followed. Such methods, by 1984, led to the full base sequence in Epstein-Barr virus (EBV) whose genome (the complete set of genes of an organism) is over 150 000 bases long. For his nucleic acid work Sanger shared the 1980 Nobel Prize for chemistry and became the first to win two Nobel Prizes in chemistry. His work has given new, surprising and detailed knowledge of both proteins and genes, and has stimulated others in this field.

SANTORIO Santorio (Sanctorius)

1561-1636

Italian physician: applied physics to medicine

A graduate of Padua, Santorio was physician to the King of Poland for 14 years before returning to Padua as professor of theoretical medicine in 1611. He was a colleague of *Galileo* and Santorio's medical research was doubtless influenced by him. Galileo worked on pendulums and thermometers, but it was Santorio who used a pendulum to compare pulse rates (no clocks were then available) and he invented the clinical thermometer in 1612 and later explained its use. He was the first to apply quantitative methods in medicine, and is best known for his work on metabolism. He examined the change in body weight with diet, sleep, activity

Santorio in his balance

and disease, and for 30 years spent much time suspended from a steelyard, weighing himself and his solid and liquid input and output and deducing the amount of 'insensible perspiration' lost through the skin and lungs.

SCHAUDINN, Fritz Richard
1871-1906

German zoologist and microbiologist: identified organism responsible for syphilis

After starting university work as a student of philology at Berlin, Schaudinn turned to science and specialized in zoology. During his short career he worked in Berlin, especially on those protozoons (notably trypanosomes) which cause some human diseases. He demonstrated the alternation of generations in Fora-

minifera, and worked out the life-cycle of the Coccidiae (scale insect). He distinguished between the amoeba causing tropical dysentry (*Entamoeba histolytica*) and its harmless relative *E. coli* which lives in the human intestinal lining; his work included experimental self-infection with both organisms. His best-known discovery, made in 1905 with the dermatologist P. E. Hoffmann, was of the pale threadlike undulating spirochaete now named *Treponema pallidum* which causes syphilis. Proof that this causes venereal syphilis was not easy and its acceptance was delayed. He also worked on malaria, proved an earlier guess that the parasite of human hookworm enters through the skin of the feet, and described many new animals first observed by him on expeditions to the Arctic.

SCHAWLOW, Arthur Leonard
1921-

American physicist: co-inventor of the laser

Schawlow's early work was at Toronto and his postdoctoral research was with *Townes* at Columbia University. The two remained in contact; Schawlow married Townes's sister. After ten years at Bell Telephone Laboratories, a professorship at Stanford followed in 1961.

Arthur L. Schawlow in 1962, with a small ruby laser

Townes and Schawlow collaborated to extend the maser principle to light by devising the laser; although the first working laser was constructed by *Maiman* in 1960. (For an account of masers and lasers see Townes's entry.) From the early 1970s Schawlow used laser methods to simplify atomic spectra and to give improved values for basic physical quantities such as the *Rydberg* constant, and extraordinarily precise values for the electronic energy levels in the hydrogen atom. Schawlow shared a Nobel Prize in 1981 for his work on laser spectroscopy.

SCHEELE, Carl Wilhelm

1742-1786

Swedish chemist: a discoverer of chemical elements (chlorine and oxygen) and of many chemical compounds

Scheele was trained as an apothecary, at a time when they made most of their own drugs and had available a range of minerals, plants and simple equipment for chemical operations. He had a passion for chemical experimentation which is probably unsurpassed; but he was unlucky in that some of his major discoveries were also made by others at nearly the same time, and they published sooner. Nevertheless his renown led to prestigeous job offers which he refused, preferring to take a series of posts as an assistant apothecary. This left him able to experiment freely in his limited leisure time, but the overwork, the poor conditions, and the absorption of hazardous chemicals may have led to his early death.

Scheele first made the reactive green gas chlorine in 1774 from hydrochloric acid and MnO_2, but the fact that it is an element only became known by *Davy*'s work of 1810. Earlier, in 1773, Scheele had shown that air is a mixture (of 'fire air' and 'foul air' as he named its components), and he made oxygen in several different ways (e.g. by heating HgO, or KNO_3, or $Hg(NO_3)_2$; or by heating MnO_2 with H_2SO_4) but his book on this did not appear until 1777. Before then, in 1774, *Priestley* had published his discovery of oxygen. The two men were similar in their skill as experimenters, in their limited interest in theory, and their adherance to the phlogiston theory.

Scheele made a variety of new acids in the 1770s (phosphoric, molybdic, tungstic, and arsenic acids) as well as HF, SiF_4, AsH_3 and other reactive and very toxic compounds. In the 1780s he made a number of new organic acids, and fairly pure hydrocyanic acid (recording its taste!). His death at 43 is unsurprising; he was a fanatical, prolific and probably unwise chemical discoverer.

SCHIAPARELLI, Giovanni Virginio

1835-1910

Italian astronomer: demonstrated that meteors follow cometary orbits; observed Martian surface features

Educated in Italy, Germany and Russia, Sciaparelli was Director of the Milan Observatory for 40 years. In 1866 he showed that meteors follow cometary orbits, and he identified the comets associated with the annual Leonid and Perseid meteor showers. In 1877 Mars made one of its closest approaches to Earth, enabling Schiaparelli to discover its southern polar ice cap, and to identify the direction of the axis of rotation. He also saw what he thought to be many dark lines criss-crossing the planet, and termed them 'canali' (channels). Schiaparelli himself believed these to be natural features, but the American astronomer *Lowell* suggested that they were irrigation features constructed by a Martian civilization (mistranslating 'canali' as 'canals'), and thus started a long controversy that was only finally laid to rest by the Mariner space probes.

SCHLEIDEN, Jakob Mathias

1804-1881

German botanist: a founder of cell theory

Schleiden studied law in Heidelberg and

practised it in his birthplace, Hamburg; but his interest in botany grew and he studied the subject at three universities, graduating at Jena in 1831. He lectured on botany there from 1839, and became a private teacher of botany after 1864.

Schleiden was a skilful microscopist, and from about 1840 good compound microscopes became available, which were largely achromatic. By 1880, thanks to improved designs by *Abbe*, oil-immersion objectives, and better sectioning and staining of specimens, the instrument reached a high point, with good resolution at magnifications up to $2000\times$. Plant cells (i.e., delimited spaces within walls) had been observed two centuries earlier by *Hooke* and others, but Schleiden's studies convinced him of their importance, and by 1838 he argued that all the various plant structures are composed of cells or their derivatives. He accurately observed many features and activities in plant cells (e.g., cytoplasmic streaming); he recognized the importance of the nucleus in cell division, but believed (wrongly) that new cells were formed by budding from its surface.

Despite some uncritical attitudes and a quick temper his ability was great; he has been named as the 'reformer of scientific botany' and he initiated *Schwann*'s work which led to their joint creation of cell theory. He was a popular writer and lecturer on a wide range of matters and frequently engaged in harsh combative debates on scientific theories.

SCHMIDT, Bernhard Voldemar

1879-1935

Estonian-German optical engineer: designer of a novel telescope system

As a young man, Schmidt had several dull jobs before he took a course in engineering, and set up his own workshop to build telescopes. He ground and polished the mirrors unaided, despite having lost his right arm in an accident with explosives. From 1926 he worked with the Hamburg Observatory staff; he was an alcoholic and died in a mental hospital.

Before his work, large telescopes gave good images only in the centre of the field; further from the optical axis the images of stars showed a tail (coma), which made making star maps difficult. Schmidt designed in 1930 a reflecting telescope with a spherical mirror, and with a smaller glass corrector plate in front, at the centre of curvature. This specially shaped aspherical plate provides the telescope with good definition over a wide field at low power. The telescope is usually used as a camera, and it revolutionized optical astronomy.

From this design other catadioptric systems were developed, such as the Maksutov, which has a spherical meniscus corrector plate; it is usefully compact, and like the Schmidt camera, combines desirable features of the reflecting and refracting telescope.

SCHMIDT, Maarten

1929-

Dutch-American astronomer: explained optical spectra of quasars as due to their relativistic velocities

Schmidt studied at the universities of Groningen and Leiden, moving to the California Institute of Technology in 1959. He became director of the Hale Observatories in 1978.

Following the identification of a 3C 48 with a faint optical object of highly unusual spectrum in 1960 by *Sandage*, Schmidt studied the spectrum of another optically identified quasar, 3C 273, and discovered that the peculiarities of its spectrum were caused by a massive red shift. The quasar appeared to be receding at nearly 16 per cent of the speed of light, leading to what is normally the ultraviolet part of the spectrum being observed in the visible region. Such high velocities are now interpreted as implying that quasars are very distant objects. Schmidt also found that the number of quasars increases with distance from Earth, a finding that provided evidence for the big bang theory for the origin of the universe rather than the rival steady-state theory.

SCHRIEFFER, John Robert

1931-

American physicist: contributed to the BCS theory of superconductivity

After studying electrical engineering and physics at Massachussetts Institute of Technology and the University of Illinois, Schrieffer started working for his PhD under *Bardeen*. Initially he worked on electrical conduction on semiconductor surfaces, but moved to superconductivity as his thesis topic. A close and fruitful collaboration with Bardeen and *Cooper* gave rise to the BCS (Bardeen, Cooper, Schrieffer) theory in 1957, for which all three shared the 1972 Nobel Physics prize (see account under Bardeen and Cooper). Schrieffer became professor of physics at the University of Pennsylvania in 1964. He has also done research on dilute alloys, ferromagnetism and surface physics.

In the formulation of BCS theory Schrieffer contributed particularly to the generalization from the properties of a single Cooper pair to that of a solid containing many pairs. Using a statistical approach he found a suitable quantum mechanical wave function which possesses the correct properties. *See photo* p.23.

SCHRÖDINGER, Erwin

1887-1961

Austrian physicist: the founder of wave mechanics

Schrödinger was the son of a prosperous oilcloth manufacturer; he was educated by a private tutor and by his father before going to the University of Vienna. After securing a doctorate in physics in 1910 he joined the staff there. During World War I he served as an artillery officer in an isolated fort, which gave him time to read physics; from 1920 he spent short periods of time at Jena, Stuttgart, Breslau and Zürich. He began to produce inspired work, and early in 1926 published a series of papers founding wave mechanics. As a result he succeeded *Planck* as professor of theoretical physics at Berlin (1927), but chose to leave once Hitler had assumed power in 1933. He moved to Oxford, but became homesick and returned to Graz in Austria in 1936. When the Germans moved into Austria in 1938 Schrödinger fled for his life, settling in Dublin, and working at the Institute for Advanced Studies created for him there as a result of the Irish leader de Valera's mathematical interests. After 17 happy years in Eire, he became a professor at the University of Vienna, having refused to return until Soviet occupation ceased. Shortly after arriving he became ill and never fully recovered.

Schrödinger began to think about the consequences of *de Broglie*'s ideas when they were published in 1924. He had postulated that any particle has a wave associated with it and the properties of the particle result from a combination of its particle-like and wave-like nature. Schrödinger and de Broglie both realised that a partial differential equation called a wave equation would describe the motion of a particle, and deduced an equation of this type. This approach of considering the wave function alone avoided the difficulties which *Bohr*'s old quantum theory of particles had involved, but was difficult to apply in practice. Schrödinger then used *Hamilton*'s method of describing particle motion, and wrote this in wave form, to give **Schrödinger's equation**. Unlike the previous equation this ignores relativistic effects, but is much easier to apply to real situations. When applied to the hydrogen atom the equation gives the correct energy levels of an electron in the atom, without the *ad hoc* assumptions of Bohr's model of the atom. These energy levels had been measured experimentally by using the lines observed in the hydrogen spectrum. For this considerable achievement he shared the 1933 Nobel Prize for physics with *Dirac*.

Schrödinger's theory was known as wave mechanics (1926), and was shown by Dirac to be mathematically equivalent to matrix mechanics devised in 1925 by *Born, Jordan* and *Heisenberg*. The combined theory, together with *Pauli*'s exclusion principle, was used by Dirac to set out quantum mechanics in virtually complete form by the year's end.

Whilst quantum mechanics had great predictive power and correctly described a wealth of previously unexplained phenomena, Schrödinger saw in it an awkward problem. Relating the wave function to the particle (for example an electron) is difficult. Born put forward the now-accepted explanation that the wave amplitude describes the probability of finding the particle at that point. Schrödinger, like de Broglie and *Einstein*, opposed this, and together they argued against a probabilistic quantum mechanics. Born's view condemns physics to describing only the likelihood of one event following another, and is not able to definitely predict cause and effect, as classical theories sought to do.

Schrödinger was an attractive man with an informal manner much liked by his colleagues and students; throughout his life he would travel everywhere with just walking-boots and rucksack, which caused him some problems in gaining entrance to the Solvay conferences for Nobel laureates.

SCHWABE, Heinrich Samuel

1789-1875

German astronomer: discovered the sunspot cycle

An amateur astronomer who observed the Sun daily in the hope of finding a new planet closer to it than Mercury, Schwabe made careful records of sunspot activity from 1826 onwards for almost half a century. In 1843 he announced his discovery of an approximately ten-year cycle in the numbers of sunspots. Although initially ignored, *von Humboldt* brought his discovery the recognition it deserved in 1851.

SCHWANN, Theodor

1810-1882

German physiologist: the major figure in the creation of cell theory in biology

Schwann went to school in Köln and studied medicine, graduating in Berlin in 1834. He stayed there as assistant to *J. Müller* for four years, when most of his best work was done. Early in this period he studied digestion, and isolated from the stomach lining the proteolytic enzyme, pepsin; it was the first enzyme to be isolated from an animal source. He went on to study fermentation and showed in 1836 (independently of *Cagniard de la Tour*) that it was a result of the life processes of the yeast cells; this led him to doubt the idea of spontaneous generation, and so he repeated and improved the experiments on this done by *Spallanzani*. He confirmed that no microorganisms appeared and no putrefaction occurred in a sterile broth to which only sterile air was admitted. His results did not prevent all belief in spontaneous generation, which persisted until *Pasteur*'s work a few years later.

Schwann's work on fermentation led to quite vicious (if comical) attacks in papers by the chemists *Liebig* and *Wöhler*, to the extent that Schwann saw no prospect of a career in Germany and in 1838 he emigrated to Belgium. There he became a mystic, solitary and depressed, and did little more in science.

He had already discovered the **Schwann cells** composing the myelin sheath around peripheral nerve axons; and he showed that an egg (whether large or small) is a single cell which when fertilized develops into a complex organism, a central idea in embryology. Schwann's most famous work, on the cell theory, began through discussions with his friend the botanist *Schleiden* who had argued that all plant structures are cells. Animal tissues are more difficult for the microscopist, being soft, of low contrast, and subject to rapid decay; and even more than plant cells, those of animals show great diversity. However, Schwann became convinced that animal tissues, like plants, are based on cells and he became, with Schleiden, a principal advocate for the **cell theory**, whose main points are that (a) the entire plant or animal is made up of cells or of substances thrown off by cells; (b) the cells have a life that is to some extent their own; and (c) this individual life of the cells is subordinated to that of the organism as a whole. This theory, well defined in Schwann's book in 1839, soon became dominant in biology; the cell has been seen ever since as a natural unit of form, of function, and of reproduction, at the microscopic level. This last dominance is summarized in *Virchow*'s phrase of 1855, 'all cells arise from pre-existing cells'. Virchow saw the study of affected cells as central to pathology and physiology.

In shaping much biological research, the theory was beneficial; but it was unfortunate that Schwann accepted the older Schleiden's erroneous idea that new cells are formed by 'budding' from a nucleus, which was to prove a false trail for many biologists for half a century. Neither of them had any notion of the formation of cells by division; and neither regarded the cytoplasm as important.

SCHWARZSCHILD, Karl

1873-1916

German astronomer: predicted existence of black holes

Schwarzschild became interested in astronomy as a schoolboy and published papers on binary orbits at 16. He became director of the Potsdam observatory in 1909. Although an excellent observational astronomer, Schwarzschild's lasting contributions have been theoretical, and were largely made during the last year of his life. In 1916, whilst serving on the Russian front, Schwarzschild wrote two papers on *Einstein*'s recently published general theory of relativity, giving the first solution to the complex partial differential equations of the theory. He also introduced the idea that when a star contracts under gravity, there will come a point at which the gravitational field is so intense that nothing, not even light, can escape. The radius to which a star of given mass must contract to reach this stage is known as the **Schwarzschild radius**. Stars that have contracted below this limit are now known as black holes.

Schwarzschild's son Martin (born 1912) is also an astronomer, distinguished for his work on the evolution of stars and galaxies.

SCHWINGER, Julian Seymour

1918-

American physicist: one of the founders of quantum electrodynamics (QED)

Schwinger was a graduate of Columbia University, New York, gaining his doctorate at age 20. Research with *Oppenheimer* at the University of California at Berkeley followed and he joined the work on the atomic bomb during 1943-45. In 1946 he became one of Harvard's youngest-ever professors.

Schwinger studied the papers by *Dirac*, *Heisenberg* and *Pauli* on the quantum mechanics of the electron, and attempted to produce a fully quantum mechanical electrodynamics which was consistent with *Einstein*'s theory of relativity. *Feynman, Dyson* and *Tomonaga* as well as Schwinger all arrived independently at a correct theory within a short time. The details of how electrons interact with electromagnetic fields were then understood for the first time. Feynman, Tomonaga and Schwinger shared the 1963 Nobel Prize for physics.

Since then Schwinger has done research on synchrotron radiation, which is the particular sort of electromagnetic radiation which is emitted when a charged particle changes speed or direction in a magnetic field.

SEABORG, Glenn Theodore
1912-

American nuclear chemist: discoverer of transuranic elements of actinide series

After he obtained his PhD in chemistry at the University of California, Berkeley, in 1937, Seaborg worked with *Lewis*, joined the staff, and became professor of chemistry in 1945. He was to be linked with the University of California for the rest of his career, with absences on government work during World War II, and from 1961 to 1971 when he was Chairman of the US Atomic Energy Commission.

The heaviest element which occurs in nature in fair quantity is uranium, with atomic number 92. In the 1930s more than

Glenn T. Seaborg in the 1940s

one research group bombarded uranium with neutrons and examined the results, and believed that elements heavier than uranium ('transuranic elements') had been formed. Then came the proposal in 1939 by *Meitner* and *Frisch* that fission had occurred; the uranium nucleus accepts the neutron and then breaks up to give two or more nuclei of middle-range mass. But in 1940 *McMillan* and P. Abelson showed that transuranic elements can in fact be made; some of the uranium nuclei struck by neutrons do not undergo fission, but form a new element, the first to be discovered beyond uranium, and which they named neptunium. From 1940 Seaborg became involved in the work, found a new way of making an isotope of neptunium (atomic number 93) and went on to extend the research by making heavier transuranic elements. Seaborg was a key figure in the work which resulted in making and identifying nine of them, from plutonium (atomic number 94) through to nobelium (102). In much of this a cyclotron was used to generate the bombarding particles, and the work was directed in part to study the basic chemistry of the new elements, and in part to produce an atomic bomb (of the first two of these, exploded in 1945, one was fuelled by uranium, and one by plutonium). Seaborg realised in 1944 that the series of elements from actinium (89) onwards, could be classed within the Periodic Table as a new transition series, akin to the lanthanides; he named the new series (now seen as numbers 89 to 103) the **actinides**. They are all radioactive; and the transuranic members (numbers 93 onwards) occur only in minute traces in nature.

SEDGWICK, Adam
1785-1873

British geologist: identified the Cambrian period

After graduating in mathematics in 1808, Sedgwick remained at Cambridge for the rest of his life, being appointed professor of geology in 1818. In 1835 he worked out the stratigraphic succession of fossil-bearing rocks in North Wales, naming the oldest of them the Cambrian period (now dated at 500-570 million years ago). In South Wales his friend *Murchison* had simultaneously worked out the Silurian system, some strata of which overlapped with Sedgwick's Cambrian system. In a celebrated dispute the two were to argue about which system these common strata should be assigned to for almost 40 years; the matter was only resolved after their deaths when C. Lapworth proposed in 1879 that the Upper Cambrian and Lower Silurian be renamed the Ordovician. Sedgwick and Murchison also identified the Devonian system in south-west England.

SEEBECK, Thomas Johann

1770-1831

Estonian-German physicist: discovered thermoelectric effect

A member of a wealthy merchant family, Seebeck went to Germany to study medicine. He qualified in 1802, but thereafter spent his time in research in physics. His best-known work was done in Berlin in 1822, when he showed that if a circuit is made of a loop of two metals with two junctions, then when the junctions are at different temperatures a current flows (e.g., if copper and iron are used, and the junctions are at 0°C and 100°C, the circuit has an EMF of about a millivolt). Seebeck himself did not grasp that a current was generated and called the effect 'thermo-magnetism'. Later it was realised that whenever two different metals are in contact, an EMF is set up whose magnitude depends on the temperature (the **thermoelectric** or **Seebeck effect**). The effect is used in the **thermocouple** for temperature measurement.

In 1834 the watchmaker J. C. A. Peltier found the converse effect; when a current is passed through a junction of two different conductors, a thermal effect occurs (heating or cooling, depending on the direction of the current, i.e., whether the current adds to or opposes the EMF of the junction). The related **Thomson** effect is the development of an EMF between the ends of a single metal rod when these ends are at different temperatures. These two effects are mainly of theoretical interest.

SEGRÈ, Emilio Gino

1905-

Italian-American physicist: discovered the antiproton

Segrè attended school and became a university student of engineering in his home city of Rome. Then in 1927 he changed over to physics, and became the first research student to work with *Fermi*, obtaining his doctorate at Rome in 1928. He rose to hold a laboratory directorship in Palermo, but was dismissed for racial reasons by the fascist government in 1938. He took a post at the University of California at Berkeley, and had an active part during World War II in the Manhattan Project to develop the atomic bomb at Los Alamos.

Segrè has the distinction of being involved in the discovery of three elements: technetium (1937), astatine (1940) and plutonium (1940). Technetium was made by using *Lawrence*'s cyclotron to irradiate molybdenum with deuterium nuclei, and was the world's first purely artificial element to be made. It is radioactive, and one isotope is much used in medical diagnosis. After the war Segrè joined in the hunt for a novel particle predicted by *Dirac*, the antiproton.

In 1955 the Berkeley bevatron proton accelerator reached the threshold energy for producing antiprotons by proton-proton collision, 6 GeV. A beam of particles

Emilio Segrè about 1946

obtained by proton collisions on a copper target contained a few antiprotons among many other secondary particles. Segrè and his group devised an apparatus and performed an experiment for detecting these antiprotons. Segrè and *Chamberlain* received the 1959 Nobel Prize for physics 'for the discovery of the antiproton'.

dissection, Semmelweis noted that his illness was closely similar to puerperal fever. He deduced that something was conveyed on the hands of the medical staff from the dissecting rooms to the patients. By insisting that they washed their hands in disinfectant, Semmelweis reduced the mortality to 1%. However, his success produced opposition rather than imitation; discouraged and persecuted he returned to his native Buda in 1850 and a few years later became insane. Ironically, he died from a septic finger infection of the same kind as his colleague in Vienna in 1847. Only after *Lister*'s success in antiseptic surgery, in the 1870s, did antiseptic procedures in midwifery become widespread.

Puerperal fever was due to a streptococcal infection, but this was not fully understood until the 1880s. Strangely, the advance in obstetrics could have been made much earlier; the procedures to avoid the fever had been proposed by A. Gordon of Aberdeen in 1795, and by the literary anatomist Oliver Wendell Holmes of Harvard in 1843, but the former was largely ignored and the latter abused.

SEMMELWEIS, Ignaz Phillip

1818-1865

Hungarian physician: pioneer in treatment of sepsis

Semmelweis graduated in medicine in Vienna in 1844, and stayed there to specialize in obstetrics, working under J. Klein in the General Hospital's obstetric wards. There 10-30% of the pregnant women died from puerperal (childbirth) fever. Semmelweis studied the records, and found that in the clinic staffed by medical students, the mortality due to the fever was three times that in the clinic staffed by midwives. He also noted that the mortality had risen since Klein's appointment as head of the unit. Then, when a colleague died in 1847 from a scalpel wound made in a post-mortem

SEYFERT, Carl Keenan

1911-1960

American astronomer: discovered Seyfert galaxies

Seyfert studied at Harvard, and subsequently held appointments at a number of American Observatories. In 1951 he became director of the Dyer Observatory at Vanderbilt University, Tennessee.

In 1943 Seyfert discovered a class of spiral galaxies which have small bright nuclei in relation to their spiral arms, and which show broad emission lines in their spectra, indicating the presence of hot gas. These **Seyfert galaxies** also emit large amounts of energy throughout the electromagnetic spectrum, from X-rays through to radio wavelengths, and are believed to be related to quasars.

SHANNON, Claude Elwood
1916-

American mathematician: pioneer of communication theory

Shannon graduated from the University of Michigan in 1936, going on to conduct research at the Massachusetts Institute of Technology before joining Bell Telephone Laboratories. In 1948, by quantifying the information content of a message and analysing its flow, he established the foundations of communication theory. **Communication theory** is concerned with the best way to transmit messages, and the ways in which the signal may be degraded or misunderstood. It is of central importance to the design of electronic circuits and computers, as well as to communications systems. Shannon has also done important work on the binary logic of digital circuits. He coined the term 'bit' for a unit of information.

SHAPLEY, Harlow
1885-1972

American astronomer: discovered structure of our galaxy

The son of a farmer, Shapley was a crime reporter on two newspapers before entering the University of Missouri, intending to study journalism; he soon changed to astronomy. In 1915, using *Leavitt*'s 'Cepheid variable' method of estimating stellar distances, Shapley was able to provide the first reasonable picture of the structure and size of our own galaxy. He studied the distribution of globular star clusters by means of the Cepheids within them, and showed that they are concentrated disproportionately in the direction of Sagittarius. This, he argued, must be the centre of our disc-shaped galaxy, and in 1920 he estimated the Sun to be about 50000 light years from the galactic centre. The overall diameter of the galaxy he believed to be about 300000 light years (both figures have since been shown to be over-estimates by a factor of three or more).

SHERRINGTON, (Sir) Charles Scott
1857-1952

English neurophysiologist: made important studies of the nervous system

A Cambridge graduate in medicine, Sherrington studied also in Germany under *Virchow* and *Koch*, researched in bacteriology and afterwards taught physiology at London and Liverpool, and at Oxford from 1913-35. He was a sports enthusiast, including Sunday morning parachute jumps (from the tower of a London hospital) among his many activities. His main work was on reflex motor activity in vertebrates, detailing the nature of muscle operation at the spinal level. He began with a close study of the knee-jerk reflex and its control, and the hind-limb scratch reflex in the dog. A whole range of concepts and words in neurology are due to him (including synapse, proprioceptor, motor unit, neuron pool and others) and his book *The Integrative Action of the Nervous System* (1906) is a classic of neurology. He continued to be an active experimenter, especially on the reflex system, until 1935, publishing over 300 papers on this.

He shared a Nobel Prize with *Adrian* in 1932. He has been called 'the William Harvey of the nervous system'.

SHOCKLEY, William Bradford
1910-

American physicist: invented the junction transistor

The son of two American mining engineers, and born in London, Shockley was educated at the California Institute of Technology and Massachusetts Institute of Technology. He began work at the Bell Telephone Laboratories in 1936, directed US anti-submarine warfare research

351

William Shockley

(1942-1944) and served as consultant to the Secretary for War in 1945.

After returning to Bell Laboratories at the end of the war Shockley collaborated with *Bardeen* and *Brattain* in trying to produce semiconductor devices to replace vacuum tubes. It had long been known that some crystals (e.g., PbS) would act as rectifiers (that is, would pass current in only one direction). However, *Fleming*'s tubes (known as valves in the UK) had replaced these. The new work showed that germanium crystals were better rectifiers, their effect depending on traces of impurity. Using a germanium rectifier with metal contacts including a needle touching the crystal they invented the **point-contact transistor** (1947). A month later Shockley developed the **junction transistor (trans**fer of current across a re**sistor**) which uses the junction between two differently treated parts of a silicon crystal; such solid-state semi-conductors can both rectify and amplify current. These small, reliable devices led to the miniaturization of circuits in radio, TV and computer equipment. Shockley, Bardeen and Brattain shared a Nobel Prize in 1956. From 1963 Shockley was a professor of engineering at Stanford.

After 1965 Shockley became a con-troversial figure through his support of the view that intelligence is largely hereditary; and that the rapid reproduction of some racial groups can damage the intelligence of the overall population.

SIDGWICK, Nevil Vincent

1873-1952

English theoretical chemist: systematizer of valence theory

Sidgwick maintained a family tradition for intellectual virtuosity by getting a First in science at Oxford, and then another First in classics two years later, a truly remarkable feat which has probably proved unrepeatable. After further study in Germany he took a post in Oxford in 1901 and kept it for his lifetime. He was an odd person in several ways; he looked middle-aged when young, and changed only slowly afterwards; his own experimental work was unimportant; his best ideas came after he was 50; and his great influence in chemistry is largely due to three books. In each of them, he brought together a mass of work by others, added his own ideas, and produced a coherent and unified account which clarified chemical ideas and pointed the way to new work. The first was his *Organic Chemistry of Nitrogen* (1910); the second was the *Electronic Theory of Valency* (1927) in which his own major contribution to chemical theory was to develop the idea of bonds in which one atom donated both electrons forming the covalent bond, a concept which gave new life to the whole chemistry of metal complexes. His last book was his *Chemical Elements and their Compounds* (1950), a vast review which he was able to produce because of the cessation of normal published research in World War II. In British science he was distinguished by his pungent wit and his wealth, and in the US he was for years the best-known British scientist.

SIEMENS, (Sir) Charles William
1823-1883

German engineer: co-inventor of the Siemens-Martin open-hearth steel furnace

Born Karl Wilhelm, Siemens was one of four remarkable brothers, all of whom were outstanding engineers. Charles came to England at the age of 20, and worked on a method of using waste heat from blast furnaces to improve efficiency, by preheating the air blast. In 1861, together with his brother Frederick, he designed an open-hearth steel furnace, which both utilized waste heat and incorporated a gas-producer, which allowed the use of low-grade coal as fuel. By the end of the 19th century more steel was produced by this method (the Siemens-Martin method) than any other. Frederick Siemens used a similar furnace in glass manufacture.

SIEMENS, Ernst Werner von
1816-1892

German electrical engineer: developed electricity generation through application of the 'dynamo principle'

Siemens was educated at Lubeck, and later at the army engineering school in Berlin, where he was imprisoned for duelling. His interests were wide-ranging—electroplating, discharge tubes to generate ozone, a standard of electrical resistance using mercury, and electrolytic refining, to name a few. He made several innovations to existing telegraphs, including seamless insulation for the wire, which enabled his company to become a leading supplier of such systems, including the London-Calcutta line in 1870. In 1867 he revolutionized electric generation by using self-generated electricity to power electromagnets (the 'dynamo principle'), doing away with the expensive permanent magnets previously used in such generators. This enabled his company to become a pioneer in the fields of electric traction and electricity generating equipment.

The SI unit of electrical conductance, the **siemens** (S) is named after him.

SIMPSON, Thomas
1710-1761

English mathematician: contributed to calculus

Simpson's life involved a series of strange episodes, but his total contribution to 18th century mathematics is substantial. Growing up in the weaving trade in the Midlands, he married at 20 to a widow of 40 (who outlived him, and drew a Crown pension for his work until her death at 102). After seeing a solar eclipse Simpson became obsessed by astrology and soon acquired a good local reputation in it, but this changed when he 'raised a devil' from a girl who then had fits, and the Simpsons left the area hurriedly. In London he combined weaving and mathematics, and his reputation in the latter secured him the professorship at Woolwich in 1743 and his FRS in 1745. He was also editor of *The Ladies Diary*. He wrote on calculus, probability, statistics, geometry and algebra, but his most enduring result is the method for finding the area under a curve known as **Simpson's Rule**. The result is exact if the curve is parabolic, and can be used as a close approximation in other cases. He also devised a method for finding the volume of any solid bounded by planes, if two of them are parallel.

SLIPHER, Vesto Melvin
1875-1969

American astronomer: discovered the general recession of other galaxies from Earth

Slipher studied at the University of Indiana, and then spent over fifty years working at the Lowell Observatory, Arizona, becoming its director in 1926.

Slipher used spectroscopic techniques to measure the very small *Doppler* shift in light reflected from the edges of planetary discs, thereby determining the periods of rotation of Uranus, Jupiter, Saturn, Venus and Mars in 1912. He extended his methods to spiral galaxies, discovering that the Andromeda galaxy is approaching our own galaxy at a speed of about 300 km s^{-1}, and went on to measure similar velocities for a further 14 spiral galaxies, almost all of which are receding from the Earth at even greater speeds. His results later led *Hubble* to propose that all galaxies (outside the Local Group, which includes the Andromeda galaxy) are moving away from one another at velocities proportional to their separation.

SMITH, Hamilton (Orthanel)

1931-

American molecular biologist: isolated and studied restriction enzymes

Smith graduated in mathematics in 1952; and in medicine in 1956 at Johns Hopkins University where in 1973 he became professor of microbiology. In the early 1970s be obtained an enzyme from the bacterium *H. influenzae* (the strain later known as Hind II) which cleaved DNA at specific sites in relation to the sequence of bases. An early example of such a **restriction enzyme** had been obtained in the 1960s from *E. coli* by W. Arber, and Smith confirmed and amplified this work before extending it to Hind II. By the late 1970s Smith and other workers, especially D. Nathans (who collaborated with Smith in some of the research) had isolated many such enzymes. By allowing the controlled splitting of genes to give genetically active fragments, the restriction enzymes allowed the possibility of genetic engineering and of DNA sequencing to be developed. Smith, Arber and Nathans shared a Nobel Prize in 1978.

SMITH, Theobald

1859-1934

American microbiologist: studied modes of transmission of cattle diseases

Smith graduated in medicine in 1883; he chose not to enter medical practice but to move into veterinary work in the new US Bureau of Animal Industry founded to combat infectious diseases in farm animals. At his parents home German was spoken, and young Smith's fluency in it gave him the advantage of being able to read the reports of *Koch* and *Ehrlich*. Smith became the leading American bacteriologist of his generation, and the first of distinction not to be trained in Europe. His successful studies on the nature and control of animal diseases began with his work on hog cholera in 1889; in 1896 he distinguished between bovine and human tubercle bacilli; and in 1893 he published his work on Texas cattle fever, showing that it is transmitted by a tick. The complex cycle of transmission he had carefully worked out was doubted by many, but was never refuted; it led both to control of the fever and to easier acceptance, within ten years, of ideas on the place of the mosquito in human malaria and yellow fever. In 1895 he moved to Harvard and in 1914 to the Rockefeller Institute, developing his work in animal pathology and in parasitology. He was an austere, hardworking, and self-effacing person; many of his peers thought him comparable as a scientist with Koch, but he carried little fame in the minds of the mass of his countrymen.

SMITH, William

1769-1839

British geologist and surveyor: pioneer of geological mapping, proposed principle of superposition

The son of a blacksmith, Smith became a canal surveyor, an occupation which gave him ample opportunity to study the varying geology of much of England and Wales. He discovered that geological strata could be reliably identified at different places on the basis of the fossils they contained, and he also proposed the **principle of superposition** – that if a strata overlays another then it was laid down at a later time. In 1815 he published the first stratigraphic map of England and Wales, at a scale of five miles per inch, following this with more detailed geological maps of over 20 counties. Although the value of his work was only recognized late in his life, he was awarded the Geological Society's highest honour in 1831, and is today considered to be the father of English geology.

SNEL, Willebrord (often spelled SNELL)

1580-1626

Dutch physicist: discovered law concerning refraction of light passing between media

Snel studied law and mathematics in a number of European universities and in 1613 succeeded his father in the new university of Leiden, as professor of mathematics. He continued to publish translations of mathematical work, but also became involved in geodesy, and has been described as 'the father of triangulation'. Starting with his own house, and the spires of town churches as reference points, he soon mapped a substantial local area. His best-known discovery, **Snell's Law** or the **second law of refraction** of light waves, was probably made in about 1621 after much experimentation. In

Willebrord Snel

modern form, it states that for light passing from one isotropic medium to another, the ratio of the sine of the angle of incidence to the sine of the angle of refraction is constant for light of a particular wavelength (see diagram); i.e., $\sin \theta_1 / \sin \theta_2 = $ constant. The law can be deduced from *Fermat*'s principle. It is found that the value of the constant is equal to the ratio of the velocity of light in material (1) to that in material (2), and this is known as the **relative refractive index**.

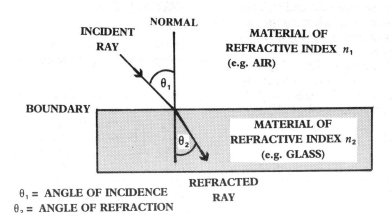

INCIDENT RAY

NORMAL

MATERIAL OF REFRACTIVE INDEX n_1 (e.g. AIR)

θ_1

BOUNDARY

MATERIAL OF REFRACTIVE INDEX n_2 (e.g. GLASS)

θ_2

REFRACTED RAY

θ_1 = ANGLE OF INCIDENCE
θ_2 = ANGLE OF REFRACTION

SNOW, John

1813-1858

*English physician: pioneer of
anaesthesiology and epidemiology*

As a very young medical apprentice Snow was sent to Sutherland to work on victims of England's first cholera epidemic, which entered through that seaport in 1831. The disease was not curable, and was often fatal, and the experience gave Snow an interest in cholera which led him to study its epidemiology in the London outbreak of 1854. He was then practising in Soho; at that time *Pasteur*'s work on micro-organisms had not appeared and the cholera vibrio was not to be described by *Koch* until 1884. Snow believed however that the disease was due to a living, water-borne organism; he had sensible views on disinfection; and he surveyed the incidence of cases and their relation to water supply, concluding that faecal contamination of Thames water was a major culprit. A plot of cases in his own parish pointed to the Broad Street pump as a focus; a sewer pipe passed close to its well; Snow persuaded the council to remove the pump handle, and dramatic improvement followed. From then on, contamination of water by faeces was seen to be a key factor in the spread of cholera.

From 1840 Snow had been interested in the physiology of respiration, and so when anaesthetic inhalation methods came into the UK in 1846, in the form of knowledge of the use of diethyl ether ($(C_2H_5)_2O$) by dental and general surgeons in the US, Snow was well placed to experiment on the new technique. He devised an apparatus for its use which gave proper control, and he divided the stages of anaesthesia into five degrees. In 1847 J. Y. Simpson introduced trichloromethane (chloroform, $CHCl_3$) as an anaesthetic in obstetrics; again, Snow applied physiological principles and devices to its use, and became an expert operator with it and the first specialist anaesthetist. As such, he was called to give it to Queen Victoria in 1853 for the birth of her seventh child,

Prince Leopold, and her use of it gave the procedure respectibility and did much to overcome religious and medical prejudice.

SNYDER, Solomon Halbert

1938-

*American pharmacologist: suggested
existence of endorphins*

Educated at Georgetown University, Snyder has worked at Johns Hopkins University since 1965. His work which led to the discovery of the body's natural pain relievers, the endorphins, began with the knowledge that some drugs are effective in very small concentration; thus the synthetic drug etorphine (an analogue of morphine) relieves pain in doses of only 0.0001 g. To be so effective, the drug must act on some highly selective receptor sites, and Snyder and C. Pert used morphine-like drugs with radioactive labels to locate these sites. Success in a difficult search came in 1973 when they reported that receptor sites are located in the mammalian limbic system, which is in a region in the centre of the brain associated with the perception of pain. Clearly these receptors have not evolved in order to accept synthetic drugs, and their existence implies that natural morphine-like substances must also exist. Within a few years such substances, **endorphins**, were found by other workers; they are highly potent analgesics (pain-relievers) and are now known to be peptides formed in the pituitary gland. Their existence may be relevant to the analgesis obtained in acupuncture.

SODDY, Frederick

1877-1956

*English radiochemist: proposed theory of
radioactive decay (with Rutherford);
pioneer theorist and experimenter in
radiochemistry*

The youngest of seven children, Soddy grew up to become a forceful, talented and eccentric individual. Two years after graduating in chemistry from Oxford, he found a job as demonstrator at McGill

University at Montreal. *Rutherford* was there as professor of physics, and his work needed a chemist. Together in 1900-3 they offered a brilliant and simple answer to the question: what is radioactivity? The **disintegration theory** proposed that heavy atoms are unstable; that such an element could undergo spontaneous atomic disintegration, losing some mass and charge from its atoms and forming a new element. The process could recur, so that a series of such changes occurred. They went on to predict that helium gas should be a decay product of radium. In 1903, working with *Ramsay* in London, Soddy used 52 mg of RaBr, collected gas from it and showed this to contain helium.

In 1913, Soddy gave the clearest of the statements of the **radioactive displacement law** which emerged about that time; that emission of an α-particle (helium nucleus) from an atom reduces its atomic number by two; whereas the emission of a β-particle (an electron) increases the atomic number by one.

It was Soddy who gave the name 'isotopes' to atoms with the same atomic number (and therefore the same chemical properties) but differing in mass. In 1920 he foresaw their value in finding the age of rocks; back in 1906 he had foreseen the use of atomic energy from uranium, which he also lived to see (1945). In 1919 he was appointed professor in Oxford. He was frustrated there in his efforts to change chemical teaching and research arrangements, and his interest in chemistry faded after his Nobel Prize award (1921). His new concern was for political and economic schemes which would ensure that the benefits of science became widely available, but he was unsuccessful as an advocate for his ideas.

SOMMERFELD, Arnold
1868-1951

German physicist: developed Bohr's theory of atomic spectra

Educated at Königsberg, he spent most of his career at Munich. He worked on a variety of problems, including gyroscopes, X-ray and electron diffraction and radio waves, but his well-known work is especially on the theory of atomic spectra. Here he developed *Bohr*'s theory of atomic structure, replacing the idea of circular electron orbits by elliptic orbits (with the nucleus at a focus) and introducing a new azimuthal quantum number; the ellipticity should result in relativistic effects being shown in the fine structure of atomic spectra, as was confirmed in some detail by F. Paschen the next year (1916). Sommerfeld was influential in physics not only for his application of relativity and quantum theory to the understanding of a variety of spectra (X-ray, atomic, and molecular spectra), but through his pupils, including *Bethe, Debye, Heisenberg, Heitler* and *Pauli*.

SORBY, Henry Clifton
1826-1908

British geologist and metallurgist: developed petrological thin section technique; and discovered the crystalline structure of steel

Sorby was the only son of a prosperous Sheffield tool manufacturer, whose death

Henry Sorby

when Sorby was 21 provided him with the means of becoming an independent scientific investigator. Working in his own laboratory he invented the technique of preparing thin sections of rocks and examining them under the microscope, enabling the constituent minerals to be examined in transmitted light (rather than the conventional study of the surface of the sample under reflected light). He also recognized the potential of the *Nicol* prism in distinguishing the different component minerals by the effect they have on polarized light. His interest in studying meteorites in this way led him to discover the crystalline nature of steel in 1863, thus founding the study of metallography.

SÖRENSEN, Sören

1868-1939

Danish biochemist: invented pH scale for measuring acidity

Sörensen studied chemistry at Copenhagen. From 1901 he was Director of the Carlsberg Laboratory, and worked on amino acids, proteins and enzymes. His fame rests on his invention in 1909 of the pH scale. The pH of a solution is defined as $\log (1/[H^+])$ where $[H^+]$ is the concentration of hydrogen ions in moles per litre. The scale is rigorous enough for physical chemists but is also useable by non-specialists, and it is universally employed. For a solution, a pH of 1 to 7 indicates diminishing acidity; 7-14 shows increasing alkalinity, and pH 7 neutrality, at 25°C. The value is measured practically by a meter with a glass electrode or by suitable indicator papers.

SPALLANZANI, Lazzaro

1729-1799

Italian biologist: pioneer of experimental physiology

Spallanzani first studied law, but his cousin Laura Bassi, who was professor of physics at Bologna, encouraged his interest in science. He became a priest and

eventually professor of natural history at Pavia; and was an enthusiastic traveller in pursuit of specimens for the natural history museum at Pavia. His other enthusiasm was experimental physiology and especially reproduction. The older biologists had largely believed (with *Aristotle*) in spontaneous generation (e.g., from mud or an animal corpse). A fellow Italian, F. Redi, had shown in the 17th century that insects developed on meat only from deposited eggs; Spallanzani showed in 1765 that well-boiled broth, hermetically sealed, remained sterile. (Despite this, it was not until *Pasteur*'s work, a century later, that the idea of spontaneous generation was largely abandoned.) He also studied digestion, which *Galen* had thought to be a kind of cooking by stomach heat, while *Réaumur* had experimented with buzzards and concluded it was solvent action. Spallanzani experimented with many animals and one man (himself) and showed that gastric juice is the active digestive agent. He was the first to observe blood passing from arteries to veins in a warm-blooded animal (the chick). He achieved artificial insemination of amphibians, silkworms, and a spaniel bitch although he did not grasp the importance of spermatozoa (which had been discovered much earlier); and he believed that the ovum contains all the parts which appeared later in the embryo. He worked on the senses of bats, and found that blinded bats could still catch insects and navigate well enough to avoid even thin silk threads. L. Jurine showed they lost their skill if their ears were covered, which was not explained until 1941 (bats use sonar). His interest in zoology was mainly in marine biology, including sponges and the *Torpedo*, and in Rotifers and Tardigrads.

SPENCER JONES, (Sir) Harold

1890-1960

British astronomer: discovered slowing down of Earth's rotation

Spencer Jones was educated at Cambridge University, becoming Chief Assistant to the Astronomer Royal at Greenwich. He later spent ten years as astronomer at the Royal Observatory at the Cape of Good Hope before being appointed Astronomer Royal. Spencer Jones organized an international project to accurately determine the Earth-Sun distance (the astronomical unit) in 1931, utilizing a close approach of the asteroid Eros, the result being a great improvement over previous values. More importantly, he discovered in 1939 that the Earth's rotation was slowing down by about a second per year, thus explaining some anomalies that had been observed in the orbits of the Moon and planets.

R. W. Sperry

SPERRY, Roger Wolcott

1913-

American neurobiologist: made important studies of brain function

Sperry was a student of psychology at Oberlin College and of zoology at Chicago, and worked in several centres before joining the California Institute of Technology in 1954 as professor of psychobiology. His ingenious experimentation has challenged previous theories of brain function and has led to new ones.

Although a mammal cannot repair a severed optic nerve, an amphibian can. Sperry studied this regeneration and found that even with obstacles in its path, the new nerve would find its way to its original synaptic connection in the brain. Again, if the optic nerve of a salamander was severed, and the eye removed and replaced after a rotation of 180°, the animal when offered food on its right side would aim to the left, showing that the fibres had remade their old functional connection.

He has done much work on the brain in higher animals. The brain consists of two similar halves (containing roughly 10^9 interconnected cells) with many nerve fibres (commissures) linking the two sides. It was well known that the two halves controlled muscles on the opposite side of the body. Sperry examined animals in which all commissures were severed to give a 'split brain', and found (surprisingly) that in many ways monkeys and cats so modified behave as if they had two brains. Human patients are sometimes commissurotomized to prevent severe epilepsy spreading, and Sperry found that such split-brain patients, although normal in many ways, show that usually the right hemisphere specializes in non-verbal processes (e.g., emotions and spatial relationships) while the left (as it has long been known) is dominant in language processing. If a split-brain person picks up an unseen object (for example, a pencil) in the left hand, the 'feel' goes to the right hemisphere; but the person could not say what was held, as 'putting it into words' calls for links with the left hemisphere. A woman shown a picture of a nude woman in her left visual field said she saw nothing, but she blushed and giggled. Sperry's results point to discrete pathways in the brain carrying specific types of information, and have implications for theories of consciousness. He shared a Nobel Prize in 1981.

STAHL, Georg Ernst

1660-1734

German chemist and physician: developed phlogiston theory of combustion

A clergyman's son, Stahl trained in

medicine at Jena, and later taught medicine and chemistry. He took a theory of combustion due to J. J. Becher and developed it well enough to dominate chemical theory for a century. The theory was that when a substance burned it was losing 'phlogiston'. This was a principle of fire, perhaps akin to heat; and the idea was used to explain what we now call the oxidation of metals, and the reduction of ores to metal. To account for the observed weight changes, phlogiston had to have negative weight. (Later, *Cavendish* and *Priestley* thought hydrogen might be pure phlogiston.) The theory was erroneous but not ludicrous. It could be made to account for a range of chemical reactions in a consistent way, and it pointed to further experiments. It was displaced, but not easily, from chemistry by *Lavoisier*'s work on oxygen, oxidation and reduction.

In medicine, Stahl's best work was on mental illness. He was one of the first to see that some mental states are of physical origin, while others are functional; and he recognized the influence of the body on the mind and vice versa.

STANLEY, Wendell Meredith

1904-1971

American biochemist and virologist: isolated the first crystalline virus

In his early years as a student Stanley's main interest was football and he planned to become a coach. However, his interest in chemistry increased and after graduating at Illinois in 1929 he worked in Germany with *Wieland*, and then joined the Rockefeller Institute at Princeton in 1931. At about that time *Northrop* proved that several enzymes are crystallizable and are proteins. Stanley set out to find if the viruses could be purified by similar methods. Viruses are infective agents, too small to be filterable like bacteria, and able to reproduce themselves in living cells. Stanley worked on the virus causing mosaic disease in tobacco plants (TMV) and in 1935 he obtained it in fine

needle-like crystals. By 1938 others found that it is a nucleoprotein. His work showed that a crystalline 'chemical' could also be 'living' (a new concept); and since its infective part is the nucleic acid portion of the molecule, the work also suggested that reproduction in living systems might be understandable in chemical terms, involving nucleic acid, as was later shown by others to be the case.

Stanley's later work in virology included the isolation of an influenza virus and the preparation of a vaccine against it, during World War II. He shared a Nobel Prize in 1946.

STARLING, Ernest Henry

1866-1927

English physiologist: pioneer of endocrinology, and of modern cardiovascular physiology

Starling was very much a Londoner, and except for short periods in Germany and during his work for the Royal Army Medical Corps on poison gases in World War I, his career was spent at University College, London. Much of his best-known work was done with his friend, brother-in-law and co-worker W. M. Bayliss, who was also a professor of physiology in the same college. Their joint work would predictably have gained them a Nobel Prize but for the war; and Starling's acid public comments on Britain's leaders largely excluded him from the honours awarded to Bayliss, including a knighthood. In their early work together, they discovered the peristaltic waves of the intestine. Then in 1902 they showed that the pancreas still produces pancreatic digestive juice when food enters the duodenum, even when all the nerves to the pancreas are cut. *Pavlov*'s work had indicated this to be a nerve-controlled process. They concluded that a chemical messenger (they named it secretin) must be carried by the blood from the duodenal wall to the pancreas, stimulating its activity. They found that an extract from the duodenum has this effect; and in 1905 Starling used the word hormone (from the Greek *hormeo*, to excite) to describe such potent biochemical messengers. They had created the subject of endocrinology, which was later to prove so fruitful. Soon it was realised that one hormone had already been found (adrenalin, by *Takamine* in 1901) and another was discovered by *Kendall* in 1914 (thyroxin), and the subject expanded strongly after 1930.

Starling's other work was largely on the cardiovascular system. Starling's **law of the heart** (1918) states that for cardiac muscle (as for voluntary muscle) the energy of contraction is a function of the length of the muscle fibres. So the more the heart is filled during diastole (relaxation) the greater is the following systole (contraction); this allows change in output without change in rate. An impared heart enlarges to maintain its output, in accord with this law, and the enlargement (detectable, e.g., by X-radiography) is an indication of heart damage.

STAUDINGER, Hermann
1881-1965

German organic chemist: the founder of polymer chemistry

Staudinger's career in chemistry began with work of a classical organic kind, and included the discovery of a new group, the ketenes, and work on the aroma agents in coffee. But in the 1920s he began to study rubber. At that time rubber and other apparently non-crystalline high-molecular mass materials were supposed to be merely disorderly aggregates of small molecules; linked with this concept, their chemistry was held in low regard. From 1920 Staudinger took the view that these polymers are giant molecules held together by ordinary chemical bonds, and frequently forming long-chain molecular strands. His view was at first strongly opposed, but he devised methods for measuring their relative molecular mass by viscometry, and chemical methods for modifying polymers, and soon X-ray studies also supported his views. When accepted, these ideas formed a philosophy for the new macromolecular chemistry – the chemistry of 'high polymers' (i.e., having high molecular mass). This has proved fundamental for an industry using synthetic polymers as rubbers, mouldable plastics, fibres, adhesives and so on. He also foresaw the importance of natural biopolymers in biochemistry, and from 1936 had some prophetic insights in that area, (e.g., 'Every gene macromolecule possesses a definite structure which determines its function in life' – correct, but not provable for another two decades). Belatedly, he received a Nobel Prize in 1953. He had then worked in Freiburg since 1926.

STEFAN, Josef
1835-1893

Austrian physicist: discovered the Stefan-Boltzmann black body radiation law

Stefan's parents were illiterate shopkeepers. After four years at the University of Vienna he became a school-teacher for seven years, researching in physics in his spare time, but in 1863 he secured the professorship of physics at Vienna, and remained there throughout his life.

A skilful experimentalist, Stefan measured the thermal conductivity of gases accurately and thereby gave early confirmation of *Maxwell*'s kinetic theory. In 1879 he considered the heat losses of very hot bodies, which were reputed to cool faster than *Newton*'s law of cooling predicted. Using *Tyndall*'s results obtained with a platinum wire made incandescent by passing a current, Stefan showed that the rate of heat loss per unit area is $E = \sigma T^4$, a relation known as **Stefan's law**. Here σ is now known as **Stefan's constant** and T is the absolute temperature. In 1884 his ex-student *Boltzmann* used the kinetic theory and thermodynamics to derive this law, and showed that it only held for bodies radiating perfectly at all wavelengths, called black bodies. It became known as the **Stefan-Boltzmann law**. Stefan used the law to make the first satisfactory estimate of the Sun's surface temperature, arriving at 6000°C for this.

STEINBERGER, Jack

1921-

American nuclear physicist: major contributor to the 'standard model' of particle physics

Steinberger went to the US in 1934 as a teenage Jewish refugee, and later studied chemistry at Chicago. In World War II he worked in the radiation laboratory at MIT, and his interest moved to physics; as a result, he worked for his PhD in Chicago on the muons present in cosmic rays. He showed that a muon decays to give an electron and two neutrinos; and he continued his work in this field with M. Schwartz and L. Lederman at Columbia University, New York, from 1959. They theorized that neutrinos should be of two kinds, the electron neutrino and the muon neutrino. In the early 1960s a new high-energy proton accelerator became available at the Brookhaven National Laboratory, which could provide enough neutrinos to test their theory. To exclude other particles, a filter was used consisting of a stack of steel plates from a scrapped battleship, and 13.5 m thick. Behind this a detector located a handful of nuclear reactions which confirmed that two kinds of neutrino exist.

Working in Europe at CERN near Geneva from 1968, Steinberger continued to use neutrinos to study nuclear forces. The current 'standard model' proposes two types of component as fundamental units of matter: the **quarks** and the **leptons**. The quarks (six kinds of them) are subject to the strong nuclear force, and they compose the heavy particles, the protons and neutrons. The leptons include three charged particles: the electron, the muon, and the tau particle; and three neutral leptons, the neutrinos each associated with one of the charged leptons. The neutrinos interact only through the weak nuclear force.

Steinberger, Lederman and Schwartz shared the Nobel Prize for physics in 1988.

STENO, Nicolaus (Niels Steensen)

1638-1686

Danish anatomist and geologist: made early studies of crystals and fossils

An anatomist by training, Steno was also interested in crystals and fossils. He showed that a pineal gland like that of man is found in other animals, and used this and other arguments to refute *Descartes*'s claim that it is the seat of the soul and uniquely human. His study of quartz crystals revealed that, although the shapes varied, the angle between corresponding faces is fixed for a particular mineral. This constancy, sometimes called **Steno's law**, is a consequence of the internal ordering of the constituent molecules in the crystal. Steno also accepted the organic nature of fossils, and recognized that sedimentary strata were laid down in former seas, having found fossil teeth far inland that closely resembled those of a shark that he had dissected. His geological sections were probably the first to be drawn.

He became a priest in 1675, was ordained a bishop in 1677, and gave up science thereafter.

STERN, Otto

1888-1969

German-American physicist: showed that magnetic fields of atoms are quantized

Stern, the son of a grain-merchant, completed his doctorate in Breslau in 1912. He travelled and attended lectures by *Sommerfeld, Lummer* and *Pringsheim*; and became a post-doctoral associate and friend of *Einstein* in Zürich. Following military service during World War I he worked with *Born* in Frankfurt on statistical mechanics.

In 1920 Stern and W. Gerlach collaborated in a historic experiment. A molecular beam of silver atoms (produced by heating the metal in a vacuum) was used to investigate whether space quantization (proposed by Sommerfeld) occurs or not. A silver atom should possess a magnetic moment (spin) and when placed in a non-uniform magnetic field should be found in two (spin-up or spin-down) configurations, so that the beam would be split into two distinct beams by such a field. Such quantum mechanical space-quantization was proved by the Stern-Gerlach experiment, and Stern was awarded the 1943 Nobel Prize for physics.

Stern took a professorship at Hamburg and set up a large molecular-beam laboratory, collaborating with *Pauli, Bohr* and P. Ehrenfest. He determined the magnetic moment of the proton, and found it to have two to three times the value predicted by *Dirac*. In 1933 Stern moved to the Carnegie Institute of Technology, Pittsburgh, but the momentum of the Hamburg laboratory was not regained and he retired early. He enjoyed luxury, good food and the cinema, and it was in the cinema that he died of a heart attack at 81.

STEVIN (or Stevinus), Simon
1548-1620

Flemish physicist and mathematician: introduced decimal notation to Europe

Stevin entered the Dutch government service, rising to the rank of Quartermaster-General to the Army, where he developed a system of sluices to defend parts of Holland from invasion by flooding them with water.

He is noted for his demonstration that hydrostatic pressure in a liquid depends only on the depth of liquid, and not on the shape of the containing vessel. In mathematics he is credited with introducing the decimal system for representing fractions, *Napier* inventing the decimal point soon afterwards. Stevin wrote an excellent book on statics, giving the law of the inclined plane. He was also an advocate of writing scientific works in the vernacular, rather than Latin, as was the custom of the day.

STIBITZ, George Robert
1904-

American computer scientist

Stibitz attended colleges in New York, emerging with a PhD in Physics from Cornell and then joining Bell Telephone Laboratories in 1930. He was there until 1941 when he moved to defence work, and from 1945 worked on the computer modelling of biomedical systems. He designed the first genuinely binary calculator in 1937, followed by a series of machines for Bell including the first multi-user machine, which was demonstrated as a remotely-controlled device in 1940 using telephone lines between Hanover (New Hampshire) and New

George R. Stibitz about 1937

York City. As well as this introduction of remote job-entry, he built the first machine capable of floating point arithmetic in 1942.

STOCK, Alfred
1876-1946

German inorganic chemist: pioneer of silicon hydride and boron hydride chemistry, and of vacuum handling methods

After graduating in Germany, Stock went to Paris in 1899 to join *Moissan*'s research group. They were a happy international team, although 'one was constantly in danger of losing one's life'. Later, as professor in Breslau, he began work in 1909 on the dangerously explosive boron hydrides; in this work he developed the vacuum-line methods so much used for volatile materials by later inorganic chemists. His work on the boron hydrides led to later work on their strange electron-deficient structures, and to their use as rocket propellants.

Stock became a victim of mercury vapour poisoning; he was not the first chemist to suffer this, but he was unusual in being aware of the cause of his illness, and from 1923 he worked on mercury poisoning and methods of avoiding it. He also devised a method for making beryllium which is used commercially; and the use of P_4S_3 in place of phosphorus in match heads is also due to him.

STOKES, (Sir) George Gabriel
1819-1903

British physicist: contributor to fluid dynamics

Educated in his native Ireland and at Cambridge, Stokes became Lucasian professor at Cambridge in 1849 and in the next half-century did much to rescue physics teaching there. He worked in most areas of theoretical and experimental physics except electricity. One of his enthusiasms was hydrodynamics and another was fluorescence, and both have laws named after him. **Stokes's law of hydrodynamics** is that the frictional force (i.e., drag) on a spherical body of radius r moving at its terminal speed v through a viscous fluid of coefficient of viscosity n is $6\pi n r v$; this holds only for a restricted range of conditions. **Stokes's law of fluorescence** states that the wavelength of fluorescence radiation is greater than that of the exciting radiation; again, the law does not always hold.

STONEY, George Johnstone
1826-1911

Irish physicist: suggested the name electron for the smallest unit of electricity

For most of his working life Stoney was secretary to Queen's University, Dublin, until its dissolution. Rightly believing that science would be simplified by a wise choice of fundamental units, he argued this in 1874 and proposed the charge on a hydrogen ion as a unit, calculating its value from the mass of hydrogen liberated on electrolysis. This idea that electricity has a 'smallest unit' was also advanced by *Helmholtz* in 1881, and ten years later Stoney introduced the word 'electron' for the unit. Later the word came to be used for the 'corpuscles' discovered by *J. J. Thomson*.

STRACHEY, Christopher
1916-1975

British computer scientist: pioneering worker on programming languages

Strachey came from a literary family (Lytton Strachey was his uncle) and was educated at Cambridge, after which he joined Standard Telephones and Cables Ltd. World War II hastened the development of electronic computers, and Strachey soon wrote some of the largest programs for them. In 1951 he joined the

National Research and Development Corporation, designing the Ferranti Pegasus computer. In 1962 he became a research fellow at Cambridge and worked on the design of the high-level language CPL, which led to the more common BCPL (Basic Computer Programming Language). He later moved to Oxford and established the Programming Research Group, working largely on a comprehensive theory of programming language semantics.

STRASBURGER, Eduard Adolf

1844-1912

German botanist: demonstrated capillary action as cause for sap rising in trees

A friend and student of *Pringsheim* and an early enthusiast for *Darwin*'s ideas, Strasburger taught at Jena and later at Bonn, and made the latter the major centre for research in plant cytology. He was the first to fully describe the embryo sac in gymnosperms (conifers) and in angiosperms (flowering plants) and to recognize the process of double fertilization in the latter. In 1875 he described the principles of mitosis, and he deduced that the nucleus was responsible for heredity, and a little later he proposed a basic principle of cytology: that new nuclei arise only from the division of existing nuclei. In 1891 he demonstrated that physical forces (e.g., capillarity) are largely responsible for the rise of sap in a tree stem, rather than physiological forces.

STURGEON, William

1783-1850

Engish inventor: much improved electromagnet design

After a few years as an apprentice shoemaker, Sturgeon joined the Army, and began to study science at night, until he became an expert on electrical instruments. After he left the Army in 1820 he became a bootmaker and itinerant teacher of science for the Army, and some schools and societies, and he published popular accounts of science such as his monthly *Annals of Electricity*. In 1821 he much improved the electromagnet by using a bar of soft iron coated with shellac varnish to insulate it from the bare wires carrying the current (*J. Henry* and *Faraday* later insulated the wires, so allowing many more turns and greater improvement in performance). For his work on electrical apparatus Sturgeon received a prize in 1825 from the Society of Arts; it consisted of a silver medal and thirty guineas. In 1836 he invented a moving-coil galvanometer, and the first commutator for a workable electric motor.

STURTEVANT, Alfred Henry

1891-1970

American geneticist: pioneer of chromosome mapping

As a boy Sturtevant drew up pedigrees for his father's farm horses, and as a student at Columbia University his older brother encouraged this interest through books on heredity. A book on Mendelism spurred his enthusiasm, since he felt that some horse coat colours could be explained on a Mendelian basis. He wrote on this to the leading American geneticist *T. H. Morgan* and in 1910 joined the group of enthusiasts in the crowded 'fly room' at Columbia working with Morgan on the genetics of the fruit fly, *Drosophila*. In 1928 Sturtevant became professor of genetics at the California Institute of Technology, where he remained, except for research visits, until his death.

In the 'fly room' he had the germ of the idea of chromosome mapping and 'went home, and spent most of the night (to the neglect of my undergraduate homework) in producing the first chromosome map . . .'. This was based on his idea that the frequency of crossing-over between two genes gives an index of their relative distance on a linear map of the genes on the chromosome. His paper of 1913 located six sex-linked genes, as deduced from the way they associated with each other; it forms a classic paper on genetics. He later developed a range of related ideas, discovering the 'position effect', i.e., the way in which the expression of a gene depends on its position in relation to other genes; and he showed that crossing-over between chromosomes is prevented in regions where a part of the chromosome material is inserted the wrong way round. The position effect was to prove of great importance in F. Jacob and *Monod*'s work on gene clusters (operons) in bacteria. Although Sturtevant's main work was in genetics (where he worked with a range of animals on an assortment of problems, including the curious effect of direction of shell-coiling in snails) he was also a knowledgeable naturalist with a special interest in social insects.

SUESS, Eduard
1831-1914

Austrian geologist: proposed former existence of Gondwanaland supercontinent

Suess was educated at the University of Prague, moving to Vienna in 1856 and becoming professor of geology there in 1861. In addition to being an academic he served as a member of the Reichstat (parliament) for 25 years. On the basis of geological similarities between parts of the southern continents, including the widespread occurrence in Africa, South America, Australia and India of the fossil fern *Glossopteris* during the Carboniferous period, Suess proposed that there had once been a great 'supercontinent' made up of the present southern continents, and he named it Gondwanaland, after a region of India. Subsequent work has established the former existence of Gondwanaland beyond doubt, and Suess's ideas, as extended by *Wegener*, led to modern theories of continental drift.

SVEDBERG, Theodor
1884-1971

Swedish physical chemist: devised the ultracentrifuge

Svedberg entered Uppsala in 1904, hoping to apply chemical methods to biological problems; he stayed in the university for life, and had fair success in his objective. His main success was in developing the ultracentrifuge, in which a centrifugal force much above gravitational force is produced, which is powerful enough to 'pull down' large molecules such as proteins. Svedberg's ultracentrifuges ran at up to 140 000 r.p.m. giving fields up to 900 000 g, and could be used to purify proteins (and other colloids) and to confirm *Staudinger's* view that these were giant molecules, of high relative molecular mass (e.g., Svedberg found relative molecular mass=68 000 for haemoglobin). Since his work ultracentrifuges have been in routine use for separating large biological molecules. He was awarded a Nobel Prize in 1926. The unit of sedimentation velocity, the **svedberg (S)**, is named after him.

SWAMMERDAM, Jan
1637-1680

Dutch naturalist and microscopist: pioneer of modern entomology, and discoverer of red blood cells

Swammerdam's father, an apothecary, had a 'museum of curiosities' and the boy helped with this and became a keen insect collector. He studied medicine at Leiden (with *Steno* as a fellow student) and graduated in 1667 but he never practised medicine, despite his father's protests and financial pressure. When only 21, he discovered the red blood cells of the frog. Also from the frog, he introduced the nerve-muscle preparation into physiology. This consists of a leg muscle with its nerve, dissected from a recently killed frog; when the nerve is stimulated, the muscle contracts. By immersing the preparation in water in a container with a narrow outlet, Swammerdam was able to show that when the muscle contracts, there is no change in its volume, contrary to earlier belief.

For the second half of his fairly short life he was a victim of mental illness, but this did not stop his skilful pioneer work on insects and their microanatomy. His minute dissections of the mayfly, bee, tadpole and snail were not surpassed until, in the 18th century, the compound microscope was much improved. His work showed the complexity of small animals (e.g., the compound eye, sting, and mouth of the bee). Much of this work was not found until 50 years after his death, when it was published as the *Bible of Nature* (1737).

SYDENHAM, Thomas

1624-1689

English physician: made early studies in epidemiology

After two months as a student at Oxford, Sydenham left to join the Parliamentary Army, and to serve in the Civil War under his older brother (who was Commander-in-Chief in Dorset). After three years he returned to his studies and graduated in 1648, but in 1651 was again in the war as a Captain of Horse. He was wounded at the battle of Worcester, and in 1655 he married and began his career as a London physician. He began there his researches on smallpox and other fevers, then prevalent in London. He pioneered the use of quinine to treat malaria, and of opium for pain relief, and iron compounds in anaemia. His scientific approach to the natural history of disease was new and valuable; he saw infections as specific entities, best treated conservatively, as described in his influential book *The Method of Treating Fevers* (1666) which is dedicated to his friend *Boyle*. He is the major 17th century clinician; 'the English Hippocrates'.

SYLVESTER, James Joseph

1814-1897

English mathematician: with Cayley, founded the theory of invariants

Sylvester was born into a Jewish family of nine children, and went to a London school and in 1828 to the new University of London, founded for dissenters. Vociferous and hot-headed, Sylvester fought back against the strong anti-Semitism which he encountered, and was sent down for threatening a fellow student with a table-knife. He returned to school in Liverpool, but was again forced to leave. Finally, with help, he was admitted to St John's College, Cambridge (1831) and became second Wrangler; however, as someone unable to accept the 39 articles of the Church of England he could not obtain a degree and only received his Cambridge MA in 1871, when this restriction was lifted. He moved to Trinity College, Dublin and gained his BA.

After a short period teaching science in London, he decided he preferred mathematics and started a disastrous few months as professor at the University of Virginia, in 1841. He resigned due to the authority's failure to discipline a student who insulted him. For some years he abandoned university life and worked in London as an actuary and then as a barrister, qualifying in 1850. Fortunately in 1850 he met *Cayley*, who rekindled his interest in mathematics, and the two became lifelong close friends. Sylvester taught private pupils, and one of the best was Florence Nightingale. He eventually got a professorship at the Royal Military Academy at Woolwich in 1855, but had to retire at 63.

Happily, he was secured as a professor in the newly-founded Johns Hopkins University at Baltimore in 1876, producing a flood of new ideas in mathematical research and teaching. In 1833, when he was over 70, he returned as a professor to Oxford; ten years later failure of his eyesight forced him to give up lecturing and move to a lonely retirement in

London. Enthusiastic and inventive to the end of his life, at 82 his talent blazed again as he worked out the theory of compound partitions.

Sylvester's mathematical style was brilliant, but not methodical, and his creativity was unfettered by rigour. With Cayley, he inspired many of the basic ideas of algebraic invariance. He also published on the roots of quintic equations and on number theory. In 1850 he coined the term **matrix** for an array of numbers from which determinants can be obtained. Invariance assumed great importance after his lifetime, as much use was made of it in quantum mechanics and relativity theory.

SZENT-GYÖRGI, Albert von

1893-1986

Hungarian-American biochemist: worked on vitamin C and on the biochemistry of muscle

Szent-Györgi had four generations of scientists in his mother's family, and in 1911 he began to study medicine at Budapest. By 1914 he had published some research on the eye, before he was called into the Austro-Hungarian army. He was soon decorated for bravery, but in order to return to his studies, he shot himself in the arm. Later he was redrafted, but again proved an awkward soldier by protesting against the treatment of prisoners. As a result he was sent to a base in northern Italy where a malaria epidemic was raging, but within weeks the war was over and he returned to complete his medical course. Afterwards he researched in five countries, and received his PhD in Cambridge for work on vitamins with *Hopkins*. Back in Hungary in the 1930s, he showed that vitamin C (the anti-scorbutic vitamin, ascorbic acid) was in fact a compound he had first isolated in Cambridge in 1928. He also showed that paprika (Hungarian red pepper) is a rich source of it; in 1937 he won a Nobel Prize (in medicine or physiology) for his work on

vitamin C. By 1935 he was working on the biochemistry of muscle; he began the work which was later developed by *Krebs* on the metabolism of muscle. He also isolated two proteins from muscle (myosin and actin) and showed that they combine to form actomyosin. When ATP (adenosine triphosphate) is added to fibres of this, it contracts. 'Seeing this artificial bundle contract was the most exciting moment of my scientific career', he wrote. This work was extended especially by *H. E. Huxley*.

He also had an exciting World War II, working for the Allies and the underground resistance. Afterwards he was offered the Presidency of Hungary, but he emigrated to the US in 1947 and directed muscle research at the Marine Biological Laboratory at Woods Hole. In the 1960s he worked on the thymus gland and on cancer, which had killed his wife and daughter. He was a man who had novel and daring research ideas; he 'thought big' and, a keen fisherman, claimed he liked to use an extra-large hook.

SZILARD, Leo

1898-1964

Hungarian-American physicist: recognized the significance of nuclear fission

A versatile and creative physicist, Szilard had an extraordinarily wide-ranging and original mind. He first studied electrical engineering, then trained in the Austro-Hungarian army during World War I, and later took a doctorate in physics at Berlin (1922). Work with *von Laue* on thermodynamics followed, and led to a paper foreshadowing modern information theory (1929). Moving to Oxford and London in 1933, and to the US in 1938, he began to work on nuclear physics at Columbia University.

In 1934 he had taken a patent on nuclear fission as an energy source, and on hearing of O. Hahn and *Meitner*'s fission of uranium (1938), he immediately approached *Einstein*, in order to write together to President Roosevelt warning him of the possibility of atomic bombs. Together with *Fermi*, Szilard organized work on the first fission reactor, which operated in Chicago in 1942. He was a central figure in the Manhattan Project leading to the atomic bomb. Szilard opposed the direct use of the bomb against the Japanese, wishing to use it in a demonstration only; and he forecast the nuclear stalemate after the war in a 1945 report to the Secretary for War.

After the war Szilard did research in molecular biology, doing experimental work on bacterial mutations and biochemical mechanisms and theoretical work on ageing and memory.

T

TAKAMINE, Jokichi
1854-1922
Japanese-American biochemist: isolated first hormone (adrenalin)

Born in the year that Japan opened its ports to the West, Takamine became a product of two cultures; brought up in the strict Samurai code, he graduated in chemical engineering at Tokyo and then at Glasgow. Back in Japan, he worked as a government scientist for four years and then opened his own factory, the first to make superphosphate fertilizer in Japan. He married an American and in 1890 went to live in the US. There he set up a laboratory to make biochemicals. In 1901 he isolated crystalline adrenalin from adrenal glands. After 1905 when *Starling* first used the word hormone to describe the animal body's 'chemical messengers' it was realised that adrenalin was the first hormone to be isolated in pure form from a natural source.

TARTAGLIA, Niccolo
c.1501-1557
Italian mathematician: found method for solving cubic equations

Tartaglia's real name was probably Fontana, but in the French attack on Brescia in 1512 he suffered sword wounds in the face which left him with a speech defect, and led to the adopted nickname Tartaglia (stammerer) thereafter. He taught mathematics in Verona and in Venice, and wrote on the mathematical theory of gunnery and on statistics, arithmetic, algebra and geometry. The array of binomial coefficients now known as *Pascal*'s triangle was first published by him; as was the first translation of *Euclid* into Italian, and of *Archimedes* into Latin. In 1535 he found a method for solving cubic equations, which he confided to *Cardano* under a pledge of secrecy. Cardano much improved and extended the method and published it (crediting Tartaglia) in his book *Ars Magna* (The Great Skill) in 1545. Their friendship ended, and controversy over priority followed, with Tartaglia emerging as the loser.

TAYLOR, (Sir) Geoffrey Ingram
1886-1975
English physicist: discovered how dislocations allow solids to deform under shear

Taylor qualified at Cambridge, and was only absent from there during the two World Wars throughout his career. From 1923 until his retirement in 1952 he held a professorship of physics. He conducted a great range of research in classical physics, always with originality, and chiefly on the mechanics of fluids and solids.

Having done major work on fluid turbulence he applied it in meteorology, aerodynamics and the planetary physics of Jupiter's Great Red Spot. In 1934 it occurred to him that metals and other crystalline solids may deform under shear because faults due to planes of atoms being 'misarranged' are propagated through the crystal. These faults he named dislocations, and their presence and movement does indeed determine how easily most solids are deformed, by comparison with the resilience of a perfect crystal.

Taylor was renowned for his experimental skill. He had some oddities: when he carried out an experiment to see whether electrons are diffracted like waves the apparatus was sealed into a light-excluding box and left untouched for two weeks, so that he could go on a sailing holiday and return to the results.

TEISSERENC DE BORT, Léon Philippe

1855-1913

French meteorologist: discovered the stratosphere

Teisserenc de Bort worked for several years as chief meteorologist at the Central Meteorological Bureau in Paris, before setting up his own observatory near Versailles in 1896. In 1902, using unmanned instrumented balloons, he discovered that above an altitude of about 11 km the temperature of the atmosphere ceases to decrease with height, and remains relatively constant. He named this part of the atmosphere the stratosphere (believing that its steady temperature was due to undisturbed layers, or strata, of air), and the region below it the troposphere (since here the temperature varies and mixing of the air takes place).

TELLER, Edward

1908-

Hungarian-American physicist: major figure in development of nuclear energy

Educated in Budapest and in Germany, Teller was one of the many scientists who left Germany in 1933. In 1935 he settled in the US, becoming professor of physics at George Washington University. In 1940 he, *Szilard* and *Wigner* met with a Government committee to discuss the possibility of an atomic bomb; afterwards he worked with *Fermi* and Szilard in Chicago on the first atomic reactor, and then in 1943 he went to Los Alamos to work on the first atomic (fission) bombs.

Edward Teller

By then, he and others had considered the possibility of a fusion bomb (H-bomb), but he discontinued this work when the war ended in 1945. However President Truman approved H-bomb production in 1950, and the work was largely guided by Teller; a successful device was exploded in 1952.

The H-bomb depends on the energy released when light nuclei are fused to give heavier nuclei, following 'priming' by a fission explosion. Much of Teller's work in the 1950s and later was concerned with the theory of nuclear fusion and its use for peaceful purposes; he also supported nuclear arms for the protective defence of the west. He served in a series of senior posts at the University of California from 1952 onwards.

TESLA, Nikola

1856-1943

Croatian-American physicist and electrical engineer: pioneer of alternating current, and inventor of the a.c. induction motor

Tesla studied engineering at Graz and Prague before commencing work with a telephone company. In 1884 he emigrated to America, where he worked for *Edison* before quarreling and setting up on his own. Soon afterward he developed the alternating current induction motor, eliminating the commutator and sparking brushes required by d.c. motors. He also made substantial improvements in the field of a.c. power transmission and generation, realizing that it could be generated and transmitted far more efficiently than the then commonly-used direct current. He patented his inventions and set up a partnership with George Westinghouse to commercialize them. His interest then turned to high-frequency alternating current, developing the **Tesla coil**, an air-core transformer with the primary and secondary windings in resonance to produce high-frequency, high-voltage output. In 1899 he used this device to produce an electric spark 135 ft long, and to illuminate 200 lights over a distance of 25 miles without intervening wires. He became increasingly interested in the possibility of transmitting power over large distances without wires, becoming something of a recluse after 1892. The SI unit of magnetic flux density, the **tesla** (T), is named after him.

THALES (of Miletos)

c. 625-c. 550 BC

Ionian (Greek) merchant and philosopher: early geometer; pioneer seeker of general physical principles underlying nature

Thales was born in Miletos (in modern Turkey) 'the most go-ahead town in the Greek world'. Thales was probably a successful merchant who visited Egypt and there learned something of Egyptian geometry; but little is firmly known of his life and achievements, despite his high reputation, and some of the many accounts of his skill lack credibility. But it is certainly possible that he developed some general theorems in geometry, understood similar triangles, and was able to find the distance of a ship from shore,

and the height of a building from its shadow. Such deductive mathematical arguments was systematised 250 years later by *Euclid*. Thales was said also to be aware of the lodestone's magnetic attraction for iron.

He believed that the Earth and all things on it had once been water and had changed by some natural process (akin to the silting-up of the Nile delta); and that the Earth as a whole was a flat disc floating in water. He offered natural (and not supernatural) explanations for phenomena such as earthquakes, and he attempted to derive theories from observed facts. He was thus a pioneer of later Greek science, and his attitudes are still with us. Later Greek thinkers gave him the highest place in their lists of wise men; and it can be argued that he is the earliest 'scientific' thinker we can name.

THEOPHRASTUS

*c.*372-*c.*287 BC

Greek philosopher and botanist: often described as 'the father of botany'

Born in Lesbos, Theophrastus studied with Plato in Athens, and then became *Aristotle*'s assistant, friend, and successor as head of the Lyceum in 335 BC. The school did well under him, and may have had 2000 students; he secured botanical information from their home areas, to add to his own observations. He wrote on many subjects, but his most important surviving books are on botany. He described over 500 plant species, and understood the relation between fruit, flower and seed, the differences between monocotyledons and dicotyledons, and between angiosperms (flowering plants) and gymnosperms (cone-bearers). Plant propagation methods, and the effect on growth of soil and climate, are also accurately described by him. His ideas were usually sound, although he believed in spontaneous generation, in accord with the views of his time.

THOMSON, (Sir) Charles Wyville
1830-1882

British marine biologist and oceanographer: postulated existence of mid-Atlantic ridge and of oceanic circulation

Educated at the University of Edinburgh, Thomson held a number of academic posts in Scotland and Ireland before being appointed professor of natural history at Edinburgh in 1870. He took part in several deep-sea expeditions, leading the five-year circumnavigational *Challenger* expedition of 1872-76, a landmark in marine exploration which resulted in the discovery of 4717 new marine species. On the basis of temperature measurements he postulated the presence of oceanic circulation, and the existence of a mid-Atlantic ridge, but the latter was not confirmed until 1925.

THOMSON, (Sir) George Paget
1892-1975

English physicist: discovered experimentally the interference (diffraction) of electrons by atoms in crystals

G. P. Thomson, the only son of *J. J. Thomson*, had an outstanding college career. He survived the first year of World War I in the infantry, and in 1915 was attached to the Royal Flying Corps to work on problems of aircraft stability. In 1919 he returned to Cambridge, working first in his father's field of positive rays. He then worked with A. Reid at the University of Aberdeen, having been appointed to a professorship there at the age of 30. They observed (in 1927) electron diffraction of electrons passing through thin gold foil, recorded on photographic plates as concentric rings of varying intensity about the incident beam. While not undertaken for that purpose they recognized the experiment as confirming *de Broglie*'s postulate of wave-particle duality. Thomson received the 1937 Nobel Prize for physics jointly with *Davisson*, who had also achieved

diffraction of electrons but by use of a nickel crystal rather than a metal foil.

In 1930 Thomson moved to Imperial College, London. During World War II he chaired the 'Maud' Committee advising the British Government on the atomic bomb, and in July 1941 reported that such a bomb could be made using separated uranium-235. The co-ordinating role on the bomb project then passed to *Chadwick*, while Thomson became scientific adviser to Canada, and then in 1943 to the Air Ministry in Britain. After the war, in 1952, he returned to Cambridge as Master of Corpus Christi College. Always known as 'G.P.', he had considerable intuition in physics.

THOMSON, (Sir) Joseph John
1856-1940

English physicist: discovered the electron

Thomson was a bookseller's son who first studied at Owens College (later Manchester University) hoping to become an engineer. Poverty caused by his father's death in 1872 led him to study mathematics, physics and chemistry instead, as he could not afford the charge then made to become an apprentice engineer. He did well and won a scholarship to Trinity College, Cambridge (1876). As a mathematician he graduated Second Wrangler (1880), and subsequently became a Fellow of Trinity College, Cavendish Professor (1884-1919, succeeding *Rayleigh*) and Master of Trinity in 1918. In modern terms 'J.J.' was an experimentalist; but his hands were clumsy, and his best work was actually performed by assistants. He was exceptionally well liked.

Thomson had carried out an excellent mathematical analysis of vortex rings in 1883 and speculation that atoms might be vortex rings in the electromagnetic 'ether' led him to investigate cathode rays (the electrical discharge emitted from an electrode under high fields in a gas at low pressure). Several German physicists

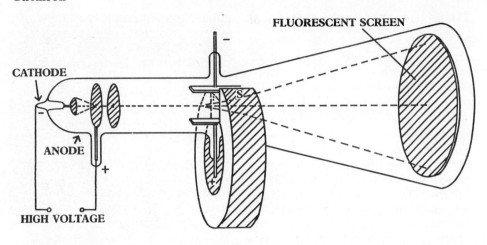

FLUORESCENT SCREEN

CATHODE

ANODE

HIGH VOLTAGE

J. J. Thomson's apparatus for finding the ratio of charge to mass (e/m) for the electron. In the evacuated tube, a high voltage applied to the cathode and anode causes cathode rays (a stream of electrons) to be emitted from the cathode. A narrow beam is selected by two small holes, and forms a bright spot on the screen. The beam is deflected by a magnetic field, but can be restored to its normal position by an electric field applied to the two horizontal plates. From the field strengths, e/m can be calculated.

believed that cathode rays were waves, and *Hertz* had tried to show that they could not be particles, because in his experiments the cathode rays were not deflected by an electric field. However, Thomson repeated the experiment in a better vacuum, in which there was no polarizable air to mask the electric field, and demonstrated that electric fields would deflect cathode rays (1897). Having shown that the rays were made up of particles, he proceeded to use their deflection under combined electric and magnetic fields to find the charge to mass ratio *(e/m)* of the particles, which did not vary from one cathode material to another. In April 1897 he revealed that he had discovered a new particle. Developing this classic series of experiments, Thomson then measured the charge *e* by allowing the particles to strike water droplets and observing the droplet's rate of fall in an electric field (see *Millikan*). He obtained the same value as the charge on a hydrogen atom, but using both results he found a mass *m* for the new particle about 1000 times lighter than hydrogen. Shortly afterwards Thomson's particle was named the 'electron' by

Stoney. Its discovery opened the way for the study of atomic structure by *Rutherford*, who succeeded him as Cavendish Professor. His device for measuring *e/m* is essentially the cathode ray oscillograph, so much used afterwards in both research and in television receivers.

Thomson also examined E. Goldstein's positive rays, and in 1912 showed how to use them to separate atoms of different mass. This was done by deflecting the positive rays in electric and magnetic fields (a method now called mass spectrometry). The method allowed him to discover that neon had two isotopes, neon-20 and neon-22, and *Aston* then developed the technique.

Thomson received the 1906 Nobel Prize for physics for research on conduction through gases. One of his achievements was to have built up the Cavendish Laboratory as the foremost in experimental physics, with seven of his research assistants subsequently winning Nobel Prizes. To his great delight his son (*G. P. Thomson*) also won a Nobel Prize for demonstrating that the electron possessed both particle-like and wave-like behaviour.

THOMSON, William (Baron Kelvin of Largs)

1824-1907

Scottish physicist and electrical engineer: pioneer of thermodynamics and electromagnetic theory; directed first successful project for a transatlantic cable telegraph

William Thomson (later Lord Kelvin) aged 28

Thomson's father had been a farm labourer who became professor of mathematics at Belfast and from 1832 at Glasgow. Two of his children became distinguished physicists and another did well in medicine. Young William studied science in Glasgow from the age of ten, and later was sent to Cambridge. He graduated when he was 21 and went to Paris to work on heat with *Regnault*, returning the next year to become professor of natural philosophy (i.e., physics) at Glasgow. He held the job for 53 years.

While still an undergraduate he gave a mathematical demonstration of the analogy between the transmission of electrostatic force, and heat flow in a uniform solid (*Maxwell* later brought this into his full theory of electromagnetism). Thomson reorganized the theory of magnetism, developing *Faraday*'s ideas, and introduced the ideas of magnetic susceptibility and permeability, and of the total energy of a magnetic system. Thomson was not only a theoretician, but put his knowledge to practical effect, showing that low voltages were better than high ones for the transmission of signals along submarine cables, and inventing the mirror galvanometer for the detection of the resulting small currents. He directed work on the first successful transatlantic cable (there had been two previous attempts), which became operational in 1866, bringing him considerable personal wealth. In 1892 be was made a baron, and chose his title from a small stream, the Kelvin, passing through the University. He was a major figure in the creation of the Institute of Electrical Engineers. He liked sailing and bought 'a schooner of 126×10^6 g' (i.e., 126 t), which prompted him to develop navigational instruments. His large Glasgow house was among the first to be lit by electricity (in 1881).

As a young man Thomson discovered *Green*'s work, then hardly known, and publicized it; he found that Green's and his own theorems gave valuable mathematical methods for attacking problems in electricity and in heat.

Thomson did much to develop heat theory. He heard of *Carnot*'s work when he was in Paris, but it was three years before he secured his paper; he then made its ideas widely known, and used and developed them further. Thomson proposed an 'absolute' scale of temperature now known as the **Kelvin** or **thermodynamic scale**; it is independent of particular substances, but corresponds practically to the *Celsius* scale with 273.16 K as the triple point of water, 0°C. The SI unit of temperature is the **kelvin (K)**. Independently of *Clausius* he formulated the **second law of thermodynamics**, which states that heat cannot flow spontaneously from a colder to a hotter body. He worked with *Joule* on the relation of heat and work (the first law of thermodynamics), and also with him found the **Joule-Thomson effect**. This is the drop in temperature shown by most gases when they emerge from a fine nozzle, as a result of the work done to pull the mutually attracting gas

375

molecules apart, and is the basis of modern methods for cooling gases for liquifaction. Thomson worked on the theory of the cooling of a hot solid sphere, and applied his theory to calculate ages for the Earth and the Sun. He recognized that his method assumed that no continuing heat supply was present: his results were about ten times lower than present values, which now take into account heat due to radioactivity which was not discovered until many years after Thomson's early work.

Thomson was an unusual scientist; his energy, enthusiasm and talent made him dominate British physics in the later 19th century, and he did much to move the focus of physics from Europe to Britain. He was always generous with ideas and in giving credit to others. His productivity was vast; 661 papers, many books and patents, covering the whole of physics (no-one since has ranged so widely) with sundry excursions into other sciences. He had some oddities, of course. He detested vector methods and gave himself much mathematical toil in avoiding them. He did not normally work on one problem for more than a month, and his results were worked out in green pocket books from which he tore sheets for publication. After his first wife died in 1870 he continued to have a great flow of ideas in physics, but he lost the ability to select good ideas from bad, and he pursued some strangely wrong notions (like the theory of the ether; and his opposition to the admission of women to Cambridge). He was probably the first scientist to become wealthy through science.

TINBERGEN, Nikolaas

1907-1988

Dutch ethologist: pioneer in study of animal behaviour

Tinbergen graduated in zoology at Leiden, and afterwards taught there, except for three years in World War II spent in a hostage camp in occupied

Nikolaas Tinbergen studying herring gulls on the Dutch island of Terschelling about 1945

Holland. In 1947 he moved to Oxford, and developed there his work on animal behaviour. The emphasis of this was to examine the patterns of behaviour shown by animals in natural conditions as well as in the laboratory; it includes work on digger wasps, arctic foxes, seals, sea birds and snails. His now-classic studies of the social habits of herring gulls, and the mating of sticklebacks, showed that key elements of behaviour follow a stereotyped pattern, and can depend largely on particular features. For example, the gull chick pecks for food at the parent's beak largely in response to a red spot on the latter. Also in these gulls, Tinbergen found that aggression between males is shown not only by calls but also by gestures, which in part seem designed to avoid actual fighting and injury. His wide-ranging work included study of learning behaviour, animal camouflage, instinct, and autism and aggression in human beings. He shared a Nobel Prize in 1973. His elder brother Jan also shared a Nobel Prize; the first awarded for economics, in 1969.

TING, Samuel Chao Chung
1936 -

American physicist: discovered the J/psi particle

Ting had an unusual upbringing, being born in the US but educated in China and Taiwan, and finally at the University of Michigan (1956-62). His work in elementary-particle physics began at the European Organisation for Nuclear Research in Geneva (CERN) and Columbia University where he became an associate professor at 29. He also led a research group at DESY, the German synchrotron project in Hamburg, and from 1967 worked at Massachusetts Institute of Technology.

Ting conducted an experiment at the Brookhaven National Laboratory synchrotron in which protons were directed onto a beryllium target, and a long-lived product particle was observed (1974). This newly-discovered particle was named the J particle; it was observed at the same time and independently by *Richter* at Stamford, who called it the psi particle. It is now known as the J/psi particle. Soon, other related particles of the J/psi family were detected, and Ting and Richter shared the Nobel Prize for physics in 1976.

TISELIUS, Arne (Wilhelm Kaurin)
1902-1971

Swedish physical biochemist: developed technique of electrophoresis for separating proteins

Tiselius was a pupil and then assistant to *Svedberg*, and like him had his career in Uppsala working mainly on proteins. Since these carry electric charges, they can be made to migrate in solution by applying an electric field. Tiselius developed this method (electrophoresis) to separate proteins, and the method has since been widely used. He showed that blood serum proteins can be separated into four groups of related proteins; they are the albumens and the α-, β-, and γ-globulins. He was awarded a Nobel Prize in 1948.

TOMBAUGH, Clyde William
1906-

American astronomer: discovered Pluto

Too poor to attend college, Tombaugh was a keen amateur astronomer and built his own 9-inch telescope. He was appointed as an assistant at the Lowell Observatory, Arizona, in 1929, and took over *Lowell*'s search for a trans-Neptunian planet; Lowell had died in 1916. After repeatedly photographing the sky along the plane of the ecliptic, and

Samuel C. C. Ting

checking for differences between successive photographs with a blink comparator, Tombaugh finally announced the finding of the new planet (Pluto) on 13 March 1930. Afterwards he continued the search for possible further planets, but although he discovered over 3000 asteroids, he found no other planets.

TOMONAGA, Sin-Itiro

1906-1979

Japanese theoretical physicist: a founder of quantum electrodynamics (QED)

Tomonaga's career was spent in Tokyo; after graduating at Kyoto University he became a professor of physics (1941) in Tokyo and then President of the University (1956).

Like others, Tomonaga started to develop a relativistic theory of the quantum mechanics of an electron interacting with a photon (1941-43). During World War II, he, *Feynman* and *Schwinger* were unaware of each other's work, and it was not until 1947 that it was realised that all three had arrived independently at solutions which were shown to be identical by *Dyson*. Tomonaga realised the value of a theory that could describe high-energy subatomic particles and he was responsible for the idea that two particles interact by exchanging a third virtual particle between them. The interaction is then like the momentum exchange when one rugby player passes the ball to another. The resulting theory is called quantum electrodynamics (QED) and for its discovery Feynman, Schwinger and Tomonaga shared the 1965 Nobel Prize for physics.

TORRICELLI, Evangelista

1608-1647

Italian physicist: inventor of the mercury barometer, and discoverer of atmospheric pressure

An orphan, Torricelli was educated by the Jesuits and by B. Castelli, for whom he worked on the dynamics of falling bodies. This led to his being appointed assistant to *Galileo*, whom he subsequently succeeded as mathematician to the court of Tuscany.

Torricelli's interests covered pure mathematics and experimental physics; he worked on conic sections and other curves, deriving the area of the cycloid. He is best remembered, however, for his discovery of atmospheric pressure, and for his invention, in 1644, of the mercury barometer. This appears to have come about from an attempt to solve the problem of why water could not be pumped out of a well more than 33 feet (≈ 10 m) deep. Deducing that the reason was that the atmosphere possessed weight, and hence exerted a pressure, he set about verifying the idea by sealing a glass tube at one end, filling it with mercury, and inverting it with the open end in a dish of mercury. He found that the height of the mercury column fell to about 760 mm, and that a vacuum was formed above it; the weight of the column was being balanced by the weight of the atmosphere. He later noticed that small variations in the height of the column were related to changes in the weather.

TOWNES, Charles Hard

1915-

American physicist: discovered the theory of the maser and produced the first working examples

Townes was the son of a lawyer and he completed his education in 1939, having attended Furman University, Duke University and California Institute of Technology. He began work at the Bell Telephone Laboratories and spent the war years developing radar-assisted bomb sights. Radar uses microwave radiation, with a frequency between that of radio and infrared light. In 1947 he joined the physics department at Columbia University. He spent 1961-67 at Massachusetts Institute of Technology and then became a professor at the University of California at Berkeley.

Beginning as early as 1945, Townes had studied the absorption and emission of photons when a molecule goes from one configuration to another. This involves very precise photon frequencies because molecular energy states are discrete and precisely defined. Thus the ammonia molecule (NH_3) may flip between two configurations rather like an umbrella blowing inside-out, but with the absorption of a very specific microwave frequency, of 1.25 cm wavelength.

In 1951, Townes realised that a wave of photons could be amplified in a practical way by the spontaneous emission process first suggested by *Einstein*. That is, if a molecule in the higher energy state is stimulated by photons of just the correct frequency, it will fall back to its lower state and emit another photon of precisely the same frequency or energy. If there are fewer molecules in the lower energy state to absorb photons than in the upper state, a net amplification results. He also recognized that if the wave is reflected back and forth in a resonant cavity, it interacts with the molecules for some time, steadily gaining more energy or amplification, and resulting in a coherent output signal consisting of a wavetrain of extremely well defined frequency.

To obtain ammonia with many molecules in the higher energy state, Townes took advantage of molecular beam techniques, separating out a beam of molecules in a high energy state with a non-uniform electric field. This 'population inversion' method, giving a majority of the high rather than low energy molecules, then provided a working amplifier and oscillator (1954). It was called a **maser** (microwave amplification by stimulated emission of radiation). A somewhat similiar idea was suggested in the Soviet Union by A. Prokhorov and *Basov*.

Masers were soon used in atomic clocks and in sensitive receivers, for example for radio telescopes and space communications. In 1958 Townes and *Schawlow* showed that an optical version of the maser (the **laser** for 'light amplication by stimulated emission of radiation') was possible, and discussed its properties and oscillation theoretically. The first operating system was constructed, however, by *Maiman* (1960) and now many versions are made.

Townes, Prokhorov and Basov were awarded the 1964 Nobel Prize for physics 'for fundamental work in the field of quantum electronics, which had led to the construction of oscillators and amplifiers based on the maser-laser principle'.

TRUMPLER, Robert Julius

1886-1956

Swiss-American astronomer: discovered interstellar light absorption

Trumpler was educated at Zürich and Göttingen. He moved to America in 1915, spending most of his career at the Lick Observatory in California. In 1930, whilst measuring the distance and size of over 300 open star clusters, Trumpler discovered that the more distant ones generally appeared to be larger than the nearer ones. Since there was no apparent reason for this, he assumed that he was observing the result of the interstellar absorption of light by dust grains, and measured the effect to be an approximately 20% decrease in brightness for every thousand light-years travelled by the starlight. His conclusions had important effects on ideas about the scale of the universe.

TSWETT, Michel (also Tsvet, Mikhail)

1872-1919

Russian botanist: developed the technique of chromatography

The son of a Russian father and an Italian mother, Tswett was educated in Switzerland and held posts in Poland and Russia.

His research was mainly on plant pigments and it was to separate these that he effectively introduced **chromatography**, although as with most inventions, precursors of success can be traced. In 1903 Tswett separated his plant leaf colours (chlorophyll a and b, carotenes, and xanthophylls) by passing the mixture, dissolved in light petroleum, down a column of powdered chalk. Distinct colour bands developed in the column, and could be easily separated with a knife. By the 1930s and especially after World War II this method of column chromatography (usually using alumina) and later its variants; notably ion-exchange, thin layers, paper chromatography, and gasliquid chromatography (both the last due to *Martin*), became essential chemical methods. Chromatography did for chemical analysis what the computer did for calculation.

TURING, Alan Mathison
1912-1954

British mathematician and computer scientist: mathematically formalized concept of the theoretical computer

After graduating from Cambridge, Turing was elected to a fellowship in 1935, visiting Princeton the following year. During World War II he did important work on code-breaking, and afterwards worked at the National Physical Laboratory and at Manchester University. In 1937 he described a theoretical computer in precise mathematical terms (the **Turing machine**), an important step which formalized the hitherto vague concept of computability. He put his ideas into practice when he supervized the construction of the ACE (Automatic Computing Engine) at the National Physical Laboratory, and at Manchester where he was assistant director of the MADAM (Manchester Automatic Digital Machine). His work on the design of such machines and the way in which they could be programmed was of great significance

in the development of the computer.

Turing was also interested in artificial intelligence, and developed a useful criterion for an intelligent machine, that it would be able to answer inquiries over a data-link in a manner indistinguishable from a human being. Turing committed suicide when prosecuted for his homosexuality, at that time a criminal offence.

TUVE, Merle Antony
1901-1982

American geophysicist: pioneer of radio techniques for ionospheric studies

Educated at the University of Minnesota and at Johns Hopkins University, Tuve was appointed to the department of terrestrial magnetism at the George Washington Institute, Washington, in 1926. He is remembered for pioneering radio techniques for studying the upper atmosphere. In 1925 he developed, together with *Breit*, an early form of radar in order to determine the height of the ionosphere. Tuve also investigated longrange seismic refraction by the upper mantle, his results subsequently providing evidence for the theory of isostasy, the process whereby areas of crust tend to float in conditions of near-equilibrium on the plastic mantle.

TWORT, Frederick William
1877-1950

English micro-biologist: discovered first virus infection of bacteria (bacteriophages)

Qualifying in medicine in London in 1900, Twort became a professor of bacteriology there in 1919. In 1915 when studying staphylococci he noticed that some cultures became transparent, and he traced the effect to an agent which was infecting the cocci. He planned to continue the work, but army service in World War I interrupted him and he did not take it up again. In 1917 F. H. d'Herelle found a similar result with some mixed cultures of dysentry bacilli, and named the infective agent **bacteriophage** ('phage'). Since then, these viruses which infect bacteria have been much studied; many strains exist, and some have proved of great value in genetic engineering.

TYNDALL, John

1820-1893

British physicist: made pioneering studies of heat, and scattering of light

Tyndall lacked a university education, leaving school to work as a surveyor and civil engineer in Ireland. He subsequently studied physical sciences at Marburg in Germany, and became first a professor and later Director of the Royal Institution.

Tyndall's early research was on diamagnetism, but he is chiefly remembered for his studies of heat. He measured the thermal conductivity of substances along their different axes, investigated the effect of radiant heat on gases, and made pioneering studies of glaciers (he was also one of the first men to climb the Matterhorn). His studies of the scattering of light by fine particles in the air and in liquids resulted in his discovery in 1859 of the **Tyndall effect**, whereby a beam of light is made visible by such scattering. Following *Rayleigh*'s work on the frequency-dependence of the scattering of light, Tyndall was the first to realise why the sky is blue: atmospheric dust particles (and density differences in the air) scatter the shorter wavelength (blue) components of sunlight to a greater degree than the longer wavelength (red) components.

U

UHLENBECK, George Eugene

1900-

Dutch-American physicist: discovered that electrons possess spin

Uhlenbeck emigrated to America once he had completed his PhD at Leiden (1927), and worked at the University of Michigan (1927-60), where he became professor of theoretical physics in 1939. From 1960 to 1974 he held a post at the Rockefeller Medical Research Centre in New York.

In 1925 Uhlenbeck and *Goudsmit* collaborated on an experiment whereby a horizontal beam of silver atoms was split by a vertical magnetic field into two components. This occurred because the electrons in the silver atoms possess spin, which is the property of having half a quantum unit of momentum directed either up or down in the applied magnetic field. The result was that the silver atoms were deflected according to their spin. This was the first observation of this purely quantum mechanical effect, and was an early piece of evidence that the new quantum mechanics was both necessary and correct.

UREY, Harold Clayton

1893-1981

American physical chemist: pioneered isotopic separation techniques and their application

Although originally a graduate from Montana in zoology, Urey soon turned to chemistry, first in industry and then at university, and following a year with *Bohr* he afterwards spent his career in chemical physics at four US universities.

In 1932 he isolated deuterium, the heavy isotope of hydrogen, and went on to devise a large-scale process for obtaining heavy water (D_2O) and to examine a range of deuterium compounds. His expertise on isotope separation gave him a critical role in World War II in the atomic bomb project (which required the separation of uranium isotopes) and afterwards in the work on securing tritium for the H-bomb. The same expertise led him to an ingenious way of measuring the past temperature of the oceans (later much developed by *Emiliani*), and to ideas on the origin of the Earth and life upon it. He believed that the Earth was formed by the cold accretion of mainly metallic particles, and that it had a primitive reducing atmosphere; and that the Moon was formed separately. Later work has given broad support for his views, developed by 1952; and the next year *Miller* in Urey's laboratory carried out successful experiments on the synthesis of organic compounds from an atmosphere on the Urey model. Urey won a Nobel Prize in 1934.

V

van't HOFF, Jacobus Henrikus
1852-1911

Dutch physical chemist: founder of stereo-chemistry

At the age of 17 van't Hoff told his mother and father, a physician, that he wished to become a chemist; their reaction was very unfavourable. Despite this, he entered Delft Polytechnic, and received his diploma in two years rather than the usual three. He went on to study chemistry in Leiden, Bonn, and Paris. He also became intensely interested in the philosophical ideas of Comte and Taine, in Byron's poetry, and in the biographies of scientists.

Back in the Netherlands, aged 22 and ready to begin his doctoral work, he published a paper which founded stereo-chemistry. It had been known since *Biot*'s work that many organic compounds are optically active (i.e., rotate the plane of polarized light). *Pasteur* had been able to relate this property, for crystalline solids, to the dissymmetry of the crystals; but interest in the organic compounds was on their optical activity in solution. Van't Hoff took up an idea of *Kekulé*'s (1867) that the four groups usually linked to a carbon atom can be expected to be equally distributed in the space around it (a 'tetrahedral' distribution; see diagram). Van't Hoff saw that if the four groups are all different from each other, they can be arranged about the carbon atom in two ways; and these two variants of a molecule are non-superimposable mirror images of each other (stereoisomers). He proposed that one form would rotate polarized light to the left, and the other form to the right. On this basis a general theory of molecular shapes could be developed; and despite some initial doubts, his ideas of stereo-isomerism were soon shown to be both correct and fruitful. The same ideas were offered independently by J. A. Le Bel soon after, but he did not develop them.

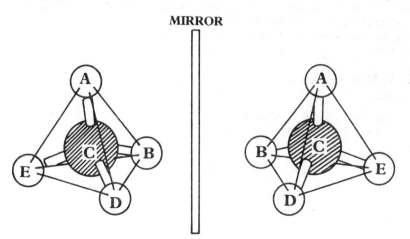

Four different atoms or groups (A, B, D, E) attached to a central carbon atom can be arranged in two different ways, which are non-superposable mirror images (the tetrahedra are imaginary)

Van Allen

At 23 van't Hoff tried for a job as a schoolteacher, but was turned down because he appeared to be a 'daydreamer'. He got a junior post in a veterinary college in 1876, but two years later took a professorship in Amsterdam until 1896, when he moved to Berlin. In the 1880s and later, his work on physical chemistry was as valuable as his stereochemistry. He studied reaction rates, mass action, transition points, the phase rule, and especially the chemistry of dilute solutions and the application of thermodynamic theory to chemistry. He was awarded the first Nobel Prize in chemistry, in 1901.

Van ALLEN, James Alfred

1914-

American physicist: discovered the magnetosphere (the Van Allen radiation belts)

Van Allen was educated at Iowa Wesleyan College and the University of Iowa. During the Second World War he served in the US Navy, helping to develop the radio proximity fuse for missiles and anti-aircraft shells. Afterwards he worked at Johns Hopkins University, and was appointed professor of physics at the University of Iowa in 1951.

Van Allen's scientific contributions have, to a large extent, reflected his war-time experiences with rocketry and miniaturized electronics. After the war, he used left-over German V-2 rockets to carry instruments to measure cosmic radiation into the upper atmosphere, and in 1958 put a *Geiger* radiation counter on the first American satellite, Explorer 1. This and later Explorer satellites revealed a region of high levels of radiation at a height of several hundred kilometres above the Earth. More detailed investigation has since shown that there are in fact two toroidal (doughnut-shaped) belts, which are created by charged particles (electrons and protons) from the Sun being trapped by the Earth's magnetic field. These **Van Allen radiation belts** constitute the Earth's magnetosphere.

Van de GRAAFF, Robert Jemison

1901-1967

American physicist: invented the Van de Graaff generator

Van de Graaff had a varied education, studying engineering at the university of Alabama, and physics at the Sorbonne and Oxford. On returning to America in 1929 he worked at Princeton and the Massachusetts Institute of Technology, becoming associate professor of physics at the latter in 1934.

Whilst a research student at Oxford, Van de Graaff realised that the conventional means of generating static electricity, the Wimshurst machine, could be greatly improved by storing the charge on a hollow metal sphere. In 1929 his first model of the **Van de Graaff generator** achieved potentials of up to 80 kV, and he subsequently built versions capable of generating millions of volts. The Van de Graaff generator has been an important tool in atomic and nuclear physics for accelerating charged particles, and in medical and industrial X-ray equipment where high voltages are required. In 1960 Van de Graaff resigned his post at MIT to become chief scientist at the High Voltage

James A. Van Allen: with a cosmic ray measurement payload for a small rocket to be launched from a balloon in the Arctic in 1952

384

Engineering Corporation, a company he had formed in 1946 to develop and market such devices.

van de HULST, Hendrik Christofell
1918-

Dutch astronomer: predicted interstellar 21-cm hydrogen emission

Educated in Utrecht and in the US, van de Hulst became director of the Leiden Observatory. In 1944 he suggested that interstellar hydrogen might be detectable at radio wavelengths, due to the 21-centimetre radiation emitted when the orbiting electron of a hydrogen atom flips between its two possible spin states. Due to the war it was not until 1951 that such emissions were first detected, by *Purcell* and H. Ewen. The technique has since proved invaluable in detecting neutral hydrogen in both our own and other galaxies, as well as in interstellar space. Since the 21-cm wavelength is not absorbed by interstellar dust, it has also enabled a much better picture of the centre of our galaxy to be built up where optical methods have failed.

van der WAALS, Johannes Diderik
1837-1923

Dutch physicist: devised equation of state for gases

Van der Waals, a carpenter's son, became a primary school teacher and a headmaster in The Hague. He trained for secondary-school work in 1866, and then studied physics at Leiden. His doctoral dissertation on the physics of gases appeared in 1873. His interest was directed to the observations of *T. Andrews* and others, who had shown that real gases deviate from the simple gas law, $pV=RT$, deduced from kinetic theory for an 'ideal' gas whose particles have no volume, and no attraction for one another. Real gases follow the law only approximately, and not at all at high pressures or low temperatures. Andrews also showed that a critical temperature exists, below which a real gas can be condensed to liquid only by pressure. Van der Waals devised a modified gas equation by introducing two new constants; a is related to intermolecular attraction, and b to the volume of the molecules themselves. The new equation of state has the form $(p+a/V^2)(V-b)=RT$, (again for one mole of gas) and with suitable values of a and b gives results in fairly good accord with observation for real gases over a range of temperatures above the critical point. He was professor of physics at Amsterdam from 1877, and was awarded the Nobel Prize for physics in 1910.

Van VLECK, John Hasbrouck
1899-1980

American physicist: major contributor to modern theories of magnetic systems

Van Vleck's father and grandfather were both eminent mathematicians. Van Vleck emerged from study at Wisconsin and Harvard to take up a post at Minnesota in 1923. He subsequently moved to Wisconsin and Harvard.

Van Vleck largely founded the modern theory of magnetism, taking *Dirac*'s quantum mechanics and working out the implications for the magnetic properties of atoms. In 1932 he published *The Theory of Electric and Magnetic Susceptibilities* which laid out the theory and which remains in use today as a classic text. In it the paramagnetic properties of atoms are discussed; the temperature-independent susceptibility is now called **Van Vleck paramagnetism**.

He also elucidated bonding in crystals and the usefulness of the crystal field and ligand field theories. These allow one to describe some features of atomic or ionic behaviour in a crystal. Furthermore, Van Vleck explained how local magnetic moment formation is assisted by electron correlation (the interaction between the motion of electrons). His wartime work resulted in showing how water and oxygen in the atmosphere give rise to absorption of radar signals.

Personally Van Vleck has been described as 'one of the few true gentlemen and scholars'; he was a quiet man with charm. In 1977 his pioneering research was recognized with a joint award of the Nobel Prize for physics.

VAUQUELIN, Louis Nicolas
1763-1829

French analytical chemist: discoverer of chromium and beryllium

As a boy Vauquelin worked in the fields with his peasant father; he did well at school, and at 14 was sent to work in an apothecary's shop, at first in Rouen and then in Paris. Soon the chemist A. F. de Fourcroy heard of his enthusiasm for chemistry and took him on as an assistant, and later as a friend and co-worker. Vauquelin rescued a Swiss soldier from a mob during the French Revolution, and as a result had to leave Paris in 1793; but he soon returned, and in 1809 he succeeded Fourcroy as professor there.

In 1797 he examined the rare, brilliant orange mineral, crocoite, and discovered in it a new metal which he named chromium. Crocoite is actually lead chromate, $PbCrO_4$, from which Vauquelin obtained Cr_2O_3, and by strongly heating this with charcoal secured the metal as a powder. The next year he studied specimens of the mineral beryl and emerald, sent to him by the mineralogist *Haüy* who suspected from their crystal forms that they are chemically identical. Vauquelin proved that this is correct, and that emerald owes its green colour to traces of chromium; both minerals are beryllium aluminosilicate. He realised that a new metal (beryllium) was present, which he was not able to isolate; this was achieved in 1828 by *Wöhler*. Vauquelin was also the first to isolate an amino acid; this was asparagine, which he got from asparagus.

VAVILOV, Nikolai Ivanovitch
1887-*c*.1942

Russian botanist and plant geneticist: pioneer of cross-breeding to improve crops

Trained in Moscow and with *Bateson* at the John Innes Horticultural Institute, at Merton in Surrey, Vavilov returned to Russia in 1914 and quickly rose to become, by 1920, director of the All Union Institute of Plant Industry, controlling over 400 research institutes in the USSR with 20000 staff by 1934. Between 1916 and 1933 he led plant-collecting expeditions all over the world, the intention being to conserve and use the valuable genetic resources in wild and cultivated plants on which crop improvement depends. He devised useful theories on where centres of genetic diversity are to be found by plant hunters. His programme was very successful, his collection of new plants reaching 250000 by 1940; it was the largest-scale enterprise of its kind and the model for later work of this sort. Vavilov supported the ideas in genetics due to *Mendel* and to *Morgan* and this was to prove fatal. The political botanist T. Lysenko, who had reverted to a Lamarckian view, resented his success; Vavilov was arrested in 1940 while plant collecting and sentenced to death after a five-minute trial. He died about two years later of starvation in a labour camp, an ironic fate for the man who did most to feed Russia during the war by improved agricultural methods. At present he is re-recognized in the USSR and the Vavilov Institute is currently named in his honour.

VENING MEINESZ, Felix Andries
1887-1966

Dutch geophysicist: pioneer of submarine gravity measurements

After graduating from the Technical University of Delft in 1910, Vening Meinesz worked on a gravity survey of the Netherlands. In 1927 he was appointed professor extraordinary of geodesy, cartography, and geophysics at Utrecht, and also professor of geophysics at Delft.

Gravity determinations can yield useful information about underlying geological structure, but very accurate measurements are necessary since the variation in gravity is small. However, for the majority of the Earth's surface, that covered by the oceans, the lack of a stable platform makes measurements by the conventional pendulum technique impossible. Vening Meinesz realised that a submarine might provide a sufficiently stable base and, with the assistance of the Dutch navy, he made the first marine gravity determinations in the Pacific in 1923. From the measurements made during a total of ten such voyages Vening Meinesz discovered a belt of negative gravity anomalies beneath the deep submarine trenches associated with island arcs. He correctly interpreted this as being due a subduction zone, i.e., a compressive down-buckling of the oceanic crust below the continental crust.

VERNIER, Pierre

c. 1580-1637

French mathematician and engineer: devised a precision measuring scale

Vernier was a military engineer in Spain. Requiring a very accurate method of measuring small distances for mapmaking, he devised in 1631 a precision scale, consisting of a moveable part with nine divisions which slid past a fixed part with ten divisions. By observing where the two marks on the two scales coincide most closely, this effectively adds another decimal place to the accuracy of the measurement. The method is a refinement of a multiple-scale device invented by the 16th century Portugese mathematician Pedro Nunez.

VESALIUS, Andreas

1514-1564

Belgian anatomist: founder of modern anatomy

A pharmacist's son, Vesalius studied medicine at Louvain, Paris and Padua. He did well, and was made professor of anatomy and surgery at Padua when he was 24. His first lectures were novel; he carried out dissections himself, instead of leaving this to an assistant while reading from a text book as was usual; and he used drawings to help his students. During the next four years, he was busy with his research on anatomy based on human dissection. His results were published in his book *On the Structure of the Human Body* (1543, the year in which *Copernicus*'s great book also appeared) which included descriptions and fine woodcuts, some by Vesalius and the rest made under his direction. The book set a completely new level of clarity and accuracy in anatomy, and made all earlier work outdated. Many structures are described in it and drawn for the first time (e.g., the thalamus) and the book also broke with tradition by its critical view of earlier work (e.g., Vesalius notes that he was unable to find a passage for blood between the ventricles of the heart, as *Galen* had assumed). At 29, with his master-work published, Vesalius became a court physician, at first to Charles V and then to Philip II of Spain. His research largely ceased. He found that Spanish doctors were Galenists, who were hostile and jealous, and he tried to recover his job in Padua. To leave Spain he needed Philip's permission, which he got by proposing a pilgrimage to Jerusalem. He probably got his job on the way to Jerusalem, but died on the return journey, in Greece.

VIÈTE, François

1540-1603

French mathematician: made many early contributions to algebra

Viète grew up in the Poitou region of

France, and in 1556 entered the University of Poitiers to study law. While practising law between 1560 and 1564 he took up cryptography and mathematics as hobbies; the former was useful when he moved to Paris in 1570 and became a court official to Charles IX. The persecution of the Huguenots forced him to go into hiding from 1584, and during this time he absorbed himself in mathematics and did work of historic importance.

After five years Henri IV succeeded Charles and Viète returned to the royal court. In the war against Spain, Viète broke the Spanish secret cipher, allowing intercepted dispatches between Philip II of Spain and his embassy to be deciphered. He was dismissed from the court in 1602 and died shortly afterwards.

Viète's mathematical research was in algebra, which he applied to solve geometrical problems. He used letters to denote constants as well as variables, and he introduced the terms 'coefficient' and 'negative'. Using algebraic methods he solved a problem that dated back to the Greek *Apollonius*, that of constructing a circle touching three given circles.

Viète published a systematic account of how to solve problems in plane and spherical trigonometry, making use of all six trigonometric functions for the first time. The cosine law for plane triangles and the law of tangents were included. He also discovered a new and elegant solution to the general cubic equation using trigonometric multiple-angle formulae. The familiar relations between the positive roots of an algebraic equation, its coefficients and the powers of the unknowns are also due to Viète. He always preferred to establish his identities and his proofs algebraically rather than geometrically, thereby setting a trend.

VINE, Frederick John
1939-1988

British geologist: co-discoverer of magnetic anomalies across mid-ocean ridges

After graduating from the University of Cambridge in 1965, Vine spent five years at Princeton before returning to England in 1970, becoming reader and later professor of environmental science at the University of East Anglia. In 1963, whilst a research student under the supervision of *Matthews*, Vine showed that the oceanic crust on either side of a mid-ocean ridge was remanently magnetized in alternately normal and reversed polarity in bands running parallel to the ridge. This, they argued, was consistent with the sea-floor spreading hypothesis proposed by *H. H. Hess* the year before, and was seen as powerful support for Hess's hypothesis (see Matthews).

VIRCHOW, Rudolf (Ludwig Carl)
1821-1902

German pathologist and anthropologist: founder of cellular pathology

Virchow graduated in medicine at Berlin, and then secured a junior post in Berlin's great hospital, the Charité. He was a skilful pathologist, who recognized leukaemia in 1845, and went on to study thrombosis, embolism, inflammation, and animal parasites. He was always politically active, and his liberal sympathies in the unrest of 1848 helped to lose him his Berlin post; but Würzburg gave him another, and seven years later he returned to Berlin as professor of pathological anatomy. He remained in politics, and as a Reichstag member opposed Bismarck so forcefully that the latter challenged him to a duel in 1865; Virchow managed to avoid this. In the 1850s Virchow took up *Schwann* and *Schleiden*'s cell theory with enthusiasm, and applied it to pathology; he saw disease as originating in cells, or as the response of cells to abnormal conditions. His ideas led to much fruitful work, aided by the improvements in microscopes after 1850 and the introduction of the microtome for making thin sections and dyes for selective staining. Modern pathology begins with him, and he became Germany's leading medical scientist.

Pasteur was his near-contemporary; however, Virchow did not enthuse over the germ theory of disease. He saw disease as a continuous change in the cells, rather than as a result only of an invasive agent (we now recognize diseases of both types, of course). Similarly he saw the theory of evolution as a hypothesis only, and voted against its inclusion in school biology.

He was an enthusiast for anthropology and archaeology and worked on the 1879 dig to discover the site of Troy. In practical politics, his efforts in public health in Berlin led to improved water and sewage purification.

VOLTA, (Count) Alessandro Giuseppe Anastasio

1745-1827

Italian physicist: inventor of the electric battery

Of an aristocratic family devoted to the Church, Volta held professorships at the universities of Como and Pavia, and after some political turbulence, became Rector of Pavia.

Following *Galvani*'s discovery in 1786 that an electric spark, or contact with copper and iron, caused a frog's leg to twitch, Volta became interested in finding the cause of the phenomenon. Experiment showed him that an electric current could be generated by bringing different metals into contact with one another, a phenomenon sometimes known as the **Volta effect**. In 1799 he succeeded in constructing a battery consisting of metal discs, alternately silver and zinc, with brine-soaked card between them. This voltaic pile produced a steady electric current, and was the first reliable source of electricity. As such it was to transform the study of the subject, and was invaluable to men such as Nicholson, *Davy* and *Faraday*. It also laid to rest the contemporary theory that animal tissue was somehow necessary for the generation of electricity. Volta himself was made a Count by Napoleon, and did little further

Alessandro Volta

work on the device. The SI unit of electric potential, the **volt (V)**, is named after him. If the work done in causing one coulomb of electric charge to flow between two points is one joule, then the potential difference between the points is one volt.

von BRAUN, Wernher Magnus Maximilian

1912-1977

German-American rocket engineer: pioneer of rocketry and space travel

The son of a baron and a former Government minister, von Braun was educated at the Zürich and Berlin Institutes of Technology. In 1932 he started working on rocket design for the German military, developing his first successful liquid-fuel rocket two years later. By 1938 he was technical head of the rocket research establishment at Peenemünde, where he was responsible for the V-2 supersonic ballistic missile used in World War II. At the end of the war he took his entire development team west in order to surrender to the American army. He subsequently became a major figure in the American space programme, designing the Jupiter rocket that put America's first satellite, Explorer I, into orbit in 1958, and being influential in the Saturn rocket that put the first man on the Moon in 1969. Von Braun resigned from NASA in 1972, feeling that the American Government was no longer strongly committed to space exploration.

von Humboldt, A. see Humboldt (Baron)

von KÁRMÁN, Theodore
1881-1963

Hungarian-American physicist: discovered Kármán vortices

Von Kármán was educated at the Budapest Royal Polytechnic University and at the University of Göttingen. He subsequently became director of the Aachen Institute, and of the Guggenheim Aeronautical Laboratory of the California Institute of Technology; he was instrumental in setting up the Jet Propulsion Laboratory at CalTech, and was a leading figure in a number of international scientific organizations.

An outstanding theoretical aerodynamicist, von Kármán discovered the two rows of vortices generated by fluid flow around a cylinder, known as **Kármán vortices**, and together forming a **Kármán vortex street**. Kármán vortices are important factors in aerodynamics, as they can create destructive vibrations. His work, which also included long-range ballistic missiles, aerofoil profiles, jet-assisted take-off, and many other aspects of flight, was instrumental in enabling the US to become a world leader in the aerospace industry.

von KLITZING, Klaus
1943-

German physicist: discovered the quantum Hall effect

Von Klitzing was born in Schroda/Posen, and studied at Braunschweig and Würzburg. He became a professor at Munich in 1980, and in 1985 Director of the Max Planck Institute, Stuttgart. In 1977 he presented a paper on two-dimensional electronic behaviour in which the quantum Hall effect was clearly seen. However few realised the significance of the measurements, and it was only when working one night at the high magnetic field laboratory in Grenoble in 1980 that von Klitzing appreciated what had occurred.

An electronic gas that is confined into a flat layer can be made by depositing a very thin layer of semiconductor upon a base material. Under a magnetic field electrons will perform circular orbits, with only particular energy states allowed (called *Landau* levels). At certain values of the field the Landau levels become filled and the conductivity and resistivity fall to zero. Kawaji had put forward a theory that the (Hall) resistance under such conditions should rise in units of h/e^2; von Klitzing realised that the resistance did rise in steps and accurately obeyed this condition. He had discovered the quantum Hall effect, and for this won the 1985 Nobel Prize for physics.

von LAUE, Max (Theodor Felix)
1879-1960

German physicist: suggested experiment to show diffraction of X-rays by atoms in crystals

Von Laue was a student of physics at four German universities, and was also an art student for two years; then he taught physics in four universities before settling in Berlin in 1919. He was to be professor of theoretical physics there until 1943, when his antagonism to the racist policy of the National Socialist party led him to resign. From 1946 he worked to rebuild German science; he was killed in a car accident, aged 81. His early work on optics gave support for *Einstein*'s relativity theory, but he is now best known for his work with X-rays.

It had been suggested that X-rays were electromagnetic waves like light but of very short wavelength, although some physicists thought otherwise. It was also believed that the atoms in crystals were in regular array, in accord with their external regularity. Von Laue realised that if both these ideas were true, then the spacing between layers of atoms in a crystal should be of the order of size (10^{-10} m) to bring about diffraction of X-rays. In 1912 he tested this idea; his technician W. Friedrich and a student, P. Knipping, passed a narrow beam of X-rays through a crystal of $CuSO_4 \cdot 5H_2O$ and obtained a diffraction pattern of spots on a photographic film placed behind it; a crystal of ZnS served even better. The experiment proved the wave-nature of X-rays, and also gave the basis on which the *Braggs* later created X-ray crystallography. Von Laue was awarded a Nobel Prize in 1914.

von NEUMANN, John (János)
1903-1957

Hungarian-American mathematician: suggested the concept of the stored-program computer

Born in Budapest the son of a Jewish banker, von Neumann was a mathematical prodigy as a child, and later became one of the most eminent mathematicians of his day. Educated at the universities of Budapest, Berlin and Göttingen, he moved to America in 1930.

Von Neumann is principally remembered for his contributions, during and after World War II, to the development of electronic computers. He is widely credited with the concept of the 'stored-program computer', whose two essential components are a memory in which to store information, and a control unit capable of organizing the transfers between the different 'registers' in memory in accordance with a program also stored in memory. All modern computers work on this principle, and are sometimes called **'von Neumann machines'**. The credit for the work (which was carried out in wartime secrecy), is now recognized not to be entirely his, however, and ought more properly to be shared with others in the development team.

He also participated in the American atomic bomb project (the Manhattan Project), and together with J. L. Tuck developed the 'high explosive lens' that was essential to its success. Apart from his wartime work he made many other contributions to mathematics, in particular to game theory, of which he was a pioneer, adapting it to real-life strategic situations including military applications. In later years he became a leading proponent of nuclear power.

W

WAKSMAN, Selman (Abraham)
1888-1973

Russian-American biochemist: isolated the antibiotic streptomycin and demonstrated its effectiveness against tuberculosis

Waksman had a difficult time as a young Jewish boy in the Ukraine, and was glad to emigrate to the US in 1910; he worked his way through his agriculture course at Rutgers College, did his PhD in California in biochemistry and returned to Rutgers, becoming professor of soil biology in 1930.

From 1939 Waksman began a systematic search for antibiotics from soil organisms. He had rich experience of such organisms, and in 1943 he isolated the new antibiotic, streptomycin, from the soil organism *Streptomyces griseius* (which he had discovered in 1915). This is active against the human tubercle bacillus and, mixed with two other compounds, it became widely used in treatment. Previously there had been no effective drug for this major killing disease, but by its use tuberculosis became a problem which had largely been solved in developed countries by the 1970s. Waksman won a Nobel Prize in 1952. He and his co-workers found a number of other antibiotics in soil organisms, including neomycin, valuable in intestinal surgery.

WALDEYER-HARTZ, Wilhelm
1839-1921

German medical scientist: gave first modern description of cancer

After studying science and mathematics, Waldeyer (as he was usually known) graduated in medicine and later taught physiology and anatomy; he moved to Berlin in 1883 and soon made his institute famous. He first used haematoxylin as a histological stain; introduced the name 'chromosome' for the rods seen in cell nuclei and which are readily stained; and he coined the name 'neuron' in neurology. His anatomical work included a description of the lymphoid tissue of the throat (the faucial and pharyngeal tonsils) known as **Waldeyer's ring**.

In 1863 he gave an account of the genesis and spread of cancer in essentially modern terms. He classified the types of cancer, and concluded that cancer begins in a single cell and may spread to other parts of the body by cells migrating from the original site through the blood or lymphatic system (**metastasis**). This implied that removal of the initial cancerous cells at an early stage could effect a cure, in contrast with the view that cancer is a generalized attack on the body and treatment is useless. This approach to oncology (the study of tumours in the animal body) became of great value when radiotherapy, and later chemotherapy were available as well as surgery in the treatment of cancerous growths.

WALLACE, Alfred Russel
1823-1913

English naturalist: developed theory of evolution independently of Darwin

Wallace left school at 14 and after a period as a surveyor became a teacher at a school in Leicester, where he met the amateur naturalist H. W. Bates. The two developed a passion for collecting, especially insects and butterflies, and inspired by *Darwin*'s account of his travels, they set out on a collecting expedition in tropical South America. After many adventures Wallace started to return to the UK, intending to sell specimens to finance their travels, but his ship was destroyed by fire at sea, with most of his specimens and records. Undeterred, he went to Malaya in 1854 on a similar expedition, and while there wrote up his ideas on species and evolution. Like Darwin, he was convinced that plant and animal species were not fixed, but show variation over time. He concluded that 'we have progression and continued divergence' of organisms, and with no knowledge that Darwin had closely similar ideas, he decided that competition and differential survival determined the path of evolution. He sent his ideas to Darwin, whose friends arranged concurrent publication in 1858; no conflict over priority occurred, the two were on the best of terms, and Wallace became by his own wish the secondary figure and a leading advocate for 'Darwinism'.

Wallace's career continued on rather mixed lines. He became an enthusiast for spiritualism, socialism, and women's rights, and he was also a founder of zoogeography; he recognized that there are some half-dozen regions each with characteristic fauna, whose separation could be linked with the geology and geography of the regions. **Wallace's line** is an imaginary line dividing the oriental fauna from the Australian fauna, and passing between the Malayan islands.

WALLIS, (Sir) Barnes Neville

1887-1979

British engineer: inventor of the 'bouncing' bomb and the geodetic lattice

Wallis was trained as a marine engineer but he spent most of his professional life at Vickers Ltd. in aeronautical design, joining them in 1913. After World War II he led their aeronautical research and development department.

Wallis's reputation is based on diverse and brilliant inventions of great practical application. He designed a very successful airship, the R100, and the geodetic lattice (a triangular lattice of great strength, which he applied to buildings and aircraft wings), which led to the Wellington bomber. This was the dominant British bomber of World War II and over 11000 were built. His most famous invention, however, was the 'bouncing' bomb, developed to enable the RAF to destroy the Möhne and Eder dams in 1943. After the war he continued to work on aircraft design, developing the principles of the swing-wing aircraft, employed in the Tornado fighter.

WALLIS, John

1616-1703

English mathematician: devised expression for π as infinite series

Wallis had a curious career. A member of a fairly wealthy family, he studied medicine and philosophy at Cambridge, was ordained in 1640 and became a private chaplain. Then in 1649 Cromwell made him Professor of Geometry at Oxford; he already had some reputation as a mathematician, but his work in deciphering intercepted letters for the Parliamentarians in the Civil War was probably more

John Wallis

influential. From about this time he began to meet with *Boyle* and others to discuss science, and these meetings led to the formation of the Royal Society in 1660 with Wallis as a founder-member.

His book *Arithmetica Infinitorum* (1655) made him famous; it is mainly concerned with series, theory of numbers, and conics, discusses infinities (he invented the symbol ∞) and includes the curious formula for $4/\pi = 3 \times 3 \times 5 \times 5 \times 7 \times 7 \ldots /2 \times 4 \times 4 \times 6 \times 6 \times \ldots$ He went on to write impressive books on mechanics and on algebra. His job continued after the Restoration and Charles II even made him a royal chaplain (he had always been a royalist, and had joined a protest against the execution of Charles I).

As well as being one of the century's leading mathematicians he wrote on a variety of subjects, and had some success in teaching deaf-mutes to speak. He was remarkably quarrelsome (he maintained a public dispute with the philosopher Hobbes for over 25 years) and the biographer Aubrey claims he was a plagiarist and that he was 'extremely greedy of glorie'.

WANKEL, Felix
1902-1988

German engineer: inventor of the Wankel rotary engine

Two types of internal combustion engine have dominated road transport; they use either the *Otto* cycle, or the compression ignition system devised by *Diesel*. Both have the inherent defect of requiring the linear reciprocating motion of a piston to be converted into circular motion, with resultant stress and limitations.

Wankel was born in the Black Forest, the son of a ranger. He never attended university, but he showed skill in engineering mathematics and an obsessive interest in vehicle propulsion; but his work on a novel engine was delayed by employment in aircraft development before World War II and later by being a prisoner of the French.

From 1929 he had in mind a novel engine using hydrocarbon fuel, and eventually made a prototype in the 1960s. The Wankel rotary engine has an approximately triangular central rotor, geared to a driving shaft, and turning in a close-fitting oval-shaped chamber so that the power stroke is applied to the three faces of the rotor in turn as they pass a single spark plug. The German car maker NSU used the engine in its RO 80 luxury saloon in the 1960s, but it showed problems of high fuel consumption and exhaust pollution; Mazda used it in sports cars in the 1980s, as have high performance motorcycle makers. Wider use of the Wankel engine is clearly possible if the above problems are fully solved; it remains the most radical innovation in its field since the familiar reciprocating internal combustion engine was developed in the 19th century.

WARBURG, Otto (Heinrich)
1883-1970

German biochemist: had an important influence on biochemistry through applying chemical techniques

Warburg was an enormously influential biochemist; his use of chemical methods to attack biological problems led him to ideas and techniques which were widely imitated, and his pupils dominated biochemistry for a generation. He first studied chemistry, at Berlin under *E. Fischer*, and then medicine at Heidelberg, qualifying in 1911. Except for the years of World War I, when he served in the Prussian Horse Guards, his life was spent in Berlin, where he headed the Max Planck Institute for Cell Physiology until he retired at 86.

Much of his work was on intracellular respiration, and from 1923 he used the **Warburg manometer** (or respirometer) in which very thin tissue slices are incubated with a buffered nutrient, and their uptake of oxygen is measured by the fall in pressure. With this he studied both normal cellular respiration and model systems, and the action of enzyme poisons (such as cyanide) and catalytic metals such as iron, and the activity of cancerous cells. From his work and that of his students (who included *Meyerhof* and *Krebs*) much information emerged on cell chemistry, enzyme action, co-enzymes and the function of nicotinamide adenine dinucleotide (NAD), cancerous cells, and photosynthesis in plant cells. He was an early user of spectroscopy as an invaluable aid to biochemical analysis. Awarded a Nobel Prize in 1931, his later career was marred by his increasingly intolerant attitude to ideas other than his own, which eventually isolated him.

WASSERMANN, August von
1866-1925

German immunologist: devised the Wassermann test for syphilis

Wassermann studied medicine in Germany, graduated in 1888, was an assistant to *Koch* and in 1910 became head of a new Institute for Experimental Therapy at Berlin-Dahlem. In 1906 he and his group devised a test for the presence of syphilitic infection at any past time in an individual's life; this **Wassermann reaction** was formerly widely used.

WATSON-WATT, (Sir) Robert Alexander
1892-1973

British physicist: pioneer of radar

Watson-Watt was educated at University College, Dundee, concentrating on physics. He remained there as assistant to the professor of natural philosophy, before joining the Meteorological Office in 1915. He subsequently became head of the radio department of the National Physical Laboratory at Teddington.

During World War I, Watson-Watt worked on the radio location of thunderstorms (detecting the radio pulses pro-

duced by lightning discharges), and developed a system capable of detecting storms several hundred miles away. In 1921 he became superintendent of the radio research station at Ditton Park, near Slough, and in 1935 proposed the development of a radio detection and ranging (RADAR) system for aircraft location. Powerful bursts of radio energy at a frequency of about 30 GHz and a duration of 10^{-5} s were transmitted, and any reflections from aircraft were detected and displayed with an oscilloscope. The time delay between transmission and receipt of the echo gave the distance to the aircraft, and the direction from which the signal was received yielded its position. Under his direction, E. G. Bowen and A. F. Wilkins quickly developed equipment capable of detecting aircraft at a range of 130 km. By the beginning of World War II a network of radar stations was in place along Britain's channel coasts, and proved to be crucial in the country's defence. Portable radar sets were soon fitted to fighter aircraft to help them locate their targets in cloud or at night.

It has to be said that Watson-Watt did not invent radar; the basic principle of the reflection of radio waves had been known for some years, but it was his foresight and direction, coupled with the demand created for such a system by wartime, that produced a working system. He led the successful team, and he led the group of seven who successfully claimed the money for the invention of radar after World War II. He was elected an FRS in 1941, and knighted in 1942. Today, radar systems are used for navigation, the safe routing of air traffic and shipping, rainfall detection, and many other non-military applications.

WATT, James
1736-1819

Scottish instrument maker and engineer: invented the modern steam engine

The son of a Clydeside shipbuilder, Watt had little formal education because of his poor health, but set up in business as an instrument maker. Whilst repairing a working model of a Newcomen steam engine, Watt realised that its efficiency could be greatly improved by adding a separate condenser, preventing the loss of energy through steam condensing to water in the cylinder. He formed a business partnership to develop the idea, improved the engine in several other ways, and in 1790 produced the Watt engine, which became crucial to the success of the industrial revolution. Soon it was being used to pump water out of mines, and to power machinery in flour, cotton and paper mills. Watt retired, a very rich man, in 1800. The SI unit of power, the **watt (W)**, is named after him; it is the power producing energy at the rate of 1 J s^{-1}.

WEGENER, Alfred Lothar

1880-1930

German meteorologist and geophysicist: proposed theory of continental drift

Educated at the universities of Heidelberg, Innsbruck and Berlin, Wegener obtained his doctorate in astronomy in 1905. Although primarily a meteorologist, Wegener is remembered for his theory of continental drift, which he proposed in 1912. Unable to reconcile palaeoclimatic evidence with the present position of the continents, he suggested that there had originally been a single 'supercontinent', which he termed Pangaea. He then provided a number of arguments to support his hypothesis that Pangaea had broken up in Mesozoic times (about 200 million years ago), and that continental drift had subsequently led to the present continental arrangement. Initially Wegener's ideas met with great hostility, largely due to the lack of any obvious driving mechanism for the movement of the continents, but the suggestion of a viable mechanism by *Holmes* in 1929, together with geo-

magnetic and oceanographic evidence obtained during the late 1950s and early 1960s, has since established plate tectonics as one of the major tenets of modern geophysics. Wegener went on several expeditions to Greenland, and it was whilst crossing the ice sheet on his fourth visit that he died.

WEIERSTRASS, Karl Wilhelm Theodor

1815-1897

German mathematician: introduced rigour into mathematical analysis

Pressed by his overbearing father, a customs officer, to study law, Weierstrass spent four unsuccessful years at Bonn, learning little law but becoming a skilful fencer and reading mathematics. Emerging in disgrace, he was sent to Münster to prepare for the state teacher's examination, and had the good fortune to be able to pursue mathematics under the guidance of C. Gudermann, whose enthusiasm at that time was that power series could be used as a rigorous basis for mathematical analysis.

Weierstrass developed this approach during his stint of nearly 15 years as a teacher in the small Prussian villages of Deutsch-Krone and Braunsberg, completely isolated from contemporary mathematical research. In 1854 he published a paper on Abelian integrals in Crelle's *Journal*, which he had written 14 years earlier. The quality and importance of this work, which completed areas that *Abel* and *Jacobi* had begun, was immediately recognized, and he was appointed a professor at the Royal Polytechnic School and lecturer at the University of Berlin in 1856.

The significance of Weierstrass's work was that he gave the first rigorous definitions of the fundamental concepts of analysis; for example a function, derivative, limit, differentiability and convergence. He investigated under what conditions a power series would converge, and how to test for this. Above all, he made great contributions to function theory and Abelian functions.

WEINBERG, Steven

1933-

American physicist: produced a unified theory of electromagnetism and the weak nuclear interaction

The son of a New York court stenographer, Weinberg was educated at Cornell and Princeton universities. He held appointments at Columbia, Berkeley, the Massachusetts Institute of Technology and Harvard before becoming professor of physics at Texas (1986).

In 1967 Weinberg produced a gauge theory (i.e., one involving changes of reference frame) that correctly predicted both electromagnetic and weak nuclear forces (such as are involved in nuclear decay) despite the two differing in strength by a factor of about 10^{10}. The theory also predicted a new interaction due to 'neutral currents', whereby a chargeless particle is exchanged giving rise to a force between particles. This was duly observed in 1973, giving strong support to the theory (now called the **Weinberg-Salam theory**). As the work was independently developed by Weinberg and *Salam*, and subsequently extended by *Glashow*, all three shared the 1979 Nobel Prize for physics.

WEISMANN, August

1834-1914

German biologist: devised theory of germ-plasm

Weismann qualified in medicine and practised for a few years before the attractions of biological research drew him to university teaching in Freiburg, a town which he greatly liked. He was a skilled microscopist, but failing sight

from 1864 eventually pushed him to become a theorist, with a special interest in heredity. Basing his ideas in part on his earlier work on the sex cells of hydrozoa, he proposed that all organisms contain a germ plasm, which he later located in what are now called the chromosomes. He saw the major events in reproduction as the halving of the chromosome number in germ-cell formation, and in the later union of chromosomes from two individuals; he suggested that variability resulted from the combination of different chromosomes. His ideas are of course broadly correct, and it is surprising that he was able in the 1880s to get so near the modern view. He was wrong in his belief that the germ plasm is unalterable and immune to environmental effects, as others were later to demonstrate.

WEIZSÄCKER, (Baron) Carl Friedrich von

1912-

German physicist: proposed theories for stellar energy generation, and for the origin of the solar system

Weizsäcker studied and later taught physics at both Berlin and Leipzig; from 1957 he was professor of philosophy at Hamburg. Independently of *Bethe* he suggested in 1938 that the energy of stars is generated by a catalytic cycle of nuclear fusion reactions, whereby hydrogen atoms are converted into helium with much evolution of energy. Then in 1944 he proposed a scheme for the origin of the solar system; this scheme developed the older ideas of *Laplace* that the Sun had been surrounded by a disc of gas, which rotated, became turbulent and aggregated to form the planets. Weizsäcker's theory (like Laplace's) failed to account for the angular momentum of the solar system, but it was developed by *Alfvén* and then by *Hoyle*, who proposed that the Sun's magnetic field could generate the required momentum.

WERNER, Alfred
1866-1919

German-Swiss inorganic chemist: founded modern theory of co-ordination compounds

Werner was born in Alsace; it was French when he was born, became German when he was four, and French again in 1919. Werner had allegiances to both French and German culture; he usually wrote in German. He lived in Switzerland from the age of 20, graduating at Zürich, and held a professorship there from 1895 until his death.

From 1892 he worked on the inorganic complexes of metals. This large class of chemical compounds had seemed confused; the sort of structure theory which had served well in organic chemistry did not appear to apply, and neither did ordinary valence rules. Werner brought a new view to them. He proposed that the central atom (usually a transition metal atom) had its normal valence, and also secondary valences which bonded it to other atoms, groups or molecules (collectively, 'ligands') arranged in space around it. This **theory of co-ordination complexes** allowed 2 to 9 ligands to be co-ordinated to the central atom; the commonest co-ordination number is 6, with the ligands arranged octahedrally. During 20 years, Werner worked out the consequences of this theory extensively, and rejuvenated inorganic chemistry as a result. Metal complexes are of great importance also in plant and animal biochemistry.

WERNER, Abraham Gottlob
1749-1817

German mineralogist and geologist: proposed Neptunist theory of geology

Werner came from a traditional mining area, and was educated at the Freiberg Mining Academy and the University of Leipzig, returning to Freiberg in 1775 as a lecturer. He is remembered for his **Neptunist theory** of the origin of the Earth, which was widely accepted for much of the 18th century. He proposed that all rocks were precipitated as sediments or chemical precipitates in a universal ocean created by the biblical Flood, and that all geological strata thus followed a universal and specific sequence. The lowest layer contained 'primitive' rocks such as granites and slates, the next higher layer included shales and fossilized fish, then followed limestones, sandstones and chalks, and finally alluvial clays and gravels. Although such a scheme fitted moderately well with the geology around Freiberg, increased knowledge of the geology of other parts of Europe revealed the flaws in his ideas, and the acceptance in its place of *Hutton*'s uniformitarian theory.

WEYL, Hermann
1885-1955

German mathematician: contributed to study of symmetry, topological spaces and Riemannian geometry

Weyl was a student under *Hilbert* at Göttingen, and on becoming a Privatdozent there, also worked with him. In 1913 he declined a professorship at Göttingen and moved to Zürich, where he worked with *Einstein*. He returned to take up the professorship when Hilbert retired in 1930, but increasing Nazi power led him to move to Princeton with *Gödel* and Einstein, retiring in 1951. As well as his outstanding mathematical work, Weyl published on philosophy, logic and the history of mathematics.

Weyl acquired from Hilbert research interests in group theory and Hilbert space and operators. Once developed, these techniques proved central to the rapidly evolving theory of quantum mechanics and the unification of matrix mechanics and wave mechanics. Weyl showed how symmetry relates to group theory and continuous groups, and how this can be a powerful tool in solving quantum mechanical problems.

When Weyl moved to Zürich, Einstein interested him in the mathematics of relativity and Riemannian geometry. In seeking to generalize this, Weyl developed the geometry of affinely connected spaces and differential geometry. Weyl anticipated the non-conservation of parity in particles, a feature that has since been observed by particle physicists working with leptons.

Weyl produced a small number of highly influential papers on number theory, proving results on the equidistribution of sequences of real numbers modulo 1. This was taken up in later work by *Hardy* and J. E. Littlewood.

WHEATSTONE, (Sir) Charles

1802-1875

British physicist: contributor to cable telegraphy

Wheatstone was privately educated, and started work in the family tradition as a maker of musical instruments. In 1834 he was appointed professor of experimental physics at King's College, London.

Much of Wheatstone's early work was concerned with acoustics and the theory of resonance of columns of air. This led him to a wider interest in physics, particularly optics and electricity. He was a prodigious inventor, and in 1838 invented a stereoscope in which two pictures of slightly differing angles of perspective could be combined to give an impression of three-dimensional solidity. In 1837 he collaborated with W. F. Cooke on a commercial electric telegraph project, which was a great success, with thousands of miles of telegraph lines being constructed. Wheatstone was responsible for several related inventions, such as the printing telegraph and the single-needle telegraph. He popularized (but did not invent) the **Wheatstone bridge**, a device invented by S. Christie and utilizing *Ohm*'s law for comparing resistance.

WHIPPLE, Fred Lawrence

1906-

American astronomer: proposed 'dirty snowball' model for comets

Whipple had a distinguished career in astronomy in California and Harvard. In 1950 he proposed that cometary nuclei consist of a mixture of water ice and dust, frozen carbon dioxide, methane and ammonia. This model, known as the 'dirty snowball' model, accounts for the fact that comets only develop their characteristic tails as they approach the Sun, when the solar wind vapourizes the volatile components in the nucleus. Radiation pressure is then responsible for the fact that the tail always points away from the Sun. Another feature of comets, their slight variability of orbital period, was also explained by the formation of an evaporated surface crust, through which jets of volatile material are sometimes ejected. Whipple's ideas were largely confirmed by observations made from space probes during the last visit of *Halley*'s Comet in 1986.

WHIPPLE, George Hoyt

1878-1976

American medical scientist

From his medical student days at Johns Hopkins, Whipple was particularly interested in the oxygen carrying pigment of red blood cells (haemoglobin) and in the bile pigments which are formed in the body from haemoglobin. Working in the University of California from 1914 to 1922, he examined the effect of diet on haemoglobin formation. To do this he bled dogs until their haemoglobin level was reduced to a third of normal, and then studied the rate of red cell regeneration when the dogs were fed various diets; he found that meat, kidney and especially liver were effective in stimulating recovery. Since the fatal human disease of pernicious anaemia is associated with red cell deficiency, it was reasonable to attempt to treat it similarly, and G. Minot and W. Murphy found in 1926 that large additions of near-raw liver in the patients diet were effective: Minot, Murphy and Whipple shared a Nobel prize in 1934. It was another twenty years before other workers isolated the active curative compound, vitamin B_{12}, and made it available for treatment and study.

Whipple spent the rest of his career at the University of Rochester, continuing to work on blood and especially on thalassaemia, a genetic anaemia due to a defect in the haemoglobin molecule, and found especially in Mediterranean races.

WHITE, Gilbert

1720-1793

English naturalist: author of first English classic on natural history

White's enthusiasm for all kinds of natural history was remarkable. He followed a family tradition by becoming a curate, and living in the family home 'The Wakes' at Selborne in Hampshire. He declined more senior posts in order to stay there, so that he could study nature in his large garden and the nearby countryside. His accounts of this were shared with friends in his letters to them; shortly before his death the diffident White was at last persuaded to edit 110 of his letters to form *The Natural History and Antiquities of Selborne*. The book so pleased its many readers that it has been in print ever since. White's keenest interest was in birds, whose song and habits he studied; other ornithologists at that time interested themselves only in plumage and anatomy. He studied mammals, bats, reptiles (especially his pet tortoise, Timothy), insects, plants and the weather. His observations gave some evidence for *Darwin*'s theory of evolution, but its main value has been to provide pleasure and inspiration to generations of naturalists. As one zoologist wrote in 1901: 'White is interesting because nature is interesting; his descriptions are founded upon natural fact, exactly observed and sagaciously interpreted'.

WHITTLE, (Sir) Frank

1907-

British aeronautical engineer: invented the jet engine

After entering the Royal Air Force as a boy apprentice, Whittle qualified as a pilot at Cranwell College and studied engineering at Cambridge. He served as a test pilot with the RAF, later working as a consultant for a number of companies. In 1977 he became research professor at the US Naval Academy, Annapolis.

Whittle's principal claim to fame has been the invention of the turbojet aircraft engine, on which he took out his first patent in 1930 while still a student. In 1936 he formed his own company to develop the concept, and in 1941 a Gloster aircraft with his engine made its first test flight. Due to the war development was rapid, and the Gloster was in service with the RAF by 1944.

WIELAND, Heinrich Otto

1877-1957

German organic chemist: carried out important work on the structure of cholesterol and other steroids

The son of a gold refinery chemist, Wieland studied and taught in several German universities before succeeding *Willstätter* at Munich in 1925. His early work was on organic compounds of nitrogen, including the fulminates; and in 1911 he made the first nitrogen free radicals. He also worked on natural products; plant alkaloids, butterfly-wing pigments (pterins), and especially the steroids. In steroid chemistry, he showed that three bile acids can all be converted into cholanic acid, which he also made from cholesterol. It therefore followed that the bile acids and cholesterol had the same carbon skeleton, and Wieland proposed a structure for this parent steroid skeleton. His first structure was shown to be incorrect, but a revised version which he and others produced in 1932 is correct.

For his steroid work he was awarded the 1927 Nobel Prize. His other work included studies on toad venom, on curare, and on biological oxidation (which he showed is often, in fact, dehydrogenation).

WIEN, Wilhelm
1864-1928

German physicist: discovered the energy distribution formula for black body radiation

Wien grew up in a farming family, and originally planned to spend his life farming. He studied briefly at Göttingen and continued his degree work at Berlin from 1884. In 1886 Wien received his doctorate for research on light diffraction and associated absorption effects, and returned to manage his parent's farm. A severe drought four years later forced the sale of the farm, and he became assistant to *Helmholtz* in Berlin. In 1900 he took up the professorship at Würzburg and after 20 years he was appointed as *Roentgen*'s successor at Munich.

In 1892 Wien began research on thermal (or black body) radiation (see *Boltzmann*) a study which initiated the transition from classical physics to *Planck*'s quantum theory. Wien showed that the wavelength λ, at which a black body radiation source at absolute temperature T emits maximum energy, obeys a law: $\lambda T = constant = 0.29$ cm K (the constant was measured by *Lummer* and *Pringsheim*). This is known as **Wien's displacement law**: in accord with it a red-hot black body on further heating emits shorter wavelength radiation and becomes white hot, as the wavelength of maximum radiation shifts from the long (red) end to the centre of the visible spectrum.

Developing this, in 1896 he produced **Wien's formula** describing the distribution of energy in a radiation spectrum as a function of wavelength and temperature. It was based on an assumption that a hot body consists of a large number of oscillators emitting radiation of all possible frequencies and all in thermal equilibrium. Interestingly, Wien's formula is well obeyed at short wavelengths but is clearly wrong for longer values, whilst *Rayleigh* produced a formula accurate at longer wavelengths but not at lower ones.

Planck gave much thought to these discrepancies, and showed that if one assumed that radiation could be emitted only in 'packets' of a minimum energy (which he called quanta), then a radiation law could be calculated which was obeyed accurately at all wavelengths. Planck published his quantum theory in 1900, aware that its assumptions had no justification in classical physics, and yet as they appeared correct, a major revolution in physical science was inevitable. Wien was awarded the Nobel Prize for physics in 1911.

WIENER, Norbert
1894-1964

American mathematician: established the subject of cybernetics

As a child Wiener showed his mathematical talent early, but his career then became erratic. At 15 he entered Harvard to study zoology; changed to philosophy at Cornell; and got a PhD from Harvard in mathematics at 19. He then studied logic briefly under B. Russell and *Hilbert*. Suffering from too rapid an education, Wiener drifted through such activities as journalism and writing encyclopedia entries before recovering his sense of purpose and obtaining a post in mathematics at Massachusetts Institute of Technology in 1919. He held this position until retirement.

Wiener began research on stochastic, or random, processes such as Brownian motion, including work on statistical mechanics and ergodic theory (which is concerned with the onset of chaos in a system). Other areas that he advanced were integral equations, of a kind now known as **Wiener integrals**, quantum theory and potential theory. As part of his war work, Wiener applied statistical methods to control and communication engineering. Extending this broadly, for example into neurophysiology, computer design and biochemical regulation, led to his founding of cybernetics as a subject. Cybernetics is the study of control and communications in complex electronic systems and in animals, especially humans.

His standing as a mathematician is hardly disputed, but his writings are hard to read and uneven in quality. As a person he was extraordinary; small, plump, myopic, playful and self-praising, he spoke many languages and was hard to understand in any of them. He was a famously bad lecturer, perhaps because his mind worked in a very unusual way.

WIGNER, Eugene Paul

1902-

Hungarian-American physicist: applied group theory to quantum mechanics and discovered parity conservation in nuclear reactions

Wigner was the son of a businessman, and took his doctorate in engineering at the Berlin Institute of Technology in 1925. He moved to Princeton in 1930 and became professor of theoretical physics there in 1938, and held this post until his retirement in 1971. He was a brother-in-law of *Dirac*.

He made major contributions in quantum theory and nuclear physics, in particular by showing the value of symmetry concepts and the methods of group theory applied to physics. In 1927 he concluded that parity is conserved in a nuclear reaction: the laws of physics should not distinguish between right and left; or between positive and negative time. As a consequence a nuclear reaction between particles and the mirror image of those particles will be identical, and this was accepted to apply to all types of reaction. However, very surprisingly *Lee* and *Ting*

identified a class of exceptions to this law of parity conservation in 1958. Reactions involving the weak nuclear force, such as beta decay when an electron is emitted from a nucleus, do not conserve parity.

Wigner's research during the 1930s mainly concerned neutrons, and he investigated the strong nuclear interaction which binds neutrons and protons in the nucleus. He showed that the force has a very short range and does not involve electrical charge. The formula describing how moving neutrons interact with a stationary nucleus was given by *Breit* and Wigner in 1936. Using this and other discoveries, Wigner assisted *Fermi* in constructing the first nuclear reactor to produce a sustained nuclear chain reaction in Chicago in 1942. For his contributions to quantum theory and applying it to nuclear physics Wigner shared the 1963 Nobel Prize for physics.

WILKES, Maurice Vincent

1913-

British mathematician and computer scientist: designed the first delay storage computer

Wilkes was educated at Cambridge, subsequently taking positions there as lecturer and director of the Mathematical Laboratory, and head of the Computer Laboratory.

After wartime work on radar and operational research, Wilkes worked on the early development of computers, leading the team which built EDSAC (Electronic Delay Storage Automatic Calculator), the first machine to use delay lines to store information. The delay lines were mercury-filled tubes with piezoelectric crystals at either end; incoming signals generated a pressure pulse which was transmitted through the mercury to the second crystal, where it was converted back into an electrical impulse. Several such devices and suitable amplification allowed an electrical signal to be stored indefinitely, an essential requirement of a computer 'memory'. EDSAC ran its first program in 1949, and was a milestone in the development of computers. Wilkes has continued to play a leading role in their development.

WILKINSON, (Sir) Geoffrey
1921-

English inorganic chemist: carried out important work on the structure of metallocene compounds and transition metal complexes

Wilkinson, born in Todmorden, Yorkshire, studied at Imperial College London. After 13 years in Canada and the US he returned to London in 1956 as professor of inorganic chemistry. While at Harvard University in 1952 he published with *Woodward* and others a paper on the remarkable compound, $(C_5H_5)_2Fe$, ferrocene. They showed that this has a structure with an iron atom sandwiched between two flat five-carbon rings. Thousands of 'sandwich type' molecules have now been made, containing other metals and other-sized rings (the 'metallocenes'); even three-decker sandwiches are known. For his work on metallocenes Wilkinson

Geoffrey Wilkinson

shared the 1973 Nobel Prize for chemistry with E. O. Fischer of Munich, who had worked independently on similar lines. Wilkinson has also done much work on transition metal complexes, and discovered the first homogeneous system for catalytic hydrogenation of C=C bonds using the rhodium complex $RhCl[P(C_6H_5)_3]_3$.

WILLIAMSON, Alexander William
1824-1904

English chemist: demonstrated chemical relationship between alcohol and ethers

Born in London, Williamson lived with his parents on the Continent and studied chemistry in France and Germany. He is remembered for the **Williamson synthesis** of ethers, in which a sodium alkoxide reacts with an alkyl halide, i.e., $RONa+R'I \rightarrow ROR'$ where R,R' are alkyl groups.

By use of this reaction (1851) the relation between alcohols and ethers became clear. As he lacked one eye and had only one useable arm his prowess as a practical chemist is surprising.

WILLIS, Thomas
1621-1675

English anatomist: made important studies of anatomy of the brain

Willis studied classics and then medicine at Oxford; for a time he served in the Royalist army in the Civil War. He was one of the small group of 'natural philosophers' (including *Boyle*) who met in Oxford in 1648-9 and who were founder members of the Royal Society of London. His main work was on the anatomy of the brain; the softness of brain tissue makes study of its circulation difficult, but Willis improved on earlier work by injecting the vessels with wax; he thus saw the ring of vessels now known as the **circle of Willis**. He also worked on fevers; and he described a type of diabetes in which the excessive urine has a sweet taste. In 1776 this was found to be due to sugar, and in the 1920s this disease (diabetes mellitus) was brilliantly explored and effectively treated by *Banting* and C. H. Best. Willis was also the first to propose that the essential feature of asthma is spasm of the bronchial muscles.

WILLSTÄTTER, Richard
1872-1942

German organic chemist: discovered the structure of chlorophyll

Willstätter was eleven when his father left Germany for New York to establish a clothing factory, following the successful example of his brothers-in-law. An expected short separation lengthened to 17 years as success came to him slowly; and it was his wife and her family who brought up his two sons. Richard's interest in chemistry was prompted by his uncle's factory for the production of carbon for batteries.

He graduated at the University of Munich, studied under *Baeyer* and gained his PhD in 1894 for work on alkaloids. He obtained a professorship at the University of Zürich (1905-12) and worked on plant pigments, quinones, and the chemistry of chlorophyll. Using the chromatographic technique developed by *Tswett* he worked out the structure of both the a and b form of chlorophyll. He showed that chlorophyll contains a single atom of magnesium in its molecule, rather as haemoglobin contains a single iron atom. His work on cocaine derivatives, begun in Munich, led to the synthesis of new medicinals and the chemical curiosity, cyclo-octatetraene. He was awarded the Nobel Prize for chemistry in 1915 for his work on plant pigments.

He returned to the Kaiser Wilhelm Institute at Berlin-Dahlem where he worked on the carotenes and anthocyanins. During World War I Willstätter worked on gas masks, and devised a filling of hexamethylene-tetramine to absorb phosgene; layered with active carbon it was effective against the gases of the time. In 1916 he succeeded Baeyer to the chair in Munich and worked on photosynthesis (with A. Stoll) and on enzymes, notably catalase and peroxidase.

In 1925 he resigned his professorship in Munich in protest against the increasing antisemitism, in particular his faculty's rejection of the appointment of *Gold-schmidt*, the geochemist, because he was Jewish. Willstätter had resigned his post at 53, without a pension, and losing the house, the status and the protection that went with it.

He was now alone, his wife had died many years before after only five years of marriage, shortly to be followed by the death of a small son. His daughter had married and was living in the US. Despite many offers of posts in other countries he wished to stay in his own country. The next few years were spent in travelling, lecturing and continuing what research he could with the help of his colleague Margarete Rohdewald, who was allowed space in the laboratory and who reported her findings to him by telephone.

It was Dr Rohdewald who in November 1938 heard that members of the National Socialist party had been requested to

Richard Willstätter

volunteer for the arrest of Jews, and warned Willstätter. He was able to avoid an immediate journey to Dachau, but he then knew he had to leave Germany to survive. He was determined to emigrate to Switzerland in a proper manner, but his patience and dignity were to be tested in the following months while he was gradually stripped of his possessions in return for his passport. With help from his former student Stoll and influential friends in Switzerland he crossed the border in March 1939.

WILSON, Charles Thomson Rees
1869-1959

Scottish physicist: inventor of the Wilson cloud chamber

Wilson left a Scottish sheep farm as a child of four, and was educated in Manchester, eventually as a biology student there. Then he went to Cambridge, did well in physics, and became a teacher in Bradford for four years before returning to Cambridge in 1896, staying there for a long career.

In 1894 he had been attracted by the brilliant cloud effects he observed from the summit of Ben Nevis, and in Cambridge he examined methods of producing artificial clouds in the laboratory by the sudden expansion of moist air. The expansion drops the temperature of the gas, and the water vapour partly condenses as droplets on the walls and on any available nuclei. Wilson showed that if filterable dust is absent, then charged ions (produced, e.g., by X-rays) will serve as nuclei. By 1911 he had devised his cloud chamber, in which the path of an ion is made visible as a track of water droplets. It was soon used to detect and examine the α- and β-particles from radioelements, and it quickly became a favourite device for particle physicists, especially in the 1920s and 1930s. It was also the predecessor of the bubble chamber devised by *Glaser* in the 1950s.

Another of Wilson's researches also began on Ben Nevis, as a result of his own electrification (his hair stood on end) during a storm in 1895. He studied electrical effects in dry and moist air; and he noted that a sensitive well-insulated electrometer shows slow leakage, by day or night, even underground; he concluded that radiation from sources outside the atmosphere might be the cause. In 1911 *V. F. Hess* studied this further, and the discovery of cosmic rays proved that Wilson was right. His interest in atmospheric electricity remained; in his long retirement in Scotland, he flew at age 86 over the Outer Isles to observe thunderstorms, and presented his last paper on this subject, aged 87. He shared the Nobel Prize for physics in 1927 for his cloud chamber.

WILSON, Edward Osborne
1929-

American biologist: creator of sociobiology

Educated at Alabama and Harvard, Wilson has taught at Harvard from 1956. He is best known for his remarkable work on social insects and its wider implications in animal behaviour and evolution. In developing his theory on the interaction

Edward O. Wilson

and equilibrium of isolated animal populations, he and D. Simberloff experimented on some small islands in the Florida Keys. They first surveyed the insect species present (75 of them) and then eliminated all insect life by fumigation. Study of the recolonization of the islands by insects over some months showed that the same number of species became re-established, confirming their prediction that 'a dynamic equilibrium number of species exists for any island'. Wilson went on to consider biological and genetic controls over social behaviour and organization in a variety of species in his book *Sociobiology: the New Synthesis* (1975) which virtually created a new subject, integrating ideas on the behaviour of a range of species from termites to man. The work has both stimulated valuable research, and provoked vigorous discussion through its extension of ideas on animal behaviour to include human cultural and ethical conduct.

WILSON, John Tuzo

1908-

Canadian geophysicist: proposed concept of the transform fault in plate tectonics, and the 'hot spot' theory for the creation of mid-ocean islands

Wilson worked for the Canadian Geological Survey before being appointed professor of geophysics at Toronto in 1946, a post he held until his retirement in 1974. Although initially a staunch opponent of continental drift, Wilson is now known for his notable contributions to plate tectonics. In 1963 he provided some of the earliest support for the sea-floor spreading hypothesis of *H. H. Hess* by pointing out that the age of islands on either side of mid-ocean ridges increases with their distance from the ridge. He subsequently suggested that there exist 'hot spots' in the mantle where plumes of mantle material rise due to convection currents, and that as the lithospheric plates pass over them

volcanic islands are formed. His other important contribution has been the concept of the transform fault, introduced in 1965, which occurs where continental plates slide past one another, rather than one sinking beneath the other in a subduction zone. Mid-ocean ridges often consist of a series of offsets connected by transform faults.

WILSON, Kenneth Geddes

1936-

American theoretical physicist: discovered the renormalization group technique for treating phase transitions

Whilst one phase or another of a physical system may be easily analysed theoretically, similar analysis of the transition between phases has always proved virtually impossible. This is because the length-scale on which physical interactions are taking place changes rapidly through many orders of magnitude. In 1974 Wilson developed the first technique able to cope with such transitions, which are called critical phenomena. An example is the onset of ferromagnetism in a magnet cooled below the Curie point, when the atoms interact with each other and become aligned over large volumes of the magnet. The distance over which ordering of atomic spins occur goes from an atomic diameter to many thousands of diameters under a very small change in temperature.

L. Kadanoff had suggested that the effective spin of a block of atoms should be found and then a renormalization (or scaling) transformation made to calculate that of a larger block made up of the small blocks. Wilson developed this method and showed how to calculate the properties of large numbers of atoms strongly interacting with each other, as in magnetic systems, metal alloys or liquid-to-gas transitions. He was awarded the Nobel Prize for physics in 1982.

WILSON, Robert Woodrow
1936-

American physicist: co-discoverer of the cosmic microwave background radiation

Wilson graduated at Rice University, Houston, and California Institute of Technology. Thereafter he took up a post at the Bell Laboratories, Holmdel, New Jersey, and became head of the radiophysics research department in 1976.

At Bell, Wilson collaborated with *Penzias* in experiments using a large radio telescope designed for communication with satellites. In 1964 they detected a radio noise background coming from all directions; it had an energy distribution corresponding to a black body at a thermal temperature of 3.5 K. The explanation given by *Dicke* and P. J. E. Peebles was that the radiation is the residual radiation from the big bang at the universe's creation, which has been cooled to 3.5 K by the expansion of the universe. This cosmic background radiation had been predicted to exist by *Gamow, Alpher* and R. C. Herman in 1948.

Wilson and Penzias together won half the 1978 Nobel Prize for physics for their work.

WINDAUS, Adolf
1876-1959

German organic chemist: major contributor to steroid chemistry

Windaus first studied medicine, but was attracted into organic chemistry by attending lectures by *Emil Fischer*. He became professor at Göttingen in 1915, and remained there. From 1901, when he was 25, he worked (like Fischer) with natural products, and became the dominant figure in unravelling the intricate chemistry of the steroid group. His successes here included especially his work on the D vitamins. He also worked on vitamin B^1; and he discovered the biogenic amine, histamine, a key compound in allergy. He won the Nobel Prize for chemistry in 1928.

WITHERING, William
1741-1799

English physician: made classic study of medicinal use of digitalis

A graduate of Edinburgh, Withering practised in Stafford and then moved to Birmingham at the suggestion of Erasmus Darwin of Lichfield (grandfather of *Charles Darwin*). He was a member of the Lunar Society (a group of Midland scientists including *Priestley*, Wedgwood and Boulton, who met monthly, at the full moon to assist their homegoing) and he was a keen botanist. Finding that an extract of herbs had long been used to treat 'dropsy' (oedema), Withering made a careful study of the matter, and found that the active herb was the foxglove; and that some cases of oedema can indeed be treated effectively with foxglove leaf extract. He gave an excellent report of this work in his classic *An Account of the Foxglove* (1785); it is modern in style, with good case histories and includes failures as well as successes. It was later found that the extract contains digitalis, which steadies and strengthens heart action and which is still used for this.

He was also a mineralogist, and witherite (barium carbonate, $BaCO_3$) is named after him. He suffered greatly from chest

William Withering

disease (probably TB) and lived for years in a controlled atmosphere, inspiring the epigram 'the flower of Physick is Withering'.

WÖHLER, Friedrich
1800-1882

German chemist: achieved synthesis of urea; first made many novel inorganic and organic compounds

Young Wöhler was not very successful as a schoolboy; his passion for chemistry distracted him from all else. He graduated in medicine, and at once moved to chemistry by joining *Berzelius* for a year. On his return to Germany he began teaching chemistry, which was to fill his life; he was professor at Göttingen from 1836 until his death. Wöhler discovered the cyanates, and in 1828 he showed that ammonium cyanate when heated gave urea: $NH_4CNO \rightarrow CO(NH_2)_2$. Now urea is a typical animal product, so that this reaction could be interpreted as marking the end of the idea of a 'vital force' essential for the chemistry of life. In fact several odd features confuse this. Wöhler's cyanate was made by a process which was not wholly inorganic. Also, J. Davy had made urea in 1812 from NH_3 and $COCl_2$ but had not realised what he had made from these truly inorganic reactants. Synthesis by *Kolbe* and by *Berthelot* in the 1840s and 1850s marked the real logical end of vitalism; but Wöhler's work in 1828 ended it in the minds of many chemists.

In 1832 Wöhler's young wife died, and to distract him, *Liebig* invited him to Giessen for some joint work. This was a study of 'oil of bitter almonds', probably suggested by Wöhler; and from the oil (benzaldehyde) they made the related acid, chloride, cyanide and amide. Structure theory was yet to come; but the two recognized that a group of atoms (the benzoyl group, C_6H_5CO) was present in all these compounds. This was the first substantial 'compound radical' to be recognized, and this recognition was the beginning of the end of a period of confusion in organic chemistry.

Wöhler first isolated aluminium and beryllium, and crystalline boron and silicon, and calcium carbide; and he saw (in 1863) the analogy between compounds of carbon and those of silicon.

In his long and valuable friendship with Liebig, Wöhler displayed none of the enthusiasm Liebig had for controversy. Wöhler had a lighter view; he was the writer of a skit on *Dumas*'s substitution theory which was published in the *Annalen* under the name S. Windler. Later he remarked that he should have given a French name such as Ch. Arlaton. He enjoyed writing and teaching even more than research, and probably taught about 8000 students in his life.

WOLLASTON, William Hyde
1766-1828

English chemist: discoverer of palladium and rhodium and pioneer of powder metallurgy

Wollaston's father's family included several scientists and physicians and he followed both interests, at Cambridge and in London. However, in 1800 he gave up his medical practice and in partnership with S. Tennant made his income from the sale of platinum and devoted his time to work in chemistry, optics and physiology. He discovered palladium in 1802 and announced this weirdly by anonymous notices offering it for sale; his discovery of rhodium (also from crude platinum ore) he announced in the usual way, in 1804. Malleable platinum had not been made previously, but Wollaston produced it by methods now basic to powder metallurgy. Not unreasonably, he did not give details of his methods until shortly before his death.

Wollaston was very inventive and wide-ranging in his scientific work, and his lasting contributions include a reflecting goniometer (for measuring crystal angles), a modified sextant, an improved microscope, and the discovery of the vibratory nature of muscular action.

WOODWARD, Robert Burns
1917-1979

American organic chemist: probably the greatest deviser of organic syntheses

Woodward's career was marked throughout by brilliance. He went to the Massachussets Institute of Technology when he was only 16, was 'sent down' for a year for 'inattention to formal studies' but nevertheless emerged with his PhD at 20. Soon he moved to Harvard, and remained there. He did major work in most areas of organic chemistry, but his most striking work was in the synthesis of complex natural products. His successes in synthesis included quinine (1944), cholesterol and cortisone (1951), lysergic acid (the parent of the hallucinogen, LSD) and strychnine (1954); the first major tranquillizer, reserpine (1956), chlorophyll (1960) and the tetracycline antibiotics (1962). The high point was the synthesis of vitamin B_{12} (cyanocobalamin) in 1971, after 10 years' work in collaboration with a team of Swiss chemists.

In each case the work was marked by the elegance and ingenuity of the synthesis, in making a valuable and highly complicated product from simple starting materials, using a large number of chemical steps. His methods frequently provided novel general syntheses of other compounds. In 1965 he developed the **Woodward-Hoffmann** rules concerning the path of a large class of addition reactions.

He had a remarkable memory, an unsurpassed knowledge of organic chemistry, and a cool wit. In many ways modest, at conferences he sported a blue silk necktie embroidered with the full formula of strychnine, which he had synthesized in 50 stages, each well planned. He was awarded the Nobel Prize in 1965.

WRIGHT, Sewall
1889-1988

American geneticist: discoverer of genetic drift

A graduate of Illinois and Harvard, Wright joined the US Department of Agriculture in 1916 where he worked particularly on stock improvement. Later he taught at Chicago, Edinburgh and Wisconsin. In his stock improvement studies his aim was to find the best combination of inbreeding and crossbreeding to achieve this. He used guinea pigs as a convenient test animal, and developed a mathematical scheme to describe evolutionary development. In his work on small isolated animal populations he found that some genes can be lost randomly, because the few individuals having them may not reproduce successfully. This loss can lead to new species without the normal processes of natural selection being involved, and is known as the **Sewall Wright effect**, a process of random 'genetic drift' which can be important in small populations.

WRIGHT, Wilbur (1867-1912) and Orville (1871-1948)

American aviators: made and flew the first successful aeroplane

The Wright brothers were a very remarkable pair indeed. Through the second half of the 19th century a number of individuals in Europe and the US had attempted flight with heavier-than-air devices but without real success, at best operating unmanned models. The Wrights, sons of a non-conformist bishop in Dayton, Ohio, and owners of a small bicycle-making firm, began to experiment in 1896. They recognized that control was as important as stability, and that systematic experimentation was needed, and settled down to a programme of wind tunnel experiments on wing sections (aerofoils) and made over 1000 flights with unmanned biplane gliders near Kitty

Hawk on the North Carolina coast. One important step was their study of buzzards in 1899, which made it clear to them that three-axis control was needed (to bank, turn, and elevate or descend) and that the bird achieved control over roll by twisting its wings.

By early 1903 they had a biplane with control achieved by warping (twisting) the wings in unison along with a rudder, and with an elevator at the front. They devised an efficient propellor and made a small (12 h.p., that is 9 kW) petrol engine, which was fitted to a new biplane, driving two 'pusher' propellors; the craft had skids and not wheels, and the pilot lay on the lower plane. On a cold windy December morning in 1903 the first controlled, powered, and manned flights were made at Kitty Hawk, two by each brother. They made two more aircraft; the last, *Flyer III* of 1905, could make figures of eight and remain airborne for half an hour. Despite French and British enthusiasm, European results were poor until Wilbur visited Europe and demonstrated their success in the year they ceased to fly, 1908. They deserve great credit; in comparison, the attempts of their predecessors seem inept, and those of their successors to be natural developments from the Wright brothers' work.

WU, Chien-Shiung

1912-

Chinese-American physicist: confirmed experimentally that parity is not conserved by the weak nuclear force

Born in Shanghai, Wu moved to the US in 1936, having completed her degree in China. Under *Lawrence* she obtained her doctorate from the University of California at Berkeley in 1940 and took up a post at Princeton. From 1946 she taught at Columbia University, becoming professor of physics in 1957.

In 1957 she developed her research on nuclear decay by emission of, beta particles, by observing that the direction of emission is closely tied to the direction of the spin of the emitting nucleus. The emission process, therefore, is not identical for a mirror image system; and the physical laws do not remain unchanged under a parity change. This extraordinary result had however been predicted by *Yang* and *Lee* who had deduced that the weak nuclear interaction would not be identical under a parity change. The results of this work were far-reaching and many basic assumptions in physics were called into question.

Wu then set out to confirm *Feynman* and *Gell-Mann*'s theory of beta decay (1958) which predicted conservation of a vector current. She confirmed this in 1963. She also observed that electromagnetic radiation that is polarized is released on electron-positron annihilation, as predicted by *Dirac*'s theory of the electron.

WURTZ, Charles Adolphe

1817-1884

French organic chemist: pioneer of organic synthesis

Wurtz's father gave him the choice of studying theology or medicine. As he wished to be a chemist Wurtz chose medicine, graduated, and diverted to chemistry. He became assistant to *Dumas* and succeeded him as professor in the École de Médicine. He was an exuberant lecturer; and his research laboratory in Paris was unique in Europe in attracting as many able young men as the laboratories in German universities. His early research was on the oxoacids of phosphorus, and he also discovered $POCl_3$.

Soon he moved to organic synthesis, where his many successes included the discovery of the first amines, from the reaction of base with an alkyl isocyanate; in this way he made CH_3NH_2 and $CH_3CH_2NH_2$. In 1855 he showed that reactive alkyl halides with sodium metal give hydrocarbons (the **Wurtz reaction**): for example, $2n-C_4H_{11}Br+2Na\rightarrow n-C_8H_{22}+2NaBr$. The reaction has been used to make very long-chain hydrocarbons from, for example, 1-iodo-*n*-pentacontane: $2C_{50}H_{101}I + 2Na \rightarrow C_{100}H_{202}$ (*n*-hectane) $+ 2NaI$. The longest-chain nonpolymeric compound now known is tetraoctacontatrictane $CH_3(CH_2)_{382}CH_3$, that is, $C_{384}H_{770}$ made in 1985.

Wurtz was a major supporter of both *Dumas*'s and *Gerhardt*'s early theories on the nature of organic compounds.

WYNNE-EDWARDS, Vero Copner
1906-

British biologist: proposed animal altruism as basis for population homeostasis control

An Oxford graduate, Wynne-Edwards taught at McGill University, Montreal, from 1930 to 1946, and thereafter at Aberdeen. In Montreal he worked on the distribution of sea birds, making four round trips by Cunarder over the Atlantic in 1933 to see the changes in species with the seasons, and began to gather the results which were to be fully developed in his book *Animal Dispersion in Relation to Social Behaviour* (1962). He proposed that animal populations use hormonal devices and social mechanisms including territoriality, dominance hierarchies, and grouping in flocks as methods of controlling population size; and that they will sacrifice their own survival and their fertility for the good of the group, whose survival depends on avoiding overuse of the available resources. This view of animal altruism provoked vigorous discussion and research in ethology and ecology; the book has been highly influential in its proposal for 'population homeostasis', and its ideas have been both criticized and developed by others including D. L. Lack, J. Maynard Smith and *E. O. Wilson*.

Vero Wynne-Edwards

Y

YALOW, Rosalyn (Sussman)

1921-

American nuclear physicist: developed radioimmunoassay method

A physicist with a special interest in radioisotopes, Yalow turned to nuclear medicine and from 1972 was Senior Medical Investigator for the Veterans Administration. Working with S. Berson in a New York hospital, she developed from the 1950s the method of **radioimmunoassay** to detect and measure peptide hormones (such as insulin) in the blood. The method has proved of great value both in locating the origin of hormones in the body, and in clinical diagnosis and treatment of a variety of diseases, and of male and female infertility. Extension of the method in the UK has led to better control of digoxin therapy in heart disease, and diagnosis of neural crest disease (e.g., spina bifida) in the foetus. The potential value of the method is great; it can be used to measure very small amounts (10^{-12} g) of any substance for which an antibody can be made. Yalow shared a Nobel Prize in 1977.

YANG, Chen Ning

1922-

Chinese American physicist: showed that parity is not conserved by the weak nuclear force

Yang is the son of a professor of mathematics, and received his college education in Kunming in China. Taking up a fellowship for travel and research in America he completed a PhD under *Teller* at Chicago. He joined the Institute for Advanced Study at Princeton in 1949. He became Director of the Institute for Theoretical Physics at the University of New York, Stony Brook in 1966.

It is Yang's work in collaboration with *Lee* which is justly celebrated as a turning point in the development of theoretical physics: they showed that the law of conservation of parity (i.e., that physical laws are unaltered in mirror-image systems) does not hold for the weak nuclear interaction (1956). The prediction was confirmed by *Wu*'s thorough experimental study, and quickly led to the award of a Nobel Prize for physics to Yang and Lee (1957).

Yang is also famous for his development of a non-Abelian gauge theory with R. L. Mills (the **Yang-Mills theory**). This proved to be an important new departure in theories of elementary particles and quantum fields.

Chen Ning Yang about 1975

Charles Yanofsky

YANOFSKY, Charles
1925-

American geneticist: experimentally verified hypothesis that DNA base sequence codes for protein synthesis

A graduate in chemistry from New York who went on to work in microbiology at Yale, Yanofsky afterwards worked at Yale and Stanford on gene mutations. His work has confirmed the idea that the sequence of bases in the genetic material DNA determines the order of the amino acids which make up proteins, including of course the enzymes which are critical to living systems. Yanofsky secured his evidence on this by ingenious experimentation using mutant strains of a bacterium; these were isolated and the positions of the mutations in the gene were mapped. Likewise, the amino acid sequences were determined in the various mutant forms of the enzyme produced by these strains. It could then be shown that the changes in amino acid sequences correspond with the mutant sites on the genetic map, in accord with the theory.

YOUNG, James
1811-1833

Scottish chemist: pioneer petroleum technologist

Young was a part-time student in Glasgow, attending 'night-school' classes in chemistry given by *Graham*; he became Graham's assistant. From 1839 he was employed in the chemical industry, and in 1848 he set up a small works in Derbyshire to purify oil from a seepage, and marketed it for lighting and as a lubricant. When after three years the seepage was exhausted he moved to Lothian in Scotland, and began to extract oil from oil shale deposits by distillation. He founded the Scottish oil shale industry, and was one of the first to apply chemical methods to oil handling.

His other ventures included a measurement of the speed of light by *Fizeau*'s method; and he gave financial support for the explorations by David Livingstone, who had been a fellow student and friend in Glasgow.

YOUNG, Thomas
1773-1829

English physiologist, physicist and Egyptologist: established wave theory of light

Young surely had one of the most acute minds of his century, but his diversity of interests, and his tendency to move to new ones rather than consolidate his ideas, caused credit for some of them to go to others. His father was a banker, and for unknown reasons the boy lived largely with his grandfather. He was a precocious child, who could read at the age of two; he had a good knowledge of five languages at 13, and of eight more oriental languages at 14. At this time a young schoolmaster also introduced him to telescope-making.

In 1792 he began to study medicine, intending to follow a friendly and prosperous uncle into his London practice, and in his first year as a medical student in

413

London he published on the physics of the eye. By neat experiments he showed that accommodation (change of focus) is a result of change in the curvature of the lens; at the same time he described and measured astigmatism; and in 1801 he devised his three-colour theory of human colour vision. He continued as a medical student, with a full social life, in Edinburgh, Göttingen and Cambridge, and in 1799 set up a practice in London. He was not very successful as a physician, perhaps because (as a friend said) his mind was usually on other matters, and he was not a success either as a lecturer at the Royal Institution. During these lectures, when discussing *Hooke*'s law in 1802, he gave physical meaning to the constant in that law, which has come to be named as **Young's modulus,** E, defined as the ratio stress/strain; here stress is the force per unit area of cross section of a material, which produces a strain measured as (change in length)/(original length). E is a measure of a material's resistance to change in length, and an average value for natural rubber would be 1×10^6 Nm^{-2} while for a mild steel $E = 2 \times 10^{11}$ Nm^{-2}.

But his major work was on the wave theory of light, which *Newton* had thought to be corpuscular and *Huygens* wave-like. Young argued in 1800-4 in favour of the wave theory and supported this by clear and detailed accounts of elegant experiments on interference due to superposition of the waves. The current view entirely supports Young's interpretation of these effects, while also using a 'corpuscular' explanation in terms of photons and quantum theory for such results as photoelectric emission.

From 1814 Young busied himself with his medical practice and with Egyptology, where his major contributions to the interpretation of the Rosetta Stone ultimately revealed the ancient Egyptian system of writing, although at the time others were given more credit for this, in part because his major work on this was published anonymously, as the entry on Egypt in a supplement to the *Encyclopaedia Britannica* for 1819.

YUKAWA, Hideki
1907-1981

Japanese physicist: first described the strong nuclear force and predicted the pi-meson

Yukawa studied at Kyoto University and took his degree there in 1929. He moved to Osaka University to take his doctorate, but returned to Kyoto for the remainder of his career, becoming Professor of Theoretical Physics in 1939.

When he was 27, Yukawa developed his theory of nuclear forces. In 1932 *Chadwick* had discovered the neutron; and Yukawa proposed a strong short-range force between protons or neutrons which overcame electrical repulsion between the protons in the nucleus without influencing the electrons in the atom. This nuclear 'exchange' force involves the exchange of a particle between the nucleons (nuclear constituents) and from the short range of the force (less than 10^{-8} m) Yukawa inferred that its mass was about 200 times that of an electron; and its charge the same as that of an electron.

In 1936 *C. D. Anderson* discovered a particle of the correct mass and called it the mu-meson; but it did not interact with nucleons sufficiently strongly to correspond with Yukawa's prediction. In 1947 *Powell* discovered another meson (the pi-meson) which did correspond with Yukawa's proposed particle, and so established his theory of the strong nuclear force.

Yukawa also successfully predicted (in 1936) that nuclei may absorb one of the innermost electrons (in the 1 K shell) and such **K capture** by a nucleus was soon observed. He was the first Japanese to be awarded a Nobel Prize, in 1949.

Z

ZEEMAN, Pieter
1865-1943

Dutch physicist: discovered the splitting of spectral lines by magnetic fields

Zeeman's experiment of 1896 proved to be a very early crucial link between light and magnetism, which also gave further identification of the electron and a basis on which to test the quantum mechanical theories of atomic structure. It was performed soon after Zeeman had graduated at Leiden (under *Lorentz*) and had become a Privatdozent at Amsterdam. He first observed that when a magnetic field was applied to sodium or lithium flames then the lines in the emission spectrum of the flame were apparently broadened; and this on inspection was due to splitting of the lines into two or three lines. Zeeman's observation agreed with results from Lorentz's classical theory of light as being due to vibrating electrons in atoms.

The normal **Zeeman effect** is shown when a spectral line splits into two with a strong magnetic field applied parallel to the light path or into three if the field is perpendicular. The old quantum theory and *Bohr*'s model of the atom could explain this. However, in general, atoms show the anomalous Zeeman effect which involves splitting into several closely spaced lines. The explanation of this required the full quantum mechanics (1925) and the concept of electron spin, due to *Uhlenbeck* and *Goudsmit* (1926). Zeeman and Lorentz shared the 1902 Nobel Prize for physics for their work on the magneto-optical properties of atoms.

Faraday had experimented in 1862 on the application of a magnetic field to emission spectra, but failed to find an effect; Zeeman succeeded, and the explanation of his results was a major step for theoretical physics.

ZHANG, Heng
78-139

Chinese astronomer and geophysicist: invented the earthquake seismograph

Zhang was born in Nanyang, Henan Province, during the Han Dynasty. He was Imperial Historian and official astronomer.

Zhang recognized that the source of the Moon's illumination was sunlight, and that lunar eclipses were caused by the Earth's shadow falling upon it. He devised a water-driven celestial globe, which revolved in correspondence with the diurnal motion of the celestial sphere. In mathematics, he calculated π as 365/116 (about 3.1466), a substantial improvement on the hitherto accepted Chinese value of 3. Perhaps his best remembered contribution, however, was to geophysics, when in AD 132 he invented an early seismograph. This was to help him locate and record earthquakes, one of his official duties as Imperial Historian. It was a bronze device almost two metres in diameter, containing a mechanism of pendulums and levers, with eight dragon figures arranged around its circumference. Strong seismic tremors caused a metal ball to be released from the mouth of the dragon facing the direction of the shock wave. It is known that the device registered an earthquake in Gansu Province in AD 138.

Norton D. Zinder in 1964

ZINDER, Norton David

1928-

American geneticist: discovered bacterial transduction

A graduate of Columbia University, New York, Zinder did graduate work with *Lederberg*, and became professor of genetics at Rockefeller University in 1964. Lederberg was the first to observe sexual union (conjugation) in a bacterium (*E. coli*); Zinder looked for it in *Salmonella*. He soon devised a valuable new technique for isolating mutants of this bacterium, but his attempt to observe conjugation led him instead to the discovery of **bacterial transduction**. This is the transfer, by a phage particle, of genetic material from one bacterium to another; the discovery has led to new knowledge of the location and behaviour of bacterial genes.

ZSIGMONDY, Richard Adolf

1865-1929

German colloid chemist: inventor of the ultramicroscope

After studying chemistry and physics Zsigmondy joined the Schott glassworks at Jena; it was through his interest in coloured glass that his work on colloids began, and this was continued through his career as a professor at Göttingen. In 1903 he made an 'ultramicroscope' in which the sample is strongly lit from one side,

against a dark background. This allowed colloid particles to be seen as points of light, even if they are smaller than the resolving power of the microscope. Such studies were of great value before the introduction of the ultracentrifuge and the electron microscope. Zsigmondy examined many colloidal solutions (especially gold sols) and deduced particle sizes, and concluded that the particles are kept apart by electrostatic charge. Colloidal solutions are of the greatest importance in biochemistry. His pioneer studies did much to advance understanding of sols, gels, smokes, fogs and foams, and he was awarded a 1925 Nobel Prize for his work.

ZU, Chongzhi

429-500

Chinese mathematician and astronomer: improved the accuracy of π, and measured the length of the year

Zu computed π to be 355/113 (about 3.1415929), a value not bettered until a thousand years later by al-Kashi and *Viète*, and also gave 22/7 as a simpler value for calculations where less accuracy was sufficient. In astronomy, he measured the length of the year to be 365.2429 days, by extensive observations of the lengths of shadows around the winter solstice, an improvement over contemporary values.

ZWORYKIN, Vladimir Kosma

1889-1982

Soviet-American physicist: invented the electronic-scanning television camera

Soon after graduating in engineering from Petrograd (now Leningrad), Zworykin spent World War I serving as a radio officer in the Russian Army. One of his teachers in Leningrad was B. Rosing who took out the first patent for a television system, in 1907; it used a cathode-ray tube as its receiver. After Russia's collapse into revolution in 1917 Zworykin emigrated to America in 1919 and joined the Westinghouse Electric Corporation. His career developed as he gained a doctorate (1926) and moved to a post with the Radio Corporation of America (1929).

Whilst at Westinghouse in 1923 he re-produced an image from a screen by dividing it into many insulated photoelectric cells which held a charge proportional to the light falling on them. An electron beam scanning the screen discharged the cells in turn, giving an electrical signal.

Zworykin then took a cathode-ray tube (invented by *Braun*, in 1897) which could produce focused spots on its fluorescent screen using electric and magnetic fields. As the beam scanned the screen the intensity of the spot varied according to the electrical signal and so could reproduce the images from his first device, so that he had a television transmitting and receiving system. By 1929 the camera had been developed to the point of practical use, and it displaced the mechanical system developed by *Baird*.

Nobel Prize Winners

Nobel Prize Winners

Physics

1901 Wilhelm C. Roentgen, German
1902 Hendrik A. Lorentz, Dutch
     Pieter Zeeman, Dutch
1903 Antoine Henri Becquerel, French
     Marie Curie, Polish-French
     Pierre Curie, French
1904 John W. Strutt (Lord Rayleigh)
     British
1905 Philipp E. A. von Lenard,
     German
1906 Joseph J. Thomson, British
1907 Albert A. Michelson, U.S.
1908 Gabriel Lippmann, French
1909 Carl F. Braun, German
     Guglielmo Marconi, Italian
1910 Johannes D. van der Waals,
     Dutch
1911 Wilhelm Wien, German
1912 Nils G. Dalén, Swedish
1913 Heike Kamerlingh-Onnes, Dutch
1914 Max von Laue, German
1915 Sir William H. Bragg, British
     William L. Bragg, British
1917 Charles G. Barkla, British
1918 Max K. E. L. Planck, German
1919 Johannes Stark, German
1920 Charles E. Guillaume, French
1921 Albert Einstein, German-U.S.
1922 Niels Bohr, Danish
1923 Robert A. Millikan, U.S.
1924 Karl M. G. Siegbahn, Swedish
1925 James Franck, German
     Gustav Hertz, German
1926 Jean B. Perrin, French
1927 Arthur H. Compton, U.S.
     Charles T. R. Wilson, British
1928 Owen W. Richardson, British
1929 Prince Louis-Victor de Broglie,
     French
1930 Sir Chandrasekhara V. Raman,
     Indian
1932 Werner Heisenberg, German
1933 Paul A. M. Dirac, British
     Erwin Schrödinger, Austrian
1935 James Chadwick, British
1936 Carl D. Anderson, U.S.
     Victor F. Hess, Austrian
1937 Clinton J. Davisson, U.S.
     George P. Thomson, British
1938 Enrico Fermi, U.S.
1939 Ernest O. Lawrence, U.S.

1943 Otto Stern, U.S.
1944 Isidor Isaac Rabi, U.S.
1945 Wolfgang Pauli, U.S.
1946 Percy Williams Bridgman, U.S.
1947 Edward V. Appleton, British
1948 Patrick M. S. Blackett, British
1949 Hideki Yukawa, Japanese
1950 Cecil F. Powell, British
1951 Sir John D. Cockcroft, British
     Ernest T. S. Walton, Irish
1952 Felix Bloch, U.S.
     Edward M. Purcell, U.S.
1953 Frits Zernike, Dutch
1954 Max Born, British
     Walter Bothe, German
1955 Polykarp Kusch, U.S.
     Willis E. Lamb, U.S.
1956 John Bardeen, U.S.
     Walter H. Brattain, U.S.
     William Shockley, U.S.
1957 Tsung-dao Lee, U.S.
     Chen Ning Yang, U.S.
1958 Pavel Cherenkov, U.S.S.R.
     Ilya Frank, U.S.S.R.
     Igor Y. Tamm, U.S.S.R.
1959 Owen Chamberlain, U.S.
     Emilio G. Segrè, U.S.
1960 Donald A. Glaser, U.S.
1961 Robert Hofstadter, U.S.
     Rudolf L. Mössbauer, German
1962 Lev D. Landau, U.S.S.R.
1963 Maria Goeppert-Mayer, U.S.
     J. Hans D. Jensen, German
     Eugene P. Wigner, U.S.
1964 Nikolai G. Basov, U.S.S.R.
     Aleksander M. Prokhorov,
     U.S.S.R.
     Charles H. Townes, U.S.
1965 Richard P. Feynman, U.S.
     Julian S. Schwinger, U.S.
     Sin-itiro Tomonaga, Japanese
1966 Alfred Kastler, French
1967 Hans A. Bethe, U.S.
1968 Luis W. Alvarez, U.S.
1969 Murray Gell-Mann, U.S.
1970 Louis Néel, French
     Hannes Alfvén, Swedish
1971 Dennis Gabor, British
1972 John Bardeen, U.S.
     Leon N. Cooper, U.S.
     John R. Schrieffer, U.S.

(*Physics* cont.)
1973 Ivar Giaever, U.S.
     Leo Esaki, Japan
     Brian D. Josephson, British
1974 Martin Ryle, British
     Antony Hewish, British
1975 James Rainwater, U.S.
     Ben Mottelson, U.S.-Danish
     Aage Bohr, Danish
1976 Burton Richter, U.S.
     Samuel C. C. Ting, U.S.
1977 John H. Van Vleck, U.S.
     Philip W. Anderson, U.S.
     Nevill F. Mott, British
1978 Pyotr Kapitsa, U.S.S.R.
     Arno Penzias, U.S.
     Robert Wilson, U.S.
1979 Steven Weinberg, U.S.
     Sheldon L. Glashow, U.S.
     Abdus Salam, Pakistani
1980 James W. Cronin, U.S.
     Val L. Fitch, U.S.
1981 Nicolaas Bloembergen, U.S.
     Arthur Schawlow, U.S.
     Kai M. Siegbahn, Swedish
1982 Kenneth G. Wilson, U.S.
1983 Subrahmanyan Chandrasekhar,
     U.S.
     William A. Fowler, U.S.
1984 Carlo Rubbia, Italian
     Simon van der Meere, Dutch
1985 Klaus von Klitzing, W. German
1986 Ernst Ruska, German
     Gerd Binnig, W. German
     Heinrich Rohrer, Swiss
1987 Georg Bednorz, Swiss
     Alex Müller, Swiss
1988 Leon Lederman, U.S.
     Melvin Schwarz, U.S.
     Jack Steinberger, U.S.

Chemistry

1901 Jacobus H. van't Hoff, Dutch
1902 Emil Fischer, German
1903 Svante A. Arrhenius, Swedish
1904 Sir William Ramsay, British
1905 Adolf von Baeyer, German
1906 Henri Moissan, French
1907 Eduard Buchner, German
1908 Ernest Rutherford, British
1909 Wilhelm Ostwald, German
1910 Otto Wallach, German
1911 Marie Curie, Polish-French
1912 Victor Grignard, French
     Paul Sabatier, French

1913 Alfred Werner, Swiss
1914 Theodore W. Richards, U.S.
1915 Richard M. Willstätter, German
1918 Fritz Haber, German
1920 Walther H. Nernst, German
1921 Frederick Soddy, British
1922 Francis W. Aston, British
1923 Fritz Pregl, Austrian
1925 Richard A. Zsigmondy, German
1926 Theodor Svedberg, Swedish
1927 Heinrich O. Wieland, German
1928 Adolf O. R. Windaus, German
1929 Arthur Harden, British
     Hans von Euler-Chelpin, Swedish
1930 Hans Fischer, German
1931 Friedrich Bergius, German
     Karl Bosch, German
1932 Irving Langmuir, U.S.
1934 Harold C. Urey, U.S.
1935 Frédéric Joliot-Curie, French
     Irène Joliot-Curie, French
1936 Peter J. W. Debye, Dutch
1937 Walter N. Haworth, British
     Paul Karrer, Swiss
1938 Richard Kuhn, German
1939 Adolf F. J. Butenandt, German
     Leopold Ruzicka, Swiss
1943 Georg de Hevesy, Hungarian
1944 Otto Hahn, German
1945 Artturi I. Virtanen, Finnish
1946 James B. Sumner, U.S.
     John H. Northrop, U.S.
     Wendell M. Stanley, U.S.
1947 Sir Robert Robinson, British
1948 Arne W. K. Tiselius, Swedish
1949 William F. Giauque, U.S.
1950 Kurt Alder, German
     Otto P. H. Diels, German
1951 Edwin M. McMillan, U.S.
     Glenn T. Seaborg, U.S.
1952 Archer J. P. Martin, British
     Richard L. M. Synge, British
1953 Hermann Staudinger, German
1954 Linus C. Pauling, U.S.
1955 Vincent Du Vigneaud, U.S.
1956 Sir Cyril N. Hinshelwood, British
     Nikolai N. Semenov, U.S.S.R.
1957 Sir Alexander R. Todd, British
1958 Frederick Sanger, British
1959 Jaroslav Heyrovsky, Czech
1960 Willard F. Libby, U.S.
1961 Melvin Calvin, U.S.
1962 John C. Kendrew, British
     Max F. Perutz, British
1963 Giulio Natta, Italian
     Karl Ziegler, German

Nobel Prize Winners

(*Chemistry* cont.)
1964 Dorothy C. Hodgkin, British
1965 Robert B. Woodward, U.S.
1966 Robert S. Mulliken, U.S.
1967 Manfred Eigen, German
     Ronald G. W. Norrish, British
     George Porter, British
1968 Lars Onsager, U.S.
1969 Derek H. R. Barton, British
     Odd Hassel, Norwegian
1970 Luis F. Leloir, Argentinian
1971 Gerhard Herzberg, Canadian
1972 Christian B. Anfinsen, U.S.
     Stanford Moore, U.S.
     William H. Stein, U.S.
1973 Ernst Otto Fischer, W. German
     Geoffrey Wilkinson, British
1974 Paul J. Flory, U.S.
1975 John Cornforth, Australian-British
     Vladimir Prelog, Yugoslav-Swiss
1976 William N. Lipscomb, U.S.
1977 Ilya Prigogine, Belgian
1978 Peter Mitchell, British
1979 Herbert C. Brown, U.S.
     George Wittig, German
1980 Paul Berg, U.S.
     Walter Gilbert, U.S.
     Frederick Sanger, British
1981 Kenichi Fukui, Japanese
     Roald Hoffmann, U.S.
1982 Aaron Klug, S. African
1983 Henry Taube, Canadian
1984 Bruce Merrifield, U.S.
1985 Herbert A. Hauptman, U.S.
     Jerome Karle, U.S.
1986 Dudley Herschbach, U.S.
     Yuan T. Lee, U.S.
     John C. Polanyi, Canadian
1987 Charles Pedersen, U.S.
     Donald Cram, U.S.
     Jean-Marie Lehn, French
1988 Johann Deisenhofer, W. German
     Robert Huber, W. German
     Hartmut Michel, W. German

Physiology or Medicine

1901 Emil A. von Behring, German
1902 Sir Ronald Ross, British
1903 Niels R. Finsen, Danish
1904 Ivan P. Pavlov, Russian
1905 Robert Koch, German
1906 Camillo Golgi, Italian
     Santiago Ramón y Cajal, Spanish
1907 Charles L. A. Laveran, French

1908 Paul Ehrlich, German
     Elie Metchnikoff, French
1909 Emil T. Kocher, Swiss
1910 Albrecht Kossel, German
1911 Allvar Gullstrand, Swedish
1912 Alexis Carrel, French
1913 Charles R. Richet, French
1914 Robert Bárány, Austrian
1919 Jules Bordet, Belgian
1920 Schack A. S. Krogh, Danish
1922 Archibald V. Hill, British
     Otto F. Meyerhof, German
1923 Frederick G. Banting, Canadian
     John J. R. Macleod, Scottish
1924 Willem Einthoven, Dutch
1926 Johannes A. G. Fibiger, Danish
1927 Julius Wagner-Jauregg, Austrian
1928 Charles J. H. Nicolle, French
1929 Christiaan Eijkman, Dutch
     Sir Frederick G. Hopkins, British
1930 Karl Landsteiner, U.S.
1931 Otto H. Warburg, German
1932 Edgar D. Adrian, British
     Sir Charles S. Sherrington, British
1933 Thomas H. Morgan, U.S.
1934 George R. Minot, U.S.
     William P. Murphy, U.S.
     G. H. Whipple, U.S.
1935 Hans Spemann, German
1936 Sir Henry H. Dale, British
     Otto Loewi, U.S.
1937 Albert Szent-Györgyi, Hungarian-
     U.S.
1938 Corneille J. F. Heymans, Belgian
1939 Gerhard Domagk, German
1943 Henrik C. P. Dam, Danish
     Edward A. Doisy, U.S.
1944 Joseph Erlanger, U.S.
     Herbert S. Gasser, U.S.
1945 Ernst B. Chain, British
     Sir Alexander Fleming, British
     Sir Howard W. Florey, British
1946 Hermann J. Muller, U.S.
1947 Carl F. Cori, U.S.
     Gerty T. Cori, U.S.
     Bernardo A. Houssay, Argentinian
1948 Paul H. Müller, Swiss
1949 Walter R. Hess, Swiss
     Antonio Moniz, Portuguese
1950 Philip S. Hench, U.S.
     Edward C. Kendall, U.S.
     Tadeus Reichstein, Swiss
1951 Max Theiler, U.S.
1952 Selman A. Waksman, U.S.
1953 Hans A. Krebs, British
     Fritz A. Lipmann, U.S.

(*Physiology or Medicine* cont.)

1954 John F. Enders, U.S.
Frederick C. Robbins, U.S.
Thomas H. Weller, U.S.

1955 Alex H. T. Theorell, Swedish

1956 André F. Cournand, U.S.
Werner Forssmann, German
Dickinson W. Richards, Jr., U.S.

1957 Daniel Bovet, Italian

1958 George W. Beadle, U.S.
Edward L. Tatum, U.S.
Joshua Lederberg, U.S.

1959 Arthur Kornberg, U.S.
Severo Ochoa, U.S.

1960 Sir F. MacFarlane Burnet,
Australian
Peter B. Medawar, British

1961 Georg von Békésy, U.S.

1962 Francis H. C. Crick, British
James D. Watson, U.S.
Maurice H. F. Wilkins, British

1963 Sir John C. Eccles, Australian
Alan L. Hodgkin, British
Andrew F. Huxley, British

1964 Konrad E. Bloch, U.S.
Feodor Lynen, German

1965 Francois Jacob, French
Andre Lwoff, French
Jacques Monod, French

1966 Charles B. Huggins, U.S.
Francis Peyton Rous, U.S.

1967 Ragnar Granit, Swedish
Haldan Keffer Hartline, U.S.
George Wald, U.S.

1968 Robert W. Holley, U.S.
H. Gobind Khorana, U.S.
Marshall W. Nirenberg, U.S.

1969 Max Delbruck, U.S.
Alfred D. Hershey, U.S.
Salvador Luria, U.S.

1970 Julius Axelrod, U.S.
Sir Bernard Katz, British
Ulf von Euler, Swedish

1971 Earl W. Sutherland, Jr., U.S.

1972 Gerald M. Edelman, U.S.
Rodney R. Porter, British

1973 Karl von Frisch, German
Konrad Lorenz, German-Austrian
Nikolaas Tinbergen, Dutch-
British

1974 Albert Claude, Luxembourgian-
U.S.
George Emil Palade, Romanian-
U.S.
Christian Rene de Duve, Belgian

1975 David Baltimore, U.S.
Howard Ternin, U.S.
Renato Dulbecco, Italian-U.S.

1976 Baruch S. Blumberg, U.S.
Daniel Carleton Gajdusek, U.S.

1977 Rosalyn S. Yalow, U.S.
Roger C. L. Guillemin, U.S.
Andrew V. Schally, U.S.

1978 Daniel Nathans, U.S.
Hamilton O. Smith, U.S.
Werner Arber, Swiss

1979 Allan M. Cormack, U.S.
Geoffrey N. Hounsfield, British

1980 Baruj Benacerraf, U.S.
George Snell, U.S.
Jean Dausset, French

1981 Roger W. Sperry, U.S.
David H. Hubel, U.S.
Tosten N. Wiesel, U.S.

1982 Sune Bergstrom, Swedish
Bengt Samuelsson, Swedish
John R. Vane, British

1983 Barbara McClintock, U.S.

1984 Cesar Milstein, British-
Argentinian
Georges J. F. Koehler, German
Niels K. Jerne, British-Danish

1985 Michael S. Brown, U.S.
Joseph L. Goldstein, U.S.

1986 Rita Levi-Montalcini, Italian-U.S.
Stanley Cohen, U.S.

1987 Susumu Tonegawa, Japanese-U.S.

1988 Sir James Black, British
Gertrude Elion, U.S.
George Hitchings, U.S.

Chronology

Chronology

This lists a number of major events in science, and notes also (in bold type) some other events of historical interest. Titles of important scientific books are given in italics; in general these surveyed earlier work in their field and also initiated fruitful advances.

c.550 BC	Anaximander proposes Earth is poised in space
c.450 BC	Empedocles proposes four-element theory of matter
c.330 BC	Theophrastus founds scientific botany
c.300 BC	Euclid systematizes geometry
c.250 BC	Archimedes founds mechanics and hydrostatics
c.200 BC	*On Conic Sections* (Apollonius)
AD 30 or 33	**Christ crucified**
43	**Romans begin conquest of Britain**
132	Zhang invents seismograph
c.825	al-Khwarizmi gives general solution for quadratic equation
c.1000	Alhazen's work in optics
c.1350	**Black Death devastates Europe**
1440	**Gutenberg introduces printing by movable type**
1498	**Columbus lands in West Indies and South America**
1519-22	**Magellan's ship circumnavigates the world; Cortez conquers Mexico**
1543	Copernicus publishes heliocentric system Versalius publishes on anatomy
1556	*De re metallica* (Agricola)
1569	Mercator's map of the world
1572	Brahe observes nova (Tycho's star)
1579	**Drake, circumnavigating the world, lands in California**
1588	**Spanish Armada defeated**
1600	Bruno burned for heresy *De magnete* (Gilbert)
1607	**English settlements in Virginia**
1608	Lippershey and Jansen make first useful telescope (3×) and offer it for military use
1609	Kepler publishes his first two laws of planetary motion

	Lippershey and Jansen make first compound microscope
1610	Galileo publishes his astronomical observations made with a telescope (30×)
1624	*Logarithmical Arithmetic* (Briggs)
1628	*De motu cordis* (Harvey)
1633	Galileo charged with heresy
1637	Descartes introduces co-ordinate geometry
1642	**Civil War begins in England** Galileo dies Newton is born
1644	Torricelli constructs mercury barometer
1646	Pascal shows air pressure drops with rising altitude
1650	Guericke makes airpump
1654	Probability theory initiated by Pascal and Fermat in response to request by gaming friends Guericke's hemispheres demonstrate pressure of atmosphere
1658	Swammerdam observes red blood cells
1660	Boyle publishes law on gas pressure-volume relation
1661	*The Sceptical Chymist* (Boyle)
1662	Royal Society founded
1665	*Micrographia* (Hooke) **Great Plague** sends Newton home from Cambridge; in 1665-6 he devises the binomial theorem, the calculus, and the theory of gravitation
1669	Bartholin describes double refraction by calcite Steno publishes ideas on mountain-building, strata, and fossils
1675	Roemer shows light has finite speed
1678	Huygens expounds wave theory of light
1687	*Principia Mathematica* (Newton)
1694	Camerarius experiments on sexuality in plants
1699	Amontons observes relation of gas pressure to temperature

Chronology

1813   Dulong discovers NCl_3 and loses an eye and two fingers in the process

1814   Fraunhofer observes dark lines in solar spectrum

1815   Biot shows that optical activity is a molecular property
Napoleon defeated at Waterloo
Gay Lussac discovers cyanogen and investigates group of cyano compounds
Smith publishes his stratigraphic map of Britain

1816   Laënnec invents stethoscope

1817   Smith shows value of fossils in stratigraphy

1818   Berzelius publishes his table of relative atomic weights

1819   Dulong and Petit find relation between specific heat capacity and relative atomic mass
Fresnel and Arago deduce that light vibrates transversely to its direction of forward movement

1820   Oersted shows that a current in a wire induces a magnetic field around it
Ampère begins work on electro-dynamics
Mitscherlich publishes law of isomorphism

1822   Seebeck discovers thermoelectric effect
Fourier suggests using mass, length and time as fundamental dimensions

1823   Olbers's paradox postulated
Chevreul deduces nature of fats, and begins use of melting point to check purity of a solid substance
Macintosh makes cotton fabric waterproof by rubberizing

1824   *Reflections on the Motive Power of Fire* (Carnot)
Flourens's work on central nervous system
Prévost and Dumas argue that sperm is necessary for fertilization
Daguerre produces 'daguerrotype' photographic plates, and announces improved version in 1839

1825   **First steam locomotive railway opened in County Durham, England, for freight**
Faraday discovers benzene

Ohm begins work which leads to Ohm's law in 1827
Balard discovers bromine

1826   von Baer begins study of mammalian ovum and embryo
Lobachevsky introduces non-Euclidean geometry

1827   Ampère's Law in electromagnetism
Brown observes movement of pollen grains under microscope
Friction matches introduced

1828   Wöhler synthesizes urea
Caroline Herschel publishes catalogue of star clusters and nebulae
Berzelius lists 'atomic weights' of 28 elements

1829   Nicol describes his polarizing prism
Quetelet analyses Belgian census statistically
Babbage writes on scientific frauds, described as 'cooking', 'trimming' and forging results

1830   *Principles of Geology* (Lyell)
Faraday begins work on electricity
J. Henry discovers electromagnetic induction

1831   Darwin begins five-year voyage on HMS *Beagle*

1833   Babbage makes his 'difference engine' for computing
Lady Ada Lovelace writes first computer program, for Babbage's 'analytical engine'
Beaumont concludes that digestion is purely chemical

1834   Wheatstone measures speed of electricity in lengths of wire

1835   Geological Survey of UK established
Morse makes model electric telegraph

1836   Baily observes Baily's beads during solar eclipse

1837   Magnus analyses blood gases and finds more oxygen in arterial blood than in venous blood, implying that respiration occurs in tissues

1838   Remak shows that nerves are not hollow tubes
Bessel measures first stellar distance

Chronology

1839 Schwann and Schleiden expound cell theory in biology

1840 **Uniform penny postage in UK**
Agassiz postulates ice ages
New Zealand colonized

1842 Doppler discovers effect named after him

1843 Schwabe finds eleven-year sun-spot cycle
Electric telegraph introduced
Joule measures mechanical equivalent of heat
Screw steamer *Great Britain* crosses Atlantic

1846 Neptune discovered by Galle

1848 **Marx and Engels publish *Communist Manifesto***
Joule estimates speed of gas molecules from kinetic theory

1849 Addison associates Addison's disease with failure of adrenal gland
Fizeau makes accurate measurement of speed of light

1850 Foucault demonstrates rotation of Earth by use of pendulum
Clausius develops thermodynamics, using 'first and second laws' as key concepts

1851 **Great Exhibition in London**
Helmholtz invents ophthalmoscope

1852 Frankland introduces idea of chemical valence

1855 Pringsheim confirms sexuality of algae
Logan and Hunt describe geology of Canada

1856 Bessemer patents steel making by 'converter'
Ferrel explains atmospheric circulation using Coriolis force

1857 Buys Ballot announces law on rotation of cyclones

1858 Kekulé's theory of organic molecular structure
Wallace sends Darwin his ideas on the origin of species, which spurs Darwin to publish his own similar ideas
Sorby shows how microscopy allows deductions on rock formation

1859 *The Origin of Species* (Darwin)
Bunsen and Kirchhoff introduce spectrum analysis

Drake drills oilwell in Pennsylvania

1860 **Lincoln becomes President of USA**

1861 Cannizzaro clarifies relation of atoms to molecules
Crookes discovers thallium
American Civil War begins
Pasteur ends debate on spontaneous generation

1862 Alvan Clark and his son discover Sirius B
Angström discovers hydrogen in Sun

1863 Waldeyer describes cancer in modern terms
Tyndall discusses greenhouse effect of Earth's atmosphere

1864 Maxwell derives equations on electromagnetism, linking magnetism, electricity, and optics

1865 Clausius introduces concept of entropy
Kekulé proposes ring structure for benzene
Loschmidt calculates Avogadro constant as 6×10^{23}

1866 **Transatlantic telegraph cable begins operation**

1867 Lister shows value of antisepsis in surgery, used by him from 1865

1868 Mendelayev describes Periodic Table

1869 T. Andrews discovers critical state for gases
Suez Canal opened
First transcontinental railway opened, in US

1870 **Franco-Prussian War**

1874 Perrault deduces that rain and snow provide supply for river water, following close study of Upper Seine
Van't Hoff advances stereochemistry
Braun uses semiconductors as rectifiers

1875 Hertwig first observes union of sperm and ovum (in sea urchin)

1876 Draper photographs solar spectrum
A. G. Bell patents telephone

1877 Manson shows insect vectors involved in some diseases

430

1878   Cailletet liquifies common gases

1879   **First electric railway exhibited, in Berlin**

1882   Mechnikov describes phago-cytosis
Ants, Bees and Wasps (Lubbock)
Flemming describes mitosis
First generating station supplying electricity to private consumers opens in New York

1884   Balmer finds sequence in hydrogen spectra (Balmer series)

1885   Galton demonstrates individuality of human fingerprints

1886   Moissan isolates fluorine

1887   Tesla makes first AC motor
Michelson and Morley show that ether is probably non-existant

1888   Hertz discovers radio waves
Nansen explores Greenland icecap

1890   Behring and Ehrlich develop diphtheria antitoxin
Hollerith punch card system used to process US census
Dewar improves insulating flask, thereafter widely used in laboratories and picnics
London Underground railway opens

1892   Weismann observes meiosis, and proposes germ-plasm theory of heredity

1893   Nansen begins *Fram* expedition to Arctic

1894   Rayleigh and Ramsay discover first noble gas, argon

1895   Roentgen discovers X-rays
Diesel invents compression-ignition engine

1896   Becquerel discovers radioactivity (of uranium)
Arrhenius calculates result of additional CO_2 on greenhouse effect
Birkeland theorizes on origin of aurora
Zeeman effect links light with magnetism experimentally
Boltzmann relates entropy to probability

1897   Buchner shows that intact yeast cells not needed for fermentation
J. J. Thomson studies electrons

1898   Curies discover activity of radium, and isolate a sample in 1902

1899   First widely used synthetic drug (Aspirin) marketed by Bayer Co

1900   J. A. Fleming invents thermionic valve
Planck initiates quantum theory
Marconi transmits radio across Atlantic
Mendel's work on heredity rediscovered
Pearson introduces chi-square test

1901   Bordet experiments on complement fixation

1902   Landsteiner describes ABO blood system
Heaviside and Kennelly find radio-reflecting layer in atmosphere
Bateson applies Mendel's laws to animals as well as plants

1903   Einthoven describes use of ECG
Wright brothers make first manned flight
Rutherford and Soddy propose that radioactivity is due to atomic disintegration, an idea widely ridiculed
Boveri, Sutton and others argue that 'hereditary factors' (later to be called genes) are located on the chromosomes

1905   Blackman demonstrates limiting factors in plant growth
Einstein's theory of special relativity; and $E=mc^2$ relation

1906   Oldham deduces existence of Earth's core
Hopkins deduces existence of vitamins
Nernst states third law of thermodynamics
Brunhes discovers past geomagnetic reversal in rocks

1907   De Forest patents triode valve (radio tube)
Pavlov publishes his work on conditioned reflexes

1908   *Inborn Errors of Metabolism* (Garrod)
First Model T automobiles made by Ford Motor Co

1909   Ehrlich begins chemotherapy, with Salvarsan

Mohorovicic describes discontinuity between Earth's mantle and crust
Blériot crosses Channel by aeroplane

1908 Kamerlingh-Onnes liquifies helium

1909 Sörensen invents pH scale of acidity

1910 Millikan measures charge on the electron

1911 Amundsen reaches South Pole
Morgan and Sturtevant plot first chromosome map
Rutherford proposes nuclear structure of atoms
C. T. R. Wilson devises cloud chamber

1912 V. F. Hess discovers cosmic rays
Wegener proposes theory of continental drift
von Laue shows that X-rays can be diffracted and so behave as waves
Henrietta Leavitt devises method for measuring stellar distances
Slipher measures speed of rotation of planets

1913 Bohr calculates spectrum of atomic hydrogen, based on his 'Bohr atom'
Russell publishes H-R diagram
Moseley shows meaning of atomic number

1914 J. J. Abel isolates amino acids from blood
World War I begins

1915 Adams identifies first white dwarf star
Twort discovers bacteriophage

1917 **Bolshevic Revolution in Russia**

1919 Eddington describes bending of light by Sun, as predicted by Einstein's general relativity theory of 1916
Rutherford discovers the proton, and artificial transmutation of elements

1920 Michelson measures first stellar diameter (other than the Sun's)
Goddard develops theory of rocket propulsion, and launches liquid fuelled rocket in 1926

1922 Banting and Best treat diabetic patients with insulin
Carrel studies white blood cells

First public radio service begins (BBC)

1924 Pauli states his exclusion principle
Appleton discovers radio reflecting layer in ionosphere

1926 First demonstration of TV by Baird
Muller discovers biological mutations induced by X-rays
Dirac unifies new quantum theory
The Theory of the Gene (Morgan)

1927 Heisenberg proposes uncertainty principle
Lemaitre initiates big bang theory of origin of universe
Electronic Theory of Valency (Sidgwick)

1928 A. Fleming discovers penicillin
Raman discovers scattering effect

1929 **First public television broadcasts begin (BBC)**
Berger introduces EEG
Hubble announces his law on recession of galaxies
Matuyama discovers remanent magnetization of rocks

1930 Tombaugh discovers Pluto

1931 Gödel proves incompleteness of arithmetic
Van de Graaff builds high voltage electrostatic generator

1932 C. D. Anderson discovers positron
Chadwick identifies neutron
Cockcroft and Walton induce nuclear reaction artificially
Deuterium isolated by Urey
Jansky announces radio emission from stars

c.1933 Ruska develops electron microscope

1934 Beebe reaches 1000 m below sea level
Joliot-Curies discover artificial radioactive isotopes

1935 Stanley obtains a crystalline virus (TMV)
Richter devises scale of earthquake strength
Bergeron proposes theory of rain precipitation
Lorenz describes imprinting in animal development

1938 Carlson makes first xerox copies

Meitner and Frisch recognize nuclear fission as explanation for Hahn's experiments

1939 Alvarez measures magnetic moment of neutron
World War II begins
The Nature of the Chemical Bond (Pauling)
Energy Production in Stars (Bethe)

1940 Beadle and Tatum begin work in bacterial genetics
Rossby discovers the atmospheric waves named after him

1942 Alfvén predicts magneto-hydrodynamic waves in plasma
First nuclear reactor begins operation, in Chicago

1943 Baade classifies stars as Population I or II

1944 Martin introduces paper chromatography
What is Life? (Schrödinger)
Principles of Physical Geology (Holmes)
Avery shows importance of DNA

1945 **First atomic bombs exploded**
Beadle and Tatum propose one-gene one-enzyme hypothesis

1946 Bloch and Purcell independently develop nuclear magnetic resonance
Lederberg and Tatum discover sexuality in bacteria

1947 pi-meson discovered by Powell
Bardeen, Brattain and Shockley develop point-contact transistor
Libby develops radiocarbon dating

1948 H. W. and H. D. Babcock detect Sun's magnetic field
Alpher, Bethe and Gamov propose scheme to explain evolution of chemical elements in early universe (α, β, γ theory)
Alpher and Herman suggest that 'big bang' should have left residue of weak radiation
Shockley develops junction transistor
Gabor invents holography
The Steady-State Theory of the Expanding Universe (Bondi and Gold)

1949 Burnet discovers acquired immunological tolerance

1950 **North Korea invades South Korea**
Barton introduces conformational analysis in chemistry

1951 Purcell detects 21 cm radiation from interstellar hydrogen
Burnet proposes clonal selection theory in immunology
The Study of Instinct (Tinbergen)
Pauling proposes some protein molecules are helical

1952 Hershey and Martha Chase prove DNA is genetic information carrier
Lederberg and Zinder discover bacterial transduction
Glaser makes first bubble chamber

1953 Watson and Crick deduce structure of DNA and its implications
Gell-Mann introduces concept of 'strangeness' in particle physics
Kettlewell shows industrial melanism in moths

1954 Backus publishes first high level programming language (FORTRAN)
Pincus introduces oral contraception
Townes devises maser
Seismicity of the Earth (Richter and Gutenberg)

1955 De Duve identifies lysosomes
Sanger determines amino acid sequence of first protein (insulin)
Thermodynamics of Irreversible Processes (Prigogine)
Segrè and Chamberlain discover antiproton

1956 Berg discovers first transfer RNA
Palade discovers ribosomes
Ewing plots mid-Atlantic ridge

1957 **First artificial satellites (Sputnik I, and II containing dog Laika) in orbit**
Meselson and Stahl verify Watson and Crick's ideas on replication

1958 *Explorer I* discovers Van Allen belts: other space probes follow
Dausset discovers human histocompatibility system
Esaki discovers tunnelling effect in semiconductor junctions

1960 Sandage and Matthews discover quasars

Maiman constructs first laser
Moore and Stein determine sequence of all 124 amino acids in ribonuclease

1961 **First men in space**
Brenner and Crick show that genetic code of DNA consists of a string of non-overlapping base triplets
Good shows importance of thymus gland in the development of immunity
Gell-Mann and Ne'eman develop scheme for classifying elementary particles

1962 Josephson discovers effect named after him
Rossi detects cosmic X-ray source in Scorpio
Venus examined by passing US space probe *Mariner 2*
Bartlett makes first noble gas compounds
H. H. Hess proposes sea-floor spreading hypothesis

1963 Cormack and Hounsfield independently develop X-ray tomography (CAT scanning)
Matthews and Vine find evidence for sea-floor spreading
Gajdusek describes first human slow virus infection

1964 Penzias and Wilson detect cosmic background radiation, providing important evidence for 'big bang' origin of universe

1965 North Sea gas discovered
Mars photographed by *Mariner 4*

1967 Hewish and Jocelyn Bell discover first pulsar
First human heart transplant

1969 **First manned lunar landing**
Edelman finds amino acid sequence of immunoglobulin G

1970 Baltimore discovers reverse transcriptase which transcribes RNA into DNA
Khorana completes synthesis of first artificial gene
North Sea oil discovered

1973 Boyer uses recombinant RNA to produce chimera

1974 J/psi particle first observed

1975 *Sociobiology* (E.O.Wilson)
Milstein produces first monoclonal antibodies

1977 Sanger describes full sequence of bases in a viral DNA
Quantum Hall effect discovered by von Klitzing

1978 Pluto discovered to have a satellite (Charon) with half Pluto's diameter

1979 Saturn and Jupiter examined by passing space probes
Antarctic meteorite (uncontaminated by Earth) found to contain traces of amino acids
Evidence from deep sea bed cores shows that all fossils absent for a period of about 100 000 years about 65 000 000 years ago; some evidence favours asteroid or comet impact resulting in fires and dust clouds cutting off sunlight as cause of destruction
Microbial fossils from W. Australia found to be 3500×10^6 years old

1981 First reusable spacecraft (space shuttle) launched and recovered
First flare (lasting ≈ 1 min) observed on a distant star
Chain of eleven carbon atoms detected in molecules in star 600 light years distant: biggest space molecule

1982 Probes land on Venus

1983 Discovery of W vector boson
Compact disc (CD) system for sound recording introduced
Navigational satellites give speed of tectonic plate movement (e.g. Europe moving away from US at ≈ 10 cm year^{-1})

1984 Details given of the deepest hole, drilled at Kola Peninsula in Soviet Arctic, and now at 12 000 m and sampling very old rocks

1985 Laser clock developed with accuracy around 1 s in 50 million years, of value to cosmologists
Increasing evidence for a black hole at the centre of our Galaxy

1986 Comet Halley investigated by space probes, and shown to have a rotating nucleus of 'dirty ice', i.e., dust with water and CO_2 ice. The probe *Giotto* passes within 605 km of the nucleus, found to be potato-shaped and about 15 km by 8 km wide

434

Voyager II examines planet Uranus, and finds strange features such as its large, oddly-shaped magnetic field and its curious satellites with 'bizarre geology'

1987   Much work done on superconductors, mainly ceramics based on copper, oxygen, barium and a rare earth metal, with critical temperatures as high as 240 K (classical superconductivity had been seen only near 0 K): and with possible uses of great interest in electronics.

Canadian astronomers find new and better evidence for planets round stars other than the Sun, and by 1988 believed the case proved

1988   Increasingly, international scientific effort directed to problems of worldwide concern, notably: ozone loss in the upper atmosphere over both poles, which allows more UV light to reach Earth with effects on weather and health; acid rain, now shown to be due as much to lightning (see p. 83) as to fuel burning, and having effects especially on plant life; and the

nature and spread of the viral disease AIDS (Acquired Immuno Deficiency Syndrome)

A major study begun by US biologists, directed to mapping all the human genes; it will take many years to complete

New knowledge of dinosaurs resulted from the discovery at one site near Egg Mountain, Montana, of fossil eggs, embryos, juveniles and adult dinosaurs

Study of human remains found in an Israeli cave shows that the human race is much older ($\approx$ 100 000 yrs) than previously thought

Boomerangs (once thought to be peculiar to Australia) have now been found in five continents; the oldest, shaped from a mammoth tusk, was found in Poland, and dates from 21 000 BC

Newton's general theory of gravitation has been re-examined; new measurements show small deviations from his law at distances up to a few hundred metres. Apparently, either the law is more complicated than Newton proposed; or a weak 'fifth force' slightly counteracts the gravitational attraction

Index

Index

Where a name is given in bold type, the scientist has an entry in the dictionary

Index

Index

Index

Index

Index

Index

Index

Index

Index

Index

Index